The BOOK of FOUR OCCULT PHILOSOPHERS

About the Author

Daniel Harms (Upstate New York) is a librarian and writer living in central New York. His major area of research is magic from antiquity to the present, especially necromancy and fairy magic. He has been published in *Fortean Times*, the *Journal for the Academic Study for Magic*, and the *Enquiring Eye*, as well as chapters for Palgrave Macmillan and Penn State Press books. Harms is also the author of two books on horror fiction and folklore

About the Illustrator

S. Aldernay (Manchester, UK) is an occultist with a background in archeology and classic literature. His previous books include *The Pentacles of Solomon* (Hadean Press, 2012) and *Tools of the Greater Key* (Hadean Press, 2015).

DANIEL HARMS

S. ALDARNAY

The BOOK of FOUR OCCULT PHILOSOPHERS

Three Centuries of Incantations, Charms & Ritual Magic

Llewellyn Publications • Woodbury, Minnesota

First Edition
First Printing, 2023

Cover design by Kevin R. Brown
Interior art by S. Aldarnay

Access to MS. Douce 116 courtesy of Bodleian Libraries, Oxford

Library of Congress Cataloging-in-Publication Data (Pending)
ISBN: 978-0-7387-6441-2

Llewellyn Publications
A Division of Llewellyn Worldwide Ltd.
2143 Wooddale Drive
Woodbury, MN 55125-2989
www.llewellyn.com

Printed in the United States of America

Also by Dan Harms

Of Angels, Demons & Spirits: A Sourcebook of British Magic

The Book of Oberon: A Sourcebook of Elizabethan Magic

The Long-Lost Friend: A 19th Century American Grimoire

Also by S. Aldernay

The Pentacles of Solomon

Tools of the Greater Key

Dedication

Ἑκάτης

Contents

Acknowledgments / xxxiv
Disclaimer / xxxv

Introduction / 1

Douce MS. 116: A Description of the Manuscript / 2

The People of Douce MS. 116 / 4
The First Occult Philosopher / 4
The Manuscript / 4
The Late Seventeenth Century / 8
Contents / 10

The Second Occult Philosopher: Thomas Harrington / 13
Thomas Harrington / 13
The Eighteenth Century / 14
Contents / 17

The Third Occult Philosopher: Olivia Serres / 19
Princess Olive / 19
The Early Nineteenth Century / 21
Contents / 22

The Fourth Occult Philosopher: Raphael / 22
Robert Cross Smith / 22
Contents / 24

The Final Owner: Francis Douce / 25

The Editor / 28

Definitions and Editorial Philosophy / 29
Defining Ritual Magic / 29
The Title / 30
Notes on Editing / 31

The Text / 35

[Chart of Alchemical Symbols] / 35

The Key to Cornelius Agrippa's *4th Book* / 36

[Astrological and Divinatory Notes] / 38

To Know the Planet That Hath Dominion in the Nativity of a Person / 38

The Beginning—with Proper Directions / 39

Some General Aphorisms [on Talismans] / 40

A Liquid from the Moon / 43

Prima Materia / 43

Alchemy / 43

[18th Century Table of Contents] / 45

A Charm to Prevent Any Man Lying with the Wife / 52

[Witch Bottle Newspaper Story] / 52

[Key to a Cipher] / 53

Incantamentum pro Nocte / 53

An Experiment to Bring the Thief Again with the Goods / 55
Coniuracio / 55

To Bind a Spirit / 57

Rules Necessary in Doing Experiments / 58

The 28 Mansions of the ☽ Rectified as Followeth / 59

The Twelve Signs of the Zodiac / 60

Prosperous Times for Any Purpose / 60

An Experiment of Invisibleness, after the Knowledge of the Ancient Philosophers / 62

The Secretness of Secrets Hid and Said by the Writer to Be True / 64

Fairies Adipisitur—To Attract a Familiar / 65

Experimentum pro Furto / 66

Experimentum pro Furto / 67

Experimentum pro Furto / 68

Experimentum Libri et Clavis / 69

Experimentum Signi Susanna ad Videndum et Su[m]endum que Volueris de Furtis et Aliis Rebus / 70

His Tribus Nominibus Obedeunt Spiritus Infernales / 71

Alia / 71

Pro Dolore Dentium Probat—For the Toothache. Proven. / 72

Alter Probat / 72

Alter Probat / 72

Habere Dominium super Spiritus / 73

To Play at Dice That Thou Shalt Not Lose / 74

[Rite of Unknown Purpose, Possibly for the Previous] / 75

Pro Furto cum LIBRO ET CLAVE / 75

[Rings of the Twenty-Eight Mansions of the Moon] / 77
- [To Make a Stream Appear] / 77
- To Make a Hart or Buck Appear with Dogs Following / 78
- To Make Men in Horns to Appear / 79
- To Make a Dervine to Appear with Branches / 80
- To Make Meadows Appear with Woods / 82
- To Make a Table with Meat Appear / 82
- To Make Trees with Fruit and without Fruit Appear / 83
- To Make Oak Trees and Birds Singing in Them Appear / 84
- That Any Man May Appear Drawing the Mast of a Ship / 85
- To Make an Elephant Appear Bearing a Castle / 85
- To Make a Castle Appear / 86
- To Make a Dragon Appear in the Air / 87
- Ad Faciendum Pecunias Revertere Tibi Iterum / 87
- To Make a Horse Carry Thee Whither Thou Wilt / 88
- To Make Pismires to Be Pence / 88
- To Make Iron Seem to Be Gold / 89

Tu omoes [?] non tagnum [?] / 89

Ut Saltent Homines / 90

Alia / 90

Pro Amore / 91

Emanuell: De Imaginibus Tractatus Pro Amore / 94

Pro Amore / 99
- Oracio ad Deum / 100
- Oracio / 102

Pro Amore / 103

Pro Amore / 106

Pro Amore / 108

Pro Amore / 111

Alia / 112

[Another] / 113

Pro Amore / 114

Conjuratio Sequ[u]nt[ur] Nominibus *Apta* [Aptis] / 115

To Obtain One's Love / 117

To Make Thy Enemy Love Thee / 117

To Make Me Love and Honour Thee / 117

To Win the Love of Any Lord or Lady / 117

To Obtain Anyone's Love / 118

[To Know If the Sick Person Is Bewitched] / 118

Pro Amore / 118
    [The Magic Square of Jupiter] / 118

[Charms for Love] / 119

[Another Jupiter Love Charm] / 119

Pro Amore / 119

[More Love Charms] / 120

Pro Amore / 120

[Another for Love] / 121

For (Ad Habendum Amorem) or Love / 122

[For Love] / 122

[For a Fever] / 122

[To Make Serpents Appear] / 122

Incantamentarum pro Nocte / 123

[For Dreams] / 124

To Make a Man Prosperous and Defend Him from All Dangers / 125

[The Wheel of Fortune] / 128

[Another System of Numerological Divination for Marriage and Children] / 130

[Whether One Shall Live or Die] / 130

Spera Pithagore / 131

Against All Enemies Visible and Unvisible, and All Power, Evil, Pestilence, and Slander / 132

To Have the Love of Any Man or Enemy—Probatum Est / 132

[To Win at Dice] / 133

[A Cure for Quartan Ague] / 133

To Be Invisible / 133

To Know How Jugglers Play / 134

To Win at Dice / 134

Pro Furto / 134

To Have Favour of Any Person / 134

Ad Sciendum qui Furte Accepte Sunt / 135

To Make Men Look Like Ghosts / 135

To Make Men Look Black / 135

To Make a Tooth Fall without Iron / 135

Pro Amore / 135

To Be Feared of Enemies / 136

Stomach and Good Devotion / Digestion / 136

A Woman in Travail / 136

Alia / 137

To Staunch Blood / 137

For Biting of a Mad Dog / 137

Of the Adder Skin / 137

Pro Amore / 139

Pro Lucro / 139

For a Child in the Mother's Womb / 140

For Worms, a Charm / 140

To Know If Gold Be under the Ground / 141

[A Protective Charm] / 141
  Crux Christi / 142

For the Pestilence / 142

Pro the Cramp / 142

Pro the Fever / 143

For the Toothache, Write in Paper as Followeth / 143

[A Collection of Charms from Scot's *Discouerie of Witchcraft*] / 143
  The Inquisitors' Trial of Weeping per Conjuration / 143
  A Charm for the Falling Evil / 144
  A Charm against Shot, or a Waistcoat to Proof / 144
  Against the Falling Evil / 145
  A Periapt or Charm, Which Must Never Be Said, but Carried about
  One against Thieves / 146
  Another Amulet / 147
  [Indulgences for Sins] / 147
  Charm / 148
  A Charm Found in the Canon of the Mass / 148
  Charm, Both [For Health and Protection] / 148
  Alter / 148
  Charm Taken out of the Primer / 149
  Charm / 149
  [For the Consecration of the Oil] / 149
  For the Falling Evil / 150

Against the Biting of a Mad Dog / 150
[Another Charm for the Same] / 151
Against the Biting of a Scorpion / 151
Against the Toothache / 151
A Charm to Release a Woman in Travail / 152
To Heal the King's or Queen's Evil, or Any Other Soreness in the Throat / 152
How to Fetch a Thorn out of Any Part of One Body, a Bone out of the Throat / 152
For the Headache / 152
A Charm to Be Said Each Morning per a Witch Fasting, or at Least before She Goes Abroad / 152
A Charm That Witches Use at the Gathering of Their Medicinal Herbs / 153
Ditto to Open Locks / 153
Ditto to Drive away Spirits That Haunt Any House / 153
For One Possessed / 154
A Charm per the Bots in a Horse / 155
Ditto against Vinegar / 155
To Enchant a Serpent / 155
[Snakes and Witchcraft] / 156
[Charms against Scorpions and Eye Troubles] / 156
A Charm Teaching How to Hurt Whom You List with Images of Wax / 156
Charm [against Torture] / 157
Counter Charms in the Saying Witches Are Vexed / 157
For Corporeal or Spiritual Rest / 157
Charms to Find Out a Thief / 157
To Put Out the Thief's Eye / 158
Enchantment / 158
Charms to Drive Away Witches / 158
Of Witches' Transportations / 159
To Spoil a Thief, a Witch, or Any Other Enemy, and to Be Delivered from the Evil / 159
A Notable Charm or Medicine to Pull out an Arrowhead, or Any Such Thing That Sticketh in the Flesh or Bones Cannot Otherwise Be Had Out / 160
Against the Quotidian Ague / 160
For All Manner of Agues / 160
More Charms for Agues / 161
For a Bloody Flux, or Rather an Issue of Blood / 161

That Person That Hath These Words about Him, Put into the Hollow of an Elder Stick, Shalt Beat Persons with Running [?] Races / 162

How to Gather a Mosaical Rod to Find Out Hidden Treasure in the Earth / 164

How to Resolve Any Question Relating to a Good or Bad Fortune / 165
The Alphabet Numbering the Letters of the Surname Me- / 165

[A Copy of a Letter Written with Gold] / 168

Ad Demonium et Maleficium Fugendum / 170

A Charm for a Fever or an Ague / 171

[To Understand How to Make Use of Any Charm or Most Amulets] / 171

To Know If You Shall Be Successful in Any Matter You Engage against Another / 172

[Astrological Tables] / 173

Numbers Attributed to the Roman Letters / 179

[Notes on Astrological Timing] / 183

[Another Numerological Alphabet] / 183

[Paracelsus on Witches and Image Magic] / 187

[Planetary Affinities] / 191

A Charm to Stop Any Bleeding / 193

To Obtain a Woman's Love / 193

Explanation of the Table, Page 78 at the Bottom / 195

[On Pacts with the Devil] / 197

Counter Charms against All Witchcrafts, and to Vex Witches / 197

[Astrological Connections between the Zodiacal Signs] / 198

[Characters of the Planets from Agrippa] / 200

De Planetarum Mensulis Earum deque Virtutibus / 201
Magic Squares / 206
This Table of ♄ in His Compass / 206
The Table of ♃ in His Compass / 207
The Table of Mars in His Compass / 208

The Table of the ⊙ in His Compass / 209
[The Table of Venus in Her Compass] / 211
[The Table of Mercury in His Compass] / 212
[The Table of the Moon in Her Compass] / 213

Night-Spell / 215

Alter / 215

When You Are in Dread of Thieves and Your Enemies / 216

Ad Ligandum Fures / 216

The Virtue of a Mandrake / 217

To Know If a Woman Be Honest or Not, or If Anyone Hath Told You a Lie or Not, per a Table / 217

Ut Saltent Homines / 218

Propter Epilipsiam G. S. / 218

To Know If the Suspected Person Hath Stolen the Things or Not / 219

To Know the Estate of Friends Far from Thee / 220

Experiment for Thieves, or Any Other Thing / 221

[To Know the Intentions of Others] / 221

An Experiment to See per Thyself, without a Boy or Companion, the Spirits under Written in a Crystal Which Will Shew the Truth without Fail of All Things Doubtful as of These, Manslaughter, Treasure Being Hid, of the State of Thy Friend Being Absent, of Secrets, of Things Lost / 221
The Consecration of the Crystal / 223
The Consecration of the Oil / 223
When the Spirit Is Entered into the Glass & c. / 224

To Cause an Angel to Appear in a Crystal Stone / 224

To Prove Theft / 225

To Make a Thief or Any Person or Persons Come Again Wheresoever You Be / 226

To Know If Any Kind of Business Shall Come to Good, Evil, or Neatly End / 228

Experiment of the Hazel Rods / 228

Pro Thesauro / 229

Whether It Be Kept or No / 230

Ante Meridiem in Die ☽ et Die ♃, a Discharge for All Manner of Spirits for the Ground / 231

Salamonis Protectria [Protectio] / 232

Experiments with the Psalms / 233
- Ad Cephal[al]agiam / 233
- Ad Mutandum ab Aliquo Quid Psalm 5 / 234
- [For Illness] / 234
- Young Child Crying / 235
- Ut Quis Secure Dormiat ab Inimiciis / 235
- Ut Bene Reciperis / 235
- Ad Fascinationem Oculorum Praeveniendum / 235
- Exaudeat Te, Deus, in Die Tribulationis, Psalm 19 / 235
- Ut Agrotus Dormiat / 236
- Against Charms or Enemies / 236
- In Prison, to Help Out / 236
- Si Fueris in Necessitatem / 236
- Ad Abortum Praeveniendum / 236
- Ad Male Somniantem / 236
- Ut Bene Recipieris / 237
- Si Velis Te Fortunatem Fore Victoriamque Obtinere / 237
- Si Fuerit in Domo tum Fuerit Commiscam / 237
- Si Incantamenta cum Maleficiis Vis Envincere / 237
- Si Vis Maritum ad Uxorem Reverti / 237
- Ad Prerudum [Puerum?] Minis Flentem et Vigilantem / 238
- Ad Inimicos Superandos / 238
- Si in Necessitatem Incideris / 238
- Ad Naufragii Timorem ex Tempestate / 238
- "In te Domine speravi," [Psalm] 70, pro Causa in Lege / 238
- Ad Amorem, Alicu[iu]s Consiliandum / 238
- Ad Inimicos Dissipandas / 239
- Ad Fascinationem / 239
- Si Vis ad Regem vel Principem Intrare / 239
- "Fundamenta Ejus," [Psalm] 86 / 239
- Ad Cephalalgiam / 239

"Domine refugium," [Psalm] 89 / 240
"Qui Habitat in Adjurato [Adiutorio]," Psalm 90 / 240
"Dominus Regnavit," [Psalm] 92 / 240
"Deus Ultionum," [Psalm] 93 / 240
"Cantate Domino [Domino Cantate]," [Psalm] 95 / 240
"Domine Exaudi Orationem Meam," [Psalm] 101 / 240
"Benedic Anima Mea, Domine," [Psalm] 103 / 241
"Confetimini, Domino," [Psalm] 104 / 241
"Confetimini, Domine," [Psalm] 106 / 241
"Paratum Cor Meum," [Psalm] 107 / 241
Ad Partum Facitandum / 241
"Laudate Pueri Dominum," [Psalm] 112 / 241
"Dilexi, quoniam," [Psalm] 114 / 241
"Credidi propter," [Psalm] 115 / 242
"Laudate Dominum Omnes Gentes," [Psalm] 116 / 242
"Beati Inmaculati," [Psalm] 118 / 242
"In Convertendo Domine," Psalm 125 / 242
"Beati [omnes] qui Tarrient [Timent] Dominum," [Psalm] 127 / 242
"De Profundis Clamavi," [Psalm] 129 / 242
Ad Male Minisque Somniantem / 242
"Memento Domine David," [Psalm] 131 / 243
"Ecce quoniam [quam] Bonum," [Psalm] 132 / 243
For Sore Eyes / 243
Ad Adulterium, "Domine," [Psalm] 138 / "Probasti Me," 138 / 243
Contra Inimicos, "Domine Clamavi," [Psalm] 140 / 243
"Voce Mea ad Dominum," [Psalm] 141 / 243
"Domine Exaudi," [Psalm] 142 / 244
Si Quis Uxorem Odiat / 244
If to Divide with Any Man / 244
"Lauda Jerusalem, Dominum," [Psalm] 147 / 244
"Laudate Dominum de Celis," [Psalm] 148 / 244
"Cantate Domino," [Psalm] 149 / 244

An Experiment of the [Shoulder] Blade or Shoulder Bone of an Ass, Hare, Cock or Hen, and per This Is Bound a Man, Woman, Beast, or Spirit, of What Kind and Condition Soever / 245

Experimentum ad Inveniendum Furem / 247

Alias / 249

An Experiment for Things Stolen, Oft Proved and Never Deceiving / 249
  [Further Elaborations on the Summoning of Sibilla] / 252
  A Licence for Sibilla to Come and Go at All Times / 254

An Experiment to Be Seen in a Crystal Stone / 255
  A Licence for Askariell with His Fellows to Depart / 257

A Prayer to Be Said before This or Any Other Experiment / 258

Ad Mensium Nimietates / 258

To Prove Theft / 258

Ut Amorem Concilias / 259

Against All Fevers / 259

Also for Any Ague or Fever / 260

For Pains in the Stomach or Heart by Witchcraft / 260

A Medicine for Persons Possessed / 260

An Incense or Fume to Drive out Evil Spirits / 260

An Oil to Anoint Persons Afflicted with Witchcraft / 261

Ad Dysenteriam / 261

Ad Partum Difficilem / 261

To Draw Out a Tooth / 261

Stolen or Lost, Whether / 262

To Know If Anyone Be Bewitched or Not / 262

Aliter, for One Bewitched / 262

[A Herb against Witchcraft] / 263

To Hurt a Witch, Thief, or Enemy / 263

To Help Any Bewitched Man or Beast / 263

Alias / 264

Another Way Approved / 264

Another Way / 264

An Experiment for This Purpose, per Friar Bacon / 265

Another per Which All Witches Are Compelled to Come and Confess Their Wicked Deeds / 266

Another Way to Help Those That Are Bewitched, or Stroken with Fairies or Otherwise / 267

Of Fairies / 268

For Fascination / 270

If the Hag or Witch Ride You or Your Cattle / 271

For Prick of a Thorn / 272

Pro Morbo Caduco / 272

For a Fairy Stroke / 272

A Receipt for Healing with Clouts / 273

To Heal All Curable Wounds with a Plate ♄ That They Shall Neither Fester, Canker, nor Corrupt while the Party Liveth / 274

For Fractures and Discoxations / 278

Experimentum qui to Ride a Long Journey / 279

Ut Sis Invisibilis / 280

Alias ut Invisibilis, Fine / 280

Of the Order and Condition of the Spirits / 281

De Natura et Formis Spirituum / 282
- Et Imprimis de Saturni Spiritibus / 282
- ♃ / 283
- ♂ / 283
- ☉ / 283
- ♀ / 284
- ☿ / 284
- ☽ / 285

Ad Habendum Vera Responsa de Omnibus Questionibus / 285

Pro Invisibilitate / 286

To Have Thy Desire of All Things Carried and Brought to Thy Hand, or, to Wit, to What Place Thou Wilt Assign / 287

[An Experiment for Love] / 289

[A Spirit of Love] / 290

A Call to Oberion / 291

Consecratio Circuli / 294

[The Summoning of Golias into a Crystal to Find a Malefactor] / 299

[The Summoning of Satan, Part 2] / 300

[The Summoning of Satan, Part 1] / 302

[The Summoning of Satan, Part 3] / 305

All These Are to Be Called into a Crystal / 306

For the Toothache / 307

A Godly Way to Have a Familiar Spirit, Which Will Tell Always Your Desire without Any Hurt or Fear / 308

[An Incense to Call Spirits] / 311

[To Make Virgin Parchment] / 311

An Experiment with Characters, with Other Manner of Writing to Be Set on Images for to Cause a Thief to Appear before You, and to Come to You in What Place Soever You Be / 312

Alias / 313

An Experiment of A Azaell / 315

Experimentum ad Inveniendum Furem Latronem / 319

Alias / 321

To Make a Thief Bring Again the Goods Which He Hath Stolen, to the Same Place or Any Other Place Whatsoever at Any Time Thou Will Appoint Him to Come / 321

[Herbs for Fever] / 323

To See a Thief in Thy Sleep / 323

Pro Amore / 324

When You Are in Dread of Thieves, or of Your Enemies / 325

[A Curious Figure] / 326

An Experiment to Talk with Spirits / 327

Invocatio Spiritus Bealphares / 329
- Sequitur Vinculum / 333

Consecratio Circuli / 334

A Prayer to Be Said before You Come out of the Circle / 336

[The Seal of Paymon] / 337

The Call [of Oriens] / 338

Aphorismum [A Selection from the Arbatel] / 340
- Character Ejus / 343
- Character / 344
- Character / 344
- Character / 345
- Character / 346
- [Character] / 346
- Character / 346

To Go Invisible / 347

Alter / 347

Alter / 347

Alter / 347

[Protection from Enemies] / 348

For the Bleeding at the Nose, or Vein, or Wound / 348

Alter / 348

To Win at Shooting / 348

To Obtain a Gift / 348

A Charm for Children / 348

For the Toothache / 349

To Go Invisible / 349

[To Be Beloved] / 349

To Play at Dice / 349

For the Falling Sickness / 351

Experiment upon Several Accounts / 351

Confessio / 365

[A Talisman for Protection and for the Circle, Part 1] / 368

[Magical Seals and Instructions] / 372

[Unknown Diagram] / 373

[On the Influence of the Planet Herschel, or Uranus] / 374

[A Talisman for Protection and for the Circle, Part 2] / 375
  [The Talisman] / 375

[Instructions for Creating the Circle, Part 1] / 375

[A Concoction to View Spirits] / 375

[Instructions for Creating the Circle, Part 2] / 376
  [Circles] / 376
  [Circles] / 377

[The Magical Roll] / 381
  [Planetary Angels and Characters] / 382
  [A Prayer of Protection] / 383
  [The Measure of Christ] / 384
  [The Three Nails of the Passion] / 385
  [A Wound of Christ?] / 386

Of a Crystal Stone / 390

Consideranda / 394

To Prove Theft / 395

An Experiment to Know Whether the Suspected be Guilty or Not, Also to Know Whether a Woman Be with Child, Corrupt in Living, or Any Such Thing Which Must Be Wrought as Followeth / 396

Oremus / 397

Alias / Experimentum Panis [Part 1] / 398

Oremus / 398

Charm for the Toothache / 399

A Charm for the Toothache or Ague That Be Wrote on a Quarter Plat of Paper in These Large Letters / 399

[The Experiment of the Bread, Part 2] / 400

Alias / 400

To Know If a Man Suspected for a Thief Be Guilty / 400

The Character / 400

The Prayer / 401

Ut Fur Consiliatur, Furtum Foyle / 401

Figura / 402

Alias / 402

Alias / 402

Figura, Alias Est Exp[erimen]t[um], Figura / 403

An Experiment to Hide Treasure under the Earth or to Leave Clothes or Any Other Thing Forth of Doors All Night / 404

[On a Night-Spell] / 404

A Bond to Bind Thieves That Have or Would Have Robbed Any Man of His Money or Goods to Cause Them Come Again, Bringing the Goods to the Right Owner, or Else to Be Taken with the Robbery / 405

To Excommunicate a Spirit for No Appearance / 405

A General Curse Following for All Spirits Both for Stone and Circle / 406

A Conjuration for the Light to Be Used in Any Work,
That Is Practised in All Cases / 409

Here Follow the Names of Certain Spirits as They Serve in Their Aptest Operation, as Hath Been Proved / 409
- Showers / 409
- For Theft and to Bring Them Again / 410
- Pro Amore / 410

Temporis Nota ad Operandum / 410

[More Names of Spirits] / 411

The Circle / 412

Experimentum Nobile Fili[ci]s Anglicum; Fern on Saint John Baptist's Even / 413

Benedictio Chartae / 413

This Most Holy Ligatum Following Shall Be Said Now or Before the Exorcism of the Fire Casting Out Devils and All Evil Spirits from Men, Women, Children, or Beasts / 414

These Following Are the Seals of the Earth / 416

[A Magical Lamen] / 418

Here Followeth the Names of the Angels of the Planets, and First of ♄ / 419

Names of the Angels That Ruleth Different Hours of the Day / 423

De Spiritu Merezium / 424

Ad Invocandum Spiritum Secrete in Camera / 428

[Times for Working] / 430
- Ad Operandi Bonum / 430
- Dies Prohibiti / 430

Ad Habendum Vera Responsa de Omnibus Questionibus / 431

For One That Is Bewitched / 432

The Figure of a Circle for the First Hour of the Lord's Day in Springtime / 433

To Explain the Week, First of the Lord's Day / 434
- Consideration of the Lord's Day / 434
    - The Angels of the Lord's Day / 434
    - The Angels of the Air Ruling on the Lord's Day / 434
    - His Ministers / 434

The Wind Which the Angels of the Air Abovesaid Are Under / 434
The Angel of the Fourth Heaven Ruling on the Lord's Day, Which Ought to Be Called from the Four Parts of the World / 434
The Perfume of the Lord's Day / 435
The Conjuration of the Lord's Day / 435
Considerations of Monday / 436
The Angels of Monday / 436
The Angels of the Air Ruling on Monday / 436
His Ministers / 436
The Wind Which the Said Angels of the Aire Are Subject To / 436
The Angels of the First Heaven Ruling on Monday, Which Ought to Be Called from the Four Parts of the World / 436
The Perfume of Monday / 436
The Conjuration of Monday / 437
Considerations of Tuesday / 437
The Angels of Tuesday / 437
The Angels of the Air Ruling on Tuesday / 437
His Ministers / 438
The Wind to Which the Said Angels Are Subject / 438
The Angels of the Fifth Heaven Ruling on Tuesday, Which Ought to Be Called from the Four Parts of the World / 438
The Perfume of Tuesday / 438
[The Conjuration of Tuesday] / 438
Considerations of Wednesday / 439
The Angels of Wednesday / 439
The Angels of the Air Ruling on Wednesday / 439
Ministers / 439
The Wind Which the Said Angels of the Air Are Subject To / 439
The Angels of the Second Heaven Governing Wednesday, Which Ought to Be Called from the Four Parts of the World / 439
The Fumigation of Wednesday / 440
The Conjuration of Wednesday / 440
Considerations of Thursday / 441
The Angels of Thursday / 441
The Angels of the Air Governing Thursday / 441
Ministers / 441
The Winds Which the Said Angels of the Air Are Under / 441
The Perfume of Thursday / 442
The Conjuration of Thursday / 442

Considerations of Friday / 442
The Angels of Friday / 442
The Angels of the Air Ruling on Friday / 442
Ministers / 443
The Wind Which the Said Angels of the Air Are Under / 443
Angels of the Third Heaven, Ruling on Friday, Which Are to Be Called from the Four Parts of the World / 443
The Perfume of Friday / 443
The Conjuration of Friday / 443
Considerations of Saturday, or the Sabbath Day / 444
The Angels of Saturday / 444
The Angels of the Air Ruling on Saturday / 444
Ministers / 444
The Wind Which the Said Angels of the Air Aforesaid Are Under / 444
The Fumigation of Saturday / 444
The Conjuration of Saturday / 445
Hours of the Day/Hours of the Night / 445
[Angels of the Seasons] / 446
Angels of the Spring / 446
The Head of the Sign of the Spring / 446
The Name of the Earth in the Spring / 446
The Names of the Sun and Moon in the Spring / 446
The Angels of the Summer / 446
The Head of the Sign in the Summer / 446
The Name of the Earth in Summer / 446
The Names of the Sun and ☽ in Summer / 446
The Angels of Autumn / 446
The Head of the Sign in Autumn / 446
The Name of the Earth in Autumn / 447
The Names of the ☉ and ☽ in Autumn / 447
The Angels of the Winter / 447
The Head of the Sign in Winter / 447
The Name of the Earth in Winter / 447
The Names of the Sun and Moon in Winter / 447
The Consecration and Benedictions, and First of the Benediction of the Circle / 447
The Benediction of Perfumes / 447

The Exorcism of Fire, upon Which the Perfumes Are to Be Put / 447
Of the Garment and Pentacle / 448
An Oration to Be Said When the Vesture Is Put On / 448
Of the Circle and the Composition Thereof / 449

Thou Mayst Call a Spirit Under per This Prayer to Appear in a Crystal Glass Held per Thy Self, a Maid, or Child / 450

The Colour of the Planets / 455

Influences of the ☽ / 455

Hours of the Day / 456

The Ring or Cup of Divination / 457

This Scheme from John Heydon's *Holy Guide*, Page 160 / 457

[Planetary Substances] / 459

The Number of the Planets and Their Characters / 460

Numbers of the Days of the Week / 460

[A Talisman for Games] / 460

Dreams / 461

To Know the Certain Hour of Any Planet / 462

[On the Olympic Spirits] / 464

[Seals for Goetic Spirits] / 467

[A Talisman for Influence] / 470

Clavicula: The Magical Ceremonies of Solomon the King / 470
Gaap's Seal / Gaap's Seal / 470
Malphas / 471
A Mighty Prince / 471
Furcas / 471
Buer, a President to Be Called When ☉ Is in ♑: / 471
Remove, an earl / 472
Dantalion, a mighty duke / 472
Decarabia, a marquis / 472

A Table of Angels Ruling Every Hour of the Day and Night, with Their Planets / 473
The Angels of the Hours / 476
A Table of the Names of the Hours / 478

[Talismans for Conjuration and Other Purposes] / 479
The Names of God / 479
The Seals of the Earth / 481

Of the Planetary Hours / 482

[Astrological Tables] / 483

To Erect a Figure / 485

Instructions [for Summoning Spirits] / 487

[Preparations for the Art] / 487

Talismans, Mysterious Figures, Images & c. / 488
The Manner to Raise a Figure Cabalistic or a Talisman in the Name and Day of One of the Seven Planets / 488
Influences / 489
Of the Working the Figures, Characters, Talismans & c. / 490
[The Grand Pentacle of Solomon] / 491
Enforcing Particulars / 492
Of the Perfume Proper for the Seven Planets Are as Follows / 493
Orations, Invocations, and Conjurations / 493
Further Remarks Respecting Sigils Amiable / 494
The Prayer / 496
The Conjuration / 496
The Spirits' Chain / 499
Conjuration for the △ Fire / 499
When the Spirits Appear / 502
Licence to Depart / 502

[Talismans for Virtues] / 503

[Magical Rings] / 504

[Various Talismans] / 505

[Untitled Poem] / 506

[More Talismans] / 507
In Hoc Vinci / 507
Prosperitas / 507

Hymn by Princess Olive / 508

[More Talismans] / 509

[William Browne's "Behold O God IN RIvers of My Tears"] / 510

Experiments for Birds, Fish, Coneys, Gathered Out of Divers Authors / 511
- A Very Good Bait to Angle / 511
- Alio / 511
- To Take Fish with Your Hand / 511
- To Take Birds with Your Hand / 511
- To Take All Manner of Fowl That Eat Corn / 511
- To Take Fish in a Pool or River / 512
- To Take Fish / 512
- To Comfort Fish to Bite / 512
- A Bait for Fish / 512
- To Take a Pike / 512
- To Take Fish with the Angle Rod / 513
- Pro Eodem / 513
- Pro Eodem / 513
- To Take Fish with Your Hand / 513
- Alia / 513
- To Take Coneys / 513
- Pro Eodem / 514
- To Take Coneys or Deer / 514
- To Take Coneys / 514
- Ad Aves Capiendas / 514
- To Take Doves / 514
- Ad Capiendas Aves, Pasceres, Cornes, et Columbas & c. / 514
- Si Vis Accipere Columbas / 515
- Ad Aves Capiendas / 515
- To Take Birds / 515
- To Take Cranes / 515
- To Take Birds / 515
- To Take Coneys / 515
- [To Frighten Cattle] / 515
- To Make Cider Fly, or to Be Smart / 515
- How to Make a Scent for Claret or White Wine / 516
- To Make a Scent for Sweet Wine / 516
- Ditto / 516

Hogshead of White That Lost Its Colour / 516
Claret That Hath Lost His Colour / 517
If Claret Be Small / 517
If Claret Will Not Wine / 517
Claret or White, If They Be Small / 517
If a Butt of Sack Have Lost His Colour / 518
If Sack Drink Eager / 518
If Sack Drink Hard, Use This for a Hogshead / 518
If Sack Drink Small, Use These / 519
To Make a Butt of Muscadine / 519
How to Make a . . . . for the Butt of Muscadine, Before Mentioned / 519
If B[r]own Bastard Be Eager / 519
If a Butt of Sack Be Cider, or Ropy or Look Brown / 520
When to Rack Rhenish Wine / 520
Wine Stink and Corrupt / 520
How to Make Hippocras for to Fill Two Gallons / 520
By Which to Make Vinegar / 521
To Make a Flavour / 521
A True Receipt to Find Any Piece of Either Spanish or French Wine / 521
To Fine Any Piece of Wine That Is Qualish or Brown, Be It What Sort Soever / 521
How to Make Wine Sweet That Stinketh, or That Hath an Ill Savour, or That Is Grown Musty / 522
How to Make a Piece of Qu[a]l[it]y Spanish Wine, Fine / 522
For Any French Wine That Comes over upon the Lee That Is Grown Brown and Faint / 523
To Make a Hugher That Is Excellent / 523
To Make Muscadel of Jeane / 523
For Bastard That Drinketh Hard Be Malmsey / 524
A Pleasant Scent or Savour for a Butt of Muscadel / 524
A Perfect Cure for the Dropsy. Probatum Est. / 524
For the Gout, as Good as Before / 525

[Quotations from Agrippa] / 525

To Distil All Manner of Flowers without an Alembic / 525

[On the Moon] / 526

Aphorisms / 532

Latin and English Names / 533

Appendix: Alternative Illustrations / 535

Bibliography / 541
Manuscript Sources / 541
Printed Sources / 542

Index / 569

Acknowledgments

This book would not have been possible without Stephanie Pope's article on the topic, which drew attention to a work that had previously gone largely unnoticed within the scholarly and occult communities. The Bodleian's Weston Library provided hours of access and permission to photograph the book, without which this work would have been impossible. Joseph Peterson called this work to my attention and gave me the first opportunity to view it via scans we ordered from the library.

Thanks to Casey Hickey for his discussion on useful fonts and to Monica Czwarno for making an extended stay in New York City possible. The Pforzheimer Collection at the New York Public Library, the British Library Maps Reading Room, David Morrison at the Worcester Cathedral Library, and the Kroch Library at Cornell provided important materials for context of what appeared within. Thanks also to Clifford Hartleigh Low for helping me try to decipher the astrological sections, Andrew Phillip Smith for his help with the Welsh passage, Jeremy Harte for insight into Bristol folklore, and Kate Leach for her translation from the Welsh and Latin. Bobby Derie gave helpful comments on the first version of this introduction, and Professor László Sándor Chardonnens gave important assistance in interpreting some curious Latin passages. I also offer my apologies to anyone whose contributions I have overlooked.

Disclaimer

The contents in this book are historical references used for teaching purposes only. The publisher and the author assume no liability for any injuries caused to the reader that may result from the reader's use of content contained in this publication and recommend common sense when contemplating the practices described in the work.

All recipes and herbal formulas are given for historical understanding and reference. Please consult a standard reference source or an expert herbalist or brewer to learn more about the possible effects of certain herbs used within spells, charms, and procedures.

Llewellyn Worldwide does not suggest, support, or condone the animal mistreatment, the animal sacrifices, or the hunting or fishing techniques detailed in this book. These practices should be viewed as a historical curiosity that has no place in our modern world—and could end up endangering the user's health and that of others. The reader may revivify ritual practices with symbolic substitutions rather than harming live animals.

Burning any substance should be conducted in a well-ventilated area, with appropriate precautions against fire having been made.

Introduction

Dan Harms

The wind howls as the small group of men trudge across the heath, the rain whipping against their long coats. Three of them heft shovels on their shoulders. Two others, stepping carefully to avoid spatters of mud on their silk stockings, pass a bottle back and forth under an umbrella. One before them holds a lantern near the ground, to illuminate the path and avoid attention. A young man walks in front, his strides uncertain in the darkness, his delicate scholar's hands gripping the two forks of a tree branch. On its far end, a length of cord wraps around a sovereign, or gold coin.

It should work, the scholar assures himself. The piece of wood—or "Mosaical rod," named after the Biblical prophet—had been cut at sunrise on the summer solstice from a hazel tree. Attaching the coin had been trickier. It had fallen off the end already, sending the young men scrambling in the grass to find it. He hoped the cord would not slip this time.

He had risked so much already for this venture. A few evenings ago, he had visited the grave of a recently deceased neighbour in the churchyard. Standing at the grave's head with his head bowed, as if praying, he had instead chanted a memorised incantation calling upon a saint to bring the dead person's spirit to him that night. He had knelt by the grave, heart racing, to scoop up dirt from the grave into a handkerchief. That night, with the handkerchief under his head, he had seen the heath in his disordered dreams.

Will they find what they seek? And if so, will anyone talk? The harsh penalties under King James's law for treasure hunting are rarely enforced—but no one wants a year in prison, punctuated with four sessions in the stocks and the jeers of the entire town. Further, the treasure trove they seek belongs to the present king. Then again, as the scholar's friends had pointed out, where is the king tonight? Certainly not in the rain on a Worcestershire heath.

The branch seems to twist in his rain-slickened hands. At his signal, the group stops. He steps back as the three men with shovels circle the piece of ground at which he pointed. One of the rich men hands the bottle to his fellow before stepping forward, covering the scholar's head with the umbrella. The scholar wipes his rain-damp hands on his shirt and pulls a thick manuscript out of a satchel. Flipping through the pages covered with his spidery handwriting, he finds the proper passage. His friend lifts the lantern, and the scholar reads the incantations to dismiss the spirits from the ground, allowing them to recover the treasure…

Did this occur? Barring the discovery of new documents, it must be considered entirely speculative—but it could have. We do have the manuscript, at least, and what it reveals is fascinating.

Douce MS. 116: A Description of the Manuscript

Whether or not Bodleian Library Douce Manuscript 116 was ever used in conjuration, its state of preservation is impressive. We know of at least four, possibly five, owners of the text over the centuries, with enough gaps between owners to suggest many more. Nonetheless, the manuscript, now in the possession of the Bodleian Library, is in excellent condition, save for the separation of the front cover from the book block.

Popular culture would have us believe that magical books are huge, thick tomes, clearly labelled and robustly illustrated. Some do meet that model, but most are small works intended to be portable and nondescript, written solely for the copyist's needs. This work lies somewhere between the two ideals, measuring 9¼ by 6¾ inches, with 445 pages of paper, with additional papers glued in in at the beginning and end, and another bifold leaf bound in at pages 428 to 431. The book was bound in plain brown leather; based on the unornamented style of binding and the extension of our second author's text to the endpapers, it happened before or during his ownership in the late eighteenth century. At a later date, an owner added gold rolls and the word "Magick" in gold to the spine.[1]

The Bodleian Library's *Summary Catalogue* describes it as "magical incantations, formulae, experiments, and drawings, in almost haphazard order," which is a fair assessment. The work is a magical miscellany, collecting material from other manuscript, printed, and possibly oral sources. The original copyist likely added materials as he found useful, in a sloppy and often careless hand. What sets Douce MS. 116 apart from other magical manuscripts is the amount of material its subsequent owners have added. Some of this amounts to side comments, glosses, decipherment of the original text, or notes to make it more useful to later owners. In addition, we also see entirely new sections appearing before or after the original material, supplementing the work with material reflecting their own philosophies of ritual magic and occult cosmology. Much of the text is in English, with passages in Latin and Welsh in the original author's work.[2]

This treasury of magical lore is not an easy one with which to work. The original copyist of the manuscript made numerous mistakes when transcribing the text,

1. Pope, "Darcke and Clowdie Speeches," 209.

2. Bodleian Library and Madan, *A Summary Catalogue of Western Manuscripts in the Bodleian Library at Oxford*, 4:527.

using the wrong word—changing "hour" to "hound," or "Aves" to "Amen"—or adding or removing letters and words, likely due to haste of copying. The page numbering, most of which is likely Harrington's work, changes repeatedly over the course of the manuscript, suggesting the author simply numbered pages without maintaining the principle that the right-hand leaf should always be odd. Errors in the text abound, with muddled words, passages scratched out, and others corrected to the extent that it is sometimes hard to tell what the authors intended.

What follows is the best version of the text I was able to create and edit, given these challenges. I hope that this edition will lead to further discussion and examination of the original manuscript, so that it may share its mysteries with a much broader audience.

The People of Douce MS. 116

The figures who owned or contributed to the work, creating layers of different usage and interpretation still visible to the readers, truly make this manuscript unique. Let's get to know them.

The First Occult Philosopher

The Manuscript

Our first author never identifies themselves, and no external evidence indicates who it might be. Two early ceremonies for finding stolen goods and protection against spirits and witches insert the initial "W." for the person's name, which might indicate that the copyist's initial was "W." or they had a recurring client with that initial.[3]

The religious background of the author remains a mystery. The repeated, but not consistent, substitution of "Amen" for "Aves" suggests that the owner was likely unaware of Catholic doctrine, but it is more likely a sign of the author's general carelessness. A better indicator might be the inclusion of an abbreviated passage from Reginald Scot's *Discouerie of Witchcraft* (1584), in which certain prayers and psalms are said before an image to grant over thirty thousand years of pardon.[4] Such a concept would have been alien outside of the Roman Catholic doctrine of purgatory, which the Church of England adopted as a key point separating their beliefs from the other faith. The inclusion of this material indicates an adherence to Catholic beliefs, while the abbreviation suggests the copyist of this book of magic didn't want the use of this particular item made explicit—a notable decision in a book concerned with the summoning of ghosts and demons.

Did our author practise magic themselves? Some people in the seventeenth century, as today, are interested out of curiosity, so this is always an important question to ask. Any determination of whether the material within a ritual magic manuscript was used is difficult; even a practicing magician might not use much of the material copied, or the person who used the magic might have come before the present copyist in the stream of transmission. Our author, in a section providing three different operations to create wax images, mentions making use of all three of them, so it seems they tried at least some of the rituals elsewhere in the book. We also see the insertion of the "W." initial mentioned previously and the mention of a place called

3. Manuscript pages 2–4.

4. Scot, *The Discouerie of Witchcraft*, 234 (book 12, chapter 9); manuscript page 63.

"Stouten Heath" in an incantation to dismiss spirits guarding treasure, where we will explore later.[5] Thus, the book has been customised toward a practitioner's interests.

No dates appear in the manuscript, but some rough idea of the period is suggested by the seventeenth-century handwriting and the contents. For example, in the section derived from the magical manual *Heptameron*, the perfume of Sunday is given as "red sanders." This indicates that this was taken from the 1665 edition of Turner's translation, given that the previous 1655 edition translates this incorrectly as "red wheat."[6] The manuscript has parallels to later works as well. A procedure for creating a "Mosaical rod" has close parallels to one published in J. M.'s *Sports and Pastimes* (1675)—which is the earliest occurrence in the Early English Books Online database and predates the first in the *Oxford English Dictionary*—but it is uncertain whether J. M. is the originator of the term.[7] Another source for some procedures is *A Whip for the Devil* (1683), an anonymous anti-Catholic polemic purporting to show the works of exorcist priests, although the manuscript has several differences from the printed version.[8] On manuscript page 383, the scribe changes a date copied from another text from 1659 to 1697, so this might be the date of copying.

We have only a few clues to the location where this book might have been written. The first is the mention of a "Stouten Heath," noted earlier. Seeking out "Stouten," "Stoughton," or "Stoulton" across the United Kingdom turns up four separate places in Leicestershire, Surrey, West Sussex, and Worcestershire. It is possible that one might find a "heath," uncultivated land covered with scrub, near each one of these places, which was referred to as "Stoughton Heath" locally—but only one, in Worcestershire, once had an explicitly named "Stoulton Heath" nearby, according to eighteenth-century maps.

Stoulton, Worcestershire, is a tiny town to the southeast of Worcester. As of this writing, it consists of a church dating back to the Norman period, several houses, a used-car dealership, and a bed-and-breakfast. To the southeast, Stoulton Heath has been cultivated and its pond drained. The former heath is now covered with placid farms and fields, along with a small, lightly forested area with trails where locals can walk their dogs. It's hard to imagine anything supernatural taking place here, but our author was, at some point, keen on investigating it to uncover riches.

Other indications also point us toward the Worcestershire area. Although the manuscript is almost entirely in English and Latin, phrases in Welsh mingle with both on multiple occasions. The author also records a Marian variation on the "out

5. Manuscript page 194.

6. Pseudo-Agrippa, *Fourth Book* (1665), 89; Pseudo-Agrippa, *Fourth Book* (1655), 89.

7. J. M., *Sports and Pastimes*, 31–32.

8. *A Whip for the Devil*, 80–85.

fire, in frost" charm, with the other known examples only being found along the Welsh border.[9]

Worcestershire has many links to famous ritual magicians, as Stephen Skinner and David Rankine have observed.[10] Two famous figures have passing connections to the region. In 1553, John Dee was presented to the rectory of Upton-upon-Severn, although he seems not to have lived there and rented it out until he lost possession of it.[11] The antiquary and magician Elias Ashmole served briefly as the excise commissioner for Worcester, arriving on December 23, 1645, and departing on July 24, 1646, when the town surrendered to Parliamentary forces.[12] This was a few years before he began investigating and collecting manuscripts on alchemy and magic.[13]

One individual with deeper ties to Worcestershire was Dee's scryer, Edward Kelley. Kelley was born in Worcester in 1555 and may have attended grammar school there before departing for Oxford.[14] On November 22, 1582, he made an excursion to Blockley, which was then in Worcestershire; the corresponding entry in Dee's diary, to which Kelley had access, was later mutilated. At Blockley, Kelley and John Husey supposedly dug at Northwick Hill, uncovering documents and a mysterious red powder, which Kelley would later credit with his success at alchemy. He returned with these items to Dee on March 22.[15] On June 5, Edward's brother Thomas came to him to tell him that Edward's wife, who had been staying at Blockley, had left her lodgings there, that he was wanted for counterfeiting, and that Husey had turned on him.[16]

Other individuals with magical ties also turn up in Worcestershire in the early modern period. The poet William Neville (1497–c. 1545) served as Worcestershire's commissioner of the police and owned extensive estates in this land through marriage. Legal challenges to this property led him to engage the services of several magical practitioners, including a Richard Jones of Oxford, and thence to accusations of treason. Jones was imprisoned in the Tower of London; he wrote from his cell that the Earl of Worcester would be willing to vouch for his freedom.[17] In the early seventeenth century, the local tutor and doctor John Lambe was prosecuted repeatedly for

9. Another possibility derives from the astrological tables, which are presumably corrected for the author's location. These might help in finding the position of the author, but without knowing the year or the methods used to calculate the houses, this would be a difficult task.
10. Skinner and Rankine, *Practical Angel Magic*, 21–22, 43–45.
11. Fell-Smith, *John Dee (1527–1608)*, 13–14, 78.
12. Ashmole, Lilly, and Burman, *Lives of Those Eminent Antiquaries*, 299–302.
13. Feola, "Elias Ashmole's Collections and Views about John Dee," 531.
14. Wood, Bliss, and University of Oxford, *Athenae Oxonienses*, 1:125.
15. Woolley, *The Queen's Conjuror*, 190–91.
16. Dee, *True & Faithful Relation*, 5–6; Woolley, *The Queen's Conjuror*, 215.
17. Klaassen and Wright, *The Magic of Rogues*, 21–55.

using magic for summoning spirits and uncovering lost objects. Prisons were more accessible to outsiders than they are today, so his cell in Worcester Castle became a popular spot for visitors who wished to see him practise magic. The authorities packed Lambe off to London, where he gained his freedom and continued in his ways until killed by a mob.[18] The Rosicrucian author John Heydon grew up and was tutored on the border between Worcestershire and Warwickshire.[19] Overall, there was little overlap between these figures' times in Worcester, yet it might indicate the existence of networks or traditions of which we know little today. Indeed, the magician William Wycherley confessed in 1549 that Worcestershire was one of four English counties with "a great nomber" of conjurors, although the source does not state his reasons for this assertion.[20]

As for Stoulton itself, Samuel Sandys (1615–85) acquired the parish in 1636.[21] Sandys would later become MP for Droitwich.[22] He committed himself to the Royalists during the English Civil War, becoming governor of Worcester and raising troops at his own expense. He incurred considerable debts to do so, and it may be that he or his family were forced to relinquish Stoulton as a result.[23] Although we may not know the timing of or reasons for this, the parish did eventually pass to a family of another famous individual: John Somers (1651–1716).[24]

Somers was born in or near, educated in, and was elected MP for Worcester, serving in addition as counsel to its cathedral. He later became Lord High Chancellor and Baron of Evesham, as well as President of the Royal Society and a noted collector whose magical manuscripts later came into the possession of Sir Hans Sloane.[25]

Could any of these individuals tied to Stoulton be our treasure hunters? Nothing exists in his published biographies that identifies Somers as having an interest in magic—although these works are mostly focused on his political career—and his handwriting seems dissimilar to that in the manuscript.[26] Sachse's biography notes his studious nature and his mastery of seven languages, including Greek and Latin,

18. Goldstein, "The Life and Death of John Lambe," 19–20.

19. Curry, "Heydon, John."

20. Foxe, Cranmer, and Nichols, *Narratives of the Days of the Reformation*, 335.

21. Willis-Bund and Page, "Parishes, Stoulton."

22. Henning, "Sandys, Samuel I (1615–85)."

23. Atkin and Worcestershire County Council, *Worcestershire under Arms*.

24. Willis-Bund and Page, "Parishes, Stoulton."

25. Chardonnens, "Magic Manuscripts from Somers and Jekyll in the Collections of the British Library," 3.

26. Chardonnens, "Magic Manuscripts from Somers and Jekyll in the Collections of the British Library," 5, 7; Sachse, *Lord Somers*.

so it is unlikely he would have copied a text with so many errors.[27] Also, Somers's legal training would have made him well aware that any hidden treasure belonged to the Crown and not to the owner of the land, although knowledge of a law does not ensure compliance.[28] The Sandys family did have multiple individuals who attended New College at Oxford, and their debts might have led some of them to delving for treasure—but certainly others in the same area would have had the same motivations. Thus, it is likely we may never know the author.

Of the people mentioned in the manuscript as sources for its material, the most notable was William Hodges, to whom the copyist attributes an anti-witchcraft procedure dating to November 18, 1652. This could have been the William Hodges, DD, of Exeter College, Oxford, who served as the Rector of Ripple from 1643 and Archdeacon of Worcester from 1645 until his death in 1675. I have not located any of Hodges's papers with this procedure, however.[29] The manuscript also refers to a "Master Boney" as a source of incantations. A husbandman named Boney Gelfe of Ripple is mentioned in the Worcester quarter session rolls in 1620, but this was at least half a century before the book's composition.[30]

The Late Seventeenth Century

In many ways, the seventeenth century was a crucial time for British magic. The greatest number of surviving magical manuscripts survive from this period. Further, the Civil War and the Protectorate brought about a pause in Crown censorship, leading to the official publication of several books, including Agrippa's *Three Books of Occult Philosophy* (1650); the *Fourth Book* falsely attributed to him, compiled with the *Heptameron* and other treatises (1655 and 1665); *Of the Supreme Mysteries of Nature* (1655 and 1660), attributed to Paracelsus; a partial edition of the *Ars Notoria* (1657); and a new edition of Reginald Scot's *Discovery of Witchcraft*, expanded with more incantations and magical lore (1665). Afterward, such publication slowed until the nineteenth century, making these works prized possessions in the libraries of cunning folk and other practitioners and aficionados of ritual magic for centuries.

Many of the practices described in these books were prohibited under the Witchcraft Act of 1604. If a person called up or interacted with an evil spirit, removed any person or portion thereof from their graves, or injured or killed anyone with magic, the penalty of the law was death. Using magic for the discovery of treasure, the discovery of lost or stolen items, or the injury of cattle or goods would lead to a year's

27. Sachse, *Lord Somers*, 14.

28. Dillinger, *Magical Treasure Hunting*, 12–13.

29. University of Oxford, *Alumni Oxonienses*, 2:724.

30. Bund, *Worcester County Records: The Quarter Sessions Rolls, Part II*, 721.

imprisonment, with four sessions on the pillory, with death for repeat offenders.[31] Although most practitioners would have been aware of the law, it was only occasionally enforced, and then usually against purported witches and not cunning folk. Between 1663 and 1699, 144 witch trials are recorded in our surviving records; although no records survive in most cases regarding the outcome, the lack of documentation of executions makes it likely that most of the accused were acquitted.[32]

Witchcraft and magic did serve a broader purpose for the religious: proof of the existence of the Divine. To fend off a perceived tide of materialism and atheism, authors such as Joseph Glanvil (*Saducismus Triumphatus*, 1681) and Richard Bovet (*Pandaemonium*, 1684) marshalled numerous accounts of witches, devils, fairies, ghosts, poltergeists, and other supernatural beings to establish the existence of a spiritual world. Even those who did believe were more likely to distinguish between magic and witchcraft as existing phenomena—as the Bible proclaimed—and the relevance of these beliefs to their lives. By the end of this period, the elite hardly took charges of magical practice seriously. In 1676 to 1682, the French court was shaken by the "Affair of the Poisons," in which accusations of poisoning, Black Masses, and other blasphemous practices reached the highest levels of the nobility. Nonetheless, the British attitude toward these events was mainly befuddlement, and some of those charged in France sought refuge across the Channel.[33]

Coupled with the hesitance of the believers was the critique and ridicule of sceptics, through which "magic would increasingly come to be associated with the ignorant, the marginalised and the ill-educated."[34] This association was not necessarily based in fact. James Scott, the Duke of Monmouth, was found to be in possession of "a manuscript of spells, charms and conjurations, songs, receipts, and prayers, all written in his own hand" at his execution in 1685.[35] Goodwin Wharton, a member of Parliament, carried on a long-term relationship with a cunning woman named Mary Parish, seeking treasure with magic and eventually becoming the King of the Fairies without ever viewing these beings.[36] Nonetheless, labelling magic as a lower-class amusement for the childish and unintelligent proved to be an effective strategy for discrediting its practitioners.

31. *Statutes of the Realm*, 5 Eliz. c. 16; ibid., I Jac. I c. 12. See also Newton and Bath, *Witchcraft and the Act of 1604*.

32. Maxwell-Stuart, *The British Witch*, 295.

33. Young, *Magic as a Political Crime in Medieval and Early Modern England*, 188–93.

34. Young, *Magic as a Political Crime in Medieval and Early Modern England*, 184.

35. Great Britain Royal Commission on Historical Manuscripts, *Third Report of the Royal Commission on Historical Manuscripts*, 41.

36. This is a vastly complex situation, on which see Clark, *Goodwin Wharton*, and Timbers, *The Magical Adventures of Mary Parish*.

Ridicule of witchcraft has always overshadowed that of ritual magic, but the anonymous *Magical Vision*, published in 1673, is a notable example of the latter. The purported author is a young lady who takes a nap after reading Dr. John Dee's works, only to be whisked away on a flying broom to a terrifying magical conjuration. After a spirit riding on an eagle and a lynx appears, the conjurer introduces himself as Cornelius Agrippa, kept alive through demonically provided elixir. The author displays knowledge of many different operations of ritual magic present in our manuscript—divination with the sieve and shears, the acquisition of seeds on Midsummer Eve for magical purposes, the creation of wax images to harm enemies, and the use of the abracadabra charm to overcome fever.[37]

Despite these trends, responses to magical works could be complicated, with both practitioners and detractors taking different perspectives on the same work. For example, Meric Casaubon published John Dee's accounts of working with spirits beginning on December 22, 1581, from the collection of Sir Thomas Cotton, as *A True and Faithful Relation* (1659). Casaubon claimed he did so out of pious motives, but John Webster later accused him of trying to insulate himself against charges of atheism while impugning Dee's reputation.[38] Casaubon succeeded in ensuring that Dee's other accomplishments would be largely forgotten for centuries—and that magic would be subject to further mockery. Nonetheless, magicians took advantage of his publication, ignoring Casaubon's rhetoric and embrace this hitherto unavailable magical material.[39]

Contents

Douce MS. 116 includes many passages from classic works of the period, both printed and manuscript: the *Three Books of Occult Philosophy*, its likely-spurious sequel the *Fourth Book*, the *Heptameron*, the *Picatrix*, the *Hygromanteia*, and the *Arbatel*. At least in some cases, these are not copied from the mid-seventeenth century English translations; they seem to be translations from the Latin texts made by another, with some passages left in Latin that were too difficult for the translator. Based on the basic errors made in the Latin elsewhere in the text, these translations were likely not the work of the scribe of Douce MS. 116. The material from the *Three Books* is more intriguing, as it includes both poorly copied material from the Latin edition and seals taken from the English language edition of 1651.[40]

37. Anonymous, *A Magical Vision*.
38. Whitby, *John Dee's Actions with Spirits: Volumes I and II: 22 December 1581 to 23 May 1583*, 101–2; Webster, *The Displaying of Supposed Witchcraft*, 8.
39. Asprem, *Arguing with Angels*, 31–32.
40. On variation among these seals, see Vârtejaru, "Planetary Characters in Agrippa."

Elsewhere, the text shows that someone in the chain of transmission was interested in consolidating the work. For example, one passage brings together the descriptions of planetary spirits from the *Fourth Book* with the corresponding functions and winds from the *Heptameron*. Much of this material originally appeared together in the mid-sixteenth century *Lucidarium Artis Nigromaticę*, with an unknown editor later separating the sections between the *Fourth Book* and the *Heptameron*. The Douce MS. 116 text, however, seems to derive from the combination of Turner's English translation of 1665 and an English-Latin Heptameron text. Our first copyist was part of a tradition in which scribes were inspired not only to reproduce the text, but also to incorporate changes they saw as improving it.[41]

One of the most prevalent sources is *The Discouerie of Witchcraft*, originally released by the gentleman, gardener, and engineer Reginald Scot. Scot's position was that the witch trials were senseless prosecutions based on the same superstitious notions that had kept the Catholic Church's influence strong before the Reformation. Toward this end, he reprinted many magical charms and ceremonies, often with mockery and sometimes alongside Catholic rituals. Our copyist takes many rituals out of the book, often omitting the Latin passages Scot has translated into English and the sections that display Scot's scepticism or ridicule.

Although it includes considerable material from printed sources, our seventeenth-century author also partook of manuscript sources. The work includes partial lists of the rings made in one of the twenty-eight mansions of the moon, pursuing a wide array of illusory purposes, previously only published as a Latin text.[42] Our enterprising magician could heal others through a spirit named Escarioth, who may be acquired by being offered herbs and kept in a box. We also have a partially incoherent ritual to create a lead plate that will allow its owner to become invisible, involving looking at an unknown constellation. One significant item is a brief account on the nature of fairies, providing information not present or only hinted at in the published works of the period, along with charms to overcome the afflictions they cause.

Two manuscripts stand out with regard to similarities in material: British Library Sloane 3850 and National Library of Scotland GD 188/25/1/3. The material in these works does not appear in the same order as in Douce MS. 116, however, and enough omissions and variations appear that neither could be said to be a direct ancestor of this work. It does attest that the rituals within were in circulation in manuscript for quite some time before being recorded here.

The manuscript has several charms to ward off witchcraft, including a lengthy one targeted at a possessed or obsessed individual. Today we usually categorise bewitchment

41. Peterson, *Elucidation*, 3.

42. For an edition of the Latin text, see Boudet, "Annulorum."

separately from possession, if we believe in either. In late seventeenth-century Britain, however, people often presented what we would describe as possession as proof of a witch's magical attack.[43] Symptoms might include fits, unnatural stiffness, hallucinations, mysterious swellings, vomiting pins and other objects, and objects flying through the air supernaturally.[44] Clerics at the time distinguished between possession and obsession, in which a person was seriously tormented and tempted through demons acting externally, although the differences between the two conditions were not always clear.[45] In 1604, the Church of England's Convocation of Canterbury adopted Canon 72, which forbade exorcism without episcopal approval—and then never bestowed said approval thereafter in England.[46] This left exorcism in the hands of ministers outside the Church, those within who chose to ignore these strictures, and those who used magical procedures to accomplish the same goals.[47]

If we accept a Worcestershire copyist for this manuscript, concerns with possession would have been a local preoccupation. Beginning in 1642, a poor Bewdley woman fell into violent fits for many years, displaying unnatural strength and foul language. Around 1646 to 1647, she was delivered, claiming to see a black dog depart from her, although she relapsed at least once thereafter.[48] The faith healer Valentine Greatrakes visited Worcester in February 1666, where he supposedly witnessed and cured multiple episodes of possession in front of huge crowds.[49] In these circumstances, it is unsurprising that a local magician might seek out rituals to resolve any future cases of possession.

The author also writes a final section of the manuscript upside down in comparison with the bulk of the text. This section includes a set of mundane recipes, with occasional instructions in cipher, for such purposes as creating different baits for fish, capturing birds, and restoring the taste, scent, or colour to wine. This sort of inversion, in which a book effectively has different material based on orientation, is typical for many domestic manuscripts of the late seventeenth century. The two orientations

43. Raiswell and Dendle, "Demon Possession in Anglo-Saxon and Early Modern England: Continuity and Evolution in Social Context," 759–60.

44. Raiswell and Dendle, 755–56; C[hamberline], *Lithobolia*, A1–B2.

45. Walsh, "The Devil's Power of Obsession," 3; Raiswell and Dendle, "Demon Possession in Anglo-Saxon and Early Modern England: Continuity and Evolution in Social Context," 758.

46. Young, *A History of Anglican Exorcism: Deliverance and Demonology in Church Ritual*, 46–52.

47. Young, 53–75.

48. Almond, *Demonic Possession and Exorcism in Early Modern England*, 15; Baxter, *The Certainty of the Worlds of Spirits*, 193–95.

49. Greatrakes, *A Brief Account of Mr. Valentine Greatraks*, 33.

of a text often serves to demarcate different types of content, as it does in Douce MS. 116.[50]

The recipes to capture birds and animals often incorporate mind-altering and sometimes toxic substances, including cannabis, opium, henbane, and belladonna. The exact source of this material is uncertain, although recipes incorporating these substances were common in medieval and early modern treatises on fishing.[51] Such recipes are not only cruel to animals, but also potentially dangerous to diners. Such material does address a recent proposal that psychotropic substances were often utilised in ritual magic yet omitted from the texts due to cultural norms.[52] It seems unlikely that the copyists of texts involving the summoning of Lucifer, Satan, and Beelzebub would have felt constrained by such considerations. This text demonstrates that at least one such individual had no trouble about mentioning such items, even if it were intended for non-magical purposes.

The Second Occult Philosopher: Thomas Harrington

Thomas Harrington

On May 24, 1806, a manuscript entitled "Key to Cornelius Agrippa's Occult Philosophy" was put up for sale by the auctioneer Thomas King, Junior, at his rooms at 36 Tavistock Street, Covent Garden. The book was one of over a thousand lots of works on "Old Songs, Ballads, History, Magic, Witchcraft, Astrology," and other topics, taken from the library of one "Doctor Thos. Harrington, decd."[53]

The name of an individual, given as "Tho. Harrtn." appears on page 49 of the manuscript alongside its numerological value, apparently to ease repeated calculations over time for a person with that name. Thus, we can be reasonably certain that Thomas Harrington was the owner of the manuscript. The slight inconsistency in the title given in the catalogue with that inside the cover—"The Key to Cornelius Agrippa's 4th Book"—is not out of bounds with the liberties the same cataloguer took with printed books in other lots.

Who was Thomas Harrington? Given how common his first name is, we should be cautious in assuming every mention of that name pertains to our author. For example, an individual of that name published of a few ballads at Bury St. Edmunds.[54] Yet this individual seems to have been accused of kidnapping a thirteen-year-old girl

50. Ezell, "Invisible Books," 59.

51. For further examples, see Berners, *The Treatise on Angling*.

52. Bennett, *Liber 420: Cannabis, Magickal Herbs, and the Occult*, ix.

53. King, *Catalogue* [...] *of Dr. Thos. Harrington*, i.

54. Harrington, "A Favourite Lesson"; Harrington, "Lord Broome's March."

the month before the auction, which hardly gives time for him to die and his estate to be auctioned off.[55] We also have an account of one "Thomas Harrington, Esqu. of Waltham-hall, Essex," who passed away on June 27, 1802, while walking in the Green Park near St. James's in London. His death notice describes him as the "author of several medical tracts," but I have had no luck in locating these sources.[56] The catalogue covers both music and medicine, but we have no guarantees that this Thomas is either of these.

The Eighteenth Century

There was no battle of knowledge and wills that led to the discrediting and dismissal of ritual magic from intellectual thought in the eighteenth century. Rather, it came about from those who sought to define the Enlightenment as the rise of logic and rationality. This narrative, often based more on rhetoric and the construction of new identities than on experimentation, consigned the study of certain "occult"—mainly non-physical or unknown—aspects of reality to the dustbin of "superstition" and ridicule. Chemists refashioned their discipline into a respectable science through the exclusion of the transformative aspects of alchemy, long associated with fraudulent practices and reliance upon the works of past authorities. Likewise, astronomy and medicine put aside the predictive elements of astrology and celestial influences to reinvent themselves as sciences. Even though astrology was still widely believed and used in religious prophecy and astrological medicine, people were more willing to downplay the influence of heavenly bodies upon the body.[57]

In his book *The Decline of Magic*, historian Michael Hunter observes that, although some early scientists became interested in accounts of poltergeists, spirits, and the like—the chemist Robert Boyle in particular—the Royal Society's records show little collective interest in the topic of ritual magic. According to Hunter, most of the opposition to magic came not from printed works, but from popular conversations about the preternatural among freethinkers and those inclined to Deism and other similar faiths.[58] Little surviving evidence can be mustered to support this theory, yet none other seems to fit. Scientists and clergy of the establishment were reluctant to endorse sceptical views, as doubts toward ghosts and witches could easily translate into scepticism about Scripture itself, yet they soon tacitly endorsed the prevailing philosophy.

55. "Whereas Thomas Harrington," *Morning Post*.

56. "[Untitled]," *London Courier and Evening Gazette*.

57. Principe, *The Secrets of Alchemy*, loc. 1503–1602; Hanegraaff, *Esotericism and the Academy*, 204–5; Campion, *History of Western Astrology, Volume II*, 2:175–90.

58. Hunter, *The Decline of Magic*, 67–85, 22–25.

Some of the most notable collectors of ritual magic manuscripts were among the sceptics. A manuscript on witchcraft at the Morrab Library in Penzance has been attributed to Thomas Rawlinson (1681–1725). The work collects reports of seventeenth-century trials, with critical comments made about the use of sleep deprivation to bring about confessions and the witch-hunters' equation of pets with familiars.[59] Sir Hans Sloane's published silence on his large collection of magical manuscripts has led to speculation that he might have practised the art himself. Nonetheless, in a letter to a French colleague, Sloane proposes that belief in magic is a condition curable via those two staples of period medicine: bloodletting and purgatives.[60]

Sloane's medical explanation seems to have been an outlier, however. Whereas ritual magic had been previously seen as a manifestation of the supernatural power of Satan, the critique in literature shifted to its potential for chicanery and fraud. This critique would prove instrumental to the reframing of "Witchcraft, Sorcery, Inchantment, or Conjuration" in the Witchcraft Act of 1735/6. This measure repealed the acts against witchcraft and magic in England and Scotland, replacing with a statute to punish fraudulent pretences of possessing such power. The Act was only enforced occasionally, yet it signalled a change in official attitudes toward those who claimed magical power.[61]

Within this atmosphere, ritual magic, along with alchemy, astrology, dream interpretation, apparitions, and many other concepts judged superstitious, ignorant, or inappropriate, came to be associated together as a singular category. This led to the definition of a new category—what came to be called "the occult" or "occult sciences" —which could be used for various purposes, including critique of the Enlightenment project, casual amusement, inspiration for fiction, or actual practice. This separation could lead to a rejection of the rhetoric of rationality and science, but in other cases the same rhetoric could be used to establish its own legitimacy. Pursuing magical operations might be "experimentation" in the spirit of science, probing gaps in the knowledge of the world could buttress occult speculation, and new topics such as mesmerism and galvanism became topics with which the "occult sciences" could be associated and justified until understanding of them deepened.[62]

For many who lived in communities where beliefs in the efficacy of witchcraft and ritual magic were still strong, these intellectual debates took a back seat to servicing those needs and desires that had been in place for centuries. Thus, the practice of the cunning folk, ritual magicians working for local communities, continued. One

59. Dearlove, "The Pretended Trial of Witchcraft," 25–28; Hunter, *The Decline of Magic*, 230.

60. Sloane, *Magic and Mental Disorder*, 8–9, 16–17.

61. Davies, "Decriminalising the Witch," 229–30.

62. Hanegraaff, *Esotericism and the Academy*, 230–39.

such individual was Duncan Campbell (c. 1680–1730), a deaf and mute man who advertised his ability to compel witches to appear to reverse their spells, his power to find lost items, and the efficacy of his talismans.[63] Another was Timothy Crowther of Skipton, a parish clerk by trade, and an astrologer and cunning person who attracted customers from miles around. His surviving recipe book includes incantations for returning stolen goods, compelling witches who hexed cattle to reverse their charms, and viewing spirits in a crystal or beryl.[64] These practitioners are only two examples in a broad network who practised across the British Isles in both rural and urban settings.

The profession had its dangers, especially for those such as Richard Walton who dealt with the criminal element. According to Walton's account, he gave astrological advice to people on various aspects of their lives, along with providing talismans to ward off witchcraft on cattle. He fell in with two horse thieves, providing advice—inadvertently, according to him—on the best time for these thefts and hearing about their plans. At one time, he even accepted money to discover a horse these men had stolen. Despite his protestations of good character, he was found guilty and executed at Warwick in 1733.[65]

When it came time for a would-be magician to find books for their practice, the selections were quite thin. *Robinson Crusoe* author Daniel Defoe entitled one of his books *A System of Magick* (1728) to attract an audience seeking "a Body of the Black Art as a Science, a Book of Rules for Instruction in the Practice, or a Magical Grammar for Introduction to young Beginners."[66] The book instead served as a highly speculative history of magical practice, whereby the Devil led astray the rational philosophers and scientists of antiquity, and today magic had no power at all. Nonetheless, Defoe's marketing strategy indicates that enough people would have bought such a book to make it a financial selling point—yet no work on actual ritual magic emerged for that market in the eighteenth century.

Eighteenth-century magicians who sought published works would rely on those from the sixteenth and seventeenth century until the very end of the century.[67] *The Conjurer's Magazine* (1791), which became *The Astrologer's Magazine* in 1793, served to disseminate astrological and, to a lesser extent, magical material on a wider basis.[68] The fourth part of Ebenezer Sibly's *A New and Complete Illustration of the Occult Sci-*

63. Campbel, *Secret Memoirs*, 17–21.

64. Dawson, "An Old Yorkshire Astrologer and Magician, 1694–1760," 197–202.

65. Wallton, *Genuine Life*, 17–20.

66. Defoe, *A System of Magick*, A3.

67. Davies, *Popular Magic*, 133–38.

68. *Conjurer's Magazine*; *Astrologer's Magazine*.

ences (1788, published together in 1794) dealt with magic at some length, lifting considerable Swedenborgian material and segments of Scot's *Discouerie of Witchcraft*.[69] Francis Barrett also borrowed considerable material from various sources when he compiled his book *The Magus* (1801).[70]

Manuscripts also played a role in this process, although the survival of such works has dropped considerably. Earlier in the century, we see them in Sloane 6481–6484, a collection including magical and Rosicrucian materials, copied by a Peter Smart and attributed to a "Dr. Rudd."[71] Nearer to the end, copies of an English translation of the *Key of Solomon*, supposedly translated from the French by Ebenezer Sibly in 1789, began to appear.[72] Although wealthy collectors often snapped up older manuscripts for their own ends, we know that Douce MS. 116 made it into the hands of not only a practitioner, but also one who further transformed it.

Contents

Whosoever Harrington may have been, he went to considerable effort to make the text useful to himself. He may have been responsible for the brown leather binding, as well as adding additional pages at the beginning and end for additional text. He paginated the work—although this was often done carelessly, as the text will show—and included a table of contents and many notes indicating sources and references to other works in his library. These included a manuscript copy of the *Fourth Book* attributed to Agrippa, a "red book" in quarto, and a "little manuscript." The numerological methods for determining good or bad fortune seem to have been popular, as he adds a chart of common English given names and their Latin equivalents in both the front and back of the book. Most of the Latin passages remain untranslated, although Harrington has added some translations of section titles.

The most notable change to the book was the insertion of a title, "The Key to Cornelius Agrippa's Fourth Book," on the new first page of the manuscript. Although the original and annotations are indebted to the *Fourth Book* for some of their contents, the work is by no means dependent upon, or able to grant many insights into, the work of pseudo-Agrippa. This is perhaps more a statement of lineage and aspiration than relation to the text.

69. Sommers, *The Siblys of London*, 160–61
70. For a breakdown of Barrett's sources, see Priddle, "More Cunning Than Folk."
71. For those of Smart's works that have been published, see McLean, *A Treatise on Angel Magic*; Skinner and Rankine, *The Goetia of Dr. Rudd*.
72. Sibley [Sibly], *Solomon's Clavis, or Key to Unlock the Mysteries of Magic*; Solomon, *The Clavis or Key to Unlock the Mysteries of Magic*.

The author's introduction on pages iii to iv is intriguing for its emphasis. Harrington writes eloquently of the importance of pursuing the art, but he also realises that a learned person of his time would be steeped in knowledge of—or at least respect for—science, have a more secular mindset, and find many of the manuscript's contents questionable or ridiculous. For this prospective reader, Harrington emphasises that a discerning and dedicated individual will certainly find "amusement" from the material within, but it might yield much more to the right person. He notes the gaps in the scientific knowledge of his day and compares the secrets of magic to the wonders yielded up by a microscope. He brings the pursuits of ritual magic and scientific knowledge into parallel, attempting to lend one's public legitimacy to the other.

Most of Harrington's references seem to be to printed works. For instance, although our first scribe used the 1665 edition of the *Fourth Book*, Harrington's annotations are taken from the 1655 edition, as listed in the sale catalogue, although he also mentions a manuscript edition of which we have no clear trace. Many of these references include errors in page numbers, indicating that he might not have had access to the original texts when he made them.

One section also includes seals and incomplete information on spirits taken from the section of the *Lemegeton* known as the *Goetia*, along with a few notes on summoning the spirits. This content is closest to Sloane 3846, although it is different enough that it must have derived from another manuscript in which part of the incantations for compelling spirits had been torn out. It is unclear why these particular spirits were chosen; they do not seem to share a function in common, and indeed some have no function whatsoever listed in the *Goetia*. At any rate, this indicates he had access to another lost manuscript.

We have three clues to the date on which these comments were written. One is a reference to a divination technique given in the *Memoirs and Anecdotes of Philip Thicknesse*, published in 1790.[73] Another matter added near the beginning also quotes a newspaper story from the *Morning Post* for May 29, 1792.[74] Elsewhere Harrington quotes from the "Love" article in the *Encyclopaedia Britannica*, including information that first appeared in the third edition of that book. A full set was published in 1797, but the first fascicles were published and issued to subscribers as early as 1788. The publication schedule for those fascicles might help us narrow down the dating of the composition of that section, at least of one section.

In the latter portions of the book, the author presents a paraphrase of many of the initial passages from the *Clavicula Salomonis*, summarised and supplemented with references to and material from the *Lemegeton*, the *Three Books* and *Fourth Book of*

73. Thicknesse, *Memoirs and Anecdotes of Philip Thicknesse*, 13–14.

74. Given the incomplete set of the archives of the *Post*, this cannot be officially confirmed.

Agrippa, and other sources. The base text here is a French and English manuscript tradition which Mathiesen classifies as the "Rabbi Solomon" grouping, due to the title given to the putative author.[75] Despite the prevalence of "Rabbi Solomon" *Keys* copied from the one in possession of Ebenezer Sibly or Sibley at the time, this book seems to have been an original translation from the French.[76] The numerous page numbers and cross-references that have been omitted indicate that Harrington never finished this project.

Based upon some of his comments and his redundancy regarding planetary metal attributions in his comments near the end, it seems likely that Harrington intended to pass this and the other manuscripts in his library off to a student. Whether he had a specific person in mind is unknown, but ultimately his goals were thwarted when his library was sold off at auction after his death. Yet this *Key* did pass on to an appreciative individual.

The Third Occult Philosopher: Olivia Serres

Princess Olive

Our next author, responsible for the poetry and musings on alchemy and talismans at the beginning and end of the manuscript, is much better known for her hotly debated claims to royalty. Attempting to write the biography of a person accused of rewriting their own history is a challenge, but I shall make the attempt.

According to the better-documented history, Olivia Wilmot was born on April 15, 1772, to Robert and Anna-Maria Wilmot. In 1780, after her father's removal from his position of county treasurer due to charges of embezzlement, her family moved to London, where she was taken in by her uncle, Dr. James Wilmot.[77] The doctor raised her at Barton-on-the-Heath in Warwickshire—a short distance from Worcestershire—and supposedly tutored her in the occult sciences.[78] Her marriage in 1791 to the painter John Serres resulted in at least three children, but it proved unhappy, and the two later separated. She earned her living as a landscape painter at the Royal Academy and the British Institution, and she was appointed to the post of landscape painter to the Prince of Wales, the future King George IV, in 1806.

Olivia became best known for her increasingly complex claims to royal lineage. At first, she claimed to be the product of a secret affair between Henry, Duke of Cumberland and younger brother of King George III, and James Wilmot's sister. Later,

75. Mathiesen, "The Key of Solomon: Toward a Typology of Manuscripts," 4–5.

76. Sibley, *Solomon's Clavis, or Key to Unlock the Mysteries of Magic.*

77. Macnair, *Olive, Princess of Cumberland*, 3.

78. Raphael, "[Untitled]," *The Straggling Astrologer.*

she elaborated on this, with her supposed mother "Olive" being the daughter of her uncle James and a Polish princess. She seems to have leveraged this into financial and social capital, with members of the royal family making comments indicating they thought her claims possible. This went so far as allowing her to travel in a carriage with the Royal Arms, until she ran out of funds to do so, and sending her a piece of the christening cake of the future Queen Victoria.[79] Still, when it came time for her or her daughter to press her claims, the courts demurred on making judgments, relying on technical arguments or their lack of jurisdiction over royal manners.

I am reluctant to dive into Ms. Serres's putative noble ancestry and associations, given their complexity and the heated debates over the evidence. Her case was mostly established via documents from her personal collection. Most of the principals who wrote the documents were deceased at the time Ms. Serres made her claims to royal pedigree. Even proponents of her royal lineage acknowledge that some of the material she presented had been forged, so the other documents in her possession must be treated with some suspicion.[80] She also became involved in other affairs involving shadowy individuals presenting documents supposedly dealing with scandalous revelations about the Royal Family to them or their representatives. The goal was for these materials to be suppressed, often with fees being paid to Ms. Serres and her associates. She also spent a great deal of time in the 1820s in debtors' prison, which would have given her a motive to seek financial relief as a member of the royal household. A role in shady affairs and profligate spending does not necessarily invalidate her claims of heredity, but it should lead to some caution. Those academics who have treated of the subject more recently have given short shrift to Olivia's claims.[81]

Ms. Serres was a prolific author, mainly in the service of presenting her claims and other exposés of royal peccadillos. Among the others, she also published several examples of sheet music, a work on the Athanasian Creed, and one book of poetry—though many more examples of the latter remain unpublished. She also published in Raphael's periodical *The Straggling Astrologer*, presenting several "astrological fragments" with commentary.[82] None of these publications translated into financial success, and she died on November 21, 1834, leaving less than £20 to her beneficiaries.[83]

79. Pendered and Mallett, *Princess or Pretender?*, 123–37.

80. Macnair, *Olive, Princess of Cumberland*, 186.

81. McWilliam, "Unauthorized Identities," 71–75; Nash, *Royal Wills in Britain from 1509 to 2008*, 113–26.

82. Serres, "Astrological Fragments [...] the First"; Serres, "Astrological Fragments [...] Fragment II"; Serres, "Astrological Fragments [...] Fragment III"; Serres, "Astrological Fragments [...] Fragment IV."

83. Macnair, *Olive, Princess of Cumberland*, 156.

The Early Nineteenth Century

Popular conceptions of nineteenth-century ritual magic often revolve around the personalities and organizations that appear late in the century: Éliphas Lévi, the Theosophical Society, the Golden Dawn, the Hermetic Brotherhood of Luxor, MacGregor Mathers, and Aleister Crowley. Nonetheless, their precursors and influences can be found in this period, with what would later be called the "occult sciences" becoming classified, commodified, and packaged as a field separate from, yet drawing legitimacy from, both religion and science.

The nineteenth century's urbanization and industrialization did not lead to an end to belief in ritual magic. These changes brought their own uncertainties and dangers, some of which could be caused or alleviated through magic. Enforcement of the 1736 Witchcraft Act was spotty, leaving cunning folk largely free to offer their services as they had before. Despite elite rhetoric and education, belief in witchcraft persisted, leading to sporadic attacks and vigilante justice on those believed to be witches.[84]

A relatively new element on the British magical scene were orders dedicated to the study and practice of the magical arts. The medieval magical manual *Liber Juratus* had mentioned a supposed magical order, and various groups of magicians did meet in the medieval and early modern eras to pursue treasure hunting and other pursuits, usually in short-term associations.[85] Still, most magical knowledge seems to have been transmitted either between individuals or through manuscripts, not through a formal school. The early seventeenth-century Rosicrucian manifestos inspired much mystical speculation, not to mention attempts to found or uncover such an organization. The eighteenth century had seen the formation of fraternal orders in Europe for esoteric purposes, ranging from Martinez de Pasqually's Élus Cöens to the German Orden des Gülden und Rosen-Creutzes.[86] Still, it would not be until the early nineteenth century that we have the first evidence of British organizations dedicated to cultivating their members' magical talents, often basing themselves on the model of Masonic lodges of various types. These might include the group of adepts that Francis Barrett sought to teach; the Mercurii, an order coalescing around the astrologer Raphael (on whom see page 22); and the Orphic Circle, in which Emma Hardinge Britten claimed membership.[87] Evidence of all of these is debatable, especially regarding the groups' sizes, members, and endurance, yet it seems that having a lodge or

84. Waters, *Cursed Britain*, 9–37.

85. Honorius, *Sworn Book*, 49–53; Klaassen and Wright, *The Magic of Rogues*, 83–116.

86. Le Forestier, *La Franc-Maçonnerie Occultiste*, 420–93; McIntosh, *The Rosicrucians*, 63–75, 97–106.

87. Harms, *Balloonists, Alchemists, and Astrologers of the Nineteenth Century*, 11–15; Mathiesen, *Unseen Worlds*, 20–26.

organization for teaching prospective adepts was now considered part of the mental model of occultism.

At the same time, a trickle of magical books appeared, including *Witchcraft Detected and Prevented* (1824), attributed to a "Member of the School of Black Art, Italy," and Raphael's compilation and expansion of the material from his *Straggling Astrologer* periodical into *The Astrologer of the Nineteenth Century* (1825). This lack of material meant that manuscripts were still significant. A thinly veiled fictional version of bookseller John Denley is presented in Bulwer-Lytton's novel *Zanoni* (1842), portraying him as a bookseller obsessed with not selling books.[88] This might have reflected Denley's workshop of copyists working to recreate beautiful manuscript editions of the *Key of Solomon* and other magical texts, and a practice of lending out books from his stock for reading or copying.[89]

Contents

Ms. Serres's contribution to the book is more limited than that of Harrington. She did record a few poems within, but she was also responsible for further expansion of the magical material. She appears to have been particularly interested in talismans, as she reproduces several she attributes to "Thetel," a "philosopher of the primitive age." "Thetel" is a variant of the more common name "Techel," which Katelyn Mesler has suggested could be either the Besal'el, the craftsman and gemcutter appointed by God in Exodus 31:2–5, or Sahl ibn Bishr, a Jewish astrologer and translator of the ninth century. A lapidary text is attributed to Thetel, but it does not seem to overlap in contents with Douce MS. 116.[90] Given that some of the diagrams here do not appear in our published editions of Techel's work, it is unknown what source she consulted for this material. In addition, she also included a small amount of alchemical material, as well as expanding the chart of English and Latin given names on the back cover with a few entries—her own being first.

The Fourth Occult Philosopher: Raphael

Robert Cross Smith

Robert Cross Smith (1795–1832) was born in Abbots Leigh, a village across the Avon gorge from Bristol. He may have worked as a carpenter in Bristol, and a Mr. Williams

88. Lytton, *Zanoni*, iii–iv.

89. University College London, Senate House Library, HPF/3C/1.

90. Mesler, "The Medieval Lapidary of Techel/Azareus on Engraved Stones and Its Jewish Appropriations," 90ff.

may have tutored him in astrology there. He made his way to London around 1822, taking up work as a clerk.[91]

His life changed through his association with George Graham, who had a long and disastrous career as a balloonist with his wife, Margaret. Graham supported him, encouraged him to take on the career of astrologer, and collaborated with him on his first book, *The Philosophical Merlin* (1822).[92] Smith took over *The Straggling Astrologer* in July 1824, which included editing the contributions Olivia Serres made to the magazine. Although the periodical was unsuccessful, it would be the first publication in which he would adopt the pseudonym "Raphael."[93] Even his publication of an anthology of its contents with new material regarding apparitions and ritual magic, *The Astrologer of the Nineteenth Century* (1825), failed to excite much interest, nor did another venture, the journal *Urania* (1825).[94] His next effort, the almanac entitled *The Prophetic Messenger*, catapulted him to astrological fame upon its release in 1826.[95]

Another of Smith's creations was the Mercurii, a band of philosophers intent on investigating astrology and other aspects of occultism. At times, he published fragments from books from the library of the Mercurii, which included the manuscripts now known as Folger Shakespeare Library V.b.26 and—as we will see—Douce MS. 116.[96] He presented what purported to be "minutes" of these meetings, which often revolve around a small group congratulating Smith on his latest predictions and occasionally breaking into spontaneous promotion for his upcoming books.[97] At least one individual—Colonel Robert Morrison, later known as the astrologer "Zadkiel"—can be been identified in these accounts. Thus, the question of how much of a working group the Mercurii truly were remains an open question.

In his publications, Smith sought to popularise not only astrology, but also the practice of ritual magic. He certainly had access to the present manuscript and made use of it in some of his later works, referring to it as an "Ancient Manuscript" in the *Familiar Astrologer* and "a Key to Agrippa" in *Raphael's Witch*, in which he describes the work as a "very ancient MSS. [sic]" and "a book of really 'wondrous lore'" from which he extracts creatively elaborated quotations of spells to round out his works.[98] A contemporary astrologer, known only as "Dixon," claimed that Smith's interest in

91. Howe, *Raphael*, 10–13; Dixon, *True Prophetic Messenger*, 86.

92. Harms, *Balloonists, Alchemists, and Astrologers of the Nineteenth Century*, 3, 5–7.

93. Howe, *Raphael*, 13–15.

94. Howe, *Raphael*, 17–18.

95. Howe, *Raphael*, 22–23.

96. Harms, Clark, and Peterson, *The Book of Oberon* [hereafter *Oberon*], 11–12.

97. Raphael, *The Familiar Astrologer*, 370–90, 451–56, 475–79,

98. Raphael, *The Familiar Astrologer*, 45; Raphael, *Raphael's Witch*, 141.

ritual magic and geomancy earned him much animosity, and that Smith had often told him "he wished he had never troubled himself with the study of these sciences to the extent that he had, as he felt certain the truth of them was very *problematical*."[99] We should not take this too seriously; his last issue of *The Prophetic Messenger* included an advertisement for *The New Astrologer of the 19th Century*, including "A COMPLETE AND FAMILIAR SYSTEM OF GEOMANCY" and "ANCIENT SUPERSTITIONS DISPLAYED, particularly those related to magical ceremonies, talismans, and divination."[100]

Little attention has been paid to Smith's efforts to blend magic with fiction. One key example is a story entitled "The Necromancers, and the Prediction," published in *The Book of Spirits and Tales of the Dead* (1827) and republished after his death under the more apt title *Tales of the Horrible* (1837). This work draws from a folktale regarding a local tower structure known as Cook's Folly, likely built in 1693 by John Cooke, in which a man is walled up inside to avoid a foretold death.[101] Smith reworks the tale in light of his magical research. The Roma fortune teller or astrologer in other versions is replaced with a necromancer. This dread wizard dwells in a cave described as similar to Burwall's Cave, a short distance from the Clifton Suspension Bridge. To meet Cooke's desire for prognostication, he and the necromancer go to the churchyard in Abbots Leigh, where the spirit "Birto"—present in *Oberon* and other early modern manuscripts—is summoned under dreadful and terrifying circumstances. It seems that Smith is here combining Bristol folklore and landscape with Gothic sensibilities and his own reading of magical manuscripts.[102]

Smith married Sarah Lucas in 1820 and was believed to have six children by the time of his death.[103] He passed on February 26, 1832, after a period in illness, sitting by the fire at home.[104] Even after his death, the name "Raphael" was taken up by a succession of astrologers who followed in his footsteps.[105]

Contents

Smith's addition to this book is a leaf inserted just before page 264, folded in half and glued into the text. The section consists of two pages on talismans; a one-page discussion of the astronomical significance of Herschel, including a note on the chart of "H. W.,"

99. Dixon, *True Prophetic Messenger*, 88.
100. Raphael, *Prophetic Messenger*.
101. Quinn, "Fact and Folly," 10; Harte, "Exotic Snakes" 10–11; "Cooke's Folly," 4.
102. Astrologer of the Nineteenth Century and Wright, *Tales of the Horrible*, 65–80.
103. Dixon, *True Prophetic Messenger*, 86.
104. Dixon, *True Prophetic Messenger*, 91.
105. Howe, *Urania's Children*, 31–32; Howe, *Raphael*, 27–35.

the president of the Mercurii; and a fourth page, on which is affixed a card with what appears to be the scribblings of a child. It is not clear what this assemblage was intended to be. Whether this book ever passed through Raphael's library, or if he simply handed off a paper to his friend Olivia, is a mystery. What we do know, however, is that the book was no longer owned by either Serres or Smith in 1829.

The Final Owner: Francis Douce

The catalogue of the bookseller John Cochran of June 15, 1829, was the first work of its kind to feature illustrations. Among its 650 items, including many manuscripts within a broad range of topics and languages, appears the following text (with no accompanying illustration):

> 413 Magic and Astrology. —A Volume of Magical Incantations and Charms. Manuscript, of the seventeenth century, with very numerous diagrams, small folio, containing upwards of 400 pages closely written,
> 2l. 12s. 6d.
>
> A volume full of strange recipes how "to bind a spirit—to bring the thief again—to attract a female familiar—to make men appear in horns—to obtain your love—to make your enemy love you—to find the virtue of mandrakes—to keep fruit from birds and your enemy in prison—to have your desire in all things," and many other wonders. There is also a treatise on Animal Magnetism, and "A Hymn by the Princess Olive," in whose possession it appears recently to have been.[106]

This is a fair list of items from the book, and it is clinched by the insertion in pencil of the catalogue number and price in the manuscript's inner back cover. From the last comment, it seems that even Cochran was unclear about what the chain of ownership between Serres and the auctioneer had been. Nonetheless, the book was picked up in this sale and made its way to its last private owner: Francis Douce.

Douce was born on July 13, 1757, the fourth and youngest child of Ellen and Francis Douce. His father was an attorney at the Six Clerks Office and expected Francis to follow him in the same profession. His son wished to pursue a life of learning and antiquarian collection instead. Although he was not permitted to attend university, he succeeded in joining the Society of Antiquaries and was permitted to read at the British Museum.[107]

106. Cochran, *A Catalogue of Manuscripts in Different Languages*, 122–23.

107. Bodleian Library, *The Douce Legacy*, vii–viii.

Seeking employment to maintain his collecting habit, Douce became employed at the British Museum's Department of Manuscripts, working to catalogue the Lansdowne and Harleian manuscript collections.[108] He chafed at the various aspects of the job, however, and resigned upon being forced to report on the activities of an employee hired against his recommendation. He resigned on April 6, 1811, listing fourteen reasons, ranging from the freezing building to the endless reports to the pompous and ineffectual committees—complaints one might still hear from librarians today.[109] Despite the trustees' efforts to bring him back, Douce remained steadfast in his decision.[110]

As it happens, Douce's lack of collecting funds might have pushed him into areas in which others did not collect, creating materials of deep value to later scholars. His house contained all manner of items, including images of the Feast of Fools, children's schoolbooks, tarot decks, nursery rhyme pamphlets, and mummies. One of his interests was the sublime, a literary mood of reaching beyond everyday consciousness that encompassed both horror and religious awe.[111] He became one of the few people to recognise the genius of William Blake during that artist's lifetime, purchasing his works and possibly even attending one of his sparsely attended exhibitions.[112] He also collected drawings of Fuseli, depictions of the mandrake, and substantial material on witchcraft and demonology—although Douce MS. 116 would be his only book-length acquisition dealing with magic itself.[113]

There is no exact entry in his notebook of acquisitions for June 1829 that indicates he received the manuscript, especially given his decision not to list individual titles in most acquisitions. The manuscript is noted in the Bodleian's manuscript catalogue as "An alchymical work of incantations, charms, tables of the planets, etc., illustrated with figures intitled Cornelius Agrippa's fourth book."[114]

Douce was childless, and speculation arose about where he might leave his collection after his death. The British Museum was a logical choice, but his history with that institution made such a gift unlikely. The matter was decided when he made a visit to the Bodleian in 1831, in the company of his friend Isaac D'Israeli. Douce was

108. Topper, "Francis Douce and His Collection," 10.

109. Bodleian Library, Douce e. 28, 2–3.

110. *The Douce Legacy*, ix–x.

111. Topper, "Francis Douce and His Collection," 35–6.

112. Stemmler, "'Undisturbed Above Once in a Lustre,'" 12.

113. Topper, "Francis Douce and His Collection," 42–5.

114. Bodleian Library, *Catalogue of the Printed Books and Manuscripts Bequeathed by Francis Douce, Esq. to the Bodleian Library*, pt. 2:18.

particularly happy that the collections others had left to the library had remained together as distinct units.[115]

Douce was not an easy person to get along with. Upon receiving a single poor review of his first book *Illustrations of Shakespeare* (1807) in the *Edinburgh Review*, Douce decided not to publish any other books for decades.[116] The Reverend Thomas Frognall Dibdin, a friend of Douce's for over a quarter century, referred after his death to "the capricious lights and shades of his character: - those crotchetty impulses, and immoveable prejudices…which peculiarly distinguished him."[117] He nonetheless did have some lifelong friends, often fellow collectors such as the sculptor and miser Joseph Nollekens, whose bequest to his friend allowed Douce, late in life, to acquire at a prodigious level.[118] He was not devoid of a brand of humour, including sarcastic labels in his scrapbooks, and Dibdin notes how Douce would "chuckle aloud" at an illustration of monstrous demons.[119]

Douce passed away on Easter March 30, 1834. In his will, he asked his friend Sir Arthur Carlisle "either to sever my head or extract the heart from my body, so as to prevent any possibility of the return of vitality" before he was laid at St. Pancras.[120] This was not necessarily an unreasonable precaution in that period, given the dangers of premature burial. In his will, he made numerous bequests, favouring his fellow collectors more than members of his family. As he had promised, he donated his extensive collection of nineteen thousand printed books and over four hundred manuscripts, prints, drawings, coins, and medals to the Bodleian. To the British Library he left a Dürer work that Nollekens left him, his impressions of monumental brasses, two annotated works, and a mysterious box that his will stated should be kept closed until 1900.[121] Official sources differ about what was inside that box, ranging from trash to an uninteresting series of materials still useful for contextualizing the collection. The box is still at the British Library, while its brass plate and contents joined the more substantive part of the collection at the Bodleian.[122]

Even though Douce's collection no longer occupies its own nook along the walls, the Bodleian has fulfilled its promise to keep the treasures of his collection alive for future generations.

115. Bodleian Library, *The Douce Legacy*, 11–12.
116. Bodleian Library, *The Douce Legacy*, xi.
117. Dibdin, *Reminiscences*, 2:777.
118. Mann, "Francis Douce as a Collector," 361.
119. Dibdin, *Reminiscences*, 2:769.
120. Bodleian Library, *The Douce Legacy*, 13.
121. Bodleian Library, *The Douce Legacy*, 13–14.
122. Bodleian Library, *The Douce Legacy*, 17; Topper, "Francis Douce and His Collection," 61.

The Editor

My first knowledge of Douce MS. 116 came through an article by Stephanie Pope in the *Bodleian Library Record*.[123] The book had garnered little attention from scholars and practitioners of ritual magic, most likely because it was the solitary work on the topic in a much more extensive and variegated collection. The benefit was that this book would be unique even to dedicated readers on ritual magic. The chief difficulty was that no one had previously paid the Bodleian Library to create a microfilm of the whole. Joe Peterson and I initially paid for a quarter of the book to be digitised, but the cost for the rest was prohibitive.

This led to a series of trips to the Weston Library to view and photograph the original. I would leave my lodgings in London early in the morning to catch a shuttle to Gloucester Green in Oxford. From there I walked up George and Broad Streets, past Balliol College and Blackwell's bookstore, until I arrived at the Bodleian's Weston Library. There, having turned over my documentation and read the traditional oath not to injure books or to set fires in the building, I would ascend to the second-story reading room. I obtained the book from the librarian, laying it on its foam supports and taking photographs—full pages, partial pages, marginal notes, the gutters next to the binding—until my back and shoulders ached. I'd finish the day with dinner at the Eagle and Child pub, where Tolkien and C. S. Lewis once relaxed, or at a less prestigious establishment, before getting on the bus. On the ride to London, I would review each photograph to make sure it was sharp and usable, making painstaking notes on reshoots if it was not.

If you said it would have been cheaper just to pay for the whole manuscript to be digitised, you're not wrong. Yet it was an experience that I would not trade.

Sometimes people ask me how I feel about the people who write these books. Our first author is unknown, so most of my emotion toward his work is frustration. With Harrington, I see a never-fulfilled wish to educate another, and I hope that any remnant of his spirit will be pleased with his work reaching appreciative readers. I feel that Serres would probably be charming, so long as I hid my wallet and didn't have to listen to her poetry. Raphael seems to need too much adulation, but I can imagine us spinning supernatural horror tales at a roaring fire. Douce is a librarian and sometimes frustrated, so I regard him with the greatest degree of sympathy, even if he'd throw me out of his home within five minutes.

123. Pope, "'Darcke and Clowdie Speeches.'"

Definitions and Editorial Philosophy

Defining Ritual Magic

As I look back at both *The Book of Oberon* and *Of Angels, Demons & Spirits*, it becomes apparent that I have never attempted to define "ritual magic," which makes up the bulk of these manuscripts. Definitions are tricky to create, even under less murky circumstances, so this should be considered a preliminary effort at best.

Early modern practitioners used terms other than "magic" to describe these rituals at the time, such as "necromancy" or "nigromancy." Yet I feel that both will be misleading for modern readers. "Necromancy" had drifted to include a larger variety of practices than simply interacting with the dead, which is both the literal meaning of the term and how it is interpreted today.[124] "Nigromancy" has no frame of reference for modern people, but its derivation from the Latin "niger" (the colour black) is likely to invoke associations with contemporary definitions of race or "black magic" that would not have been part of its original intent. Even at the time, neither term was used enough to justify denoting the entire corpus of texts that include this material.

Other authors have used labels such as "Solomonic" or "Cyprianic," referring to some of the most famous authors of this material. This is problematic for a few reasons. First, most researchers would agree that these books were written under pseudonyms, creating an initial layer of confusion. Second, I am unconvinced that the group of treatises attributed to "Solomon" or "Cyprian" are more similar with each other than to works not attributed to them. Those familiar with the proliferation of treatises on various topics attributed to Hermes Trismegistus will immediately see the echoes with the indiscriminate use of the word "Hermetic."

A more recent and effective attempt has been Bernd-Christian Otto's work at sketching out the field of "Western learned magic."[125] Although much of the material within this book might derive from the corpus that Otto outlines, the "learned" aspect, in which a privileged literate elite is responsible for its transmission and practice, is a problematic label when examining early modern or later material.[126] On one hand, the intellectual elite were losing confidence in the reality and theory of the topic; on the other, magic gained in popularity through vernacular literature and became the province of middle and lower-class adherents outside scholarly circles. Referring to such magic as "learned" in this period is likely to lead to misinterpretation of its era and its believers and practitioners.

124. Láng, *Unlocked Books*, 41–42.

125. Otto, "Historicising 'Western Learned Magic.'"

126. Otto, 180. Otto points out that the sixteenth century is where the "learned" label becomes problematic.

To remove us from this morass, I will be using "ritual magic" to describe much of the content of this book. To help readers conceive of what sets this apart from other spiritual practices, I would like to set out the following tendencies among the material that these books cover:

- It is often transmitted through writing.
- The primary source of its language is Christian liturgy and tropes, including Biblical figures, saints, and prominent figures; written and oral narratives; and particular sacraments and rituals, often used in ways that are outside of orthodox praxis.
- The agents it calls upon are intermediate beings—angels, demons, fairies, planetary spirits, the dead, or other intelligences—who are usually coerced and commanded into service rather than entreated or worshiped.
- Its aims are usually based on instrumental goals of an individual, rather than spiritual progress or community concerns.

This is not to say that this is a perfect definition. It omits the inclusion of ideas derived from Arabic, Greek, Hebrew, and other learned traditions; the similarities to the techniques of exorcism; the overlap in definition with sanctioned individual prayer; and the usage of names of God causing effects by virtue of their own power. It gives short shrift to talismanic magic, along with other qualities such as length, timing, atmosphere, tools, materials, and other aspects that others might find important. I'm sure some readers will be raising other objections and concerns. At the same time, I feel that this idea of "ritual magic" is a good place to start the conversation.

Yet even "ritual magic" is an insufficient term to describe the entirety of the present book. Some content overlaps with what readers will likely define as astrology, astrological magic, alchemy, household remedies, devotional works, and poetry, among other categories. The copyists were not concerned with niceties of definition when they compiled the manuscript, so we should not expect strict adherence to these boundaries.

The Title

Some manuscripts of magic are clearly recognised by title as part of a given textual tradition with numerous exemplars. This manuscript is not one of them. Thomas Harrington's title, *The Key to Cornelius Agrippa's Fourth Book*, reflects his aspirations for the work more than the contents of the manuscript. The publishers and I did not want to give readers the impression that this was a direct commentary on the *Fourth Book* when it is an entirely different work. The spine title on the binding, "Magick," is much worse, of course.

What sets this book apart from other manuscripts is the accretion of work from each of the scribes. Whereas in other ritual magic works an owner might confine themselves to glosses or pagination, in Douce MS. 116 each scribe has added material to the text, often substantially, that reflects their particular time, place, and interests. With that in mind, we decided to name the text in honour of those four figures.

Notes on Editing

This manuscript falls into a category that Margaret Ezell refers to as "badly behaving books," to which both *The Book of Oberon* and *Of Angels, Demons & Spirits* also belong.[127] Its owners did not think of it as a work with an audience of more than one or two people. It runs against our sensibilities as readers used to legible type, logical layout, and clearly defined sections and topics. One ritual does not always follow another, later material is inserted into the margins or the body of earlier text, and where one rite ends and another begins is ambiguous.

The book represents a challenge to you as a reader. You'll be engaging with something outside your ordinary reading experience—which, given the topic, you're probably predisposed to doing already. What I outline here are my efforts to help: adding headings, clarifying wording, splitting the text into different sections to reflect breaks where later text intrudes, and much more. This can only go so far before it breaks the basic organization of the text, so I'm hoping you'll be willing to meet me halfway to experience a different sort of work.

Abbreviations: In most cases, these have been expanded.

Ampersands: Expanded into "and" or "et," save with regard to "& c." ("and so forth").

Brackets, square: These are used to indicate page numbers and editorial insertions into the text. If preceded by *italics*, the bracketed text is a correction of the original.

Catchwords: Words at the bottom of each page used to collate the text, or, in this case, to make the book look more professional. These have been removed, save when the copyist omits them from the text on the following page.

Ciphers: I've left the original cipher in the headers and the body of the text (but not the table of contents), moving the decipherment to the footnotes. The ciphers contain non-standardised spelling, omitted letters, unclear characters, and mistakes, so the cipher and the decipherment will not be character-by-character accurate.

Duplicate words and phrases: Removed, save for words of power in incantations.

127. Ezell, "Invisible Books," 65.

Fonts: The following fonts are used to indicate different authors in the book:

Hand 1 (unknown): Arial
Hand 2 (Thomas Harrington): Palatino Linotype
Hand 3 (Olivia Serres): **Rockwell**
Hand 4 (Raphael): Silentium Pro Roman II
Hand 5 (Francis Douce Scribe): Bodoni MT
My own text, such as this introduction, the bibliography, and the footnotes, are in Minion Pro.

Headings: Many of these appear in the manuscript. A heading entirely in brackets indicates that it is my own addition. In some cases, I have split the heading from text on the same line that is clearly part of the main body of the text.

Indented text: Short magical phrases and talismans, or translated text from Latin.

Italics: Used to indicate subheadings within a ritual, incorrect items in the main text followed by bracketed phrases to indicate corrections, or book titles within the text.

Latin passages: If such a translation is not provided in the original, I provide either a short translation in the footnotes or, for those instances that form distinct paragraphs, an indented translation following the Latin. Page numbers within translated passages might have moved slightly; see the Latin passage for an accurate placement of the page numbers. Some common phrases that may not always be translated:

Fiat: "Let it be done."
In nomine Patris et Fili et Spiritus Sancti: "In the name of the Father, and of the Son, and of the Holy Ghost."
Probatum est: "It is proved."
Vel: "or."
See also "per" and "pro," on page 34.

At some points, it is difficult to make out what a given Latin passage is saying. This is usually due to mistakes or omissions in the original. This has been corrected through reference to other texts when possible.

Line breaks: Removed or inserted for ease of reading. Sometimes sections in the original will run together on the same line, which makes for difficult reading.

Manuscripts: Full or partial editions of manuscripts listed in the footnotes are as follows:

Bayerische Staatsbibliothek Clm 849: Kieckhefer, Richard. *Forbidden Rites*. University Park: Pennsylvania State University Press, 1998.

Biblioteca Medicea Laurenziana Plut. 89 sup. 38: Johnson, Brian, trans. *Necromancy in the Medici Library: An Edition and Translation of Excerpts from Biblioteca Medicea Laurenziana, MS Plut. 89 Sup. 38*. West Yorkshire, UK: Hadean Press, 2020.

Bodleian Additional MS. B.1.: Klaassen, Frank F. *Making Magic in Elizabethan England*. University Park: Pennsylvania State University Press, 2019.

British Library Additional Manuscript 36,674: Legard, Phil, and Alexander Cummins, eds. *An Excellent Booke of the Arte of Magicke*. London: Scarlet Imprint, 2020.

British Library Sloane 3824: Ashmole, Elias, and David Rankine. *The Book of Treasure Spirits*. London: Avalonia, 2009.

British Library Sloane 3847: Peterson, Joseph H., trans. "Sloane 3847: The Clavicle of Solomon, Revealed by Ptolomy the Grecian." Esoteric Archives. 1999. http://www.esotericarchives.com/solomon/sl3847.htm.

British Library Sloane 3850: Peterson, Joseph H., ed. "Sloane 3850: Tractatus et Experimenta Magica." CD-ROM. 2007.

British Library Sloane 3851: Gauntlet, Arthur. *The Grimoire of Arthur Gauntlet*. Edited by David Rankine. London: Avalonia, 2011.

Cambridge Additional 3544: Foreman, Paul. *The Cambridge Book of Magic: A Tudor Necromancer's Handbook*. Edited by Francis Young. Cambridge: Francis Young, 2015.

Wellcome 4669: Skinner, Stephen, and David Rankine, eds. *A Collection of Magical Secrets* [...] Translated by Paul Harry Barron. London: Avalonia, 2009.

Marginalia: The text has a great deal of marginal contents, and these are noted in the footnotes when relevant. Harrington sometimes inserts a gloss near the first author's writing to clarify a reading; these additions have been omitted.

Missing letters and words: Added when they can be easily determined. I've been more conservative with the Latin text than the English on this account.

Misspellings and non-standard spelling: Corrected to today's English with British spellings. This includes minor adjustments regarding singular or plural, or subject-verb agreement.

Numbers in text: Usually written out, in English or Latin as appropriate for the surrounding text.

Page numbers, manuscript: Included and extrapolated from the surrounding material, although these are not always accurate. Sometimes Harrington fails to check for the proper page number, leading to some redundancies or missed numbers. I have followed his numbering for the most part, although I have inserted missing ones when they are consistent with his overall scheme.

Per: Latin for "by" or "through," occasionally used as "from."

Pro: Latin for "for," used infrequently.

Punctuation: Thoroughly modernised. Sentences in works such as this are much longer than those to which modern readers are accustomed. When necessary, a sentence may be interrupted in such a way that the next segment is a sentence beginning with a conjunction, such as "And" or "But."

Question marks within brackets: Indicate places where the text is illegible or indecipherable.

Red text: Harrington uses such ink on occasion to emphasize particular points. It is reproduced wherever it appears in the MS.

Supernumerary words (duplicate words unnecessary within the passage's context): These were omitted in the main text but included in incantations. Also see "Catchwords" on page 31.

Underlining: Indicates text underlined in the original.

Voces magicae: Magical words of power. These have been capitalised for consistency. Inconsistencies in magical names, even within the same ritual, have been left uncorrected.

Welsh passages: Translated thanks to Kate Leach, with the conjectural Welsh included in the main text and the translation of the Welsh and Latin elements in the footnotes. Our notes in these sections are labelled as "KL" and "DH."

The Text

[Inside front cover]

The Wheel of Fortune [pp.] 49, 50 & 51
Text for Tryon 1 Cor 8 Chap 13[128]

[Chart of Alchemical Symbols][129]

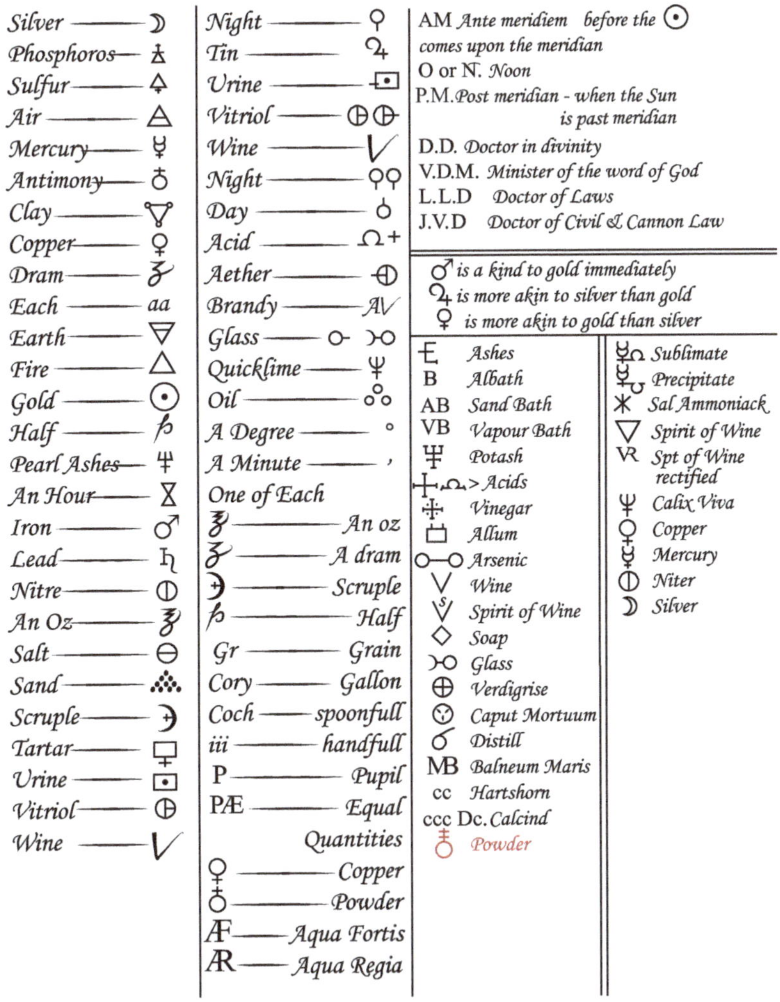

128. *Text...13*: The Bible passage seems to be 1 Corinthians 8:13 (KJV): "Wherefore, if meat make my brother to offend, I will eat no flesh while the world standeth, lest I make my brother to offend." This would seem to be a reference to the vegetarianism of Thomas Tryon (1634–1703), a noted author and advocate of healthy lifestyles.

129. An abridged version of a chart appearing in Valentine, *The Last Will and Testament of Basil Valentine*, B5. The book is Lot 856 in King, *Catalogue* [...] *of Dr. Thos. Harrington*, 27.

Douce
MS
116

[i]

Auvol L J G.[130]

usiqqwafba abs be eng tl obeg sbe real bar[131]

1640 Appendix N1[132]

The Key to Cornelius Agrippa's *4th Book*

In nomine Dei.[133]

Reason is the power of separating truth from falsehood in all propositions within the reach of our understanding; and reason is the same in God, with this difference: that his knowledge is infinite, and all creatures finite or limited.

Who makest angels thy spirits, and thy ministers a flaming fire.[134]

To do honour, glory, and praise to God, and good to our neighbours, was man created thereby to enjoy eternal life, but evildoers to distinction, therefore in all and to all do good and eschew evil and willingly hurt no man, for man and angels of all creatures do glorify for God and for thy profit, and to do the good if you fear, as obey, love, and serve the Lord, to whom be all glory, world without end. Amen.

If there be no such things as witchcraft, all legislators, juries, witnesses, nay, and hundreds of witches and wizards themselves who have died for it and at their execution confessed themselves guilty of the charge, have acted unaccountably. Saul, Job, Mary Magdalene & c. have confessedly been under supernatural power.

Divine Philosophy is not harsh or crabbed, no dull fools suppose, but sweet and musical as is Apollo's lute.[135]

It will meet thee waking, sleeping, sailing, travelling, by night and by day, when thou speaketh or keep silence, for on all things is impressed the image

130. *Auvol L J G*: The significance of these lines is unknown.

131. *Usiqqwafba…bar*: Deciphered: "Huttinson not or pass my lord for any one."

132. Four books in Harrington's sale catalogue date to 1640, but one cannot be found, and the other three seem not to have an appendix of appropriate content.

133. *In…Dei*: Translation: "In the name of God."

134. Psalm 104:4.

135. "How charming is divine Philosophie! / Not harsh, and crabbed as dull fools suppose, / But musicall as is Apollo's lute"—Milton, *A Maske Presented at Ludlow Castle*, 17.

of God. And God is in all and everywhere, and no place is hid, but at all times found and seen, if you rightly seek him with faith and truth, to whom be glory, honour, might, majesty, and dominion with laud and thanksgiving now and forever, without end. Amen. Good God save me.[136]

Animal magnetism consists in the following rules: first, self-abstraction; second, attention; third, intention; fourth, affection or desire; fifth, sympathy; sixth, volition willing and power to have [illegible]; seventh, confidence,[137] in all which wisdom and ability are absolutely requisite with perseverance, for the science is wholly founded on the principles of sympathy and antipathy philos [illegible].

136. Similiar to Everard, *Divine Pymander*, 136. For more, see Pope, "'Darcke and Clowdie Speeches,'" 215, 235–36.

137. This appears to be part of the teachings of the mesmerist John Holloway. See Martin, *Animal Magnetism Examined*, 62.

[ii]

[Astrological and Divinatory Notes]

Latin Names[138]
Jacobus—Jacob
Abraham—Abrahamus
Daniel—Daniel
Edward—Edwardus
Thomas—Thomas
Richard—Richardus
Sarah—Sara
Elizabeth—Elizabetha
Mary—Maria
Monday—Luna ☽ silver
Tuesday—Martis ♂ iron
Wednesday—Mercury ☿ [quick]si[lv]er
Thursday—Jovis ♃ pewter
Friday—Veneris ♀ tin
Saturday—Saturni ♄ lead
Sunday—Sol ☉ Gold

☿ joyeth in the first house, ☽ in the third, ♀ in the fifth, ♂ in the sixth, ☉ in the ninth, ♃ in [the] eleventh, ♄ in the twelfth.[139]

Lead and silver are <u>earthly</u>,
Quicksilver is <u>waterish</u>,
Copper and tin are <u>airy</u>, and
Gold and iron <u>fiery</u>.

♂ and ☉ are fiery; ♃ and ♀ airy; ♄ and ☿ watery; ☽ earthy and watery.

To Know the Planet That Hath Dominion in the Nativity of a Person

1	*2*	*3*	*4*	*5*	*6*	*7*	*8*
A	*B*	*C*	*D*	*E*	*F*	*G*	*H*
9	*0*	*20*	*0*	*4*	*50*	*60*	*70*
I	*K*	*L*	*M*	*N*	*O*	*P*	*Q*
10	*0*	*100*	*200*	*300*	*400*	*500*	
R	*S*	*T*	*V*	*X*	*Y*	*Z*	

Take the number of every letter of the Christian name of the party inquiring, and the like of their parent's name. Apply them to the letters of the table (above) and their figures, then bring the several numbers into one sum total, and then divide by 9. And then, if 1 or 4 remains, it denotes the ☉ to have dominion in the nativity, promising long life and riches.

If 7 or 2,—the ☽; your life will be inconstant and changeable
If 9—♂; troubles, fears, and strife
If 5—☿; wealth but not keep it
If 3—♃; riches and favour
If 6—♀; successful love
If 8—♄; sullen bad fortune

The under table contains the names of the angels of the signs. Under one of these signs every man is born; therefore, if he knows his ascendant, the table will shew him his angel that governs him.[140]

♂	♀	☿	☽	☉	☿	♀	♂	♃	♄	♄	♃
♈	♉	♊	♋	♌	♍	♎	♏	♐	♑	♒	♓
Fire	*Earth*	*Air*	*Water*	*Fire*	*Air*	*Earth*	*Water*	*Fire*	*Earth*	*Air*	*Water*
Aiel	*Tual*	*Glae*	*Cael*	*Ol*	*Voil*	*Joel*	*Iosel*	*Hu~saige*	*Cavio~jah*	*Angul*	*Patile*

138. For the use of this material, see material on manuscript page 434 and the rite on manuscript page 105.

139. The "joys" are the astrological houses associated with a given planet. Brennan, "The Planetary Joys and the Origins of the Significations of the Houses and Triplicities."

140. A similar table appears in the *Ars Paulina*. Peterson, *The Lesser Key of Solomon*, 133.

[iii]

The Beginning—with Proper Directions

The form, manner, apparatus, and appendages for the beginning of this business may be seen at large in the folio Key of Rabbi Soloman,[141] with directions also relative to the talisman, which in brief are to procure a metal similar to the planet to attend to the favourable days of the moon and see her well aspected, as also the planet from which you are principally affecting the business, and, if possible, the planet which ruled at your birth should be in good aspect. Most of the orations & c. in this book are taken from the *Fourth Book* of Cornelius Agrippa and seem very faithfully translated. More of these invocations & c. may be found in the Quarto Red Book,[142] and after all it will be found that some expense, much patience, not a little trouble, and very great study is necessary to procure only one certainty, which is amusement, if you should be partial to these researches, but there is assuredly something extremely injurious, in many of the schemes, and if there appears a degree of infatuation in the mysterious parts, yet many things exceeding curious will be discovered by a candid liberal mind. Many of the prayers are devote[143] and excellent, and some astonishing truths will be found relative to the influences of the planets & c. All studies may be carried so far; was the dross sifted from this by a learned and discerning unprejudiced philosophic hand, some invaluable discovery perhaps might be made, was the researcher to stop and turn back because he met with an absurdity. Such an explorer would never bring satisfaction to himself or any useful discoveries to his country. No harm can arise here if the good accrues this balloon of the mind, will never precipite[144] its appointed secrets [?] from any great heights. In a word, attend, be diligent, search, and try, and the disposition of the person necessary for this performance is such that if you do not already attain it, the possession thereof alone will in some measure compensate for your pleasing pains, as it is absolute necessary that you should be sober, religious, cleanly, judicious, learned, just, and free from all kind of dissipations, charitable, and honourable [?].

141. A "Ray of Rabby Salomon; Astrology from the French" is lot 1083 in Harrington's catalogue. King, *Catalogue* [...] *of Dr. Thos. Harrington*, 36.

142. *Quarto Red Book*: Unknown manuscript source.

143. *Devote*: Devout.

144. *Precipite*: Precipitate.

[iv]

The operator must possess genius, be conversant in most sciences, particular in astronomy, and be free from uncandid prejudices and avarice. He must be firm and courageous yet patient, humble, polite, sincere, and respectful. The possession of these qualities alone will make a good beginning—nor let the crude hasty ideas of absurdity, presumption, or impossibility deter you, because we do not immediately comprehend, we are not to disbelieve; perhaps faith will make us whole. We feel the wind, but we cannot tell its component parts, nor tell today from whence it shall blow tomorrow. We know our blood circulates, but from where does it derive its first impulse, spring, or continued force? An automaton may be moved by spring and weights, but we are curious automatons, fearfully and wonderfully made. We know the trembling needle turns to the north, but what attracts it there? Can we tell the source of its attraction? We see the sun and feel its power and know its influence, as it will attract a whole pond of water, but we know not how that divine body is supplied with heat. The moon has influence on the tides. Epidemic disorders are influences on the human mind and bodies, but by what means we know not. If a polypus[145] is cut in many pieces, each piece becomes a distinct polypus, by what operation we know not. Each mouldy grain of sand viewed through the microscope affords a complete visitation of trees, herbs, and even flowers. If therefore we cannot account for those great truths, let us not be too precipitate in condemning or censuring other abstruse matters because we cannot comprehend or account for them. Let us be candid and not mistake our own imbecilities for errors in silence. Let us firmly, fully, and impartially try and examine and prove, then reject the fallacious and improve the permanent. If we make a discovery, we add our useful mite to society. If we detect a falsity, delusion, or imposition, we shall be affable to draw the veil from before the eyes of the misguided and prevent honest minds falling dupes to false science and groundless, absurd, fallacious, though perhaps originally priestly and artful whims.

[v]

Some General Aphorisms [on Talismans]

[1.] The seven planets are said to have great virtues in their own proper metals only, as the ☉ upon gold, ☽ on silver, ♀ on copper, ♃ on tin, ☿ on quicksilver, ♂ on iron, ♄ on lead.

145. *Polypus*: A cephalopod or other aquatic invertebrate.

2. Observe that the moon has favourable direction to the planet which you are working under, and that planet is not in its detriment. Also attend to its day and hour.

3. In the beginning of every work, be especially attentive to the aspects and strength of the planets, and whatever angel you call, be sure the planet that rules and influences him be in good aspect, strong, or exaltation, and better if above the Earth.

4. In forming talismans & c., you must have some knowledge in astrology, or it cannot be performed, nor any of the arts contained in this book, for the dignity and strength of the planets are absolute necessary to be known. Therefore, a table of their dignities and debilities should be before you and may be found in most astrologic books. A short one follows to shew the houses of the planets:

♄	♃	♂	☉	♀	☿	☽
♑ ♒	♐ ♓	♈ ♏	♌	♉ ♎	♊ ♍	♋

5. In making sigils, talismans, & c., I should think a plate formed of plaster of paris or virgin wax and coloured according to the colours of the planet, [for] which see page 365, might answer.

6. In making sigils, talismans, & c., the artist should often repeat during the operation what 'tis making for, with all some well-turned serious energetic prayer.

7. In gathering herbs or preparing medicines to cure, first pray unto God that he would inspire thee with his grace, whereby thou mayst bring the end thou desirest for the praise and glory of God and benefit of thy neighbour.

[That] a spirit can act upon bodies is plain from every man's own experience who finds that he alone wills also and moves his body—Reason is the power of separating truth from falsehood.

[vi]

[blank]

[vii]

A Liquid from the Moon

When the moon is at the full, take a clean sponge, and with it a tin glass such as will burn a paper with the rays of the sun, and obtain the full force of the ☽ upon the sponge, and a moisture like milk will be obtained—a liquid or divine quality—if penetrated with philosopher knowledge.

Prima Materia

This Mercury of the Philosophers has created a diversity of opinions and more perplexity than all other things common with the sun or gold or philosopher's stone. It is said to partake of the astral qualities or nature of the oculus mundi and luna. It is declared to be a celestial and a terrestrial sulphur—replete with foulness and a penetrating pungent power.

Query if the dew is not this heavenly and earthly sulphur—which fully of night

[viii]

to the crux of fruitfulness to the earth, full dispersed ever at sunrise, again spread and expends itself in regions of light, and nitrous extension unembodied with the elements it descended from, and per triply in the fiery and aerial and watering comports by the elements every day till it again descend, and the earth with unmoved action, life, intention, and agency incomprehensible.

☉—☿ dew—Hermetically sealed and kept three months in constant heat, will cause a corruption from which shall arise a new soul—or magnetite—and read Basil Valentine and Flamel with deep and [pro]found attention.—Olive

[ix]

Alchemy

+ Esteem the proper period for the composition of ☉ and ☿[146]

To find ☿ and yet to retain its spent and penetrative quality is to possess an agent infallible, immutable, and efficient. The soul of gold is eternal; it never dies, and conjunct well its part—subtiled[147]—incorporated and warm—it sends forth its hidden strong evening [?] in its progeny beyond computation or belief!—My opinion is founded on the philosophical nourateds [?] of

146. Sideways on the page.

147. *Subtiled*: Made thinner or more fluid.

Jabir, Solomon, + Basil Valentine, Flamel, and Hermes, which induce myself to say—

This sun's conjunction shall bestow
Wits, fame—wonders great below +
A mighty mystery there doth lie—
Which shall a world of wealth supply
Twice the soul and life unite
And one of a penny—glorious bright
Shall reveal—the golden art
Which will the soul or ☉ impart

[x]

O mighty wonder—seen below—
O new life—a stream doth show—
Of endless riches!—Matter seen
In a new—and glorious mien—
The spirit then, the tin most grant
Does a regeneration want—
And—transmuting as it goes.
Around a calculation throws
Sublime!—known to very few
And those to power and wisdom true!
Where less profane not secrets given
But sound keep—the gifts of heaven!
Devoutly bearing to that shrine of grace
Where wisdom finds a lasting place
These thoughts of mine pray accept
From missing science long has kept
New who writes—with grateful hurt
that serves such comfort does missort [?].
Olive—

[xi]

[18th Century Table of Contents][148]

Animal magnetism 1st leaf

Index

Page

Animal magnetism 1st leaf

Incantation 1

To bring the thief again 2

To bind a spirit 3

Rules for beginning experiments 4

The mansions of the moon 5

Prosperous times 6

Invisibility 7

The secretness of secrets 10

To attract a female familiar 11

Experiment relative to theft or 13

treasures hid 14

15

Charm for diseases 16

17

To stop the stream of a river 20

To make a hart or buck appear 20

To make men appear in horns 21

To make a vine with branches appear 22

To make meadows and woods appear 23

A table with meat & c.

Oak trees and birds singing 24

A man drawing the mast of a ship and elephant 25

A castle and dragons in skin 26

A horse to carry thee and iron, gold 27

To obtain their love and to make 43[149]

thy enemy love thee and do 45

To make a man prosperous 48

and defend him from all danger

The Wheel of Fortune 49

A do and a do 50–51[150]

To have restut[151] of any one 52

and to be invisible & c. & c. 53

To make a tooth full, & for a 55

good digestion, a woman's travail & c. 55

For wounds in the head, disputation, & c 56

For a child in the mother's womb 57

If gold be hid in the ground 58

For the pestilence 59

148. This is the original table of contents that Harrington assembled, with no changes made. It indicates his own priorities and interests, as much material is passed over in silence.

149. The intervening pages are in Latin, suggesting that Harrington was not overly familiar with that language.

150. *A do and a do*: The same as the above.

151. *Restut*: Not in OED.

A charm against falling evil and shot 60
Do against thieves and an amulet 63
Charms against biting of mad dog 66
Scorpions, woman in labour 67
Do for toothache, headache, witch & c.
Charms to open locks, drive away 69
spirits, gather herbs & c. & c. & c. & c. 70
71
72
Of witches & c. 88–89 73
Charms for agues 75
To find out hidden treasures 77
A magical alphabet and table of good 79
and bad fortune
A table from the *Shepherd's Calendar* 81
A variety of astrologic houses 82
Invocations 92
A table of aspects 93
Seals, letters, characters of Saturn 95
and all the planets 98
Intelligence and characters 100
of all the planets
To know if truth or a lie is told 105
and the virtue of mandrakes
To know the state of friends afar with an egg 107
and for theft or any other thing
To see of spirit in a crystal glass 108
To prove theft and find the thief 111
To know if any kind of business 113
shall come to good or evil
& experiments of hazel rods
A discharge for all manner of spirits 116
Against charms or enemies and to 120
help out of prison
A fascination and to make melons grow 122[152]
To keep fruit from birds 124
and the enemy in prison 125
Experiment from the Psalms 126
To bind a spirit & c. 127
For things stolen—approved 130
To raise a spirit and lay the same 130
135
The spirit to appear in the crystal stone 136
A licence for spirits and their 140
followers and a prayer

152. The melons charm is found on the following page.

[xii]

To cure diseases, against theft 141
Also ague, fever, and dysentery 142
Draw out teeth, recover
stolen goods, & c. 143
And for witchcraft—approved 144
From 144 to 148 on witches 148
Fairies 149
Fascination 153
For prick of a thorn, a cattle 154
bewitched, & c.
Charms, receipts, & c. 296 155
To heal wounds 157
For fractures and dislocations 161
For a long journey 162
Invisibility and spirits 164
The nature, order, and condition 167
of all the spirits and the planets 168
To have your desire in all things 171
To call Obreon[153] 174
and other spirits to page 187
Toothache and to have 188
an obedient familiar
To bring the thief again 205
To see the thief in thy sleep 208
A curious figure 211
To talk with spirits 212
Invocation 215
The circle and character 219
The prayer 221
The call 224
Invisible 235
Obtain a gift, win at shooting 235
Bleeding at the nose or wound
A charm for children 236
Experiments on several accounts 233
and these continue to pass 264
Schemes and characters 265 to 268
for a woman's delivery 273
Crystal stone and figure 284
Prayers and invocations 285
The circle 289
To know if a woman be with 292
child, a bad liver, & c. & c.
A bond to bind thieves 301
To excommunicate a spirit 303
A curse 304
Names of the spirits 312
Seals of the earth + 314
Names of the angels of the planets 317
A table of names of the angels
that 321
rules the different lords of the day
A figure for the first hour Lord's
day 332
Conjuration for Monday 337
To Wednesday and to Saturday 348

153. *Obreon*: A misspelling for Oberion. For another eighteenth-century misspelling, see Wellcome 4669, II.25–8.

Hours of day and night when begin
+ 349

Colour of the planets 365

Planetary hours of day and night 366

The ring and cup of divination 367

A table of all the angels and 379
planets ruling every hour,
both for day and night

Seals and figures for various 382
purposes

For one bewitched 331[154]

Instructions for beginning the 388
principal of this work

A length of planetary hours 384

Essential dignities and detriments
of all the planets 384

Animal magnetism 1st Leaf

154. This is out of sequence, indicating that Harrington passed over it and then decided to add it after many pages.

[xiii]

[blank]

[xiv]

[blank]

[xv]

[blank]

[xvi]

A Ch197 to Prevent Any 712 Hy38g w3th the Wif2[155]

After the 1ct 4f c43t348, wip2 the p282s immediate, and when Q [?] is rolled up in a piece of linen b59932d under the th92sh4ld as long as 'tis b59932d, so long h3s p282s no effect. Only them that has ch197d h37, and will not be freed from the ch197 till 'tis removed from the thresh45ld. Contrary let the party b598 728st951 to ashes mixed with urine. Make a figure of a p931p5s;[156] if not ashes enough to make it, take some dirt which has p12t 5p48 and carefully dry the 371g2 he has thus 71d2 and keep it in a dry place. So long as keeps it, so long will the shot h166 sh49t from any other 718 and will have stoppage in the 59382 when about to 72dd2l, and is cured by anointing the body with the gall of a crow mixed with oil of sesamum.[157]

[Witch Bottle Newspaper Story][158]

The following magical incantation is taken from the Morning Post, May 29, 1792:[159] A farmer at Uxbridge[160] haved[161] a fine horse suddenly taken with a kind of wanton madness different from any disorder usual to horses, so that, after having tried every method of cure and the animal growing worse and useless, the farmer was recommended to shoot him. Just as he was loading for that purpose the piece, the horse suddenly recovered and nothing ailed him. But at that very instant a fine mare, who had been perfect well before, was immediately taken as the horse had been, but upon putting some of her

155. *A Ch197... Wif2*: Deciphered: "A Charm to Prevent Any Many from Lying with the Wife." Parts of this passage were in cipher, for which the key can be found on manuscript page 1, but it seems to have been used inconsistently. I have attempted the most logical rendering of the passage possible.

156. *P931p5s [priapus]*: The form of a phallus, although it could also be used for a statue of the god Priapus often placed in gardens.

157. *Sesamum*: Sesame.
The passage deciphered: "After the act of coition, wipe the penis immediate, and when it [?] is rolled up in a piece of linen buried under the threshold as long as 'tis buried, so long his penis [shall have] no effect. Only them that has charmed him, and will not be freed from the charm till 'tis removed from the threshold. Contrary, let the party burn menstrua to ashes mixed with urine. Make a figure of a priapus; if not, ashes enough to make it, take some dirt which has peat upon, and carefully dry the image he has thus made, and keep it in a dry place. So long as keeps it, so long will the shot fall short from any other man and will have stoppage in the urine when about to meddle, and is cured by anointing the body with the gall of a crow mixed with oil of sesamum."

158. A witch bottle is a magical device intended to reverse witchcraft cast on a person or animal, although the reasoning behind this ritual is not given here. See Harms, *Witch Bottles: Steel and Glass*.

159. *Morning Post, May 29, 1792*: No copy of the paper from this date is known to have survived.

160. *Uxbridge*: Town in west London.

161. *Haved*: Owned.

water in a bottle with a quantity of crooked pins therein and placing all in the midst of the fire, the bottle burst with vast explosion [that] threw the pins about with that force. The mare directly recovered, and both animals continued perfectly well and useful.

[1]

[Key to a Cipher]

a e i o u l m n r
1 2 3 4 5 6 7 8 9

Incantamentum pro Nocte[162]

"As thou, O Lord, didst stop and stay (for thy chosen people) the Red Sea,
Wanting their course, till they passed Pharaoh's force,
And of Joshua's invocation the moon stood still and made a stay
The sun abode and stayed in Gideon, all that day;
So I pray thee stay, each one that seek my good's confusion,
Make them to stand still without any corporeal motion,
Whilst my hand a sign doth make, a sign for them their way to take.
O thou that art the king of bliss, mighty Jehovah, grant me this,
In the name of the Father, and of the Son, and of the Holy Ghost." (Scribe it)
After:

"In *nove* [nomine] + Patris + et Filii + et Spirit + Sancti, amen. Thieves, thieves, thieves, stand ye still in the name of the Trinity, and for the passion of Jesus Christ, and for his death, and his uprise,[163] and for the names of Matthew, Mark, Luke, and John. Also I charge you if you stand still, still I come to you, if any thieves hither come my goods for to steal, the Holy Ghost be there before then for to let, I bind the thieves that hither come as hard in his stead, as did St. Bartholomew ye find with a hair upon his head,[164] that none of you pass away, till tomorrow that be day, and till I myself do come you to; and give you leave for to go.

162. Translation: "Incantation for Night."

163. *Uprise*: Resurrection.

164. *St. Bartholomew…head*: A motif that seems to largely originate in magical texts. See Roper, *English Verbal Charms*, 94. See also Harms, Clark, and Peterson, *Oberon*, 178, and manuscript page 240.

"Irrual super eos, formido et panas, magnitudine bractii timor. fiant immobile, quasi lapis, donec pertransant populus tuus iste quem possedisti.[165] Obscurantur oculi eorum ne videant, et doria eorum semper mearva offende super eos, iram tuam, et furor vie tua comprehendet eos.[166] In nomine Patris et Filii et Spiritus Sancti, amen.

"Disparibus meritis pendunt tria corpora remus
Dismas et Gismas dedie demina potestas
Alla petit dismas set tendit infina germas
Nos et res nostra conservat dimina potestas,"[167]

"Three bodies with unequal blame hang on crosses,
Dismas and Gesmas, with the divine power in the middle;
Dismas seeks the highest, but Gesmas strives toward the lowest.
The divine power protects us and our goods."

165. *Irrual...possedisti*: This is a transformed version of Exodus 15:16 in the Vulgate: "inruat super eos formido et pavor; in magnitudine brachii tui fiant immobiles quasi lapis, donec pertranseat populus tuus, Domine, donec pertranseat populus tuus iste quem possedisti." Translation from KJV: "Fear and dread shall fall upon them; by the greatness of thine arm they shall be as still as a stone; till thy people pass over, O Lord, till the people pass over, which thou hast purchased."

166. *Obscurantur...eos*: A transformed version of Psalm 68:24–25 in the Vulgate: "obscurentur oculi eorum ne videant, et dorsum eorum semper incurve; effunde super eos iram tuam, et furor irae tuae conprehendat eos." English translation from KJV Psalm 69:23–4: "Let their eyes be darkened, that they see not; and make their loins continually to shake. Pour out thine indignation upon them, and let their wrathful anger take hold of them."

For anti-theft charm with these two verses and the one cited previously, see Bodleian Rawlinson D.252, 121r–v (order reversed); Argentine, *De Praestigiis et Incantationibus*, 181; Klaassen, *Making Magic in Elizabethan England*, 41; Lecouteux, *Dictionary of Ancient Magic Words and Spells*, 185.

167. *Disparibus...potestas*: Original (corrected): "Disparibus meritis pendunt tria corpora ramis / Dismas et Gesmas, medio divina potestas / Alta petit Dismas, sed tendit infima Gesmas / Nos et res nostra conservat divina potestas.

The "Dismas et Iesmas" charm type, dating back to the early fourteenth century, is usually used for protection against theft, although some versions are to ward off the effects of torture. Definition and commentary: Roper, *English Verbal Charms*, 103–4. Examples: Hunt and Benskin, *Three Receptaria from Medieval England*, 2; "Rawlinson D.252," 121r; Hunt, *Popular Medicine in Thirteenth-Century England*, 77, 94; Roper, *English Verbal Charms*, 104; Argentine, *De Praestigiis et Incantationibus*, 180–81; Weyer, *De praestigiis daemonum*, 547; Scot, *The Discouerie of Witchcraft*, 259 (book 12, chapter 17); Klaassen, *Making Magic in Elizabethan England*, 42–43; Schönbach, "Eine Auslese Altdeutscher Segensformeln," 49–50; Oxford, Bodleian Library, Ashmole 1378, 62, 77; Delrío, *Disquisitionum Magicarum Libri Sex*, 767; Briggs, "Some Seventeenth-Century Books of Magic," 452; Peterson, "Le Grand Grimoire"; *Petit Albert*, 113; Thiers, *Traité des Superstitions*, 1:365; Rankine and Barron, *The Complete Grimoire of Pope Honorius*, 203; Leitão, *Opuscula Cypriani*, 373; manuscript pages 103, 282. In several of these, this appears with one or both of the Biblical passages given above.

In nomine Patris et Filii et Spiritus Sancti, amen.

Saint John's wort, carried about one, proven to [prevent] being hurt, either by witches or devils.

"Adiuro vos fures ex parte dei et pro sanguine Jesu Christi ut non me pertubatis. + Tola + Falla + Tetragrammaton + Jesus Palnato."

> "I adjure you, thieves, from the part of God, and by the blood of Jesus Christ, that you will not disturb me. + Tola + Falla + Tetragrammaton + Jesus Palnato."

[2]

Leave the foresaid [with] the Latin unsaid, for the great peril that might happen to the thieves, that thou sayst them. At "leave"—at this word—"give you leave for to go," and then say three Pater Nosters, three Aves, and one Credo, in the worship of the Father, and of the Son, and the Holy Ghost, and St. Bartholomew and all saints.

Without doubt, if this be said by a faithful man, this night-spell is as profitable by day or by night.

An Experiment to Bring the Thief Again with the Goods[168]

Upon a Monday or Wednesday, the work must have a Mass of the Holy Ghost [said] before the sunrise. Then take virgin wax pure and clear, and make thereof a circle[169] as hereafter followeth, and say first against the east, then against the west, then against the south, and last the north.

Coniuracio[170]

"O you, Sheltion, Uperion, Batheryone, and Matherione, whose names and signs be there written, I conjure and exorcise you, by the living God, and by the true God, and by the holy God, and by all the holy names of Jesu Christe, unto whom all patriarchs and prophets do call, and he helpeth them, and by the excellent name of God + Tet[r]agrammaton, and by all the names

168. This experiment, in which four spirits are invoked to return stolen goods, appears in several other manuscripts. For analysis, see Harms, Clark, and Peterson, *Oberon*, 179–83. For examples, see Harms and Clark, *Of Angels*, 125–27; British Library Sloane 1727, 50r–51r; Sloane 3824, 16r–20r; Sloane 3853, 73v–74v; Bodleian Rawlinson D.252, 103r–107r; Cambridge Additional 3544, 41–44; National Library of Scotland GD188/25/1/3, 103–6; Wellcome Institute 110, 99v; Dawson, *History of Skipton*, 392–93; manuscript pages 206–7.

169. *Circle*: A wax plate, as specified later.

170. Translation: "Conjuration."

of God, which may be seen or said, and by the virtue of blessed Peter, and by the virtue of any saint, by the order of angels and archangels of God, by cherubim and seraphim, and by all special orders, by prophets, patriarchs, apostles, evangelists, disciples, innocent martyrs and confessors, holy monk eremites,[171] virgins, and widowers, and by all the saints of God, and by the virtue of God, per heaven, earth, sun, moon, astrea,[172] and deepness of the sea, that whosoever he be in fire or water, in earth or in the air, that you together do bring in one place him or them the same stolen such a thing of W., and that you make him come again with the goods of W.," (and name the thing stolen) "such a day, such an hour, and such a place, and that you, per the power of the king, obey and fulfil my desire and will, without hurt of body or soul of him or them, and by all the holy names of God, O Saviour Jesus Christ, *Mesras* [Messias], Sother, Emanuell, Sabauth, Andonay, Obey, Oon, Tet[r]agrammaton, Anamizapta, Elefore, I conjure by all the foresaid names of God that you rest not in fire, in water, in earth, or air, until you have

[3]

brought him or them which such a thing or things, unto such a place, such an hour" (naming them) "if which if you do not, I condemn to everlasting fire, there to remain till you have fulfilled my will, per the power of their characters, and per Sathan your king, unto whom you owe obedience, and per all the high clemency of and per your Monday plays,[173] and by Lucifer, and per the virtue of all herbs, and all trees and stones, and by the virtue of the bonds of King Solomon, and per celestial, terrestrial, and infernal power, and by him that shall come to judge both the quick and the dead, and the world with fire, fiat, + fiat, + fiat."

And if he come not the day and hour appointed, then bury all the said plates in the ground and recite the work in the morning, at noon, or at night and the next day following. Thou shall not fail of thy purpose.

171. *Eremites*: Hermits.

172. *Astrea*: Likely *astra*, "stars." See Harms, Clark, and Peterson, *Oberon*, 180.

173. *Monday plays*: Possibly a reference to Plough Monday plays, performed on the first Monday after Epiphany. Metzler, "The Plough Monday Plays."

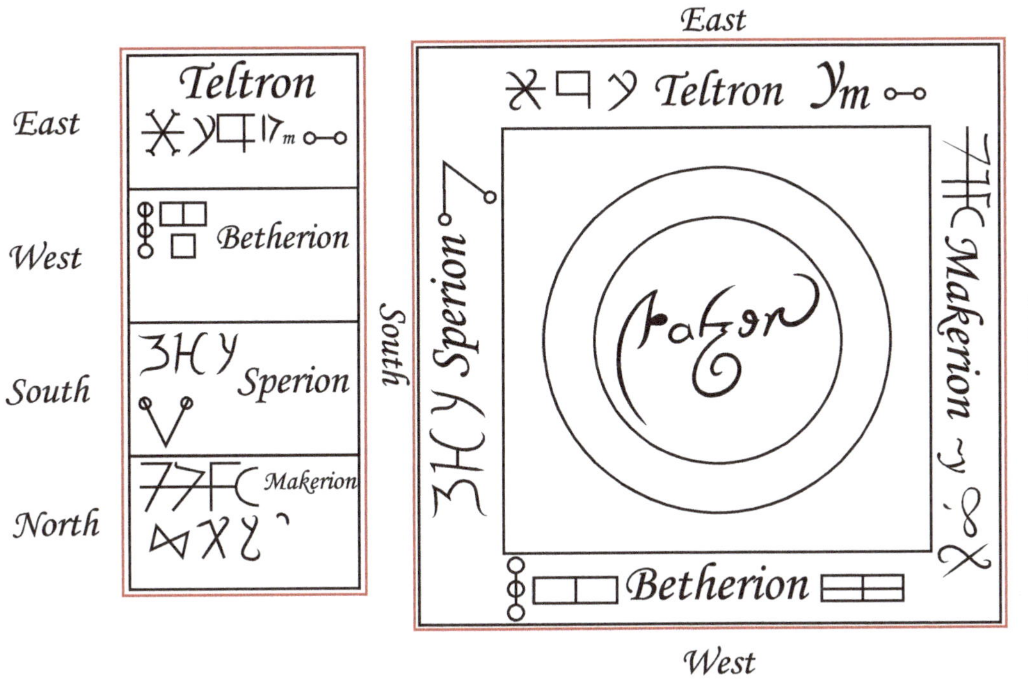

To Bind a Spirit

"I conjure you spirits, Gibor, Tibolato, Petron, et Tribo, by the power of the Father and of the Son and the Holy Ghost, by these holy names of God Tet[r]agrammaton, Sabarathagla, and Bason, and per all the names of God which Solomon bound all the spirits into a glass, per all the rules, ink, and signs, and divisions in the high air that God the highest hast made, ordained, and assigned you to obey unto, that you all bind and labour this spirit or witch that hath troubled or do hurt or trouble W.

[4]

"I charge you, per all those names aforesaid, and per all the names of God, that this spirit, or spirits, witch or witches, or whatsoever, they be expelled, extinct, and put away, and that they have no more power on W., neither to hurt, harm, trouble, or vex him anymore, in any way. Thus bind I you, by the names above reserved, and in the name of the Father, the Son, and the Holy Ghost, (Amen)."

Then say Pater Noster, Ave Maria, et Credo and thy *cominauciarem* [conjuration] three times.

See No. V of the aphorisms at the beginning of this book and prayer behind the frontispiece of Cornelius Agrippa's *Fourth Book*.[174]

Rules Necessary in Doing Experiments

In the beginning do good work, pray, and fast, and give alms and deeds, and absent yourself from the world.

Secondly, have a secret, clean place, wherein is no stirring, nor going of men nor *womb* [women], and that no man can scare you.

Thirdly, that you call such into your company that be wise, discreet, and virtuous, and no babblers, for the telling of the science doth but find it, and hethest[175] the virtue thereof.

Fourthly, is that you provide all things new or clean washen, but new is best to wear upon you.

Fifthly, you must have a familiar[176] priest to consecrate all your instruments, and he must be virtuous and a good lynar,[177] and also he must have good understanding that he may consecrate truly.

Sixthly, provide all things to make all things as parchment, metals, censes,[178] instruments, sword, pencils, knife, silks, inks, collars, gold with other things, as is necessary to provide before you begin.

The seventh rule is, you must be confessed, clean from sin actual and venial.

The eighth is, before you begin any work, go to mass church[179] and hear a Mass of the Holy Ghost and a memory[180] of Our Lady with a memory of angels and all priests.

[5]

The ninth is, the master must be bathed, his nails pared, so that in all things he must be clean, inwardly and outwardly, and write nor grave any thing, but

174. This does not appear to be present in the published editions of pseudo-Agrippa, although I have not been able to view these due to COVID restrictions at this time of writing. If it is not, it may indicate a manuscript edition.

175. *Hethest*: A variant of "havest," dating to sixteenth-century southwest England or pre-seventeenth century Scotland.

176. *Familiar*: Friendly.

177. *Lynar*: Harrington glosses this as "liver," or one who lives in a particular way.

178. *Censes*: Incense. The original has "sencis."

179. *Mass church*: A Catholic church.

180. *Memory*: A short prayer or portions of a service inserted into a service of another sort—in this case, the Mass of the Holy Ghost.

it ought to be written and graven in such times and hours as the experiment doth firm[181] her.

Finally, do nothing but in good signs, wherein astronomy must there help, and that will not avail, and always let it be in the increase of the ☽, in any case or for any cause.

The 28 Mansions of the ☽ Rectified as Followeth[182]

The first beginneth at the 19 grade 26 m of ♈ and is called—Genell

2 at the 2 grade 17 m of	♉	voc: Enediel[183]
3 at 15 grade 9 m of	♉	voc: Amiriell
4 at 28 Ditto 0: m	♉	voc: Azachiel
5 at 10 Ditto 52 m	♊	voc: Gabiel
6 at 23 Ditto 43 m	♊	voc: Dirachiel
7 at 6 Ditto 35 m	♋	voc: Seheliel
8 at 109[184] Ditto 26 m	♋	voc: Amnediel
9 at 2 Ditto 17 m	♌	voc: Bardiel
10 at 15 Ditto 9 m	♌	voc: Ardefiel
11 at 28 Ditto 0: m	♌	voc: Reael
12 at 10 Ditto 42 m	♍	voc: Abdisnel
13 at 23 Ditto 43 m	♍	voc: Lacerieb
14 at 6 Ditto 35 m	♎	voc: Ergedial
15 at 19 Ditto 26 m	♎	voc: Atzaliel
16 at 2 Ditto 17 m	♏	voc: Azeruel
17 at 15 Ditto 9 m	♏	voc: Aedriel
18 at 28 Ditto 0 m	♏	voc: Egibiel
19 at 10 Ditto 52 m	♐	voc: Amtiel
20 at 23 Ditto 42 m	♐	voc: Kiriel
21 at 6 Ditto 35 m	♑	voc: Bethnael
22 at 19 Ditto 26 m	♑	voc: Geliel

181. *Firm*: Confirm or affix.

182. Despite Harrington's following comments, these seem to be similar to those in Agrippa and other sources, with some errors. Agrippa, *De Occulta Philosophia Libri Tres*, 470–71 (book 3, chapter 24); Peterson, "Liber Juratus Honorii, or The Sworne Booke of Honorius." The first house is to start at the beginning of Aries, so this makes little sense.

183. This and the following four names were one higher in the manuscript, with their true locations indicated by lines drawn in after the fact.

184. *109*: Likely should be 19 degrees.

In page 285, *Third Book* Cornelius Agrippa[185] are the virtues and names of the twenty-eight mansions of the ☽, but they totally differ from this. Perhaps these [are] the names of the angels or spirits, and Cornelius Agrippa's of the stars.

[6]

23 at the 2 grade 18 m of	♒	voc: Requiel
24 at 15 ditto 9 m	♒	voc: Abrimael
25 at 28 Ditto 0 m	♒	voc: Aziel
26 at 10 Ditto 52 m	♓	voc: Catrigiel
27 at 23 Ditto 43 m	♓	voc: Altremel
28 at 6 Ditto 35 m	♈	voc: Ammiel

The Twelve Signs of the Zodiac[186]

♈ *Malchideel*	♉ *Asmodel*	♊ *Ambriel*
♋ *Muriel*	♌ *Verchiel*	♍ *Hamaliel*
♎ *Zuriel*	♏ *Brachiel*	♐ *Avalachiel*
♑ *Plannael*	♒ *Cambiel*	♓ *Berchiel*

Prosperous Times for Any Purpose

Compare this with page 285 of *Third Book* Cornelius Agrippa's, page 304 and of the same book.[187]

The ☽ being in the head of ♈, work for love of virgins and to provoke blood, and to build castles and fortresses.

The ☽ being in the belly of ♈, work for love of lords[188] and ladies, and to call angels to come before you, and work for invisibility.

The ☽ being in the tail of ♈ and in the head of ♉, work for love of all women, and call angels to come before you.

The ☽ being in the belly of ♉, call angels, and work for images and invisibility.

The ☽ being in the tail of ♉ and in the head of ♊, conjure and [make] images for love.

185. *Third...Agrippa*: 1651 edition.

186. For other sources, see Agrippa, *De Occulta Philosophia Libri Tres*, 470 (book 3, chapter 24); Peterson, "Liber Juratus Honorii, or The Sworne Booke of Honorius." Agrippa gives the final five as Barbiel, Adnachiel, Hanael, Gabiel, Barchiel.

187. These page numbers correspond to the chapter in the 1561 Agrippa dealing with the twenty-eight mansions of the moon, and the images on which they are based (book 2, chapters 33 and 46). The list here does not parallel that in Agrippa, however; compare instead to British Library Sloane 3850, 168v–169v. Bracketed words in this section come from that source.

188. *Lords*: Left out in Sloane 3850.

The ☽ being in the belly of ♊, work for love of men and women.

The ☽ being in the tail of ♊ and in the head of ♋, work for love and to get wisdom.

The ☽ being in the belly of ♋, work enchantments and to make destructions.

The ☽ being in the tail of ♋ and in the head of ♌, work enchantments and work for to make discord.

[7]

The ☽ being in the belly of ♌, work to bind an ill tongue and slanderers [and] for love.

The ☽ being in the tail of ♌ and in the head of ♍, work for love and invisibility.[189]

The ☽ being in the belly of ♍, work for love and invisibility.

The ☽ being in the tail of ♍, work for slanders and discord.

The ☽ being in the head of ♎, work for love and losses, enchantment, and conjure spirits.

The ☽ being in the belly of ♎, work for losses and enchantments, and call spirits in the west part.[190]

The ☽ being in the head of ♏, work for losses, bonds, love, and make conjurations.

The ☽ being in the belly of ♏, work for love.

The ☽ being in the tail of ♏ and in the head of ♐, bind men and women, conjure enemies, and call angels.[191]

The ☽ being in the head of ♑, work for hatred.

The ☽ being in the belly of ♑, work to conjure enemies.

The ☽ being in the tail of ♑ and in the head of ♒, work for love, losses, enchantment, and contrary.

The ☽ being in the belly of ♒, work for enmity, bind, and conjure.

The ☽ being in the tail of – and in the head of ♓, work for hatred and invisibility.

The ☽ being in the belly of ♓, work for enmity, losses, enchantment.[192]

189. *Work...invisibility*: Sloane 3850: "Work for slander and discord." The copyist of Douce MS. 116 seems to have accidentally read the following item.

190. The working for the tail of Libra is missing here and in Sloane 3850.

191. The workings for the belly and tail of Sagittarius are missing here and in Sloane 3850.

192. The workings for the tail of Pisces are missing in both documents.

An Experiment of Invisibleness, after the Knowledge of the Ancient Philosophers

Socrates, of all philosophers after the mind of Donat,[193] doth excellently entreat of invisibleness, that which or go into a castle invisible and by this art only. Therefore, dear brethren, when you desire with one accord to work secretly in the time Lazn I the ☽ calezare[194] on the i of ♊ or the 13 or 17 or 19 or 21.[195] Go to a hill of anigtte,[196] for in that time they gather the chief of part of their

[8]

living wherewith they live and are nourished by the space of the holy year, for then ☉ hath great power in so much that the herbs and all green things receive their power. Mark this and prove it to be true, that either the twelfth or fourteenth day the fowls do rest from their labour, for these days they do not labour, not per any knowledge of their own judgment but per nature of themselves and of the time present. And on these days aforesaid, take warm water with you, and to go to a hill of amytte,[197] and, with your water, you may expulse and drive them away from their place, and then take their eggs and break them in a mortar and dried in the ☉, and then meddle[198] the dust with honey, and keep it diligently until you have need thereof. And the 1st day of ♋ or the 7 or 15 or 17, with the said ointment anoint thy eyes, and that night about one of the clock, at the first singing of the cock, and turn the 6 eastward after the order of the great charge, and stand or kneel unto; thou shalt see in the firmament such a sign of such stars formed on this fashion as followeth.

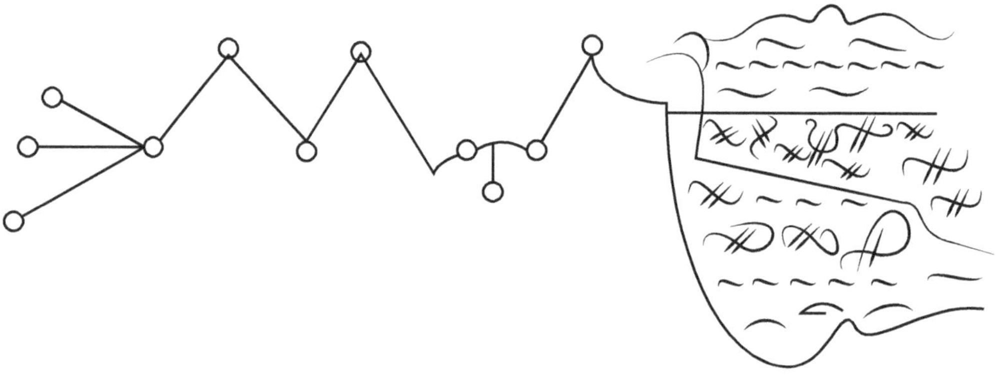

193. *Donat*: A short treatise, which a copyist has apparenty misinterpreted as a personal name.

194. *Lazn…calezare*: Unknown significance.

195. Marginal notes on next page: "1 of 3 is the 5th day of July / 13 of 3 is the 6 day of July and 17 of December / 17 of 3 is the 20 day of November / 19 of 3 is 30 day of August / 21 of 3 is the 31 [sic] of February."

196. Harrington notes "perhaps Emmet," or ants.

197. Harrington notes "perhaps Emmet."

198. *Meddle*: Mix.

This sign the astronomers in Arabia do call it Wasud,[199] that which is as much say as a marvellous secret of signs. The eyes that which receipt such brightness of the anointing, the element not hindering, but the eye should see unreasonable beholding the

[9]

least star that doth waver in the fiery heaven. And then as he shall stand, beholding the said sins, and the said stars with great diligence, or, if there be more than yourself, let everyone have a plate of lead the breadth of his hand, and let him lay it under his right foot. And whilst he stand and earnestly behold the said stars, let it be so that you see any other secret sign, do either move or appear about them, as a green cross, or a red circle, or a brass triangle, that which be visible shewed at all times, but not always, in like manner sometimes a cross, only sometimes a circle, sometimes a triangle, bearing redness in his order. And when you see any of those signs, then take up the plate of lead from underfoot and with an instrument of steel, grave upon it the sign that reigneth, and by and per after divide the plate of lead in four parts, and in the four parts with your instrument of steel, grave such sign as followeth:

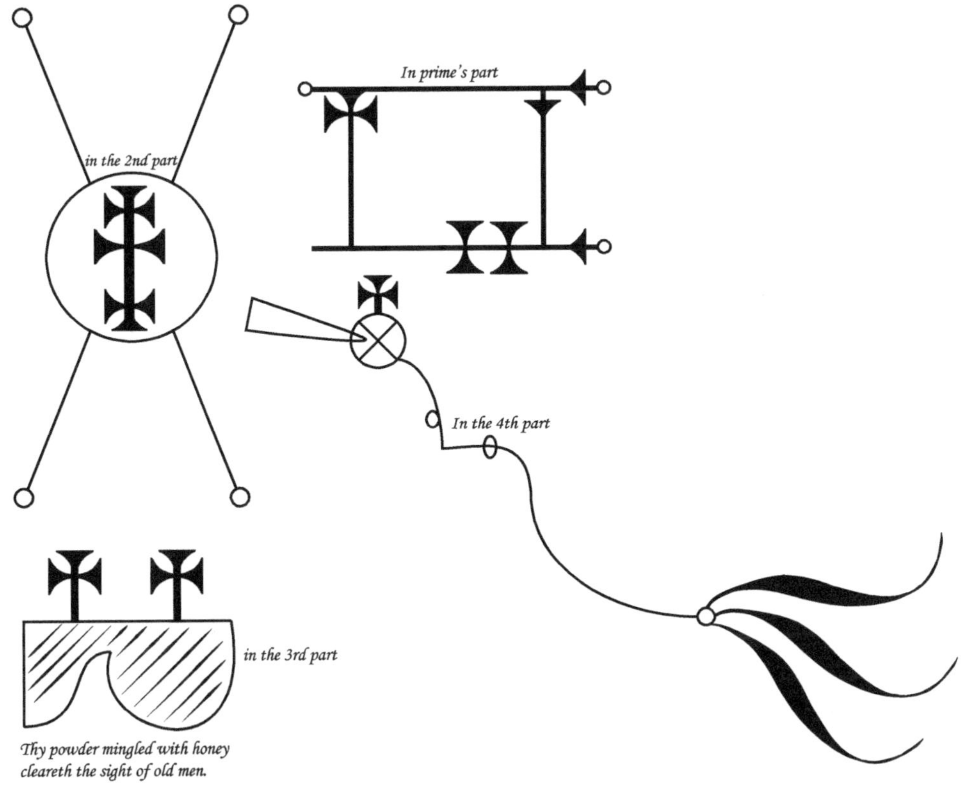

199. *Wasud*: Uncertain.

[10]

Then he shall keep these plates, thus written or engraven, clean wrapped in a silk cloth, and the next night following, come again to the same place, and that which sheweth thee the chief brightness in heaven, write or grave with the instrument in either of the foresaid plates, and when you have done this, lay them up and keep them clean. And so when thou art disposed to be invisible, take the first plate and put it upon thy breast, and the second on thy back behind, and the third upon thy right arm, and the fourth upon thy left arm, and then thou shalt be invisible to all men's sights or warrant, and when that thou will be seen of men, take away the plate of from the aforesaid place. But in any wise lay them up secretly, and keep them clean, for this be of effect. For according to the wise men, in heaven is power to be and not to be, power to be is always, and his power as the power not to be, but the dignity of sign, to defer much in there. Therefore any man Christian men have wrought every year, and ndnalonslye at the gate Pisanentes, a Gadeseron cud pisone cum de legis nuntacionem,[200] and this may be done without sin.

The Secretness of Secrets Hid and Said by the Writer to Be <u>True</u>[201]
Take a lapwing and slay him on the Wednesday in the hour of ☿, and a vessel made of box,[202] with a knife made of brass, and beware he sheds no blood beside the vessel, but keep all the blood in the dish or vessel well covered, and set it in a private place, where no man cometh but thyself, and look that no man see the vessel with the blood but thyself, ne[203] nor come where it is, and you should not see it be nine days from thy sight. Then look thereto and uncover it, and you shall see the blood full of worms, then cover the vessel again, till another nine other days be gone. Then look thereto again, and thou shall see but one worm. Then take the meat of dates,

[11]

and kernels of walnuts and of almonds and figs, and bray them altogether, and make a paste thereof as round as a ball, and in the midst of it a hole, and cover the vessel therewith from the air at all times and set it again till another nine days then under the vessel, and you shall see a chicken in likeness of

200. *Ndnalonslye…nunctacionem*: Uncertain; it appears to be a garbled Latin passage.

201. For similar experiments, see BL Sloane 1727, 18–19; Sloane 3846, 111r; Bodleian Ballard 66, 13–15; e. Mus 238, 1r; Cambridge Additional 3544, 56–57; National Library of Scotland GD188/25/1/3, 102–3; Harms, Clark, and Peterson, *Oberon*, 366–369; Harms and Clark, *Of Angels*, 171.

202. *Box*: Harms, Clark, and Peterson, *Oberon*, 368, has "braay"; Harms and Clark, *Of Angels*, 171, has "box."

203. *Ne*: Than.

a lapwing. Slay it and put it on a spit and roast it, and make the fire of date stones, and walnut shell, and as it roasteth, keep the grease that droppeth thereto.

And when you will work into any work of philosophy, anoint thy face and thine eyes with the grease, and you shall see spirits face to face and what they do. They shall not hide their doings from thee, and they shall seem unto you as they were men and your fellows, and you shall hear them and speak with them, and ask of them what you will, and they shall tell you, and they shall hide nothing from your presence, and you need not to be adoubted,[204] for this is without doubtless true, without dread of God. For by this was our science first found. Also, when you will no longer see, then wash your face with water that swallows were sodden[205] in, under secret. Fin.

Note that this vessel must be made on Wednesday under ☿ and the knife of brass, and if thy experiment must be done under ☿ on the Wednesday.

Fairies Adipisitur[206]—To Attract a Familiar[207]

This is said to have been proved.

You may work after this sort, for the fair maidens, the night before the new ☽, the night after, or the same night, or night before the full ☽, the night of the full ☽, or the night after, go to the house where fairies do use. Provide you a fair bucket clean washed, full of fair water, and set it by the chimney side or where fire is made, and hang a fair new towel by, or fair washed,

[12]

and so depart your way until the morning. Then be you the first that shall come to the bucket before sun rising, and take your bucket to the light. If you find upon the water a white rime,[208] like raw milk or grease, take it up with a silver spoon, and put it into a clean saucer.

Then the next night following, come to the same house again, before the 11 of the clock, making a good fire with sweet wood, and setting upon the table board a new towel or clean washed, a upon it three fine l[oaves] of manchet,[209] three knives with white hafts new, a new cup full of new ale, then

204. *Adoubted*: Frightened.

205. *Sodden*: Moistened.

206. *Adipisitur*: Probably "adipiscitur," or "he/she summons."

207. For similar experiments, see British Library Sloane 3851, 129r; Harms and Clark, *Of Angels*, 291–92.

208. *Rime*: Harrison adds "scum."

209. *Manchet*: A light-coloured bread of fine quality.

set yourself per the fire in a chair, your face towards the table, and anoint your face with the said oil or cream before named. Then you shall see come in by these the fairy maids, and as they pass per with beckoning their heads to you, and as they do to you, (so you do) the like to them, but say nothing. Suffer the first, whatsoever she be, to pass by, for she is malignant, but to the second or third, which you like best, reach forth your arm and pluck her to you, and with few words, ask her where she will appoint a place to meet with you the next morning, for to assoyle[210] such questions as you will demand of her. Then, if she grant you, suffer her to pass to her company till the hour appointed, missing her not, at the hour appointed and place. Then will the other, in thy time that you are talking, go to the table, and eat of it that is there. Then will they depart from you, and as they obey you, do you the like, saying nothing, but let them depart quietly. Then when your hour cometh to meet, say[211] to her your mind, for she will come then alone, then covenant with her for all matters convenient for your purpose, and she will be always with you. Of this assure yourself, for this has been proved.

[13]

Experimentum pro Furto[212]

Take silver foil some, and the white of an egg together, and shave the wall with a knife, and make an eye  and their names about the eye with these characters. And when they be written, call them all to the eye, and ask them if they will restore the theft. If they say nothing, repeat these names, "Nabbas, Rabbas, Bellaman, Mayfa, Retha, fac te apparere, fure, qui hanc rem subtraxit magnas apamen ales."[213] Hoc dicto,[214] call one of them and make one look in the eye, saying,

210. *Assoyle*: Dismiss, although Harrington's interlinear reading of "answer" seems better.

211. *Say*: Harrington adds above "open."

212. Translation: "Experiment for Theft." This is the Eye of Abraham, an anti-theft magical experiment. For further examples and similar operations, see Betz, *The Greek Magical Papyri*, 102; Buzzetta, "Fragments of a Jewish Magical Tradition in the Library of Giovanni Pico Della Mirandola," 96–97; Stallcup, "The 'Eye of Abraham' Charm for Thieves"; Benati, "Painted Eyes, Magical Sieves, and Carved Runes," 207–13. Many of the items in this work differ from the examples in Stallcup especially in regard to the brevity of the incantations.

Harrington's table of contents promises experiments for treasure hunting in the next few pages, but nothing seems to work for that topic.

213. *Fac...ales*: Translation: "Make yourself to appear, thief, who carried off this thing, you will nourish the magnates Apamen [?]."

214. *Hoc dicto*: Translation: "After saying this."

"Domine Jesu Christe, qui cuncta creasti ex nihilo, et *hosem* [hominem] de limo terrae formasti, et oculos Tobia ex tua bonitate excecasti, et eos iterum ex tua pietate restituisti, te *supplicat* [supplico] exoro, ut si iste homo sit hominis rei culpabilis, sic enim digneris, obsecrasti, Domine, Tobia."

> "Lord Jesus Christ, you created all things out of nothing, and made man out of the mud of the earth, and blinded the eyes of Tobit out of your goodness, and you restored these again through your love, I induce you, I beseech, that if this man be guilty of this thing of man, thus truly you may deign, you beseeched [...],[215] Lord, Tobit."

Hoc dicto,[216] hang a nail of copper or of cypress tree, and put it on the eye, and strike on it with a hammer. And if he be guilty, he shall weep; strike the second time, he shall cry; and he strike it three times, his eyes shall fall out.

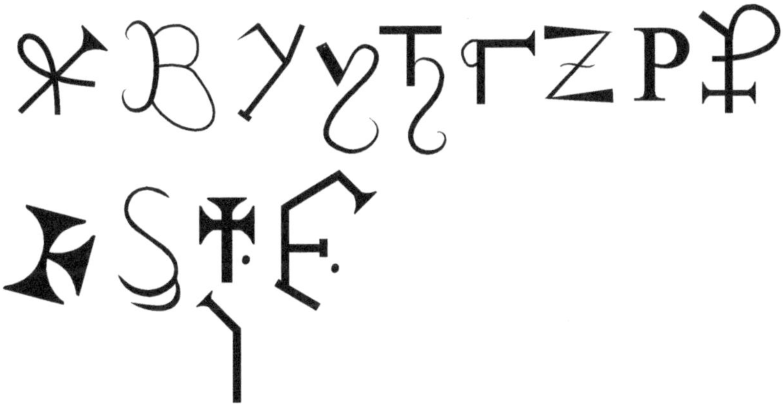

Experimentum pro Furto[217]

Take silver foil and temper it with a glyre[218] of an egg, ground together, and take a stick of cypress, and paint on a wall an eye with one end and write with the other end about the eye what he have, painting aforesaid these four names, "Malbeas, Nabbas, Colceram, Battenay." Then get a nail of pure copper, and stretch the eyes in the black with the nail sharp, and say these words aforesaid:

"Conjuro nos spiritus ut faciatis furem apparere et *apparire* [aperire] os suum recognoscere furtem qua quaerimus."

215. We seem to be missing part of the text here, describing the effect that striking the eye will have on the thief.

216. *Hoc dicto*: Translation: "this having been said."

217. Translation: "Experiment for Theft." Another instance of the Eye of Abraham.

218. *Glyre*: White part of an egg

> "Malkeo, Nabbas, & c. I conjure you, spirits, that you make the thief to appear and to open his mouth to admit the stolen thing which we seek."

Then rehearse his name that thou wilt do thy cast unto,

[14]

et statim clamabit.[219] Grind thy foil and thy glyre upon a marble stone, and therewith make the eye and the names as it is hereafter.

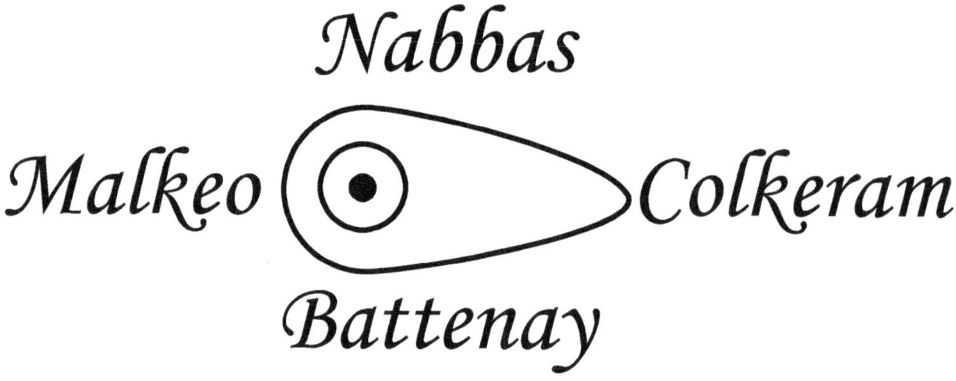

Experimentum pro Furto[220]

First take silver foil and temper it with the glyre of an egg ground together, and take a stick of cypress, and paint on a wall an eye with the one end, and write with the other end about the eye with the same painting aforesaid these four names, Malkeo, Nabba, Colkeram, Battenay. Then get a nail of pure copper, and trench the eye in the black, with your nail sharp, and say these words aforesaid:

"Conjuro nos, spiritus, ut faciatis furem apparere et *apparire* [aperire] os suum et recognoscere furtem quae querimus."

> "Malkeo, Nabbas, Is, I conjure you, spirits, that you make the thief to appear and to open his mouth and to admit the stolen thing which we seek."

219. *Et...clamabit*: Translation: "And he will shout immediately."

220. Translation: "Experiment for Theft." Another Eye of Abraham.

Then rehearse his name that thou wilt do thy cast unto, et statim clamabit.[221] Grind thy glyre, and thy foil upon a marble stone and therewith make the eye, and the names as it is hereafter.

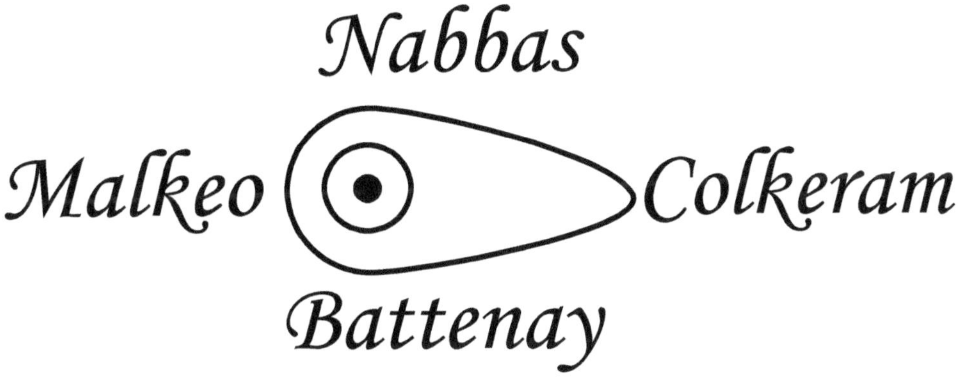

Experimentum Libri et Clavis[222]

To perform this experiment by the book and key to find treasure, it will be necessary also to have a Latin psalter or prayer book.

First take a psalter and a key which hath a cross ward, and put the key into the book upon these seven verses: "Tu vero odisti,"[223] and six following, that which be in the Psalms, next after "Miserere mei, deus,"[224] and say these, saying, "The key before and the book, in nomine Patris et Filii et Spiritus Sancti, amen. I conjure thee, book and key, that thou shew unto us the very truth if there be any treasure hid in this place, where this earth in the pipe of this key[225] comes from, and the virtues of the Father, and of the Son, and of the Holy Ghost

221. *Et…clamabit*: Translation: "And he will cry out immediately."

222. Translation: "Experiment of the Book and Key." An experiment of clidomancy or cleidomancy. For other examples, see Braekman, *Middeleeuwse Witte en Zwarte Magie*, 332–36; Klaassen and Wright, *Magic of Rogues*, 108; Foxe, Cranmer, and Nichols, *Narratives of the Days of the Reformation*, 332–33; Historical Manuscripts Commission, *Report on Manuscripts in Various Collections*, 7:53; Benati, "Painted Eyes, Magical Sieves, and Carved Runes," 187–88; Harms and Clark, *Of Angels*, 140, and manuscript pages 19 and 292.

223. *Tu vero odisti*: Vulgate, Psalm 49:17. English (KJV Psalm 50:17): "Seeing thou hatest…" This and the following six verses include condemnation of one for consorting with thieves, indicating that this treasure-hunting procedure is a modified anti-thief procedure.

224. *Miserere mei, deus*: Vulgate, Psalm 50:3: "Have mercy on me, O Lord." The verses stated come before this one.

225. *Pipe of this key*: The operation calls for a key pipe, or a key with a hollow shaft as part of the opening mechanism.

[15]

"and persons in trinity, and by the virtue and strength of the blessed milk that Our Lord Jesus Christ took of his blessed mother, Mary the virgin, per the virtue and truth of the twelve apostles; per the virtue of the patriarchs, prophets, martyrs, confessors, and virgins; and per the virtue and truth of all the angels in heaven, and per the virtue of all the earth, and all things in the earth, and per the virtue of the sea, and all that swimmeth therein, and per the virtue of every sacrament ordained per God's hand, and by the truth of every experiment that ever was wrought, per the virtue of all words that be in this book, and in all books of the holy scripture, to shew the very truth whether there be any gold or silver hid in this earth, or in the place from whence thy earth cometh."

Then take the book, and the key, and lay the wards[226] of the key upon the verse with the said earth, and bind the book together fast, and hold it *two men* [with their] longest fingers, and say, "I charge the book and the key, by the virtue of all the charges that I lay unto thee before this time. And if there be any gold or silver hid in the aforesaid place, where that this earth cometh from, that you shew us the true knowledge anon, without any tarrying, by and per, per the virtue of these verses following, and per all these holy names of God, + On + Te[tra]gramaton" + and a and p a ut supra, and r.[227] Finis.

Experimentum Signi Susanna ad Videndum et Su[m]endum que Volueris de Furtis et Aliis Rebus[228]

Scribe in quinta die Lunae, hora 2 imaginem in carta virgina vel in *comina* [lamina] plumbi, et postea qua die volueris, lica circa pollicem dextrum pueri cum filo serice, *bubeo* [lubricato?] oleo olive. *Vacto* [vade?], et in loco quo volueris, tempore serene ac circa meridiem puer sit *feminis* [femini?] et sedeat dorsum ejus versus solem, ita quod umbra

[16]

capitis cadat super pollicem pueri et dicas tu sic, "Volo ex parte dei, ut videas istum furtem et furem ei," septies vel novies quacunque rem aliam volueris habere. (Sequitur figura.)

On the fifth day of the moon, in the second hour, write the image in virgin paper or on a plate of lead, and afterward, on the day you will

226. *Wards*: The distinctive teeth of the key.

227. *A and p…r*: Likely intended to signify an Ave, a Pater Noster, and a Creed.

228. Translation: "Experiment of the Sign of Susanna for the Viewing and Recognizing of What You Desire Regarding Theft and Other Matters."

desire, tie a silken string around the right thumb of the boy, the nail having been slickened[229] with olive oil, and in what place you desire, in a calm time around noon, the boy should be placed on your thigh,[230] and he should sit with his back to the sun, so that the shadow [16] of your head may fall on the thumb of the boy, and you should say seven or nine times, "I desire on behalf of God that you should see this theft and the thief," that being any other thing you will desire to have. The figure follows

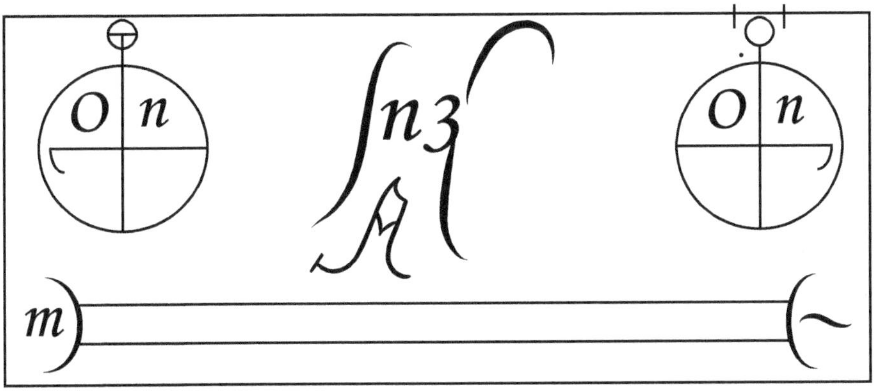

Agenus Tetragramaton Semiforas

His Tribus Nominibus Obedeunt Spiritus Infernales[231]

Alia[232]

229. *Slickened*: Conjectural.

230. The reading here is conjectural, but other procedures involve placing the boy between the magician's legs: Bayerische Staatsbibliothek Clm 849, 103v; Cambridge Additional 3544, 8, 27; Experiment 8b; British Library Sloane 3851, 40r; Harms and Clark, *Of Angels*, 142; Reynes, *The Commonplace Book of Robert Reynes*, 169.

231. Translation: "By These Three Names, the Infernal Spirits Will Obey."

232. *Alia*: Translation: "Another."

Pro Dolore Dentium Probat For the Toothache. Proven.[233]

[Take] a hazel wand of one year's growth, and write first this name Tetragramaton, and then both the names of the patient upon the same stick, and in writing say a Pater Noster, then "In nomine Patris et Filii et Spiritus Sancti," and so prick every vowel in all thy writing with a knife or pin, but for O and U you must prick them twice. But before you prick them, say these words, Te + tra + gra + ma + ton, and then you must write it with crosses, and then say this:

[17]

"I conjure thee, blood and or gout, or whatsoever thou be, that thou disease no more this man, a creature of God, N., and that thou go from him. I conjure and charge thee per the virtue of the Father, and the Son, and the Holy Ghost, and per the virtue of thy word Tetragramaton."

And then prick the vowels and before is said, then burn the stick.

Alter, Probat[234]

Write these words, "Maria, Emamel, Aminany, Zapta,[235] Setz, Goitz," and use the ceremonies before the last recited, having that before thou prick the vowels, thou must deliver the patient a knife to prick the said sore teeth withal; but he must give it you again and not whip the point thereof, but with the said point prick the vowels (ut supra), et dic ut supra, et procul dubio sanabit. Sepe probatum.[236]

Alter, Probat[237]

"It. a. ab. hurste ge baldare garret," write this on a paper or a hazel stick and the patient names, and this done, cross every vowel with your pen as before or knife, and throw the said paper or stick into the fire, and say 3 soe ne 3 a i credo,[238] et eodem tempore sanabitur.[239]

233. For other toothache charms involving pricking the mouth or gums, see BL Sloane 3850, 157r–v; Johnson, *Svartkonstböcker*, 253, 259, 274, 287, 296, 313, 590. As specified later in the charm, this charm may also be used for gout, bleeding, and other illnesses.

234. Translation: "Another, It Is Serviceable."

235. *Emamel, Aminany, Zapta*: Most likely "Emmanuel, Ananizapta."

236. *(Ut supra)…probatum*: Translation: "as above, and say as above, and it will heal at a distance with[out] doubt. It is often proved."

237. Translation: "Another, It Is Serviceable."

238. *3 soe…Credo*: Likely intended to be "three Pater Nosters, three Aves, one Creed."

239. *Et…sanabitur*: Translation: "and it will be cured at that very time."

Habere Dominium super Spiritus[240]

Si vis habere *domine* [dominium] super *eos* [omnes] spiritus, et maxime super Beal, qui est meorum qui dant vera responsa quod sit omni die et hora fac imaginem de recenti cera ad similitudinem huius pedibus condistartis et disperge eam cum aqua qua virtit circa rota molendini pro tres dies. Hoc facto, unge eam cum sangine albe galline in fronte et in pectore et in pedibus quarto die post scribe in pectore sigillum ☉ is qui est sic,

[18]

 in dorso, sigillum ☽ ae, sic — ...Die vero 5o, suffumiga eam cum herba thuris. Deinde pone eam sub aqua currente pro quattuor dies. Postea, fode eam in loco 3 vel 4 [dies] cum tribus *dentis diusax* [denariis diversarum] *momentarium* [monetarum] dicens:

> If you desire to have dominion over all spirits, and especially over Beal, who is of mine spirits that give good responses in all days and hours, make an image of fresh wax in his likeness, with feet extended, and sprinkle it with water that turns around a millwheel for three days. This done, anoint it with the blood of a white cock on the forehead, breast, and feet. On the fourth day after, write the seal of the ☉, which is thus: [18]  and the seal of the ☽ on the back, thus: 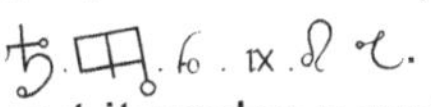. On the fifth day, suffumigate it with frankincense, then put it under running water for four days. Afterward, bury it in a place for three or four days with three pennies of different mints,[241] saying:

"Coniuro vos, Boal, Arriel, Darriel, Thorion, per creatorem celi et terra et per eos virtutes ejus, et per caput regis viri, et per eos principies vestros, ut consecretis mihi/nobis imaginem istam et felificetis ut respondeat in veritatem de *nobis* [omnibus] quae per orbis *quesiere* [quaeserem] ab ea."

> "I conjure you, Boal, Arriel, Darriel, Thorion, by the creator of heaven and earth, and by all his powers, and by the head of the king of man, and by your princes, that you should consecrate that image for me/ for us I have made, that he answer truthfully regarding all things of the world that I might ask from it."

240. Translation: "To Have Dominion over Spirits." Compare to Sloane 3850, 26r.

241. *Mints*: Could also be different denominations.

Et sit ibi 3 diebus. Tercia die, veni ad locum, et iterum asperge imaginem cum sanguine columbe et postea quere quid vis et dabit vera responsa et si moram fecerit in responsione, dic,

> And it should remain there three days. On the third day, go to the place and again sprinkle the image with dove's blood, and afterward ask what you will, and it will give a true response. And if it makes to delay in response, say:

"Coniuro te, Boal, cujus imaginem est hac, et exorcizo te per N caput regis tuae et per Periel, Dariel, Threfon, Merion, ut loquaris mihi veritatem de omnibus quae *quaesivere* [quaeserem]."

> "I conjure thee, Boal, whose image is here, and I exorcise thee, by N., the head of your king, and by Periel, Dariel, Threfon, Merion, that thou tell me the truth of all things that I might ask."

Et proculce eam virga conili unius anni, et statim respondebit tibi. Deinde defer in domum tuum imaginem, et pone in loco mundo et secreto, et cum vis aliquid facere, interroga eam diligenter et dabit responsa vera. Hoc secretum noli alicui revelare ut sis sapiens.

> And thresh him with a branch of hazel[242] of one year's growth, and it will respond immediately to you. Then carry the image off to your home, and place it in a clean and secret place, and when you wish to do something, ask it diligently, and it will give you a true response. Do not reveal this secret to anyone, that you may be wise.

To Play at Dice That Thou Shalt Not Lose[243]

Take the nail of the right hand of a man that is dead and write this in virgin parchment.

> Deviserunt + vestimenta mea et super vestem meam miserunt sortem[244]

242. *Hazel*: A highly conjectural reading.

243. See manuscript page 57.

244. *Deviserunt…sortem*: Vulgate Psalm 21:19, without the "sibi" after the first cross. Translation (KJV Psalm 22:18): "They part my garments among them, and cast lots upon my vestures." This passage, foretelling the events of the Passion, is particularly appropriate for an amulet to win at dice.

And wrap the nail in the same writing on Twelfth Day,[245] and cause the Mass of Three Kings Coloniae[246] to be said on it, and then take and bind it about thy arm and place it as thou play. Take the dice in this hand, and say thy conjuration: "I conjure you, dice, per all the points that is in you, and per this nail, and per his spear, and per

[19]

his vestment upon that which they did cast lots, that you made me always to win of any creature, per him that which shall come to judge both the quick and the dead, and the world per fire. In the name of the Father, and of the Son, and of the Holy Ghost. Amen, amen."

[Rite of Unknown Purpose, Possibly for the Previous]

Write these letters following in a piece of paper and then blot out all the vowels and inri.[247]

i l a b e e s e n t e a b e e r u r
h u r s e g e b a l l a g a r e t t e } *& then Burn it.*

inri
wnzrf ✠ *fiwfg*　　*Hunc similis* ⁜

Pro Furto cum LIBRO ET CLAVE[248]

Dic devote:

Say with devotion:

"In nomine Patris et Filii et Spiritus Sancti. Amen. O Gell, Eliel, Elezel, Agla, Elpanton, rex, craton, Jesus nazarenus, estote in adiutorium virum et verum. *Perficitite* [perficite] *apertione* [operationes] actionesque nostras, quasimas, Domine, aspirando peruenni et adjuvando prosequere ut et [sic] cuncta nostra operatio a te semper incipiat et pro te cepta chiefs fineatur, pro Christum dominum virum. Amen. Jesus Christum, quo fructas, venas, et corda, antequam

245. *Twelfth Day*: Epiphany.

246. *Three Kings Coloniae*: The Three Kings of Cologne, or the Three Wise Men.

247. Cipher in illustration: "James saith." *Hunc similis*: Translation: "Similar here."

248. Translation: "For Theft, with BOOK AND KEY." For other examples of theft detect with the book (often a Bible or psalter) and key, see manuscript pages 292.

fiant. Domine deus qui dixisti solus, qui nosti o[mn]ia, tu es panis vivus quot de coelo descendit, domine, qui es alpha et omega, per sanctissum *nomine* [nomen] tuam, Tetragramaton, per merita et intercessions tuorum apostolorum, et licet nos peccatores simus memoriam tamen tuam imploramis qui Siprosona, cuius nomen est supra cartam, reus sit hominis furti ut nobis demonstrare digneris in virtutem tuam, per librum et clavem virtutem, et si non sit reus non moveatur, oc rogamus per inseperabilem trinitatem, Patrem et Filium et Spiritum Sanctum, et quemadmodum satuisti quinque hominum millia, a panibus et a piscibus da nobis in hac re plena et profecta veritatem demonstrare digneris per spiritum deum verum tuum."

"In the name of the Father and of the Son and of the Holy Ghost. Amen. O Gell, Eliel, Elezel, Agla, Elpanton, king, creator, Jesus of Nazareth. You all are our true and living help. Complete our labours and actions, we ask, O Lord. I arrived with hopes, and thou shalt accompany with assistance, that our entire labour may always begin from thee, and our commands are concluded.[249] Jesus Christ, by whom fruits, veins, and souls were made, Lord God, who alone spoke, who knows all things, you are the living bread that came down from heaven, Lord, you are alpha and omega, by your most holy name, Tetragrammaton, by the manifested kindnesses and intercessions of your apostles, and it is permitted that we sinners should be in your memory. We beseech thee that Siprosona, whose name is on the paper above, if the criminal would be the person who did the theft, that you would deign to show us in your virtue, by the power of the book and key, and if he should not be the criminal, it would not move, and we ask by the inseparable Trinity, Father and Son and Holy Ghost, and, in the manner you fed five thousand people by loaves of bread and fish, give us in this matter fulfilled and completed, may you deign to show the truth, by thy true spirit of God."

Dic ter hoc versiculum:

Say this little verse three times:

"Si videbas furem currebas cum eo, et cum adulteris portionem ponebas tuam."[250]

249. *You all...concluded*: Much of this translation is conjectural.

250. *Si...tuam*: A slight modification of Vulgate Psalm 49:18. Translation (KJV Psalm 50:18): "When thou sawest a thief, then thou consentedst with him, and hast been partaker with adulterers." See manuscript page 292.

[20]

[Rings of the Twenty-Eight Mansions of the Moon][251]

See page 285, 2nd Book of the *Three Books*, Cornelius Agrippa[252]

There be twenty-eight mansions of the ☽ per that which she goeth her course, per day and per nighttime.

[To Make a Stream Appear][253]

In the first mansion, on the day and hour of the ☽'s course, a silver ring is to be made hollow without a stone, in the which hollowness let there be put virgin parchment in which is written these four names of angels, "Pharap, Giaray, Inney, Bayacy,"[254] the which names must be written in virgin parchment with the blood of an eel. This done and the hole stopped, keep it, and the next day in the morning, upon the bank of some river, opening the hole of the ring against the east and, kneeling on thy knees, say this orison following:[255]

"+ O Lord God Almighty, which doth see from the heavens, beholdest all privy places, per whom the living that be alive doth live and they that die do die, and that which didst drown the people of King Pharoah in the sea, and didst make a well to spring out a stone, I desire and pray thy great goodness, that what day or hour I shall require these four spirits whose names be enclosed in this ring, that they make one stream of mus[256] for to appear, and that incontinently."

This being said and done, touch the water with the ring, making therewith this sign or token.

251. A shorter version of a longer text, detailing up to forty rings, that dates back to the fifteenth century. For an edition of the most complete text, see Boudet, "Annulorum." I have not noted every of the variations in the incantations from this text, and there is considerable disparity between the characters here and in Boudet's edition. A partial English translation appears in Sloane 3850, 169v–174v.

252. This page in the 1651 English translation of Agrippa, *Three Books of Occult Philosophy*, begins his discussion of the twenty-eight lunar mansions.

253. Boudet, 271–72. Harrington mislabels this as "To stop the stream of a river" in the original table of contents.

254. *Pharap…Baracy*: Boudet has "Pharai, Murath, Baroy," and provides other manuscript variants for those and the names below.

255. Boudet's edition adds that the ring should be fumigated with frankincense.

256. *Stream of mus*: Unknown significance. Boudet has "flumen," or "river."

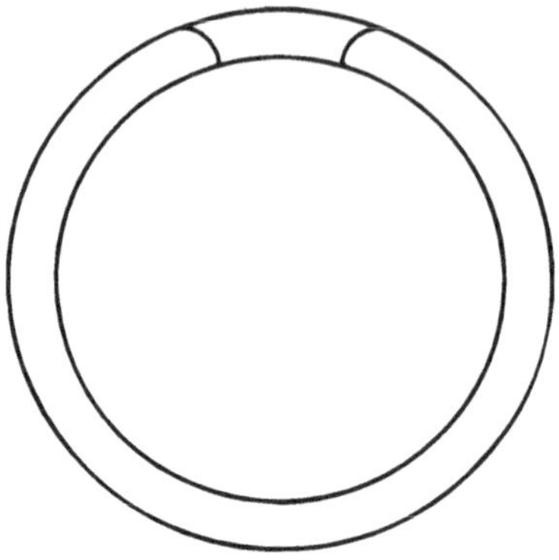

That done, wrap the ring in a fine cloth of lawn[257] or in clean white sendal,[258] and keep it clean, and when that thou will work, touch the ring with the spittle, saying this:

"O ye spirits whose names be here enclosed, I charge you per him unto whom you owe principally to obey, that you incontinently do work that thing that I desire that he do, that is to arear[259] a flood of stream between me and these persons."

Then you must open the engine[260] of the ring, and as long as it is open, so long the flood or stream shall run for the space of three hours and then shut it, and incontinently the water will be gone.[261]

To Make a Hart or Buck Appear with Dogs Following[262]

In the second mansion, cause a ring to be made of silver, hollow, within that which

[21]

hollowness may be closed with virgin parchment, in that which must be written with the blood of a hart or buck, or of a hound,[263] these four names following, "Anuam, Carsial, Varrical, Varsian."[264] This ring made and the hole stopped, the next day in the morning, into the entering[265] into some wood,

257. *Lawn*: Fine linen.

258. *Sendal*: Either a silken or linen material.

259. *Arear*: Build.

260. *Engine*: Instrument.

261. *Then you must...gone*: This paragraph not in Boudet.

262. Boudet, "Annulorum," 272–73.

263. *The blood...hound*: Boudet's edition specifies that both must be mixed together.

264. *Anuam...Varsian*: Boudet: "Anna, Heasil, Sorphail, Vacerail."

265. *Entering*: Entrance.

subfume the ring with myrrh,[266] holding the hole open against the wood, saying this orison:

"O Lord God almighty, which doth see from the heavens, and beholdest all privy places, by whom the living that be alive do live, and that die do die, and that which did make a great wood, that whatsoever day or hour I shall require that these four spirits whose names be enclosed in the ring do make a hart or buck appear and two dogs following him, before whose sight I shall desire."

This being done and said, touch the ground with the ring, making this sign:

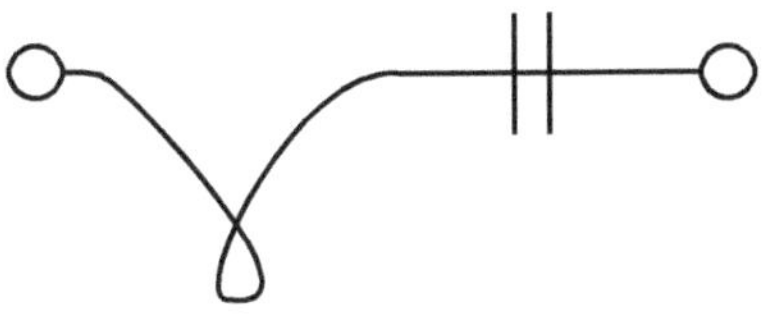

That done, wrap it [in] green silk, and keep it very clean, and when thou wilt work, touch the ring with thy spittle, and say thus:

"O the spirits whose names be here enclosed, I charge you per him unto whom thou ought principally to obey, that you incontinently do work the thing that I desire you do, that is to cause to appear to all men's sights a hart or buck with two dogs following him."

And anon the thing that was spoken, thou shall see per the space of three hours.[267]

To Make Men in Horns[268] to Appear[269]

In the third mansion, cause to be made a golden ring hollow, within that which hollowness thou mayst put virgin parchment, in that which be written with the blood of a man these names following: "Admolita, Alibeat, Urciferi, Obtablait."[270] The ring being thus made, keep it, and the next day in the morning, in the entering into some field, suffumigate it cum ossibus mortui

266. *Myrrh*: Boudet adds aloe.

267. *And anon…hours*: Not in Boudet.

268. *Horns*: Based on Boudet and what appears below, this should be "in harness," or in armour.

269. Boudet, "Annulorum," 273.

270. *Admolita…Obtablait*: Boudet: "Anelim, Alibeat, Estade, Boad, Bartifari."

hominis,[271] and kneeling on thy knees against the entral[272] of the field, say thus:

"O Lord God almighty, which dost see from the heavens and beholdest all privy places, per whom the living that be alive do live, and they that be dead do die, and he which didst make mankind unto thy likeness and similitude,

[22]

"I desire and pray thy great goodness, that, in whatsoever day or hour I shall touch this ring with my spittle, these spirits whose names be enclosed in the ring make men in harness to appear incontinently."

This done, touch the ground with the ring, making thy sign:

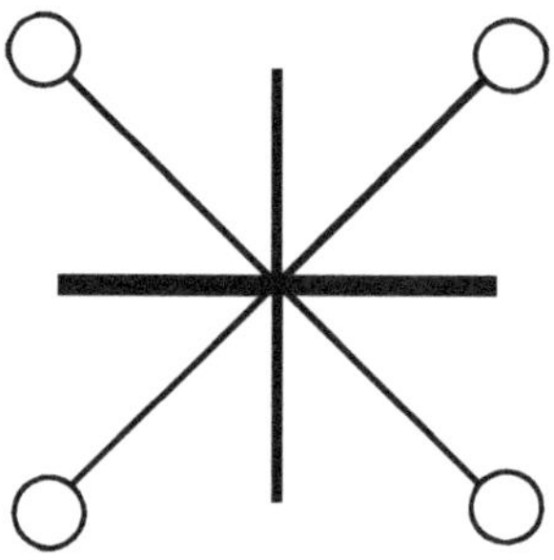

Then wrap it up in the fine black silk and keep it clean. And when you will work, touch the ring with thy spittle and say thus:

"O ye spirits whose names be written within, written and enclosed, I charge you per him unto whom you owe principally to obey, that thou work that my desire is."

This said, thou shalt see marvellous things, as it were, harness-men[273] fighting together.

To Make a Dervine[274] to Appear with Branches[275]

In the fourth mansion, cause to be made a ring of gold, hollow, in which hollowness may be put virgin parchment, wherein is written with ink made of

271. *Cum...hominis*: Translation: "With the bones of a dead man." Boudet's edition has the teeth of a dead man.

272. *Entral*: Entrance.

273. *Harness-men*: Technically, the carrier of a soldier's armour, but here the one wearing this armour.

274. *Dervine*: Apparently vine, in this context.

275. Boudet, "Annulorum," 274.

thorns these four names following, "Barbada, Bacatu, Fascra, Ciauliarug."[276] The ring being thus made,

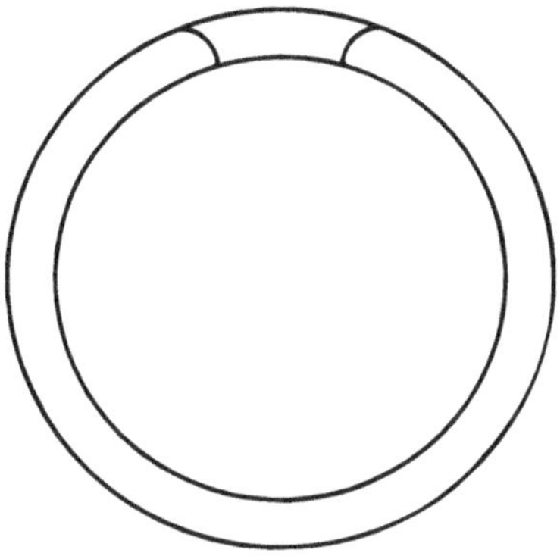

keep it, and in next day in the morning, in the entering of some vineyards, suffume[277] it with vines of the same, and say against the east this orison:

"O Lord God almighty, which dost see from the heavens and beholdest all privy places, I desire and pray thy great goodness, that in whatsoever day or hour I shall touch this ring with my spittle, these spirits whose names within written be enclosed in this ring do make a vine with grapes and with branches garnished to appear incontinently."

Then touch the ground, and with the ring make thy sign:

Then wrap it clean in green silk, and keep it clean, and when you will work, touch the ring with thy spittle, say thus:

"O the spirits whose names be enclosed ut supra,[278] that you do work the thing that I desire to have, that is a vine to appear here, with grapes garnished with branches," and by and per there shall appear.

276. *Barbada…Ciauliarug*: Boudet: "Hiradi, Hatiarie, Fastur, Craulyaruy."

277. *Suffume*: To consecrate with incense from below.

278. *Ut supra*: Translation: "as above."

[23]

To Make Meadows Appear with Woods[279]

In the fifth mansion, cause a ring to be made of copper, hollow, & c. Within the hollowness you must put in virgin parchment wherein be written[280] these four names, "Osturcios, Betradandi, Hamnscadan: Patzunfici."[281] The ring thus made, in the next morning, suffume it. At the entering of some meadow with a herb called sonsiane nemorie,[282] and inclining the head towards the meadow, say this orison:

"O Lord God almighty, which dost see from the heavens, and that which did make all green herbs, grass, and flowers growing on the earth, I desire and pray thy goodness, that, in whatsoever day or hour I shall touch this ring with my spittle, these spirits whose names be here enclosed may make to grow a wood with green meadows before my sight, and all other sights that I shall will, and that they do that incontinently."

This done, touch the ground with the ring, making this sign

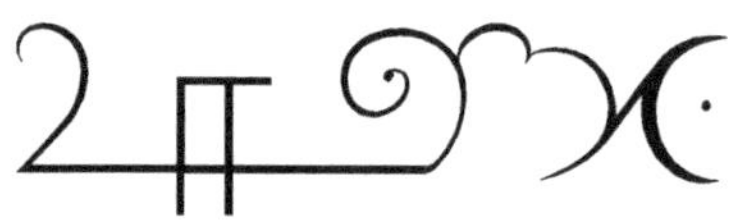

Then wrap the ring in a fine linen cloth and keep it clean. And when you will work, touch the ring with your spittle, saying this:

"O ye spirits whose names be enclosed, I charge you per him unto whom you ought principally to obey, that incontinently thou do make that I desire," and per and per there shall meadows appear with woods.

To Make a Table with Meat Appear[283]

In the sixth mansion, cause to be made a ring of tin,[284] hollow, & c., and on the parchment within to be enclosed, write these four names with the blood of an ——[285] or neat,[286] "Adariat, Perdegramma, Caudae, Rupasca,"[287] and

279. Boudet, "Annulorum," 275.

280. *Written*: Boudet's edition states this should be in the blood of a green lizard.

281. *Osturcios...Patzunfici*: Boudet: "Osturies, Bragandi, Iucamilchada, Pachimisca."

282. *Sonsiane nemorie*: Unknown, although nemorie translates as "of the woods." Sloane 3850: "sensian or nemorie." Boudet's edition has hay.

283. Boudet, "Annulorum," 275–76.

284. *Tin*: Boudet's edition has silver and lead alloyed.

285. Line in original.

286. *Neat*: A cow or bull, confirmed in Boudet.

287. *Adariat...Rupasca*: Boudet: "Bardari, Acer, Predogam, Magandarui, Hastapulo."

in the entering of some kitchen, perfume it with the brain of a swine, and inclining,[288] say this orison:

"O Lord God almighty who dost see from the heaven, and behold all privy places per whom the living do live, & c., and that which didst make manna fall down from the heavens,[289] I desire and pray thy great goodness, that in whatsoever day or hour I shall touch this ring with my spittle, these spirits whose names be enclosed may make a table with delicate meats,

[24]

for to appear, and that they do that incontinently."

This done, touch the ground with the ring making this sign:[290]

Then wrap it in fine linen cloth, and when you wilt work, touch the ring with thy spittle, saying, "O ye spirits, whose names be written here enclosed in this ring, I charge you per him unto whom you ought principally to obey, that you do work incontinently that thing that I desire to have done, that is, a table garnished full of dishes with delicate meats may appear here." Per and per, and there shall appear a table full.

To Make Trees with Fruit and without Fruit Appear[291]

In the seventh mansion of the ☽, cause to be made a hollow ring[292] & c., and therein enclosed, written on virgin parchment, these four names, "Caucze, Ystay, Amaneczax, Fastarie."[293] This ring made, perfume with lignum aloes in the entering of some orchard, saying:

"O Lord God almighty, who dost see from the heavens, and beholdest all private places & c., and that which didst make the trees and all growing herbs, I desire and pray thy goodness that, in whatsoever hour or time I shall touch this ring with my spittle, the spirits whose names be in thy ring enclosed may

288. *Inclining*: According to Boudet, the head.

289. *And that which...heavens*: Not in Boudet.

290. Intertextual note: "non stet," "it should not remain."

291. Boudet, "Annulorum," 266–67.

292. *A hollow ring*: Boudet's edition notes the substance as iron.

293. *Caucze...Fastarie*: Boudet: "Cambristay, Anurecha, Farastario."

make green trees, without fruit and with fruit, for to appear, and that they do it incontinently."

This done, touch the ground with the ring, making this sign:

Then wrap it in yellow silk, and when thou wilt work, do as is aforesaid in the chapter before, and say, "O ye spirits whose names be within written, enclosed in this ring, I charge you & c., that trees with fruits and without fruits may appear."

To Make Oak Trees and Birds Singing in Them Appear[294]

In the eighth mansion, make a ring of the root of firm oak, in that which write this name "Barioth."[295] The ring made, suffume it with oak leaves. In the entering of some wood, saying,

"O Lord God almighty, who dost see from the heavens and beholdest all private places, per whom the living that be always do live, and the dead do die,

[25]

I desire and pray thy great goodness, that in whatsoever hour or day I shall touch this ring with my spittle, these spirits whose names be within closed may make the oak with leaves, and birds sitting on them, may appear, and that they do it incontinently."

That done, touch the ground with the ring and make this sign:

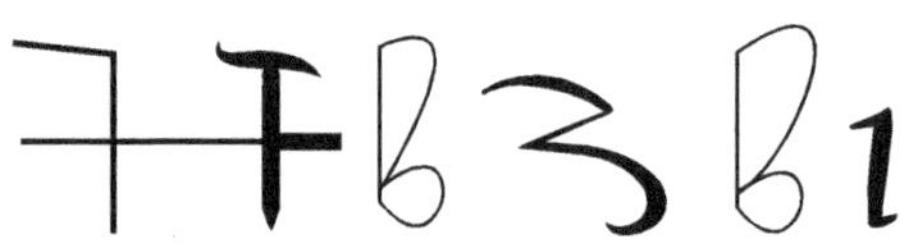

[Wrap] in green silk;[296] when thou wilt work, fac ut supra te.[297]

294. Boudet, "Annulorum," 277.

295. Boudet lists these: Rariath, Barath, and Beroth.

296. *[Wrap] in green silk*: Not in Boudet.

297. *Fac ut supra te*: Translation: "Do as above."

That Any Man May Appear Drawing the Mast of a Ship[298]

In the ninth mansion, make a hollow ring, and write in virgin parchment and enclose these names of spirits, "Cixlen, Tidimat, Bauros, Benculsioth,"[299] in the ring & c. At the entering of some mill, suffume it with the grains of diverse corn,[300] saying thus:

"O Lord God almighty, which dost see from the heavens and beholdest all private places, and that which didst work all marvelous things, I desire and pray thy great goodness that in whatsoever hour or time I shall touch this ring with my spittle, these spirits whose names be within closed may make that one may appear drawing after him a ship[301] or a mill, and that they do it incontinently."

That done, touch the door or the ground next to the door,[302] making this sign:

And [keep] the ring in the leather of a mouse skin, and work when you will. Fiat.

To Make an Elephant Appear Bearing a Castle[303]

In the eleventh mansion, make a ring of ivory not hollow, and write in it this name, "Fermagon."[304] The ring made, touch the gate of some castle and suffume it with incense and the hairs[305] of a man's head that is alive,[306] saying,

"O Lord God almighty, who didst see from the heavens," & c., ut supra,[307] "and that which didst bear Abacub[308] per one hair of his head,[309] I desire

298. Boudet, "Annulorum," 278, as an experiment to show a mouse dragging a millstone behind it.
299. *Cixlen...Benculsiot*Boudet provides "Trellari, Yenuat, Bournes, Bournay, Syeth."
300. Boudet's version states grain, perhaps wheat.
301. Not in Boudet.
302. Boudet's version specifies the millpath near the water.
303. Boudet, "Annulorum," 279.
304. Boudet: "Fervagitim."
305. Original: "Eares." Sloane 3850 has "heares."
306. Other manuscripts have ivory or frankincense, as well as the hairs of a living man.
307. Translation: "As above."
308. Likely Habakkuk; see Daniel 14:33–6.
309. Not in Boudet.

and pray thy great goodness, that in whatsoever hour or time that I shall touch this ring with my spittle, this spirit whose name is written enclosed may make that one elephant, bearing a castle, may appear, and that you do it incontinently."

That done, touch the ground making this sign:

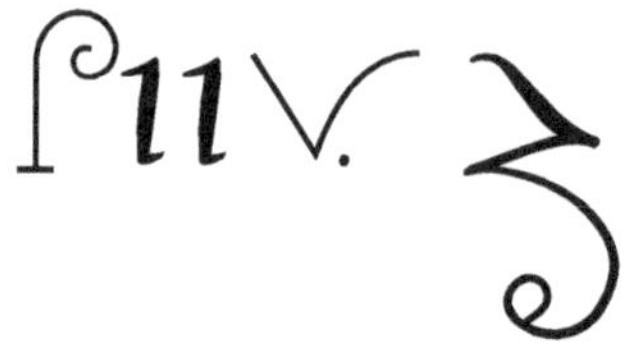

Then wrap it in a box of ivory * when you will work. Fac ut supra.[310]

[26]

To Make a Castle Appear[311]

In the fourteenth mansion, make a hollow copper ring. Write in common or in virgin parchment these names, "Origo, Calibit, Beandinet, Fimiricti."[312] This ring made, touch the door of some castle, and fume it with fresh milk,[313] saying:

"O Lord God almighty, which dost see from the heavens and beholdest all private places, & c., and I desire and pray thy great goodness that, in whatsoever hour or time I shall touch this ring with my spittle, these spirits whose names here be within enclosed may make a castle to appear in some distant place to whose sight I shall desire, that they do it incontinently."

That done, touch the ground making this sign:

Then wrap it in a black cloth when you will work. Do as is here aforesaid, and there shall appear a castle afar off.

310. *Fac ut supra*: Translation: "Do as above."

311. Boudet, "Annulorum," 281.

312. *Origo…Fimiricti*: Boudet: "Goralidio, Brandamiroth, Staurioci."

313. *Milk*: Boudet indicates lime.

To Make a Dragon Appear in the Air[314]

In the twelfth mansion, make a copper ring hollow, and write in virgin parchment these names, "Dermmat, Barcilana, Cauenpria, Coriet."[315] That ring made, suffume it, in the entering of some meadow, with the blood of some dragon sting,[316] [say]:

"O Lord God almighty, who dost see from the heavens and beholdest all privy places & c., I desire and pray thy great goodness, that in whatsoever hour or time I shall touch this ring with my spittle, these spirits whose names be here enclosed may make that a great horrible dragon may appear in the air, and that they do incontinently."

And touch the ground making this sign:

And wrap it in fine linen cloth,[317] and when you will work, do as aforesaid and there shall happen, & c.

Ad Faciendum Pecunias Revertere Tibi Iterum[318]

In the sixteenth mansion of the ☽, take as many pence as be necessary for thee, and bind them in a lawn cloth that is yellow and clean, and suffume it with viscus quarci,[319] saying thus:

"O Lord God almighty, which dost see from the heavens and beholdest all private places & c., I desire and pray thy great goodness that in whatsoever hour or time

[27]

"I shall touch this & c., with my spittle, these spirits, whose names be within enclosed may make these pence, which I shall expend, may return again unto me, and that they do that incontinently."

314. Boudet, "Annulorum," 280.

315. *Dernmmat…Coriet*: Boudet: "Dominath, Boriatiacali, Evapria, Teriath."

316. *Dragon sting*: Boudet: "sanguine draconis," or dragon's blood incense.

317. *Fine linen cloth*: Boudet's edition specifies that this should be white.

318. Translation: "To Make Money Return to You Again." Boudet, "Annulorum," 282.

319. *Viscus quarci*: Oak mistletoe.

And when thou wilt lay out thy pence, say thrice very secretly, "Griberi, Doliarimerat, Fracradi, Geerin,"[320] and without doubt thy pence that thou didst lay out and spend shall restore again unto thee. Nota quod hae mansis sit quando ☽a sit in 20 grad Libre et 52 minuta.[321]

To Make a Horse Carry Thee Whither Thou Wilt[322]

In the twenty-fifth mansion & c., write and enclose these names,[323] "Gariot, Fortimelich, Hunamalich."[324] The next day mane,[325] suffume it[326] with the hoof of a horse and viscus quarci, saying:

"O Lord God almighty, which dost see from the heavens, and beholdest all privy places, & c., I desire and pray great goodness that, in whatsoever hour or time I shall touch thy ring with my spittle, these spirits whose names be within closed may make that a horse or any other beast in the twinkling of an eye may carry me whithersoever I will, and that they do it incontinently." And when thou wilt work, do as is aforesaid.[327]

To Make Pismires[328] *to Be Pence*[329]

In the twenty-seventh mansion, make a hollow ring of lead, and write and enclose these names, "Flegur, Manopall, Martalio."[330] The next day mane, suffume it with viscus quarci at the mammets,[331] saying thus:

"O Lord God almighty, who dost see from the heavens and beholdest all privy places & c., I desire and pray thy great goodness that, in whatsoever hour or time I shall touch this ring with my spittle, these spirits whose names be herein enclosed may make that ants or pismires may seem to be pence, and that they do it incontinently," as above.[332]

320. *Gribardi...Geerin*: Boudet: "Gubridali, Harmuroch, Fratradrith, Gormi."

321. *Nota...minuta*: Translation: "Recognise that this should be done when the ☽ is in the twentieth degree and 52nd minute of Libra." This line is not in Boudet.

322. Boudet, "Annulorum," 285.

323. *Enclose these names*: Boudet's edition encloses them in a ring of alloyed silver and lead.

324. *Gariot...Hunamalich*: Boudet: "Gariech, Fictimetim, Amanbilch."

325. *Mane*: In the morning.

326. *Suffume it*: Boudet's edition notes this should be at an entrance to a stable.

327. Boudet's edition adds that it should be wrapped in a new green fine cloth.

328. *Pismires*: Ants.

329. Boudet, "Annulorum," 286.

330. *Flegur...Martalio*: Boudet: "Yligai, Macipal, Mare, Marcalia."

331. *Mammets*: Possibly the fairies. In Boudet, this is done at a place with many ants. Other definitions include an idol or a puppet.

332. *As above*: Original "ut supra."

To Make Iron Seem to Be Gold[333]

In the twenty-eighth mansion, make a hollow ring of gold and write and enclose these names, "Pergor, Naith." The next day in the morning, suffume it with viscus quarci in the entering of the chamber, saying, "O Lord God

[28]

almighty & c., I desire and pray, great goodness, that in whatsoever hour or time I shall [touch] this ring with my spittle, these spirits whose names be within enclosed may make that iron to appear to the people most precious gold, and that they do that incontinently, & c."

When thou wilt work, touch the ground with the ring, and the iron shall appear to be most precious gold to the sight of & c.

Tu omoes [?] non tagnum [?][334]

Accipe vellem *veritri* [ventri] canis et conficiatur ad modum pellis pelli [sic?] parior. Postea, scribe in pelle ad sanguine nigrae columba nomen illius quem volveris ligare. Postea, eas ad locum ubi consuetus est mingere, et cum recesserit, accipe de terra super qua mixerit, et dum accipias, dic:

> Take the skin of a dog's belly, and it should be prepared in the way suitable to a hide. Afterward, write the name of the one you desire to bind on the skin with the blood of a black dove. Then go to the place where he is accustomed to urinate, and after he has left, take the earth over which he has urinated, and at the time you take it, say:

"Ego ligo terram ista in nomina 72 et per virtutem istorium, Alaby, Sadalaos, Jennefatos, Numel."

> "I bind this earth in the seventy-two names, and by their power, Alaby, Sadalos, Jennefatos, Numel."

Et tunc pone terram illam in pellem pecam et liga fortiter cum filo filata a virgine, dic:

> And then place that earth in a piece of the hide, and bind strongly with a thread spun by a virgin, and say:

"Ego te, N., ligo ut non possis mingere, donec terram istam dissolva."

333. Not in Boudet.

334. This is entirely corrupt.

"I bind thee, N., that thou shalt not be able to urinate until this earth dissolves."

Scias procul dubio cum fuerit terram ligata nunque minget, nec aliquis poterit eam solvere per aliquam artem ni tu solus, et cum vis dissolvere, disliga illam terram in eo loco ubi acceptisti, libabitur.

You should know beyond doubt that, as long as the earth remains, he will never urinate, and no one will be able to release him through any technique, save you alone. And when you would dissolve, unbind the earth in that place where it was taken, and he will be freed.

Ut Saltent Homines[335]

Sic [scribe] hac *nonerca* [nomina] in pergameno vel papiro cum penna et sanguine babonis, et pone sub limine domus et omnes intrantes saltabimus vidi [?].

Write these names on parchment or papyrus[336] with a pen and the blood of an owl,[337] and place it under the threshold of the house, and all entering will dance:

Elex + bex + mex + thasia + nuncia + stavi + mili +

Et rite operatio fiet.
And the work will be done duly.

Alia[338]

Sic [Scribe] haec:
Write these things:

Pondula + Tripes + Nepos + Sitor + Regnum + Celi[339] + Pliphes + Ludula +

in cera virginiea, et pone sub limine domus dicendo incantationem huic experimento apta. *Probant* [probatum?], vel hac verba:

335. Translation: "So that men may dance." Compare to Sloane 3850, 154r.

336. *Papyrus*: This word could also signify paper.

337. *Of an owl*: "Babonis" means "of a baboon," but Sloane 3850, 154r, bears out the reading as "of an owl."

338. *Alia*: Translation: "Another."

339. *Tripes…Celi*: These words might be read as "Three-legged + Grandson + Sitor [Sator?] + King + of Heaven."

in virgin wax, and place it under the threshold for the door, saying the attached to this experiment—it is proved—or these words:

Hastas, Misanas, Clier, Bater, Casia, Vas, Max

ad [sic] sanguinem vesperontillionis modo praedicto.
with the blood of a bat, in the way aforesaid.

[29]

Pro Amore[340]

Accipe radicem valeriam, arridam factam, sub brachio per duas dies. Tunc des ei bibere.

Take valerian root, having been dried, under your forearm for two days. Then give it to her to drink.[341]

Accipe flores rosmariae et suspende circa collum in bisso. Tum fige osculabis vel & c.

Take rosemary flowers and hang them around the neck in linen or silk. Then fasten it, you will kiss, and so forth.[342]

Accipe helenam companam arridam factam, et des a vulveri bibere.

Take the flowers [?] of helenam,[343] having been dried, and give it in the woman to drink.

Accipe tria corda of[344] reremise, et fac in pulverem tuum pene et suum mulieris, et amabit te. Pones iterim in aqua, et si pedit *fundum* [fundo] *redigem* [redige] in *voluerem* [volueris], et da in potu.

Take ten drams of the heart of reremise,[345] and make it into powder, [and apply] to your penis, and the private parts of the woman, and she will love you. On the other hand, you will put it in water, and if it settles to the bottom, collect it in whatever you wish, and give it in a drink.[346]

340. Translation: "For Love."

341. For a similar rite, see Cambridge Additional 3544, 66.

342. For rosemary as an agent expressing or bringing about love, see Watts, *Dictionary of Plant Lore*, 325.

343. *Helenam*: Probably helenium, or elecampane.

344. *Of*: English in the original.

345. *Reremise*: Bats.

346. Thanks to Joseph Peterson for his help with the passage.

In dipli, cape canem venere accensum, et obseres eam 9 dies in cubiculo, et post 9 dies mactabit eam ejusque jecur siccabis in furno, et cum velis uti cape magnitudinem pisae et da a bibendum aut edendum et sic ardenter ut ultro te reget; amabit probatum.

> In [?],[347] take a dog aroused with love, and confine it in your chamber for nine days, and after nine days you will kill it and you will dry its liver in a furnace, and when you desire to use it, grab a large amount of it, and give through drinking or eating, and thus it will ardently rule *you* [her] wantonly. She will love you. It is proved.

Est queda massa carnis in fronte pulli equini. Eam acceipe a aqua quam primum poteris, et arridam fac in furnes, et in pulvere ministra alicui in potu & c.

> There is a certain lump of flesh in the forehead of the foal of a horse. Take it from water that you should drink first, and dry it in ovens, and give it in powder to someone as a drink, & c.[348]

Combure cor columbe et [da] eam mulieri ut bibat.

> Burn the heart of a dove, and give it to a woman, that she may drink it.

Currat[349] sanguis gallinae columbae in potionem, et pone potionem in eum sanguine[m] per 24h et postea da mulieri, et provocat.

> Let the blood of a rooster and a dove be combined into a potion, and put the potion in that blood for twenty-four hours, and afterward give it to a woman. It arouses her.

Accipe[350] baldmoney[351] and diagalanga,[352] two ounces ana.[353] Make it into powder and give it to be drink, et provocat.[354]

347. "Dipli" is unknown.

348. This is the hippomanes, a traditional component in many different varieties of love potion. Forbes, "The Social History of the Caul," 503–5.

349. *Let...be combined*: Conjectural translation.

350. *Accipe*: Translation: "Take."

351. *Baldmoney*: Gentian.

352. *Diagalanga*: A medicinal concoction of honey and galangal.

353. *Ana*: Translation: "of each."

354. *Et provocat*: Translation: "and it arouses."

Recipe sanguinis e *alti* [cani] albi unciae[355] ii et tantandem ejus cerebri, algas [et cerebri] Algasel, sanguinis humani unciae iiii. Cum istis simul mixtis, incorporalis quem volueris suffumiga, nam eijus spiritus erga te *monebit* [movebitur] in amore.

> Take two ounces of the blood of a white dog, and as much of its brain, and four ounces [of the brain of] a gazelle and human. With these mixed and united together, suffumigate the one you want; for her spirit will be moved in love toward you.[356]

Accipe cerebri de algazel unciae v, sanguinis leopardi uncia i, coaguli *lepax* [leporum] unciae ii. Omnia ista insimul misce et optime incorpora, et ex ista mixtura des parum in potu aut cibo cui volueris, et amaberis ab ea.

> Take five ounces of gazelle brain, one ounce of leopard's blood, and two ounces of hare rennet. Mix all these together at the same time, and amalgamate it very well, and give a very small part from this substance in the drink or food to whom you love, and they will be enamoured of you.[357]

Accipe cerebri columbi albi ejusque sanguinis et sangui[ni]s aquile ana unciae ii, coaguli leporis uncia i, cerebri *estarii* [asturis] uncia i. Ista insimul misce et bene incorpora, et dabis ex eo in cibo, et ab eo amabis

> Take two ounces of the brain of a white dove, and of its blood, and the blood of an eagle; one ounce of hare rennet; one ounce[358] of brain of a goshawk. Mix these at the same time, and amalgamate it well, and you should give in food from this, and they will be enamoured with you from it.[359]

Accipe sanguinis galli sanguinis *leprodi* [leopardi], coaguli *lepox* [leporis] uncia 1; sanguinis humani unciae ii. Omnia simull incorpora et *adde eis in forbii* [cum eis addas euphorbii] uncia i; *cujusque cum hac consettone subfumigabis*

355. *Unciae*: The abbreviation for "ounce" appears in the original, but this is written out for ease of understanding.

356. This is a mangled version of a recipe from the *Picatrix*. Latin: Pingree, *Picatrix*, 156. English: Attrell and Porreca, *Picatrix*, 199.

357. Latin: Pingree, *Picatrix*, 156. English with commentary: Attrell and Porreca, *Picatrix*, 199.

358. *One ounce*: *Picatrix* has one-half.

359. Latin: Pingree, *Picatrix*, 156. English with commentary: Attrell and Porreca, *Picatrix*, 199–200.

[quemcumque autem cum ista confectione suffumigas], ab eo diligeris et ejus spiritus et voluntates erga te *monebitur* [movebuntur].

> Take one ounce of the blood of a cock, the blood of a leopard, and hare rennet; and two ounces of human blood. Amalgamate them all at the same time, and add an ounce of euphorbia to these. Whosoever you suffumigate with this compound, you will be loved by that one, and their spirits and wills shall be stirred toward you.[360]

Accipe sanguinis passeris ejusque cerebri ana uncia i; sanguinis humani unciae iiii; [sanguinis] *nunscipat* [muscipule] et ejus cerebri ana uncia i; *enforbis* [euphorbis] uncia i. Misceantur et da in potu [cui volueris].

> Take one ounce each of the blood of a sparrow, and its brain; four ounces of human blood; one ounce each of the blood of a cat and its brain; and one ounce[361] of euphorbia. They should be mixed together, and give them to the one you desire in drink.[362]

[30]

Accipe sanguinis galli rubrei ejusque cerebri ana unciae iiii; coaguli leporis, sanguinis columbae, sanguinis cattion unciae ii; euforbii uncia i. Misceantur omnia et suffumiga quem volueris cum eodem.

> Take four ounces each of the blood of a red cock,[363] and of its brain; two ounces of hare rennet, dove blood, and cattion[364] blood; one ounce of euphorbia. They all should be mixed, and suffumigate the one you desire with it.[365]

Emanuell: De Imaginibus Tractatus Pro Amore[366]

Accipe tegulam in die ♀ et hora, et pratrach in ea imaginem aninsuis, ad stilo veluti scribit, modo quo sequitur, dicendo sic:

360. Latin: Pingree, *Picatrix*, 156–57. English with commentary: Attrell and Porreca, *Picatrix*, 200.

361. *One ounce*: *Picatrix* has one-third.

362. *Take one ounce…you desire*: Latin: Pingree, *Picatrix*, 157. English with commentary: Attrell and Porreca, *Picatrix*, 200.

363. *Cock*: *Picatrix* has "dog."

364. *Cattion*: *Picatrix* has "rooster."

365. *Take four ounces…with it*: Latin: Pingree, *Picatrix*, 157. English with commentary: Attrell and Porreca, *Picatrix*, 200.

366. Translation: "A Treatise on the Images for Love." For other versions, see Braekman, *Magische Experimenten*, 38–40; Harms and Clark, *Of Angels*, 159; Folger X.d.208, 1r–1v.

Take a stone roof tile, in the day and hour of ♀, and carve[367] an image on it of the one you love,[368] just as you will write with a pencil, in the manner that follows, saying:[369]

"N. filia N., facio hanc imaginem ad similitudinem et *forniam* [formam] tuam."

"N., daughter of N., I make this image in thy likeness and form."

Ita dum sculpis, dicas:

While you carve, say:

"O domina ♀ splendida lucidissima stellarum, amore plena, adjuva me."

"O Lady ♀, splendid and most brilliant of the stars, help me with plentiful love."

Et postquam impleveris formam cum nominibus et characteribus sicut infra intra. Facies ignem de carbonibus ignites, et accipe tegulam in manum et pone faciem tuam ad meridiem, et *dies* [dic] hanc oracionem.

And after cover the form within with the names and characters below. Make a fire of burning charcoal, and take the tile in your hand, and put your face toward the south, and say this prayer:

"Omnipotens sempiterne deus, qui in principio creasti caelum et terram, mare et quae in eis sunt, qui Adam et Euam ad similitudinem tuam formasti, et eos in paradisum terrestriem misisti, et eis ne de ligno vitae comederent praecepisti, qui incredulem angelum propter *subias* [superbiam] ad tartara misisti, qui Susanna de falso *erie* [crimine] liberasti, et *Inadithe* [Iudithe] de manu Holoferni, et *Damielem* [Danielem] de lacu leonum, et tres pueros de camino ignis *ardentem* [ardentis], Jonam de ventre ceti liberasti, et Adam de profundo inferno precioso sanguine tuo redemisti, Paulum de mare et Petrum de vinculis liberasti, te supplex pii deus pater invoco et deprocor, quatenus me quere[nte], pulsante super alios spiritus in 4 orbis partibus, viz., Astrot Godras, Arot Unno ut de deus invente voluntatem meam impleant et preceptis meis obediant, qui vivis et regnas et imperas eum, deo patre et filio et spiritu sancto. Amen."

367. *Carve*: Conjectural.

368. *Of the one you love*: Conjectural, based upon what follows.

369. *Take a stone…saying*: Some of this is conjectural, based on the sources given previously.

"Almighty everlasting God, who in the beginning created heaven and earth, the sea, and all things in them, who formed Adam and Eve in your likeness, and sent them into the paradise of the lands, and ordered them that they might not eat from the tree of life, who sent the disobedient angel to Tartarus for his pride, who freed Susanna from false accusation, and Judith from the hand of Holofernes, and Daniel from the lions' den, and the three youths from the furnace of burning fire, and freed Jonah from the belly of the whale, and redeemed Adam from the lower depths with your precious blood, and freed Paul from the sea and Peter from bonds, I invoke and pray to thee, holy God the Father, entreating so that, with me asking and you impelling the other spirits in the four parts of the world, viz., Astrot, Godras, Arot, Unno, that, having found thee, O God, they may fulfil my will and obey my commands, thou who livest and reignest and rulest, with God the Father and the Son and the Holy Ghost. Amen."

[31]

Posthac ponas faciem tuam versus miridie, dic:

Afterward, place your face toward the south, say:

"O princeps meridionalis Astrot, coniuro te cum omnibus sociis tuis in collegio *exuntibus* [existentibus], qui potestatem habentes ad amorem per A Ω, primum et novissimam, Abres vel Abies, Rubeus vel Rubres, Teste vel Caste, Eli, Messias, Sabaoth, Adonay, Sother, Emmanuel. Coniuro vos pro anunciatione Jesu Christi, gubernat, per coelum et terram, per mare et omnia que in eis sunt, et per quattuor ventos et quattuor *elemata* [elementa], per septem planeta, per coelum maximum est, per virtutem istius summi *nomine* [nominis] *Tegragaton* [Tetragrammaton], quod in fronte tulit *auream* [Aaron], et caput vestri principis et regis *Tuciferi* [Luciferi], et per eius coronam quae religatus est in inferno, et per eis *pritates* [principates] infernalis et quibus poteris coniurari et ex ne[ces]sitari suffiendi, a prop[ri]o loco vestro meridionali recedatis iam et sine mora eatis ad N. filia N. et ita credentitur et ardenter eam in amore meum inflammatis sicut ista figura facta ad formam et similitudinem ejus ardebit et inflamabit in igne isto sic abeatis et calefacite et inflamate cor et corpus N. filia N. in amorem meum ita quae nullo momento possit ducare, neque quiescere dormiendo vigilando, jacendo, stando, sedendo, qualitercumque monendo qui est semper in et de cogitet et in in amore mei ardeat, et sic durando donec ad me veniet vel mittatur et totam *voluatur* [voluntatem] meam adimplet et nullam grannem mihi inferendo." ✠.

"O prince of the south, Astrot, I conjure thee with all thy associates present in thy company who have power for love, by Alpha and Omega, first and last, Abres or Abies, Rubeus or Rubres, Teste or Caste, Eli, Messias, Sabaoth, Adonay, Sother, Emmanuel.[370] I conjure you all for the sake of the annunciation of Jesus Christ. He governs[371] by heaven and earth, by the sea and all things that are in them, and by the four winds and the four elements, by the seven planets, by the heaven that is highest, by the virtue of that most high name *Tegragaton* [Tetragrammaton], that Aaron bore on his chest, and by the head of your prince and king Lucifer, and by his crown who was bound in hell, and by his infernal principalities, both by which you may be conjured and out of which you may be compelled, that you withdraw from your place in the south now, and without delay go to N., daughter of N., and that you all kindle her trustingly and hotly in my love, just as this image, made in her form and likeness, will burn and kindle in this fire, thus shall you all go and both heat and inflame the heart and body of N., daughter of N., into my love, so that in no moment of hers she can think or rest, sleeping, waking, standing, sitting, in such a manner, and with reminding her that she is both thinking and burning in love of me, and remaining thus until she will come or be sent to me and complete all my will and causing me no burden." ☩.

☽ silver, ♀ copper, ♂ iron, ♄ lead, ☿ quicksilver, ☉ gold, ♃ tin
Who makest angels thy spirits and thy ministers a flaming fire.

Istam conjuraconem dices ad 4 *pater* [partes] orbis, primo ad Astrot versus meridiem, 2o ad vimon versus orientem, 3o ad Aret versus borealem, 4o ad Godras versus occidentem, et ita *conicabis* [conicies] per 3 dies 4 vel 5 dies in qualibet die, ter, sicut scilicet in mane, meridie et crepusculo, et qualibus vice oratione ad predictam conjuraconem quater repetila, ut dictum est.

You will say this conjuration to the four regions of the world, first to Astrot toward the south, second toward Vimon to the east, third to Aret to the north, fourth to Godras in the west, and thus you should do for three, four, or five days, three times each day, thus, namely, at dawn, noon, and evening, and with some prayer said four times in place of the aforesaid conjuration, as it is said.

370. *Abres…Emmanuel*: Braekman: "abios abics rubeus rubet caste hely messias sabaoth adonay sother emanuel."

371. *Gubernat*: Braekman: "et per passionem eius per resurrexionem eius per aduentum eius domini nostri ihesu Christ." Translation: "and by his passion, and by his resurrection, and by the arrival of our Lord Jesus Christ."

[32]

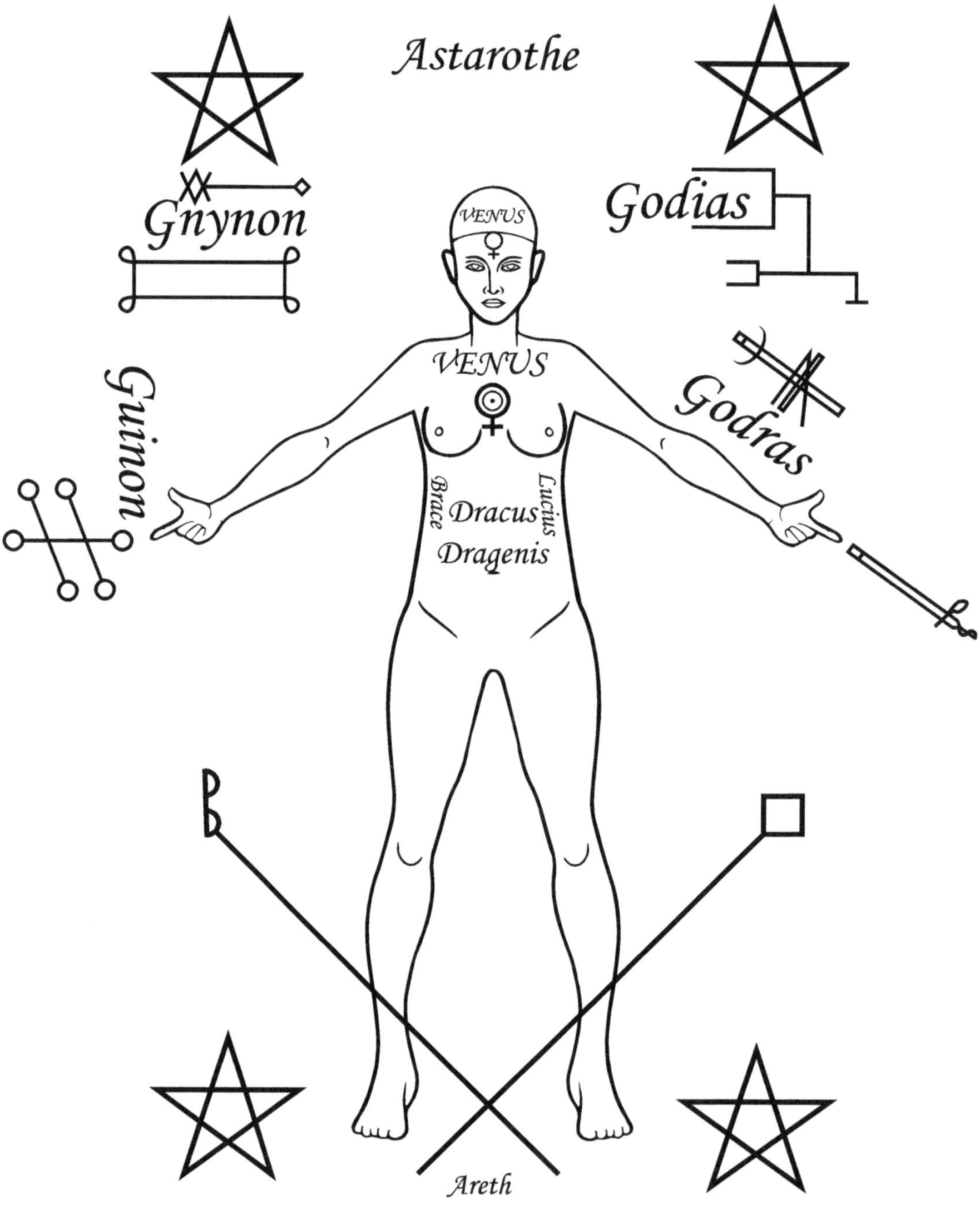

This image belongs to the experiment last before.

[33]

Pro Amore[372]

Accipe pergamenum virginem amplitudinis manus tuae [?] die ☉, ☽ crescente, et prima hora diei, depinge *unam* imaginem tui similem & in nomine tuo, et vide quod ille diei sit nullius mundi *superbleas* [super eas], et tunc die veneris, explana eam, et in hora prima diei fac imaginem alteram ad similitudinem M cujus amore desideras, tunc recipe sanguinem de tuo digito medio manus sinistre, et scribe cum eo nomen tuum super imaginem tuam et super altera imagine nomen M et inter ambas, scribe Sathan, Lucifer, Dentalien. Plica imagines ad invicem ita quod tua sit directa super *altam* imaginem, et tunc predicto illo die, pone sub planta pedis tui intra calligas et cutem, et ibi jaceat per 3 dies et quotidie, dic istam conjura[tione]m ad horam prima nona vespere ut sequitur.

> Take virgin parchment of the width of your hand, in the day of the ☉, with the ☽ waxing, and in the first hour of the day, draw an image of your likeness and in your name, and see that on this day that nothing of the world may come over them.[373] And then on a Friday, spread it out, and in the first hour of the day make another image in the likeness of M., whose love you desire. Then take blood from your middle finger of your left hand, and write with it your name on your image, and the name of M. on the other image, and between both, write, "Sathan, Lucifer, Dentalien."[374] Fold these images toward each other, so that yours is placed over the other, and then, on the aforesaid day, place it below the soles of your feet, between your footwear or hose and your skin, and it should lie there for three days, and each day say this at prime, nones, and vespers,[375] as follows:

"Coniuro te, Sathan, te, Lucifer, te, Dentalis, qui estis *prencipis* [principes] *barrati* [barathri], qui fecestis Adam et Evam in paradiso per fraudulentissimum ingenium virum peccare. Coniuro vos per Patrem et Filium et Spiritus Sanctum, per quattuor *evangilestas* [evangelistas], cum vos proprietates quas dominus h[ab]et in caelo, et in terra, et in inferno, in mari, in alto abisso.

372. Translation: "For Love."

373. *May come over them*: Conjectural.

374. *Sathan…Dentalien*: These are three of the four demons cited elsewhere in an operation for theft. Harms and Clark, *Of Angels*, 221.

375. *Prime, nones, and vespers*: Canonical hours, with prime being the first hour of the morning, none the early afternoon, and vespers at sunset.

Coniuro vos per inseparabilem trinitatem et indivisibilem unitatem, et per *Christum* [Christi?] dei excellentissimum nomen Tetragamaton. Ego vos conjuro, Sathan, Lucifer, Dentalis, quod eatis ad et non dimittatis eam aliquo modo quiescere ut dormiendo nec vigelando, comedendo, nec bibendo, stando, sedendo, nec somniando, sed faciatis cor ejus in amore mea semper fixum, et in amore meo eam inflamantem ut ferrum ab igne inflamantum est, ut in omnibus et per omnia secundum posse *sron* [?] omnes voluntates meas faciat, et ad hoc faciendum vos cogat virtus illius sublimis, qui solo verbo cuncta *caevit* [creavit]. Amen."

> "I conjure thee, Sathan; thee, Lucifer; thee, Dentalis, who art the lords of hell, who madest Adam and Eve to sin in paradise through the most deceitful nature of men. I conjure you all, by the Father, and the Son, and the Holy Ghost, by the four evangelists, with you, the qualities that the Lord possesses in heaven, and on earth, and in hell, in the sea, and in the depths of the abyss. I conjure you all by the inseparable trinity and indivisible unity, and by the most excellent name of God Christ, Tetragrammaton. I conjure you all, Sathan, Lucifer, Dentalis, that you go to and not release her to rest in any way, neither sleeping nor waking, eating nor drinking, standing nor sitting, or dreaming, but that you make her heart always unwavering in my love, and her enflamed in my love, as an iron is heated from the fire, that in all things and by all things after she be able to meet all my desires, and the power of the exalted one, who with one word created all things, may summon you for the purpose of doing this. Amen."

Oracio ad Deum[376]

"Domine Jesu Christe, rex gloriose, rex invictus, Jesu mitiss, te deprecor et rogo ut des eis non modo licentiam sed p[otes]tatem mittendi eam N in amorem meum, sed etiam hos inbeas at imperas eum ardere et inflamare amore mee, *excaeleconem* [excaecationem] nullam ponendo, sed quod

[34]

"moveat et preveniat in amorem meum ita quod amore indissolubili me diligat ferventissime. Amen. Fiat. Fiat. Fiat."

> "Lord Jesus Christ, glorious king, unconquerable king, mild Jesus, I pray and ask you that you give these not only licence but power, send-

376. Translation: "Prayer to God."

ing her, N., into my love, but also you should seek these, but order her to burn and enflame in my love, placing no blindness, but that [34] she rouse herself and approach in my love, so that she may love me with indestructible love most fervently. Amen. Let it be done, let it be done, let it be done.

"Coniuro vos, Sathan, Lucifer, Dentalis, per omnes virtutes et potestates Christi. Coniuro vos per angelos et arcangelos & c. Conuiro vos per amorem quo deus dilexit omnes sanctos, per amorem quo illi dilexerunt illum, et per amorem quo Maria, mater Domini *verus* [veri] Jhesu Christi, dilexit filium suum, et per amorem quo deus dilexit illam. Coniuro vos per amorem quo deus dilexit Johannem exangelistam, et per amorem quo ipsi *dilexerunt* [dilexit] illi eum eo. Vos coniuro per confessores, martires, virgines, viduas, et sanctas *invocentes* [innocentes]. *Cum* coniuro vos per beatum mariam, matrem domini viri Jhesu Christi, et ejus virginitatem. Conjuro vos per virginitatem omnium *virginem* [virginum], per amens passionis omnium martirum, per merita omnia omnium *confessionum* [confessorum], patriarcharum, et prophetarum, et per eorum no[m]i[n]a et dicta et facta. Coniuro ad eam vos per omnes sanctos et sanctas dei, ut faciatis N. in amore meo *indesinentur* [indesinenter] ardere et inflamare. Coniuro vos per passionem domini nostri Jesu Christi, per coronam spineam qua fuit coronatus, per columnam quam legatus fuit, per *virgis* [virgas] quibus verberatus, per opprobrium quibus maculatus fuit, per sanctissimum crucem in quae crucifixus fuit, per lanceam *in* [et] clavis quibus perforatus fuit. *Cum ad* [coniuro?] et constringo vos per aquam et sanguinem ejus per vulnera ejus, et per aquam baptismatis et *sanguinis* [sanguinem] redemptionis. *Ego* [coniuro] vos per totam conjurationem *predicit* [praedictam?] & pro virtutem ejus et per o[mn]ia no[m]i[n]a dei summi, effabilia et *infessabilia* [ineffabilia], quibus patriarchae, prophetae, et apostoli oraverunt et eos exaudivit. *Com* [conjuro] denique vos. O Sathan, o Lucifer, o Dentalis, in virtute dei ut eatis ad N et faciatis cor et corpus ejus indisinentur amore arderem, ita quod, per amoris fervore, nihil mihi denegare possit. Ite, ite, ite, o Sathan, o Lucifer, o Dentalis, et rapite inflamate, ardete, N. in amorem meum, ita ut me absente

[35]

"pro [sic] *presentere* [praesente] me ante omnia ferventissime diligat. Fiat, fiat."

"I conjure you all, Satan, Lucifer, Dentalis, by all virtues and powers of Christ. I conjure you by the angels and archangels, & c. I conjure you by the love with which God loved all saints, by the love that they loved him, and by the love that Mary, mother of the true Lord Jesus Christ, loved her son, and by the love that God loved her. I conjure you by the love that God loved John the Evangelist, and by the love that he loved him. I conjure you by the confessors, martyrs, virgins, widows, and holy innocents. I conjure you by the Blessed Mary, mother of the Lord of man, Jesus Christ, and his virginity. I conjure you by the virginity of all virgins, by the 'amens' of the suffering of all martyrs, by all the merits of all the confessors, patriarchs, and prophets, and by their names, both spoken and done. I conjure you all to her by all male and female saints of God, that you should make N. to burn and kindle in my love unceasingly. I conjure you all by the passion of our lord Jesus Christ, by the crown of thrones by which he was crowned, by the column to which he was tied, by the rods by which he was beaten, by the dishonour with which he was polluted, by the most holy cross on which he was crucified, by the lance and nails by which he was pierced. I conjure and bind you by his water and blood, by his wounds, and by the water of baptism and blood of redemption. I conjure you all by the whole aforesaid conjuration, and by its power, and by all the names of the highest God, effable and ineffable, by which patriarchs, prophets, and apostles prayed, and he heard them. At last, I conjure you all, O Sathan, O Lucifer, O Dentalis, in the power of God, that you go to N. and make her heart and body to burn ceaselessly with love, so that, by the heat of love, she will be able to deny nothing to me. Go, go, go, O Sathan, O Lucifer, O Dentalis, and kindle, burn N. quickly in my love, so that, being removed from or [35] present with me,[377] that she should love me most fervently before all others. Let it be done, let it be done."

Oracio[378]

"Domine Jesu Christi, te deprecor et rogo ut des eis licentiam et *pietatem* [potestatem] ut possint suadere, N. cuibus signum, nomen, et imago porto sub planta pedis mei, ut me amet. Amen."

377. *Being removed...me*: Conjectural.

378. Translation: "Prayer."

> "Lord Jesus Christ, I beseech and ask thee that thou givest licence and power to these, that they are able to urge N. to love me, whose sign, name, and image I place below the soles of my feet. Amen."

Deinde conbure imagines cum thure et aromatibus et *dicam* [dicas] *Plalmum* [Psalmum], "Attollite portas principes vestras," sic.

> Then burn the images with frankincense and spices, and say the psalm, "Attollite portas principes vestras,"[379] thus.

Pro Amore[380]

Accipe cera virginea et formes imaginem ad similitudinem cujus amare desideras, dicendo:

> Take virgin wax, and shape an image in the likeness of she you desire to love thee, saying:

"Ego facio te, imaginem, in nomine N. et te stabilio in forma ad finem, ut omne illud quod te facio pati *patiatner* [patiatur?] N., per amore meo. Lucifer, Sathan, Belzebub sitis adiutores mei ad hoc complere."

> "I make thee, image, in the name of N., and I appoint thee in the form to the end that every thing that I make you to suffer, N. may suffer through my love. Lucifer, Sathan, Belzebub, may you be my helpers to complete to this end."

Cum facias diligenter quocunque die volueris, si melior est dies ♀ ☽ crescente et existente in signo calido, qui ista imago facta est vi ad tollerandum supplicandum. Et tunc scribes in fronte imaginis nomen M. in altissimo loco capitis figura ista 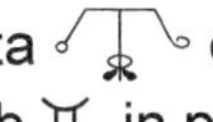 et hoc nomen, Sathan in dextra auricula, Lucifer, in sinistra, Belzebub ♊, in pectore ♀ et ista nomina Perenell, Aperyes, Filiat, Disdros Me Nec Hic, Probalnea, Protalion, Cubras, super dexteram latus Paymon, As Monday, et supra sinistram latus, Egin, Poet, Amaymon, et postea scindas

379. *Attollite...vestras*: Vulgate Psalm 23:7 and 23:9. English translation (KJV Psalm 24:7): "Lift up your heads, O ye gates." The intent here might be for the magician to read 23:7–10.

380. Translation: "For Love."

ventrem et scribe hos exsequentes cum carbonibus in pergamento virginea, et impenas in ventre dicendo:

> Although you may do this assiduously in whatsoever day you desire, it is better if in the days of ♀, ☽ waxing and visible in a hot sign,[381] that this image is made with power for exalting and praying. And then you will write on the forehead the name M., on the crown of the head this figure 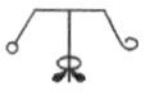 and this name, Sathan, on the right ear, Lucifer on the left, Belzebub ♊, on the chest ♀, and these names: "Perenell, Aperyes, Filiat, Disdros, Me Nec Hic,[382] Probalnea, Protalion, Cubras"; on the right side Paymon[383] As Monday[384] and on the left side Egin, Poet, Amaymon, and after that cut open the stomach and write these following with charcoal on virgin parchment, and place them in the stomach, saying:

"Ite, vos omnes ad N., et calefacite eam in amore meo,"

> "Go, you all, to N., and make her burn in my love."

Et propt[er]ea reclude ventrem, et scribe super illum quod scidisti "Draco, Braciget," in femore dextro, "Belial, Ascarothe, Saltem," in sinistro femore, "Sakunas, Galtim, Baltim," et postea liga

[36]

imaginem cum uno pilo gaballi per collum, et cum volueris habeas ignem de carbonibus vinis et calefacias imaginem se vide sis ne fundat guttabant. Postea intingas imaginem in urina de puro masculo et postea recaleface et punge imaginem cum *acto* [acie], dicens:

> And therefore open the stomach again, and write on it, that you cut open, "Draco, Braciget." Then write on the right thigh, "Belial, Asca-

381. *Hot sign*: Aries, Leo, Sagittarius.

382. *Filiat…Hic*: One possible reading would be "Filia, desideres me nec hic," or "Daughter, love me not them."

383. *Paymon*: Spirit associated with the west. For other references to Paymon, see Bayerische Staatsbibliothek Clm 849, 30r; Bodleian Aubrey 24, 29r; British Library Additional 36,674, 11r; Sloane 1727, 29; Sloane 3824, 16v; Sloane 3847, 32v; Sloane 3850, 70r–v; 124v; Leipzig University Library Cod. Mag. 41, 43; Harms, Clark, and Peterson, *Oberon*, 194 et passim; Harms and Clark, *Of Angels*, 106–7, 198; Rosen and Thorndike, *The Sphere of Sacrobosco and Its Commentators*, 404; Peterson, *The Sixth and Seventh Books of Moses*, 148; Peterson, "Index of Angel Names, Magical Words, and Names of God," (Paimon/Paymon); Faust, *Magia Naturalis et Innaturalis*, 63; Vârtejaru, "The Book of the Seven Rings of the Planets of Messalah"; Scot, *The Discovery of Witchcraft*, 218–21; Aster, *Hereditary*.

384. *As Monday*: Most likely "Asmoday" is intended here.

rothe, Saltem," and on the left thigh, "Sakunas, Galtim, Baltim." Afterward bind [36] the image with a stake of a gallows around the neck, and when you desire, make a fire out of coals of grapevines, and heat the image. Watch to make sure it is not melting or dripping. Afterward soak the image in the urine from a chaste man, and afterward heat it again, and puncture it the image with a sharp object, saying:

"♂, ignis malefactionis, *adjuvare* [adjuva] me et nos. Lucifer, Belzebub, Sathan, Egin, Poet, Amaymon, Asmoday, Venue, Diraco, Brucius, Sathanas, Galtim, Belial, Astarothe, Saltim, Baltim, coniuro vos omnes per infinitam virtutem dei Patris et Fili et Spiritus Sancti, per quatuor reges in caelis regnantes, per omnia ista nomina On, El, Eley, Eloy, Sabaoth, Adonay, et per istos, ex [sic?] et per omnia nomina quae sunt in ista imaginem sic illa crucietis et pungatis sic illam [non] dormiat vel vigilat, et meum amorem cordi illius. Fugite, et cor et corpus et animam suam faciatis ardere et sudare et illam faciatis reminisci de me et de delectatione mea quatenus, non possit dormire nec quiescere donec veniat ad me loqui et *obsculari* [obscurari] os meum et compleat volutatem meam. Et nunc vos omnes, coram ad me, constringo vos per potestatem quam dedit vobis deus altissimum, ut quemadmodum ista imagino crutiatur, sic illam ad cuius similitudinem ha facta est *crucifate* [cruciate]."

"♂, fire of stolen goods, help me and us. Lucifer, Belzebub, Sathan, Egin, Poet, Amaymon, Asmoday, Venue, Diraco, Brucius, Sathanas, Galtim, Belial, Astarothe, Saltim, Baltim, I conjure you all by the infinite virtue of God the Father, Son, and Holy Ghost, by the four kings ruling in the heavens, by all these names, On, El, Eley, Eloy, Sabaoth, Adonay, and by these, and by all the names that are on this image. As you shall torment and puncture this, so she shall not sleep or wake, and my love of this heart...[385] Go, and make her heart and body and soul to burn and sweat, and make her to remember me and my pleasure so long, that she cannot sleep nor lie still until she come to me to speak and to be blinded by my mouth, and she shall fulfil my will. And now, I constrain you all, face to face to me, by the power that the highest God gave to you, that howsoever this image is tormented, thus it is done to torment her through the likeness of her."

385. Apparently a verb is missing here.

Tu hoc facies ternis vicibus, et eris voti copes.

You should do this three times in succession, and you will be satisfied.

Pro Amore[386]

Fac imaginem de cera virginea in nomine quae amas et baptiza in aqua, ad baptizandum idonea, dicendo:

Make an image in virgin wax in the name of her you love, and baptise it in water fitting for baptism, saying:

"Baptizo te in nomine Patris et Filii et Spiritus Sancti. Amen."

"I baptise thee in the name of the Father and of the Son and of the Holy Ghost. Amen."

Cum aliis baptizandis ritibus. Quibus peractis, scribe in fronte nomen M. quam desideras et nomen tuum in pectore imaginis, in capite venus karacter. Hoc facto, accipe quatuor acus novas et earum unam pungere in dorso adversus umbilicum; altam in leve latere iuxta cor; tertiam in latere dextro, 4th supra umbilicam. Tum scribe in sinistra latere, Sicare, dextro vero Gratnel,

[37]

super umbilicum Asmodeus, in dorso Mammot. Hisce rite et tempore conveniente fabricatis, dicas quam pure ac denote poteris:

With other ceremonies of baptism. With these finished, write on the forehead the name M. who you desire, and your name on the chest of the image, on the head the character of Venus. This done, take four new needles and plunge one of these into the back across from the navel, another in the left side near the heart; the third into the right side; the fourth over the navel. Then write on the left side, "Sicare"; on the right, "Gratnel"; [37] above the navel, "Asmodeus"; on the back, "Mammot." Speak solemnly, and with these made at an appropriate time, say as plainly and devoutly as possible:

386. Translation: "For Love."

"Coniuro vos, spiritus qui habetis *protate* [potestatem] et virtutem provocandi amores. Conjuro, adjuro, et constringe vos spiritus Sicate, Gratnel, Mammoy, Asmodeus per infinitam partem dei Patris, qui est *diminitate* [divinitatem] per immensam potentiam dei filii, qui est humanitatem et per potestatem cuncti potentem dei, spiritus *scantti* [sancti], qui suo ambitu circuit universum mundum. Ego vos conjuro per sanctissimum nomen dei, Tet[r]agramaton, ut in unum conveniatis ubi, ubicunque sitis et ne quem scite, per deum vivum, per deum verum, per deum sanctum, donec satisfecistis animi mei desiderum. Venite, venite igitur ab oriente Galhinos, et ab hoc occidente Imbroson, ab astra Memiatha, et ab boriali Thimeramet, venitis. Venite, convenite, inquam, et ite ad N filia N, et inflamate eam in amorem meum. *Experite* [experimini] potentiam vestram, et efficite ut totaliter in amore meo ardeat. Hoc ut faciatis, vos coniuro per pritatem dei qui dixit et facta sint omnia, ut ne sinatis N. ullo loco aut ullo momento temporis quiescere, sed semper de me cogitet, me solum ardenter amet, incendatur meo amore, ita ut nec dormiat, nec edat, donec ego petitum fero. Hoc ut officiatis, vos spiritus S. G. M. A., coniuro, contestor, et constringo per omnia nomina summi et altiique dei per virtutem caeli et terrae. Coniuro vos ad omnia et sine fallacia compleatis animi mei desiderium."

> "I conjure you all, O spirits who have power and virtue for provoking loves. I conjure, adjure, and bind you all, O spirits Sicate, Gratnel, Mammoy, Asmodeus, by the boundless power of God the Father, who is divinity, by the endless power of God the son, who is humanity, and by the strong power of all God the Holy Ghost, who travels around the entire world in its revolution. I conjure you by the most holy name of God, Tet[r]agramaton, so that you gather all together wheresoever you may be, and know her not,[387] by the living God, by the true God, by the holy God, until you satisfy the will of my soul. Come, come, therefore, Galhinos out of the east, and Imbroson out of the west, Memiatha from the south, and Thimeramet from the north, you all come. Come, gather, I say, and go to N. daughter of N. and inflame her in my love. Test your power, and cause that she may burn entirely in my love. As you do this, I conjure you by the power of God who spoke and all things were done, that you not permit N. to rest in any place or any moment of time, but she will think of me always, she will love me alone hotly, she should be burned by my love, so that she may neither sleep

387. *And know her not*: Unclear in the original.

nor eat, until I make my request. As you oppose this, O you spirits Sicare, Gratnel, Mammoy, and Asmodeus, I conjure, I invoke, and I bind you by all the names of the highest and most exalted God, by the power of heaven and earth. I conjure you for all things, and you should fulfil the desire of my soul without deceit."

His tempore oppertune rite et debito, ordine finitis. Strue tibi ignem in nomine ejus, et super ignem pone salum cum gravis sinapis. Prius protracte in igne imaginem, super quam pone super eam carbones ardentes adversus quas. Calefac imaginem ceream et dic quemadmodum compositio haec tumet et saltet sic:

[Having said] these things at a convenient time and solemnly, you finish in the appointed order. Build a fire for you in her name, and put salt water with strong white mustard on it. Bring the image to the fire, and place burning coals near it. Warm the wax image, and say thus as this mixture swells and dances:

"*Officite* [efficite] ut N. sic accensa in amore meo, fiat, fiat, fiat. Vos etiam coniuro, angeli quatuor ventorum, Gathinos, Smabathan, Saym, Atheizen, Nemigatha, Thimi, Miratin, Beclachim, Achamaytymon, Ramet, ut hoc desiderium animi mei perficiatis, per dominum verum Iesum Christem. Amen."

"Make it so that N. may be so kindled in my love. Let it be done, let it be done, let it be done. I also conjure you all, angels of the four winds, Gathinos, Smabathan, Saym, Atheizen, Nemigatha, Thimi, Miratin, Beclachim, Achamaytymon, Ramet, that you carry out this desire of my soul, by the true god Jesus Christ. Amen."

[38]

Pro Amore[388]

Accipe ceram virgineam, et confice imaginem in novilunio, et scribe in fronte imaginis Iris, cum hoc caracteres  et in vertice Scibilla, cum hoc caracteres , et in sincipite Azaria cum hoc caracteres 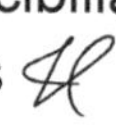 et in corde imaginis scribe nomen tuum cum his nominibus Eliazare, Megalagia, cum his

388. Translation: "For Love." For other examples, see Bodleian Additional B.1, 1r–2v; Rawlinson D.252, 69v–71v; BL Sloane 1727, 24–28; Sloane 3846, 38r–39v, 41r–42v; Harms and Clark, *Of Angels, Demons, and Spirits*, 270–72; Bellhouse, *A Complete System of Magic*, 32–37. Only the Rawlinson manuscript also suggests the image could be used for love, and although the creation of the image has many similarities, the prayers and spirits called upon here are quite different from those used in other sources.

caracteres  p. 21 b. i. et in dorso adversum cor hoc caracteres 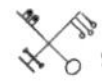, tunc cape imaginem in manu dicens:

> Take virgin wax, and produce an image in the new moon, and write on the forehead of the image "Iris," with these characters , and on the crown of the head, "Scibilla," with these characters 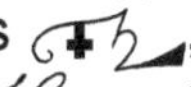, and on the front of the head[389] "Azaria" with these characters , and in the heart of the image write your name with these names, "Eliazare, Megalagia," with these characters , p. 21 b. i.,[390] and in the back against the heart these characters . Then take the image in your hand, saying:

"O Deus omnipotens, tua ineffabilia bonitate te obtestor ut misericordia digneris consedere mi amore N. (quam ego amo) ut me ante omnes et ante omnia amet atque desiderat. Hoc rogo et *simmis* [summis] precibus obtestor pro amore unius unigeniti filii tui salvatoris Jesu Christi qui *lecum* [tecum] vivit et *regnant* [regnat] in gloria, in secula seculorum. Amen."

> "O God omnipotent, I beseech thee, in thy unutterable goodness, that thou deignest in mercy to overwhelm N. in love for me (whom I love), and she will love and doth desire me before all people and all things. I ask this and I beseech through the highest prayers, for the sake of the love of thy one only-begotten son, the saviour Jesus Christ, who lives and rules with thee in glory, world without end. Amen."

Tunc dicas 3 pater noster et 3 ave maria et unum credo, postea dicas Psalm "Deus tu conversus vivificabus nos et plebs tua letabitur in te."

> Then say three Pater Nosters, and three Ave Marias, and a Creed, after which you should say the Psalm "Deus tu conversus vivificabis nos, et plebs tua letabitur in te."[391] [Then say]:

"Orem, omnipotens et sempiterne Deus, conditor, rex *viris* [vivis]. Te suplex rogo ut imbeas hos tuos ministros, Amael, Michael, Grabriel, Captiel, Satquiel, Samuel, Raphael in his meis operibus conatis et negotiis meis preceptis, ac mandatis in omnia obsequi per virtutem tuam qui verbo tuo cuncta creasti: et ut hac N. me ardentissime diligat ut propter hoc tibi et nomino tuo detur laus et gl[or]ia in sepiterna secula, amen."

389. *On the front of the head*: The Latin is ambiguous about where on or in the head this is.

390. *p. 21 b.i.*: The page reference does not seem to correspond with this manuscript.

391. *Deus te…letabitur in te*: Vulgate Psalm 84:7. Translation (KJV Psalm 85:6): "Wilt thou not revive us again: that thy people may rejoice in thee?"

> "Let me speak, omnipotent and everlasting God, author, living god. On bended knee I ask thee that that thou seekest these thy ministers Amael, Michael, Grabriel, Captiel, Satquiel, Samuel, Raphael, for attempting these my works, ordering my affairs, and commanding in everything to gratify by your power, who created all things with your word, and so with this N. may love me ardently, so that through this is given praise and glory to thee and in thy name in perpetuity. Amen."

His devote dictis, accipe imaginem in una manu et in altera virgam ejus arboris dicitur a white thorne, et imaginem versus ignem tenendo dicas, ut sequitur coniurationem:

> Having said these things solemnly, take the image in one hand, and in the other a wand of that tree—it is called a white thorn[392]—and holding the image against the fire, say the conjuration as follows:

"Coniuro vos angelos dei omnipotentissimi Anael, Michael, Grabniel, Captiel, Sutquiel, Sammuel, Raphael, per virtutem et *pritatem* [potestatatem] dei Patris, dei Filii, et dei Spiritus Sancti. Item conjuro vos, spiritus, per omnia haec nomina *quacum* [quam] in hoc opere non iacere Alpha, et Ω, Agla, Tegramaton, Sadai, Adonai, Diah, et Elohim, Sabaothe, Gibor, Eloha, Vedaath, Iod, Quanton, Craton, Alhanudos, Messcas, Emanuel, Jesus Christ. Conjuro, adiuro omnia, et constringo vos,

[39]

"Anael, Michael, Grabniel, Captiel, Sutquiel, Sammuel, Raphael, P., omnia haec nomina et per infinitam virtitem horum onnoy [nominum?] ut haec N., quod amo, in quocumque loco sit, pro nos et pretatim viram ita sit excitata, ut per vim horum *tactum* [factum] incitetur et impellatur in amorem meum, quemadmodum ego hanc imaginem predictam hac virga tango, ita ut amoris mei ardere, nec die, nec nocte quiescat, sedendo, stando, eendo, dormiendo, aut edendo: de me et meo amore cogitare, donec *volutari* [voluntatem] ac *disiderio* [desiderium] *meo* [meum] satisfecerit. Hoc vobis (o preci spiritus) impero per virtutem *infinita* [infinitum] et *pretatem* [potestatem] imensam domini nostri Jesu Christi salvatoris et redemptoris humani *gumris* [generis] qui vivit cum deo patrem et spiritem sancto per omnia secula seculorum, amen."

392. *A white thorn*: These words are English in the original. One hypothesis is that the incantation was translated from English back into Latin at some point, with the author being unaware of the proper word. Another would be that it was given in English for future readers who might not know a Latin term.

"I conjure you all, angels of most omnipotent God, Anael, Michael, Grabniel, Captiel, Sutquiel, Sammuel, Raphael, by the virtue and power of God the Father, God the Son, and God the Holy Ghost. Again I call you, spirits, by all these names I have not uttered in this work: Alpha, et Ω, Agla, Tegramaton, Sadai, Adonai, Diah, and Elohim, Sabaothe, Gibor, Eloha, Vedaath, Iod, Quanton, Craton, Alhanudos, Messcas, Emanuel, Jesus Christ. I conjure, I adjure all, and I constrain you, and [39] Anael, Michael, Grabniel, Captiel, Sutquiel, Sammuel, Raphael,[393] all these names, and by the infinite power of these names, that this one N., whom I love, in whatsoever place she may be, for us all,[394] and this woman may thus be summoned, that she, by the power made of these, may be hastened and stimulated in my love, as I touch this aforesaid image with this wand, so as to burn in my love. She may rest neither day nor night, sitting, standing, going, sleeping, or eating, to think of me and my love, until she fulfils my will and desire. Here I command you all, O spirits, to my request, by the infinite strength and boundless power of our Lord Jesus Christ, saviour and redeemer of the human race, who lives with God the Father and the Holy Ghost, world without end. Amen."

Omnibus rite factis, recita quinquies conjuraconem predictum, primo in *virtute* [vertice], secundo in fronte, tertio in pectore, quarto in occipite, quinto in dorso, tangendo caracteres in ea parte scriptos cum virga. Hoc quotidie feceris donec impetraveris.

With all this done, recite the aforesaid conjuration five times, first, on the top of the head; second, on the forehead; third, on the breast; fourth, on the back of the head; fifth, on the back, touching the characters written on each part with the wand. Do this every day, until you achieve your end.

Pro Amore[395]

Hora ♀ ☽ in ♐, fac imaginem de cera virginea per illa quam habere volueris, et scribe in eam nomen et caracter ♀ et calefac eam ad lentem ignem et

393. The original gives these as a string of abbreviations expanded here and includes the initial "P." at the end. This might have been added accidentally, or it may signify a previous version with another spirit name.

394. *For us all*: Conjectural. I have not found another version of this ritual with this incantation.

395. Translation: "For Love."

dum calefit, verita nomina angelorum leonis quae sunt Belferiel, Anerium vel Aeroy, Facison, Charathion, vel Ger Dicham, et nomina angelorum veneris, Penel, Aries, Fyliath, Diseros, Mechymn, Prebal, Neptaban, Othis, Aprops, Ciriael, Eaicham vel Garliam, Comosnay, et dic aliquam conuiractionem convenientem.

Make an image of virgin wax of her whom you desire to hold, in the hour of ♀, with the ☽ in ♐, and write the name and character of ♀, and warm it at a slow fire. And when it is warmed, [write] these revered names of the angels of Leo, who are Belferiel, Anerium or Aeroy, Facison, Charathion or Gerdicham, and the names of the angel of Venus, Penel, Aries, Fyliath, Diseros, Mechymn, Prebal, Neptaban, Othis, Aprops, Ciriael, Eaicham or Garliam, Comosnay, and say some suitable conjuration.

Alia[396]

Fac imaginem de cera virginea hora ♀ sub domino ♐ et scribe in ea caracteres Jovis  et caracteres arietis  et suspende imaginem in aliquo loco ut a vento agitetur, sed dum scribis caracteres no *laceantur* [iaciantur] nomina angelorum sagitarii that[397] Brandel, Zedroteyl, Rubibian, et nomina angelorum veneris, Penel, Aries, & c., ut supra hac. Accipe ranas *aquinas* [aquaticas], et eas concoque in oleo communi et, cum ipso oleo et filo vel iunco, fac candelam in quae scribas nomen ejus quam amas cum his caracteribus sequentibus. Quo facto, pone candelam in vestibus mortui vel *onisi* [ossi?] hominis ut ardeat et statim sine dubio veniet. 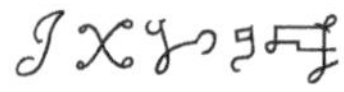

In the hour of ♀, under the ruler ♐, make an image of virgin wax, and write on it the characters of Jupiter  and the characters of Aries 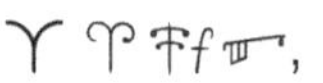, and suspend the image in some place where it may be agitated by the wind, but while you write these characters, the names of the angels of Sagittarius, viz., Brandel, Zedroteyl, Rubibian, and the names of the angels of Venus, Penel, Aries, & c., should be spoken, so as above. Take water frogs, and boil these in common oil, and, with that oil and a thread or rush, make a candle, on which write

396. Translation; "Another." For descriptions of similar rites, see Hartlieb, *Das Buch Aller Verbotenen Künste*, 90–91; Agrippa, *Three Books of Occult Philosophy* (1651), 311 (book 2, chapter 49).

397. *That*: English in the original.

the name of her who you love with the characters following. This done, place the candle in the clothes of a dead person, or on the bone of a man, and she may burn, and she will come to you immediately and doubtlessly. 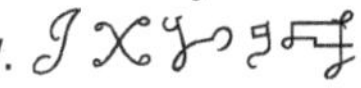

[40]

[Another][398]

Take virgin wax from the bees at such time as the ☽ is not of the full per a week or more, and keep it till the next Saturday after the full ☽. And that day make a candle of it, and write about it these words with the blood of thy little finger, "X Alifesta + Atemihelt + Bararthethyel, + Abesis, + Arex." Then write the woman's name whom thou desirest, and then say this conjuration:

"I conjure you which was sent into the second vessel, which Solomon did seal. I adjure you per the womb of the Blessed Virgin Mary, and by all things which are under heaven and in heaven contained, that you make N. to obey to my will and to me."

That which conjuration said, light the candle and put it out, and go to the church, and lay it under the door sill privily that it be not perceived, and let it lie till the priest go and come over it. Then take it up and put in under thy left arm, till it take some of thy sweat, and say, "Even as the candle is made warm per my heat, so let N. be made hot per my love," and if she be nigh she will send to thee, but keep thee away and speak not with the messenger, but make thyself busy and strange[399] till he be gone. Then hold thy candle unlight[400] in thy hand, and say the conjuration before said. And if the party do not come, light thy candle quickly and put it out again quickly, and so do often chiefly about the twilight in some secret place, with saying the conjuration, and though the whole world say nay, she will come to thee. But take heed the candle do not burn out, and the spirits' names about it, for so you may kill her. Therefore take heed that none of the names burn in the candle.

This may be done at all times, except the new of the ☽.

398. For another example, see British Library Sloane 3850, 150v.

399. *Strange*: Distant and reserved.

400. *Unlight*: Unlighted.

Pro Amore[401]

Die Jovis et hora ejus ante omnis ortum,[402] with the ☽ being towards the full, standing towards the east, dic:[403] "In the name of the Father have I sought, in the name of the Son have I found thee, in the name of the Holy Ghost I gather thee, in nomine Patris et Filii et Spiritus Sancti, & c."

[41]

Tunc dic Patrem Nostrum, Avem et Credo septies, circumendo herbam. Tunc dic:

> Then say a Pater Noster, an Ave, and a Creed seven times, circling the herb. Then say:

"I conjure thee, vervain, per the Father, Son, and Holy Ghost, one God omnipotent, and per the nativity of the Son, his circumcision, presentation, passion, and precious death, and per his glorious resurrection and ascension, per the blessed Trinity, per the heavens, per the names of the most holy, Agla, + Eledo, + Ely, + Zan, + Cell +, and per all the names of God, per the Mother of our Lord Jesu Christi, per her virginity, and per the commission of her Son, and per his holy birth, and her purification, per all the power of God in heaven and earth, and per all the names of God, heavenly, earthly, and infernally, that while I have thee in my hand or mouth, whomsoever I shall touch or kiss be ready in all things to consent to my will, in the name of the Father, and of the Son, and of the Holy Ghost. Amen. I conjure thee, vervain, that thou have full power, virtue, and strength to make men, women, and maids to love me, and especially S.S. so much to love me, that she have never lust to do anything until she be consented unto me, and that she be ready always to help me and fulfil my desire without delay or distance.

"Also I conjure thee, vervain, per the sufferance of God the Father omnipotent, which in the beginning made and created all things, per his Son and per the Holy Ghost, which came from the Father to the Virgin Mary in likeness of a dove, and the flood Jordan did sanctify, and per the Virgin Mary which brought forth the son of God for the salvation of mankind, per John Baptisti, and per all the orders of angels, per the 30,000 archangels, per the

401. Translation: "For Love." For similar rituals, see Thompson, *The Mysteries and Secrets of Magic*, 209–10; Cambridge Additional MS. 3544, 60; and manuscript page 53.

402. *Die Jovis…ortum:* Translation: "On the day and hour of Jupiter, before everyone rises."

403. *Dic*: Translation: "Say."

twelve Apostles, per the four evangelists, by the twenty-four seniors[404] which stand before the presence of God, and per these names of God, + Eloy, + Sabaothe, + Adanay + Emamuell, + Tetragramaton + and per all the miracles of God, per his holy sacrament,

[42]

"and per all that can be spoken, and per all that cannot be spoken, that whatsoever I shall touch or kiss, having thee in my mouth or about me, may neither eat nor drink, nor do anything that shall do her good, till she have consented unto my will, but that her heart may burn in my love as wood burneth in the fire, to that which I call to help me O Lord Jesu Christi, who liveth and reigneth, God with the Father and the Holy Ghost, to whom be all honour, glory, and praise forever and ever. Amen."

Then touch whom thou wilt upon the bare[405] with it, and thou shalt have whatsoever thou desirest.

Conjuratio Sequ[u]nt[ur] Nominibus ***Apta*** [Aptis][406]

"Primum te creatorem pomi ex omnino per omnipotentem tuam creationem." Deinde:

> "Thou, first creator of the apple entirely out of…[407] by thy omnipotent creation." Then [say]:

"O vos spiritus, coniuro vos et contestor per illum qui dixit et facta sunt, omnia cuius iussa movent montes *terribilia* [terribiles?] tremunt. Vos etiam conjuro et contestor per extremum diem judicii, ut faciatis sine mora eam quae hoc ponum comederit, ite, in meo amore ardere ut nunquam nec ullo loco quiescat donec voluntati mea satisfecerit. Fiat, fiat, fiat."

404. *Seniors*: Elders.

405. *Bare*: The bare skin.

406. Translation: "A Conjuration, with the Suitable Names Following." Spells that require the delivery of an apple to a prospective lover date back to ancient Greece and can be found in many manuscripts throughout Europe. For examples, see Faraone, *Ancient Greek Love Magic*, 69–78; Biblioteca Medicea Laurenziana Plutei 89 sup. 38, 66v–67r, 298v; British Library Sloane 1315, 118r; Sloane 3847, 35r; Sloane 3850, 149r, 150r, 151v, 152r; Sloane 3851, 140r–v; Cambridge Additional 3544, 60, 62; Lecouteux, *Book of Grimoires*, 100, 103; Harms, Clark, and Peterson, *Oberon*, 548; Harms and Clark, *Of Angels*, 264; Gaster, "English Charms of the Seventeenth Century," 376; Briggs, "Some Seventeenth-Century Books of Magic," 456; Gal, Boudet, and Moulinier-Brogi, *Vedrai Mirabilia*, 259, 269, 270, 281; Thompson, *The Mysteries and Secrets of Magic*, 208–9; *Petit Albert*, 16–17; Johnson, *Svartkonstböcker*, 349, 351, 363–64, 424, 525, 540, 562, 606; Bang, *Norske Hexeformularer og magiske Opskrifter*, 506; Ohrt, *Danmarks Trylleformler* (1917), 2:103, 113, 117, 129.

407. *Thou…out of…*: The nouns in this section are in the accusative and genitive cases, suggesting the manuscript is missing some words.

"O all you spirits, I conjure and appeal to you by he who spoke and all things were done, whose commands set in motion and the dreadful mountains shake. I also conjure and appeal to you by the last day of judgment, go, that you should make her who ate this apple to burn in my love without delay, that she may rest never nor in any place, until she might satisfy my will. Let it be done, let it be done, let it be done."

Vel sic:

Or thus:

"Coniuro vos per deum verum, per deum vivum, per deum sanctum, per illum qui venturus est judicare vivos et mortuos, per illum qui dixit et facta sunt omnia, ut ita *opatis* [operatis] in illa quae hoc ponum gustaverit ut nunquam quiete dormiat, nec edat, nec bibat, nec sedeat, donec omnino [desiderio?] meo satisfecerit. Fiat."

"I conjure you by the true God, by the living God, by the holy God, by him who will come to judge the living and the dead, by him who said and all things were done, that so you should work to affect within her who should taste this apple, that she may never sleep with rest, nor eat, nor drink, nor sit, until she may fulfil my [desire] entirely. Let it be done."

"Conjuro te, *ponum* [pomum] per ista nomina quae in te sint scripta, ut si qua de te comederit volunta[te]m meam impleat." Et da ei.

"I conjure you, apple, by these names that are written on you, that if she would eat from you, she would fulfil my will," and give it to her.

Ante omnis ortum,[408] take an apple with a red side, before it falls. With a sharp stick, write in it any of three of these names following.

[43]

+ Aleo, + Doleo, + Delaton, +[409]
+ Grax, + Crux, + Cenerax, +
+ Rea, + Comilici, + Lucifer, +[410]
+ Elite, + Elitese + Simel, +

408. *Ante omnis ortum*: Translation: "Before everyone rises."

409. + *Aleo...Delaton,* +: For another apple charm with these words, see BL Sloane 3851, 140r.

410. + *Rea...Lucifer* +: Sloane 3851, 140r: "Reacamo Lise Lucifero."

Satanas, Raguel, Dencalion,
Dedia, Sculpa, Dracon,[411]
Eliet, Elital, Tiniel,
Sorday, Abrothe, Altra,
Gys, Salbeo, Ebaseb,
Ganfrite, Tetragramaton, Agios,[412]
Cosma, Obrotz, Sorday,[413]
Silmo, Baruth, Tetragramaton,
Ewal, Satuel, Eliel, cum nominibus *viris* [viri],[414]
Flagla, Datharm, Fisamus,
Ganfrit, Mase, Ruel, Elande, Mertarus, Scalprutus, Marotus, Tetragramaton,
Cum sanguine talpae hec nomina sequentes,[415] Saglas, Dathar,
Mosesisamis,[416] Amore Ysagnel
Faro Faraanto Melcatria, in schedula pargamenti virginei si scribantur et tenentur in ore cum osculareris, provocante eundem.[417]

To Obtain One's Love

Write these letters in the bath[418] of thy hand, and what woman thou shalt touch with thy feet, she shall love thee: e e e e z y y s q. q q m. m. m. b. b. b.

To Make Thy Enemy Love Thee

Write these names in thy right hand. Touch thy enemy upon the bare flesh. Hagrernet, Gratny, Galpha, Gabrick, Sambio.

To Make Me Love and Honour Thee

Have these letters always about thee.

u. r. h. L. K. o. n. n. t. m. i. r. o.

To Win the Love of Any Lord or Lady

Have about thee these letters: r. e. a. K. S. m. q. o. que. p. e. p. e.

411. *Dedia...Dracon*: Sloane 3851, 140v: "Dedia Calpa Draco."
412. *Ganfrite...Agios*: Sloane 3851, 140r: "Gausuite + + I Tetragrammaton J B Sceltagus."
413. *Cosma...Sorday*: Sloane 3851, 140r: "Causma, Abroth, Sordaye."
414. *Cum...[viri]*: Translation: "With the name of the man."
415. *Cum...sequentes*: Translation: "These names following, with the blood of a mole."
416. *Saglas...Mosesisamis*: Sloane 3851, 140v: "Saglaff Dather Mos Fileimes."
417. *In schedula...eundem*: Translation: "On a small leaf of virgin parchment; if you draw [these] and hold it in your mouth when you might kiss her, stirring her up."
418. *Bath*: Unknown.

To Obtain Anyone's Love

Write these names in an apple and give them to eat: b. r. u. b. r. z. n. Ω. Statim non obstabit voluntate tua,[419] vz. ujlt sri mx itz thy his nmlyur.[420]

[To Know If the Sick Person Is Bewitched][421]

To know if the sick person is bewitched, hold melted lead over him and pour into a basin of water. If the figure of an image is on the lead, that party is bewitched.

[44]

Pro Amore[422]

Sculpe hoc signum in lamina argentea die ♃ et hora ejus, luna cressente, et suffumiga eum cum odorifere ligno et omnes te amabunt citissimi, et si quid peteris a muliere eris voti compos. Probat erat.

> In the day and hour of ♃,[423] with the moon waxing, carve this seal in a silver lamen, and suffume it with fragrant wood, and all will love you most swiftly, and if you are asked anything by a woman, you will be master of your wish. It was proved.

[The Magic Square of Jupiter][424]

16	3	3	13	♀
5	10	11	9	♀
9	6	7	12	
4	15	14	1	

419. *Statim…tua*: Translation: "Immediately she will not oppose your will."

420. *Ujlt…nmlyur*: Apparently in a different cipher than what appears elsewhere. I have not been able to decipher it.

421. A technique of molybdomancy, or divination via molten lead dropped into water.

422. Translation: "For Love."

423. Venus would seem to be a better match, but Jupiter is elsewhere also noted for works of love. Sloane 3850, 152v.

424. This square for Jupiter is slightly inaccurate.

[Charms for Love]

Agnus castus[425] is an antidote against love, having the power of weakening the generative faculty. Also sprinkling the dust in which a mute has rolled herself, or tying toads in the hide of a beast newly slain, or amulets of minerals or herbs. See Love in the *Britannica Encyclopedia*.[426]

[Another Jupiter Love Charm][427]

"Scribe hoc sequens signum ZZ in pergameno virgineo et tange quem vel quam velis, et hanc figuram ante ⊙ is ortum, et si non possis tangere, saltem narra et sequetur te. Quo probes tangas canem."

> "Write the sign following ZZ on virgin parchment, and touch he or she you desire, and make this figure before the ⊙ rises, and if you are not able to touch them, at least tell them, and he or she shall follow you. You should touch a dog, so that this is proved."

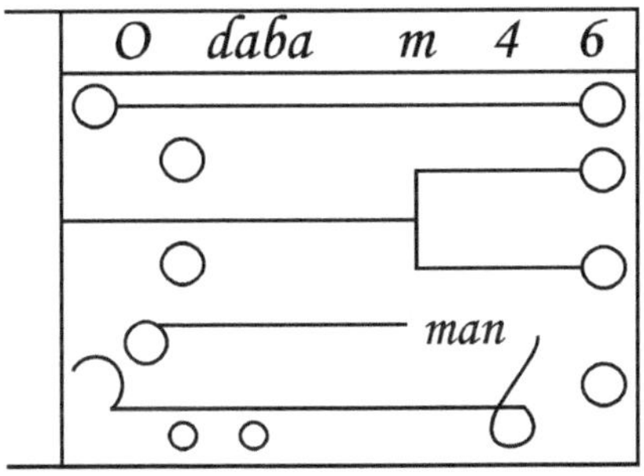

Pro Amore[428]

Accipe tria crines ejus et fillum factum in die ♀ virginis macere et ceram virgineam, et inde fac candela, et scribe in ea haec nomina, Tiblo, Tible, Lata, Pean, Tibe, et cum vis ut M. veniat, accende candelam et veniat.

> Take three of her hairs, and a thread made by a virgin on the day of ♀, and virgin wax, and thereafter make a candle, and write these names on it, Tiblo, Tible, Lata, Pean, Tibe,[429] and when you wish that M. should come, light the candle, and she should come.

425. *Agnus castus*: *Vitex agnus-castus*, or chasteberry.

426. This material first appeared in the third edition. Macfarquhar and Gleig, *Encyclopaedia Britannica*, 10:303.

427. Compare to Harms, Clark, and Peterson, *Oberon*, 547; Harms and Clark, *Of Angels*, 117; manuscript page 141.

428. Translation: "For Love." See Sloane 3850, 166r.

429. *Tiblo…Tibe*: Sloane 3850: "Tibon, Libola, Peteron, Tibo."

[More Love Charms][430]

The brain of a calf and the blood of doves promote love.

The ingredients used by the antients to promote love were the hippomanes,[431] cantharides,[432] the jynx,[433] insects bred from putrefaction, the fish remora,[434] and lizard. The brains of a calf, the blood of doves.

Pro Amore[435]

Accipe ceram virgineam et fac imaginem in die ac hora ♀, dicendo:

In the day and hour of ♀, take virgin wax and make an image, saying:

"Hanc imaginem protraho in amorem meum, in nomine Patris et Fili et Spiritus Sancti."

"I produce this image in my love, according to my love, in the name of the Father, and of the Son, and of the Holy Ghost."

Hoc facto, scribe super caput vel in fronte imaginis Elmalim, in dextere latere ♀ U in sinistro ♃ in dextero tuo [sic] pede ⊙ in sinistro ♄. Tum pone imaginem versus ignem, dicendo:

This done, write over the head or on the forehead of the image Elmalim, on the right side ♀ U, on the left ♃, on the right foot ⊙, on the left ♄. Then put the image near the fire, saying:

"⊙, Elmalim, Rerus ♃ ⊙ ♄ audi me, ut h[ab]e[a]m *pretate* [potestatem] supra N. filia N. quam amo. Date mihi, quaeso, ut ad omnia mihi consentiat, nec ullo alio, donec voluntati meae satisfecerit. Hoc rogo per virtutem istius signi ♀, ut sicut hac cera liquescit, ita sine ullo modo N. ardeat in amore meo. Fiat, fiat, fiat. *Apes cerea* [amen, amen?]."

"⊙, Elmalim, Rerus, ♃, ⊙, ♄, hear me, that I should have power over N., daughter of N., whom I love. Give to me, I beseech, that she might agree to me, all things considered, and not in any other, until she fulfils

430. Macfarquhar and Gleig, *Encyclopaedia Britannica*, 10:303.

431. *Hippomanes*: See manuscript page 29.

432. *Cantharides*: The dried remains of the *Cantharis vesicatoria* beetle, better known as "Spanish fly." Although used as an aphrodisiac, it is a poisonous substance.

433. *Jynx*: *Jynx torquilla*, or the wryneck bird.

434. *Remora*: A fish from the Echeneidae family, notable for its mouth like a suction disc, which it uses to attach to larger fish.

435. Translation: "For Love."

my desire. I ask this by the power of this sign ♀, that as this wax melts, so N. will burn in my love without limit. Let it be done, let it be done, let it be done. Amen, amen."

[45]

[Another for Love][436]

Accipe tria crines capitis cuiusvis et fac imaginem de cera virginiea, et in ipsa pone pilos predic[tos], *prea* [praescribe?] non in pectore et in fronte imaginis et in dextero pede Goalls vel (ut potu) Goliathe, et in sinistra manu, Belzabub et in dextera, Leclamat, in sinistro pede, Sathan. Hoc rite facto, dicas:

Take three hairs from the head of whomsoever you wish, and make an image from virgin wax, and into it put the aforesaid hairs. Do not write on the breast or on the forehead of the image, and on the right foot [write] "Goalls," or (as I reckon) "Goliathe," and on the left hand, "Belzabub," and on the right, "Leclamat," and on the left hand, "Sathan." These things done with solemnity, you should say:

"Conjuro vos per Patrem et Filium et Spiritum Sanctum, et per haec illa sancta nomina, Agla, A, et Ω, Tetragramaton, et per virtutem omnium nominum summi et individui dei, et per virtutem angelorum et archangelorum, per thronos et dominationes, per caelum et terram, et per omnia quae in eis sunt contenta, ut faciatis N. filia N. ardere in amore meo, sicut fluit cera ista a facio ignis, ut nullo loco aut tempore quiescat, neque stando, sedendo, dormiendo, edendo, bibendo, vigilando, eundo, currendo, sessando, donec ad meam voluntatem proficiendam venerit. Fiat, fiat, fiat."

"I conjure you all by the Father and the Son and the Holy Ghost, and by these holy names, Agla, A and Ω, Tetragramaton, and by the power of all names of the highest and indivisible God, and by the power of angels and archangels, by thrones and dominions, by heaven and earth, and by all things that are enclosed in them, that you make N., daughter of N., to burn in my love, just as this wax flows from the face of the fire, that she may rest at no place or time, neither standing, sitting, sleeping, eating, drinking, waking, walking, running, or loitering, until she shall come, so she may accomplish my will. Let it be done, let it be done, let it be done."

436. See manuscript pages 54 and 208.

For (Ad Habendum Amorem) or Love[437]

In the 20th mansion of the ☽, make a hollow ring of silver, and in virgin parchment, write and enclose these names therein, "Faccigrat, Pimlbe, Cliody, Husbreth."[438] That ring made, suffume it in the entering of some meadow with the hairs of some woman, saying, "O Lord God almighty, who dost see from the heavens and beholdest all private places, per whom all the living that hath life do live, and they that die do die, I desire and pray, thy great goodness, that in whatsoever hour or time I shall touch this ring with my spittle, these spirits whose names be enclosed may make that I may have the love of women, and that they do it incontinently."

Wrap it in a linen cloth, and when he will work, do as is aforesaid in the beginning of the book.

[For Love]

On St. James even[439] at afternoon, take and put in a fine linen cloth your seeds,[440] some after some, till you have done all.

Take oil olive and put into a goose-quill, and put therein some of your seeds, and make a close stop of fine cloth, lapped in wax, and when you are disposed, let some of the oil drip in the base of your hand, and then take her per the hand, with your hand, and rub the base of your hand on the back of her hand, et *amababit* [amabit].[441] Probatum est.

[For a Fever][442]

Decoction of agrimony—good in a low fever.

[To Make Serpents Appear][443]

'Tis said the skin of a serpent lighted in a lamp makes serpents appear. 98. *3 Book* Cornelius Agrippa.

437. Harrington's translation brackets the Latin title here. See also Boudet, "Annulorum," 284.

438. *Faccigrat...Husbreth*: Boudet: "Herebreth, Fartigrat, Permisbret, Noch."

439. *St. James Even*: July 24. This probably is a mistaken reference to St. John's Eve, or June 23, which has a tradition connected with seeds collected on the date. See manuscript pages 311–12.

440. The exact plant from which the seeds are taken is not stated, but picking a plant on St. John's Eve is a common ingredient in many folk charms. For several European examples, see Frazer, *The Golden Bough*, 11:45–75. A good candidate for the plant might be the fern, the "seed" of which is said to be collected on St. John's Eve. For an example, see manuscript pages 311–12.

441. *Et amababit [amabit]*: Translation: "and she will love thee."

442. Agrimony is not known to have any medical effect on fevers.

443. Agrippa, *Three Books of Occult Philosophy* (1651), 98 (book 1, chapter 49).

[46]

Incantamentarum pro Nocte[444]

"In nomine Patris et Filii et Spiritus Sancti, amen. The Holy Ghost bless us; the Father, the Son, and the Holy Ghost be with us, to the blessed Trinity and all Christ's apostles, and to all the archangels and angels, and to all the holy order of angels, cherubins and seraphins, I bequeath this place all about, and all my goods within and without, to the blessed Trinity, that is one God and persons three, and to St. John the Evangelist that was the true disciple of Jesus Christ, that no thieves away it take, but keep it holy, St. John, for Mary's sake, that they not here one foot go, but keep them still, O blessed Trinity, through the virtue of thy godhead, that hath created heaven and earth and all things contained therein, and per the virtue of his painful passion, that he suffered here in his manhood for our redemption, and per his holy name Jesus, and per all the names of God that be for to be spoken, and that be not to be spoken, and per the name that is above all names wherewith God created all things, and per the virtue of his blessed body in form of bread, and per the virtue of every Mass that ever was said, both more and less, and per the virtue of words, herbs, stones, and grass, and per all the names afore rehearsed, I charge you per all apostles and evangelists Mark, Matthew, Luke, and John, and per all the mighty powers of God, and per the glorious ascension of our Lord Jesus Christ, and per all the names and miracles of the apostles, martyrs, confessors, and virgins, I charge you, keep them or him still here, I charge you seven planets ♄ ♃. ♂. ☉. ♀. ☿. ☽. I charge you twelve signs, Aries, Taurus, Gemini, Cancer, Leo, Virgo, Libra, Scorpio, Sagittarius, Capricorn, Aquarius, and Pisces. I charge you all to them or him still here, per all the miracles of God, and of his apostles and of all holy martyrs, and per all their virginity of our Blessed Lady, and per the virginity of all holy virgins, that they pass no foot away, until he have told every stone in the way, and every water drop in the sea, I pray you all that it be so, and that you bind them also hard, as did St. Bartholomew the Devil with the hair of his beard. Thieves, thieves, thieves, stand

444. Translation: "Incantation for Night."

[47]

"you still per the virtue of the blessed Trinity, and per the virtue of the passion of Christ, and of all the virtues before rehearsed, and per the virtue of his death and burial, and his uprise and ascension, and per his coming at the dreadful day of judgment to judge the quick and the dead. Also I bind you with the great name of God, Tetragramaton, until tomorrow that I come and speak with them in my manner, I charge you all it [that] it so be, per the virtue of the blessed Trinity, that is, Lord of mighty hosts. Amen."[445]

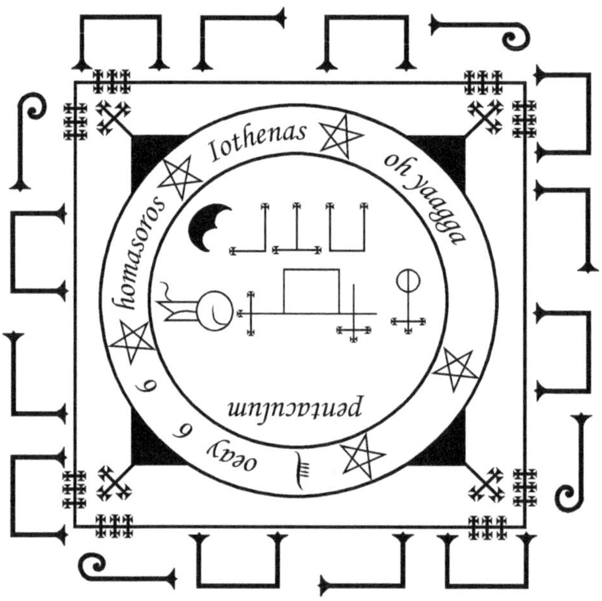

This circle you must make in the four corners of the house, orchard, or any place, or in that which any of your goods are.

[For Dreams]

The seeds of flax and fleawort powdered and smelled, to occasion prophetic dreams.[446]

445. Compare the following diagram to Harms, Clark, and Peterson, *Oberon*, 501.

446. Bacon, *The Works of Francis Bacon, Lord Chancellor of England, A New Edition*, 4:502.

[48]

To Make a Man Prosperous and Defend Him from All Dangers[447]

"Massias + Sother + Emanuell + Adonay + Unitas + Trinitas + Veritas et Omnipotens + Miserico[r]s + Redemptor + Eternitas + Creator + Ihesus + Homo + *Vision* [Usion] + Salvator + Origo + Unitas + Tetragrammaton + Athanatos + Yskiros + Mediator + Alpha + Omega + Primus et Novissimus + Panton + Craton + Ysus + *Aguns* [Agnus] + Ovis + Vitulus + Serpens – Aries + Leo + Vermis + Columba + Claritas + in nomine Patris + et Filii + et Spiritus + Sancti + Heli + Heli + Lamazabathani + quod significant, "Deus meus, deus meus, *quaere* [ut quid] derelequisti me?" + Jasper fert mirrham + Melchi thur + Balthazar aurum + haec tria qui secum portabit nomina regum + solvitur a morbo Christi pietate caduco + deus Abrahamem + deus Isaac + deus Jacob + o breve per virtutem omnium sanctorum + Jhesu Christi et istorum verborum + Jhesu Christi et passionis Jhesu Christi et omnique vulnerum + Jhesu Christi et quinque gaudiorum Sancte marie et omnium sanctorum + angelorum et + archangelorum + et duodecem appostolorum defende me die ac nocte.

> "Messiah + Saviour + Emanuell +[448] My Lords + Unity + Trinity + Truth and Omnipotent + Compassionate + Redeemer + Eternity + Creator + Jesus + Man + Essence + Saviour + Source + Unity + Tetragrammaton + Undying + Powerful + Mediator + Alpha + Omega + First and Last + Everything + Strength + Ysus + Lamb + Sheep + Bull-Calf + Serpent – Ram + Lion + Worm + Dove + Splendor + in the name of the Father + and of the Son + and of the Holy + Ghost + Heli + Heli + Lamazabathani + which means, "My God, my God, why hast thou forsaken me?" + Jasper brought myrrh + Malchus, frankincense + Balthazar, gold + he who will carry with him the three names of the Kings + is released from the falling illness through the compassion of Christ + God of Abraham + God of Isaac + God of Jacob + O amulet, by the power of all the saints + of Jesus Christ and of those words + of Jesus

447. An example of the Prière de Charlemagne variant of the Heavenly Letter, or Himmelsbrief, tradition. Hebing, "The Textual Tradition of Heavenly Letter Charms in Anglo-Saxon Manuscripts," 211–12. The prayer here is best known from the *Enchiridion*; for an English translation, see Cecchetelli, *Crossed Keys*, 151–52. See other examples in Bodleian Additional B.1., 18r–19r; BL Sloane 121, 183v–184r; Scot, *The Discouerie of Witchcraft*, 231–33; Skinnebach, "Haptic Prayer, Devotional Books, and Practices of Perception," 100. For context, see Klaassen, *Making Magic in Elizabethan England*, 69; Harms and Clark, *Of Angels*, 87.

448. Other sources insert "Sabaoth +" here.

> Christ, and of the passion of Jesus Christ and of all the wounds + of Jesus Christ and of the five joys of Blessed Mary, and of all saints + of the angels and + of the archangels + and of the twelve apostles, ward off me both day and night...[449]

"Vigilando + dormiendo + stando + sedendo + ambulando + ab insidiis diaboli et a subitat[ion]e a morte et a periculo mortis ignis et aquae ab *inimicicis* [inimicis] meis et a caduce morbo a pesce maris et peri[culi]s et omnibus infirmatibus + Christus imperat + Christus ab omni malo me defendat + per crucis hoc signum fugiat procul omne malignum + et per eudem signum solvetur quodque benignum + per signum sancte crucis de inimicis viris, liberes nos, deus noster + crux Christi, conforta me + crux Christi, inebria me + crux Christi, guberna me + crux Christi, conforta me + sanguis Christi, sana me + passio Christ defende de vii peccatis mortalibus + In manus tuas domine comendo spiritum meum. Redemisti me, domine deus veritatis. Amen.

> "Waking + sleeping + standing + sitting + walking + from all the snares of the devil and from sudden death, and from danger of death of fire and water, from my enemies and from the falling illness, from the fish of the sea and dangers and all illnesses + Christ rules + Christ, defend me from every evil + by this sign of the cross, fly away, every wicked one + and by the same sign every good one will be released + by the sign of the holy Cross, free us, our God, from hostile men + cross of Christ, strengthen me + cross of Christ, inebriate me + cross of Christ, guide me + cross of Christ, strengthen me, + blood of Christ, restore me + passion of Christ, defend from the seven deadly sins + Into your hands, O Lord, I commend my spirit. You redeemed me, Lord God of truth. Amen.

449. The text has a break at this point, but the next section directly flows into it.

[49]

"+ Jesus Nazarenus, crucifixus rex, Judeorum, filii dei, miserere mei. Amen. Mattheus, + Marcus + Lucas, Johannes + Amen. In nomine Patris, + et Filii + et Spiritus + Sancti. + Amen."

> "+ Jesus of Nazareth, crucified king of the Jews, son of God, have mercy on me. Amen. Matthew, + Marcus + Luke, John + Amen. In the name of the Father + and of the Son + and the Holy + Ghost. + Amen."

St. Leo, Pope of Rome, wrote this write[450] to King Charles of France, saying "Whoso[ever] bear the same about him should be defended from all perils and dangers and sudden death."

450. *Write*: Document.

[The Wheel of Fortune][451]

Number of the day of the Week
Sunday—26
Monday—17
Tuesday—15
Wednesday—25
Thursday—11
Friday—17
Saturday—26

N.B.[452] In the *Holy Guide* by John Heydon, page 101, is this his circle & c.? Fact.[453]

See page 51 and 368 and page 78—It should be proved whether the number of the day and shape on 368 is not best.[454]

451. This, and the examples on the following pages, are a divinatory method dating back to the fourth century, attributed to various authors, including Apuleius, Democritus, Petosiris, Pythagoras, and others. Although condemned in ecclesiastical works, many physicians found it an easy means to give a patient's prognosis. For some examples, see Betz, *The Greek Magical Papyri in Translation, Including the Demotic Spells*, 165–66; Chardonnens, *Anglo-Saxon Prognostics*, 181–222; Edge, "Licit Magic or 'Pythagorean Necromancy'?"; Harms, Clark, and Peterson, *Oberon*, 175–77.

452. *N.B.*: Nota bene, or take note.

453. This device does not appear in any edition of Heydon's *Holy Guide* examined, let alone on this page.

454. On the following illustration, it is not clear what the "Funds" abbreviation was supposed to signify. It also appears on the next manuscript page.

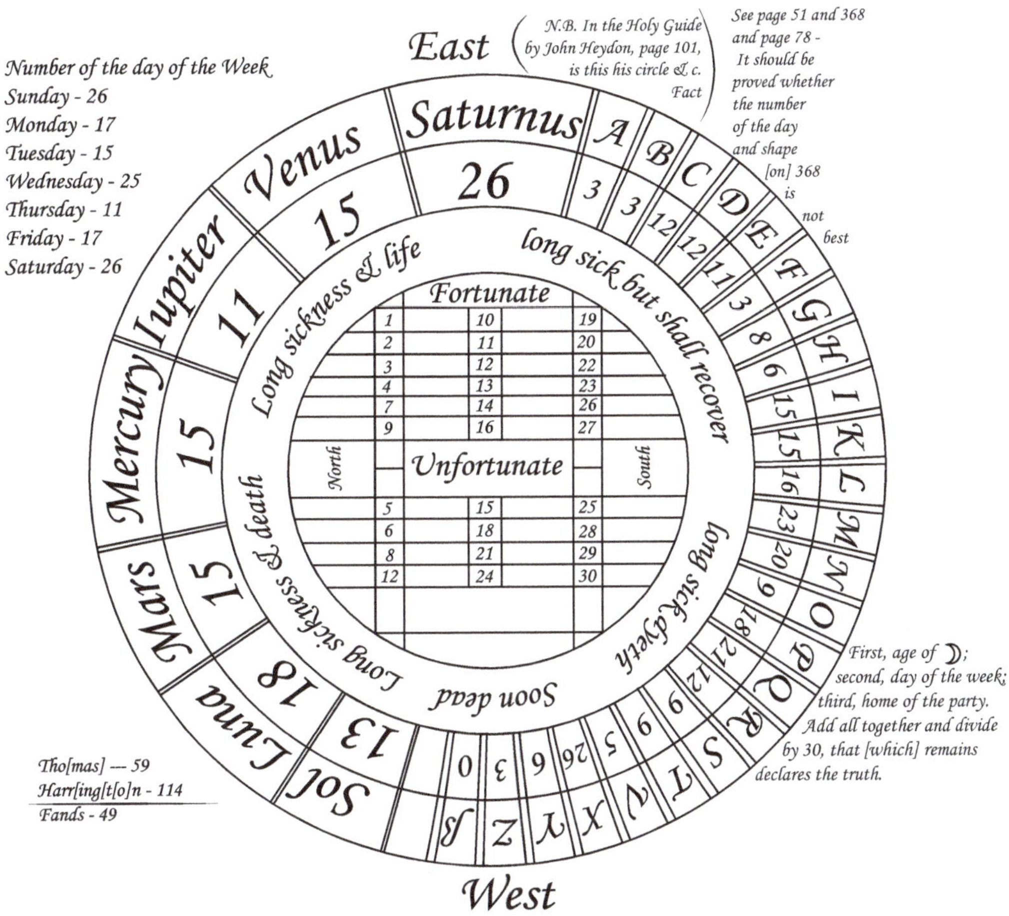

First, age of the ☽; second, day of the week; third, home of the party. Add all together and divide by 30, that which remains declares the truth.[455]

Gather per these numbers, thus take the age of the ☽, the day of the week, and the name of the party (or thing). These being gathered together, divide them per thirty, and then take the number above 30, and that shall declare the truth. See the tables page 78.

See more of the explanation over leaf

455. In the left margin opposite this is: "Tho'—59 / Harrtn—114 / Funds—49." The first two represent abbreviations of the name "Thomas Harrington." The latter may be a reference to a location, and if this is read as "Funds," the numbers match, although this does not seem to correspond to a known person or location.

[50]

[Another System of Numerological Divination for Marriage and Children]

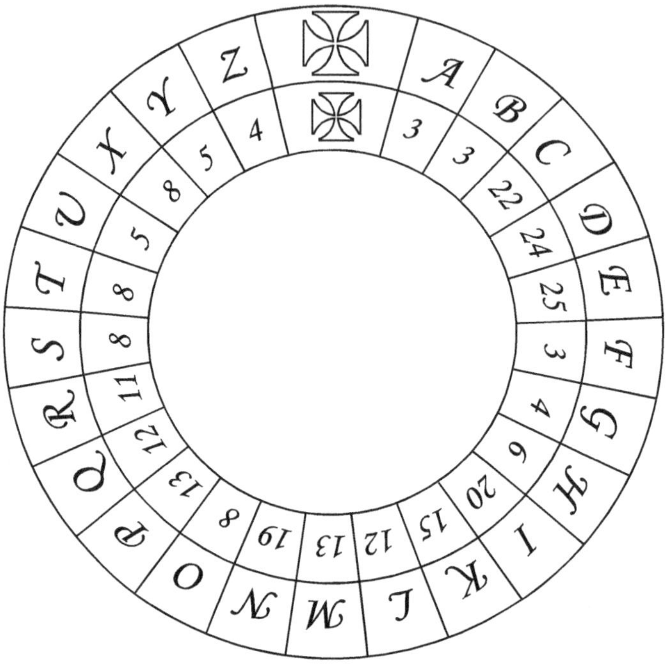

To know what shall be the first child of any man or woman married together, and likewise whether of them shall die first, and what all the rest of their children shall be, or they shall have any more: First take the father's names and the mother's name, and if the number be above nine, or twice nine, or thrice & c., then part it still per nine, and look what is above nine declareth the truth. If the number above nine be even, it betokeneth the man shall die first and a man child, odd the contrary. To know the rest of the children, take the first child's name with the number that was above 9 and then still divide it per nine as aforesaid; then take the next child's name with the residue of the other, & c. But if the numbers will not reach to nine, then add thereto nine and then divide it per nine as aforesaid.

[Whether One Shall Live or Die]

The sphere followeth on the other next leaf is to know whether one shall live or die, win in battle, or have the upper hand in law, or, if one fly his country, whether he shall return again, then take the number of the day he fell sick (went to fight, or to the law, or fled his country), with the age of the ☽ and also his name. Then those three being numbered, divide it per by thirty, and if that number light above it, it betokeneth life, victory, upper hand in law, or return home; if it light beneath it, betokeneth the contrary.

[51]

Spera Pithagore[456]

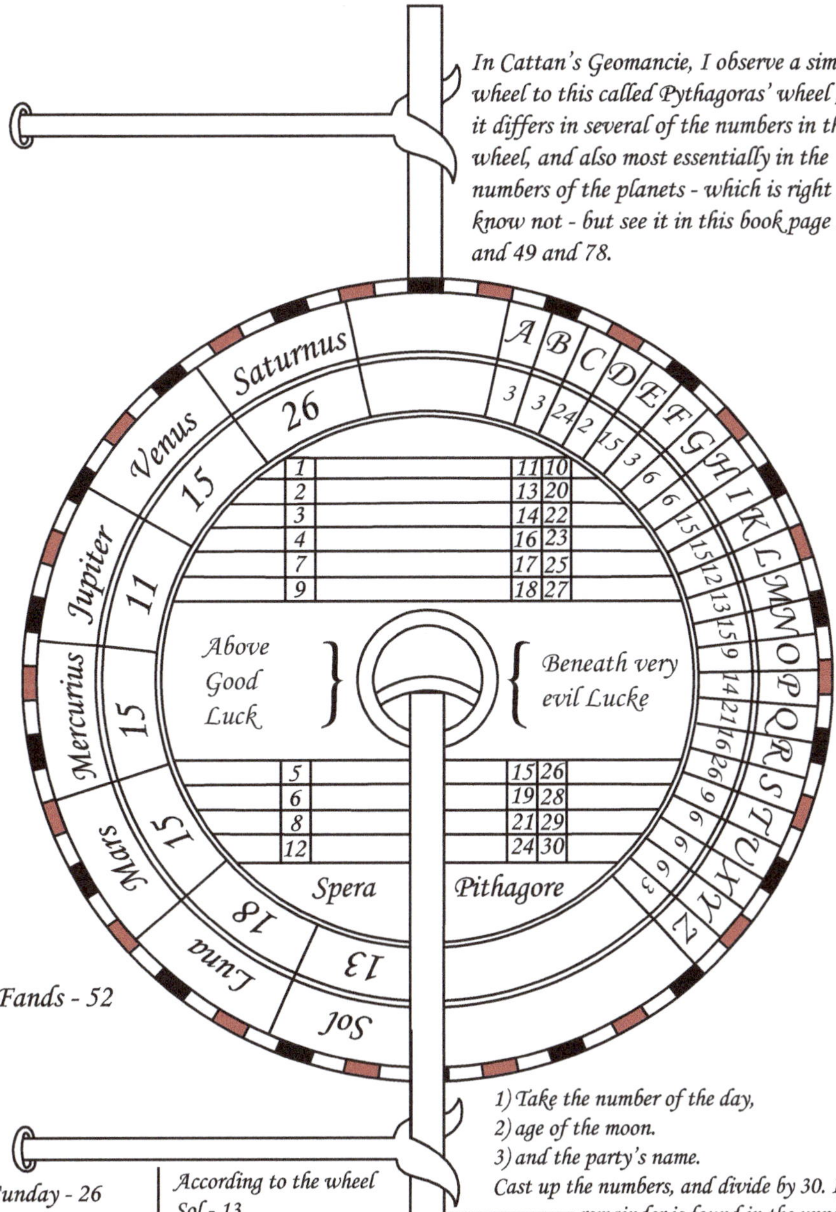

In Cattan's Geomancie, I observe a similar wheel to this called Pythagoras' wheel, but it differs in several of the numbers in the wheel, and also most essentially in the numbers of the planets - which is right I know not - but see it in this book page 368 and 49 and 78.

Fands - 52

1) Take the number of the day,
2) age of the moon.
3) and the party's name.
Cast up the numbers, and divide by 30. If the remainder is found in the upper part of the wheel, good; lower part, bad.
See opposite
See four tables, page 78

Sunday - 26	*According to the wheel*
Monday - 17	*Sol - 13*
Tuesday - 15	*Luna - 18*
Wednesday - 25	*Mars - 15*
Thursday - 11	*Mercury - 15*
Friday - 17	*Jupiter - 11*
Saturday - 26	*Venus - 15*
	Saturn - 26

456. Translation: "Sphere of Pythagoras." Cattan, *Geomancie* (1591), 260.

[52]

Against All Enemies Visible and Unvisible, and All Power, Evil, Pestilence, and Slander[457]

Carry with thee these letters in a white linen cloth, because Oyson, the angel of God, brought them to king Carolus when he went to the wars and bade him on God's behalf that he should take with him these here following:[458]

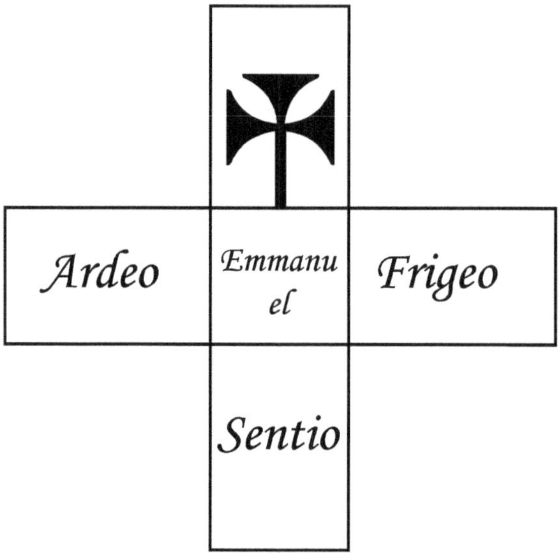

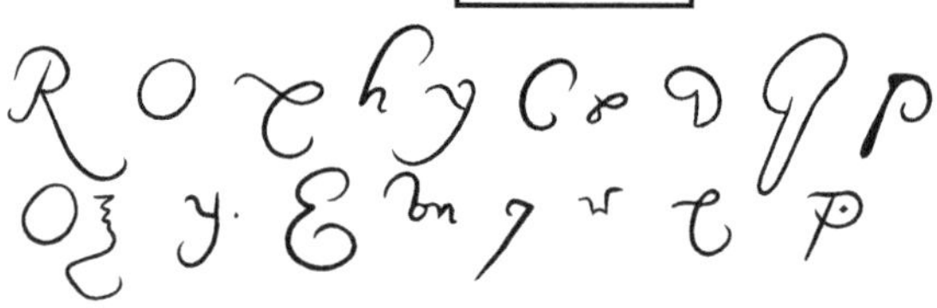

To Have the Love of Any Man or Enemy—Probatum Est

Write in paper, and sew it in red leather, and put it on thy right arm, saying, "I would have the love of such a man," and then name him, and he shall favour thee. Make these figures:

457. For other examples, see National Library of Scotland, GDD 188/25/1/3, 43; manuscript page 142. This appears to be a reappropriated charm for fever.

458. *Ardeo...Sentio*: Translation: "I burn, Emanuel, I freeze, I feel." For two twelfth-century charms, one of which is inscribed on a lead cross, see Olsan, "Writing on the Hand in Ink: A Late Medieval Innovation in Fever Charms in England," 29; Skemer, *Binding Words*, 80.

[To Win at Dice]

Scribe hac nomina, per aleas: Salic, Talic, Satael, sanguine vespe[ri]tilionis in vola manus et pricii aleas.

> Write these names in the hollow of the hand, by the dice, with the blood of a bat and [you will succeed at] dice games of value: Salic, Talic, Satael.

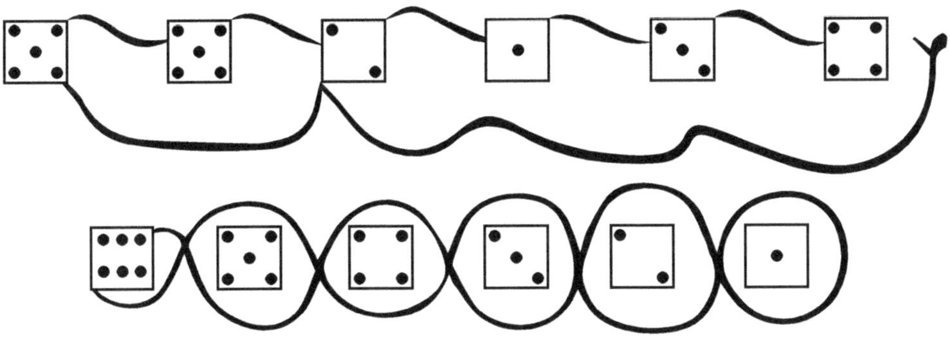

[A Cure for Quartan Ague]

Quartan agues, 'tis said, may be cured by tying the paring of the nails in a linen bag, and fastening it to the neck of a live eel, and let him go. 102, *3 Book*, C[ornelius] A[grippa].[459]

[53]

To Be Invisible[460]

Take the inward bowels of a whelp within. Shard[461] off nine days, and mingle it well with earth, then set beans in the sun grounds,[462] and when they be ripe, put every bean in the mouth one after another, and have a glass in thy

459. Agrippa, *Three Books of Occult Philosophy* (1651), 102 (book 1, chapter 51).

460. One of many such rituals, accounts of which appear across western Europe, in which beans or peas are grown in an animal or human skull in order to bring about invisibility. Examples: Peterson, *Grimorium Verum*, 48–49; Lecouteux, *Book of Grimoires*, 162; Veiga, "Sob a Capa Negra," 63; Martin, *Witchcraft and the Inquisition in Venice, 1550–1650*, 99; Barbierato, "Magical Literature and the Venice Inquisition from the Sixteenth to the Eighteenth Centuries," 164; Ravaisson-Mollien, *Archives de la Bastille: Documents Inédits*, 10:333; Burnett, "The Conte de Sarzana Manuscript," 6–7; Jones and Olsan, "Takamiya MS 61: A Book of Experiments," 105–6; Dillinger, *Magical Treasure Hunting*, 97; Muyard, "Un Manuel de Sorcellerie en Basse Bretagne au XVIIIe Siècle," 294; Clark, *Goodwin Wharton*, 28–29; Leitão, *The Sorcerer's Treasure*, 82; Leitão, *Opuscula Cypriani*, 436; Johnson, *Svartkonstböcker*, 258, 329, 424, 571.

461. *Shard*: Break into pieces.

462. *Sun grounds*: Possibly a sun pan, a depressed area of ground where items were left in the sun.

hand, and when thou canst not see thyself in the glass, keep the beans in a clean cloth.

To Know How Jugglers[463] Play[464]

Take herbs called hart's tongue[465] before he begin to play, and say this upon the herb: "Justiciam loquiminam in eo,"[466] & c.

To Win at Dice

Take three leaves of mouse-ear,[467] et scribe hac tria nomina super eum:[468] "Galpha, Gata, Offra." When thou hast writ them, bind *aft 6* [about the] little finger hence.

Pro Furto

Scribe hac letteras in cera virginiea:

Write these letters in virgin wax:

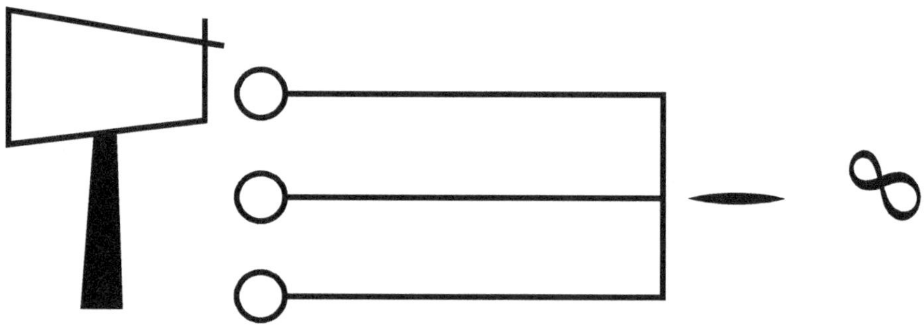

Et pone subter caput tuum et in somne videbis fures.

And place them under your head, and you will see the thieves in your sleep.

To Have Favour of Any Person

Take vervain after the full of the ☽ when it beareth flowers, + before ☉ rise, going about then, say seven Pater Nosters, seven Amen,[469] and in taking it up, (say) "I require thee, vervain, in the name of the Father, and of the Son,

463. *Jugglers*: Stage magicians and entertainers.

464. For another example, see National Library of Scotland GD 188/25/1/3, 46.

465. *Hart's tongue*: Usually ferns of the *Scolopendrium* genus, especially *Scolopendrium vulgare*.

466. *Justiciam...eo*: Quote of unclear source. It might reflect Vulgate Psalm 57:2: "Si vere utique iustitiam loquimini recta iuidcate filii hominum."

467. *Mouse-ear*: A number of different plants appear under this name.

468. *Et scribe...eum*: Translation: "And write these three names on them."

469. *Seven Amen*: Seven Aves?

and Spiritus Sancti, in nomine Patris,[470] that everything in this world may love me as long as I bear thee about me."

Ad Sciendum qui Furte Accepte Sunt[471]

Scribe haec ipsa, "Magnus deus," et "cantabilis nimis," cum hac 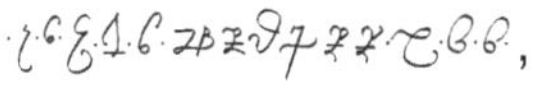, et pone sub capite tuo cum dormire velis et in somne apparebit.

> Write these words, "Magnus deus"[472] and "Cantabilis nimis"[473] with this 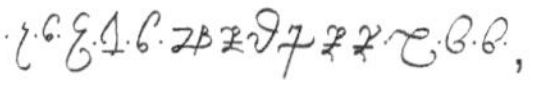, and place it beneath your head when you desire to sleep, and he will appear in your sleep.

To Make Men Look Like Ghosts

Put aqua vitae brandy[474] in a chafing dish of hot coal and a little bay salt, and light it.

To Make Men Look Black[475]

Take oil olive in a lamp, and put thereto shell of the cuttlefish. Give part of glass and light it.

[54]

To Make a Tooth Fall without Iron[476]

So make powder of a green lizard, and meddle[477] it with oil, and touch the sore tooth with the powder with thy finger, or with a quill, and anon it shall fall out. Take ivy leaves and bray[478] them or burn them, and lay to the tooth or gum of ivy, & c.

Pro Amore[479]

Take three hairs of her head, and take a thread spun on the Friday of a maid, that never she had to do with man, and make these a candle of virgin wax,

470. *Spiritus…Patris*: Translation: "Of the Holy Ghost, in the name of the Father."

471. Translation: "For Knowing What Things Were Taken by Theft." This heading appears at the end of the previous line, indicating the transcriber might not have understood its meaning.

472. *Magnus Deus*: Translation: "Great God."

473. *Cantabilis nimis*: Translation: "Worthy to be sung without measure."

474. *Aqua vitae brandy*: Brandy would be an acceptable example of these distilled spirits.

475. Pliny and Jones, *Libri XXVIII–XXXII*, 550–51 (book 32, chapter 52).

476. For similar charms, see Breverton, *The Physicians of Myddfai.*

477. *Meddle*: Mix.

478. *Bray*: Crush into powder.

479. Translation: "For Love." See manuscript pages 45 and 208.

and it must be four square, and write with the blood of a mole or sparrow the name of the said woman, and put it to burn there as it shall not drop on the earth, and wheresoever she be, she will come, sliding over the candle.

To Be Feared of Enemies

"O celandine, here have I thee found in the name of Jesus Christ. I take thee from the ground, in the name of the Father, and of the Son, and of the Holy Ghost, one blessed Trinity, work thou thy wondrous operations that God hath given thee, that as long as I thee about him[480] shall bear, all his enemies, both bodily and ghostly, may greatly him fear."

This herb must be gathered on Lammas day early in the morning before the sun rise with three Pater Nosters and three *Amen* [Aves] and Credo, with a fasting.

Stomach and Good Devotion / Digestion[481]

To know whom the fault of the connection is that, cause that man or woman to piss in diverse vessels of earth, and probatum, bran[482] or malt in the vessels, in which pot engendereth worms in it, is the default.

A Woman in Travail[483]

As soon as thou comest to the door, set thy foot near the threshold and say thus, "In nomine et Patris et Filii et Spiritus Sancti." After say, "St. Anne bare Mary, Mary bare Jesus, our saviour, Elizabeth bare John the Baptist,"[484] and say this, "In nomine, *f. & d & Ss* [Patris et Filii et Spiritus Sancti]. Amen." Also give

[55]

her vervain in cold water to drink, and she shall be delivered.

480. The magician switches here from first to third person.

481. This is misleading; the charm that follows is to determine which of a couple is infertile. Trotula, *Medieval Woman's Guide to Health*, 169.

482. *Bran*: Boil in bran water.

483. *Travail*: Childbirth.

484. *St. Anne…Baptist*: A truncated version of the *peperit* charm, used since the ninth century to alleviate the pains of childbirth. This and the one following may be the only ones known in English. On the genre, see Elsakkers, "In Pain Your Shall Bear Children (Gen 3:16): Medieval Prayers for a Safe Delivery"; Jones and Olsan, "Takamiya MS 61: A Book of Experiments"; Harms, Clark, and Peterson, *Oberon*, 526.

Alia[485]

"Blessed Anne bare St. Mary, the Maker of our Lord Jesus Christ; Mary bare the same Jesu Christi, the son of God, through the armachacone[486] of archangel Gabriel; per this nativity, per the belief that Christian men and women may be delivered from death and all evil perils. Holy Mary, Mother of God, and all holy angels, and all holy martyrs, and all holy confessors, and all holy virgins, pray for this woman their servant, M."

To Staunch Blood[487]

Take the name of the man or woman, and go to the church, and say thee this charm, and look you say it before nobody:

"In nomine Patris & c., when Our Lord Jesu Christ was done on the cross, then came Longens and smote him with a spear into his side. Blood and water came thereout of the wound, and he wiped his eyes with the blood and he saw anon through the virtue that God did there. I conjure thee, thou blood that camest out of the Christian NL, that thou stanch, in nomine Father et Son et Spiritus Sancti." Say this 3, and at every time Pater Noster and Ave, and look that you name the person every time.

For Biting of a Mad Dog[488]

Ribo, Ribas, Rimos, Rimas, Opulusque Orens Alibus Venis Ranis, Opimusque Nare, Qaure, Scare,[489] Remis, Pamis, Opinusque.

Of the Adder Skin[490]

John and Paul in the city of Alexander found a book called *Salus Vitae,*[491] wherein were written twelve experiments of the adder skin, and the author was a philosopher called Alcanus, and affinitely[492] these experiments to be true.

485. Translation: "Another." Corrected from "alea," a game of dice, in the original.
486. *Armachacone*: Unknown—"annunciation" seems likely.
487. An example of the Longinus charm against bloodletting, dating back to the thirteenth century. Roper, *English Verbal Charms*, 112–13.
488. Attached to the conclusion of the previous charm. Most of this is unreadable.
489. *Nare, Qaure, Scare*: See "[Another Charm for the Same]" on page 151.
490. These treatises on snakeskin, attributed to John Paulinus in other manuscripts, date back to the thirteenth century and forward into the nineteenth. Discussion: Johnsson, "Les 'Experimenta Duodecim Johannis Paulini'"; Thorndike, *A History of Magic and Experimental Science During the First Thirteen Centuries of Our Era*, 2:794–95. Examples: Grohmann, *Aberglauben*, 1:81; Johnson, *Svartkonstböcker*, 229, 255; Bellhouse, *A Complete System of Magic*, 38–39; Thorndike, *Michael Scot*.
491. *Salus Vitae*: Translation: "The Preservation of Life."
492. *Affinitely*: Probably an error for "definitely."

When the ☽ shall be increasing in the first degree of ♋,[493] then ☽ standing in the same degree, make in powder the skin of an adder with fire, upon a hot tile stone, and keep this powder diligently.

[56]

The first experiment is that if any man be wounded in the head, put in the wound part of this powder, and within three days he shall be whole.

The second: spring[494] the powder among the seer's head, and as long as this powder is thereon, he shall not be hurt of any man.

The third: meddle the powder with water and therewith wash thy face, and thou shalt be fearful[495] of all thy enemies, and thy enemy shall fly from thee.

The fourth: spring this powder in the bed straw of thy enemy, and he shall forsake his houth[496] with all his servants.

The fifth: if a man be called to counsel, let him put the powder under his feet, and whatsoever he spoke or say, he shall be heard.

The sixth: if a man dispute in any science, put of the powder in his mouth or under his tongue, et non erit convictus.[497]

The seventh: if a man doubt him of things to come, spring of the powder on his head, and hold it or bind it with a clean cloth, and lay him to sleep, and he shall see in his sleep what manner, thing, or wise[498] shall befall thereof.

The eighth: if thou wilt know the poverty[499] of a man, cast the powder on his breast when he is asleep, then ask him what thou wilt, and he will tell thee.

The ninth: bind of this powder in thy servant's cloth when he goeth on thy message; he shall do it faithfully.

The tenth: put of the powder in a platter or dish made of a tree and set in on the table, and if there be a venom on the table, that powder shall spring about as if it were blown with wind.

The eleventh: if a man bear this powder in his hand, he shall be loved greatly of women.

493. ♋: Other manuscripts refer to Aries.

494. *Spring*: Sprinkle.

495. *Fearful*: Likely causing fear, and not full of fear, in this context.

496. *Houth*: Likely an error for "house" or "hearth."

497. *Et...convictus*: Translation: "And he will not be overcome."

498. *Wise*: Mode.

499. *Poverty*: Destitution or meanness.

The twelfth: if a leper[500] use this powder in his meat, the sickness shall not increase further.

Also, bind this powder on the belly of a woman that travails,[501] and she shall be delivered quickly. Also put on thy powder on a tooth that aches, and it shall do away that ache also. Put also the powder on a sore called noli me tangere[502] and it will abate the ache and heal it.

[57]

Pro Amore[503]

Take virgin's wax from the bees at the new of the ☽, and keep it till next Sabbath day, and upon the day, make a candle of the same wax, which being made, write round about with the blood of your ring finger the names of these spirits, "Alpho, Gesta, Enuell, Baratiel, Obessiel, Aiel," and after write the name of the woman whom you love, which being done, say, "I conjure you spirits which were shut in the glass vessel which[504] did seal, I adjure you per the womb of the Virgin, and per all things that are in heaven and earth, that you enforce M. to obey me and to accomplish my will." Which when thou hast said, light the candle, and forthwith do it out, est sone.[505]

Pro Lucro[506]

Write this hereunder written, and take the nail of a dead body, and keep the writing about thee.

Demi serunt vesitnenta mea est[507]

After say on a Mass of the Three Kings either on Twelfth Day[508] or any other day upon the writing and the nail, and take what dice soever thou shalt play withal, and say as followeth:

500. *Leper*: Original: "leopard," but "leper" is consistent with other manuscripts.

501. *Travails*: Suffers in childbirth.

502. *Noli me tangere*: "Touch me not," a condition causing ulcers to form, believed to be made worse by handling. See Wallis, *Medieval Medicine: A Reader*, 345, 548.

503. Translation: "For Love."

504. Perhaps the name "Solomon" was omitted here.

505. *Est sone*: This should probably be "it is done."

506. Translation: "For Riches." See manuscript pages 18–19.

507. Probably meant to be Psalm 21:19, "Diviserunt sibi vestimenta mea, et super vestem meam miserunt sortem"; KJV Psalm 22:18: "They part my garments among them, and cast lots upon my vesture."

508. *Twelfth Day*: Epiphany, the day the Three Wise Men visited Jesus.

"I conjure you dice, per all the points and pimples that are on you, and per the passion of Our Lord Jesus Christi, and per all his sorrow's great pain, per his nails, and per his cross, and per his vestments, upon which they did cast lots, that you make me not lose in any manner wise, but upon my own will, but always to win of everybody and of all creatures, in the name of him that shall come to judge the world on the last day."

For a Child in the Mother's Womb[509]

When thou comest to the house where the woman is, set thy right foot on the threshold and make a sign of the cross, and say, "In *nominis* [nomine] Patris et Filii & c. Amen.

"Anna *petit* [peperit] Sammuel, Elizabeth praecursorem, Maria dominum salvatorem, et tu, mulier, fac quid in te est. O infans quicunque es aut masculus aut femina, veni foras, Christus te vocat, Christus regnat te, vocat, Christus imperat, ut cito exeas foras, veni ad baptismum."

> "Anna gave birth to Samuel, Elizabeth to John the Baptist, Maria to the Lord Saviour, produce anything that is in you. O infant, whoever you are, whether man or woman, come forth. Christ calls you, Christ rules you, he calls, Christ rules, that immediately you go forth, come to baptism."

Dic ter, et Pater Noster ter et Ave Maria ter,[510] and she shall be well.

For Worms, a Charm[511]

"In nomine Patris & c. Right as Our Lord Jesus Christ *dd* [delivered] Job from nine worms, so I do *dd* [deliver] thee N. from nine worms to eight, from eight to seven, per seven to six, per six to five, per five to four, per four to three, per three to two, per two to one, per one to never a one, in nomine Patris et Filii & c." Det; dicatur ter.[512]

509. See discussion of the *peperit* charm, manuscript page 54.

510. *Dic ter...Maria ter*: Translation: "Say three times, and a Pater Noster three times, and an Ave Maria three times."

511. A diminishing charm, in which a condition diminishes in intensity as the number of items in the charm does. For discussion, see in particular Roper, *English Verbal Charms*, 112; also, Davies, "Healing Charms in Use in England and Wales 1700–1950," 25–26; Halpern and Foley, "The Power of the Word: Healing Charms as an Oral Genre," 912.

512. *Det, dicatur ter*: Translation: "It delivers; it should be said three times."

[58]

To Know If Gold Be under the Ground[513]

Take the juice of milfoil, *al* [or?] yarrow, and powder of alum and copperas, and the filing of fine copper, and mix it altogether. Then take an elder stick, and get out the pith, and then fill it with the aforesaid, and then close the ends of the stick with wax, and lay it on the ground when the sun ☉ is set (for the sun takes away the virtue of it). And if there be but so much gold within two feet of the place where thou layest it, as may weigh the stick four times, it will draw the stick in eight hours' times, and so the stick shall remain set or lying over the place where the gold is hid. And to verify and prove this hid gold, where thou wilt lay the stick, so thou shall prove it.

[A Protective Charm][514]

Almighty God wrote this example with his own hand, and sent it per an angel to King Abagor,[515] saying that whosoever say, read, or have it upon him shall not be slain, neither with fire burnt, nor with water be drowned, nor the Devil or any evil man or thing may do him harm that day.

513. National Library of Scotland GD 188/25/1/3, 49.

514. The "Crux Christi" prayer. See Hagen, "Crux Christi Sit Mecum: Devotion to the Apotropaic Cross," and manuscript page 62.

515. *King Abagor*: King Abgar V Uchama of Edessa, the purported author of a letter to Christ whom Christ supposedly answered, both likely third-century forgeries. Ehrman, *Forgery and Counterforgery*, 375–79, 468–71.

Crux Christi[516]

"+ Crux Christi + sit *super* [semper] mecum + crux Christi est quam *super ardoro* [semper adoro] + crux christ de vera salus + Crux Christi superat gladium + crux Christi soluit vincula mortis + crux Christi et arma invisibilii, + crux Christi o via veritas, + super crucem *diminam* [divinam] *aggrediere* [aggrediar] + crux Christi impedit omnem malum + crux Christi dat omnem bonum + crux Christi aufert penam eternam, + crux Christi salve me + crux Christi super [me, et] ante me et poste me et *aquae* [ubique] *Anteamis* [antiquis] hostis *fingis* [fugis] ubi vides me. Amen."

> "+ May the Cross of Christ + be with me always + The Cross of Christ is that which I revere always + The Cross of Christ, of true health + The Cross of Christ overcomes the sword + The cross of Christ dissolves the bonds of death + The Cross of Christ and the unseen weapons + Cross of Christ, O the way, the truth + I will also approach the divine cross + The Cross of Christ hinders every evil + The Cross of Christ grants every good + The Cross of Christ takes away eternal punishment + Cross of Christ, save me + The Cross of Christ above [me, and] before me, and after me and in every place, the foe of old flees when you see me. Amen."[517]

[59]

For the Pestilence

"Per signum taro + a peste et fame, libera nos, Jesu Christi. Hic est titulum e *treemphant* [triumphalis] + Jesus Nazarenus, rex Judeorum. Cruce venit et, domine, homo sanctus est."

> "By the sign of the cross[518] + from pestilence and famine, free us, Jesus Christ.[519] This is the triumphal inscription: + Jesus of Nazareth, king of the Jews. He comes with the cross, and, Lord, the man is holy."

Pro the Cramp

"Poco, Parre, Zelo, Zedica, Zeysezey, in nomine Patris et Filii et Spiritus Sancti, amen."

516. Translation: "The Cross of Christ."

517. The latter part is reconstructed from Hagen, "Crux Cristi Sit Mecum."

518. *Of the cross*: Conjectural.

519. *From pestilence…Jesus Christ*: Taken from the Litany of the Saints.

Pro the Fever[520]

"*Ad* [ante] portas Jerusalem jacebat S. Petrus, et *supervemiem* [supervenit] Jesus. Dixit ei, 'Petre!' Petrus respondit, 'Domine, iaceo de febre male,' et dixit ei Jesus, 'Surge et dimitte illam,' et dimissa febre, continuo surrexit et, recepta sanitate, secutus est Jesus. Tunc Petrus oravit eum dicens, 'Obsecro te, domine, ut quicunque hec verba secum scripta portabit, non possit ei nocere febris ne frigora.' Dixit ei Jesus, 'Tibi sicut petisti.' Fiat, fiat, fiat. Amen."

> "Saint Peter was lying before the gates of Jerusalem, and Jesus came upon him. He said to him, 'Peter!'[521] Peter answered, 'Lord, I lay prostrate from an evil fever.' And Jesus said to him, 'Get up and send it away.' And, with the fever sent, he got up immediately, and his health being regained, he followed Jesus. Then Peter pleaded with him, saying, 'I beseech you, lord, that whosoever will carry these words written with them, neither fever nor chills may be able to harm them.' Jesus said to him, 'For you, as you ask.' Let it be done, let it be done, let it be done. Amen."

For the Toothache, Write in Paper as Followeth[522]

"In the name of God, amen. *Borse* ✠ *Uri* ✠ *Marse* ✠,"[523] then second, the party's name, and let the party look precisely on the paper, and cast it in the fire, and say nre[524] in Latin or English.

[A Collection of Charms from Scot's *Discouerie of Witchcraft*]

The Inquisitors' Trial of Weeping per Conjuration[525]

"I conjure thee per the amorous tears which Jesus Christ our saviour shed upon the cross for the salvation of the world; and per the most earnest and burning tears of his mother, the most glorious virgin Mary, sprinkled upon his wounds late in the evening; and per all the tears, which every saint and elect

520. An example of the "Ante portas Jerusalem" charm against fever. Discussion: Roper, *English Verbal Charms*, 124–25; Skemer, *Binding Words*, 106, 189; Olsan, "Writing on the Hand in Ink," 15–16, 41. Examples: Giacosa, *Magistri Salernitani*, 368; Holthausen, "Rezepte, Segen, und Zaubersprüche aus zwei Stockholmer Handschriften," 79–80; Priebsch, "Segen aus Londoner Handschriften," 16; Heinrich, "Ein Mittelenglisches Medizinbuch," 167, 220; Ohrt, *Danmarks Trylleformler* (1917), 2:201.

521. A common insertion at this point is Jesus questioning Peter about what ails him.

522. Compare to Aubrey, *Miscellanies*, 107.

523. *Borse*...*Marse*: Aubrey: "Mars, Hur, Abursa, Aburse."

524. *Nre*: A Pater Noster?

525. Scot, *The Discouerie of Witchcraft*, 29 (book 2, chapter 7).

vessel of God hath poured out here in the world, and from whose eyes he hath wiped away all tears; that if thou be without fault, thou mayst pour down tears abundantly; and if thou be guilty, weep in no wise. In the name of the Father, and of the Son, and of the Holy Ghost, amen."

And note (witch) that the more you conjure, the less she weepeth.

[60]

A Charm for the Falling Evil[526]

These virtues under these verses are contained in a periapt or tablet, to be continually worn about one, called Agnus Dei,[527] which in a little cake, having the picture of a lamb, carrying off a flag on the one side, and Christ's head on the other side, and is hollow, so as the Gospel of St. John[528] written in fine paper, is placed in the concavity thereof, and it is thus compounded or made:

Balm virgin wax and holy water, an Agnus Dei make
A gift than which name can be greater, I send thee for to take
From fountain clear, the same have issue, in secret sanctify;
'Gainst lighting it hath sovereign virtue, and thunder crash beside.
Each heinous sin it wears and wasteth, even as Christ's precious blood,
And woman, while your travails lasteth, it saves it is so good.
It doth bestow great gifts and graces on such as well deserve:
And born about in noisome places, from peril doth preserve;
The force of fire whose heat destroyeth, it breaks and bringeth down;
And he or she that this enjoyeth—no water shall them drown.

A Charm against Shot, or a Waistcoat[529] *to Proof*[530]

Before the coming up of these *Agnus Deis*, a holy garment called a waistcoat per necessity was much used of our forefathers, as a holy relic & c., as given per the pope or some archconjurer, who promised thereby all manner of immunity to the wearer thereof, insomuch as he could not be hurt with any shot, or other violence, and otherwise, that women that would wear it should have quick deliverance. The composition thereof was in this order following.

526. Scot, *The Discouerie of Witchcraft*, 230–31 (book 12, chapter 9). This version omits the Latin in the original.

527. *Agnus Dei*: A round seal of wax with a lamb and cross placed on it, consecrated by the pope. Scot included this mention in his book to raise comparisons with magical amulets.

528. *Gospel of Saint John*: Likely the first chapter.

529. *Waistcoat*: A men's garment for the torso, worn for various purposes.

530. *Proof*: To make impervious. For this ritual, see Scot, *The Discouerie of Witchcraft*, 231 (book 12, chapter 9).

[61]

On Christmas Day at night, a thread must be spun of flax per a little virgin girl, in the name of the Devil, and it must be per her women, and also wrought with the needle. In the breast or forepart thereof, must be made with needlework two heads, on the head of the right side must be a hat and a long beard; the left head must have on a crown, and it must be so horrible, that it may resemble Beelzebul, and on each side of the waistcoat must be made a cross.

Against the Falling Evil[531]

Moreover, this ensuing is another excellent[532] charm of theirs, whereby the falling evil is presently remedied.

Gaspar fert myrrham, thus Melchior, Balthasar aurum,
Hac tria qui secum portabit nomina regum,
Solvitur a morbo christi pietate caduco.

Gaspar with his myrrh began the presents to unfold.
Then Melchior brought in frankincense, and Balthazar brought in gold.
Now he that of these holy kings the names about shall bear,
The falling ill, per grace of Christ, shall never need to fear.

This is a true copy of the holy writing that was brought down from heaven per an angel to Saint Leo, pope of Rome, and he did bid him take it to King Charles, when he went to the battle at Ronceval.[533] And the angel said that what man or woman beareth this writing about them with good devotion, saying every day three Pater Nosters, three Aves, and one Creed, shall not that day be overcome of his enemies, either bodily or ghostly; neither shall be robbed or slain per thieves, pestilence, thunder, or lightning, either shall be hurt with fire or water, nor cumbered[534] with spirits, neither shall have displeasure of lords and ladies.[535] He shall not be condemned with false witness, nor taken with fairies,

531. Scot, *The Discouerie of Witchcraft*, 231–33 (book 12, chapter 9).

532. *Excellent*: A substitution for "counterfet" in Scot.

533. *King Charles...Ronceval*: The Battle of Roncevaux Pass in 778, at which Charlemagne escaped Basque forces.

534. *Cumbered*: Overwhelmed.

535. For an example of a "Letter of Charlemagne" from a Worcestershire source, see Baugh, *A Worcestershire Miscellany*, 154.

[62]

or any manner of axes, nor yet with the falling evil. Also, if a woman be in travail, lay this writing upon her belly; she shall have easy deliverance, and the child right shape and Christendom,[536] and the mother purification of the holy church, and all through virtue of these holy names of Jesus Christ following:

+ Jesus + Christus + Messias + Soter + Emmanuel + Sabbaoth + Adonay + U[n]igenitus + Majestas + Paracletus + Salvator noster + Agiros Iskiros+ Agios + Adanatas + Gasper + Melchior + et Balthasar + Mattheus + Marcus + Lucas + Johannes

The Epistle of our S. Saviour, which Pope Leo sent to King Charles, that whosoever carry the same about him, or in what day soever he shall read it, or shall see it, shall not be killed with any iron tool, or be burned with fire, nor be drowned with water, neither any evil man or other creature may hurt him. The cross of Christ is a wonderful defence + the cross of Christ be always with me + the cross is it which I do always worship + the cross of Christ is true health + the cross of Christ doth loose the bonds of death + the cross of Christ is the truth and the way + I take my journey upon the cross of the Lord + the cross of Christ beateth down every evil + the cross of Christ giveth all good things + the cross of Christ taketh away pains everlasting + the cross of Christ save me + O cross of Christ be before me, and behind me, and upon me + because the ancient enemy cannot abide the sight of thee + the cross of Christ save me, keep me, govern me, and direct me

[63]

+ Thomas bearing this note of thy divine majesty per Alpha + Omega + first + and last + midst + and end + beginning + and first begotten + wisdom + virtue.

A[537] Periapt or Charm, Which Must Never Be Said, but Carried about One against Thieves[538]

"I do go, and I do come unto you, with the love of God, with the humility of Christ, with the holiness of our blessed Lady, with the faith of Abraham, with the justice of Isaac, with the virtue of David, with the might of Peter, with the constancy of Paul, with the word of God, with the authority of Gregory, with

536. *Christendom*: Baptism.

537. The author omits the word "Popish" from Scot here.

538. Scot, *The Discouerie of Witchcraft*, 233 (book 12, chapter 9).

the prayer of Clement, with the flood of Jordan, p p p c g e g a q q q[539] est p t i k a b g l k 2 a x t g t b a m g 2 4 2 1 q p x c g k q a 9 9 p o q q r. Oh only Father + Oh only Lord + and Jesus + passing through the midst of them + went + in that name of the Father + and of the Son + and of the Holy Ghost +."

Another Amulet[540]

Joseph of Arimathea did find this writing upon the wounds of the side of Jesus Christ, written with God's finger, when the body was taken away from the cross. Whosoever shall carry this writing about him shall not die any evil death, if he believe in Christ, and in all perplexities[541] he shall soon be delivered. Neither let him fear any dangers at all. Fons + Alpha et Omega + Figa + Figalis + Sabbaoth + Emmannuel + Adonai + O + Neray + Elay + Ihe + Rentone + Neger + Salve + Pangeton + Commen + A + G + L + A + Mattheus + Marcus + Lucas + Johannes + + +

Titulus triumphalis + Jesus Nazarenus rex Judeorum + ecce dominicae crucis signum + fugite partes adversae, vicit Leo de tribu Iuda, radix David, Alelujah, kyrie eleeson Christe eleeson, pater noster, ave maria, et ne nos [inducas in tentationem], et veniat super nos salutare tuum, oremus.

> The triumphal inscription + Jesus of Nazareth, king of the Jews + behold the sign of the Lord's cross + flee, evil forces + the lion of the tribe of Judah, the root of David, conquers. Alleluia, Lord have mercy, Christ have mercy, our Lord, Hail Mary, and [lead] us not [into temptation], and he should come upon us to greet your own, we pray,"[542] & c.

[Indulgences for Sins][543]

Dic:[544]
5 Pater Nosters
5 Aves
1 Credo
Granted
37,522[545]

539. *Q*: This single instance of the letter not in Scot.

540. Scot, *The Discouerie of Witchcraft*, 233–34 (book 12, chapter 9). For a description of a similar charm, see Skemer, *Binding Words*, 249.

541. *Perplexities*: Troubles.

542. Translation not in Scot.

543. Scot, *The Discouerie of Witchcraft*, 234 (book 12, chapter 9).

544. *Dic*: Translation: "Say."

545. This is probably intended to be the number of years of pardon in purgatory that the prayer grants. According to Scot, the number of years should be 32,755 years. The author's inclusion of this without the explanatory text might indicate Catholic sympathies.

[64]

Charm[546]

"Signum sanctae crucis, defendat me a malis presentibus, preteribus, et futuris, interioribus et exterioribus."

> "May the sign of the holy cross defend me from all evils, present, past, and future, within and without."

A Charm Found in the Canon of the Mass[547]

"Hac sacro sancta commixtio corporis et sanguinis domini nostri Jesu Christi fiat mihi, omnibusque sumentibus, salus mentis et corporis, et ad vitam promerendam, et capessendam, praeparatio salutaris." That is, "Let this holy mixture of the body and blood of our Lord Jesus Christ, be unto me, and unto all receivers thereof, health of mind and body, and to the deserving and receiving of life, an healthful preparative."

Charm, Both [For Health and Protection][548]

Let holy water be, both life and health to me.
When Martin's name is sung or said
Let heretics fly as men dismayed.[549]

Alter[550]

It makes her soldiers excellent, and crowneth them with victory,
Restores the lame and impotent, and healeth every malady.
The devils of hell in it conquereth, releaseth from imprisonment,
Newness of life it offereth, it hath all at commandment.
O cross of wood incomparable, to all the world most wholesome,
No wood is half so honourable in branch, in bud, in blossom.
O medicine which Christ did ordain, the sound save every hour,
The sick and sore make whole again, by virtue of thy power.
And that which man's unableness, hath never comprehended,
Grant per the name of holiness, it may be fully ended.

546. Scot, *The Discouerie of Witchcraft*, 234 (book 12, chapter 9). The copyist omits "A Papisticall" at the beginning of the title. A charm in the National Library of Wales found in Aberhafesp over a pigsty carries a similar inscription. Nottingham, *Welsh Border Witchcraft*, 31–32.

547. Scot, *The Discouerie of Witchcraft*, 234 (book 12, chapter 9).

548. Scot, 234 (book 12, chapter 9). The original title in Scot is "Other papisticall charmes." The copyist omits the Latin versions of both charms.

549. Our copyist omits Scot's comments on the burning of heretics.

550. Translation: "The Other." Scot, *The Discouerie of Witchcraft*, 236 (book 12, chapter 9). This is the second English part of an English and Latin incantation entitled "A charme of the holie cross" in Scot.

[65]

Charm Taken out of the Primer[551]

"Omnipotens + Dominus +[552] Christus + Messias," + with thirty-four names more, and as many crosses,[553] and then proceedeth in this wise:

"Ista nomina me protegant ab omni adversitate, plaga et infirmitates corporis et animae, plene liberent et assistent in auxilium ista nomina regum, Gasper & c., et duodecim Apostoli (videlicet) Petrus & c., et quattuor evangelista, (videlicet) Mattheus & c.: Mihi assistent in omnibus necessitatibus meis, ac me defendant et liberent ab omnibus periculis, et corporis et animae, et omnibus malis praeteritis, presentibus, et futuris."

> "May these names protect me from every suffering, injury, and infirmities of body and soul; may these names of the kings, Gasper & c., and the twelve apostles, namely Peter & c., and the four evangelists, namely Matthew & c., free and aid me completely. They will help me in all my needs, and may they defend and free me from all dangers of both body and soul, and from all evils past, present, and future."

Charm[554]

"Aperi os, et ibi imperenam stercus."[555]

[For the Consecration of the Oil][556]

Three breathings crosswise, (able to make a queasy stomach spew) nine mumblings, and three curtsies, saying thereunto, "Ave sanctam oleum," ter, "ave sanctum balsamum,"[557] and so the Devil is thrust out, and the Holy Ghost let into the place.

551. Scot, *The Discouerie of Witchcraft*, 236 (book 12, chapter 9). For more analysis, see Klaassen, *Making Magic in Elizabethan England*, 26, 70.

552. *Omnipotens + Dominus +*: Translation: "Omnipotent + Lord +"

553. *With thirty-four...crosses*: These names are not provided here, but this is the passage from the York Primer: "Sother + Emmanuel + Sabaoth + Adonay + Unigenitus + Via. Vita. Manus. Homo [+] Usion. Saluator. Alpha et Ω. Fons. Origo. Spes. Fides. Charitas. Oza. Agnus. Ouis. Vitulus. Serpens. Aries. Leo. Vermis. Primus. Nouissimus. Rex. Pater. Filius. Spiritus sanctus. Ego sum. Qui sum. Creator. Eternus. Redemptor. Trinitas. Unitas. Clemens. Caput. Otheotecos. Tetragrammaton." Wordsworth, *Horae Eboracenses*, 126.

554. Scot, *The Discouerie of Witchcraft*, 238 (book 12, chapter 10).

555. Scot translates this roughly as "Open thy mouth and I will put in a plumme," indicating it is intended as satirical. Scot's reading of "plum" is better translated as "excrement."

556. Scot, *The Discouerie of Witchcraft*, 239 (book 12, chapter 11). This is an extract from Scot's dismissive critique of Catholic service, as the parenthetical comment near the beginning suggests.

557. *Ave...balsamum*: "Hail holy oil," (three times), "hail holy balsam."

For the Falling Evil[558]

Take the sick man per the hand, and whisper these words softly in his ear: "I conjure thee per the sun and moon, and per the Gospel of this day delivered per God to Hubert, Giles, Cornelius, and John that thou rise, and fall no more." * Otherwise: drink in the night, at a spring, water out of a skull of one that hath been slain. * Otherwise: eat a pig killed with a knife that slew a man. * Otherwise, as followeth:

"Ananizapta[559] smiteth death, whilst harm intended be,
This world An[an]izapta say, and death shall captive be
An[an]izapta, O of God, have mercy now on me."

[66]

Against the Biting of a Mad Dog[560]

Put a silver ring on thy finger, within that which these words are graven, + Habay + Habar + Heber[561] +, and say to the person bitten with a mad dog, "I am thy saviour, lose not thy life," and then prick him in the nose thrice, that at each time he bleed. * Otherwise: take pills made of the skull of one that is hanged. * Otherwise: write upon a piece of bread, Irioni, Khiriora, Esser, Blunder,[562] Feres; and let it be eaten per the party bitten. * Otherwise: "O rex gloriae Jesu Christe, veni cum pace: in nomine Patris Max, in nomine Filii Max,[563] in nomine Spiritus Sancti Max:[564] Gasper, Melchior, Balthasar + Prax + Max + Deus I max +."[565]

558. Scot, *The Discouerie of Witchcraft*, 242–43 (book 12, chapter 14). Just before this, Scot writes, "There be innumerable charmes of coniurers, bad physicians, lewd surgians, melanchalike witches, and couseners, for all diseases and greefes; speciallie for such as bad physicians and surgions knowe not how to cure, and in truth are good stuffe to shadow their ignorance, whereof I will repeate some." The copyist of Douce MS. 116 omitted the Latin version of the final charm.

559. *Ananizapta*: Magical word found in various protective charms, dating back to the fourteenth century, often for epilepsy. Jones and Olsan, "Middleham Jewel: Ritual, Power and Devotion," 262–68.

560. Scot, *The Discouerie of Witchcraft*, 243 (book 12, chapter 14).

561. *Heber*: Scot has "Hebar."

562. *Blunder*: Scot has "Khuder."

563. *Max*: This and the following instance is "prax" in Scot.

564. *O Rex…Max*: Translation: "O king of glory, Jesus Christ, come in peace, in the name of the Father Max, in the name of the Son Max, in the name of the Holy Ghost Max."

565. Scot includes the following, which our copyist cuts: "But in troth this is verie dangerous; insomuch as if it be not speedilie and cunninglie prevented, either death or frensie insueth, through infection of the humor left in the wound bitten by a mad dog: which bicause bad surgions cannot cure, they have therefore bled foolish cousening charmes."

But Dedenous[566] in his herbal saith that the herb allyson[567] cureth it. That herb, hanged at a man's gate or entry, preserveth him and his cattle from all enchantment, or bewitching.[568] He is overtaken with folly.[569]

[Another Charm for the Same][570]

Quare fare nare
Fare quare hare
Nare quare fare[571]

Against the Biting of a Scorpion[572]

Say to an ass secretly, and, as it were, whispering in his ear, "I am bitten with a scorpion."

Against the Toothache[573]

Clarify[574] the gums in the grief,[575] with the teeth of one that hath been slain. * Otherwise: Galbes, Galbat, Galdes, Galdat * Otherwise: A Hab Hur Us, & c. * Otherwise: at sacring[576] at mass, hold your teeth together and say, "Os non comminuetis ex eo."[577] * Otherwise, "Strigiles falcesque dentatae, dentium dolorum persanate: O horsey-combs and sickles that have so many teeth, come heal me now of my toothache."

566. *Dedenous*: Rembert Dodoens (1517–1585), a botanist from Flanders.
567. *Allyson*: At this time, used in a non-specific sense to describe a plant based on the power to cure rabies. See OED, "alyssum."
568. Dodoens, *A Nievve Herball*, 107.
569. *He is...folly*: This is a dismissive statement not in Dodoneus, but added by Scot, and left in by our copyist.
570. This charm is included in the margin, with a bracket pointing to the previous header.
571. Not included in Scot, but positioned next to the section heading in brackets. For a parallel ritual, see National Library of Scotland GD188/25/1/3, 97. A similar charm is noted for curing hogs, with "Sare, Nare, Fare, Fare, Nare, Sare," being written on an apple or piece of cheese and fed to them (Howell, *Complete Collection of State Trials*, 5:721). We have a similar charm for ague noted from Holcombe (Wickham, *Records by Spade and Terrier*, 146). For an example for an unspecified purpose, see Bodleian MS 163, 14v.
572. Scot, *The Discouerie of Witchcraft*, 244 (book 12, chapter 14).
573. Scot, *The Discouerie of Witchcraft*, 244 (book 12, chapter 14).
574. *Clarify*: Scot has "Scarify."
575. *Grief*: Sore, pain, or wound.
576. *Sacring*: The consecration of the bread and wine.
577. *Os...ex eo*: "Mouth, you will not crumble out of this."

[67]

A Charm to Release a Woman in Travail[578]

Throw over the top of the house, where a woman in travail lieth, a stone or any other thing that hath killed three living creatures; namely, a man, a wild boar, and a she-bear.

To Heal the King's or Queen's Evil, or Any Other Soreness in the Throat[579]

First, touch the place with the hand of one that died an untimely death. * Otherwise, let a virgin fasting lay her hand on the sore, and say, "Apollo denieth that the heat of the plague can increase, where a naked virgin quenched it," and spit three times upon it.

How to Fetch a Thorn out of Any Part of One Body, a Bone out of the Throat[580]

Saint Blaze's day;[581] to wit, "Call upon God, and remember S. Blazes." This Saint Blaze could also heal all wild beasts that were sick or lame, with laying on of his hands, as appears in the lesson read on his day, where you shall see that matter at large.

For the Headache[582]

Tie a halter about your head, wherewith one has been hanged.

A Charm to Be Said Each Morning per a Witch Fasting, or at Least before She Goes Abroad[583]

"The fire bites, the fire bites, the fire bites; hog's turd over it, hog's turd over it, hog's turd over it. The Father with thee, the Son with me, the Holy Ghost between us both to be," ter.[584] Then spit over one shoulder, and then over the other shoulder, and then three times right forward.

578. Scot, *The Discouerie of Witchcraft*, 244 (book 12, chapter 14).

579. Scot, *The Discouerie of Witchcraft*, 244 (book 12, chapter 14).

580. Scot, *The Discouerie of Witchcraft*, 244 (book 12, chapter 14). The copyist has replaced Scot's "A charme read in the Romish church, upon saint Blazes daie, that will" with "How to." The charm's beginning also omits Scot's reiteration of the purpose of the charm, and his attribution of it to Catholicism.

581. *Saint Blaze's day*: February 3. Saint Blaze is known for removing a fishbone from a boy's throat.

582. Scot, *The Discouerie of Witchcraft*, 245 (book 12, chapter 14). For other instances, see Davies and Matteoni, *Executing Magic in the Modern Era*, 64.

583. Scot, 245 (book 12, chapter 14).

584. *Ter*: Translation: "Three times."

[68]

A Charm That Witches Use at the Gathering of Their Medicinable Herbs[585]

"Hail be thou holy herb, growing on the ground!
All in the Mount Calvary, first wert thou found.
Thou art good for many a sore, and healeth many a wound.
In the name of Sweet Jesus, I take thee from the ground."[586]

Ditto to Open Locks[587]

As the herb called Aethiopides[588] will open all locks, if all be true that enchanters say, with the help of certain words. Also be there charms also and periapts which, without any herbs, can do as much; as, for example, take a piece of wax crossed in baptism, and do but print certain flowers therein, and tie them in the skirt of your shirt, and when you would undo the lock, blow[589] twice therein, saying, "Arato Hoc Partiko Hoc Maratarykin, I open this door in thy name, that I am forced to break as thou breaketh hell gates, in nomine Patris et Filii et Spiritus Sancti."

Even with gutta[590] put before, the lock would open.

Ditto to Drive away Spirits That Haunt Any House[591]

Hang in every of the four corners of your houses this sentence written upon virgin parchment: "[a] omnis spiritus laudet dominum: [b] mosen habent et prophetas: [c] exurgat deus et dissipenter."[592]

585. Scot, *The Discouerie of Witchcraft*, 245 (book 12, chapter 14). For more examples of this charm, see Briggs, "Some Seventeenth-Century Books of Magic," 454–55.
586. After this item, the copyist skips three items clearly intended as jokes aimed at credulous practitioners.
587. Scot, *The Discouerie of Witchcraft*, 246 (book 12, chapter 14).
588. *Aethiopides*: A variety of sage.
589. The Harrington comment in the line that follows this section should be inserted here.
590. *Gutta*: A type of gum.
591. Scot, *The Discouerie of Witchcraft*, 246–47 (book 12, chapter 14). For other examples of this "Paracelsian charm," see Labouvie, *Verbotene Künste*, 118; Member of the School of Black Art, Italy, *Witchcraft Detected and Prevented*, 43; Bellhouse, *A Complete System of Magic*, 13.
592. The three superscript letters also appear in Scot's original 1584 edition, with each corresponding with the sources cited on the next page. After this, three charms for possession are omitted, as is the sourcing of it to a 1515 book published at Rome and Avignon, and Scot's ridicule thereafter.

Psalm
150[593]
Luke
16[594]
Psalm
64[595]

For One Possessed[596]

"Obsecro te, Jesu Christi," & c. that is, "I beseech thee, O Lord Jesus Christ, that thou pull out of every member of the man all infirmities, from his head, from his brain,[597] from his back, from his breast,[598] from his heart, from his stomach, from his sides, from his flesh, from his blood,[599] from his sinews, from his marrow,[600] from his skin, and from every joint of his members," & c.[601]

593. *Psalm 150*: Psalm 150:6. Translation (KJV Psalm 150:6): "Let every thing that hath breath praise the Lord."
594. *Luke 16*: Luke 16:29. Translation (KJV): "They have Moses and the prophets."
595. *Psalm 64*: Should be Psalm 67:2. Translation (KJV Psalm 68:2): "Let God arise, let [his enemies] be scattered."
596. Scot, *The Discouerie of Witchcraft*, 248 (book 12, chapter 14). Scot's original heading is "Another charme or witchcraft for the same."
597. The copyist omits the following from Scot: "from his forhead, from his eies, from his nose, from his eares, from his mouth, from his toong, from his teeth, from his jawes, from his throte, from his necke..."
598. Omitted here from Scot: "from his paps."
599. Omitted here from Scot: "from his bones, from his legs, from his feete, from his fingers, from the soles of his feete."
600. *Sinews...marrow*: These two are reversed from the order in Scot.
601. A paragraph is omitted from Scot, who goes on to ridicule this charm and provide another requiring a Host.

[69]

A Charm per the Bots[602] *in a Horse*[603]

You must both say and do thus upon the diseased horse three days together before the sun rising: "In nomine pa+tris et fi+lii et spiritus + sancti, exorcizo te, vermen, per deum pa + trem et fi+ ilium et spiritum + sanctum"; that is, "In the name of God the Father, the Son, and the Holy Ghost, I conjure thee, O worm, per God the Father, the Son, and the Holy Ghost, that thou neither eat nor drink the flesh, blood, or bones of this horse, and that thou hereby mayst be made as patient as Job, and as good as [Saint] John the Baptist, when he baptised Christ in Jordan. In nomine pa + tris, et fi + lii, et spiritus + sancti," and then say three Pater Nosters and three Aves, in the right ear of the horse, to the glory of the Holy Trinity. Do + minus, fi + lius, spiri + tus, Mari + a.[604]

Ditto against Vinegar[605]

That wine wax not eager, write on the vessel, "Gustate et videte, quoniam suavis est dominus."[606]

To Enchant a Serpent[607]

"I conjure thee, O serpent, in this hour, per the five holy wounds of our Lord, that thou remove not out of this place, but here stay, as certainly as God was born of a pure virgin." * Otherwise: "I conjure thee in nomine Patris, et Filii, et Spiritus Sancti; I command thee, serpent, by our Lady Saint Mary that thou obey me, as wax obeyeth the fire, and as fire obeyeth water, that thou neither hurt me nor any other Christian, as certainly as God was born of an immaculate virgin, in which respect I take thee up. In nomine Patris, et Filii, et Spiritus Sancti. Eli lash eiter, eli lash eiter, eli lash eiter."

[70]

* "Otherwise. O vermin, thou must come, as God came unto the Jews." * Otherwise: L. Vairus[608] saith that serpens quernis frondibus contacta, that a

602. *Bots*: Worms or maggots.

603. Scot, *The Discouerie of Witchcraft*, 248 (book 12, chapter 14).

604. *Do + minus...Mari + a: Translation*: "Lo + rd, s + on, spi + rit, Mar + y."

605. Scot, *The Discouerie of Witchcraft*, 249 (book 12, chapter 14).

606. *Gustate...suavis*: Vulgate Psalm 33:9. Translation (KJV Psalm 34:8): "O taste and see that the Lord is good."

607. Scot, *The Discouerie of Witchcraft*, 254–55 (book 12, chapter 15).

608. *L. Vairus*: Leonardus Vairus (1540–1603), author of *De Fascino Libri Tres* (1583).

serpent touched with oak leaves dieth and stayeth even in the beginning of his going, if a feather of the bird ibis be cast or thrown upon him, and that a viper smitten or hut[609] with a reed is astonished, and touched with a beechen branch, is presently numb and stiff.

[Snakes and Witchcraft][610]

Serpents and snakes [and their][611] skins exceed all other creatures per witchcraft and enchantment.[612]

[Charms against Scorpions and Eye Troubles][613]

If any see a scorpion and say this word, "Bud," he shall not be stung or bitten therewith. These two Greek letters Π and A, written in a paper and hung about one's neck, preserve that party from blearedness.[614]

A Charm Teaching How to Hurt Whom You List with Images of Wax[615]

N.B. Your mind must be fixed, on that party all the time (abstract) you are making the figure.

Make an image in <u>his name</u> whom you would hurt or kill of new virgin wax. Under the right arm-poke,[616] place a swallow's heart, the liver under the left. Then hang about the neck thereof a new thread and a new needle pricked into the member which you would have hurt, with the rehearsal of certain words, which is fitting to be omitted.[617] Otherwise: sometimes these images are made of brass, and then the hand is placed where the foot should be, and the foot where the hand, and the face downwards. * Otherwise: for a greater mischief, the like image is made in the form of a man or woman, upon whose head is written the

609. *Hut*: Scot: "hot." Hit?

610. Scot, *The Discouerie of Witchcraft*, 255 (book 12, chapter 15).

611. *And their*: Added from Scot for clarity.

612. *And enchantment*: Added by the copyist.

613. Scot, *The Discouerie of Witchcraft*, 256 (book 12, chapter 16).

614. *Blearedness*: Dimming of the eyes.

615. Scot, *The Discouerie of Witchcraft*, 257 (book 12, chapter 16).

616. *Arm-poke*: Armpit.

617. *Which…omitted*: Scot: "which for the avoiding of foolish superstition and credulitie on this behalfe is to be omitted. And if they were inserted, I dare undertake they would do no harme, were it not to make fooles, and catch gudgins." A "gudgin" was a bait fish, or a gullible individual.

[71]

certain name of the party, and on his or her ribs these words: Ailif, Casyl, Zazel, Hit Mel Meltat, when the same must be buried.

Charm [against Torture][618]

As the milk of our Lady was luscious to our Lord Jesus Christ, so let this torture or rope be pleasant unto mine arms and members.

Counter Charms in the Saying Witches Are Vexed[619]

"Eructavit cor meum verbum bonum, dicam cuncta opera mea regi."[620] Otherwise: "Domine, labia mea aperies, et os meum annunciabit veritatem [laudem tuum]."[621] Otherwise: "Contere brachia iniqui rei, et lingua maligna subvertetur."[622]

For Corporeal or Spiritual Rest[623]

In nomine Patris up and down, et Filii et Spiritus Sancti upon my crown;
Crux Christi[624] upon my breast; sweet lady, send me eternal rest.

Charms to Find Out a Thief[625]

The means how to find out a thief is thus: Turn your face to the east and make a cross upon crystal with oil olive, and under the cross write these two words: Saint Halen.[626] Then a child that is innocent and a chaste virgin, born in true wedlock and not base begotten, of the age of ten years, must take the crystal in his hand. And behind his back, kneeling on thy knees, thou must devoutly and reverently say over this prayer thrice: "I beseech thee, my lady Saint Halen, mother of King Constantine, which did find the cross whereupon Christ died, per that thy holy devotion and invention of the cross, and per the same cross, and per the joy which thou conceivest at the finding thereof,

618. Scot, *The Discouerie of Witchcraft*, 259 (book 12, chapter 17). This is one of several charms in this section.

619. Scot, *The Discouerie of Witchcraft*, 260 (book 12, chapter 17).

620. *Fructavit…regi*: A modification of Vulgate Psalm 44:2. Translation (KJV Psalm 45:1, modified): "My heart is inditing a good matter: I will speak of all things which I have made touching the king."

621. *Domine…veritatem*: A modification of Vulgate Psalm 50:17. Translation (KJV 50:15, modified): "O Lord, open thou my lips; and my mouth shall shew forth the truth."

622. *Contere…subvertetur*: "Destroy the arms of unjust criminals, and a wicked tongue will be overthrown." This is similar to Vulgate Psalm 9:36.

623. Scot, *The Discouerie of Witchcraft*, 260 (book 12, chapter 17).

624. *Crux Christi*: Translation: "Cross of Christ."

625. Scot, *The Discouerie of Witchcraft*, 261 (book 12, chapter 17). See also manuscript page 110.

626. *Halen*: Helen in Scot.

[72]

and per the love which thou bearest to thy son Constantine, and per the great goodness which thou dost always use, that thou show me in this crystal whatsoever I ask or desire to know. Amen."

And when the child seeth the angel in the crystal, demand what you will, and the angel will make answer thereunto. Memorandum,[627] just at sun rising, when the weather is fair and clear.

To Put Out the Thief's Eye[628]

Read seven psalms[629] with the litany, and then must be said a horrible prayer to Christ and God the Father with a curse against the thief. Then, in the midst of the step of your foot, on the ground where you stand, make a circle like an eye and write thereabout certain barbarous names, and drive with a cooper's hammer or adze into the midst thereof a brazen nail consecrated, saying, "Justus es domine, et justa juditia tua,"[630] then the thief shall be bewrayed[631] per his crying out.

Enchantment[632]

Certain priests use the hundred and eighth Psalm[633] as an enchantment, or at the least wise saying, that against whomsoever thou pronounce it, they cannot live one whole year at the utmost.

Charms to Drive Away Witches[634]

The first way is to nail a horseshoe at the inside of the outmost threshold of your house, and so you shall be sure no witch can have power to enter thereinto. Otherwise: the triumphant title to be written crosswise, in every corner of

627. *Memorandum*: "It is to be remembered."

628. Scot, *The Discouerie of Witchcraft*, 262 (book 12, chapter 17). Another example of the Eye of Abraham charm (see manuscript page 13).

629. *Seven psalms*: Seven Penitential Psalms, or Vulgate Psalms 6, 31, 37, 50, 101, 129, 142.

630. *Justus...tua*: A modification of Vulgate Psalm 118:137. English (KJV Psalm 119:137, modified): "Righteous art thou, O Lord, and righteous is thy righteousness."

631. *Bewrayed*: Revealed as an evil-doer.

632. Scot, *The Discouerie of Witchcraft*, 266 (book 12, chapter 17).

633. *Hundred and Eighth Psalm*: Probably a reference to Vulgate Psalm 108, which is Psalm 109 in other versions. For more on the usages of this psalm, see Rankine and Barron, *The Book of Gold*, 191–92.

634. Scot, *The Discouerie of Witchcraft*, 266–67 (book 12, chapter 18).

[73]

the house, thus:

Jesus + Nazarenus + Rex + Judeorum +

Memorandum you may join therewithal the name of the Virgin Mary or of the Four Evangelists, verbum caro factum est.[635] * Otherwise: in some places they nail a wolf's head on the door. Otherwise: hang garlic up upon the roof of the house, for to keep away witches and spirits. * Otherwise: perfume made of the gall of a black dog, and his blood besmeareth on the posts and walls of the house, driveth out of the doors devils and witches. Otherwise: the smoke of sulphur, the herb called mullein, longwort, and moly are excellent against enchantment, every one of them.

Of Witches' Transportations[636]

The fat of young children, and seeth it with water in a brazen vessel, reserving the thickest of that which remaineth boiled in the bottom, which you lay up and keep, until occasion serveth to use it. Then put hereunto eleoselinum, aconitum, frondes populeas,[637] and soot.

To Spoil a Thief, a Witch, or Any Other Enemy, and to Be Delivered from the Evil[638]

Upon the Sabbath day before sunrising, cut a hazel wand, so saying: "I cut thee, O bough, of this summer's growth, in the name of him whom I mean to beat or maim." Then cover the table and say, "+ In nomine Patris + et Filii + et Spiritus Sancti +" ter,[639] and striking thereon, say as followeth (English[640] it he that can), "Broche Myroch, Esenaroth + Betu + Baroch + Ass + Maaroth +." And then say, "Holy Trinity, punish him that hath wrought this mischief, and take it away per the great justice

635. *Verbum...est*: "The word was made flesh" (John 1:14).

636. Scot, *The Discouerie of Witchcraft*, 184 (book 10, chapter 8).

637. *Eleoselinum, aconitum, frondes populeas*: Smallage, aconite, and poplar foliage.

638. Scot, *The Discouerie of Witchcraft*, 269 (book 12, chapter 18). For commentary, see Klaassen, "Three Early Modern Magic Rituals to Spoil Witches." Other examples: Weyer, *De Praestigiis Daemonum*, 524; Albertus Magnus, *Egyptian Secrets*, 19; Stehle, "Volkstümliche Feste, Sitten, und Gebräuche im Elsass, 1892," 181; Harms and Clark, *Of Angels*, 174.

639. *Ter*: Translation: "Three times."

640. *English*: To translate a passage into English.

[74]

"Eson + Elion + Emaris, Ales Age," and strike the carpet with your wand.

A Notable Charm or Medicine to Pull out an Arrowhead, or Any Such Thing That Sticketh in the Flesh or Bones Cannot Otherwise Be Had Out[641]

Say three several[642] times kneeling: "Oremus; preceptis salutaribus [moniti]," [643] Pater Noster, Ave Maria. Then make a cross, saying, "The Hebrew knight strake our Lord Jesu Christ, and I beseech thee, O Lord Jesu Christ + per the same iron, spear, blood, and water to pull out this iron: in nomine Patris + et Filii + et Spiritus Sancti. +" [644]

Against the Quotidian Ague[645]

Cut an apple in three pieces, and write upon the one, "The Father is uncreated"; upon the other, "The Father is incomprehensible"; upon the third, "The Father is eternal." [646] * Otherwise, write upon a mass-cake[647] cut in 3 pieces, "O ague to be worshipped"; on the second, "O sickness to be ascribed to health and joys"; on the third, "Pax + max + fax +" [648] and let it be eaten fasting. * Otherwise: paint upon three like pieces of mass-cake, "Pater pax + Adonai + filius vita + Sabbaoth + spiritus sanctus + Tetragramaton[649] +." Eat it as aforesaid.

For All Manner of Agues[650]

Join two little sticks together in the midst, being of one length, and hang it about your neck in the form of a cross. * Otherwise: for this disease, the Turks put within their doublet

641. Scot, *The Discouerie of Witchcraft*, 270 (book 12, chapter 18).

642. *Several*: Separate, distinct.

643. *Oremus…[moniti]*: Translation: "Let us pray. Having been reminded of the saving commands…" This passage is recited in the Mass, before the priest recites the Pater Noster.

644. *The Hebrew knight…sancti +*: A variant of the Longinus charm, usually used to staunch blood. Roper, *English Verbal Charms*, 112–13. The reference here to the "Hebrew knight" is another attempt to shift blame from the Romans to the Jewish people for Christ's death.

645. Scot, *The Discouerie of Witchcraft*, 270 (book 12, chapter 18). The quotidian ague is a fever recurring daily.

646. For a fifteenth-century version of this charm, see Hunt, *Popular Medicine in Thirteenth-Century England*, 91.

647. *Mass-cake*: The wafer consecrated in the Mass, referred to in a derogatory sense.

648. Compare to Johnson, *Svartkonstböcker*, 237.

649. *Pater…Tetragramaton*: Translation: "Father, peace + Adonai + Son, life + Sabbaoth + Holy Ghost + Tetragramaton."

650. Scot, *The Discouerie of Witchcraft*, 270 (book 12, chapter 18).

[75]

a ball of wood, with another piece of wood, and strike the same, speaking certain frivolous words. * Otherwise, certain monks hanged scrolls about the neck of such as were sick, willing them to say certain prayers at each fit, and at the third fit to hope well.

More Charms for Agues[651]

Take the party per the hand and say: "Aeque facilis sit tibi hac febris, atque Mariae virgini Christi partus.[652] * Otherwise: wash with the party, and privily say this psalm, "Exaltabo te, Deus meus, rex," & c.[653] * Otherwise: wear a piece of a nail about your neck taken from a cross and wrapped in wool. * Otherwise: drink wine wherein a sword hath been drowned that hath cut off one's head. * Otherwise: let the urine of the sick body made early in the morning be softly healed nine days together, continually till all be consumed into a vapor. * Otherwise: "Fecana, Cageti, Daphnes, Gebare, Gedaco, Gebali stant, sed non stant Phebas, Hecas, et Edas."[654] Every one of these words must be written upon a piece of bread and be given in order one day after another to the sick body, and so must be cured.

For a Bloody Flux, or Rather an Issue of Blood[655]

Take a cup of cold water, and let fall thereinto three drops of the same blood, and between each drop, say a Pater Noster and an Ave. Then drink to the patient and say, "Who shall help you?" The patient must answer, "Saint Mary." Then say you, "Saint Mary, stop the issue of blood." * Otherwise: write upon the patient's forehead with the same blood, "Consummatum est."[656]

651. Scot, *The Discouerie of Witchcraft*, 271 (book 12, chapter 18). The copyist only includes part of this chapter.

652. *Aeque...partus*: Translation: "May this fever be as easy for you as the birth of Christ of the Virgin Mary."

653. *Exaltabo...rex*: Vulgate Psalm 144.

654. Scot has "Hedas." The whole translated: "Fecana, Cageti, Daphnes, Gebare, Gedaco, Gebali stand firm, but Phebas, Hecas, and Edas."

655. Scot, *The Discouerie of Witchcraft*, 273 (book 12, chapter 18).

656. Latin: "It is finished."

[74bis]

* Otherwise, say to the patient: "Sanguis, mane in te, sicut fecit Christus in se; sanguis, mane in tua vena, sicut Christus in sua paena; sanguis, mane fixus, sicut Christus quando fuit crucifixus,"[657] ter.[658] * Otherwise as followeth:

In the blood of Adam, death was taken +
In the blood of Christ, it was all to shaken +
And by the same blood I do thee charge,
That thou do run no longer at large.[659]

* Otherwise: "Christ was born at Bethlehem, and suffered at Jerusalem, where his blood was troubled. I command thee per the virtue of God, and through the help of all saints, to stay even as Jordan did, when John baptised Christ Jesus, in nomine Patris + et Filii + et Spiritus Sancti +" * Otherwise, touch that part and say, "De latere ejus exivit sanguis et aqua."[660] * Otherwise, "In nomine Patris + et Filii + et Spiritus Sancti + & c., Chimrat, Chara, Sarite, Confirma, Consona, Imohalite." * Otherwise: Sepa + Sepaga + Sepagoga + sta sanguis in nomine Patris + Podendi + et Filii + Podera + et Spiritus Sancti + Pandorica + pax tecum,[661] amen."

Gvng Crefba Gvng Ungv Gvrfr Ib[e]qf nobhg Vwz;
Chg Wa Wagb gvr Ubhygbi bs na Ryqre Fgwpx,
Funyq Orng Crefbaf iwgv Evvawat Enprf[662]

"Te[tra]gramaton, + Adonay, + *Alga* [Agla], + Craton, + Saday, + I conjure, + confirm these spirits, per the resurrection of our Lord Jesu Christ, + Te[tra]gramaton, + Adonay, + Algramay,

657. *Sanguis...crucifixus*: "Blood, remain in you, just as Christ did in himself; blood, remain in your vein, just as Christ in his punishment; blood, remain fixed, just as Christ when he was crucified." For more on the "Stans sanguis in te" charm, see Roper, *English Verbal Charms*, 121–22.

658. *Ter*: Translation: "three times."

659. *In the blood of Adam...large*: The "In sanguine Adae" charm. See Roper, *English Verbal Charms*, 109–10.

660. *De latere...aqua*: "Blood and water went forth from his side." A reference to John 19:34.

661. *Sta sanguis...tecum*: "Stay, blood, in the name of the Father, + Podendi + and of the Son + Podera + and of the Holy Ghost + Pandorica + peace with you."

662. Deciphered: "That Person That Hath These Words about Him, Put In / Into the Hollow of an Elder Stick, Shalt Beat Persons with Running [?] Races."

[75bis]

"+ Saday, + Sabaoth + Phanaboth, + Panthon, + Craton, + Neupmalon + & c., and per their virtues and powers, and per all their names which God gave power to man, both to speak or think; so per their virtues and powers, I conjure thee that thou shalt fulfil my request at all times. I conjure thee per the excellent name of Jesu Christ, A and Ω, per his nativity, resurrection, and ascension, and per the golden girdle which girded the loins of our Lord Jesu Christ, and per the two-edged sword which John saw proceed out of the almighty, and so thee to be torn and cut in pieces with that sword, and to be condemned into everlasting pain, where the fire goeth not out. I conjure thee[663] per these names, Cados, Cados, Cados, + Eschereie, Eschereie, Eschereie, Hakim, Ya, strong founders of the world, per Cantine, Yam Jarnice, Amis, Ralboch, Saback, Berisay, All Naim, and per the name Adonay, who created all fishes and living creatures in the water, birds upon the face of the earth, in the fifth day, and the name of the angels serving the sixth host, before Pastor, an holy angel. I conjure and bind thee per the omnipotent God which commanded the angel St. Michael to drive Lucifer out of heaven, with a sword of revengeance,[664] and to fall from joy to pain. I conjure thee per all angels, archangels, thrones, dominations, principates, potestates, virtutes, cherubim, and seraphim, and per all their virtues and powers. I conjure thee per Mic[h]ael, + Gabriel, + Samael, + Raphael, + Sachiel, + Anael, + Cassiel, + great and powerful angels which are chief ruler and governor over all the days in the week, that for me you all labour, and suffer me not to be overcome, but that I may always entertain my enterprise, and fulfil my request at all times, when I have this or bear it about me.

[76]

"Satael, Amabiel, + Miel, Serapiel, + Castiel, Asasiel + Rachiel, Sachiel, + Machatan, Uriel, + Dardiel, Haralapall, + Michael, Samael,[665] + upon pain of everlasting condemnation, to be sussisting[666] and obedient, fulfil my request, and preceding me at all times. I conjure you per the Holy Trinity and all your virtues and powers, the four evangelists, Mattheus, Mark, Luke, and John,

663. Compare to the Conjuration of Thursday in de Abano, "Heptameron."

664. *Revengeance*: Revenge.

665. Angels of the days of the week, from Tuesday to Monday, likely originating in Byzantium and appearing in such sources as the *Sworn Book* and the *Heptameron*. For other examples, see Honorius, *Sworn Book*, 17–22; Cambridge Additional MS. 3544, 12; Peterson, *Elucidation*, 46, 86, 144.

666. *Sussisting*: Likely "subsisting," or maintaining.

and the twelve apostles, and per him who shall come to judge both the quick and the dead, that you fail me not. If you [do, you] shall enter into the place where there is no remedy of rest, but everlasting horror and pain, there dwelling a place where there is pain upon pain, daily, horribly, and lamentably, thy pains there to be augmented as the stars in the heavens and as the gravel and sand in the sea, and thou shalt answer at the day of judgment. I conjure thee per the innocent martyrs, confessors, per the virtue of herbs, stones, words, and glass. I charge per the seven planets, ♄, ♃, ♂, ♀, ☿, ☽, and ⊖ and per your hours, and per the twelve signs ♈, ♉, ♊, ♋, ♌, ♍, ♎, ♏, ♐, ♑, ♒, and ♓, and by all the powers, virtues, and commands aforenamed, and by the cross of our Lord Jesus Christ, and per the innocent lamb and per the virtue of every ass, to fulfil at all times my enterprise and to sussist me upon pain of condemnation in hell fire."

Which person saying three Aves, three Pater Nosters, three Creeds. Fiat, fiat fiat. Vale, vale, vale.[667]

Gvwf iebhtug wa hertwa cnepuzrag wf orfg; irg hbe Ibh na ryqre fgwpx, gnxr gvr ewar bs, znxr wg ubggbi, & ebhy grwf cncre hc, & chg wg wayb gvr ubyybi of ynr fgwpx, & fgbe wg iwgu hwetwa cnepuzrag & pneel wg nobhg ura Ibl ehaar.[668]

[77]

How to Gather a Mosaical Rod to Find Out Hidden Treasure in the Earth[669]

It must be gathered on a certain day of the summer solstice and a sprout of one year's growth, and it must be chosen forked like a V or in the form of a Y. It must be a clean red hazel. The best time is a little before the sun rises, and if ☿ be well dignified and posited, you may gather them on any Friday, for it is to be noted when the ☉ entered ♋, that is when the woods and plants have most force. Being thus gathered, when thou wouldst make use of it, hang at the single end what pieces of metal soever, and let it be made fast at the end with a little cord. Take the two ends of the fork in both your hands, and hold it steadfast towards the heavens, and the other end towards the earth, and in this manner when you are in a place, with a design to find somewhat hidden, be it gold, silver, or any other metal, if that which is in the earth be

667. *Vale...vale*: Translation: "Farewell, farewell, farewell."

668. *Gvwf...ehaar*: Deciphered: "This wrought in virgin parchment is best; get for you an elder stick, take the rind off, make it hollow, and roll this paper up, and put it into the hollow of the stick, and store it with virgin parchment, and carry it about when you run."

669. The first known reference to the "Mosaical rod" appears in J. M., *Sports and Pastimes*, 31–32. Most of this is a paraphrase from J. M.'s work.

more noble, then that which is made fast to your wand, that on the wand will bend towards its superior, as acknowledging its superiority, but when you make use of it, say with devotion the charge, and your expectation will be answered.

How to Resolve Any Question Relating to a Good or Bad Fortune

To do this, you must observe the day of the week in which the question was made. Secondly, the numerical letters of the surname of the party that inquires, numbering them by this following alphabet. Thirdly, the ☽'s age from her change to the day.

The days of the week are to be numbered thus, as follow	*Sunday* — — —	*26* — — — —
	Monday — — —	*17* — — — —
	Tuesday — —	*15* — — — —
	Wednesday — —	*29* — — — —
	Thursday ——	*11* — — — —
	Friday — — —	*17* — — — —
	Saturday — — —	*26* — — — —

1 day of the week, 2 letter.
First, day of the week; second, letters of the surname; third moon, age.

[78]

The Alphabet Numbering the Letters of the Surname Me-

Let him which hath understanding compute the number of the name of the Beast which is the number of a man...[670]

A	B	C	D	E	F	G	H
3	3	22	24	25	3	7	6
I	K	L	M	N	O	P	Q
15	5	4	24	15	9	14	21
R	S	T	u w V	X	Y	Z	Page 248 Cattan differs
13	9	8	5	6	3	3	

670. *Let him...man...*: Revelation 13:18. The reference in the table should be Cattan, *Geomancie* (1591), 248.

There is a table of this kind in page 599 of the *Shepherd's Calendar*,[671] which I have inserted here page 81. It differs from this. Which is correct, I know not. See page 81.

For an example, whether you shall recover in a suit of law or no, first I consider the day of the week supposing it to be Thursday[672] which gives the number 11, secondly the surname of the person that make the question. As suppose it to be Swift, I find per examining the alphabet. S. 9. W 10. I 15 F 3. T 8., all which added together, makes 45. Lastly, I find per my Almanac the ☽ was ten days old at the time of the question was propounded; the day of the week gives in number:

Thursday	11
Surname	45
Age of the ☽	10
	66

The number of the days of the other side back of this leaf

All these being added together makes sixty-six, which, dividing it per thirty, the remainder six, which looking into the table following you find bad fortune, this table shews whether it be good to take a voyage to sea or not; whether at such a time it be good to use merchandise. If a man shall be fortunate in city or country, if marry or not, if rich or not, if a thing stolen shall be recovered, if you shall win at gaming, whether such a horse shall win the race, and so all your demands which you desire, you shall be resolved.

Page 160 in the *Holy Guide*[673] has this table but Number 44 in the good and 28 in the bad. All the other accords with this.

This table is as in the *Book of Knowledge*:[674]

671. Harrington's catalogue cites a "Shepherd's Kalendar, and Mosaic Wand of Hidden Mysteries, wood cuts, rare" from 1659. I have found no sign of such a work in library collections, or any edition of the calendar that would have such a page number. King, *Catalogue [...] of Dr. Thos. Harrington*, 24.

672. See manuscript page 51.

673. This does not appear on this page in Heydon's work. Heydon, *The Holy Guide*, 160.

674. This does not appear in the 1729 edition of the *Book of Knowledge* referenced elsewhere.

1 7 3 2 14	*How to use this Table see page 54* *Good*	11 16 9 13 17	*The table of Numbers see page 84* *Fortune*	20 19 26 10 22 27 28 23		4 6 5 8 12	*How to use this Table is Blot shown page 92* *Bad*	15 21 18 ~~23~~ 24	*Fortune*	25 29 ~~27~~ 30

See another table to know if truth or a lie is told (page[675]).

675. This is blank.

[79]

[A Copy of a Letter Written with Gold][676]

A copy of a letter written with gold per Jesus Christ, found under a stone near a town called Isander Joy, per the commandments or working of our Lord Jesus Christ. In the foot of a cross, from the town of Isander Joy in a village called Marcondyt was found a great stone, red and large, whereon was graved these words, "Blessed be he that can turn me," which words were carried to the next village, the people labouring to turn the stone but could not. Then did they all fall to prayers, desiring God to shew them the meaning of it. Then they passed through six pikes with crosses and banners. Oftentimes they assigned to turn the stone, but all in vain. They could not move it until a child of six years of age came thither and turned it, and under the stone was found a letter written with gold, and it was carried to Isander-Joy, which attained to the lady, personage, or madam. This is it, which was written in the letter:

"The commandments of our Lord Jesus Christ, sent per the angel Gabriel, in the year of Our Lord 1392. You shall say, one to another, they that work on the sabbath day shall be excommunicated of me, Jesus Christ. I do command you that, on the Sunday you go to church with good devotions, with prayers and supplications, desiring of me forgiveness of your sins. I command you, that you should do no manner of work on the Sunday. And I command you that you keep my commandments and steadfastly believe them, for this is written with my own hand. If you do not believe, but forget my commandments, I tell you I myself will blot you out of all that / [you] have, and do not marvel that I be angry with you, for I have given six days to labour and travel, and the seventh day I myself did rest. And on that day, you shall go to church and take your children with you, that they may hear and observe my words, and if you chasten your children and teach them my commandments, I will give you manifold gifts and long life on earth; your lands shall be replenisheth and fruitful of all trees, and all grace and blessings, shall come upon you. But if you do the contrary,

676. The Sunday epistle, a written charm promising benefit to those who keep the Sabbath holy. For more on the Sunday epistle, see Skemer, *Binding Words*, 104–5; Hebing, "The Textual Tradition of Heavenly Letter Charms in Anglo-Saxon Manuscripts," 212.

[80]

"you shall be accursed of me; I will bring upon you lightning and thunder, with hunger and want, and greater hurt I will send unto your works until I have destroyed you all. You shall leave work on the Saturday at five of the clock until Monday. You shall do no manner of work, but only desire forgiveness of sins, and I will that you fast five Fridays, for the bloody wounds, which I suffered for your sins on the cross. Furthermore, you shall not take gold nor silver unjustly, nor scorn my commandments. You shall love them with a true heart and cause my commandments to be kept. You shall believe steadfastly that this was written with my own hand and spoken with my own mouth, and so doing I will send you comfort. But they that will say against this and bear false witness, and not accomplish my commandments, and they that have wherewithal to give alms and do it not, I will curse them. And they that be not baptised, cause them to come to the church and be baptised. And they that murmur at this writing and do not believe that this was written with my own hand and spoken with my own mouth shall be accursed of me. The man that shall write a copy thereof and keep it without teaching shall be accursed of me, and you shall have wonders until the day of judgment, which shall be very shortly. If you doth chasten your children and cause them to keep my commandments, you shall be unblessed[677] of me. And whoever shall write a copy of this letter, and cause it to be published abroad, if he have as many sins as there be stars in the sky, they shall be forgiven, if he have true repentance for his sins. But if you shall not believe things but be against my commandments, I will send black worms which shall destroy you and your children, and also your goods. And whosoever shall write a copy of this letter and keep it within his house, no naughty spirit shall enter therein, neither lightning nor thunder, neither plague nor pestilence, nor any other thing to hurt him. Furthermore, is any woman great with child, have a copy

677. *Unblessed*: Blessed?

[81]

"of this about her, she shall straight be delivered. And, observing my commandments, all goodness and all gladness shall be in the house where this copy shall be."

Ad Demonium et Maleficium Fugendum[678]

Avis pica, assata vel elixata comesta, sanitatem reddit *velocitis* [velociter] infirmanti[bu]s, et incantatione ligatos solvit, et pro[s]p[er]itatem tribuit.

> The bird magpie, eaten roasted or boiled, will bring back health from enfeeblement quickly, and it releases the bonds from incantations, and it bestows prosperity.

Item, in chalamo sub limine hostii impleatur [vel] avellana vacua argento vivo, et ponatur sub uincali: vel ligetur ad caput, vel *fachim* [faciem] mulieris, vel sub limine hostii ubi intrat *maleficiatis* [maleficorum], Solvit maleficium. "*Constantis* [Constantini]."

> Also, below the threshold of the door, an empty hazelnut or a reed should be filled with quicksilver, and it should be placed under the magician's pillow,[679] or it should be tied to the head or the face of the woman, or under the threshold of the door where the magician enters. It dissolves witchcraft. "Of Constantine."

Item, sanguis canis, linitis in omnibus *pietatibus* [parietibus] domus, in qua est, maleficium tollit.

> Also, the blood of a dog, smeared on all walls of the house in which the witchcraft is, lifts it.

Item, arthemesia super limen domus suspensa, facit, ut nullum maleficium noceat *ille domum* [illi domui]. Occidam.

> Also, mugwort hung over the threshold of the house makes it so that no witchcraft may do harm to that house. I kill.

[Item,] suspendent ypericon ad limen hostii.

> [Also,] they should hang St. John's wort on the threshold of the door.

678. Translation: "For the Flight of Demons and Witchcraft." This content seems to be taken from sixteenth-century printed versions of the treatise *Remedies against Magic*. Due to the corruption of the text, it likely passed through multiple copyists before it reached our manuscript. For a critical edition and translation of this treatise, see Rider, *Magic and Impotence in the Middle Ages*, esp. 215–28.

679. *The magician's pillow*: The Latin in Douce MS. 116 is uncertain, so this is taken from Rider.

Item, si tecum portaveris radicem brioniae, omnia maleficia a te fugient.

Also, if you may carry the root of briony with you, all witchcrafts will fly from you.

Item, si vir *portendit* [portaverit] cor cornicis *majis* [maris], et uxor eis, cor feniellae, semper bene convenient.

Also, if a man carries with him the heart of a male raven, and his wife carries the heart of a female raven, they will always couple well.[680]

A Charm for a Fever or an Ague[681]

"When Jesus went up to the cross to be crucified, the Jews asked him, saying, 'Art thou afraid, or hast thou the ague?' Jesus answered and said, 'I am not afraid, neither have I the ague or fever.' Amen. Sweet Jesus, amen. Sweet Jehova, amen." Probatum est.

[To Understand How to Make Use of Any Charm or Most Amulets]

Ewtug your punez hrel cynla, gung gur yrggref znl gbhpv bar nabgvre. Gvra phg bs rhrel jbeq sebz gvng iewgwat, fb gvng bar jbeq znl abg gbhpv gvr bgvrd, gvra gnc gubfr ibeqf hc wa fwgx, fb chg wg nobhg gvr cnegl arpx.[682] Probatum est.

680. The reading of "feniellae" here is taken from other sources in the genre. Rider, *Magic and Impotence in the Middle Ages*, 23.

681. A version of the "Crux Christi" fever charm, based upon an anti-Semitic historiola. Discussion: Roper, *English Verbal Charms*, 101–3. Example: Hohman, *The Long-Lost Friend*, 78–79.

682. *Ewtug…arpx*: Deciphered: "Write your charm very plain, that the letters may touch one another. Then cut off every word from that writing, so that one word may not touch the other, then *tap* [wrap] those words up in silk, so put it above the party's neck.

To Know If You Shall Be Successful in Any Matter You Engage against Another

This is taken from the Shepherd's Calendar. I know not which is correct – this or page 78.

A	B	C	D	E	F	G	H
13	3	22	25	22	3	7	6
I	K	L	M	N	O	P	Q
20	1	10	33	13	8	13	7
R	S	T	V	X	Y	Z	
13	9	8	2	6	6	4	

If you would know whether you shall have the advantage against your adversary in any matter of introverse,[683] suit of law, love, racing, gaming, bargaining, or the like to do this consider the names of each party, put the Christian names into[684]

683. *Introverse*: Looking inward spiritually or mentally.

684. *Into…*: Picks up on page 175 (at the bottom of manuscript page 82).

[82]

[Astrological Tables][685]

Januarius habet 31 dies et tot figuram incipiendus a 20 ad 21 us.

January possesses 31 days, and so many figures beginning from 20 to 21 [?].[686]

Circumcisio domini.[687] Something similar to these houses are to be[688] found in Coley's *Key to Astrology*; perhaps these are from them.[689]

685. The numbers in the tables that follow are miniscule, and the individual numbers are often unclear or even corrected. This represents our best attempt to show them.

686. *Januarius…us*: Translation: "January possesses 31 days, and so many figures beginning from 20 to 21 [?]."

687. *Circumcisio domini*: Translation: "The circumcision of the Lord."

688. The rest of this title is found on page 83.

689. *Coley's Key to Astrology*: Coley, *Clavis Astrologiae Elimata: Or a Key to the Whole Art of Astrology, New Filed and Polished, in Three Parts* […]. These are not taken from that source.

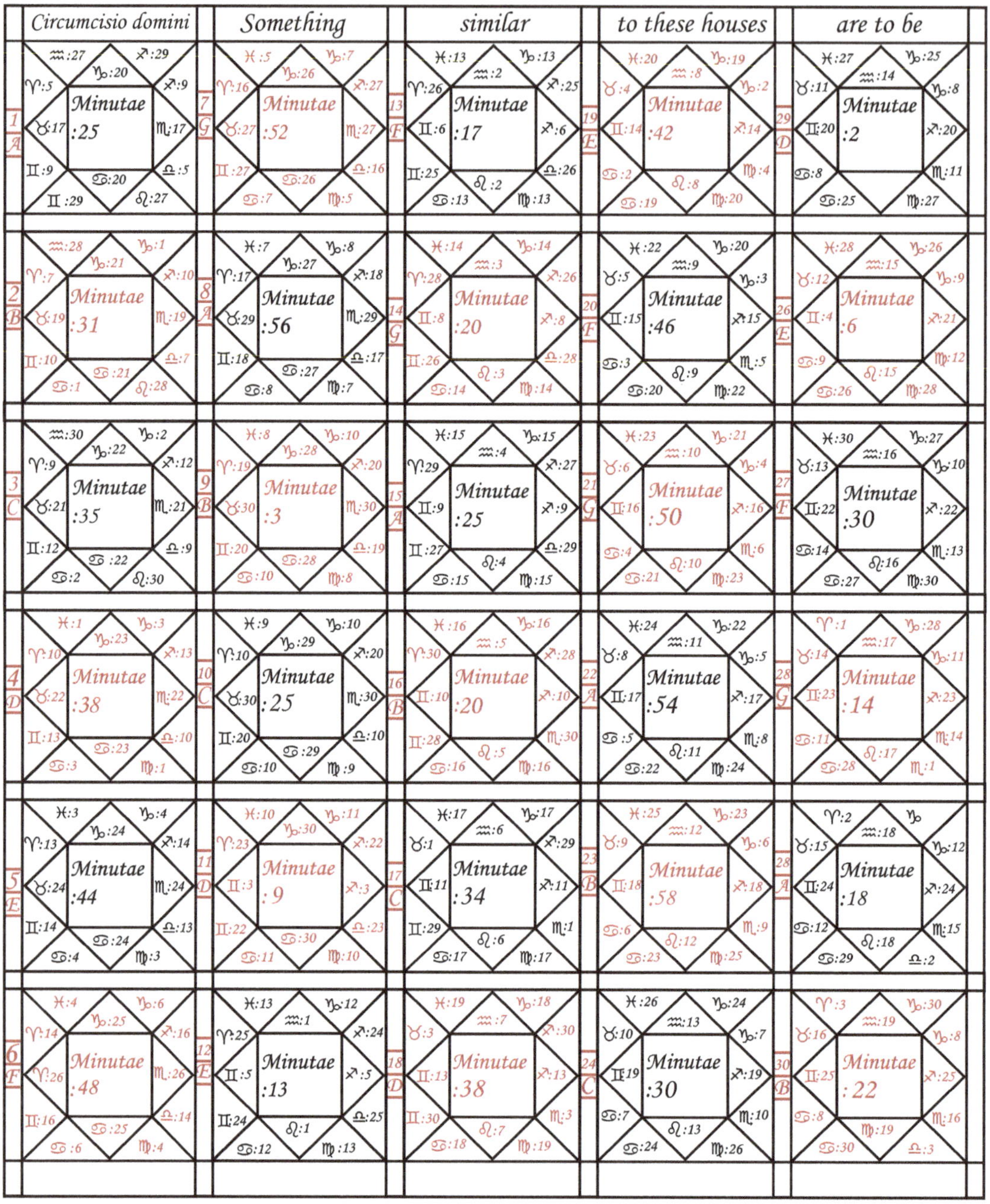
Circumcisio domini
Something
similar
to these houses
are to be
1 A: ♒:27 ♐:29 ♑:20 ♈:5 ♐:9 ♉:17 Minutae :25 ♏:17 ♊:9 ♎:5 ♋:20 ♊:29 ♌:27
2 B: ♒:28 ♑:1 ♑:21 ♈:7 ♐:10 ♉:19 Minutae :31 ♏:19 ♊:10 ♎:7 ♋:21 ♋:1 ♌:28
3 C: ♒:30 ♑:2 ♑:22 ♈:9 ♐:12 ♉:21 Minutae :35 ♏:21 ♊:12 ♎:9 ♋:22 ♋:2 ♌:30
4 D: ♓:1 ♑:3 ♑:23 ♈:10 ♐:13 ♉:22 Minutae :38 ♏:22 ♊:13 ♎:10 ♋:23 ♋:3 ♍:1
5 E: ♓:3 ♑:4 ♑:24 ♈:13 ♐:14 ♉:24 Minutae :44 ♏:24 ♊:14 ♎:13 ♋:24 ♋:4 ♍:3
6 F: ♓:4 ♑:6 ♑:25 ♈:14 ♐:16 ♈:26 Minutae :48 ♏:26 ♊:16 ♎:14 ♋:25 ♋:6 ♍:4
7 G: ♓:5 ♑:7 ♑:26 ♈:16 ♐:27 ♉:27 Minutae :52 ♏:27 ♊:27 ♎:16 ♋:26 ♋:7 ♍:5
8 A: ♓:7 ♑:8 ♑:27 ♈:17 ♐:18 ♉:29 Minutae :56 ♏:29 ♊:18 ♎:17 ♋:27 ♋:8 ♍:7
9 B: ♓:8 ♑:10 ♑:28 ♈:19 ♐:20 ♉:30 Minutae :3 ♏:30 ♊:20 ♎:19 ♋:28 ♋:10 ♍:8
10 C: ♓:9 ♑:10 ♑:29 ♈:10 ♐:20 ♉:30 Minutae :25 ♏:30 ♊:20 ♎:10 ♋:29 ♋:10 ♍:9
11 D: ♓:10 ♑:11 ♑:30 ♈:23 ♐:22 ♊:3 Minutae :9 ♐:3 ♊:22 ♎:23 ♋:30 ♋:11 ♍:10
12 E: ♓:13 ♑:12 ♒:1 ♈:25 ♐:24 ♊:5 Minutae :13 ♐:5 ♊:24 ♎:25 ♌:1 ♋:12 ♍:13
13 F: ♓:13 ♑:13 ♒:2 ♈:26 ♐:25 ♊:6 Minutae :17 ♐:6 ♊:25 ♎:26 ♌:2 ♋:13 ♍:13
14 G: ♓:14 ♑:14 ♒:3 ♈:28 ♐:26 ♊:8 Minutae :20 ♐:8 ♊:26 ♎:28 ♌:3 ♋:14 ♍:14
15 A: ♓:15 ♑:15 ♒:4 ♈:29 ♐:27 ♊:9 Minutae :25 ♐:9 ♊:27 ♎:29 ♌:4 ♋:15 ♍:15
16 B: ♓:16 ♑:16 ♒:5 ♈:30 ♐:28 ♊:10 Minutae :20 ♐:10 ♊:28 ♏:30 ♌:5 ♋:16 ♍:16
17 C: ♓:17 ♑:17 ♒:6 ♉:1 ♐:29 ♊:11 Minutae :34 ♐:11 ♊:29 ♏:1 ♌:6 ♋:17 ♍:17
18 D: ♓:19 ♑:18 ♒:7 ♉:3 ♐:30 ♊:13 Minutae :38 ♐:13 ♊:30 ♏:3 ♌:7 ♋:18 ♍:19
19 E: ♓:20 ♑:19 ♒:8 ♉:4 ♑:2 ♊:14 Minutae :42 ♐:14 ♋:2 ♍:4 ♌:8 ♋:19 ♍:20
20 F: ♓:22 ♑:20 ♒:9 ♉:5 ♑:3 ♊:15 Minutae :46 ♐:15 ♋:3 ♏:5 ♌:9 ♋:20 ♍:22
21 G: ♓:23 ♑:21 ♒:10 ♉:6 ♑:4 ♊:16 Minutae :50 ♐:16 ♋:4 ♏:6 ♌:10 ♋:21 ♍:23
22 A: ♓:24 ♑:22 ♒:11 ♉:8 ♑:5 ♊:17 Minutae :54 ♐:17 ♋:5 ♏:8 ♌:11 ♋:22 ♍:24
23 B: ♓:25 ♑:23 ♒:12 ♉:9 ♑:6 ♊:18 Minutae :58 ♐:18 ♋:6 ♏:9 ♌:12 ♋:23 ♍:25
24 C: ♓:26 ♑:24 ♒:13 ♉:10 ♑:7 ♊:19 Minutae :30 ♐:19 ♋:7 ♏:10 ♌:13 ♋:24 ♍:26
29 D: ♓:27 ♑:25 ♒:14 ♉:11 ♑:8 ♊:20 Minutae :2 ♐:20 ♋:8 ♏:11 ♋:25 ♍:27
26 E: ♓:28 ♑:26 ♒:15 ♉:12 ♑:9 ♊:4 Minutae :6 ♐:21 ♋:9 ♍:12 ♌:15 ♋:26 ♍:28
27 F: ♓:30 ♑:27 ♒:16 ♉:13 ♑:10 ♊:22 Minutae :30 ♐:22 ♋:14 ♏:13 ♌:16 ♋:27 ♍:30
28 G: ♈:1 ♑:28 ♒:17 ♉:14 ♑:11 ♊:23 Minutae :14 ♐:23 ♋:11 ♏:14 ♌:17 ♋:28 ♏:1
28 A: ♈:2 ♑ ♒:18 ♉:15 ♑:12 ♊:24 Minutae :18 ♐:24 ♋:12 ♏:15 ♌:18 ♋:29 ♎:2
30 B: ♈:3 ♑:30 ♒:19 ♉:16 ♑:8 ♊:25 Minutae :22 ♐:25 ♋:8 ♏:16 ♍:19 ♋:30 ♎:3

Latin[690] in the nominative case singular. [Let] us suppose Peter is contending with Paul; set down Petrus and Paulus, and so of any other name. Then according, as the alphabet directs, join unto every letter of the name proposed the figure of figures under the letter as they hand in order. Then cast up on the numbers to each party by itself and, being put together, proceed to divide by nine, so doubt not to find (the division being made) what remains to the one party or to the other and this gives a light of the victor and the vanquished. If it so happens that, in the division of the whole nine, nothing remains then, take[691]

690. Picks up from page 172 (the end of manuscript page 81).

691. *Take*: Picks up at the end of manuscript page 83.

[83]

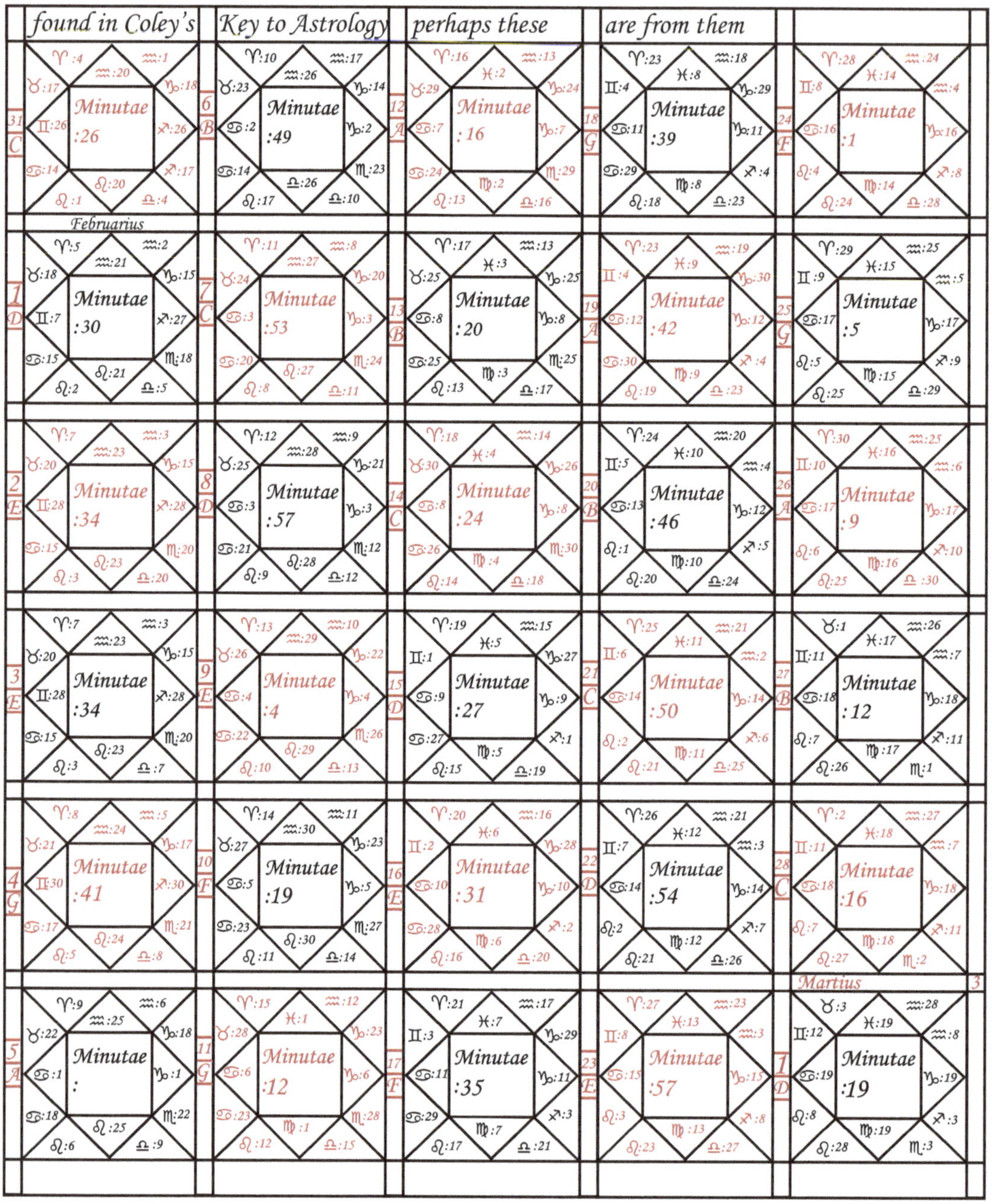
found in Coley's Key to Astrology perhaps these are from them
31 C
Minutae :26
6 B
Minutae :49
12 A
Minutae :16
18 G
Minutae :39
24 F
Minutae :1
Februarius
1 D
Minutae :30
7 C
Minutae :53
13 B
Minutae :20
19 A
Minutae :42
25 G
Minutae :5
2 E
Minutae :34
8 D
Minutae :57
14 C
Minutae :24
20 B
Minutae :46
26 A
Minutae :9
3 E
Minutae :34
9 E
Minutae :4
15 D
Minutae :27
21 C
Minutae :50
27 B
Minutae :12
4 G
Minutae :41
10 F
Minutae :19
16 E
Minutae :31
22 D
Minutae :54
28 C
Minutae :16
Martius 3
5 A
Minutae :
11 G
Minutae :12
17 F
Minutae :35
23 E
Minutae :57
1 D
Minutae :19

P 13	*Sum*	☾	*P 13*	
e 13	*67*	☿	*a 1*	*Sum 37*
t 8	*makes*	♂	*u 2*	*makes 4*
r 13	*7 times 9*	☉	*l 10*	*times 9*
u 2	*Remains 4*	♄	*u 2*	*Remains 1*
s 9		♃	*s 9*	

1		3	5	7	9
2		1	4	7	8
3	*He that*	2	5	6	9
4	*shall*	1	3	7	8
5	*Overcome*	2	4	5	9
6	*is of*	1	3	6	8
7		2	4	5	8
8		1	3	6	7
		2	4		8

the last number of nine to serve for your purpose, and thus you begin, according to this table with the names mentioned, as by the same rule you may do with any other. And by this rule, the planets give their favourable influence to Peter as having four to one—that is three odds to give him a good lot. But to make this more manifest, take the under table according to the

[84]

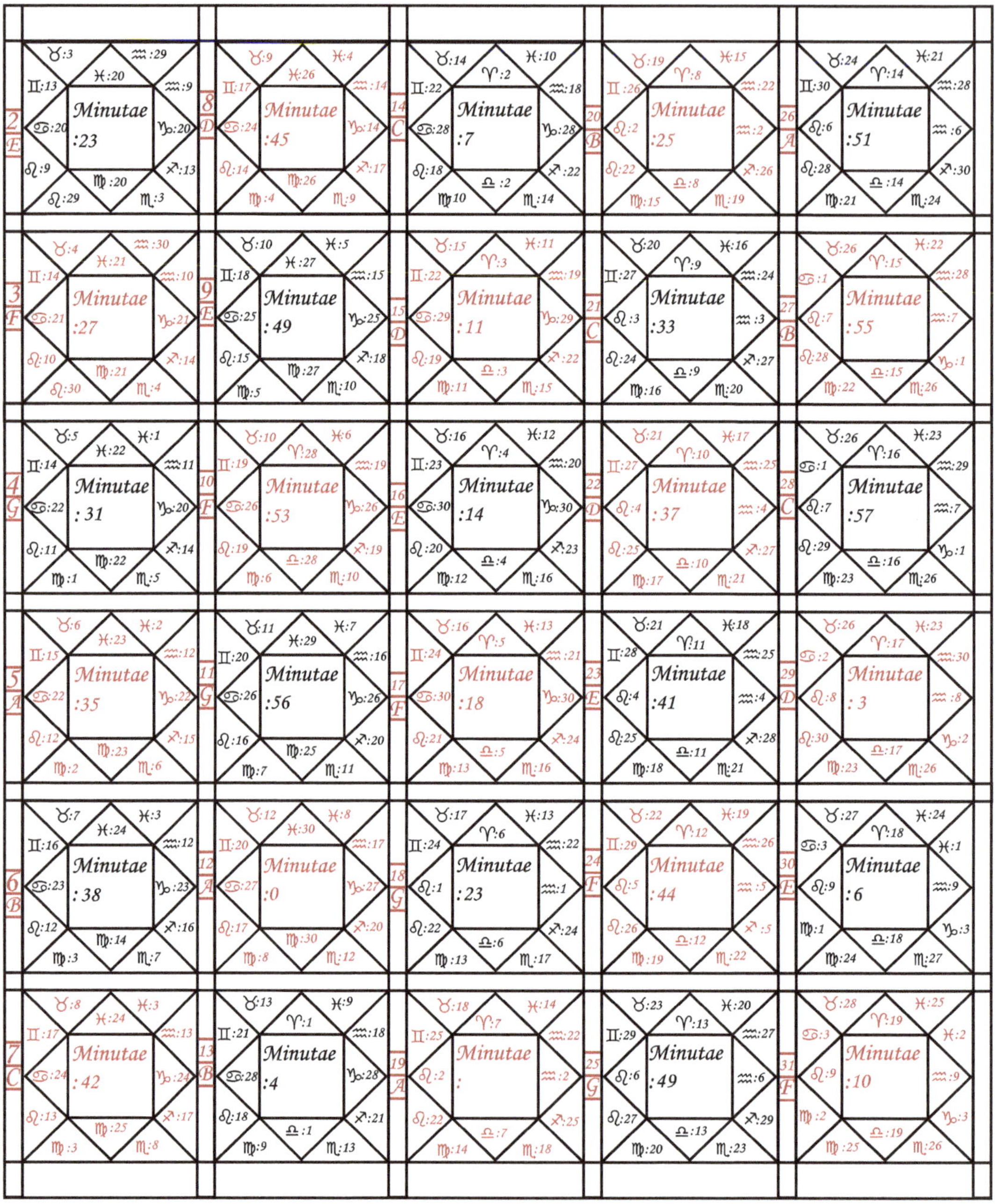
2 E
Minutae :23
8 D
Minutae :45
14 C
Minutae :7
20 B
Minutae :25
26 A
Minutae :51
3 F
Minutae :27
9 E
Minutae : 49
15 D
Minutae : 11
21 C
Minutae :33
27 B
Minutae :55
4 G
Minutae : 31
10 F
Minutae :53
16 E
Minutae :14
22 D
Minutae : 37
28 C
Minutae :57
5 A
Minutae :35
11 G
Minutae :56
17 F
Minutae :18
23 E
Minutae :41
29 D
Minutae : 3
6 B
Minutae : 38
12 A
Minutae :0
18 G
Minutae : 23
24 F
Minutae : 44
30 E
Minutae : 6
7 C
Minutae : 42
13 B
Minutae :4
19 A
Minutae :
25 G
Minutae : 49
31 F
Minutae :10

foregoing rule.

The table of the back of this leaf and in the *Shepherd's Calendar*.

Numbers Attributed to the Roman Letters

1	2	3	4	5	6	7	8	9	10	20	30	40	~~50~~	60
A	B	C	D	E	F	G	H	I	K	L	M	N	O	P
70	80	90	100	200	300	400	500	600	700	800	900			
Q	R	S	T	U	X	Y	Z =	I	V	HI	HV			

Cattan in his *Geomancie* page 255 [692] has exact the same table as this, which is taken from the last leaf of Cornelius Agrippa's *Three Books*.[693] 'Tis here in manuscript page 236. Cattan says it will discover what planet hath dominion at the birth of any person. The rule is as follows: take the numbers (see the first leaf of this book) of every letter of the proper names

692. This table appears in both editions of Cattan, but not on page 255 in either. Cattan, *Geomancie* (1591), 238; Cattan, *Geomancie* (1608), 260.

693. Such a chart does not appear in the 1651 English edition of Agrippa, *Three Books of Occult Philosophy*. It is possible that it is specific to Harrington's own copy, which was sold with a lot of "very curious Almanacks." King, *Catalogue* [...] *of Dr. Thos. Harrington*, 37.

[85]

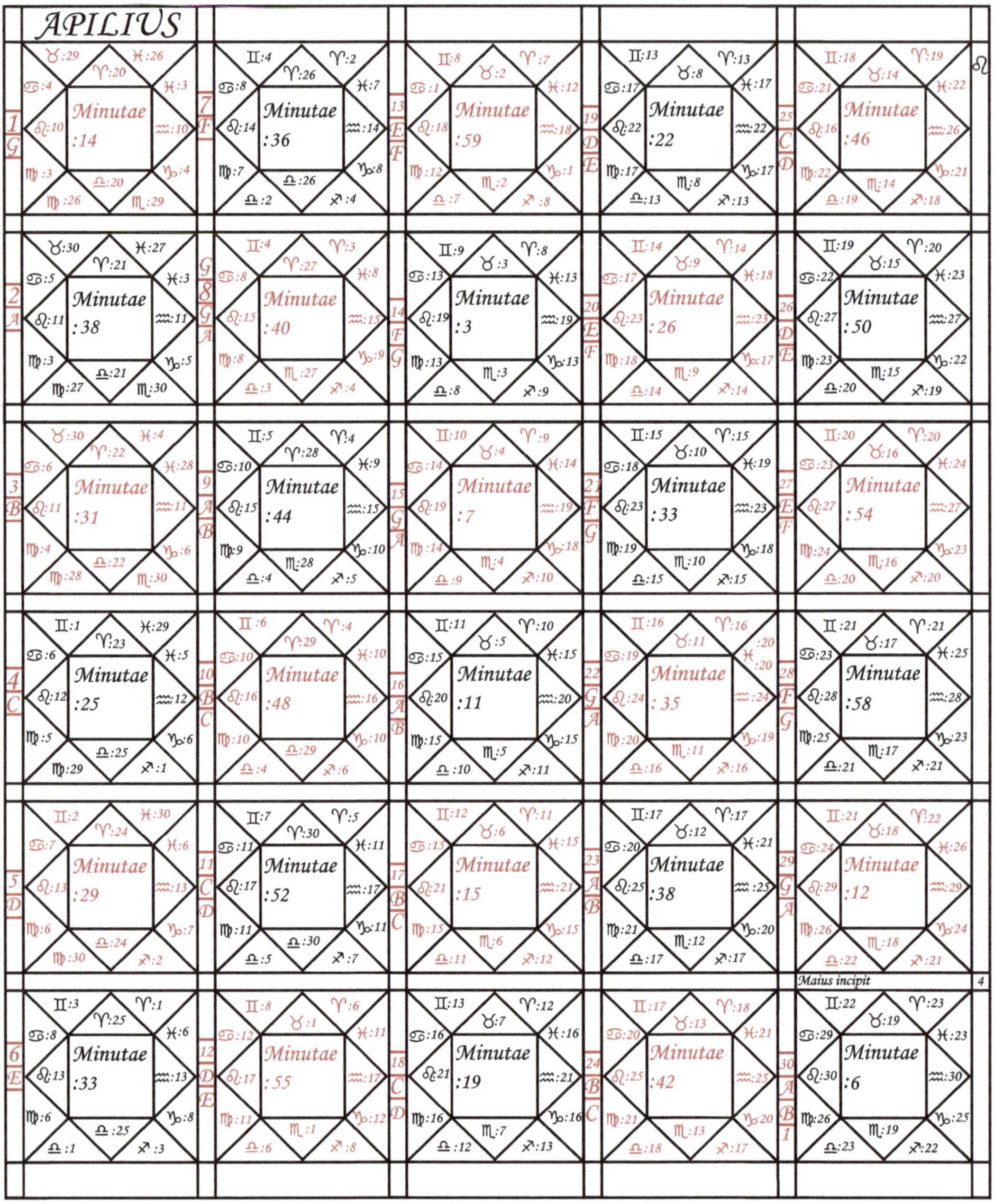
APILIUS
1 G Minutae :14
2 A Minutae :38
3 B Minutae :31
4 C Minutae :25
5 D Minutae :29
6 E Minutae :33
7 F Minutae :36
G 8 G A Minutae :40
9 A B Minutae :44
10 B C Minutae :48
11 C D Minutae :52
12 D E Minutae :55
13 E F Minutae :59
14 F G Minutae :3
15 G A Minutae :7
16 A B Minutae :11
17 B C Minutae :15
18 C D Minutae :19
19 D E Minutae :22
20 E F Minutae :26
21 F G Minutae :33
22 G A Minutae : 35
23 A B Minutae :38
24 B C Minutae :42
25 C D Minutae :46
26 D E Minutae :50
27 E F Minutae :54
28 F G Minutae :58
29 G A Minutae :12
30 A B 1 Minutae :6
♌ 5
Maius incipit
4

of the party you desire to know, and of his or her father and mother by the alphabet above said, adding all the said numbers into one total sum. Then divide the same by nine, and if one or four remain, it sheweth the planet ☉ to have dominion; if two or seven, the ☽; if three, ♃; if five, ☿; if six, ♀; eight, ♄; nine, ♂. In like manner is known under which of the twelve celestial signs any person is born: sum together that person's name [and those of] his father and mother as aforesaid, and divide the sum total by twelve. Then if one remain, it signify ♌; two, ♒; three, ♑; four, ♐; five, ♋; six, ♉; seven, ♈; eight, ♎; nine, ♏; ten, ♍, eleven, ♓; twelve, ♊. If only twelve remain, it must be ♊.

[86]

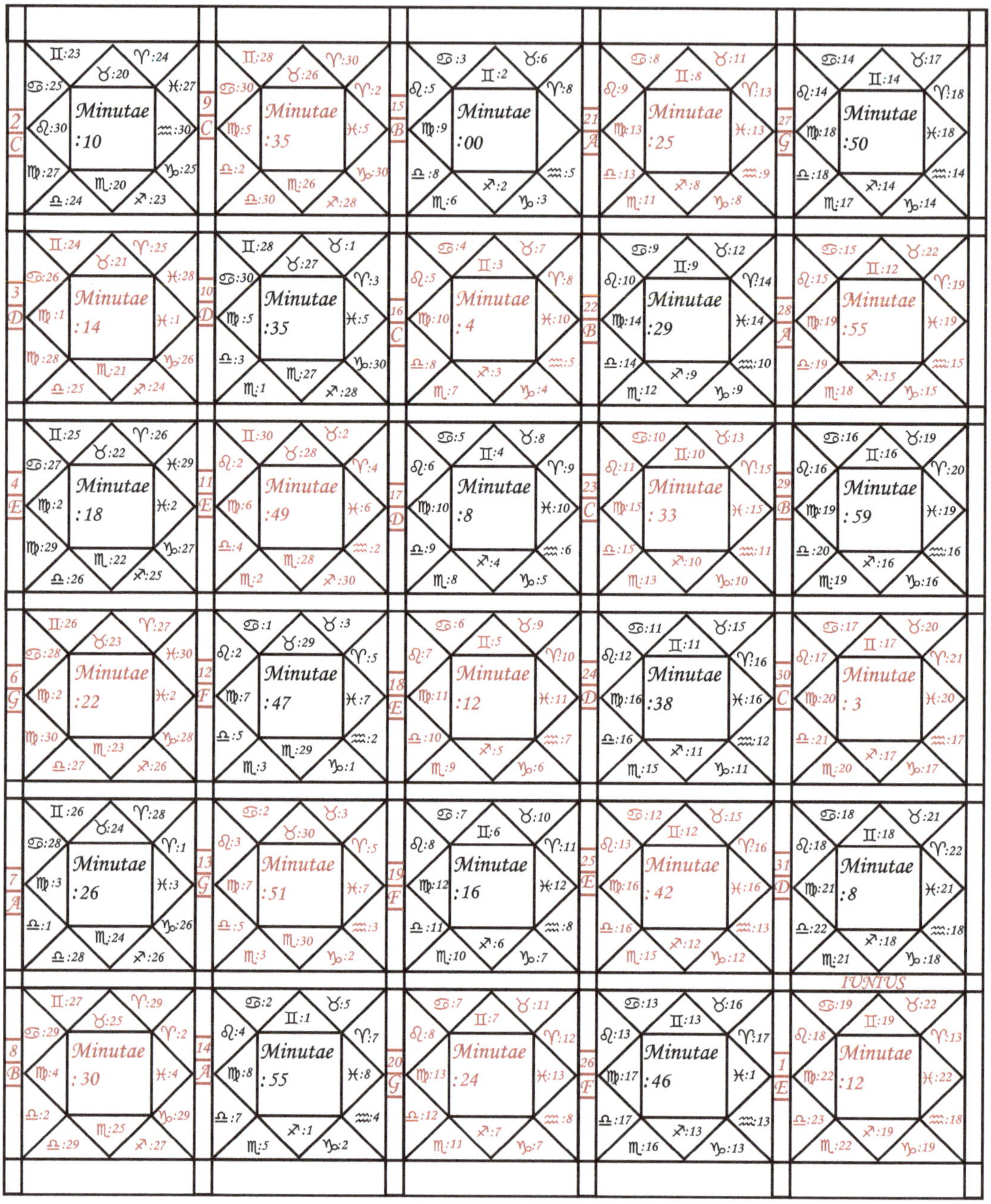
2 C
Minutae :10
9 C
Minutae :35
15 B
Minutae :00
21 A
Minutae :25
27 G
Minutae :50
3 D
Minutae :14
10 D
Minutae :35
16 C
Minutae :4
22 B
Minutae :29
28 A
Minutae :55
4 E
Minutae :18
11 E
Minutae :49
17 D
Minutae :8
23 C
Minutae :33
29 B
Minutae :59
6 G
Minutae :22
12 F
Minutae :47
18 E
Minutae :12
24 D
Minutae :38
30 C
Minutae :3
7 A
Minutae :26
13 G
Minutae :51
19 F
Minutae :16
25 E
Minutae :42
31 D
Minutae :8
8 B
Minutae :30
14 A
Minutae :55
20 G
Minutae :24
26 F
Minutae :46
IVNIUS
1 E
Minutae :12

[Notes on Astrological Timing][694]

The moon entering ♓, with no bad aspect from ♄, is a proper time to make the talisman and characters under this constellation, if favourably influenced by ☿, ♃, or ♀, the infallible influence for honour, good fortune for play.

This from Cattan, see 78 and 81.

N.B. The first hour (in every season) of the day of every country is to be assigned to the sun rising, when he appeareth rising in the horizon, and ♄ first hour of ♄ night is to be the thirteenth hour from the first hour of the day.

[Another Numerological Alphabet]

A	B	C	d	G	A	G	H
J	K	L	M	N	O	P	Q
20	1	10	23	12	8	13	27
a	b	c	d	g	A	G	H
1	3	22	24	23	3	7	6
R	S	T	U	X	Y	Z	
13	9	8	2	6	3	4	

694. Neither the 1591 nor the 1608 edition of Cattan's *Geomancie* includes this material on these pages.

[87]

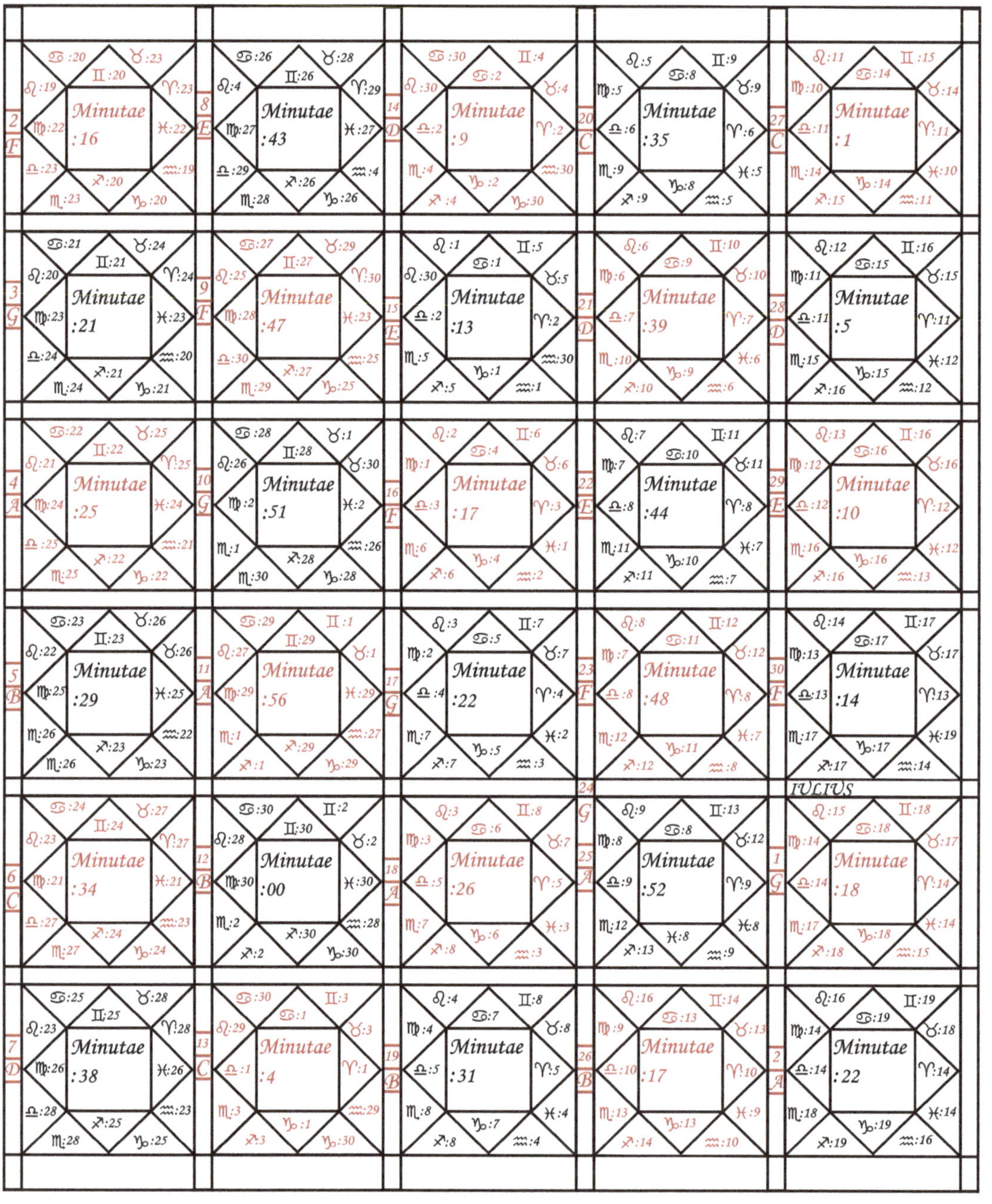
2 F
Minutae :16
8 E
Minutae :43
14 D
Minutae :9
20 C
Minutae :35
27 C
Minutae :1
3 G
Minutae :21
9 F
Minutae :47
15 E
Minutae :13
21 D
Minutae :39
28 D
Minutae :5
4 A
Minutae :25
10 G
Minutae :51
16 F
Minutae :17
22 E
Minutae :44
29 E
Minutae :10
5 B
Minutae :29
11 A
Minutae :56
17 G
Minutae :22
23 F
Minutae :48
30 F
Minutae :14
6 C
Minutae :34
12 B
Minutae :00
18 A
Minutae :26
24 G
25 A
Minutae :52
IVLIVS
1 G
Minutae :18
7 D
Minutae :38
13 C
Minutae :4
19 B
Minutae :31
26 B
Minutae :17
2 A
Minutae :22

[blank]

[88]

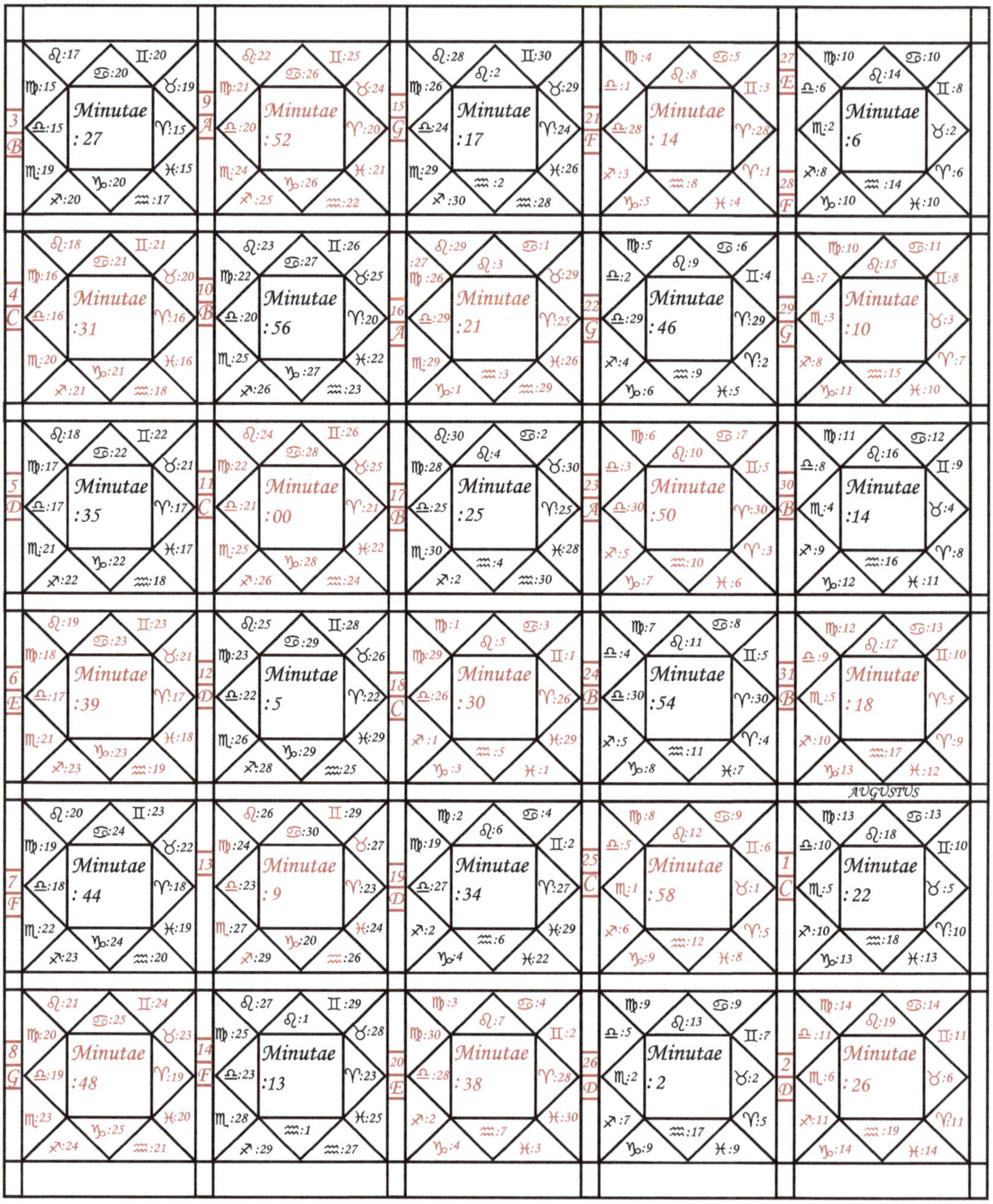
3 B ♌:17 ♊:20 ♋:20 ♍:15 ♉:19 ♎:15 Minutae : 27 ♈:15 ♏:19 ♓:15 ♑:20 ♐:20 ♒:17
9 A ♌:22 ♊:25 ♋:26 ♍:21 ♉:24 ♎:20 Minutae :52 ♈:20 ♏:24 ♓:21 ♑:26 ♐:25 ♒:22
15 G ♌:28 ♊:30 ♌:2 ♍:26 ♉:29 ♎:24 Minutae :17 ♈:24 ♏:29 ♓:26 ♒:2 ♐:30 ♒:28
21 F ♍:4 ♋:5 ♌:8 ♎:1 ♊:3 ♎:28 Minutae : 14 ♈:28 ♐:3 ♈:1 ♒:8 ♑:5 ♓:4
27 E 28 F ♍:10 ♋:10 ♌:14 ♎:6 ♊:8 ♏:2 Minutae :6 ♉:2 ♐:8 ♈:6 ♒:14 ♑:10 ♓:10
4 C ♌:18 ♊:21 ♋:21 ♍:16 ♉:20 ♎:16 Minutae :31 ♈:16 ♏:20 ♓:16 ♑:21 ♐:21 ♒:18
10 B ♌:23 ♊:26 ♋:27 ♍:22 ♉:25 ♎:20 Minutae :56 ♈:20 ♏:25 ♓:22 ♑:27 ♐:26 ♒:23
16 A ♌:29 ♋:1 ♌:3 :27 ♍:26 ♉:29 ♎:29 Minutae :21 ♈:25 ♏:29 ♓:26 ♒:3 ♑:1 ♒:29
22 G ♍:5 ♋:6 ♌:9 ♎:2 ♊:4 ♎:29 Minutae :46 ♈:29 ♐:4 ♈:2 ♒:9 ♑:6 ♓:5
29 G ♍:10 ♋:11 ♌:15 ♎:7 ♊:8 ♏:3 Minutae :10 ♉:3 ♐:8 ♈:7 ♒:15 ♑:11 ♓:10
5 D ♌:18 ♊:22 ♋:22 ♍:17 ♉:21 ♎:17 Minutae :35 ♈:17 ♏:21 ♓:17 ♑:22 ♐:22 ♒:18
11 C ♌:24 ♊:26 ♋:28 ♍:22 ♉:25 ♎:21 Minutae :00 ♈:21 ♏:25 ♓:22 ♑:28 ♐:26 ♒:24
17 B ♌:30 ♋:2 ♌:4 ♍:28 ♉:30 ♎:25 Minutae :25 ♈:25 ♏:30 ♓:28 ♒:4 ♐:2 ♒:30
23 A ♍:6 ♋:7 ♌:10 ♎:3 ♊:5 ♎:30 Minutae :50 ♈:30 ♐:5 ♈:3 ♒:10 ♑:7 ♓:6
30 B ♍:11 ♋:12 ♌:16 ♎:8 ♊:9 ♏:4 Minutae :14 ♉:4 ♐:9 ♈:8 ♒:16 ♑:12 ♓:11
6 E ♌:19 ♊:23 ♋:23 ♍:18 ♉:21 ♎:17 Minutae :39 ♈:17 ♏:21 ♓:18 ♑:23 ♐:23 ♒:19
12 D ♌:25 ♊:28 ♋:29 ♍:23 ♉:26 ♎:22 Minutae :5 ♈:22 ♏:26 ♓:29 ♑:29 ♐:28 ♒:25
18 C ♍:1 ♋:3 ♌:5 ♍:29 ♊:1 ♎:26 Minutae : 30 ♈:26 ♐:1 ♓:29 ♒:5 ♑:3 ♓:1
24 B ♍:7 ♋:8 ♌:11 ♎:4 ♊:5 ♎:30 Minutae :54 ♈:30 ♐:5 ♈:4 ♒:11 ♑:8 ♓:7
31 B ♍:12 ♋:13 ♌:17 ♎:9 ♊:10 ♏:5 Minutae : 18 ♈:5 ♐:10 ♈:9 ♒:17 ♑:13 ♓:12
AUGUSTUS
7 F ♌:20 ♊:23 ♋:24 ♍:19 ♉:22 ♎:18 Minutae : 44 ♈:18 ♏:22 ♓:19 ♑:24 ♐:23 ♒:20
13 ♌:26 ♊:29 ♋:30 ♍:24 ♉:27 ♎:23 Minutae : 9 ♈:23 ♏:27 ♓:24 ♑:20 ♐:29 ♒:26
19 D ♍:2 ♋:4 ♌:6 ♍:19 ♊:2 ♎:27 Minutae :34 ♈:27 ♐:2 ♓:29 ♒:6 ♑:4 ♓:22
25 C ♍:8 ♋:9 ♌:12 ♎:5 ♊:6 ♏:1 Minutae :58 ♉:1 ♐:6 ♈:5 ♒:12 ♑:9 ♓:8
1 C ♍:13 ♋:13 ♌:18 ♎:10 ♊:10 ♏:5 Minutae : 22 ♉:5 ♐:10 ♈:10 ♒:18 ♑:13 ♓:13
8 G ♌:21 ♊:24 ♋:25 ♍:20 ♉:23 ♎:19 Minutae :48 ♈:19 ♏:23 ♓:20 ♑:25 ♐:24 ♒:21
14 F ♌:27 ♊:29 ♌:1 ♍:25 ♉:28 ♎:23 Minutae :13 ♈:23 ♏:28 ♓:25 ♒:1 ♐:29 ♒:27
20 E ♍:3 ♋:4 ♌:7 ♍:30 ♊:2 ♎:28 Minutae : 38 ♈:28 ♐:2 ♓:30 ♒:7 ♑:4 ♓:3
26 D ♍:9 ♋:9 ♌:13 ♎:5 ♊:7 ♏:2 Minutae : 2 ♉:2 ♐:7 ♈:5 ♒:17 ♑:9 ♓:9
2 D ♍:14 ♋:14 ♌:19 ♎:11 ♊:11 ♏:6 Minutae : 26 ♉:6 ♐:11 ♈:11 ♒:19 ♑:14 ♓:14

[Paracelsus on Witches and Image Magic][695]

Witches make and form likenesses of some man they conceive in their own mind, and do stick a nail in the sole of his foot, and after this manner hurt the man, that he invisibly feeleth the pain of a nail in his feet, and is tormented, and cannot go till the nail is removed out of the image's foot, which being drawn away, the man is healed. Fixing a nail in the teeth, or any part of the images, give pain in the part to those extended.

Curative: Those who are bewitched cannot be cured any better than by hurting again the same place afflicted, that is, by making, through faith and imagination, such a like member that to hurt, or else a whole image out of wax, which he shall either anoint or bind up with plasters where the hurt is, is a present help for that person in whose name it shall be made, and the harm shall leave. But if he be so bewitched

695. Paracelsus, *Of the Supreme Mysteries*, 85–89. Harrington's copy is listed as Item 683 in King, *Catalogue* [...] *of Dr. Thos. Harrington*, 22. Several portions of the original have been omitted.

[89]

3 E E
Minutae :30
8 D
Minutae :53
14 C
Minutae :26
20 B
Minutae :9
26 A
Minutae :17
4 F F
Minutae :34
9 E
Minutae :57
15 D
Minutae :20
21 C
Minutae :12
27 B
Minutae :5
5 G
Minutae :38
10 F
Minutae :1
16 E
Minutae :24
22 D
Minutae :46
28 C
Minutae :8
5 A
Minutae :41
11 G
Minutae :5
17 F
Minutae :27
23 E
Minutae :50
29 D
Minutae :12
6 B
Minutae :45
12 A
Minutae :8
18 G
Minutae :31
24 F
Minutae :54
30 E
Minutae :16
SEPTEMBER
7 C
Minutae :49
13 B
Minutae :12
19 A
Minutae :35
25 G
Minutae :57
1 E
Minutae :19

that he is in danger to lose an eye, his hearing, or be otherwise impedited.[696] Let then be made an image of the whole body, so that, with a firm faith, upon which image let the intent of your imagination be firmly fixed, and afterwards let the whole image be consumed with fire in due order. Pains which witches occasion by tumours, dartings,[697] prickings & c. in the flesh or body is cured by bruising oak leaves, celandine, and mixing with powder of coral and binding to thee, or bound in a bag about the centre of a man, cures in twenty-four hours. Whatever is extracted should be buried in an oak or elder and fixed with a wedge towards the east. Per Paracelsus, *Occult Philosophy*, page 87 and 89.

696. *Impedited*: Impeded.

697. *Dartings*: The acts of piercing with a dart.

[90]

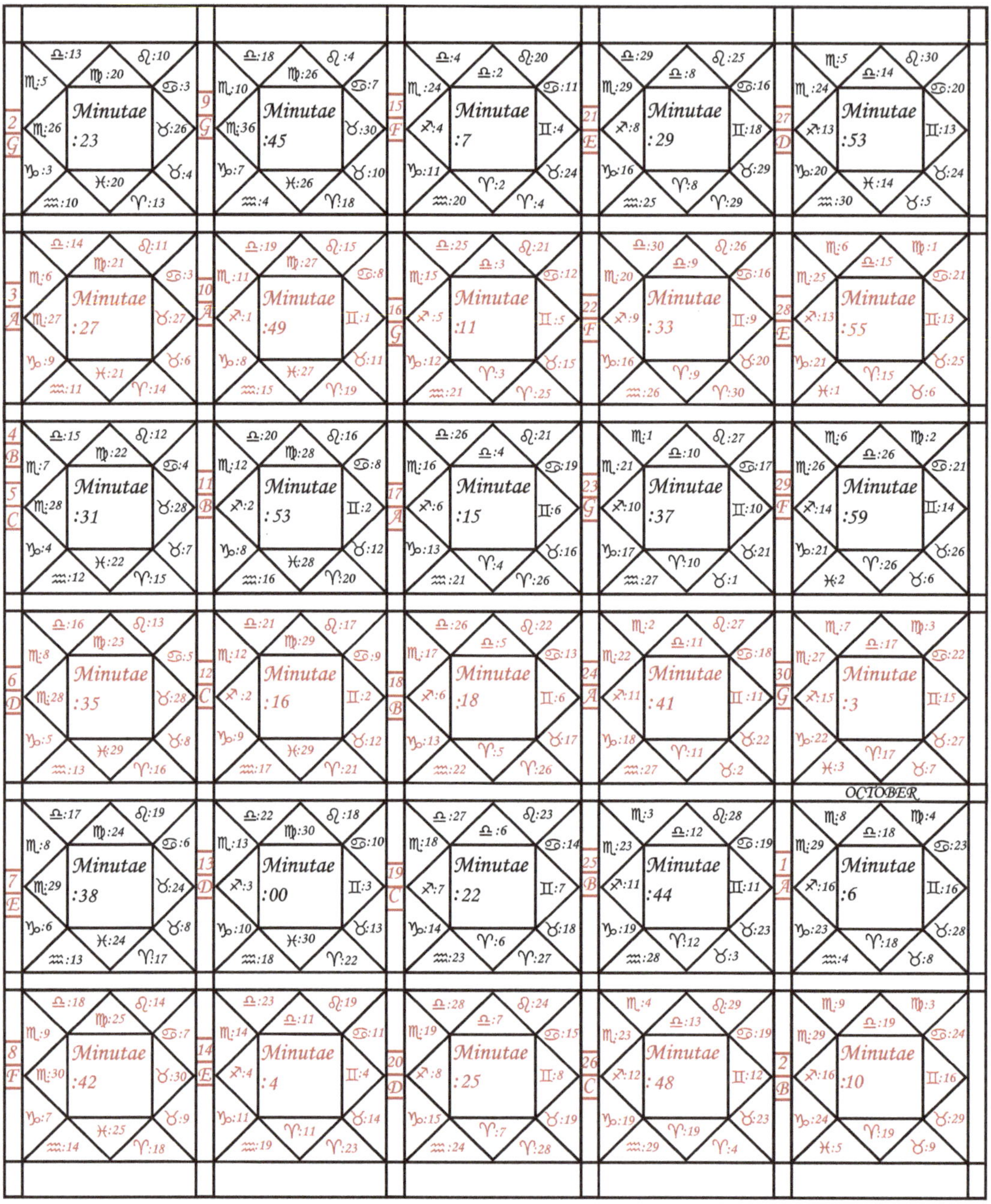
2 G ♎:13 ♌:10 ♍:20 ♏:5 ♋:3 Minutae :23 ♏:26 ♉:26 ♑:3 ♉:4 ♓:20 ♒:10 ♈:13
9 G ♎:18 ♌:4 ♍:26 ♋:7 ♏:10 Minutae :45 ♏:36 ♉:30 ♑:7 ♉:10 ♓:26 ♒:4 ♈:18
15 F ♎:4 ♌:20 ♎:2 ♋:11 ♏:24 Minutae :7 ♐:4 ♊:4 ♑:11 ♉:24 ♈:2 ♒:20 ♈:4
21 E ♎:29 ♌:25 ♎:8 ♋:16 ♏:29 Minutae :29 ♐:8 ♊:18 ♑:16 ♉:29 ♈:8 ♒:25 ♈:29
27 D ♏:5 ♌:30 ♎:14 ♋:20 ♏:24 Minutae :53 ♐:13 ♊:13 ♑:20 ♉:24 ♓:14 ♒:30 ♉:5
3 A ♎:14 ♌:11 ♍:21 ♏:6 ♋:3 Minutae :27 ♏:27 ♉:27 ♑:9 ♉:6 ♓:21 ♒:11 ♈:14
10 A ♎:19 ♌:15 ♍:27 ♋:8 ♏:11 Minutae :49 ♐:1 ♊:1 ♑:8 ♉:11 ♓:27 ♒:15 ♈:19
16 G ♎:25 ♌:21 ♎:3 ♋:12 ♏:15 Minutae :11 ♐:5 ♊:5 ♑:12 ♉:15 ♈:3 ♒:21 ♈:25
22 F ♎:30 ♌:26 ♎:9 ♋:16 ♏:20 Minutae :33 ♐:9 ♊:9 ♑:16 ♉:20 ♈:9 ♒:26 ♈:30
28 E ♏:6 ♍:1 ♎:15 ♏:25 ♋:21 Minutae :55 ♐:13 ♊:13 ♑:21 ♉:25 ♈:15 ♓:1 ♉:6
4 B 5 C ♎:15 ♌:12 ♍:22 ♏:7 ♋:4 Minutae :31 ♏:28 ♉:28 ♑:4 ♉:7 ♓:22 ♒:12 ♈:15
11 B ♎:20 ♌:16 ♍:28 ♋:8 ♏:12 Minutae :53 ♐:2 ♊:2 ♑:8 ♉:12 ♓:28 ♒:16 ♈:20
17 A ♎:26 ♌:21 ♎:4 ♋:19 ♏:16 Minutae :15 ♐:6 ♊:6 ♑:13 ♉:16 ♈:4 ♒:21 ♈:26
23 G ♏:1 ♌:27 ♎:10 ♋:17 ♏:21 Minutae :37 ♐:10 ♊:10 ♑:17 ♉:21 ♈:10 ♒:27 ♉:1
29 F ♏:6 ♍:2 ♎:26 ♏:26 ♋:21 Minutae :59 ♐:14 ♊:14 ♑:21 ♉:26 ♈:26 ♓:2 ♉:6
6 D ♎:16 ♌:13 ♍:23 ♏:8 ♋:5 Minutae :35 ♏:28 ♉:28 ♑:5 ♉:8 ♓:29 ♒:13 ♈:16
12 C ♎:21 ♌:17 ♍:29 ♋:9 ♏:12 Minutae :16 ♐:2 ♊:2 ♑:9 ♉:12 ♓:29 ♒:17 ♈:21
18 B ♎:26 ♌:22 ♎:5 ♋:13 ♏:17 Minutae :18 ♐:6 ♊:6 ♑:13 ♉:17 ♈:5 ♒:22 ♈:26
24 A ♏:2 ♌:27 ♎:11 ♋:18 ♏:22 Minutae :41 ♐:11 ♊:11 ♑:18 ♉:22 ♈:11 ♒:27 ♉:2
30 G ♏:7 ♍:3 ♎:17 ♏:27 ♋:22 Minutae :3 ♐:15 ♊:15 ♑:22 ♉:27 ♈:17 ♓:3 ♉:7
OCTOBER
7 E ♎:17 ♌:19 ♍:24 ♏:8 ♋:6 Minutae :38 ♏:29 ♉:24 ♑:6 ♉:8 ♓:24 ♒:13 ♈:17
13 D ♎:22 ♌:18 ♍:30 ♏:13 ♋:10 Minutae :00 ♐:3 ♊:3 ♑:10 ♉:13 ♓:30 ♒:18 ♈:22
19 C ♎:27 ♌:23 ♎:6 ♏:18 ♋:14 Minutae :22 ♐:7 ♊:7 ♑:14 ♉:18 ♈:6 ♒:23 ♈:27
25 B ♏:3 ♌:28 ♎:12 ♏:23 ♋:19 Minutae :44 ♐:11 ♊:11 ♑:19 ♉:23 ♈:12 ♒:28 ♉:3
1 A ♏:8 ♍:4 ♎:18 ♏:29 ♋:23 Minutae :6 ♐:16 ♊:16 ♑:23 ♉:28 ♈:18 ♒:4 ♉:8
8 F ♎:18 ♌:14 ♍:25 ♏:9 ♋:7 Minutae :42 ♏:30 ♉:30 ♑:7 ♉:9 ♓:25 ♒:14 ♈:18
14 E ♎:23 ♌:19 ♎:11 ♏:14 ♋:11 Minutae :4 ♐:4 ♊:4 ♑:11 ♉:14 ♈:11 ♒:19 ♈:23
20 D ♎:28 ♌:24 ♎:7 ♏:19 ♋:15 Minutae :25 ♐:8 ♊:8 ♑:15 ♉:19 ♈:7 ♒:24 ♈:28
26 C ♏:4 ♌:29 ♎:13 ♏:23 ♋:19 Minutae :48 ♐:12 ♊:12 ♑:19 ♉:23 ♈:19 ♒:29 ♈:4
2 B ♏:9 ♍:3 ♎:19 ♏:29 ♋:24 Minutae :10 ♐:16 ♊:16 ♑:24 ♉:29 ♈:19 ♓:5 ♉:9

[Planetary Affinities]

☿, ♃, the ☉, and ☽ are friends to ♄, ♂ and ♀ enemies to him. All the planets besides ♂ are friends to ♃; also, all besides ♀ hate ♂. ♃ and ♀ love the ☉; ♂ and ☿ and the ☽ are enemies to him. All beside ♄ love ♀. ♃, ♀, and ♄ are friends to ☿; the ☉, ☽, and ♂ his enemies. ♃, ♀, and ♄ are friends to the ☽; ♂ and ☿, her enemies. See page 37, 3 *Books* Cornelius Agrippa.[698]

698. Agrippa, *Three Books of Occult Philosophy* (1651), 37 (book 1, chapter 17).

[91]

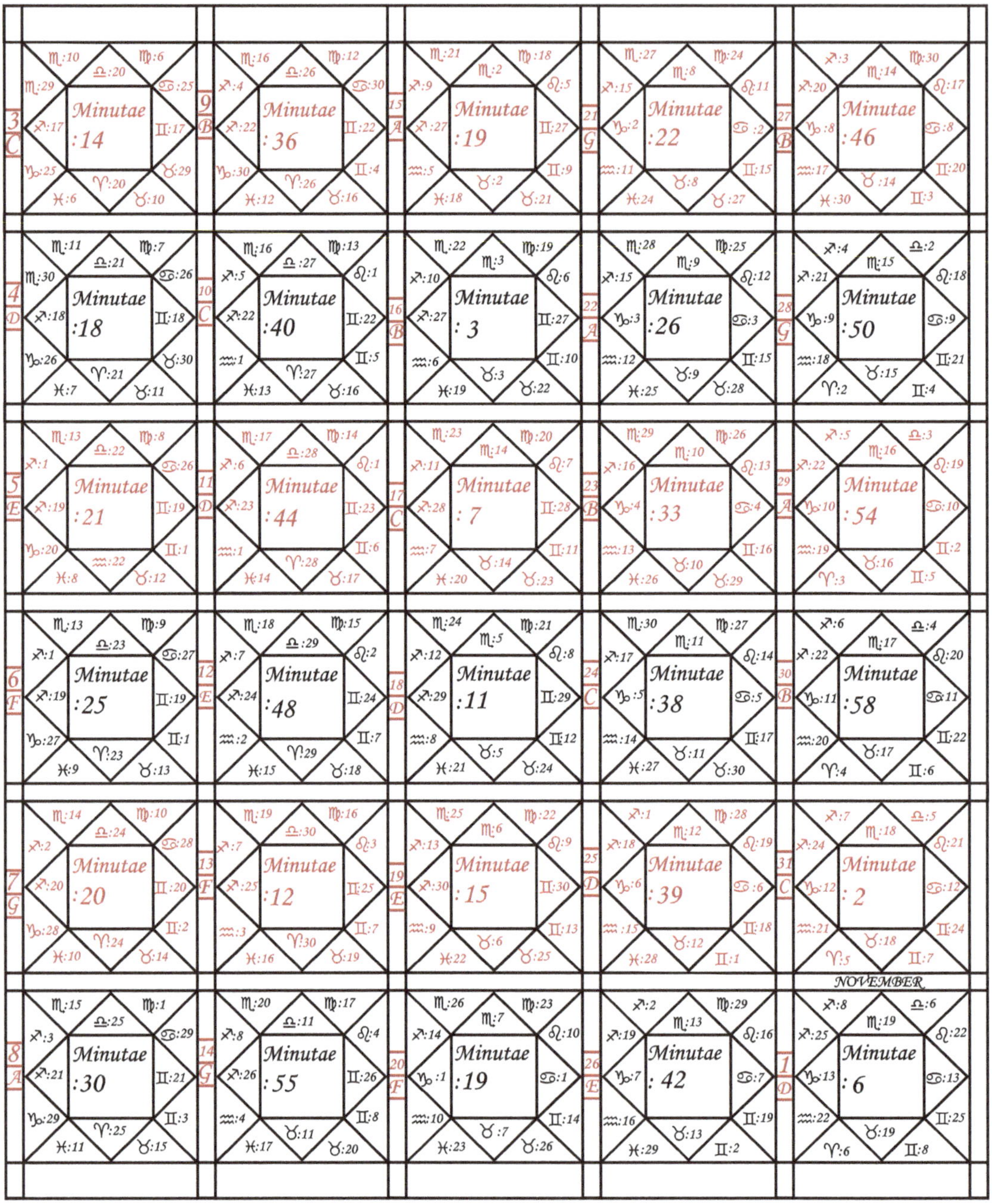
3 C
Minutae :14
9 B
Minutae :36
15 A
Minutae :19
21 G
Minutae :22
27 B
Minutae :46
4 D
Minutae :18
10 C
Minutae :40
16 B
Minutae : 3
22 A
Minutae :26
28 G
Minutae :50
5 E
Minutae :21
11 D
Minutae :44
17 C
Minutae : 7
23 B
Minutae :33
29 A
Minutae :54
6 F
Minutae :25
12 E
Minutae :48
18 D
Minutae :11
24 C
Minutae :38
30 B
Minutae :58
7 G
Minutae :20
13 F
Minutae :12
19 E
Minutae :15
25 D
Minutae :39
31 C
Minutae : 2
NOVEMBER
8 A
Minutae :30
14 G
Minutae :55
20 F
Minutae :19
26 E
Minutae : 42
1 D
Minutae : 6

A Charm to Stop Any Bleeding[699]

To be repeated three times:

Sanguis mane in te,
Sicut fecit Christus in se,
Sanguis mane in tua vena,
Sicut Christus in tua paena,
Sanguis mane fixus,
sicut Christus quando fuit crucifixus.

To Obtain a Woman's Love

An image must be made in the hour of ♀ of virgin wax in the name of the beloved, whereupon a character is written and is warmed at a fire, and in doing thereof the name of some angel must be mentioned.[700] Some here only made a heart in wax and punished the party by running pins & c. therein, perhaps in particular as people colour [?] it.[701]

699. Another example of the "Sanguis mane" charm, noted and translated manuscript page 74bis.

700. Scot, *The Discouerie of Witchcraft*, 257 (book 12, chapter 16).

701. Scot, *The Discouerie of Witchcraft*, 258 (book 12, chapter 16).

[92]

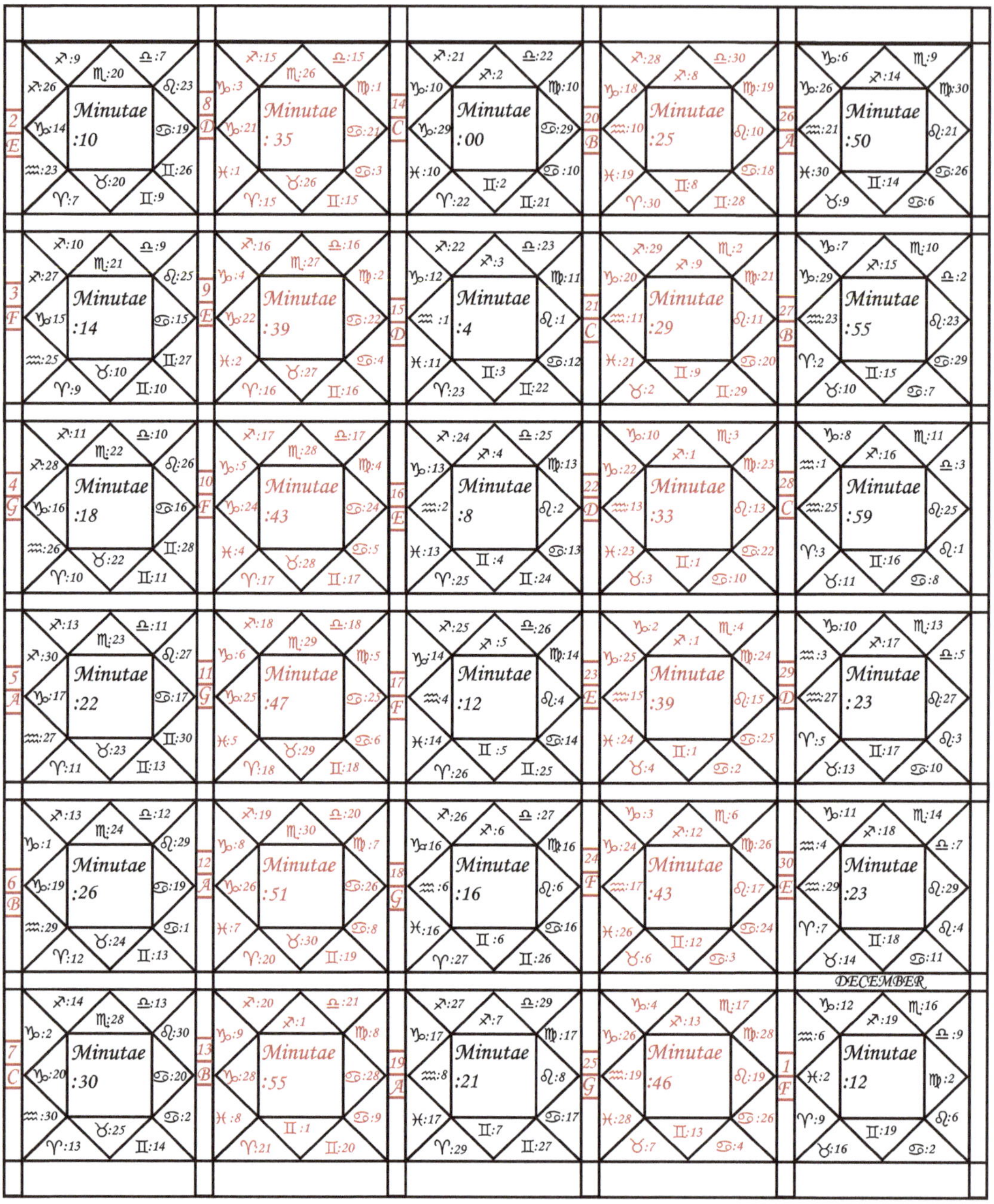
2 E
Minutae :10
8 D
Minutae : 35
14 C
Minutae :00
20 B
Minutae :25
26 A
Minutae :50
3 F
Minutae :14
9 E
Minutae :39
15 D
Minutae :4
21 C
Minutae :29
27 B
Minutae :55
4 G
Minutae :18
10 F
Minutae :43
16 E
Minutae :8
22 D
Minutae :33
28 C
Minutae :59
5 A
Minutae :22
11 G
Minutae :47
17 F
Minutae :12
23 E
Minutae :39
29 D
Minutae : 23
6 B
Minutae :26
12 A
Minutae :51
18 G
Minutae :16
24 F
Minutae :43
30 E
Minutae :23
7 C
Minutae :30
13 B
Minutae :55
19 A
Minutae :21
25 G
Minutae :46
DECEMBER
1 F
Minutae :12

Explanation of the Table, Page 78 at the Bottom[702]

First choose any figure you think proper. Write it over and under it the number of the day (as in page 84). Then take the number you shall find in said table, under the first letter of your Christian name. Add these three numbers together into one sum, and divide them by thirty, and observe if the remainder is among the good or bad fortune, and so judge the issue of any question you may propose. See this in the said *Book of Knowledge*, page 50.

702. This does not seem to correspond to the 1726 edition of the Erra Pater *Book of Knowledge* noted elsewhere.

[93]

2 G
♑:14 ♏:17 ♐:20 ♒:8 ♎:11 ♓:4 Minutae :16 ♍:4 ♈:11 ♌:8 ♊:20 ♉:17 ♋:14
8 F
♑:22 ♏:26 ♐:26 ♒:20 ♎:24 ♓:20 Minutae :43 ♍:20 ♈:24 ♌:20 ♊:26 ♉:26 ♋:22
14 E
♒:1 ♐:5 ♑:2 ♓:2 ♏:6 ♈:5 Minutae :9 ♎:5 ♉:6 ♍:2 ♋:2 ♊:5 ♌:1
20 D
♒:10 ♐:14 ♑:8 ♓:14 ♏:18 ♈:21 Minutae : 35 ♎:21 ♉:18 ♍:14 ♋:8 ♊:14 ♌:10
26 C
♒:19 ♐:22 ♑:14 ♓:26 ♏:29 ♉:5 Minutae : 1 ♏:5 ♉:29 ♍:26 ♋:14 ♊:22 ♌:19
3 A
♑:15 ♏:19 ♐:21 ♒:10 ♎:13 ♓:6 Minutae :21 ♍:6 ♈:13 ♌:10 ♊:21 ♉:19 ♋:15
9 G
♑:24 ♏:28 ♐:27 ♒:22 ♎:26 ♓:22 Minutae :47 ♍:22 ♈:26 ♌:22 ♊:27 ♉:28 ♋:24
15 F
♒:3 ♐:6 ♑:3 ♓:4 ♏:8 ♈:8 Minutae : 13 ♎:8 ♉:8 ♍:4 ♋:3 ♊:6 ♌:3
21 E
♒:11 ♐:15 ♑:9 ♓16 ♏:20 ♈:23 Minutae : 39 ♎:23 ♉:20 ♍:16 ♋:9 ♊:15 ♌:11
27 D
♒:20 ♐:23 ♑:15 ♓:28 ♐:1 ♉:7 Minutae : 5 ♏:7 ♊:1 ♍:28 ♋:15 ♊:23 ♌:20
4 B
♑:16 ♏:20 ♐:22 ♒:12 ♎:16 ♓:9 Minutae :5 ♍:9 ♈:16 ♌:12 ♊:22 ♉:20 ♋:16
10 A
♑:25 ♏:29 ♐:28 ♒:24 ♎:28 ♓:24 Minutae : 51 ♍:24 ♈:28 ♌:24 ♊:28 ♉:29 ♋:25
16 G
♒:4 ♐:8 ♑:4 ♓:6 ♏:10 ♈:11 Minutae : 17 ♎:11 ♉:10 ♍:6 ♋:4 ♊:8 ♌:4
22 F
♒:13 ♐:16 ♑:10 ♓:19 ♏:22 ♈:26 Minutae :44 ♎:26 ♉:22 ♍:19 ♋:10 ♊:16 ♌:13
28 E
♒:22 ♐:24 ♑:16 ♈:30 ♊:2 ♉:9 Minutae :10 ♏:9 ♊:2 ♍:30 ♋:16 ♊:24 ♌:22
5 C
♑:18 ♏:22 ♐:23 ♒:14 ♎:18 ♓:11 Minutae :29 ♍:11 ♈:18 ♌:14 ♊:23 ♉:22 ♋:18
11 B
♑:26 ♐:1 ♐:29 ♒:26 ♎:30 ♓27 Minutae : 5=6 ♍:27 ♈:30 ♌:26 ♊:29 ♊:1 ♋:26
17 A
♒:5 ♐:9 ♑:5 ♓:8 ♏:12 ♈:13 Minutae : 20 ♎:13 ♉:12 ♍:8 ♋:5 ♊:9 ♌:5
23 G
♒:14 ♐:18 ♑:11 ♓:21 ♏:14 ♈:28 Minutae :48 ♎:28 ♉:14 ♍:21 ♋:11 ♊:18 ♌:14
29 F
♒:23 ♐:26 ♑:17 ♓:1 ♐:4 ♉:11 Minutae : 14 ♏:11 ♊:4 ♎:1 ♋:17 ♊:26 ♌:23
6 D
♑:19 ♏:23 ♐:24 ♒:16 ♎:20 ♓:14 Minutae : 34 ♍:14 ♈:20 ♌:16 ♊:24 ♉:23 ♋:19
12 C
♑:28 ♐:2 ♐:30 ♒:28 ♍:2 ♓30 Minutae :7 ♍:30 ♉:2 ♌:28 ♊:30 ♊:2 ♋:28
18 B
♒:7 ♐:11 ♑:6 ♓:10 ♏:14 ♈:16 Minutae : 26 ♎:1 ♉:14 ♍:10 ♋:6 ♊:11 ♌:7
24 A
♒:16 ♐:19 ♑:12 ♓:23 ♏:26 ♈:30 Minutae : 52 ♎:30 ♉:26 ♍:23 ♋:12 ♊:19 ♌:16
30 G
♒:24 ♐:27 ♑:18 ♈:2 ♐:6 ♉:13 Minutae : 18 ♏:13 ♊:6 ♎:2 ♋:18 ♊:27 ♌:24
7 E
♑:21 ♉:25 ♐:25 ♒:18 ♎:22 ♓:17 Minutae :38 ♍:17 ♈:22 ♌:18 ♊:25 ♏:25 ♋:21
13 D
♑:29 ♐:4 ♑:1 ♒:30 ♏:5 ♈:3 Minutae :4 ♎:3 ♉:5 ♌:30 ♋:1 ♊:4 ♋:29
19 C
♒:18 ♐:13 ♑:7 ♓:12 ♏:16 ♈:18 Minutae :31 ♎:18 ♉:16 ♍:12 ♋:7 ♊:13 ♌:18
25 B
♒:18 ♐:20 ♑:13 ♓:25 ♏:27 ♈:3 Minutae :57 ♎:3 ♉:27 ♍:25 ♋:17 ♊:20 ♌:18
31 A
♒:26 ♐:28 ♑:19 ♈:4 ♐:7 ♉:15 Minutae :22 ♏:15 ♊:7 ♎:4 ♋:19 ♊:28 ♌:26

[On Pacts with the Devil]

Agrippa says that the words used by those in compact with the Devil to invoke him and to succeed in what they undertake are as follows: Dies, Mies, Jesquet, Benedoefet Dourina Enitamaus.[703]

Counter Charms against All Witchcrafts, and to Vex Witches[704]

"Eructavit cor meum verbum bonum dicam cuncta opera mea regi." Or these: "Domine labia mea aperies et os meum annunciabit veritatem [laudem tuum]."—Or this: "Contere brachia iniqui rei et lingua maligna subvertetur" (Psalm the 44).

703. This seems to first appear in reference to Agrippa in the treatise "De Speciebus Magiae Ceremonialis quam Goetiam Vocant," attached to Agrippa's works in the *Opera omnia* published pseudonymously under the "Beringos brothers" imprint. Here it is used during coscinomancy, or sieve and shears divination, not spirit summoning. Agrippa, *Opera*, 487–88.

704. A repeat of content given under the heading "Counter Charms in the Saying Witches Are Vexed," manuscript page 71. Translations of these charms may be found there.

[93bis]

[Astrological Connections between the Zodiacal Signs]

Explanation: from ♈ to ♊ is a sextile aspect, or 60 degrees distant, en each sign being 30 degrees distant. From ♈ to ♊ are two signs, or [a] six[th] part of a circle being a sextile ✶ From ♈ to ♑ are three signs distant, or D90 degrees as part of a circle. The above sextile is friendly, but this quartile unfriendly □ &c. &c. DFrom ♈ to ♎, oppositional.

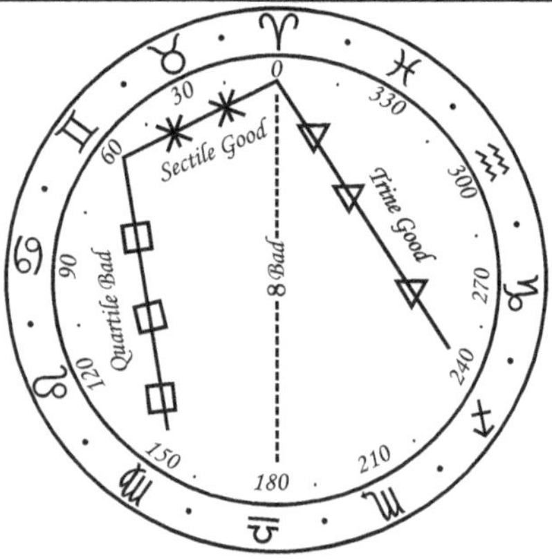

			Degrees	
Conjunction	☌	*indifferent Aspect*	0	*Parts of a Circle*
Opposition	☍	*Malign Aspect*	180	*1/2 of a Circle*
Trine	△	*Benign Aspect*	120	*3d Part of a Circle*
Quadrate	□	*Malign Aspect*	90	*4th Part of a Circle*
Sextile	✶	*Friendly Aspect*	60	*6th Part of a Circle*

The angles between two planets in conjunction are nothing; in sextile, 60; quartile, 90; in trine, 120; in opposition, 180 degrees.

[94]

III Stars

♈	1	2	3	4	5	6	7	8	9	10	11	12	13	14	15	16	17	18	19	20	21	22	23	24	25	26	27	28	29	30
♉	1	2	3	4	5	6	7	8	9	10	11	12	13	14	15	16	17	18	19	20	21	22	23	24	25	26	27	28	29	30
♊	1	2	3	4	5	6	7	8	9	10	11	12	13	14	15	16	17	18	19	20	21	22	23	24	25	26	27	28	29	30
♋	1	2	3	4	5	6	7	8	9	10	11	12	13	14	15	16	17	18	19	20	21	22	23	24	25	26	27	28	29	30
♌	1	2	3	4	5	6	7	8	9	10	11	12	13	14	15	16	17	18	19	20	21	22	23	24	25	26	27	28	29	30
♍	1	2	3	4	5	6	7	8	9	10	11	12	13	14	15	16	17	18	19	20	21	22	23	24	25	26	27	28	29	30
♎	1	2	3	4	5	6	7	8	9	10	11	12	13	14	15	16	17	18	19	20	21	22	23	24	25	26	27	28	29	30
♏	1	2	3	4	5	6	7	8	9	10	11	12	13	14	15	16	17	18	19	20	21	22	23	24	25	26	27	28	29	30
♐	1	2	3	4	5	6	7	8	9	10	11	12	13	14	15	16	17	18	19	20	21	22	23	24	25	26	27	28	29	30
♑	1	2	3	4	5	6	7	8	9	10	11	12	13	14	15	16	17	18	19	20	21	22	23	24	25	26	27	28	29	30
♒	1	2	3	4	5	6	7	8	9	10	11	12	13	14	15	16	17	18	19	20	21	22	23	24	25	26	27	28	29	30
♓	1	2	3	4	5	6	7	8	9	10	11	12	13	14	15	16	17	18	19	20	21	22	23	24	25	26	27	28	29	30

Astrologers maintain that the deluge was owing to a conjunction of all the planets in Capricorn, and the conflagration will be occasioned by their conjunction in ♋ Cancer, whence they foretell the end of the world.[705]

A ✶ is friendship, though imperfect. A conjunction is good with good planets & p. contra. A □ square, imperfect trinity. —A △ trine, true concord, love, and friendship. An ☍ opposition is an aspect of perfect hatred and the worst.

705. Chambers, *Cyclopædia*, 1:307.

[95]

[Characters of the Planets from Agrippa][706]

The seals, Letters & Characters of Saturn

Characters of ♃

Ditto ♂

Ditto ☉

Ditto ♀

Ditto ☿

Ditto ☽

If thou dost desire to attract virtue from the sun, gain love, get honour, and several other things, as plants, vegetables, metals, stones, and animals & c., these characters are chiefly to be used; as the number of the stars is known to God alone, so also their effects and seals upon these inferior things (upon any account you may form).[707]

706. Characters below are based upon the English 1651 edition of the *Three Books*. For an examination of the variations, see Vârtejaru, "Planetary Characters in Agrippa."

707. Agrippa, *Three Books of Occult Philosophy* (1651), 69–70 (book 1, chapter 34).

[96]

De Planetarum Mensulis Earum deque Virtutibus[708]

[Harum] prima *tabula* Saturni [Saturno adsignata] ex quadrato ternario *constant* [constat] continens numeros particulares, 9 et in qualibet linea 3 *quaque suum* [quaquaeversum], et per utrumque diametrum *constinentes* [constituentes] *25* [quindecim], tota autem *numerum* [numerorum] *simia* [summa], O quadraginta quinque *hinc* [huic] ex *diminis* [divinis] no[min]ibus praeficiantur praedictos mundos implentia nomina, cum intelligentia ad bonum, et demonio ad malum Elicit[ur]que ex eisdem *mundis* [numeris] signaculum sive caracter Saturni et spirituum ejus, quales inferius suae tabulae adscribemus. Dicant hanc tabulam fortunato Saturno in laminam plumbeam sculptam *adimvarem* [adiuvare] partum, reddere hominem *tutam* [tutum] et potentem atque praestare successus peticionum apud principes et potestates; si vero infortunato Saturno fiat impedire edificia et plantationes et consimilia hominem dejicere ab honoribus et dignitatibus gignere rixas et *discondias* [discordias] et dispergere *exeicitus* [exercitus].

> The first of them is assigned to Saturn, and consists of a square of three, containing the particular numbers of nine, and in every line three every way, and through each diameter making fifteen. Now the whole sum of numbers is forty-five. Over this are of divine names set such names as fill up the numbers with an intelligency to what is good, with a spirit to what is bad, and out of the same numbers is drawn the seal, or character of Saturn, and of the spirits thereof, such as we shall beneath ascribe to its table. They say that this table being with a fortune Saturn engraven on a plate of lead, doth help to bring forth, or birth, and to make a man safe, and powerful, and to cause success of petitions with princes, and powers: but if it be done with an unfortunate Saturn, that it hinders buildings, plantings, and the like, and casts a man from honours, and dignities, and causes discords, and quarrellings, and disperses an army.[709]

708. Translation: "Of the Tables of the Planets and Their Virtues." Taken from Agrippa, book 2, chapter 22. English translation is taken from Agrippa, *Three Books of Occult Philosophy* (1651), with normalised capitalisation and spelling. For a scholarly Latin edition, see the 1992 edition edited by Compagni. For a modern translation, see Agrippa, *Three Books of Occult Philosophy* (2021), 2:38–41.

709. *The first…army*: Translation from Agrippa, *Three Books of Occult Philosophy* (1651), 239–40 (book 2, chapter 22).

Secunda [dicitur] Tabula Jovis, *quo* [quae] constat *quatrinario* [quaternario] in se ducto, continens *mundos* [numeros] particulares sex-decem et in quavis linea atque diametro 4 *constinentes* [constituentes] 34, *hominum* [omnium] autem *fumam* [summam] 136. Et praesunt illi nomina divina cum intelligentia ad bonum, cum *demonum* [daemonio] ad malum, et *eliater* [eliciter] ex ea characteres Jove potente *dum antequam* [dominanteque] argenteae laminae fuit impressa, conferre lucrum, et *dimitias* [divinitas], gratiam et amorem, pacem, et concordiam hominum, et placare inimicos, confirmare honores, et dignitates, et concilia, et *disiobnere* [dissolvere] maleficia, si in corallo insculpta fuerit.

> The second is called the table of Jupiter, which consists of a quarternian drawn into itself, containing sixteen particular numbers, and in every line, and diameter four, making thirty-four. Now the sum of all is 136. And there are over it divine names with an intelligence to good, with a spirit to bad, and out of it is drawn the character of Jupiter, and the spirits thereof. They say that if it be impressed upon a silver plate with Jupiter being powerful, and ruling it, it conduceth to gain, and riches, favour, and love, peace, and concord, and to appease enemies, to confirm honours, dignities, and counsels, and dissolve enchantments if it be engraven on a coral.[710]

Tertia tabula ad Martem spectat, *qui* [quae] quinario quadrato constituitur *complectos* [complectos] *mundos* [numeros] 25 et ex his in quovis latere et diametro 5, qui faciunt sexaginta quinque et omnium *sumam* [summa] est 325. Et praesunt illi nomina *dimina* [divina] cum *intelligentiam* [intelligentia] ad bonum, et demonia ad malum et illiciter ex ea character martis *eius spiritum* [et spiritum eius]. Haec fortunato Martem in lamina ferrea aut

[97]

ense *insculpta* [sculpta] potentem facit in bello, et iudiciis, petitionibus, et tiribilem [terribilum] adversariis suis, et victoriam praestat adversus hostes: et si in lapide corneola sculpta sit, *stringet* [stringit] sanguinem et *inestrum* [menstrua]: si vero infortunato Marte sculpatur in lamina eris rubric, impedit edificia, dejicit potentes a dignitatibus, [et honoribus et divitiis, generat] discordiam et lites et odia hominum et bestiarum, generet [sic], fugat apes et columbas et pisces, impedit molendina, et infortunat euntes ad venaciones,

710. *The second…coral*: Agrippa, *Three Books of Occult Philosophy* (1651), 240 (book 2, chapter 22).

et praelia et generat sterilitatem in viris et mulieribus et ceteris *animalibus* [animantibus], adversariis[que] omnibus timorem incutit et ad reverentiam exhibendam compellit.

> The third table belongs to Mars, which is made of a square of four containing twenty-five numbers, and of these in every side and diameter five, which make sixty-five, and the sum of all is 325. And there are over it divine names with an intelligence to good, with a spirit to bad, and out of it is drawn the character of Mars, and his spirits. These with Mars being fortunate, being engraven on an iron plate, or [97] sword, makes a man potent in war, and judgments, and petitions, and terrible to his enemies, and victorious against them; and if engraven upon the stone correola, it stops blood, and the mestrues; but if it be engraven with Mars being unfortunate, on a plate of red brass, it hinders buildings, casts down the powerful from dignities, honours, and riches, and causeth discord, strife, and hatred of men, and beasts, chaseth away bees, pigeons, and fish, and hinders mills, and renders them unfortunate that go forth to hunting, or fighting, and causeth barrenness in men and women, and other animals, and strikes a terror in all enemies, and compels them to submit.[711]

Quarta tabula solis et quadrato senario *constat* [constituta est] et continent *mundes* [numeros] 36 quorum 6 in quotibus latere et diameter producunt 111 et *sumam* [summa] omnium sexcentum sexaginta sex. *Praesant* [praesunt] illi nomina *dimina* [divina] cum intelligentia ad bonum, et *demoniae* [daemonio] ad malum, et eliciuntur ex ea characteres solis et spiritum eius. Haec fortunato Sole in lamina aurea sculpta reddit, gestantem gloriosum, amabilem, gratum, potentem in omnibus operibus, et comparat hominem regibus et princi[pi]bus, *denans* [elevans] cum ad sublimia fortunae fastigial, impetrare faciens quicquid voluerit. Sole autem infortunato, facit tyrannum superbum, ambitiosum, inexplebilem et malo fine termenatum.

> The fourth table is of the sun, and is made a square of six, and contains thirty-six numbers, whereof six in every side, and diameter, produce 111, and the sum of all is 666. There are over it divine names with an intelligency to what is good, and spirit to what is evil, and out of it are drawn characters of the sun, and of the spirits thereof. This being engraven on a golden plate with the sun being fortunate, renders him that wears it to

711. *The third...submit*: Agrippa, *Three Books of Occult Philosophy* (1651), 240 (book 2, chapter 22).

be renowned, amiable, acceptable, potent in all his works, and equals a man to kings, and princes, elevating him to high fortunes, enabling to do whatsoever he pleaseth: but with an unfortunate sun, it makes a tyrant, and a man to be proud, ambitious, unsatisfiable, and to have an ill ending.[712]

Quinta tabula veneris est, constans septenario in se ducto, *mundis* [numeris] videlicet 49 quorum 7 in omni latere et diametro constituunt 175 et summa *omnia* [omnium] 1225. Et praesunt illi nomina *dimina* [divina] cum intelligentia ad bonum, et demonio ad malum, et elicitur ex ea characteres veneris et spirituum ejus. Hac fortunata venere in lamina argenti sculpta, consiliat concordiam, *dicint* [dirinit] lites, *targitur* [largitur] amores mulierum, *apud* [confert] ad conceptum, pellit sterilitatem, reddit potentes in coitu, et dissolvit maleficia, et pacem *gumral* [generat] in[ter] virum et mulierum, et quoruncunque animalium et pecorum greges copioso partu *secundat* [foecundat]; et posita in *columbam* [columbari] multiplicat

[98]

columbas confert *adulsas* [adversas] omnes agritudines *malanchollia* [melancholias], et *gegenerat* [generat] laeticiam,et gesta[ta] fortunat itinerantes; quod si infortuna[ta] Venere in ere *formantur* [formetur] omnibus praedictis contraria facit.

The fifth table is of Venus, consisting of a square of seven drawn into itself, viz., of forty-nine numbers, whereof seven on each side and diameter make 175, and the sum of all is 1225. And there are over it divine names with an intelligency to good, and spirit to evil; and there is drawn out of it the character of Venus, and of the spirits thereof. This being engraven on a silver plate, Venus being fortunate, procureth concord, endeth strife, procureth the love of women, conduceth to conception, is good against barrenness, causeth ability for generation, dissolves enchantments, and causeth peace between man, and woman, and maketh all kind of animals and cattle fruitful; and being put into a dove-house, causeth an increase [98] of pigeons. It conduceth to the cure of all melancholy distempers, and causeth joyfulness, and being carried about travellers makes them fortunate. But if it be formed upon brass with an unfortunate Venus, it causeth contrary things to all that hath been above said.[713]

712. *The fourth...ending*: Agrippa, *Three Books of Occult Philosophy* (1651), 240–41 (book 2, chapter 22).
713. *The fifth...said*: Agrippa, *Three Books of Occult Philosophy* (1651), 241 (book 2, chapter 22).

Sexta tabula ☿ est, in octonario in se ducto resultans, *mundos* [numeros] *contimens* [continens] 64 quorum octo in quovis latere et per utrumque diametrum faciunt 260, et summa omnium 2080. Et praesunt illi nomina *dimina* [divina] cum intelligentiam ad bonum, et demonio ad malum, et elicitur ex ea characteres Mercurii et spirituum ejus. Et si fuerit mercurio fortunato sculpta in argento. vel stanno vel aere citrino, vel inscripta in pergameno virgineo, reddit gestantem gratum, fortunatum ad impetrandum quicquid voluerit, confert *tucum* [lucrum] et pellit inopiam, confert memoriam et intellectum et divinationem, et noticiam occultorum per somnia; et si fuerit mercur]us infortunatus, facit his omnibus contraria.

> The sixth table is of Mercury resulting from the square of eight drawn into itself, containing sixty-four numbers, whereof eight on every side and by both diameters make 260, and the sum of all 2080, and over it are set divine names with an intelligency to what is good, with a spirit to what is evil, and from it is drawn a character of Mercury, and of the spirits thereof; and if it be with Mercury being fortunate engraven upon silver, or tin, or yellow brass, or be writ upon virgin parchment, it renders the bearer thereof grateful, and fortunate to do what he pleaseth: it bringeth gain, and prevents poverty, conduceth to memory, understanding, and divination, and to the understanding of occult things by dreams, and if it be an unfortunate Mercury, doth all things contrary to these.[714]

Septima tabula Luna est, constans et *nenenario* [novenario] in se multiplicato, ha[ben]s *mundos* [numeros] 81 in quolibet latere, et *diametro* [diametrum] 9, producentes 369, et omnium summa est 3321. Et praesunt illi no[mi]n[a] *dimina* [divina] cum intelligentiam ad bonum, et demonio ad malum voluntatem [sic], et eliciuntur ex ea characteres Lunae et spirituum ejus. *Bles* [haec] fortuna[ta] Luna in argento sculpta facit, gestantem gratum, amabilem, jucundum, alacrem, honoratum, auferens omnem militiam et malum voluntatem; praestet securitatem in *itinerem* [itinere] et profectum divitiarum, et corporis sanitatem, et pellit inimicos et alias res *nocinas* [nocivas], de quocunque loco volueris, et si ☽ infortunata fiat in lamina plumbea, ubicunque [fuerit] *sublimata* [subhumata], *infortunatur* [infortunat] locum illum et habitantes et conversantes in eo, [similiter naves, fontes, flumina, molendina; et infortunat omnem hominem, adversus quem rite facta fuerit], *et facit eos*

714. *The sixth…these*: Agrippa, *Three Books of Occult Philosophy* (1651), 241–42 (book 2, chapter 22).

[faciens illum] *profuges* [profugum] de terra *ex* [et] de patria sua, contra *vos* [quos] fuerit *sabiccala* [fabricata].

> The seventh table is of the Moon, of a square of nine multiplied into itself, having eighty-one numbers, in every side and diameter nine, producing 369, and the sum of all is 3321. And there are over it divine names with an intelligency to what is good, and a spirit to what is bad. And of it are drawn the characters of the moon, and of the spirits thereof. This fortunate moon being engraven on silver, renders the bearer thereof grateful, amiable, pleasant, cheerful, honoured, removing all malice, and ill will. It causeth security in a journey, increase of riches, and health of body, drives away enemies and other evil things from what place thou pleasest; and it if be an unfortunate moon engraven in a plate of lead, where ever it shall be buried, it makes that place unfortunate, and the inhabitants thereabouts, [as also ships, rivers, fountains, mills, and it makes every man unfortunate, against which it shall be directly done,] making him fly from his country, and that place of his abode where it shall be buried, and it hinders physicians and orators, and all men whatsoever in their office, against whom it shall be made.[715]

Magic Squares[716]

This Table of ♄ in His Compass

4	9	2
3	5	7
8	1	6

Saturn

The square of three belongs to ♄ four to ♃, five to ♂, six to the ☉ seven to ♀, eight to ☿, nine to the ☽.

ד	ט	ב
ג	ה	ז
ח	א	ו

The square of three belongs to ♄, four to ♃, five to ♂, six to the ☉, seven to ♀, eight to ☿, nine to the ☽.

715. *The seventh…made*: Agrippa, *Three Books of Occult Philosophy* (1651), 242 (book 2, chapter 22). Bracketed areas indicate omitted sections from the Latin in the manuscript.

716. What I present here are the manuscript's squares in all their flawed glory, in hope that these errors might allow us to identify other manuscripts from the same tradition. Those seeking accurate reproductions should consult Agrippa.

[99]

Divine names answering to the number of Saturn 3. abt—9. Hod. 15; Jah, 15; Hod, 45. Jehovah extended.
45. Agiell. The intelligence of ♄
45. Zazell. The spirit of ♄

The Table of ♃ in His Compass

The Table of ♃ in His Compass

4	14	15	1
9	7	6	12
5	11	10	8
16	2	3	13

Jovis

In Hebrew notes

ד	יד	טו	א
ט	ז	ו	יב
ה	יא	י	ח
יו	ב	ג	יג

Of Jupiter *Intelligence of ♃* *Spirit of ♃*

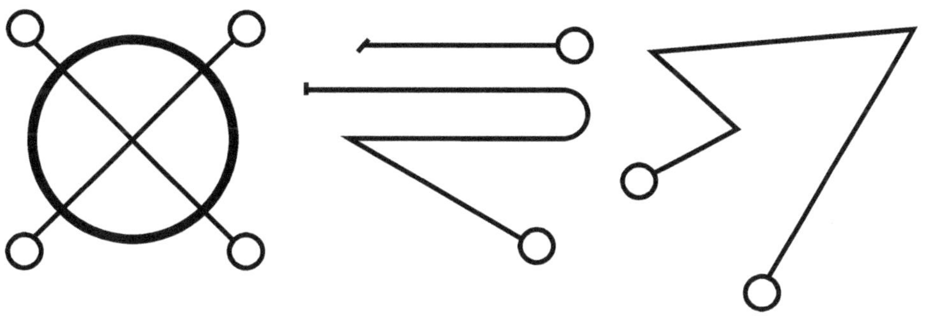

Divine names answering to the number of ♃

4. *Abab* [Abba]
16 34 . El ab.
16[717]

136: Iophiel: The intelligence of Jupiter.
136. Hismael: The spirit of Ditto.

717. The published editions of Agrippa provide no English text here but do include the Hebrew words הוה and אהי.

[100]

The Table of Mars in His Compass

The Table of Mars in his Compas

11	24	7	20	3
4	12	25	8	6
17	5	13	21	9
10	18	1	14	22
23	6	19	2	15

Mars

In Hebrew notes

יא	כד	ז	כ	ג
ד	יב	כה	ח	ו
יז	ה	יג	כא	ט
י	יח	א	יד	כב
כג	ו	יט	ב	יה

Of ♂ Seals & Characters

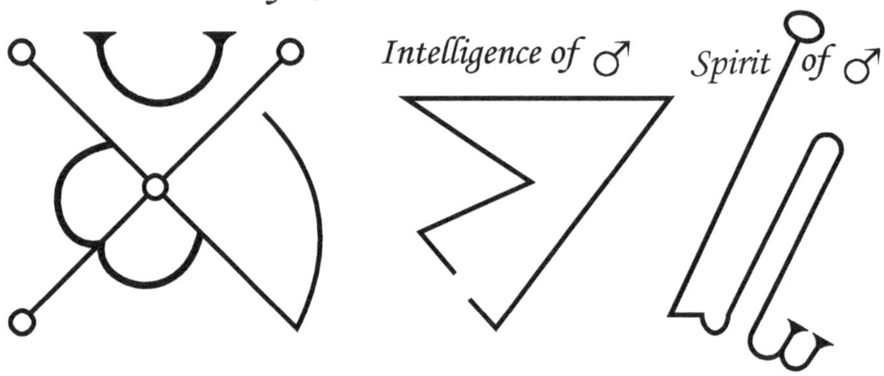

♂ Divine names answering to the number of Mars
5 he hath the letter of the Holy name ה

25		
65	Adonay	
325	The intelligence of ♂	Graphiel
325	The spirit of ♂	Barzabel

The Table of the ☉ in His Compass[718]

The table of the ☉ in his Compas

32	3	34	35	1
11	27	28	8	30
14	16	15	23	14
26	22	21	17	23
29	10	9	26	12
5	33	4	2	31

Sol

In Hebrew notes

ו	לב	ג	לד	לה	א
ז	יא	כז	כח	ח	ל
יט	יד	יו	יה	כג	כד
יח	כ	כב	כא	יז	יג
כה	כט	י	ט	כו	יב
לו	ה	לג	ד	ב	לא

[101]

Sol

Intelligence ☉

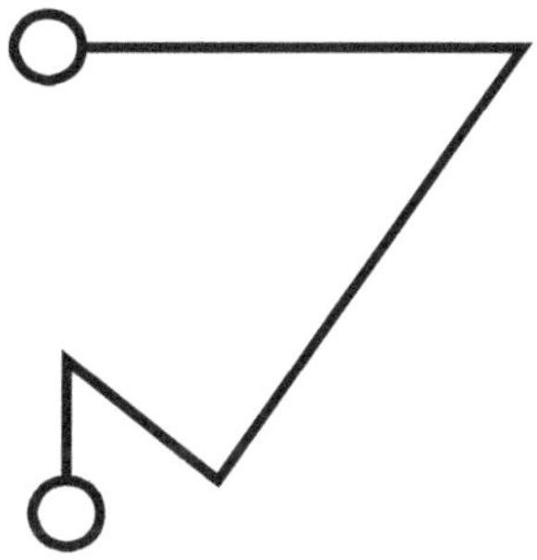

Spirit of ☉

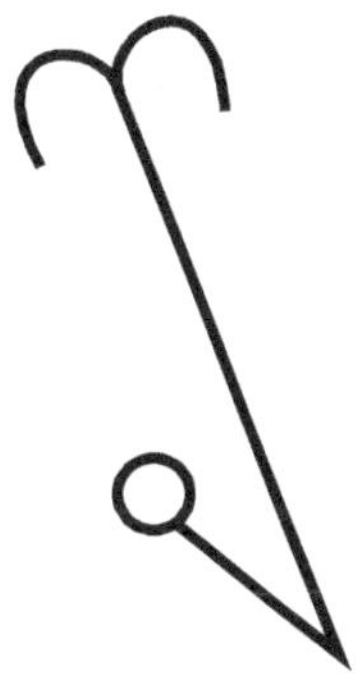

Names answering to the number of the sun
6 Vau, the letter of the holy name
6 He extended, the Letter of the holy name
56 Eloh. 111 Nachiel—The intelligence of the sun
666 Sorath—The spirit of the sun.

718. This magic square has accidentally omitted the left-hand column.

The Table of Venus in his Compass

22	47	16	41	10	25	4
5	23	48	17	42	11	29
30	6	24	49	18	36	12
13	31	7	25	43	19	37
38	14	32	1	26	44	20
21	38	8	33	2	27	45
46	15	40	9	34	3	28

In Hebrew Notes

כב	מז	יו	מא	י	לה	ד
ה	כג	מח	יז	מב	יא	כט
ל	ו	כד	מט	יח	לו	יב
יג	לא	ז	כה	מג	יט	לז
לח	יד	לב	א	כו	מד	כ
כא	לח	ח	לג	ב	כז	מה
מו	יה	מ	ט	לד	ג	כח

of Venus *Intelligence of ♀*

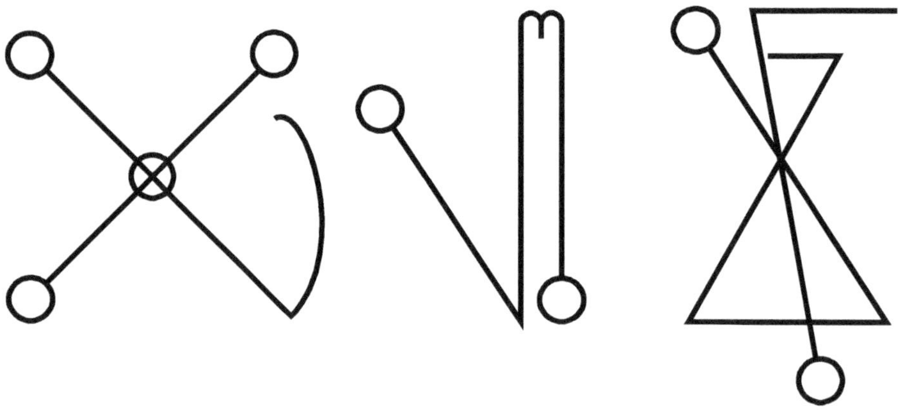

[102]

[The Table of Venus in Her Compass]

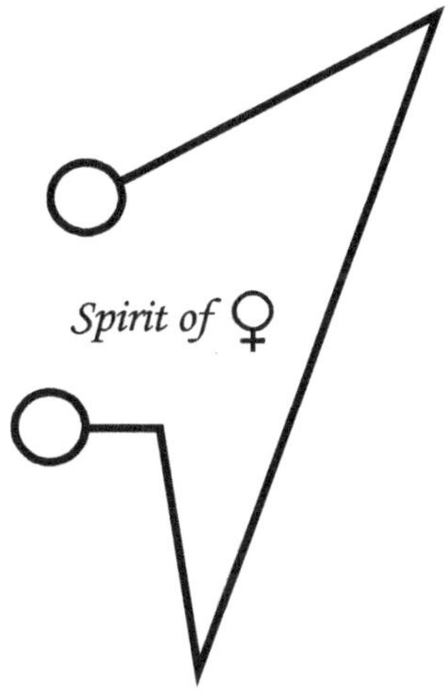

names answering to the number of Venus

.7	49 Hagiel—the intelligence of ♀
157	Kedemel—the spirit of ♀
1252	The Seraphim—the intelligences of ♀

[The Table of Mercury in His Compass][719]

The Table of Mercury in his Compass

8	58	59	5	4	62	63	1
49	15	14	52	53	11	10	56
41	23	22	44	45	19	18	45
32	34	38	29	25	38	39	25
40	26	27	37	36	30	31	33
17	47	45	20	21	43	41	24
9	55	54	12	13	51	50	16
64	2	3	61	60	6	7	57

☿

The sixth last word of the sixth line downwards is placed in the fifth and the fifth line and in the 6

In Hebrew Notes

ח	נח	נט	ה	ד	סב	סג	א
מט	יה	יד	נב	נג	יא	י	נו
מא	כג	כב	מד	מה	יט	יח	מה
לב	לד	לח	כט	כה	לח	לט	כה
מ	כו	מה	כ	כא	מג	מב	כד
יז	מז	כז	לז	לו	ל	לא	לג
ח	נה	נד	יב	יג	נא	נ	יו
סד	ב	ג	סא	ס	ו	ז	נז

of ☿

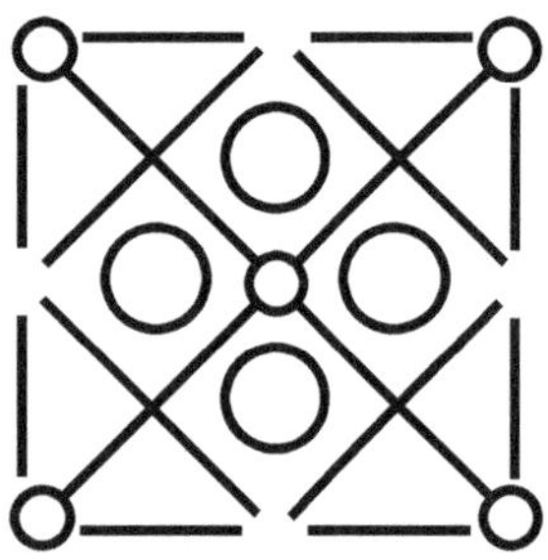

Intelligence of ☿

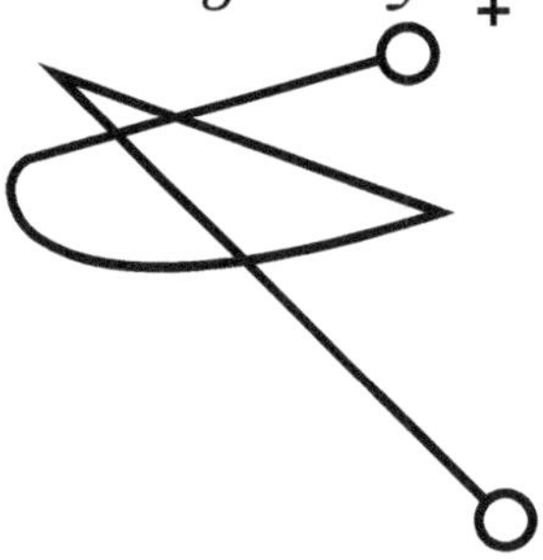

Spirit of Mercury

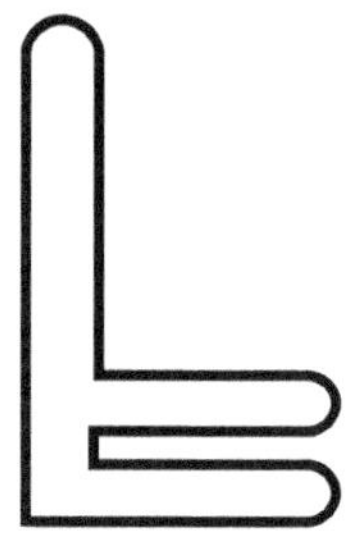

Names answering to the number of Mercury

8	Asboga—eight extented
64	Din 64 Doni
260	Ctitiel—the intelligence of ☿
2080	Taphtharath—the spirit of ☿

719. The illustration of the intelligence of Mercury that follows is tilted in such a manner to indicate it comes from the English language text. Agrippa, *Three Books of Occult Philosophy*, 249 (book 2, chapter 22).

[102bis]

[The Table of the Moon in Her Compass][720]

The Table of the ☽ in Her Compass

37	75	29	70	21	62	19	45	5
6	35	79	30	71	22	63	14	46
47	7	39	80	31	72	23	55	15
16	45	8	40	81	32	64	24	56
57	17	49	9	41	73	33	68	25
26	55	18	50	1	42	74	34	66
67	27	59	10	51	2	43	78	35
36	68	19	60	11	52	3	44	76
77	28	69	20	61	12	53	4	45

In Hebrew Notes

לז	עה	כט	ע	כא	סב	יג	מה	ה
ו	לה	עט	ל	עא	כב	סג	יד	מו
מז	ז	לט	פ	לא	עב	כג	נה	יה
יו	מה	ח	מ	פא	לב	סד	כד	נו
נז	יז	מט	ט	מא	עג	לג	סח	כה
כו	נה	יח	נ	א	מב	עד	לד	סו
סז	כז	נט	י	נא	ב	מג	עח	לה
לו	סח	יט	ס	יא	נב	ג	מד	עו
עז	כח	סט	כ	סא	יב	נג	ד	מה

Of the Moon

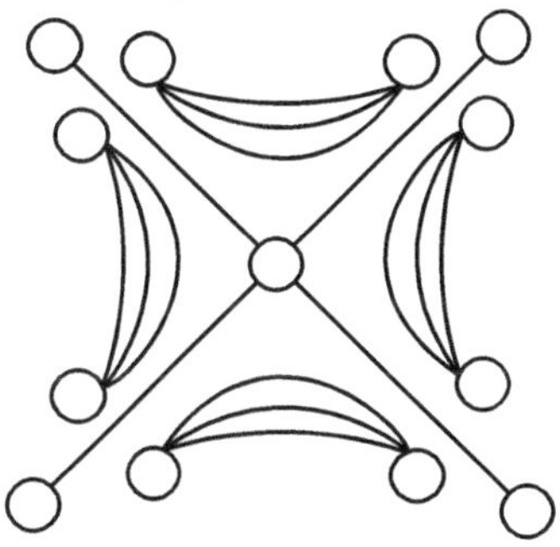

Of the Spirit of the Moon

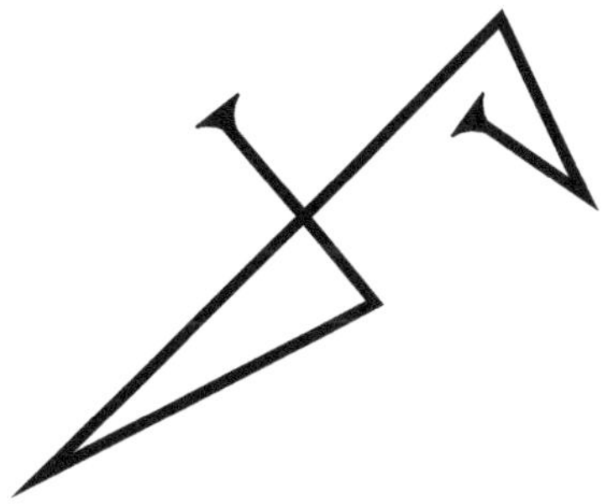

Of the Spirit of the Spirits of the ☽

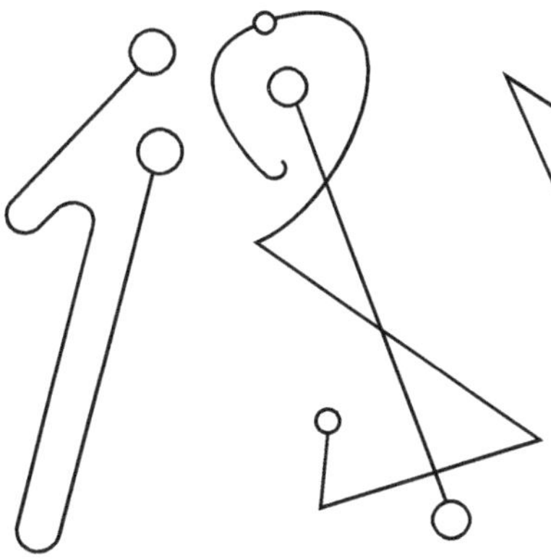

Of the Intelligences of the Intelligences of the ☽

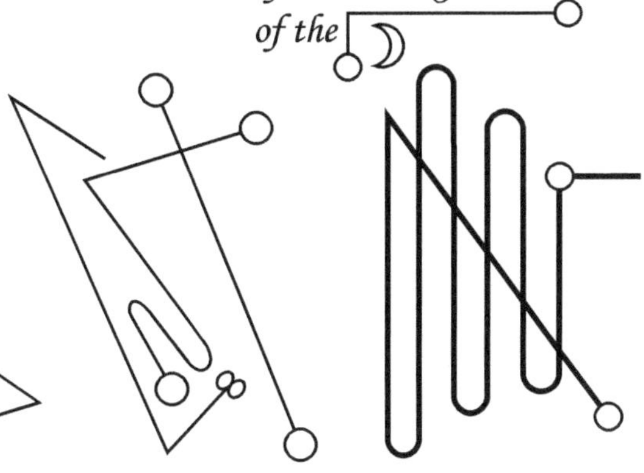

Names answering to the number of the moon

720. Some of the errors on this table are present in the English Agrippa, instead of being errors of the copyist.

Hod

9 Hod—eight extended

81 Elim 369 Hasmodai—the spirit of the ☽

3321 Schedbarscemoth Schartathan the spirit of the spirits of the ☽

3321 intelligence of the intelligences, of the ☽ Malcha, betharsisim hed beruah Schehakim

[103]

Night-Spell[721]

"On three crosses made of tree, three dead bodies did hang. Two were thieves, the third were Christ's, and who in our belief is Dismas et Gismas, Christ amidst them, was Dismas to heaven, went Gismas to hell, was sent Christ that died on the rood for Mary's love. Save us and our good within and without, and all this place about, and though the virtue of his might, let no thief enter in this night, no farther upon this place which I myself go upon, but at my bidding, they be bound to all things I bid them do. Stark be their sinews therewith and their limbs mightless,[722] and their eyes sightless, deadliness and doubt them be close round about, as a wall wrought of stone, so be the cramp in the toe, a cramp and croaking and faint in their failing footing. The night of trinity, save these goods and me, in the name of Jesus Christ betokening[723] the holy and the holy benedicite[724] all about our goods be, within and without, and this place round about." Dic[725] Pater Noster, five Aves, five Creeds, in honorem quinque plagarum Christi et duodecem apostolorum.[726]

Alter[727]

"To the Holy Ghost, I bequeath my goods that in place are set,
And to the Father and the Son, all thieves that come to let,[728]
If any thieves do hither come, my goods away to fetch,
The Holy Ghost be them, before, because them to be let,
And make them here still to abide, till I again do come,
Though the virtue of the Holy Ghost, the Father, and the Son.
Now I go my way a while, betide what may betide.
If any thieves shall hither come, here they shall abide,
Though the great virtue of St. Mark, St. Matthew, Luke, and John,
The holy four Evangelists according, all in one.

721. An example of the "Dismas et Iesmas" charm. Roper, *English Verbal Charms*, 103–4; this manuscript, pages 1 and 232.

722. *Mightless*: Weak.

723. *Betokening*: Presaging, showing.

724. *Benedicite*: A blessing, especially at the table.

725. *Dic*: Translation: "Say."

726. *In honorem…apostolorum*: Translation: "In honour of the five wounds of Christ and of the twelve apostles."

727. *Alter*: Translation: "The Other." Compare Sloane 3160, 137v–138r.

728. *Let*: Prevent.

I bind you thieves, which come so fast, do your way assure
As did St. Bartholomew the Devil with his long beard so hoar.
Thieves, stand you still, if you to fetch my goods do enterprise
By virtue of Christ his Cross, his passion and uprise,[729]
And per the night of the Holy Ghost, the Father, and the Son,
Still that you stand as any stone, till I again do come,

[104]

"This place is set in Christ's cross, and in Saint Mary's field,
No thieves that come shall hence away, but fast their bodies yield.
Christ which was born at Bethlehem and offered at Jerusalem
And baptised in the flood Jordan, and suffered with a crown of thorns,
Save all the goods that herein is, that thereof nothing I do miss,
Neither within, near, nor without, of this place comfort round about.
Saint Peter said thieves send about, Saint Paul hath said they shall not out,
Their hands I hast, their feet I fetter, whether they be worse or better,
Their tongues I close till morrow day, until I bid them go away."

Dic[730] Pater [Noster], three Aves, three Creeds.

When You Are in Dread of Thieves and Your Enemies[731]

Say, "Sanctus Jesus autem transiens per medium eorum ibat,"[732] and also keep verses of the Psalter three times: "*Irruat* [inruat] super eos formido et *favor* [pavor] in magnitudine brachii tui, fiant immobiles quasi lapis donec pertranseat populus *tuorum* [tuus], Domine, et populus iste quem redemisti me?"[733]

Ad Ligandum Fures[734]

Go to the place from whence a thief hath stolen any thing, and write the names of the suspected persons in parchment, and put the same under the

729. *Uprise*: Resurrection.

730. *Dic*: Translation: "Say."

731. This charm first appears in the works attributed to Sir John Mandeville, although the word "Sanctus" is not included in the beginning. Mandeville, *Boke of Iohn Maunduyle*, 47. See manuscript page 210.

732. *Sanctus…ibat*: Vulgate Luke 4:30, modified. Translation (KJV, modified): "But holy Jesus, passing through the midst of them, went his way."

733. *Irruat…Domine*: Vulgate Exodus 15:16, modified at the end. Translation (KJV, modified): "Fear and dread shall fall upon them; by the greatness of thine arms they shall be as still as a stone; till thy people pass over, O Lord, and your people which thou hast redeemed."

734. Translation: "For Binding Thieves." Raphael would later publish this as an extract from an "Ancient Manuscript." Raphael, *The Familiar Astrologer*, 45.

threshold where he or they went out. And then make four crosses on the four corners or posts thereof, and then go your way saying, "Thou thief, which hath stolen and taken away such a thing N. from this place, Abraham, per his virtue and power God gave him, call thee back again; Isaac per his power stop thee in the way; Jacob make thee go no farther, but bring it again, and Toby[735] per his power and virtue, and also per the grace and might of the Holy Ghost, force thee to come again into this place, and that neither Solomon let thee, nor David bind thee, but that the same, through Christ our Lord, do cause thee presently and without stay to come again into this place, and bring thee the N. with thee. Fiat, fiat, fiat. Cito, cito, cito,[736] in nomine Patris et Filii et Spiritus Sancti. Amen."

[105]

The Virtue of a Mandrake[737]

Whosoever can get any of this rare creature shall have continual joy without sorrow, wealth without want, and be warded from all evil and sudden death and mischance. He shall never be robbed nor killed, but overcome all his enemies in what nature soever. This is plainly proved.

To Know If a Woman Be Honest or Not, or If Anyone Hath Told You a Lie or Not, per a Table[738]

Take the woman's name, and her mother's name [in] Latin,[739] and add fifteen to the names, and divide them per nine, and if the product is even, she is honest; odd, dishonest.

A	*B*	*C*	*D*	*E*	*F*	*G*	*H*	*I*	*K*	*L*	*M*	*N*	*O*	*P*	*Q*	*R*	*S*	*T*	*U*	*X*
10	*2*	*22*	*4*	*14*	*6*	*10*	*7*	*18*	*10*	*11*	*12*	*4*	*14*	*6*	*16*	*8*	*18*	*10*	*2*	*12*

Y	*Z*
4	*14*

For the lie, write his name in Latin, and the day he told it, and add the number of the letters above together, and divide them per seven, If the product be odd, untrue; even, true.

735. *Toby*: Raphael's version has "Joseph."
736. *Cito*: Translation: "Quickly."
737. Reprinted as a passage from the "MSS. Key to Agrippa." Raphael, *The Familiar Astrologer*, 233–34.
738. Reprinted in Raphael, *Raphael's Witch*, 141.
739. For Latinised names, see the chart at the very end of this book.

Ut Saltent Homines[740]

Write in cera virginae, on virgin wax "+ Epos + Medula + Centus + Sedula," unosque [?] sub limine et fiet donec auferatur.[741]

Propter Epilipsiam[742] G. S.

"In nomine dei, amen. In principio erat verbum, [et verbum erat apud Deum], et Deus erat verbum."[743]

Scribas usque ad hoc verbum,[744] "comprehenderunt."[745] [Then:]

"'+ N + In nomine Patris, hoc scriptum facio + in nomine Filii, hoc scriptum continuo + in nomine Spiritus Sancti, hoc scriptum concludo + N + Ananizapta & c. +' Tunc:[746] '+ N + Jasp[er] fert mirrham, & c.,'[747] 'ut ulterius invenies in hoc libro, ubi hanc literam N *offenderus* [ostendens][748]; stat per nominibus paticulis totiusque conscribere debes, tum proxime pergas ut sequitur.'[749] + N + Robam, Malaron, Macharon, Magoll, Rabale, Machare, Vagen, Polaza, Kanop, Garnael Talamite, Azaga, Sebamay, Alcarice; Malxipe, + N + Ely + Adonay + Tegramaton + Sophyr + Mechat + Raba + Satyr + Alpha, + Satonay + Durissimus + Achor + Diclary + Elchior + Necior, + Bibas + N + Alma, Chorus Domini, *Paracletas* [Paracletus], Messias, Hosanna, Hosanna Hosana, Christus vincit + Christus regnat + Christus et [sic] imperat, + Christus dignus per virtutem hujus scripti, defende me, N.,

740. Translation: "So That Men May Dance."

741. *In cera…auferatur*: Translation: "On virgin wax '+ Epos + Medula + Centus + Sedula,' and place it under the threshold, and it will be done until it is taken away.

742. Translation: "For Epilepsy."

743. *In nomine…erat verbum*: The latter part is from Vulgate John 1:1, with the omitted section added in brackets. Translation (KJV 1:1, modified): "In the beginning was the Word, [and the Word was with God], and the Word was God."

744. *Scribas…verbum*: Translation: "You should write until this word."

745. *Comprehenderunt*: That is, Vulgate John 1:1–5.

746. *+ n…& c.*: Translation: "+ N + In the name of the Father, I begin this writing + in the name of the Son, I continue this writing without interruption + in the name of the Holy Ghost, I complete this writing + N. Ananizapta & c. Then: "For the likely cham implied by "Ananizapta," see manuscript page 65.

747. *+ N.…& c.*: Translation: "+ N + Jasper brought myrrh, & c."

748. This refers to the material on manuscript page 48, although the letter "N." does not seem to appear alongside this passage."

749. *Ut ulterius…sequitur*: Translation: "as you will find further above in this book, where this letter N. is showing; It stands with the sections with names. And you should write all of these, then next continue as follows."

[106]

"+ N + ab omni malo ab sede ad Gehennam, Vadasuall, Giel, Verbim, per signum sanctae crucis + in nomine dei + Emanuel, + + + Amen."[750]

You must first put it into this writing, some of the secundine[751] skin, with a few roots of daffodils, then wrap it up and sow it a small silk bag to hang about the party's neck, who must precisely forebear eating on Fridays.

To Know If the Suspected Person Hath Stolen the Things or Not[752]

First write all the names of the suspected persons per himself in a several[753] piece of parchment. Then close them up in a little ball of stiff clay. Then take a piece of chalk therewith, and make a circle on a plain table, making a cross within it, and write therein "Agla" in the day and hour of ♄. Then set a basin of a fair water in the midst of the circle, into which put the balls with the names, and crossing the water over with these words, "In nomine Patris et Filii et Spiritus Sancti, amen." Then, looking into the water, say this conjuration three times, and if his name be there which hath done the feat, the ball will break, and the name will swim aloft on the water, and whereper you may perfectly know him.

"I conjure thee, water, per the living God, per the holy God which, per the hand of the prophet Elizaus, didst make sweet the water infected with bitterness. I conjure [thee], water, per the blessed lamb of God, our only dear saviour, the only begotten son of the most high God, who turned water into pleasant sweet wine, at the marriage in Cana in Galilee. I conjure thee, water, per him which said and defended Peter from sinking and drowning. I conjure thee, water, per these holy names of God, Messias, Sater, Emanuel, and per the virtue and power of the inestimable word of God, Te[tra]gramaton, and per these holy names of God, Agla and Adonai, Homousion, and per the virtue and power of the holy Blessed Virgin Mary, mother of our Lord Jesus Christ, and per all other words and sayings per that which he mayst

750. *Christus vincit…amen*: Translation: Christ conquers + Christ rules + Christ commands + worthy Christ, by virtue of this writing, defend me, N. [106] "+ N + from every evil from the seat to Gehenna, Vadasuall, Giel, Verbim, by the sign of the Holy Cross + in the name of God + Emmanuel, +++ Amen."

751. *Secundine*: Placental.

752. For the closest version, see Sloane MS 3846, 43r–44r. For other versions, see Sloane MS 3846, 71v; Sloane 3851, 55r–v; Cambridge Additional 3544, 46–7; Kittredge, *Witchcraft in Old and New England*, 192–93; Harms, Clark, and Peterson, *Oberon*, 417; Harms and Clark, *Of Angels*, 116–17. For the condemnation of the process by the 1287 Synod of Exeter, see Wilkins, *Concilia Magnae Britanniae et Hiberniae*, vol. 2, 162.

753. *Several*: Distinct.

be constrained, that thou wilt manifest unto me and to my fellows the truth of whom committed this theft, if that his name be contained amongst these suspected persons, so many as be guilty cast up from the rest that they may swim aloft, that I or we may

[107]

"know who hath done this fact. Per this we enterprise this experiment, per this plain and manifest token. But if the name of suspected person and guilty in this deed be not contained here, I conjure and constrain thee per the eternal God, and all his holy names, to keep and detain them under, that we may not argue, suspect, blame, or condemn any without just and lawful cause. Dear Lord, grant this be done, quickly, quickly, quickly. Amen."

This must be said three times. and if the name swim not per the time you have so said, you must say "Quicunque vult,"[754] & c., and "Deus deorum dominus"[755] with three Pater [Nosters], three Aves, and one Creed, in the worship of the Father, the Son, and the Holy Ghost. Without doubt, if the name be there, it will swim atop; else, not.

To Know the Estate of Friends Far from Thee[756]

Take an egg which was laid on a Thursday and in a such a day of the ☽ when the ☽ is seven, ten, or twenty, or, as some will, seven, twelve, or twenty days old. Then anoint the egg with oil olive, and go into a dark house where the beams of the ☉ shineth, and then say,

"I conjure thee, egg, per the living God, the creator of all things, and per the virtue which moves in the heavens and in the earth, and per all things which God created, that thou certify and assure me, how N. of M. doeth, and in what state he is in."

Then look upon the egg towards the beams of the ☉, and thou shalt see the likeness of another, and if he be well, whose state you would know whether he be dead or recovered of his sickness, in the elevation you shall see as before, and you shall know it of a certain.

754. *Quincunque vult*: The Athanasian Creed.

755. *Deus...dominus*: Vulgate Psalm 49.

756. For other examples, see Marathakis, *The Magical Treatise of Solomon or Hygromanteia,* 121, 200.

Experiment for Thieves, or Any Other Thing

First make a little coffin[757] of barley flour and water in form of a custard,[758] one inch broad or less, and put therein some good oil olive, and let a child look therein, holding it in your hand, east and west, with this form written thereon as followeth, and repeat the words beneath very often, and they shall appear, the truth of all your desire

[108]

[To Know the Intentions of Others]

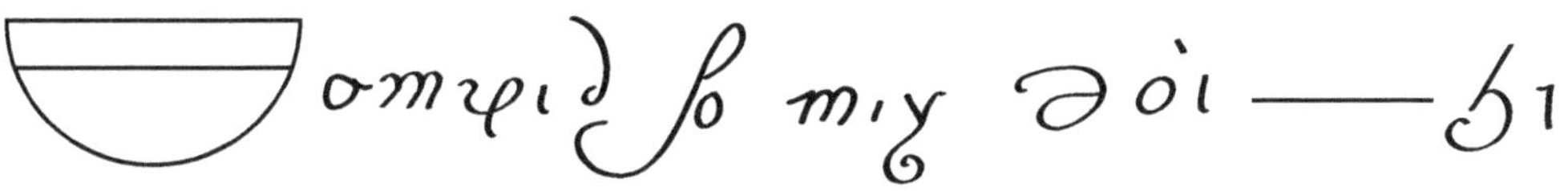

By this rule before set down, he that can understand the use thereof may know what business any one hath with him or cometh about to ask for before he speech with him.

An Experiment to See per Thyself, without a Boy or Companion, the Spirits under Written in a Crystal Which Will Shew the Truth without Fail of All Things Doubtful as of These, Manslaughter, Treasure Being Hid, of the State of Thy Friend Being Absent, of Secrets, of Things Lost[759]

First say this prayer:

757. *Coffin*: This can be used both in today's sense, and as a pie crust.

758. *Custard*: Probably an open sort of pie in this sense.

759. For further examples, see Sloane 3846, 37r–v; Harms, Clark, and Peterson, *Oberon*, 533–37, Harms and Clark, *Of Angels*, 136–38, and manuscript page 136.

"Lord Jesus Christ, let thy virtues and mercies appear, which made all things with thy right hand, God of Abram, of Isaac, and Jacob, God of Ely or Haly and Toby, which didst deliver the three children Sidrach, Misach, and Abedenigo, which didst deliver Tecta out of the wars, Margaret out of pain, and Susanna from her false accusers, Daniel out of the lion den, which didst heal the man lying sick on the palsy, and didst heal the woman of Canaan of her bloody issue, which didst vanquish devils and didst raise Lazarus from death, which didst preserve Abraham in his age, and suffered him to see thee in the true Trinity, grant, I beseech thee, I may see these spirits, without hurt: Alkaley, Walcates, Mucon, Mucriton, Balto, Bosco, that they appear to me in this crystal stone, and may shew me the truth of things past, present, and to come hereafter, when I do ask them, and they being bound per the power may fulfil all my desire, which with God the Father, God the Son, and God the Holy Ghost liveth and reigneth, & c. Amen."

NB: Go on; this under line should not have been drawn.[760]

Then hold the stone a little while in a piece of hart's leather in thy right hand towards the ☉, but take care thou be not polluted with love seven days before, and say,

"In the name of the Holy Trinity, the Father, the Son, and the Holy Ghost, and of the high deity, I look upon this stone."

[109]

And then say:

"I conjure ye, Alkates, Walcates, Muron, Mucriton, Bosco, et Bafeo[761] vel Balko, which do inhabit the woods, that ye be ready to fulfil my precepts in obeying my will. I conjure ye, Alcates, Walcates, Muron, Macriton, Balco, et Bosco, per the Father, the Son, the Holy Spirit, per him which is A and Ω, per the dreadful day of judgment, per the merits of all saints, per the terrible and unspeakable names of God, that thou, Alcates, come without stay or let into this crystal stone in thy proper person and in a decent form, bearing on thy head a crown, and that shew unto me thy self, and bring thy fellows with thee, and that I may see them transformed in man's shape, per all the virtues of God, and do that which I shall command you. And further, I conjure thee

760. The original copyist accidentally drew a dividing line here.

761. The original scribe tries to correct this name with superscript text, but it's unclear what spelling they would prefer.

per the Blessed Virgin Mary the Mother of God, and per all saints of God, and per all things which are in heaven, in earth, in the sea, in hell, and all things which are procreate or made, I condemn thee (or you) into hell, Alkates, Walkates, Muron, Mucriton, Balko, and Bosco, per the virtues of our Lord Jesus *S.* [Christ], the son of almighty God, and per the names of all saints, and I command you to be cast into everlasting fire, unless you come quickly and fulfil my desire."

Thus done, if he or they come, ask what you will, and they will shew it; if they will not, say:

"I conjure Alcates, Walcates, Maron, Mucriton, Balko, Bosco, into the everlasting fire of hell, per the virtue of the true and living God, and per the power that God hath given you, that you be always bound in hell with fiery chains and suffer the pains of fire, until you appear unto me in this stone, neither fearing and hurting me, but to fulfil my mind."

If they will not appear the first day thou call them, call the second and the third day, and they shall come and answer truly to all thy requests. And take heed thou do not presume to thy work on a holy day, or in cloudy weather, because it may not be done but when the ☉ may be seen. Thou must be void from sin if thou do wilt do it, and most especially from the secrets of women, and from women that are corrupt.

[110]

The Consecration of the Crystal

"I conjure and exorcise thee, crystal stone or glass, per the head corner stone, which is a right stone, which is the holy mother of the church, and per that Christ which is a rock, and is called a stone, that the spirit entering into thee, though the virtue given to thee of God, he may not have power to lie nor deceive me in the things which I will ask him, in nomine Patris, et Filii, et Spiritus Sancti. Amen."

The Consecration of the Oil

"Coniuro te, oleum, per setum[762] *baptismum* [baptismatis] dei, et per illum setum quod tres mariae portaverunt ad sepulchrum Christi, ut sis tenax in pollice istius pueri N. quod non noceatur insidiis vel dolis diabolicus, in nomine Patris et Filii et Spiritus Sancti. Amen."

762. *Setum*: I cannot find this word anywhere, so I am translating it based upon context.

"I conjure thee, oil, by the oil of the baptism of God, and by the oil that the three Marys carried to the tomb of Christ, that you may be steadfast in the thumb of this boy N., that he may not be harmed by diabolic snares and artifices, in the name of the Father, and of the Son, and of the Holy Ghost. Amen."

When the Spirit Is Entered into the Glass & c.

"I conjure thee, crystal, per the virtue per which the stones rent graves did open and many saints did rise, and appear that thou so part thy self in the mids, or midst, that per thee, and in thee, all things may be discerned, seen, and perceived, and heard of N. .N., which we court to hear and see, per and of the angel we have adjured, viz. Salmomon[763] or any other, in nomine Patris et Filii et Spiritus Sancti. Amen."

To Cause an 1 + O L U[764] to Appear in a Crystal Stone[765]

Turn into the east and make a cross with the holy oil on a crystal stone, or under the cross, write "Sancta *Halena* [Helena]." Then take a child lawfully begotten in matrimony under ten years old, or thereabouts, and let him hold the crystal in his right hand behind his back. Then, kneeling on thy knees, shall, with great devotion and reverence, say and rehearse this prayer following three times:

"Deprecor te, domina *setam* [sancta] *Helenam* [Helena], mater regis *Constantim* [Constantini], qui crucem domini nostri Jesu Christi invenisti, et per illam sanctissimam devotionem et inventionem crucis, et per illam sanctissimam crucem, per illum *gradium* [gaudiam] quod habuisti *quanum* [quando] illam sanctissimam crucem invenisti, et per illam dilectionem quam verax [circa] filium tuum [regem] Constantissimum [Constantinum]

[111]

"habuisti, et per *illam summam* [illa summa] bona quibus frueris *interim* [aeternaliter], ut *digneris* [debeas] dimonstrare mihi in hoc crystallo quicquid peto et scire cupio. Amen."

763. *Salmomon*: A likely corruption of King Solomon. Summoning Solomon would not have been unknown to magicians of this period; Sir Humphrey Gilbert and John Davis recorded a series of rites that involved conversations with his spirit. Legard and Cummins, *An Excellent Booke*, 119ff.

764. Deciphered: "Angel."

765. Cardano, *De Rerum Varietate*, 640. For Scot's version, see manuscript pages 71–72.

"I pray to thee, holy lady Helen, mother of King Constantine, who found the cross of our lord Jesus Christ, and by that most holy piety and discovery of the cross, and by that most holy cross, and by that joy thou hadst when thou foundest that most holy cross, and by the love that thou hadst [111] for thy son Constantine, and by those highest goods that thou enjoyest eternally, so thou shouldst show to me in this crystal whatsoever I ask and desire to know. Amen."

Digneris vel sit debeas.[766]

Now when the child doth see the angel, answer to him truly and effectually. This must be done ortu ☉ apparenti, celoque sereno.[767]

To Prove Theft

Write these characters in paper, and then wrap this writing into red sealing wax, and upon the wax make three crosses, saying to every cross, "Bricii, Benisci, Bricii, Breve, Bricii, Bevisci." This being well done, lay the wax under thy head when thou goest to bed, and thou shalt dream of the thief and shall find the thing stolen.

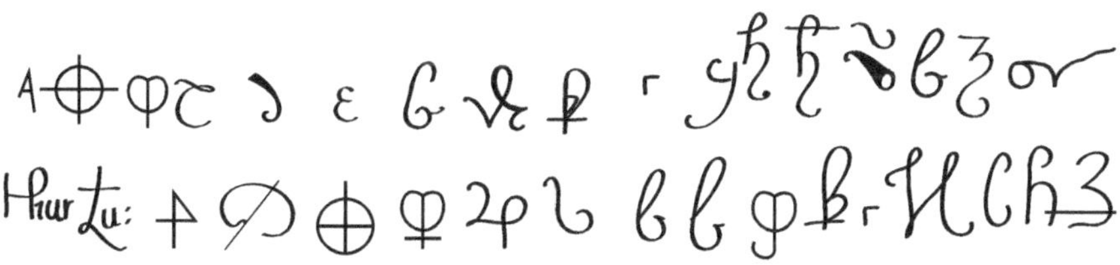

When you have covered the writing with the characters abovesaid, make three crosses on the wax with the party's knife that owneth the goods stolen, saying these words at making of every cross, "Bricii, Rani-bricii, Benisti, Bricii," bene et pone sub capite.[768]

766. *Digneris...debeas*: Translation: "'Digneris' should be 'debeas.'" This is a copyist's minor correction of the above.

767. *Ortu...sereno*: Translation: "with the sun being seen rising, and with the sky serene."

768. *Bene...capite*: Translation: "well, and place it beneath the head."

To Make a Thief or Any Person or Persons Come Again Wheresoever You Be[769]

First look that the  be in ♓, then mark the new ☽ while the ☽ is in the sign, and the first Monday after the new ☽, the ☉ being in ♓, take virgin wax or parchment which never touched fire nor water, and make -1 = i o l o[770] like the proportion of a *Man q: Wopan* = *1* + *é o 6* = *1* +[771] so that thou mayst have them at all times at thy pleasure, and if in wax, it must be made per the heat of the ☉. Thus done, write in the 7 6 11 + L i -[772] of one of them this word Iris with thy character  in the n b o + L[773] of the r c l -[774] Sibilia or Ulicia with this  and in the middle of the r L i m[775] this word Aziria, with this character 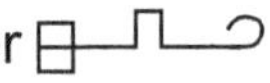 in the < u L i △ C or r i n c,[776]

[112]

these: Elemer, Emalagra, sr Malagria, with these characters , and make his characters following in the \ I \ Ω L back against the r 1 v c heart. Now, when thou wilt work, make a fire of dry sticks of eglantine, then take the - l = o l △[777] in hand, but beware  they consume not, in peril of thy self, and say this oration following:

"O God, ruler of all things, unto whom no secrets are hidden, we humbly beseech thy might that the thief that hath committed this theft thou wilt vouchsafe to bring again to us. Through the sin of this theft, he may desire to come to worthy penance and repentance, though Christ our Lord, amen. Almighty and everlasting God, the true discerner of all things both manifest and hidden, unto whom no secrets are unknown, I humbly beseech thee that, per calling upon thy holy names, thou wilt command thy clean spirits Sabaoth, Uriel, and Rogaell, to obey unto my precepts and commandments in this my

769. For other examples, see BL Sloane 1727, 24–28, 52; Sloane 3845, 38r–39v, 41r; Bodleian Additional B.1, 1r–2v; Rawlinson D.252, 69v–71v; Harms and Clark, *Of Angels*, 270–71; manuscript page 193. Most of the ciphers are deciphered immediately thereafter or nearby by Harrington. I have rendered the enciphered passages as best as I can without turning all into an unwieldy separate image. It bears noting that Harrington's readings are borne out in comparison with other works.

770. Harrington inserts above, "two images 2 images like the proportion."

771. Harrington inserts above, "man & womman."

772. Harrington inserts above, "forehead."

773. Harrington inserts above, "crowne."

774. Harrington inserts above, "head."

775. Harrington inserts above, "head."

776. Harrington inserts above, "breast or heart."

777. Deciphered: "image."

work, that the thief coming to me may openly confess his fault and civil[778] deed before us, wheresoever we shall be, either in this place or elsewhere, that in thy holy church we may give thanks and laud to thee, through thy son, our lord Jesus Christ, who liveth and reigneth with thee in the unity of the Holy Ghost, world without end. Amen."

Then say thy prayers with this verse following: "O Lord, quicken us, and thy servant shall rejoice in thee." Then hold your work before the fire, and say,

"I command and call you angels, Sabaoth, Uriel, and Ragael. Pray you, per the power of the right God the Father, the Son, and the Holy Ghost, and of the names of God that I now call upon, that you do help me, Ego sum qui sum[779] A et Ω, the first and the last, per Agla, and per these holy names of God Te[tra]gramaton, and per the name of Jesus, per virtue whereof and all knees do bow and obey, in heaven, and in earth, and in hell, and the voice of heaven in which you are, that you

[113]

"force and constrain this thief which hath stolen these things, in what place soever he, she, or they be, per the virtue of these characters that are hereon written in all places of his body as in on this -I = I O L[780] which now I strike," and strike it with eglantine, "so that he rest not day nor night, sitting, going, sleeping, waking, eating, or drinking, and that his heart in coming to me melt and warm as this o I 4[781] doth [in] all the fire, until he come again and confess his fault. In nomine Patris et Filii et Spiritus Sancti, amen."

Use this daily till he come, and say it first in the crown of the head, and after on the back, etc., and if he be in the whole universe, he will come in a fortnight. You must keep this 4 = I O L[782] in a clean linen cloth, and in a clean chest, and as it happeneth, so will it happen to the thief.

Tried and proved true not only on thieves, brought again in three days, but also to call spirits in a glass found effectual.[783]

778. *Civil*: Pertaining to members of the community.

779. *Ego sum qui sum*: Translation: "I am that I am."

780. Deciphered: "image."

781. Deciphered: "wax."

782. Deciphered: "image."

783. *But also...effectual*: This is not mentioned in other instances of the ritual.

To Know If Any Kind of Business Shall Come to Good, Evil, or Neatly End[784]

Let him take a psalter closed between his two hands,[785] and make the sign of the cross in his forehead, and think of the business, [and say]:

"In nomine Patris et Filii et Spiritus Sancti, Domine, labia mea aperies & c. Ostende nobis, Dominus, misericordiam tuam, et salutare tuam da nobis."[786]

> "In the name of the Father, and of the Son, and of the Holy Spirit, Lord, open my lips & c. Show us, O Lord, your mercy, and give us your deliverance."

Then open the psalter and look on the right side, and that first letter of the upmost line shall shew his effect. Of the letters, some be very good:[787] 7, a, b, e, i, o, l, m, p, q. The very evil are c, d, f, g, h, k, x. The mutely[788] are these: r. n. s. t. y. v. z.

Experiment of the Hazel Rods

Let them be of one year's growth, then say, "In the name of the Father I have sought thee, in the name of the Son I have found thee, in the name of the Holy Ghost I cut thee." Cut them both at one stock.[789] If you do so, say, "*Principe* [in principio] erat verbum," & c.,[790] and then say Pat[er Nosters] three, Aves three, Creeds three. Then say,

"O Lord, hear my prayer, and let my cry come unto thee,

784. This is a late version of a "mantic alphabet," a procedure typically used to divine the meaning of dreams. Other texts may attribute the procedure to a prophet or philosopher, particularly Joseph, and might give particular significance to each letter. Given that the seventeenth-century scribe includes other rituals for dream divination, the lack of any mention of dreams was probably a change made earlier in the chain of transmission. See Chardonnens, "Mantic Alphabets in Medieval Western Manuscripts and Early Printed Books"; Chardonnens, "Mantic Alphabets in Late Medieval England, Early Modern Europe, and Modern America."

785. Other examples state this should occur in a church.

786. *In nomine…nobis*: Translation: "In the name of the Father, and of the Son, and of the Holy Spirit, Lord, open my lips & c. [Psalm 50:17]. Show us, O Lord, your mercy, and give us your deliverance [Psalm 84:8]."

787. In other sources, the individual letters are given more specific meanings than simply good or bad.

788. *Mutely*: Uncertain—it could mean that these letters are quiet on the question asked.

789. *Stock*: Trunk or stalk.

790. *Principe…& c.*: John Chapter 1.

[114]

"O God, in whose providence and position no thing goeth amiss or is deceived, we humbly bless thee thou will put away all our infirmity and grant all things that annoy be profitable, through Jesus Christ our Lord. Amen."

Then when thou wilt have the operation, then say, "In nomine Patris et Filii et Spiritus Sancti. Amen. O God in whose providence," & c. Then say:

"I conjure you this day, one year's hazel rods of one year's growth, by the unspeakable names of God + Edy + Elgay + Ousion, + Te[tra]gramaton, + that you bring me to the place without fraud where any treasure is hid, and per these holy names be that you bow not in vain, in nomine Patris et Filii et Spiritus Sancti. Amen. I conjure thee, hazel rods of one year's growth. per the virtue of the Three Kings of Culleyn,[791] Gassiar, Melchio, Balthazar, the like, as these three rods, being wise and prudent men, were led per the star were that found Christ, so I command you that you bring us to the place where treasure is."

Write on the rods the names above written.

Pro Thesauro[792]

"O most great and glorious God, I, humble, beseech thee, though I be a most wretched and miserable sinner conceived and born in sin and iniquity, yet vouchsafe for thy dear son Christ Jesus's sake, in whom thou art well pleased, to reveal the truth unto me concerning this hidden treasure, that neither temptations of the Devil hinder me, nor any suggestions of ♄[793] prevail against me, but that, per the virtue and power of these thy blessed names, I may obtain and bring my purpose to good effect: + Agla, + On, + Te[tra]gramaton, + Sabaoth, + Adonay, + Panton, + Craton, + Jesus, + Enamuel, + Sedebin, or Sedekin, + Messias, + Medicina + Jehovah, + Elos, + Elohim, + Xusi, + Pucer, + and per O other thy blessed names, I, humble, beseech thee to exalt

791. *Three Kings of Culleyn*: The Three Wise Men or Magi, for whom Cologne was a site of popular devotion.

792. Translation: "For Treasure."

793. *Suggestions of* t: In light of what appears below, perhaps lead.

[115]

"me that no temptations hinder me in my work, but that, thy glorious name compelling them, these rods may draw to no other metal but only to ☉ and ☽.[794] Grant this for thy own glorious name's sake, and per thy dear son's sake our lord. Amen.

"O thou wicked and envious traitor ♄ and all thy complices,[795] I charge thee, per Jesus Christ the blessed son of God, to depart hence with all thy subtlety and suggesting, and that thou have no power to tempt or hinder this business who I have now in hand, Christus vincit, Christus regnat, Christus imperat, Christus nos in pace benedicat.[796] Amen."

Let one help you to hold the rods at the small ends, you holding the great ends betwixt your foremost fingers and your thumbs of both your hands, and as they watch and draw, so follow that way still, or else go as far the contrary side, and then next on the third side, and lastly to the fourth side so you may draw inward to a head, and per that means find the place direct, and when you draw down to the earth direct, you have your purpose. And ever as you work, say as followeth: "Auribus tuis precipice,"[797] psalm first, "How long wilt thou forget me, O Lord?" per "How long wilt thou hide thy face from me?" Second, "How long shall I take counsel within myself, having weariness daily in my heart, how long shall mine enemy be exalted above me?" Third, "Behold and hear me, O Lord God; lighten mine eyes that I sleep not in death." Fourth, "Lest mine enemy say I have prevailed with him, and they that effect me, rejoice when I slide." Fifth, "But I trust in thy mercy, mine shall rejoice in thy salvation; I will sing to thee, Lord, because he hath dealt so loving with me."[798]

Whether It Be Kept or No[799]

Make two circles about the place, and say "De profund[is]" & c.,[800] "Misere[re] mei, Domine," & c.[801] If it remove, it is kept; else not.[802]

794. ☉ and ☽: Gold and silver.
795. *Compli[ce]s*: Associates.
796. *Christus vincit…benedicat*: Translation: "Christ conquers, Christ rules, Christ commands, may Christ bless us in peace."
797. *Auribus…precipe*: Likely Psalm 5, "Verba mea auribus percipe…"
798. KJV Psalm 13:1b–6. This is close to the KJV but does not follow it exactly.
799. Likely a reference to whether a treasure is guarded by spirits.
800. *De profund[is]*: Vulgate Psalm 129.
801. *Misere[re] mei…*: Vulgate Psalm 50:3.
802. In magical treasure hunting, typically incantations are used to fix the treasure in place. This seems to map more to the folk magic procedure of avoiding mentions of God while digging, lest the spirits take away the treasure.

[116]

Ante Meridiem in Die ☽ et Die ♃,[803] a Discharge for All Manner of Spirits for the Ground[804]

"O thou spirit or spirits that keep this ground or place and treasure herein contained, I conjure you and charge you per all the mighty power and strength of the Holy Ghost and of the blessed Trinity, that you depart from this place or ground and treasure. O you spirits, or thou spirit, I charge and command you per the power and strength of the almighty God, the Father of heaven and earth and all therein contained, and per the virtue and dignity of Jesus Christ, his only son our saviour, co-equal with the Father and the Holy Ghost, and per all the three persons in the Trinity, that you depart from this place, ground, or treasure, and that you do not return till we have had our will and desire.

"I conjure and command you, O ye spirits, per the virtue, strength, and power of our lord and saviour Jesus Christ, king of glory, and per the virtue and love of the Holy Ghost, and per all the strong mentions of Jesus Christ, king of all goodness, per the virtue and of his mercy, and per the virtue of the love of my saviour Jesus Christ, the only son of the living god, per the virtue of his obedience, when he was made equal with the Father of the Holy Ghost, in the majesty of his strength and power, that you depart from this place or ground.

"I conjure you, O ye spirit of spirits, per the fearful hour of him which shall come to judge both the quick and the dead, and the world with fire and brimstone, and moreover I command you, ye wicked spirits, per him to whom all kings do bow, both in heaven, earth, and hell, that you depart from this place of ground, and that you come not near it till that we have taken our wills, desires, and commands.

[117]

"I conjure, O ye spirits, per hellfire, and per all the pains, that thou or you depart from this place or ground a hundred miles, through the virtue and strength of the cross, which was on the Cross, that you be drawned,[805] stretched, and nailed with the most cruel pains of hell, except that thou or you depart, per and per without delay.

803. Translation: "Before Noon on Monday and Thursday."

804. For another example, see Harms and Clark, *Of Angels*, 274–75.

805. *Drawned*: Drawn or stretched.

"I conjure thee, thou spirit or spirits, per the great pains which Christ Jesus suffered, when he was on the cross, that in like manner, O thou spirit or spirits be nailed and pained in hell fire, which always shall burn yet never be quenched, and the curse of God the Father, the Son, and the Holy Ghost descend and tarry upon you, so that you shall have never ease or rest, and as the spear painfully pierced the most precious side of our saviour Jesus Christ, even so be thou spirit or spirits painfully pained, so that you from this day forth shall never rest in ease, and all thunder, lightning, with all the most horrible pains of hell fire, descend and tarry upon you, and the word of death, with all the torments of hell, descend and tarry upon you, and envenom you forevermore, except you depart incontinently from this place and ground, and not to come near it per the space of a hundred miles, until we have taken our wills, minds, and pleasures of this earth and ground."

Salamonis Protectria [Protectio][806]

"In nomine Domini Nostri Jesu Christi, in potentia altissima signo sacro, signo crucis + me defendat, ut spiritus adventus me ledere offendere vel infestare no valeat, ipso adjuvante protegente et defendente, cui caelestia, terrestria, et infernalia flectantur. Amen. Salva me, Domine, et salvus ero, quoniam salus mea es tu et gloria mea omnibus diebus vitae meae + Ag[i]os, + Athanatos, + Christus vincit, + Christus regnat, + Christus vivet, + Christus benedicit me. Ad spiritus depell[endum]

[118]

"meque adjuvat in omnibus in captis meis. Amen.

> "In the name of our Lord Jesus Christ, by the holy sign in the highest power. He may defend me + by the sign of the Cross, that the coming spirit not be able to hurt, injure, or disturb me, with him helping, protecting, and guarding to whom all heavenly, earthly, and hellish things kneel. Amen. Save me, O Lord, and I will be saved, because you are my health and my glory in all days of my life. + Ag[i]os, + Athanatos, + Christ conquers + Christ reigns + Christ will live + Christ blesses me. He helps me in the expulsion of spirits [118] and in all things in my capacities. Amen.

"Benedicat me imperialis majestas + protegat me immensae *divinata* [divinitas], + custodiat me sempiterna deitas, + foveat mihi gloriosa *vintas* [unitas],

806. Translation: "The Protection of Solomon." Compare to Cambridge Additional MS. 3544.

+ defendat me immensae trinitas, + dirigat inaestimabilus bonitas, + regat me potentia patriis, + vivificet me sapientia filii, + illuminet me virtus spiritus *sanctus* [sancti], + A et Ω + deus et homo sit mihi famulo tuo vocatio ista salus et protectio. Amen.

> "May the imperial majesty bless me + may the endless divinity protect me + may the eternal deity keep me + may the glorious unity assist me + may the boundless Trinity defend me + may the inestimable goodness guide me + may the power of the Father rule me + may the wisdom of the Son restore me to life + may the power of the Holy Ghost illuminate me + alpha and omega + God and man, may the calling be for me, your servant, health and protection. Amen.[807]

"O all ye spirits of fairies whatsoever that do inhabit this ground and keep this treasure therein enclosed, I charge and command you to depart away per the space of an hundred yards, and leave the treasure behind, without hurting me or any fellow or any other creature whatsoever, and this I charge you to do without any illusions, frights, or fears, per all the most holy names of God + Soter, + Te[tra]gramaton, + Adonay, + Sabaoth, + Eloy, + Emanuel + and that you quietly and patiently leave this treasure for our comfort to the honour and glory of almighty God, the good of his church, and our profit. Amen."

Say this three times over with three Paters, three Aves, and one Creed in honey of the blessed Trinity.

[Experiments with the Psalms][808]

Ad Cephal[al]agiam[809]

Write this Psalm, "Domine quid multiplicati sunt" 3 unto "exaltans caput meum"[810] with these characters in hora ☉ and bind them to his head, to be safe.

807. *Beneficat...Amen*: This prayer is derived from a prayer identified elsewhere as "A gode belsyng + whan ye goe forth on a message or yournay + say thys." Wordsworth, *Horae Eboracenses*, 88.

808. A partial list of the *Sefer Shimmush Tehillim*, a Hebrew treatise on the magical uses of the Psalms. It has parallels in three published texts, most closely following Rankine and Barron, although it does not map perfectly to any one of them. Rebiger, *Sefer Shimmush Tehillim*; Rankine and Barron, *The Book of Gold*; Peterson, *The Sixth and Seventh Books of Moses*.

809. Translation: "For Headache." "Cephalalagiam" is derived from the Greek. Rebiger, *Sefer Shimmush Tehillim*, 82–83; Rankine and Barron, *The Book of Gold*, 26; Peterson, *The Sixth and Seventh Books of Moses*, 175.

810. Vulgate Psalm 3:3–4.

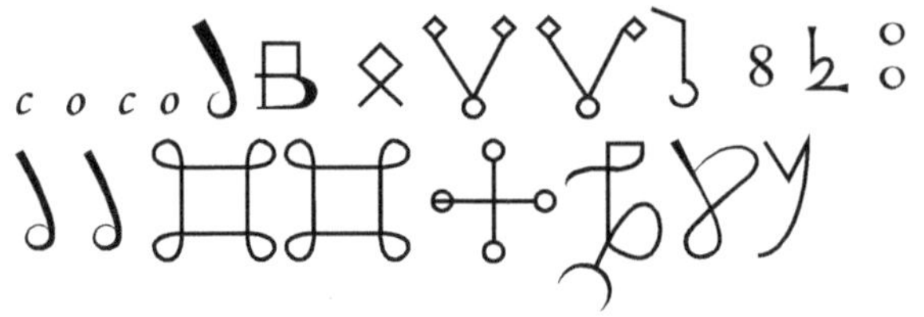

Ad Mutandum ab Aliquo Quid[811] *Psalm 5*[812]

"Verba mea auribus precipe Domine." Read this psalm thrice over oil of roses unto "in eternum"[813] and carry

[119]

these subscribed[814] characters in a new shell in hora ♃ ♋, mixed them with the oil, and with it anoint thy face, et quicquid *rogaremus* [rogaberis], concedetur tibi.[815]

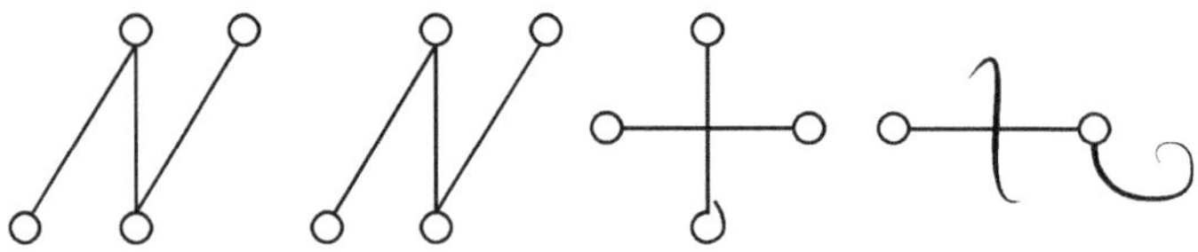

[For Illness][816]

If one be sick, "Domine deus meus in te speravi,"[817] Psalm 7. Write these characters in a new pot in hora ☉, and fill it with fair water, and read this psalm seven times upon the water per seven days together, and after, wash the patient therewith.

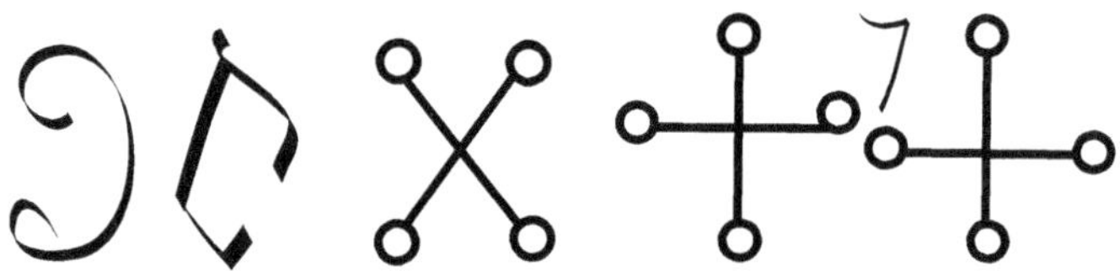

811. Translation: "For Changing the Mind of Anyone [?]."
812. Rebiger, *Sefer Shimmush Tehillim*, 84–85; Rankine and Barron, *The Book of Gold*, 30; Peterson, *The Sixth and Seventh Books of Moses*, 176.
813. Vulgate Psalm 5:2–12.
814. *Subscribed*: Written below.
815. *Et quicquid…tibi:* Translation: "and whatsoever you will ask, it will be granted to you."
816. In other versions, a similar operation is used to vanquish one's enemies using water. Rankine and Barron, *The Book of Gold*, 35; Peterson, *The Sixth and Seventh Books of Moses*, 178.
817. Vulgate Psalm 7:2.

Young Child Crying[818]

"Domine Domine n[oste]r," Psalm the 8th. Write this psalm and bind it upon his arm, and he shall sleep.

Ut Quis Secure Dormiat ab Inimiciis[819]

"Usquequo Domine" Psalm 12. Say this unto "nequaquam dicat inimicas,"[820] et non nocebitur a furibus.[821]

Ut Bene Recipieris[822]

If thou goest into a city or great person, read, "Domine quis habitat, & c.," Psalm 14, as thou enterest, and bear these characters in virgin parchment about thee.

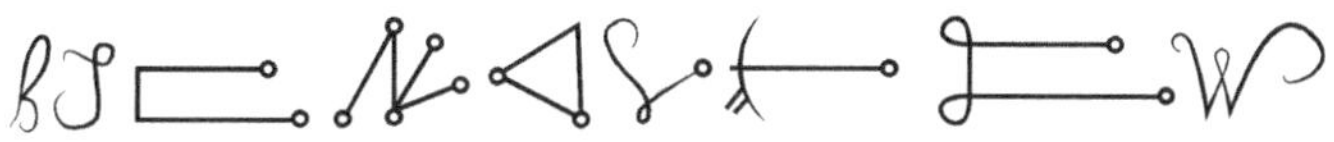

Ad Fascinationem Oculorum Praeveniendum[823]

"Conserve me, Domine," Psalm the 15th. Write this Psalm, with these characters, and bear upon thee.

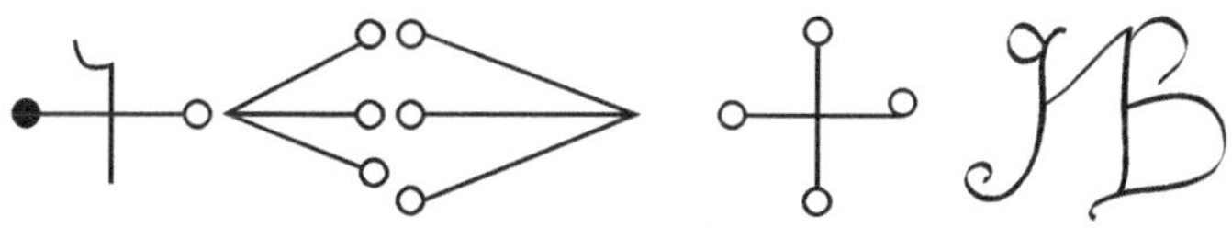

Exaudeat Te, Deus, in Die Tribulationis, Psalm 19[824]

Read it three times every morning to have God's blessing. If you read it over a sick party, if he be recoverable; he shall find safe or die quickly. Write these characters in virgin parchment, suffumigate it with mastic, and bear on thee for the former. 

818. Rebiger, *Sefer Shimmush Tehillim*, 89; Rankine and Barron, *The Book of Gold*, 37; Peterson, *The Sixth and Seventh Books of Moses*, 179.

819. Translation: "That Anyone May Sleep Safely from One's Enemies." Rankine and Barron, *The Book of Gold*, 46; Peterson, *The Sixth and Seventh Books of Moses*, 180.

820. Vulgate Psalm 12:1b–5. "Nequaquam dicat inimicas" should be "nequando dicat inimicos."

821. *Et non...furibus*: Translation: "And one will not be harmed by thieves."

822. Translation: "That You Will Be Received Well." Rankine and Barron, *The Book of Gold*, 50; Peterson, *The Sixth and Seventh Books of Moses*, 180.

823. Translation: "For Preventing Fascination of the Eyes." Rankine and Barron, *The Book of Gold*, 52.

824. Rankine and Barron, *The Book of Gold*, 59.

[120]

Ut Agrotus Dormiat[825]

"Ad te Domine levavi," Psalm 24. Write this psalm in virgin parchment and bind it to his head.

Against Charms or Enemies[826]

"Judica me Domine quoniam in nocentia" & c., Psalm 25.

In Prison, to Help Out[827]

"In te Domine speravi," [Psalm] 30. Say this every day three times to "In miserere mei, Domine, quoniam tribulor,"[828] and three times in the night, and bear these characters.

Si Fueris in Necessitatem[829]

"Iudica Domine nocentes," [Psalm] 34. Read it seven times. If to go before a prince or thine enemy, write and bind to thy right arm to be delivered.

Ad Abortum Praeveniendum[830]

"Dixit *sinistras* [scelus]," [Psalm] 35. Write the psalm and bind it to her right arm.

Ad Male Somniantem[831]

"Dixi custodiam," [Psalm] 38. Write this psalm, and when he goes to bed, put it under the right side of his head.

825. Translation: "That a Sick Man May Sleep." Rankine and Barron, *The Book of Gold*, 70.

826. Rankine and Barron, *The Book of Gold*, 71.

827. Rankine and Barron, *The Book of Gold*, 80.

828. Vulgate Psalm 30:2–10.

829. Translation: "If You May Be in Need." Rebiger, *Sefer Shimmush Tehillim*, 109; Rankine and Barron, *The Book of Gold*, 87; Peterson, *The Sixth and Seventh Books of Moses*, 188.

830. Translation: "For Preventing Miscarriage." Rankine and Barron, *The Book of Gold*, 89.

831. Translation: "For Dreaming Poorly." Rankine and Barron, *The Book of Gold*, 94.

Ut Bene Recipieris[832]

"Quemadmodum," [Psalm] 4[1]. Write this psalm and bind it to thy right arm, vel "Deus judicium tuum."[833]

Si Velis Te Fortunatem Fore Victoriamque Obtinere[834]

"Omnes gentes plaudite," Psalm 46. Write this and carry it upon thee, and say it seven times, "Aday volumque obsequents."[835]

Si Fuerit in Domo tum Fuerit Commiscam[836]

"Magnus Domine et laudabilis," Psalm 47. Write this with  these characters, and put under thy head when thou goest to bed, and thou shall see the thief, as thou sleepest, enter in.

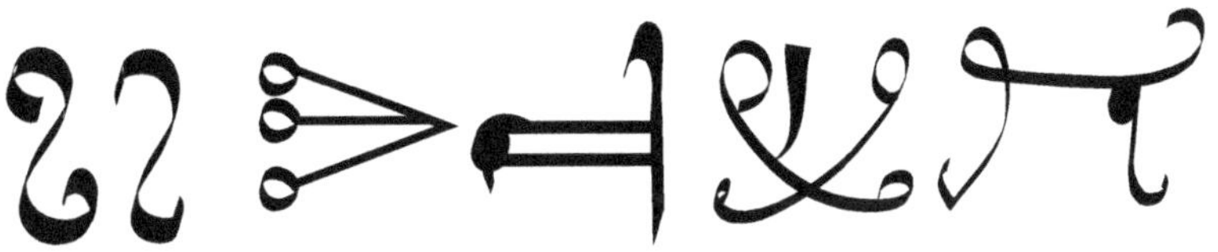

[121]

Si Incantamenta cum Maleficiis Vis Envincere[837]

"Si veri utique," Psalm 57. Say this psalm seven times, and no man can hurt thee or any such thing.

Si Vis Maritum ad Uxorem Reverti[838]

"Exaudi deus deprecationem meam," Psalm 60. Write these characters with the blood of a white cock, saying this psalm three times over them, and bind them in the right arm.

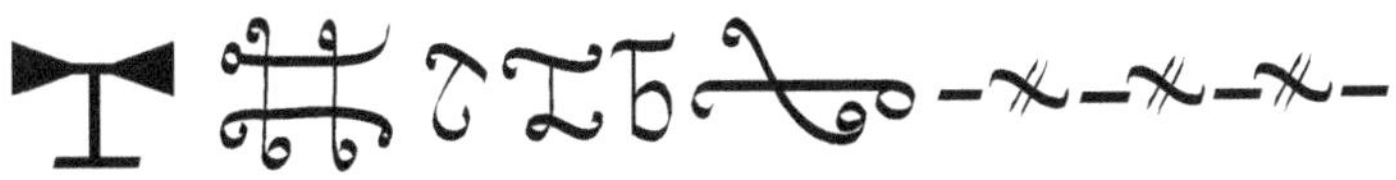

832. Translation: "That You Will Be Received Well." Peterson, *The Sixth and Seventh Books of Moses*, 189.

833. Vulgate Psalm 71.

834. Translation: "If You Should Desire to Obtain Fortune and Victory for Yourself from Abroad." Rankine and Barron, *The Book of Gold*, 104.

835. *Aday....obsequents*: Unknown. It does not seem to be a corruption of any line in the psalm.

836. Translation: "If He Will Go in Your Home, then He Will Be Screwed [?]." Rankine and Barron, *The Book of Gold*, 106.

837. Translation: "If You Wish to Overcome Incantations with Witchcrafts." Rankine and Barron, *The Book of Gold*, 120.

838. Translation: "If You Desire a Husband to Return to His Wife." Rankine and Barron, *The Book of Gold*, 124.

Ad Prerudum [Puerum?] Minis Flentem et Vigilantem[839]

"Deus deus meus," Psalm 62. Write this psalm in virgin parchment and bind it on the child's arm.

Ad Inimicos Superandos[840]

"Exaudi deus orationem meam," Psalm 63. Write these characters in virgin parchment saying this psalm three times over them, and bind them on thy right arm.

Si in Necessitatem Incideris[841]

"Te decet hymnas," Psalm 64. Say this psalm three times daily, et ab illis *liberabilis* [liberabis]."[842]

Ad Naufragii Timorem ex Tempestate[843]

"Salvum me fac deus quoniam," Psalm 68. Read this psalm three times, and there shall be a great calm, so that thou mayst safely arrive at the haven of thy desire.

In te Domine speravi," [Psalm] 70, pro Causa in Lege[844]

If thou goest to law with anyone, say this psalm before thou enter to the judge, and thou shalt overcome thy adversary.

Ad Amorem, Alicu[iu]s Consiliandum[845]

Psalm 72, "Tu[846] bonus Israel Deus." Write this psalm in his name whose son thou desirest, and his name, & his etc.,[847] and bind in thy right arm.

839. Translation: "For a Child Not Crying or Staying Awake." Rankine and Barron, *The Book of Gold*, 126.
840. Translation: "For Overcoming Enemies." Rankine and Barron, *The Book of Gold*, 127.
841. Translation: "If You Come into Need." Rankine and Barron, *The Book of Gold*, 128.
842. *Et ab…liberabis*: Translation: "And you will be freed from these."
843. Translation: "For Fear of Shipwreck from Tempest." Rankine and Barron, *The Book of Gold*, 136.
844. Translation: "For a Case in Law." Rankine and Barron, *The Book of Gold*, 138.
845. Translation: "For Love and Counseling of Anyone." Rebiger, *Sefer Shimmush Tehillim*, 141.
846. *Tu*: This word does not appear in either of the Vulgate Psalm variants I have seen.
847. *Etc.*: This interpretation of the abbreviation here is speculative.

[122]

Ad Inimicos Dissipandas[848]

Write this psalm, "Ut quid deus repulisti," 73, and the name of the enemies with these characters. Put them into the fire; they shall be dissipated abroad anon.

 or this, three this way 

Ad Fascinationem[849]

"Voce mea, ad Dominum clamavi," Psalm 76. If any be witched, write this psalm in the new of the ☽ upon a piece of glass and wash away the writing with holy water and give the bewitched to drink, and he or she shall be safe, per God's assistance.

Si Vis ad Regem vel Principem Intrare[850]

"Quam dilecta tabernacula," Psalm 83. Write this usque ad[851] "Respice in facione, Christi tui,"[852] and bind it upon thy right arm, ut honorifice ut [sic] recipiaris.[853]

"Fundamenta Ejus," [Psalm] 86[854]

Write this psalm with these characters with the blood of a dove, and suffumigate it with mastic and hyleates,[855] and bind upon thy right arm, and thou shalt be without all likeness, as long as thou bearest it on thee.

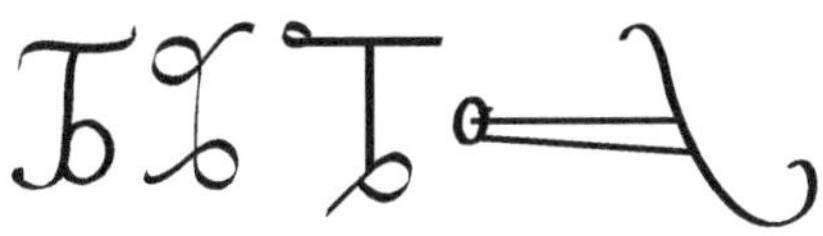

Ad Cephalalgiam[856]

"Misericord[ias] Domini in eternum," [Psalm] 88. Write this psalm in paper and bind on his head that is sick, and he shall be whole and read it over holy water, and sprinkle the house, ut divina benedictio restet ibi.[857]

848. Translation: "For Dispersing Enemies." Rebiger, *Sefer Shimmush Tehillim*, 141; Rankine and Barron, *The Book of Gold*, 144. The diagrams given in the latter are different.
849. Translation: "For Witchcraft." Rankine and Barron, *The Book of Gold*, 148.
850. Translation: "If You Desire to Appear before a King or Prince." Rankine and Barron, *The Book of Gold*, 155.
851. *Usque ad*: Translation: "Without interruption to."
852. Vulgate Psalm 83:2–10.
853. *Ut…recipiaris*: Translation: "So you will be received with honour."
854. Rankine and Barron, *The Book of Gold*, 158.
855. *Hyleates*: Unknown. *The Book of Gold* has aloe wood.
856. Translation: "For Headache." Rankine and Barron, *The Book of Gold*, 161.
857. *Ut…ibi*: Translation: "So that divine blessing may remain there."

[123]

"Domine refugium," [Psalm] 89

If thou sow milliens[858] or cucumbers in the garden, write this psalm and characters, and bury it in the midst of the garden, and they shall prosper therein.

"Qui Habitat in Adjurato [Adiutorio]," Psalm 90[859]

Write this psalm in paper with the blood of a dove; suffumigate it with lignum aloes and dry roses, and bear on thee, and thou shalt be safe from wicked spirits and their powers, wild beasts, forethinking,[860] and naughty eyes, and fear per night going. It prevails against fear in children if they carry it on them.

"Dominus Regnavit," [Psalm] 92[861]

If thou wilt build a house, read this psalm upon holy water, and it shall be a great blessing. Also, it profiteth against noise; if thou write and bury it in the four corners of thy house or garden, they will go your way.

"Deus Ultionum," [Psalm] 93[862]

Read this psalm seven times every day, and thine enemies shall fly from and fear thee.

"Cantate Domino [Domino Cantate]," [Psalm] 95[863]

If thou hath any matter against rich and wealthy men, and they have asked a council against thee, and will grant thee nothing, say this psalm in the evening seven days, and write it and their names, and bind it upon thy arm, and boldly ask of them what thou wilt, and they shall give it thee.

"Domine Exaudi Orationem Meam," [Psalm] 101[864]

Say this psalm before thou depart out of thy house, and thou shalt find joy.

858. *Milliens*: Melons.

859. Rebiger, *Sefer Shimmush Tehillim*, 155–56; Rankine and Barron, *The Book of Gold*, 164.

860. *Forethinking*: A plot or contrivance.

861. Rankine and Barron, *The Book of Gold*, 171. The purpose here is different.

862. Rankine and Barron, 172; Peterson, *The Sixth and Seventh Books of Moses*, 200.

863. Rankine and Barron, *The Book of Gold*, 175.

864. Rankine and Barron, *The Book of Gold*, 182.

[124]

"Benedic Anima Mea, Domine," [Psalm] 103

If thou hast a fruitful tree, and it be hurt of birds, write this psalm in paper and hang it in the tree, and no bird shall abide therein.

"Confetimini, Domino," [Psalm] 104[865]

If a man be long imprisoned, write this psalm and bind it in his arm, and say it[866] times every day to be soon delivered.

"Confetimini, Domine," [Psalm] 106[867]

To keep thy enemy long in prison, read this in the prison before him.

"Paratum Cor Meum," [Psalm] 107[868]

If thou wilt go to the king or prince, read this psalm before thou go to him, and fear not.

Ad Partum Facitandum[869]

"Dixit Dominus Domino meo," Psalm 109. Write this Psalm unto "Luciferum genui te,"[870] and bind it to her thigh, and she shall soon be delivered without much pain or property.

"Laudate Pueri Dominum," [Psalm] 112[871]

If any man's cattle die, read this psalm seven times upon holy water, and sprinkle it in his house, and his beasts and substance shall multiply.

"Dilexi, quoniam," [Psalm] 114[872]

Write this psalm unto "Custodiens *pueror* [parvulos],"[873] and suffume it with musk and the tytoal,[874] and bind it on a child's arm to preserve and heal from all evil.

865. Rankine and Barron, *The Book of Gold*, 186.
866. The space is blank in the original.
867. Rankine and Barron, *The Book of Gold*, 188.
868. Rankine and Barron, *The Book of Gold*, 190.
869. Translation: "For Easing a Birth." Rankine and Barron, *The Book of Gold*, 193.
870. Vulgate Psalm 109:1b–3.
871. Rankine and Barron, *The Book of Gold*, 197.
872. Rankine and Barron, *The Book of Gold*, 200.
873. Vulgate Psalm 114:6.
874. *Tytoal*: Uncertain. *The Book of Gold* has aloe, along with mastic.

"Credidi propter," [Psalm] 115

Write this to, "vincula mea,"[875] and bind it to the thigh of one in chains to deliver him.

[125]

"Laudate Dominum Omnes Gentes," [Psalm] 116

If thou wilt be without drunkenness, read this psalm over wine that thou wilt drink.

"Beati Inmaculati," [Psalm] 118[876]

If anyone be sick, read this psalm over him and suffume him with mastic, and he shall be whole.

"In Convertendo Domine," Psalm 125[877]

If thou wilt sow wheat or any other seed, read this psalm over the seed seven times, and sow the seed, per and per, and God's blessing shall remain in that field.

"Beati [omnes] qui Tarrient [Timent] Dominum," [Psalm] 127[878]

Write this Psalm unto "sicut vitis abundans,"[879] and bury it at the root of the vine tree, and it shall bear presently.

"De Profundis Clamavi," [Psalm] 129[880]

Write this psalm on paper and bury it in the corners of the field to preserve it from all harm.

Ad Male Minisque Somniantem[881]

If a man dream much, write this psalm, and bind it to his arm: "Domine non est *exaultem* [exaltatem]," [Psalm] 130.

875. Vulgate, Psalm 115:1b–7.

876. Rankine and Barron, *The Book of Gold*, 207. That example is more protective than curative, although both include fumigation with mastic.

877. Rankine and Barron, *The Book of Gold*, 216.

878. Rankine and Barron, *The Book of Gold*, 219.

879. Vulgate Psalm 127:1b–3a.

880. Rankine and Barron, *The Book of Gold*, 221.

881. Translation: "For Dreaming Poorly and Little."

"Memento Domine David," [Psalm] 131[882]

Write this psalm unto "viduam ejus,"[883] and bind it a fisher's net, and he shall catch many fishes.

"Ecce quoniam [quam] Bonum,"[884] *[Psalm] 132*

Read this psalm over oil of roses, and anoint thy face, and all persons shall receive thee honourably.

For Sore Eyes[885]

Say this psalm seven times over oil of roses, and anoint thy face, and he shall be whole.

[126]

Ad Adulterium,[886] *"Domine," [Psalm] 138*
"Probasti Me," 138[887]

Say this psalm seven times every day, and God shall bring thee to penance and shew mercy on thee.

Contra Inimicos,[888] *"Domine Clamavi," [Psalm] 140*[889]

Say this psalm seven times, and thou shalt escape safe from them through God's assistance and help.

"Voce Mea ad Dominum," [Psalm] 141[890]

Say this psalm seven times, and write these characters, and hang in the air. And if thy servant run away, they shall return anon, and if one be imprisoned, say this psalm every unto, "Educ de custodia animam meam."[891]

882. Rankine and Barron, *The Book of Gold*, 223.

883. Vulgate Psalm 131:1b–15a.

884. This might be due to confusion with Psalm 135:1, "Confitemini Domino quoniam bonus."

885. This must be a psalm between 133 and 137. Nothing in the other sources matches up with regard to procedure and purpose.

886. Translation: "For Adultery."

887. Rankine and Barron, *The Book of Gold*, 230.

888. Translation: "Against Enemies."

889. Rankine and Barron, *The Book of Gold*, 232.

890. Rankine and Barron, *The Book of Gold*, 233.

891. Vulgate Psalm 141:2–8a.

"Domine Exaudi," [Psalm] 142[892]

If any fall into trouble or necessity, let him say this psalm seven times every day unto, "Eripe me de inimicis meis, Domine, ad te confugi,"[893] & c., to be delivered.

Si Quis Uxorem Odiat[894]

"*Exalto* [Exaltabo] te, deus meus," [Psalm] 144. Say this psalm seven times over the oil of roses, and anoint the woman's bread, and write it, and bury it before the woman's gate, and he shall return to her. And if thou read this psalm seven times over oil of roses, and anoint the face of one that is sick, and they shall be whole anon.

If to Divide with Any Man

"*Laud omnia* [Lauda anima] mea Dominum," [Psalm] 145. Read this ten times, and thy part shall be good.

"Lauda Jerusalem, Dominum," [Psalm] 147[895]

Read this psalm eight times every evening in thy house, and evil spirits and all fantasies will go away, and the blessing of God abide.

[127]

"Laudate Dominum de Celis," [Psalm] 148

If thou have an orchard, say this psalm seven times in that place, and God shall multiply therein, and the blessing of God be there.

"Cantate Domino," [Psalm] 149[896]

if any woman be sick, say this psalm seven times over good oil and anoint her, and she shall be well.

892. Rebiger, *Sefer Shimmush Tehillim*, 199; Rankine and Barron, *The Book of Gold*, 234.

893. Psalm 142:1b–9.

894. Translation: "If Someone May Hate His Wife." Rankine and Barron, *The Book of Gold*, 236.

895. Rankine and Barron, *The Book of Gold*, 240, 241.

896. Rankine and Barron, *The Book of Gold*, 242.

An Experiment of the [Shoulder] Blade or Shoulder Bone of an Ass, Hare, Cock or Hen, and per This Is Bound a Man, Woman, Beast, or Spirit, of What Kind and Condition Soever[897]

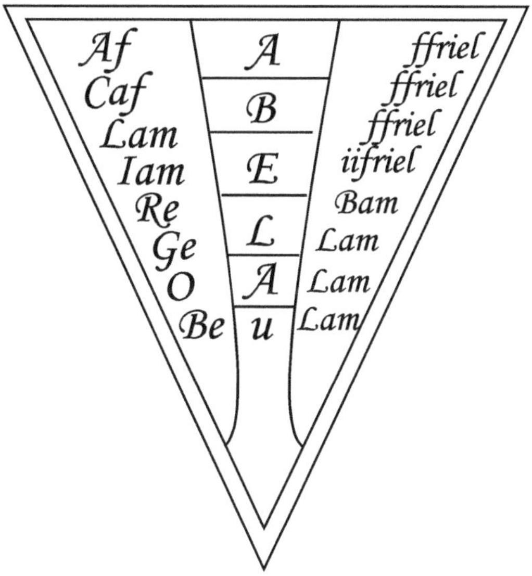

Write these names in the scapula of [a beast] as aforesaid, or in a pure tin plate, as one saith, as in the example following. And if thou wilt bind a spirit, write his name ins[er]t[ed] between B and EE.[898] Suffume it with mastic and aloes, saying,

"I conjure you Otfriel [?], Caffriel, Lamfriel, Iamfriel, Rebam, Gelam, Olam, Belam,[899] that all ye compel the spirit which hath power to do this which I desire to come unto me in a fair form, and to fulfil all things humbly that I command."

If thou wilt find a man, write his name betwixt B. E. L., and thou must have white thorns, or sweet-brier, or else reeds which he came, and put them in a new earthen pot, and a little above put the scapula. Make a fire per little and little, saying,

"I conjure you, Afriel, Cafriel, Lamfriel, Iamfriel, Rebam, Gelam, Plam, Belam, per the living and true God, which hath created you, and formed Adam,

897. This ritual is used for power over people or spirits. For similar rituals, see Bayerische Staatsbibliothek Clm 849, 32r–33r; Sloane 3850, 28r–v. Harms and Clark, *Of Angels*, 131–35.

898. *EE*: Should be "E."

899. *Otfriel…Belam*: *Of Angels*: "Asiell, Casiell, Lamfriel, Iamfriell, Palam, Herlam, Olam, Bolam." Bayerische Staatsbibliothek Clm 849: "Asyel, Castiel, Lamisniel, Rabam, Erlain, Belam." British Library Sloane 3850: "Affriel, Caffriel, Lamfriell, Iamfriell, Rebam [?], Gelam, Olam, Belam."

[128]

"and Eve, which hath put a border into the sea which it may not pass, and hath established the dry land in midst thereof, which maketh his angels spirits and his ministers flame of fire, which knoweth all things past, present, and to come, as if you were present and at hand, which hath the key of hell and death, and is the first and last, beginning, and ending, A and Ω, which liveth and was dead, and he hath risen again, and is called + Te[tra]gramaton + I conjure you again, per his most glorious name whose virtue no heart doth know, but he alone, which is the word of God, and per these holy names of God, + Eloy, + Sabaoth, + Elim, + Adonay, and per all his names, and per all his omnipotent power, and per all the powers of heaven, earth, air, fire, and sea, and per the virtue of all herbs, stones, fish, and living cattle, fowls in the air. Item, I conjure you per the Father, Son, and Holy Ghost, and per its trinity and its unity, and per the crown of thorns which our Lord Jesus Christ wore upon his head, and per the milk of the blessed virgin Mary, and all the holy names of God, I command you that, quickly and without delay, that you bring the heart and the whole cogitation of N. into my love, that he be kindled and wax whole over, as this scapula waxeth hot per reason of this fire, that he may neither sleep nor take any rest, per113 fervventing[900] of my love, until he come unto me and accomplish my desire."

And if thou will have a woman, write her name betwixt L. and A., and do as before, and she will come, and if a beast thou wilt bind, write his name between A. and U., and his colour, and thou mayst bind him that he depart not from the place wherein he is as long as thou wilt.

[129]

You must write the party's name upon the crest in the middle of the shoulder bone, and must set the bond above upper, or over the heat of the fire, that it be not burned, for it must not be burned alive.

900. *Ferventing*: Heating.

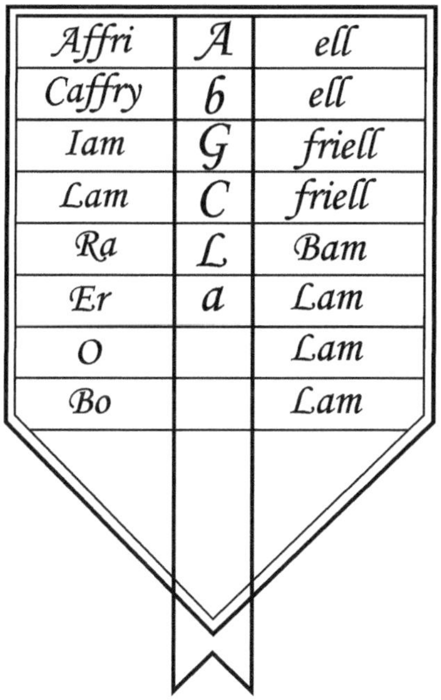

You must make a shield of virgin wax and write in it the words as you see, and set it against the fire, that it may melt softly, and read this conjuration aforesaid three times in horam[901] ♀, naming her whom you work for, and ever after she will fulfil all your requests. Probatum est.

Experimentum ad Inveniendum Furem[902]

Scire cupiens furem rei ablato, vadat in crepusculo noctis ad sepulchrum cujusdum mulieris infra 30 dies prius transactos mortes, inclimansque ad caput ejus tumuli, succedentia nomine, voce submissa, non sine attentione, dicat

> If one desires to know the thief of a stolen thing, they go in the evening to the tomb of some woman having died within thirty days, and bending toward the head of the grave, approaching saying the name in a low voice, not without attentiveness, one should say:

"Zernae, Zernae, Zernae, quae hic jaces in caria Abra, Cadra, Sabra. Conjuro te, amina cujus cadaveris N tunc sepultae, per deum sancti Samuel,

901. *In horam*: Translation: "In the hour."

902. Translation: "Experiment for Discovering a Thief." See the following rite and those at manuscript 196–204. For a discussion of other examples, see Harms, "'Thou Art Keeper of Man and Woman's Bones': Rituals of Necromancy in Early Modern England."

prophetae, omnipotentem et per omnia sancta nomina ejus et per ejus majestatem et virtutem incomprehensibilem *mei unsam* [immensam] precipis, et mando tibi ut petes *habuisque* [habebisque?] *licentiones* [licentia] ea qui detinent te, hoc nocte veniendum ad me et uni agentium sine mora, sine terrore, et sine laesione, placida et tranquilla ad me et in veritatem reveles mihi furem hujus rei ablata (viz. N. vel similis et hic rem nominibus) quod quidem si fueris promitto tibi quod 3 Missas intra triduum per remissionem peccatorum tuorum celebrari faciam. Ego iterum te rogo, moveo, et adjuro ut hac nocte in somnis clarissime study [?]. In nomine Patris et Filii et Spiritus Sancti. Amen."

> "Zernae, Zernae, Zernae, she who lies here in decay, Abra, Cadra, Sabra, I conjure you, soul of that cadaver N. afterwards buried, by the omnipotent God of holy Samuel, the prophet, and by all these holy names and by his majesty and boundless and incomprehensible power that you order, and I command you that you will ask and have these licences that held you, coming this night to me and to one agent without delay, without terror, and without injury, calm and tranquil, and may reveal to me in truth the thief of this carried-off item (viz, N. or similar, and here the thing with its names) that assuredly if you are, I promise to you that I will have celebrated three Masses for remission of your sins within three days. Again I ask, stir, and adjure you that [I will see it] this night most clearly in dreams. In the name of the Father, and of the Son, and of the Holy Ghost. Amen."

[129bis]

And after having said, "De profundis"[903] twice, this experimenter went home and laid under the bolster upon which he should sleep, some of the earth of the grave, then he went to bed, and in his sleep came the spirit of the dead woman, shewing him the thief, the manner of stealing, and you the place where it then stay hid. It did also shew the marks and signs and which the thief might be known and so vanished. He swore this to be true, and said that hereper one might know of treasure hid, things past, present, and to come, and if any do not whatsoever. But above all things he that will work any thing hereper must be clean in conscience, contrite, and confessed, and the dead party such a one as you think in hope of salvations. When you go to a man's

903. *De profundis*: Vulgate Psalm 129.

grave, say, "In the mass, gender,[904] Zerne, Zerne, Zerne," mutantur mutanda.[905] You may translate and say in English as before.

Alias[906]

First bless thee and stand at the head of the grave, and call "M., M., M.,"[907] and said standing still, "O Saint S., Saint S., E. E.,[908] as thou art keeper of man and woman's bones, and at this time keepest the bones and body of this man to whom I do call, I charge, and command, and also conjure you per the virtue, might, and power of the Lord Jesus Christ, per his nativity, per his resurrection and ascension, and per his strength, power, and might, and also per the virginity of Our Lady the blessed virgin St. Mary his mother, and per the virtue of heaven and earth, that thou appear to me, thy mightiness, in the fair form of a man, not fearing or hurting me, or any other creature,

[130]

"tell me such treasure as is hidden in (Gosling Sellert[909] and Stouten Heath[910]), and bring me safely to it, as thou takest to be saved and not damned at the dreadful day of judgment."

Then take some of the mould[911] of the grave and keep it a fair linen cloth, and when thou sleepest in bed, lay it under thy right ear.

An Experiment for Things Stolen, Oft Proved and Never Deceiving[912]

First, the man must say this psalm 51, "Miser[er]e me" & c., et "Deus misereatur nostri" & c.[913] per, and then this prayer following:

904. *Gender*: Referring at the time to an offspring, a particular group of people, or men or women as a group. The sense in which it is used here is uncertain.

905. *Mutantur mutanda*: Translation: "And accordingly, being changed, they are changed."

906. Translation: "Another."

907. *M., M., M.*: Likely saying the name of the dead person three times.

908. *Saint S.…E. E.*: This might be the dead person's name, but why the initials have changed is uncertain.

909. *Gosling Sellert*: Conjectural, and unknown. Finding this location or person could narrow the potential author or location of the original manuscript.

910. *Stouten Heath*: See introduction.

911. *Mould*: Earth, in this context.

912. For other examples, see Bodleian Rawlinson D.252, 13r–14v, 92r–94v; British Library Sloane 3318, 95r–96v; Cambridge Additional 3544, 7–10; Harms, Clark, and Peterson, *Oberon* 538–41.

913. Vulgate Psalm 66.

"O God, which didst send thy Holy Ghost upon thine apostles, send thy holy spirit upon this maculate[914] child. Clarify his mind that his spirit may certify us of the thing or things which we demand, that he hath no power to lie, but that he may overcome all spirits, and aspectally[915] this quiet spirit Sibilla, that she may answer to all our requests[916] per this maiden child and maculate."

Then the minister,[917] laying his hand on the child's head, must say:

"O child, I conjure thee per our Lord Jesus Christ, and of the Blessed Virgin his mother, and of St. John the Baptist, and per the virginity of St. Katherine and St. Margaret, and per the virginity of St. Lucy, and per the virginities and sacraments, per the baptism and per the cup of our Lord, that thou hast power to see and understand the revelations of spirits, to constrain and bind them to come and satisfy the will of thy master, per our Lord Jesus Christ the son, which with the Father and Holy Ghost, liveth and reigneth, one God, world without end. Amen."

[131]

Then let the master say to the candle, holding[918] the child's right hand:

"I conjure thee, candle by the immaculate light, and per the virtue of our Lord Jesus Christ, per the virtue of his mother, and per the virtue of St. John the Baptist, per his head, and per the virginity of St. Mark, of St. Cicely,[919] and of St. Barbara, and per St. Agnes, and per the living God and true God, that thou have power to receive Sibilla, a spirit to be called per Our Lord Jesus Christ."

Then let the master say, taking the right hand of the child with the candle therein:

"Rootha vel Roatha, Athole, Tronda, Marma, Rutilla,[920] I coniuro te Sibella[921] per facismatem catecam, per brolum magnaminum, per marcilium magnum magnati, per magnam sufflanciam, per consuetudinem optimam, per

914. *Maculate*: Stained or soiled. This should likely be "immaculate," both here and below.

915. *Aspectally*: Visibly. The author likely meant "especially."

916. *To...requests*: This replaces material marked out, which is "this to all our repeats [?]."

917. *Minister*: It is possible that this term could signify a Protestant minister.

918. *Holding*: Remaining [in].

919. *St. Cicely*: St. Cecilia, known for her efforts to maintain her virginity.

920. *Rootha...Rutilla*: Sloane 3318: "Rothea. Altolle. Crowyda. Morina. Rutilia."

921. The spelling of this name will change multiple times during this ritual.

candelam sacram, per corpora mortuorum, per inferni sedes, et per has constellationes Matua, Sonalker, et Velpor, quod subito in hanc candelam venias palam, et pulveris et tenebrarum *explem* [expertem]. Propera, Sibella, in hanc candelam venire per summum dei nomen *Tegragramaton* [Tetragrammaton]."[922]

If she come not, the master must say:

"Reotha, or Roatha, Athole, Tranda, Marma, Ratilla, Sibilla. I conjure thee per farismates, Catera, per Grottas magnanimus, et per Marcelline, magnum, magnati, per great sufflincia, per the best custom, per the holy candle, and per all the dead bodies, per the seats in hell, and per the constellations, Matua, Somalphar, and Vese,[923] that thou come in this candle without delay."

[132]

Ask the boy what he seeth. If she come not, let him say after his master:

"O Lady Sibilla, I, humble, beseech and desire thee that thou fulfil the will of my master, N., and that thou appear in the goodly shape of a woman."

And she come not, let the master say this following with the child:

"I conjure thee, Sybilla, per the virginity of our Lord Jesus Christ, per the virginity of his mother, and per the virginity of St. Baptist, and per his head, and by the virginity of St. John Evangelist, and per the virginity of St. Catherine, of St. Mark, St. Cicely, St. Lucy, St. Barbara, and St. Agnes, and per the living and true God, per the virginity and all the sacraments, per the baptism and cap of our Lord, that thou come into this candle without let."[924]

And if she come not, let the child say after his master:

"All these things aforesaid shall be for thy damnation, unless thou come quickly into this candle."

Let the child say the last words in his mother tongue, beginning here: "O Lady Sybilla..."

922. *Rooatha... Tegragramaton*: Some of the above is translated below, although part of that is clearly too garbled to be understood. A parallel passage in Sloane 3318 is no clearer. What is not translated below is the section from "et pulveris" on: "free from both toil and darkness. Hasten, Sibella, to come into this candle, by the greatest name of God, Tetragrammaton."

923. *Matua... Vese*: Unknown.

924. *Let*: Hindrance.

And when she cometh, the master must bid the child will her to sit, that she be comely clothed, and bid he clothe her in better clothing, and when she hath so done, let the master say what he will before her that is good, and she will shew him with signs and writings of this Tetragramaton all that you shall ask, and when she depart, let the master say:

"Peace, be between thee and thine, between me and mine, and go to the place to these predestinate,[925] until I call thee another time, and be thou ready to me and obedient in all things and points." Finis.

[133]

[Further Elaborations on the Summoning of Sibilla][926]

Figure of the breastplate for the master to wear in the conjuration of Sibella, formed on this manner.

First make a circle about thee with chalk, and having this figure written in parchment on thy breast, sit down with the child, setting him before thee with the candle in his hand. Begin as aforesaid, and always begin this work in the new of the ☽, and in the hour of ♃, and the ☉ and ☽ to be one of the inhabited signs as ♋, ♐, or ♓. Call hereper night, if may be; then is the best time.

If she will not appear for all aforesaid, then say as follows, rehearsed the words on your breast:

"Sorthie, Sorthia, Sorthios, I conjure thee Sibella, O gentle virgin of fairies, per the mercy of the Holy Ghost, and per the dreadful day of doom, and per your virtues and powers, I conjure thee Sibella, O gentle virgin of fairies, per all the angels of ♃ and their characters and virtues, and per all the spirits of ♃ and ♀, and their characters and virtues, and all the characters that be in

925. Indecipherable text marked out here.

926. What follows is adapted from Reginald Scot's *Discouerie of Witchcraft*, in order to serve the candle-burning rite. I have left most other omissions and other minor changes unnoted. Scot, *The Discouerie of Witchcraft*, 405–8.

the firmament, and per the king and queen of fairies, and their virtues, and per the faith and obedience thou bearest unto them. I conjure thee, Sybilla, per the blood that came out of the lord and saviour Jesus Christ crucified, and per the opening of heaven, and per the renting of the veil of the temple, and per the darkness of the sun in the time of his death, and per rising up of the dead in the time of his resurrection, and per the virgin

[134]

"Mary, mother of our Lord Jesus Christ, and per the unspeakable name of God, *Tegtaramaton* [Tetragrammaton], I conjure thee, Sybilla, O blessed beautiful virgin, per all the rial[927] words aforesaid. I conjure thee, Sybilla, per all virtues, to appear in this candlelight[928] before us, visible in the form and shape of a handsome woman, in a bright shining vesture, white, adorned, and garnished most fair, and to appear to us quickly without deceit or tarrying, and that thou fail not to fulfil my will and desire effectually, for I will choose thee to be my blessed virgin and will have common conference[929] with thee. Therefore make haste and speed to come unto me, and appear as I said before. In the name of the most high and almighty God,[930] to whom be all honour and glory for ever and ever. Amen."

Thus done and ended, if she come not, repeat the conjuration till she come, for doubtless she will come, and being come,[931] bind her thus:

"I conjure thee, Sybilla vel Sibilia, per God, per God the Father, the Son, and God the Holy Ghost, three persons and one God, and per the Blessed Virgin Mary, the mother of our Lord Jesus Christ, and per all the whole and holy company in heaven, and per the dreadful day of doom, and per all angels, archangels, thrones, dominations, principes, potestates, virtues, and powers. I conjure thee and bind thee, Sybilla, that thou shalt not depart out of this candlelight[932] wherein thou art appeared, nor yet to alter thy shape, unless I give thee licence to depart. I conjure thee, Sybella, per the blood that ran out of the side of our lord and saviour Jesus Christ crucified, and per the virtue

927. *Rial*: Royal.

928. *This candlelight*: Scot has "that circle."

929. *Conference*: Scot has "copulation" here.

930. *In the name…God*: Added by copyist.

931. This omits Scot's recommendation to fumigate with frankincense.

932. *Candlelight*: Scot has "circle."

thereof. I conjure thee, Sybella, to come to us and appear at all times visible, as the conjuration of words

[135]

"here written in this book. I conjure thee, Sybella, O blessed virgin of fairies, per the opening of heaven and per the rending of the veil of the temple, the darkness of the ☉ in the time of his death, and per the rising of the dead, per his glorious resurrection, and per the unspeakable name of God, Tetragramaton, and per the king and queen of fairies, and per their virtue, I conjure thee Sybella to appear before the conjuration be read over[933] times, and that visible to appear as the conjuration leadeth written in this book, and to give me good counsel at all times, and how to come to treasure hidden in the earth, and all other things that are to me pleasure, and fulfil my will without any deceit or tarrying, nor yet that thou shalt have any power of any body or soul, earthly or ghostly, nor yet to perish so much as one hair of my head. I conjure thee, Sybella, per all the rial words and real aforesaid, and per the virtues and powers, I charge and bind thee per the virtue thereby to be obedient to me and all the world aforesaid, and this bond to stand between thee and me upon pain of everlasting condemnation. Fiat, fiat, fiat. Amen."

A Licence for Sibilla to Come and Go at All Times

"I conjure you, Sybilla, that art come hither here before me or us per the commandment of thy God and mine, that thou shalt have no power in going and coming to me, imagining any evil per or in any manner of ways in the earth, above the earth, or under the earth, of evil doings to any person or persons, I conjure and

[136]

"command thee, sister, per all the rial words and virtues that be written in this book, if thou shalt not [go to] the place from whence thou comest, but shall remain peaceably, invisibly, and look thou be ready to come unto me when thou art called per any conjuration of words that be written in this book, to come I say at my commandment, and to answer unto me truly and duly of all things, my will quickly to be fulfilled. Vade in pace, in nomine Patris et Filii et Spiritus Sancti. Amen. Laus Deo."[934]

933. Scot's "four" is omitted here.

934. *Vade…Deo*: Translation: "Go in peace, in the name of the Father and of the Son and of the Holy Ghost. Amen. Praise (be) to God." The last sentence is not in Scot.

An Experiment to Be Seen in a Crystal Stone[935]

Take a crystal stone or glass, most clean without cross, wrap about it a piece of hart's leather, saying, "In the name of the Holy Trinity and of the high Deity. Amen."

Then hold the crystal in the beam when the ☉ is most bright, at the hottest of the day, and say this conjuration subsequent, and per and per you shall see the spirit, peradventure appearing himself, then say to him:

"I conjure thee per the virtues of all things aforesaid that thou depart out of this crystal, and bring with thee thy fellow in my honest and decent form apparelled, some in blue, some in yellow, & c."

For sometimes he cometh alone and hiding his head, sometimes in a cloak, sometimes in a gown. Command him or them, if you work for theft, to go out of the crystal, and that they come again, bringing or representing the form or shape of the thief, or thieves, and things stolen, or which shall be stolen, et fiat,[936] and he will bring with him the thieves, and will shew them with his finger, and their names if thou wilt. Also thou mayst ask and be certified[937] of treasure hid

[137]

under the ground, how thou mayest have it, when it was laid there, where it was, whether he be alive or dead that laid it there, and you may be certified of parents, friends, or enemies, being far or near distant, or what other thing you will require.

The conjurations follow:

"I conjure Ceton, Munton, and Marciterton, which do inhabit the woods. I conjure thee and thy fellows, that you be ready at my commandment in ministering and serving me to fulfil my desire, & c.," altera nec non melior.[938]

935. See manuscript page 108. For other examples, see British Library Sloane 3846, 34r–v; Sloane 3853, 217v–219r; Harms, Clark, and Peterson, *Oberon*, 534–38.

936. *Et fiat*: Translation: "And let it be done."

937. *Certified*: Be made certain.

938. *Altera...melior*: Translation: "Another, and not better."

"I conjure thee, Askariel, Abilon, or Beall, in the name of the Father + and of the Son, + and of the Holy Ghost +, which is A + and Ω + the beginning + and ending + per the fearful day of judgment, per the virtue of the living God, per his speakable and unspeakable names, that thou, Alcariel, that thou come into this crystal or glass, quickly, without stay, in thy proper person, in decent form, having on thy head and crown, and shew thyself visible to me, and to them that are about me, and bring with thee thy fellows, that we may see them plainly at my desire and conjurations, and per all other that I shall command thee, and if thou wilt not do so, N., per the virtue of the almighty God and all saints, condemn thee, Askariell, into hell under everlasting fire until the latter day of doom. Fiat, fiat, fiat. Amen. That unless thou do come unto me and answer all my demands and do all that I shall command you, and always without stay do obey my precepts in all hours and times to certify my requests.

[138]

"I conjure thee, Askariel, per the twelve patriarchs, per the twelve apostles, per the twelve prophets and their preaching, per the forty seniors, their thrones and harps, per their stairs, per their victory and seal, and per the seat of the majesty, per the throne of God, per the voice and thundering which goeth out of the throne of God, per the passion of martyrs, per the merits of confessors, per the holy priests, per the holiness of widows and virgins, and per all things that laud and praise God, that thou come into this crystal or glass, and answer to all my demands, and do all that I shall command thee, and always, without stay, do obey my precepts, in all hours and times, to fulfil my requests.

"I conjure thee, Alkarell, per him which is A and Ω, the beginning and ending, and per these holy names of God, El, + Ely, + Theos, + Adonay, + Tetragramaton, + Messias, + Sother, + Emanuell, + Jesus, + Ferce, + Fortis, + Solus, + Unigenitus, + Via, + Vita, + Veritas, + Manus, + Homousion, + Primogenitus, + Sapia, + Virtus, + Cinis Imago, + Panis, + Filos, + Vitis, + Mens, + Janua, + Petra, + Lapis, + Augutaris, + Angelus, + Sponsus, + Pastor, + per Pata, + Sacerdos, + Immortalis, + Dominus, + Deus, + Panton, + Craton, + O Ausion,[939] that thou come into this crystal or glass, and answer justly and truly to all my demands, and do all that I shall command thee, and

939. *O Ausion*: The first letter is unclear in the original.

always, without stay, do obey my precepts, at all hours and times, to certify my requests.

"I conjure thee, Alkariel, bind, and adjure thee, per the godhead of the Father, per our Lord Jesus Christ,

[139]

"the Son, and per his incarnation, baptism, fasting, and per his humility whereper he washed his disciples' feet, per his cross and passion he suffered, and per the crown of thorns he bore on his head, per the nails wherewith his hands and feet were pierced, per the spear that wounded his side, per the water and blood that gushed out of his side, per the sweet calling wherewith he called upon his father, and per his soul which he commanded into his hands when he died, and per the virtue wherewith the covering of the temple was divided, the ☉ was obscured, and darkness was made, the graves opened, and many holy bodies did rise—per these and all things aforesaid, I conjure thee, Askariell, and command that thou and thy fellows come into this stone or glass in this hour, per and per, without any delay or let in thy proper person, and in a comely man's shape, bearing on thy head a crown, and shew thyself plainly and visibly to me and to all that stand here, without any deceit of any man, or having power to hurt us either in body or soul, or any other thing or part whatsoever, and not to depart out of my commandment until thou hast given a true answer unto me of all my demands, without lie or deceit or subtility, being adjured per him that shall come to judge the quick and the dead, and the world with fire."

This done, and they come not at first, say this conjuration three times, and they will come, per and per, and certify thy requests.

[140]

A Licence for Askariell with His Fellows to Depart

"Now give thy ways, Askariell, with thy fellows, to your predestinate places where God hath appointed you, until I call you again in pain of damnation, and the curse of God the Father, the Son, and the Holy Ghost, descend and tarry upon you, unless you return quickly and without tarrying whensoever I call you, whether it be in field or town, house or habitation, or what place else soever, so be it, so be it, so be it. Amen."

A Prayer to Be Said before This or Any Other Experiment

"O merciful and everlasting Lord God, which madest both heaven and earth, and in the mightiness of thy arm did measure them, O glorious God, that sitteth on the cherubim and seraphim in light of lights which frailty of nature cannot obtain. O worthy, to whom be praises for ever and ever, I most humbly beseech thee, of thy everlasting mercy and goodness, to give me grace, virtue, and power to constrain thy spirits, to constrain thy spirits, to constrain thy spirits, that they may truly and faithfully, without fraud, shew to me all such things as I shall at any time or hour command them, and also do all such things or hour as I bid them. Grant this, O merciful Lord, through the power of thy unspeakable name Tetragramaton, and per the wonderful name, power, and virtue of our Lord and saviour Jesus Christ."

[141]

Ad Mensium Nimietates[940]

Take a goblet full of wine, and say over it this psalm seven times, "Miserere mei deus quoniam conculcavit,"[941] and then give her the wine to drink, and the grief shall shortly cease.

To Prove Theft[942]

Take a pair of shears and stick them fast in the rim of a sieve or riddle,[943] which thou and another must hold betwixt thy longest fingers' ends, and standing in a line for more certainty, lest there should be any deceit wrought against the truth per any invisible enemy, the one of you standing in the east, the other right west, and so per the book and key. Then hold up the sieve betwixt you and say as followeth:

"If N. hath stolen or taken any that goods of M. or had away part of them, dies mies gesetret bine defect dona da Mose."[944]

Say this three, seven, or nine times, naming both the loser and suspected persons' names, and without doubt, if he or such have the thing or did the deed, the shear will turn off your fingers, otherwise stand still. Probatum.

940. Translation: "For a Superfluity of Menses."

941. Vulgate Psalm 55:2. Rankine and Barron, *The Book of Gold*, 118.

942. An example of coscinomancy, divination with shears and sieves. See also Braekman, *Middeleeuwse Witte en Zwarte Magie in het Nederlands Taalgebied*, 334–36.

943. *Riddle*: A circular sieve made of wires.

944. *Dies mies...*: For other instances, see British Library Lansdowne 1203, published in Mathers and Peterson, *Key of Solomon the King*, 40–41: "Dies mies yes-chet bene done fet Donnima Metemauz"; Weyer, *De praestigiis daemonum*, 196: "dies, nues, ieschet, benedoefet, donuina, enitemaus."

Ut 1=EnL=[945] Concilias[946]

Write this character in virgin parchment in hora ♀

Touch a dog, for experiment's sake. N.

Ut mulier te sequitur, scribe in manum sinistrum sigillum istum, eamque tangeris ante ⊙ ortum vel ei monstra quicquid in palma scripsisti et si volueris probare tange canem.

> So that a woman follows you, write on your left hand this seal, and touch her before ⊙rise, or show her whatsoever you wrote on your palm. If you desire to prove this, touch a dog.

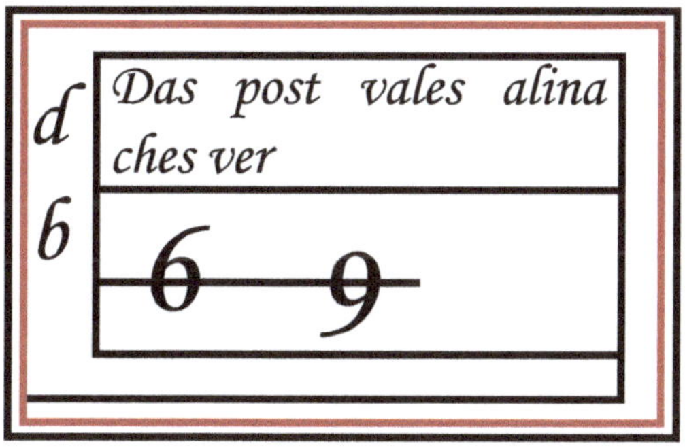

[142]

Against All Fevers[947]

Make such a cross of lead as followeth with the words therein, and the name of the fever, and then hang it about the neck of the sick party when he shaketh, and the same shall soon depart from him.

945. Deciphered: "Amorem."

946. Translation: "So That You Procure Love." For other examples, see Harms, Clark, and Peterson, *Oberon*, 547; Harms and Clark, *Of Angels*, 117; manuscript page 44.

947. See manuscript page 52.

Also for Any Ague or Fever[948]

This word "Abracadabra" must be written, diminished letter per letter, according as in this table following in virgin parchment and hanged about the party neck, and it shall help under God.

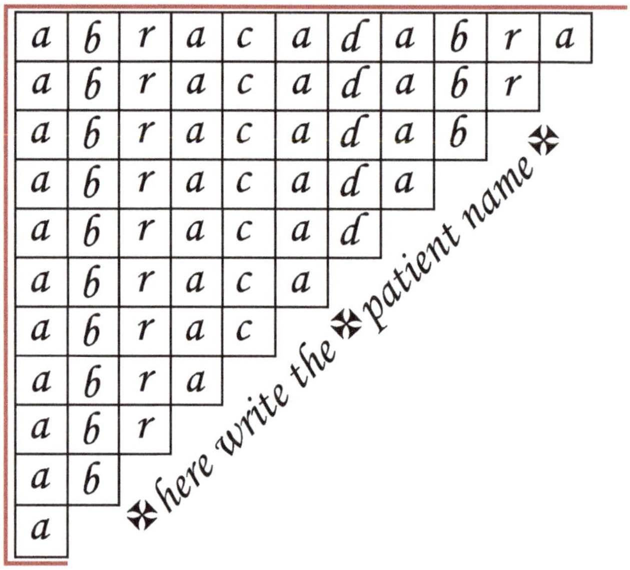

For Pains in the Stomach or Heart by Witchcraft[949]

First purge with oil and honey. Then take the following: white hellebore, one dram; St. John's wort, one oz.; sugar, two drams; frankincense, a dram. Boil in wine or water to one ½[950]—give a few spoonful three or four times a day. If [the patient] do well, add more hellebore.

A Medicine for Persons Possessed[951]

Take broom flowers, St. John's wort, horehound, ivy, and rue, each two ounces. Boil to half, and give a cup full frequent to the patient.

An Incense or Fume to Drive out Evil Spirits[952]

Take galbanum and sulphur, of each one dram; roots of asafoetida, birthwort, St. John's wort, and rue, of each one dram; for a pomander.[953]

948. For other examples of this charm, see Serenus Sammonicus, *Liber Medicinalis*, 48–49; Agrippa, *De Occulta Philosophia Libri Tres*, 432 (book 3, chapter 31); Harms and Clark, *Of Angels*, 160.
949. Similar to *A Whip for the Devil*, 81, although some of the proportions have changed.
950. *Boil…½*: Based on *A Whip for the Devil*, boiling until half the substance is gone.
951. *A Whip for the Devil*, 82.
952. *A Whip for the Devil*, 85. The recipe here has been cut down to a third.
953. *Pomander*: A sweet-smelling substance (not in this case) to perfume an area, or the container in which it was kept.

An Oil to Anoint Persons Afflicted with Witchcraft[954]

Take rue, sage, and dill, three handfuls;[955] boil all in oil, and anoint the possessed therewith.

Ad Dysenteriam[956]

Write these letters following, and tie under thy pecten.[957] Thou shalt be whole, and if thou wilt not believe, write these letters upon a knife, and thrust it into a pig, and in blood shall come forth.

[143]

Ad Partum Difficilem[958]

Write the words on a long piece of parchment as a girdle, and bind it about her middle or body:

"Ave, + recipit + Alua, + Elisabeth, + Johannem, + Sator, + Arepo, + Tenet, + Opera, + Rotas +"[959]

And give her hisse[960] and betony to drink, and she shall be delivered without danger and child come to Christendom,[961] per God's help.

To Draw Out a Tooth[962]

Take chalk and mark upon a post as many teeth as have been in thy mouth, and at the sore tooth, make a mark, and then take a nail of iron, and drive upon the sore tooth into the post with a hammer, saying these words following: "Ultera,

954. *A Whip for the Devil*, 80.

955. *A Whip for the Devil* adds ashes of olive wood and holy water, "each of a sufficient quantity."

956. Translation: "For Dysentery." Compare to National Library of Scotland GD 188/25/1/3, 50.

957. *Pecten*: Pubic area.

958. Translation: "For Difficult Birth." A derivative of the *peperit* charm, on which see manuscript page 54. For a fourteenth-century version of this charm, see Hunt, *Popular Medicine in Thirteenth-Century England*, 367. See also National Library of Scotland GD 188/25/1/3, 46.

959. *Sator…Rotas*: The famous magical square commonly used in all manner of charms. For discussion, see Vinel, "Le Judaïsme Caché du Carré SATOR de Pompéi"; Skemer, *Binding Words*, 116–17; Stein, "Das Sator-Quadrat: Magie, Mystik und Wissenschaft."

960. *Hisse*: Hyssop.

961. *Christendom*: Baptism.

962. National Library of Scotland GD 188/25/1/3, 46.

Butera, Urtera, Bustera, Gustera, Ostera, Ostnandra,[963] in nomine Patris et Fillii et Spiritus Sancti. Amen."

Stolen or Lost, Whether[964]

Write these words following and put the writing under thy head sleeping; it shall appear:

"+ Agris, + Agios + spiritus sanctus sit cum famulo dirio tuo"[965]

vel

Write these letters in virgin wax:

d. b. e. b. te. l. f. t. p. r. b.

and lay it under thee, et videbis somnio.[966]

To Know If Anyone Be Bewitched or Not[967]

You must hold molten lead over the sick body's stomach as he lieth on his back, and pour it through the bow of a pair of shears into a porringer[968] or bowlful of fair water, which he most hold with his hands upright on his breast. And then, if there any appear upon the lead an image or like of a hart

[144]

or living creature, the party is bewitched. Then melt that same again the next day, and do as before, and use it so daily till the same lead be wasted to dross, and the sick person shall amend.

Aliter[969] for One Bewitched[970]

Take a horseshoe, and heat it red hot in the fire, then take it forth and lay upon it a handful of broom with a little hair of the party's neck, and sprinkle his or her water on the hot horseshoe, and say, "And it pleased God, I would

963. *Ultera...Ostnandra*: GD 188/25/1/3: "Utera batera ushera bustera gustera ostenda ost Nandra."

964. National Library of Scotland GD 188/25/1/3, 47.

965. *Agris...tuo*: Translation: "+ In the fields + holy [Greek] + Holy Spirit, may you be with your faithful [?] servant."

966. *Et...somnio*: Translation: "And you will see in dreams."

967. An elaboration of the procedure in Scot, *The Discouerie of Witchcraft*, 276 (book 12, chapter 18). See also GD 188/25/1/3, 50.

968. *Porringer*: A bowl with a handle.

969. Translation: "Another."

970. For other charms involving horseshoes, see McIlwaine, *Minutes of the Council and General Court of Colonial Virginia*, 112; Blagrave, *Blagrave's Astrological Practice of Physick*, 154; Hand, *Popular Beliefs and Superstitions from North Carolina, 4874–8569*, 443; National Library of Scotland GD 188/25/1/3, 51.

the witch that hath done this deed were as hot burning as this horseshoe." And immediately the hag shall come and cry out and ask why you do so. This was taken out of a very old manuscript, and hath been often proved true on my knowledge.—William Hodges,[971] November 18, 1652.

[A Herb against Witchcraft]

N.B. Amara dulcis[972] is a magical herb good against witchcraft.

To Hurt a Witch, Thief, or Enemy[973]

Upon the Sabbath day in the morning, before ☉rise, gather a young hazel rod, saying, "I cut thee, O thou hazel bough of this year's growth, in the name of him or her[974] I mean to beat or maim." Then cover the table with a carpet,[975] saying, English it he that can,[976] "+ Drocks + Mydocy + Esenaroth, + Becu, + Baroch, + Ass, + Maaroch, + Holy Trinity punish him, that hath wrought this mischief, and take it away per thy great justice, + Eson, + Elion, + Emaris, + Ales, + Age, +," and strike the carpet with the wand.

To Help Any Bewitched Man or Beast[977]

First, if it be a Christian, lay him upon a bed, kneel down, and kneeling down per the bed, take a hazel wand of one year shoot, so long as the patient can spare. Then make therewith the sign of the cross upon his heart,

[145]

and say three Creeds, three Pater Nosters, and three Aves, and at each time say these words, naming the party in this wise following:

"N., God save thee. Three biters have bitten thee with heart, tongue, and eye, three better they boot shall be: the Father, the Son, and the Holy Ghost in Trinity. Say, amen. Lord Jesus Christ, I beseech thee, send boot and help, for holy Charity. Amen."

971. *William Hodges*: See introduction.

972. *Amara dulcis*: *Solanum dulcamara*, or bitter nightshade, a poisonous plant.

973. Scot, *The Discouerie of Witchcraft*, 269–70 (book 12, chapter 18). Bodleian Additional MS. B.1. 25r. See also Harms and Clark, *Of Angels*, 174.

974. *Or her*: Not in Scot.

975. *With a carpet*: Not in Scot.

976. *English it he that can*: Suggesting that these are untranslatable magical words.

977. The three bitter biters charm, dating back to the fourteenth century. See Harms and Clark, *Of Angels*, 265, 267, the next three charms, and manuscript page 148 for more examples. For analysis: Roper, *English Verbal Charms*, 125–27.

Alias[978]

"Three biters hath thee bit, the heart, the eye, the tongue; three better shall be thy boot, thou Father, the Son, the Spiritus Sancti. Amen."

Another Way Approved[979]

"If three evils hath thee, N. bit all, at that the most three goods shall be thy change, the Father, the Son, and the Holy Ghost, three persons and one God in Trinity. Give this in heart, health, and boot, in the way of charity and mercy. Amen." Then say,

* "God that was in Bethlehem born,
And baptised in the water of Flum[980] Jordan,
The water was wild, the water was wood,
The child was meek, the child was good,
He smote the water, still it stood,
So cease this grief, this pain, this woe,
That out of this person may be seen go
Out of thy heart, thy flesh, thy sinews, thy veins,
Thy bones let it consume and wear of ones,
Per the virtue of the Holy Trinity. Fiat, fiat, fiat. Amen."

Say this three or nine times together, naming the party's name or beast, then say three Pater Nosters, three Aves, and three Creeds, worship of the Holy Trinity, and the party shall presently amend, if not past all help.

Another Way

"I ask health and boot of my lord and saviour Jesus Christ, in the way of Charity, which art called per

[146]

"these[981] three secret names, + Agla, + On, + Tetragramaton, +, for this person that is grieved with a witch and grief, that if three shrews have thee bit, with either eye, heart, or tongue, three gods shall be thy boot: the Father, the

978. Translation: "Another." See the previous charm for commentary.

979. The "Flum Jordan" charm. For discussion, see Harms and Clark, *Of Angels*, 265; Hohman, *Long-Lost Friend*, 74, 82. For this particular variation, see NAS GD188/25/1/3, 51, and manuscript pages 153 and 155.

980. *Flum*: Stream or river.

981. This is a catchword from the previous page not present on this one.

Son, and the Holy Ghost. Amen." Likewise, you must now begin as before at this mark, * "God that was in Bethlehem born."

An Experiment for This Purpose, per Friar Bacon[982]

Take the patient's water, and put into it one dram of oil papal, and set it on a fire, or seethe it well. Then take a pair of tongs red hot out of the fire, and thrust them therein in the hour of ♄ and ♂, and say as followeth:

"I conjure N., thee witch or witches, wicked spirit or wicked spirits, per the living God, the true God, the holy God, and per the birth of Jesus Christ, and holy, godly doctrine and wonderful works that he did upon the earth, and per his burial, resurrection, and ascension, and per all powers that are erected and contained under the throne of God, and per all the powers pronounced per me.

"I conjure thee, N., witch or witches, or wicked spirit or spirits, and per all other powers that you are subject unto, that you depart from this M. in peace and unity, and never to vex him or her any more, per any kind of your diabolical powers, earthly or ghostly, upon everlasting condemnation in hellfire for your wicked deeds, to be tormented with the fiery darts of Arnus,[983] signed with a mark upon your breast, whereper you may repent and amend your wicked lives. Fiat, fiat, fiat. Amen."

When this is done, the witch will come to you or someone of your house to beg or borrow something, but let her have nothing,[984] but say,

"Depart from my house or ground, thou wicked person, in the name of the Father, the Son, and the Sancti Spiriti, and the holy cross of Jesus Christ be between thee and me, from this time forth and for evermore. Fiat, fiat, fiat. Amen."

[147]

If your cattle be bewitched, cut some of the hair of the tails and tips of the ear of them, and, having bound them in a piece of paper, burn it in the fire, and say the aforesaid conjuration, and name the sick cattle.

982. For another rite attributed to a "Friar Bacon" for the same purpose, see Harms and Clark, *Of Angels*, 175–76.

983. *Arnus*: Avernus?

984. *When this…nothing*: The witch's physical appearance after an anti-witchcraft charm is common in popular accounts. The usual instruction for the charmers is to say and exchange nothing during the encounter.

Also for bread: if it will not bake, take the bag or sack when it come from the mill, and say, "Like as Simon did bear the heavy cross of Jesus, so bear thou, witch or witches, my heavy strokes." Then beat the bag, saying, "In the name of the Father, and of the Son, and of the Holy Ghost. Amen."

And your drink be bewitched, thrust a pair of hot tongs in it, and say the conjuration. Give not, neither lend any thing to them, and they are rewarded per their wickedness, according to their desserts. Probatum est.

Another per Which All Witches Are Compelled to Come and Confess Their Wicked Deeds[985]

First in the new of the ☽ being in some airy sign as ♊, ♎, ♒, on a Saturday, in the hour of ♄, take a piece of parchment and write the picture of any witch whom you suspect, writing in the forehead , and then take a sharp bodkin, and all to prick the picture's breast and head, and read the conjuration following.

"I conjure N., witch, per the living God, the true God, the holy God, and per all patriarchs, prophets, martyrs, confessors, and all other holy people which follow the lamb of God, and per all angels, archangels, thrones, dominations, principalities, powers, cherubim, and seraphim, and per the four elements, the fire, the earth, the air, the water, and per the thirty thunders and lightnings as in Capthorn, Sade, Daleth,[986] and per the seven planets, ♄, ♃, ♂, ☉, ♀, ☿, ☽, and per the twelve signs ♈, ♉, ♊, ♋, ♌, ♍, ♎, ♏, ♐, ♑, ♒, ♓, and per all powers pronounced before, I conjure thee,

[148]

"witch, wheresoever thou be within seven miles of this place, no rest to have out of pricking pains, sleeping or waking, until thou do come into this pool of water, and therein to confess to me some part of thy wicked deeds that thou hadst done to N. M. or any other, per the virtue of the Holy Trinity. Fiat, fiat, fiat, Amen."

985. For another example, see Harms and Clark, *Of Angels*, 175–76.

986. *Capthorn, Sade, Daleth*: *Of Angels* has "Sem, Caph, Tan, Sade, Dalleth."

Another Way to Help Those That Are Bewitched, or Stroken with Fairies or Otherwise[987]

"If three biters have bitten thee, N. M., through teeth, tongue, heart, eye, I pray God three betters may mend thee, the Father, the Son, and the Holy Ghost, I leave the same both more or less, with all the virtues of the Mass, now God the Father, God the Son, and God the Holy Ghost, as followeth hereafter."[988]

And note if this form of prayer may be said for many other diseases, for fevers, and for aches and lameness wheresoever.

Wherefore you shall always have a staff in readiness[989] to use at all times in your hand. Beginning thus, first make the sign of the cross on the first end of the staff, then measure three measures with your arm, that is, three times the meet length from your elbow to the end of your foremost finger. Then make that length on the staff, with a knife or the like. Thus do nine times in all, that is three times three, ever still as you may say the prayer. And if the staff be longer or shorter in the measuring and saying of nine times, then it is that disease you do it, or else not. And per this, you may find per what witch the party, and what is the disease. Then begin again and measure the staff other nine times, still saying the prayer for the diseased person, till the measure be meet of length, or at first, and so shall the party have health, and be cured, else not,

[149]

for you ought not to give over till it come to even measure again. But take care in mind to alter your style as for lameness aforesaid: "If N. be taken with any manner of ache or lameness in his arms or legs, I beseech almighty God be his help and amend him, and I leave the same," and as aforesaid in the beginning, if for a fever or ague, "If N. M. be troubled with an ague or fever, I pray and beseech almighty God to be his help and put it from him, & c."

Also, for a stroke with a planet, "If a planet have stroke N. M. I beseech almighty God to help amend him, I leave & c." Now the stroke of a planet is naught else but this man being born in the world in a certain hour and time, whereper he is made fortunate or unfortunate, according to the common courses of the stars, which hath great power over all creatures, and according to the celestial and natural influences (ex dei voluntate[990]) are the cause

987. See National Library of Scotland, GD/188/25/1/3, 58–59.

988. See manuscript page 145.

989. For a similar procedure, see Thomas, *Religion and the Decline of Magic*, 217–18.

990. *Ex dei voluntate*: Translation: "By the will of God."

of good or evil fortunate to the child then born (exempli gratia),[991] when in fortunate planets be in angles, and the ☉ and ☽ applying unto them corporally or ☍ in signs. The party then born will halt or have the loss of some member, and chiefly the ☽ being with the ☋ in these signs: ♈, ♉, ♋, ♍, or ♑, or the beginning or end of the signs.

Of Fairies[992]

But to come to the purpose concerning those creatures which common peoples like, thus of what nature and condition they be, and also what qualities they have hereby shall appear. Therefore know this, that first they were created all things of God, and having once sinned

[150]

with the prince of pride, both he and they were cast down to the earth; the chief captain went before, and they followed, and as it seemeth their fault being not so great as the rest, of their punishment is the less. Truly they are spirits, and not such as some men and women imagined them to be, who thought them to be some kind of people which live here on earth,[993] who are begotten and born one of another, and eat and drink as we do, and, when they die, are buried in the earth as we are. Now surely these people are much deceived in them who call them in the name fairy-folk, which live in an isle or country of themselves, having a king and queen to govern them, who are amongst us many times invisible, and steal meat from the butcher's, bread from the baker's, which, through their policy,[994] cannot be missed, and that fairy women have been delivered of children in men's houses, which all indeed are but mere illusions, deceptions, and vices. They say they can enrich a man whom they affect, and have power to hurt and kill whosoever displeaseth them, and which they came into any place where they thought fairies used to be, as gardens, meadows, where green rings of grass, where many green traces are to be seen, which they call the fairies' board. Then they vied to say these words: "With your leave," or, "With your leave, fair lady, give me leave safe to go, and safe to come." Much more you may per-

991. *Exempli gratia*: Translation: "For example."

992. Parallel in National Library of Scotland GD 188/25/1/3, 61–65. A modernised translation of this section can be found in Dan Harms, "Of Fairies: An Excerpt from a Seventeenth-Century Magical Manuscript," Folklore 129, no. 2 (2018), 192–98.

993. This runs counter to the thesis put forth by the most famous work on fairies, Kirk's *Secret Commonwealth*. Kirk, *Occult Laboratory*, 77–106.

994. *Policy*: Stratagem.

ceive when they still put in this prayer, which is to be said nine times together with the measure of the staff as aforesaid, for the health and help of them that are stroked therewith:

"If the fairy fall have stroken N. M., Almighty God bless him, now fair be they, and foul be we, and that fathers' and mothers' blessing be with them, and the sweet

[151]

"king of fairies lead them, and the queen of fairies feed them, I leave (or lay) the same, both more or less, with all the virtues of the Mass. Now God the Father, God the Son, and God the Holy Ghost, three persons and one true God in trinity. Take this same grief and disease away from thee, N., amen. For sweet St. Charity."

Further understand [there are] four kinds of fairies:

- the white, which are airy and have sometimes power to make men sickly and unhealthful, yet nevertheless with them is little hurt to us;
- the black are terrestrial and very malignant and deadly, for who are stroken with them do never recover; this kind seldom or never shew themselves about the earth;
- the red fairies are not so evil, yet they have power to hurt and kill, whosoever they strike is hardly cured, and that per great pains per the help of God, for they have been seen wandering up and down in several places, but always very sadly, without any mirth;
- the green fairies do commonly frequent houses, gardens, green meadows, and such places, having power to do good and evil to men or women, as to enrich or to imperish,[995] to hurt those offending them, but not so much as ye former, who are stroken of these, per God's grace, being taken in time, are ever curable.[996]

Finally these fairies, which some call elves or nymphs, are clean spirits desiring to be in houses or elsewhere that are kept with cleanly people. To such they give gifts of rewards, [to those] which, in respect of them, brush, sweep, and garnish their rooms, setting fair and fresh water in place with fair firelight. Many

995. *Imperish*: Injure.

996. I have turned this paragraph into a list, for ease of reading.

[152]

times, they leave them money, which they find on the hearth of the chimney, or in their shoes, or other places, as it hath been reported. They are very familiar with whom they shew themselves to, and very desirous of their company, filling their ear with rare music, they are to shew themselves with sweet and mild behaviour, with dances and much mirth. Their stature is like little children, most beautified and fair, using many illusions.

Further a certain friend of mine, who in his youth was much conversant with them and beloved of them, signified unto me, as far as I could perceive, that his stature was about five quarters[997] high. He said they were a people living on the earth invisible, as he supposed. I asked if they were of flesh and blood bone, as we are; he said no. Then I asked if they did eat such meal and drink such drink as we do; he said no, but that they eat some kind of food. To this I conclude they were spirits, but he would often say, "God save us and fear fall them." I asked if he were afraid of them; he answered no. Then I replied, "Why say you so?" "Because," quoth he, "we are not to talk of them."

Thus you may partly perceive their qualities, what they be, and how some are illuded.[998] To be brief, those which are those that are stroken say a prayer to help them thus: "In nomine Patris et Filii et Spiritus Sancti, amen. I ask health of body and limbs for N.," that which prayer you shall find hereafter in this book.[999] Also, if anyone be hurt in leg, foot, or arm, then first make the sign of the cross on the ground with your hand, saying, "In nomine Patris et Filii et Spiritus Sancti, amen," then again the same on the sore and grieved place, say as followeth, stroking the grief still downwards often with your right hand, "In the name of the Father, and of the Son, and of the Holy Ghost, from the ground thou cameth,

[153]

"and to the ground thou shalt vanish in God's name." Do so often, and apply on the place a plaster or poultice, made with pure oatmeal, sheep's suet, and sage, and red cow's milk, and the party shall be whole per God's help shortly.

For Fascination[1000]

"In the name of the Father, and of the Son, and of the Holy Ghost, three persons and one God in trinity, amen. I, N. M., ask help and boot of our lord and

997. *Quarters*: One-fourth of an ell or yard.

998. *Illuded*: Deceived.

999. See manuscript page 155.

1000. See manuscript pages 145, 155; National Library of Scotland GD 188/25/1/3, 65–66.

saviour Jesus Christi for I P ox,[1001] which is grieved with an ache and grief, that if three evils have been bit with eye, with tooth and tongue, and though all, at the most, three goods shall be his boot: the Father, the Son, and the Holy Ghost, three persons and one God in trinity. Give thy heart, heal them, the way of mercy and charity, amen, that all names and ache and woe out of this creature, whatsoever it may seem, go out of his heart, his flesh, and his blood and bones, that it may consume and wear at once, per the virtue of the holy Trinity. Jesus that was in Bethlem born, and baptised in the water of flem[1002] Jordan. The water was wild, the water was wood, the child was meek, and the child was good. He blessed the water, and still it stood. Then ceased the Lord God the wild flood, and as he ceased, the wild flood to cease, this grief, this pain, this ache, this woe, that out of his hurt it may soon go, out of his flesh, & c. * as above.[1003] Of this, Jesus Nazarenus, rex judeorum,[1004] saviour of all them that put your trust in thee, deliver us from all our enemies, now and evermore, amen. Jesus, Jehovah, Messias, Tetragrammaton, Emanuel, Amen."

[154]

Say this aforesaid five or nine times, and at every Pater Noster, and lastly a Creed. This is a perfect cure (under God) for man or beast.

If the Hag or Witch Ride You or Your Cattle[1005]

Say when you lay you down, three times together, with one breath: "Arint[1006] thee, witch; arint thee, witch; arint thee, witch! Thou shall merit her rest, nor row[1007] three kings' lands, till thou hast come them all through."

1001. *I P ox*: Unknown; it may signify the patient's name.

1002. *Flem*: Possibly derived from "flumen," meaning "river."

1003. See manuscript pages 145 for the rest.

1004. *Jesus...judeorum*: Translation: "Jesus of Nazareth, King of the Jews."

1005. See National Library of Scotland GD 188/25/1/3, 66. The first part of this likely refers to sleep paralysis, often seen as being caused by a hag or witch who would "ride" the person or animal at night. See Davies, "Hag-Riding in Nineteenth-Century West Country England and Modern Newfoundland."

1006. *Arint*: Probably "begone," a word first known from the 1608 edition of *King Lear*: "he met the night mare and her nine fold bid her, O light and her troth plight and arint thee, witch, arint thee." Shakespeare, *M. William Shak-speare* [...] *King Lear*, G2v. Later editions have other spellings; see Shakespeare, *King Lear*, 280 (act III, scene 4, line 120).

1007. *Row*: Stir up.

For Prick of a Thorn

"Christ was the first one that ever thorn was prick upon,
Whose flesh did neither beal[1008] nor blow,
so I pray God thy never do."

Pro Morbo Caduco[1009]

Write, with the blood of the patient's little finger, these verses following, and hang it about the party's neck: "Jasper fert myrrhum, thur *Melatrior* [Melchior], tria nomina regum solvitur a morbo Domini pietate caduco."[1010] You may say these words before these verses, though they do well without: "Purget et mundet et *manint* [muniat] nos, titulus triumphalis, Jesus Nazarenus crucifixus rex.[1011] *Adeorum* [Amen]."

Vel:[1012]

Write these words following in fair paper: "+ Pater est Alpha + et Ω, + Filius est, + salus, + vel vita, + Spiritus, + Sanctus, + est medicina dei,[1013] + Jaspar, + Melachior, + Balthasar, +." If you must put hereto, "Thur, myrrh, et auri eum et panum illi."[1014] Then wrap it up, and hang it about his neck, ut prius.[1015]

[155]

For a Fairy Stroke[1016]

"In nomine Patris, et Filii, et Spiritus Sancti, amen. I get health of body and limbs for N. that is grieved with lack and grief, that if any evil spirit of the air, earth, water hath come unto him, either standing, going, sitting, sleeping, or awaking, or per any other manner of way, either the white, black, red, or green spirits that hath shot into him any wild wind, wild water, or wild blood,

1008. *Beal*: Boil?

1009. Translation: "For Epilepsy."

1010. *Jasper...caduce*: Translation: "Jasper brought myrrh, Melchior frankincense, the three names of the king, one is released from the falling sickness with compassion of God." A mangled version of the Three Kings charm; on which see manuscript page 61.

1011. *Purget...rex*: Translation: "May the triumphal inscription, Jesus of Nazareth, the crucified king, purify us and clean us and protect us." For a sixteenth-century French text, see Duffour, "Heures Anciennes d'Auch," 128.

1012. *Vel*: Translation: "or."

1013. + *Pater...dei*: Translation: "+ The Father is Alpha + and Ω, + the Son is + deliverance, + u L life, the + Holy + Spirit + is the medicine of God."

1014. *Thur...illi*: Translation: "Of frankincense, myrrh, gold, and bread for him." This is quite mangled.

1015. *Ut prius*: Translation: "As above."

1016. See National Library of Scotland GD 188/25/1/3, 93–94.

per any manner of way. I ask heartily of our lord and saviour Jesus Christ, that it may consume away all downwards, nothing upward, all outward, and nothing inward, from the crown of the head to the sole of the feet, into the ground, all grief, pain, his ache, his woe, that from the earth did come to the earth, it may you gain, in the name of the Father, and of the Son, and of the Holy Ghost, amen. Jesus, that was born in Bethlem and baptised in the water of flem Jordan,[1017] the water was wild, the water was wood, when our Lord Jesus was baptised in the water stood still, for thou our Lord God the wild flood did cease, and he caused the wild flood to rest this grief, this pain, this ache, this woe, that from the earth did come, so to the earth it may go, in the name of the Father, and of the Son, and of the Holy Ghost, amen. I coniuro te [per] virtutem[1018] Jehovah, Emanuell, Messias, Tetragramaton." Tunc dicas[1019] three Pater Nosters, three Aves, and a Creed.

[156]

A Receipt for Healing with Clouts[1020]

First in the morning, say this prayer, kneeling on thy knees:

"O high Jehovah, most holy and glory Trinity, whose kingdom is everlasting power and infinite, have mercy upon me, most wretched creature, and grant to me thy holy spirit, Escarioth,[1021] may always be ready with me, for the benefit and help of all painful, sick, and afflicted creatures that put your trust in thee, and although I be a most wretched and wicked sinner, not worthy to look up to heaven, yet per the tender mercy of our lord and saviour Jesus Christ, forgive me and sanctify me that I may be pure to have thy holy angel, Escarioth, to be aiding, assisting, and remaining with me for the benefits of thy poor creatures, that they, receiving health, may give thee praise and glory. Grant this, O merciful Father, for Jesus Christ's sake, thy only son, our Lord and saviour Jesus Christ. Amen."

Then, having a new clean box in your hand, gather rosemary, thyme, hyssop, and winter savoury,[1022] and in gathering them, say thus:

1017. See manuscript pages 145 and 153.

1018. *I coniuro...virtutem*: Translation: "I conjure thee [by] the power."

1019. *Tunc dicas:* Translation: "Then say."

1020. *Clouts*: Cloths. See GD 188/25/1/3, 88–90.

1021. *Escarioth*: Iscariot, especially in texts in the Catalan language. It is also reminiscent of the spirit Scariot, which William Wycherley called into a crystal. Foxe, Cranmer, and Nichols, *Narratives of the Days of the Reformation*, 333.

1022. *Winter savoury*: *Satureja montana*. This was grown in England at the time on a limited basis.

"Escarioth, I charge thee per the virtue of the composition of these herbs which I offer to thee, that thou remain in thy full virtue in this box ready at my service, and I do further command thee per the holy Trinity, and per all the heavenly powers, thrones, dominations, angels, and archangels, to work my desire for the good of mankind, that were, I shall put my hand to my composition, I command thee to work my desire in healing and restoring, so I close thee with these saviours to contentions + Ah + Jehovah, + Manoth, + Adonay, + Sother, + Eloy, + Tetragramaton, + Ω, + Amen, + fiat, + fiat, + fiat, +."

[157]

And when you minister to any grief, fold a very fine clean cloth, so that it may have a cross on it, and then open your box and say, "In nomine Patris et Filii et Spiritus Sancti. Amen. Escarioth, surge et perde."[1023] Then when you have put your thumb unto the box, and after striking your thumb on the cloth, say as followeth, making a cross with your thumb at every word: "+ Eskarioth, + A, + Jehovah, + Adonay, + Sother, + Eley, + Manoth, + Emanuel, + Tetragramaton, + Ω, + Amen." Say this three times in the cloth, and three times on the place where the grief is. Then say the cloth thereon, and let continue twelve hours, and, in like manner, lay to a new again. Probatum est.

To Heal All Curable Wounds with a Plate ♄[1024] That They Shall Neither Fester, Canker,[1025] nor Corrupt while the Party Liveth

First make a square plate of ♄ in each corner, a cross, and one in the midst, and at making each cross, say the  Pater Noster until thou come unto "panem," and say all the prayer out to the end, and do see at making each cross, so that there be five Pater Nosters and five Aves in the honour of the five wounds that our Lord Jesus Christ suffered on the cross, and say this oration over the plate:

"Vulnera quinque dei sint medicina mei, *pei* [pie] crux et Christi passio.[1026] Sweet Jesus Christ, as merits as thou sufferedst five wounds in thy holy body

1023. *Surge et perde*: Translation: "Rise and destroy."

1024. ♄: Of lead.

1025. *Canker*: Infect.

1026. *Vulnera...passio*: Translation: "May the five wounds of God be my medicine, O holy cross and passion of Christ." For other examples, see Hunt, *Popular Medicine in Thirteenth-Century England*, 89, 95, 98, 226, 287; Olsan, "Writing on the Hand in Ink," 31; Forbes, "Verbal Charms in British Folk Medicine," 297; Chardonnens and Hebing, "Two Charms in a Late Medieval English Manuscript at Nijmegen University Library," 191; Lecouteux, *Dictionary of Ancient Magic Words and Spells*, xii–xiii, 85–86; MacLeod and Mees, *Runic Amulets and Magic Objects*, 132.

for all sinners, as verily keep this man. N. thy servant, from this sickness and all other sicknesses in the same,

[158]

"the Father," & c., five Pater Nosters, five Aves.

And look that the plate touch not the earth after the blessing, and renew it not till three days be over, and then wash the wound with juice of rue small,[1027] and having wept it, lay on the plate again, and afterwards remove it each day, and having wept it, lay it on without washing, and at each time you and the sick must say Pater Nosters five, and five Aves in honour of before and the five joys of our Lady. If it chance to fall to the ground, say all your oration and prayers as at beginning and lay it to again. It is good for fevers and all old sores, and note that the first oration must be said over the cross, and this over the cross:

"Coniuro te, *dolorem* [dolor], ut per istum salvum crucem, et per carnem pro nobis super crucem passam, per sanguinem Jesu defusum, ne nectas ibi *famulo* [famulum], N. quam recipiat sanitatem in aliquo membro vel in isto hora; te *dolorem* [dolor], per tres salvas dei per quod Christus passus fuit mortem propter nos super crucem, et lavit nos ab omnibus peccatis *maris* [nostris], etc.[1028] Liberet hunc famulum tuum ab omni dolorem. Amen."

> "I conjure thee, pain, so that by that uninjured cross, and by the flesh suffering for us on the cross, by the blood pouring out of Jesus, and thou not confinest there thy servant, N., who should regain their health in any member or in that hour; O thou pain, by the three salves of God, by which the suffering Christ was dead on the cross on our behalf, and he washed us from all our sins, etc. He will free this your servant from all pain. Amen."

"O most blessed glorious holy Trinity, three persons and one true God, take this infirmity, grief, and disease clean utterly away from N. for the merits, death, and passion of Christ Jesus, and as thou dost put virtue in thy holy word, and in all things, namely in words, water, wind, herbs, earth, wood, and stone & c. So put virtue in these my words, good Lord, I most humbly beseech thee, for Jesus Christ's sake, and for his holy namesake. O most merciful Father, grant

1027. *Rue small*: Possibly *Thalictrum simplex*, small meadow-rue.

1028. *Etc.*: See Vulgate Revelation 1:5.

[159]

"him health of body and soul, for in the name of Christ Jesus, thy only beloved son, our lord and saviour, do we trust and believe, which name Jesus is the name of health, as is far above all other names. And Jesus never faileth them that steadfastly believe in him and faithfully call upon him; he strengtheth, healeth, and recovereth all those that put the trust in him and seek to him for help. Therefore, Jesus, per thy holy name's sake, and for thy great mercy and pity, as verily help N. and amend him, and like as the water stood still, and the wild flood did cease and rest, so rest this impediment, this grief, this pain, this act, this disease, this woe, that from N. it may soon go and depart. I most humbly and heartily desire and beseech thee, O Lord Jesus Christ, that this affliction, infirmity, grief, and disease may waste and consume and wear away from N., all downward and nothing upward, all outward and nothing inward, from the top of the head to the soles of the feet, and never more grow, nor increase or wax greater in this, nor in any place or part of N., but always waste and to consume away lesser and lesser, till it be clean gone from him, in nomine Patri et Filii et Spiritus Sancti. Amen."

Say this oration, first three times with the patient,[1029] and last of all one Creed. Then say this following five times together, five times together with five Pater Nosters, and then last of all one Creed.

"Whatsoever humour thou be, in God's behalf, Jesus Christ, then Jesus Christ thee, per the blessed cross that Jesus was done on not per force, Jesus Christ thee with those nails

[160]

"three, that Jesus was nailed on a tree, Jesus Christ, thee with the crown of thorn that was put on Jesus's head with scorn, Jesus Christ, thee with the blessed blood, that Jesus bleeded upon the rood,[1030] Jesus Christ, thee per the wounds five that Jesus suffered in his life, Jesus Christ, thee with the sharp spear that lungs to Jesus hurt can bear, Jesus Christ, thee nevertheless, per all the virtues of the mass in honour of Saint Mary, Saint

1029. Patient: Marginal comment by original scribe appears to be "Pater," reflected in GD 188/25/1/3, 83.

1030. *Rood*: Cross.

Bokinleph,[1031] and Saint Apolin,[1032] and St. Petronil,[1033] that thou waste and consume, depart, and wear away from this place and from every part of N., through the great mercy of goodness of God, and never hereafter increase and wax great in this place and in any part of N. anymore, but ever still lesser and lesser, till thou be clean worn away and departed from this place, and in every part of him, in nomine Patris & c.," Pater Noster, Aves in five, Creed. "Now I pray God and beseech our blessed Lady, Saint Mary, the Mother of God, and Saint Kesler,[1034] and Saint Kester's mothers, to pray for us, to send this disease away from thee N...."

(Here name the disease whatsoever, whether it be any of these following, or any other disease, saying, "This wen or wart," "this cancer," or wolf,[1035] noli me tangere,[1036] King's evil, sephirus,[1037] fistula, scrofula, glandula, bubo, carbunculae, ulcer, ringworm, or any other thing that groweth or increaseth in any one.)

"God save thee, N., and preserve thy life, thy heart, thy stomach, thy brains, thy liver, thy lights, thy bowels, thy will and gall, flesh, blood, veins, sinews, & c., and cursed be this disease. Let it consume and wear away at once from this person N., per virtue of the holy Trinity. Fiat, fiat, fiat, in nomine Patris et Filii et Spiritus Sancti. Amen."

Or, "Wen, vanish away in God's name, Ise had nine children and now he hath but eight," so repeat it

[161]

over forward, till "he have none."[1038]

Then make a ring about it, and cross with your finger saying, "In nomine Patris, & c., as thou didst come, so do thou fade and want, consume, and wear away from N., from every part and place from him, and thou humour or tumour, the chief cause of this infirmity, grief, and disease, I most humbly pray and beseech almighty God that thou mayst cease forever, and

1031. *St. Bokinleph*: Unknown.

1032. *St. Apolin*: Likely St. Apollonia, a third-century saint believed to relieve toothache.

1033. *St. Petronil*: Likely St. Petronilla, a first-century Roman Christian.

1034. *St. Kesler*: Possibly St. Christopher, although the gender is incorrect..

1035. *Wolf*: Ravenous hunger.

1036. *Noli me tangere*: "Touch me not," a condition causing skin ulcers.

1037. *Sephirus*: A hard swelling or tumour.

1038. For a similar charm, see manuscript page 57.

never hereafter vex nor trouble him anymore. In the blood of Adam, death was taken, in the blood of Christ it was overcome, and per the same blood, I do thee charge that thou run no longer at large.[1039] Stay, humour; stand, humour; stop, humour; and nevermore increase or trouble any place or part the body or limbs, of N. anymore, in nomine Patris & c. Christus vincit, Christus regnat, Christus imperat."[1040] Pater Noster, Aves, Creed one.

For Fractures and Discoxations[1041]

Say as followeth, three times together.

"Now God the Father, God the Son, God the Holy Ghost in Trinity. Send boot and help for N." (here name the party, and the member or thing you pray for), and then say, "St. Bright[1042] [had?] a hunting rod; then his foot stumbled and fell, and put a bone out of the feet of his foot. Then down he alight, to set the joint right and straight,[1043] per the help of God Almighty, God set bone to bone, and bone to other, joint to joint, and joint to other, sinew to sinew, and sinew to other, rein to rein, and rein to other, blood to blood, & c., water to water, & c., flesh to flesh, & c., skin to skin, & c., hair to hair, & c., knee to knee, & c., better to better, worse and worse, and all their

[162]

"in their true proper places, nature, form, and manner as you were there before, Lord God, I most humbly beseech thee, for thy great mercy and pity, say amen, Lord Jesus Christus, I beseech, send boot and help for sweet Saint Charity." Pater, Ave, and Creed.

1039. The "In sanguine Adae" charm. See manuscript page 75.

1040. *Christus vincit…imperat*: Translation: "Christ conquers, Christ reigns, Christ commands."

1041. *Discoxations*: Likely "dislocations." This charm is a variant on the Second Merseburg Charm, dating back to the tenth century. Beck and Cottin, *Die Merseburger Zaubersprüche.*

1042. *Saint Bright*: Likely Saint Bridget, or Bride.

1043. *Stright*: Straight, left uncorrected here for poetic effect.

Experimentum qui[1044] to Ride a Long Journey[1045]

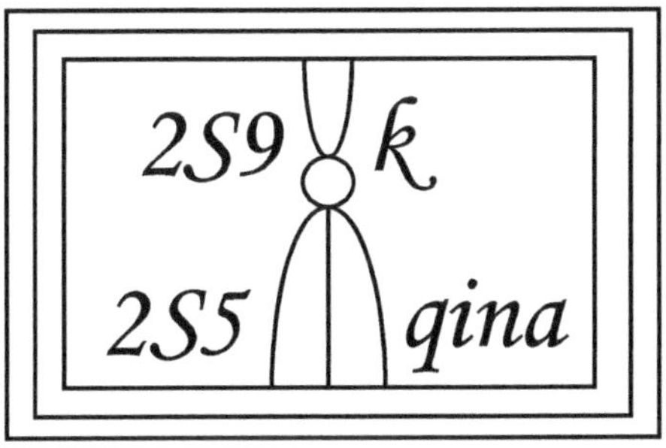

Whensoever thou wilt ride a long journey in one night, write with the blood of a bat in the evening upon the door of an house not habitas te[1046] these Hebrew names, "Deda, Elpa, Scolpa,"[1047] and say also "Eo"[1048] & c., and then go thy way, and about the space of a hour after, return thither again, and thou shall find a horse ready prepared, and when thou wouldst get upon him, put thy foot[1049] into the stirrup, saying:

"I conjure thee, thou good horse, per the creator of all things, who made all things of naught, per the living God, per the true God, per the holy God, that thou have no power to hurt me neither in body, nor in soul, or any other things, but unto such a place, such an hour, me safely bring."

And name thee [the place] and the hour, and then thou mayst get upon him safely, but thou [should] not bless thee, for then he will fly away. Note also that thou must have with thee Solomon's seal. And when thou comest to the place where thou wilt alight, and take off the bridle, and hide it under the ground, and when thou wilt have him come again,

[163]

take the bridle and shake it as hard as thou canst, and he will come to thee, and when thou wouldst get up, put thy foot in the stirrup, saying the conjuration aforesaid, and as long as thou hast the bridle, he will come when thou wilt.

1044. Translation: "Experiment."

1045. For a close parallel, see Bayerische Staatsbibliothek Clm 849, 36r–v. For discussion, see Kieckhefer, *Forbidden Rites: A Necromancer's Manual of the Fifteenth Century*, 54–57.

1046. *Not habitas te*: Translation: "[Where] you do not reside."

1047. *Deda, Elpa, Scolpa*: Clm 849: "Tuditha, Stelpha, Alpha, Draco, Mariodo, Ypation."

1048. *Eo*: Possibly "co," or "conjuration" abbreviated.

1049. Clm 849 specifies the left foot.

Ut Sis Invisibilis[1050]

"Accipe *rata* [cattae?] pellem, ante quinque dies ante aquam vialit, et in ea scribe sanguine vespertilionis notam *sequentiam* [sequentum] cum charectarum, Algatha, Pirgistas, Grimm, Plarata Irelpel.

> Take the skin of a cat; let it hang in front of water five days beforehand, and write on it the following note with the characters "Algatha, Pirgistas, Grimm, Plarata, Irelpel," with the blood of a bat, [and say:][1051]

"Invoco vos, innominatos spiritus, et coniuro ut hoc experimentum diratibas sine [?] ut inter omnes ubicunque sivi passim esse invisibilis."

> "I invoke you, unnamed spirits, and I conjure that you fulfil [?] this experiment without..., that I may be invisible among all, wherever and everywhere."[1052]

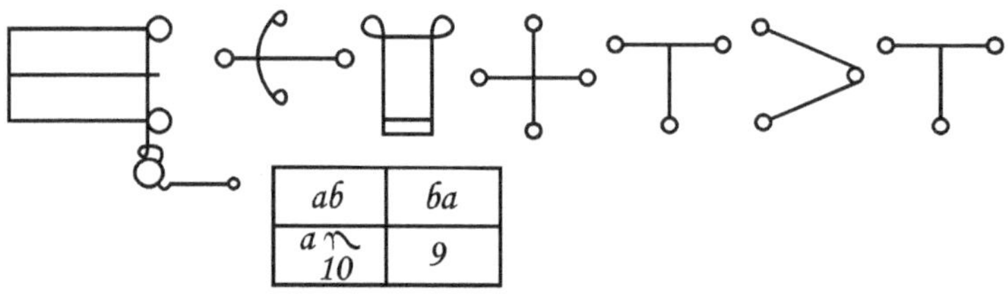

Alias ut Invisibilis,[1053] Fine[1054]

Take the water of fennel, and go unto an anthill, and say thus nine times, putting down every time of the water on the hill saying,

"Conjuro te, Belzabub, per *hostem* [nostrum] Domin[um] verum Jesum Christi, ut reddas mihi lapidem per *qui* [quem] *ne* [sic?] eam invisibilis."

> "I conjure thee, Belzabub, by our true lord Jesus Christ, that thou handest over to me the stone by which I may be invisible."

1050. Translation: "So That You May Be Invisible."

1051. Translation is conjectural.

1052. Translation is conjectural.

1053. Translation: "Another for Invisibility."

1054. For other anthill invisibility charms, see British Library Sloane 3850, 145r; Zingerle, "Segen und Heilmittel aus einer Wolfsthurner Handschrift des XV. Jahrhunderts," 324; Luther, *Werke*, 1:401; Ryan, *The Bathhouse at Midnight*, 199; Johnson, *Svartkonstböcker*, 277.

Then look immediately after, and thou shalt find a stone of diverse colours, which thou must bear in thy right hand. Idem with hot water; as soon write, it should be done, and with a piece of lead whereon is written

[164]

these words, "Athatos, Ryros, Thean, Panton, Craton," wear it under your left foot.

Of the Order and Condition of the Spirits[1055]

There be nine degrees of spirits, and the first order be called false gods, because they do usurp the name of the true God, and would be worshipped for the true God, desiring sacrifices and adorations. Humfiem Beskebub princeps.[1056]

Of the [second] order be the spirits of lies which, enluring[1057] men, do make then prophesy dreams of things to come, and expound dreams, deluding men, et princeps horum est Python.[1058]

Spirits of the third order be called vasa *minignitutis* [iniquitatis] et vasa irae,[1059] because they be the inventors of mischief and all evil arts. As Plato witnesseth, the spirit Theulus was the inventor of play at dice, whereof grows much mischief, et princeps eorum Belial.[1060]

Spirits of the fourth order be called ultores scelerum, et princeps eorum Asmodeus.[1061]

Of the fifth order be called spirits praestigiatores, beguiling spirits, which imitate working of miracles and obeying to naughty, and delude men to reduce the people per their miracles from the true God, et princeps eorum est Satan.[1062]

Of the sixth order aeriae potestates, the airy spirits which send thunder and lightnings, pestilence, and other evils, et princeps dictus Miririm.[1063]

1055. A condensation of Agrippa, *De Occulta Philosophia* (book 3, chapter 18). The wording in this section does not follow the published English text, suggesting it is a copy of another author's partial translation. Some Latin phrases defined immediately thereafter have been left untranslated.

1056. *Humfiem...princeps*: Conjectural translation of "*Beskebub* [Beelzebub] is their leader."

1057. *Enluring*: Enticing.

1058. *Et...Python*: Translation: "And their prince is Python."

1059. *Vasa...irae*: Translation: "Vessels of iniquity and anger."

1060. *Et...Belial*: Translation: "And their prince is Belial."

1061. *Ultores...Asmodeus*: Translation: "avengers of evil, and their prince is Asmodeus."

1062. *Et...Satan*: Translation: "And their prince is Satan."

1063. *Et...Miririm*: Translation: "And their prince is called Miririm."

[165]

The spirits of the eighth[1064] order are *ceimisatores* [criminatores] sive exploratores *belleris* [bellicos], et princeps eorum est Astaroth.[1065]

Spirits of the seventh order be called furiae, furies, which do make discord, wars, and mischief amongst men, et princeps eorum est Apollion vel Abadton.[1066]

Ditto of the ninth order, which are called tempters, and these are present at all times with every man, et princeps *horum* [eorum] est Mammon.[1067]

De Natura et Formis Spirituum[1068]

Et Imprimis de Saturni Spiritibus[1069]

The nature of the spirit of ♄ is to sow discord, hatred, and evil cogitations, to give a man leave,[1070] as much as he will, to kill any man or lame any creature. At first they will appear with a long, thick body, with an angry countenance having four faces, one in the hinder part of the head, and another in the fore part, made after the manner of a beak. Also, in both the knees doth appear eyes. They are of a black colour yet shining. They will appear, [as it] were, familiarly, like a king with a great beard riding upon a dragon, like an old man with a beard; or like an old woman leaning upon a staff; like a hog; like a dragon or owl. Their motions are with great winds, with a shew of earthquake. The sign of their coming is with earth, whiter than snow. Spiritus aeri diei saturni subjiciuntur vento Africae.[1071]

1064. *Eighth order*: Note the seventh order appears directly below.

1065. *Ceimisatores...Astaroth*: Translation: "Accusers or warlike spies, and their prince is Astaroth." "Bellicos," or "warlike," is not in Agrippa.

1066. *Et...Abadton*: Translation: "And their prince is Apollion or Abadton."

1067. *Et...Mammon*: Translation: "And their prince is Mammon."

1068. Translation: "Of the Nature and Appearances of the Spirits." What follows is a combination of material on the planetary spirits from both the *Fourth Book* of pseudo-Agrippa and the *Heptameron*. This is at least partially adapted from the English texts.

1069. Translation: "And First, of the Spirits of Saturn."

1070. Peterson notes that the Latin editions have "plumbum," or the metal lead. Peter de Abano, "Heptameron." The same error appears in Turner's edition.

1071. *Spiritus...Africae*: Translation: "The spirits of the air of Saturday are subject to the southwest wind."

[166]

♃

The nature of the spirits of Jupiter is to get the love of a woman, to make men glad and pleasant, to pacify strifes, to make enemies friends, to heal the sick and infect the whole, to carry and fetch things that are stolen. They do appear with a choleric and sanguine body, on an indifferent stature, with a horrible motion, with a pleasant sight, with a courteous speech, in colour like unto rusty iron. More familiarly, they appear like a king with a drawn sword, riding upon a hart; like a man with a sceptre in a long raiment; like a maid with a laurel crown set with flowers; like a bull, hart, peacock, golden[1072] garments, a sword, or box tree. Their motion is with lightning and thunder; the sign of their coming is men appearing about the circle, with a shoe are devoured as lions.[1073] Spiritus aeris diei Jovis subjiciuntur austro.[1074]

♂

The nature of the spirits of ♂ is to make wars, murders, burning per fires, death, infirmities, to give health, and two thousand soldiers for a time. They do appear with a long, choleric body, a filthy aspect with a red colour, and with horns almost like the horns of an hart, and claws of a griffin; they will roar like a mad bull. Their familiar forms be these: a king armed, riding upon a wolf, a man armed; a woman holding a shield in her buttock;[1075] a goat; a horse; a hart;[1076] red garment; whole multitudes. Their motion is like burning fire; the signs of their coming is thunder and lightning about the circle. Spiritus aerie diei ♂ subiciuntur subsolano,[1077]

[167]

☉

The nature of the spirits of Sol is to give gold, jewels, carbuncles, riches, favours, and good soil; to make peace amongst men; to give honour; to take

1072. *Golden*: Other versions have "azure."

1073. *With a shoe…lions*: Translation: "Who in appearance will be devoured by lions."

1074. *Spirits…austro*: Translation: "The spirits of the air of Thursday are subject to the south wind. "

1075. *Buttock*: Other versions have "thigh."

1076. *Hart*: The Turner translation, derived from the edition of the Beringos brothers, has "stag," but "raven" is consistent with earlier Latin editions. See Peterson, "Heinrich Cornelius Agrippa: His Fourth Book of Occult Philosophy."

1077. *Spiritus…subsolano*: Translation: "The spirits of the air of ♂ are subject to the east wind."

away and bring infirmities. [They] do appear with a great body, red and thick, with a golden colour springled,[1078] as it were, with blood. Their familiar forms be these: a king with a sceptre riding upon a lion; a crowned king; a queen with a sceptre; a bird; a lion; a cock; yellow and golden vesture; a sceptre; a tail. Their motion is shining of the heaven; the sign of their coming is to make the caller sweat. Spiritus aerie diei Solis subjiciuntur vento Borea.[1079]

The nature of the spirits of ♀ is to give money, to stir men, and make them luxury, to make enemies friends per luxuries, to make marriages, to entice men to the love of women, to bring and take away infirmities, and to do all things which are to be done per motion. They do appear with a fierce[1080] body of an indifferent stature, with an amiable and pleasant aspect, with a white and green colour, imbrothered,[1081] as is it were, with gold. Their familiar forms be these: a king with a sceptre riding upon a camel, a maid gorgeously apparelled, a naked maid, a she-goat, a camel, a dove, vestments white or green, shewers,[1082] or like the herb savine.[1083] Their motion is like a bright star. The sign of their coming is maids playing about the circle, which will entice the worker to play. Spiritus aeris diei ♀ subjiciuntur *Zelphero* [Zephiro].[1084]

[168]

☿

The nature of the spirits of ☿ is to give all kind of metals, all earthen things, and to shew things present, past, and to come; to please judges, and to give victory in battles; to make perfect experiments to teach and make plain all decayed sciences; to change one kind of metal into another upon conditions;

1078. *Springled*: Sprinkled.

1079. *Spiritus…Borea*: Translation: "The spirits of the air of Sunday are subject to the north wind."

1080. *Fierce*: Latin editions have "pulchro," "fair."

1081. *Imbrothered*: Embroidered.

1082. *Shewers*: Latin editions have "flores," "flowers."

1083. *Savine*: *Juniperus sabina*, connected with Venus as a highly toxic contraceptive and abortifacient. Watts, *Dictionary of Plant Lore*, 344–45.

1084. *Spiritus…[Zephiro]*: Translation: "The spirits of the air of ♀ are subject to the west wind."

to take away and bring infirmities to every man, or decay[1085] them; to bind or lose spirits; or to open locks. They will often appear with a body of middle stature, cold, moist, and fair, with a pleasant speech, like to an armed soldier with a bright colour. Their particular forms be these: a king riding a bear; a fair young man; a woman with a rock;[1086] a dog; a bear; a pie;[1087] a garment of diverse colours; a twig; a staff. Their motion is like a silver cloud; the sign of their coming is, they bring horror and fear to the caller. Spiritus aeris diei ☿ subjiciantur Africo.[1088]

☽

The nature of the spirits of the ☽ is to give money, to carry things out of one place into another, to give swift horses, to tell men secrets present and past. They appear with a great, soft, phlegmatic body in colour like to a black cloud, with a full countenance, red eyes full of water, with a bald head, and with teeth like to boar's teeth. Their familiar forms be these: a king with a bow and arrows riding upon a buck, a little boy, a woman like a hunter with bow and arrows, a cow, a doe, a goat, a garment green or silver coloured,

[169]

an arrow, or many feet.[1089] Their motion is like the foaming of the sea; the sign of their coming is great rain about the circle. Spiritus aeris diei ☽ subjiciuntur Zephero.[1090]

Beware of some that do write the characters and the names of the spirits in paper or parchment, and then burn it in powder and giveth to drink to obtain their devilish purpose.

Ad Habendum Vera Responsa de Omnibus Questionibus[1091]

Prima antequam hoc facias, debes esse vere penitens et confessus, et in prima die jejuna in pane et aqua. Post ea in die mercurii sero in hora mercurii, hora intrandum dormitum solis, sis in camera, tace, et ardeat lucerna, et stando, *sic* [dic] ista verba:

1085. *Decay*: Cause to lose prosperity.

1086. *Rock*: Latin editions have "colum," "distaff."

1087. *Pie*: Magpie.

1088. *Spiritus…Africo*: Translation: "The spirits of the air of ☿ are subject to the southwest wind."

1089. *Many feet*: Latin editions have "multipes," "millipede."

1090. *Spirits…Zephero*: Translation: "The spirits of the air of ☽ are subject to the west wind."

1091. Translation: "For Having True Answers for All Questions." For other examples, see Harms, Clark, and Peterson, *Oberon*, 528; Bodleian Rawlinson D.252, 99r–100r; British Library Sloane 3318, 55v, 64v–65r, Sloane 3850, 157v; below, manuscript page 330–31.

First, before you do this, you should be truly penitent and confessed, and fast on the first day on bread and water. After that on the day of Mercury, on the hour of Mercury in the evening, at the hour of the sun setting, be silent in your chamber, and a lamp should burn there. And standing, say these words:

"Sanctus, sanctus, sanctus, Deus Jesus Christus in die *mercurius* [mercurii] fuit perditus ac traditus. Sanctus, sanctus, sanctus, Deus, Jesus Christus in die Jovis fuit captus, temptatus *est* [et] flagellatus. Sanctus, sanctus, sanctus, Deus Noster, Jesus Christi in die veneris fuit suspensus, flagellatus, et sepulitis, Sanctus, Sanctus, Sanctus Deus, cum sanctis tuis, mitte mihi nuncium qui dabit mihi vera responsa de quibuscunque eum interregabo."

"Holy, holy, holy God, on Wednesday Jesus Christ was lost and handed over. Holy, holy, holy God, on Thursday Jesus Christ was seized, tested, and whipped. Our holy, holy, holy God, on Friday Jesus Christ was hung, whipped, and buried. Holy, holy, holy God, with your saints, send a messenger to me who will give true answers to him regarding whatsoever I will ask him."

Haec verba dic tribus vicibus, et postea vade dormitum ad lectum tuum, et cito post vigilia, invenies hominem barbatum in specie hominis senis, et primo interroga nomen ejus diligenter, et post ea, quere de omnibus qui volueris scire.

Say these words three times, and afterward go to sleep in your bed, and immediately after awakening, you will find a bearded man in the likeness of an old man, and first ask his name diligently, and after this, ask regarding all things that you desire to know.

[170]

Pro Invisibilitate[1092]

First say this Psalm nine [times] "Quicunque vult," & c.;[1093] "Salvum me, fac deus quoniam defecit sanctus," & c.;[1094] "Deus in nomine tuo," & c.;[1095] "Salvum me, fac deus intraverunt aquae";[1096] and "Miserere mei, deus secun-

1092. Translation: "For Invisibility." For a French parallel, see Peterson, *Grimorium Verum*, 44–45. For more examples of similar rites, see Harms, "Spirits at the Table," and manuscript pages 188–92.

1093. *Quicunque...*: The Athanasian Creed.

1094. *Salvum...*: Psalm 11.

1095. *Deus in nomine...*: Psalm 53.

1096. *Salvum...*: Psalm 68.

dum," & c.[1097] Then take a large fair tile-stone, and lay charcoal thereon, and tinder the charcoal with a candle of virgin wax, and go three times about the fire, with the candle burning in thy hand, saying these words: "Panton, Craton, Maveton, Iwereston, Manton, Diaton, Tetragramaton." Then set upon the fire a pan with water, and wash thy body clean with the same, and see thy bed be made with clean sheets, fast per the fire. And lay thee down and say these words, "Crothe, Crothea, Crothees," three times.

"In nomine Patris et Filii, & c. Conjuro vos tres sorores, Meillya, Catillya, Sybillia, in nomine Patris & c., ut veniatis visibiliter in judicia mea, et ne noceatis mihi, et portetis vobiscum signum per quod possum fieri invisibilis quando mihi placuerit, et statim recedatis a presentia mea; nec habeatis potestatem mihi nocendi."

> "In the name of the Father, and of the Son, & c. I conjure you three sisters, Meillya, Catillya, Sybillia, in the name of the Father & c., that you should come visibly in my judgment, and you should not hurt me, and you shall bear with you the seal-ring by which I shall be able to be made invisible when it might please me, and you should immediately leave from my presence; nor should you have power for hurting me."

Do all these things on the second day as thou didst on the first day; except water washing thee, but on the third day, do all things as on the first day, and when thou art upon thy bed, cover thy face with handkerchiefs, that is thine, that thou mayest

[171]

see though it, and three will come to thee. Then say thou, "Crothe, Crothea, Crotheon," three times, and one of them will put a ring on thy finger that thou mayest go invisible, and this must be done three days at the beginning, or else three last days of [1098]. Finis.

To Have Thy Desire of All Things Carried and Brought to Thy Hand, or, to Wit, to What Place Thou Wilt Assign

First take the blood of a buck, and keep it in a vessel of glass, and thou wilt do this experiment at the first, beginning the Wednesday or the Friday after the prime,[1099] and go barefooted all that day, and fast the three days. After the ☉ is down, take parchment of a black cat's spine, and write these names

1097. *Miserere...*: Psalm 50.

1098. Text missing. The *Grimorium Verum* does not have a parallel passage.

1099. *Prime*: Early morning church office.

following: "Aldiater, Belleracke, Bellonay, Hallahallynza, Saluzem," and wind therein three pence of diverse money, and bind it in a silk thread, that which should be deeped[1100] in thy own blood, and going barefoot, put it in the earth. Then make the Pantacle of Solomon, and write these words or names therein before written, "Aldiacor, & c.," with the buck's blood, and see it be pegged upon a window or door. Before sacrifice, rehearse these words or names thrice, "Aldiacor" & c. Write the name of the thing which thou wouldst have carried with ink in four places about the pentacle, and go thy

[172]

way precisely, and come again in the morning before ☉ rise, and thou shalt find that thou asketh. And from that time and day forward, whensoever thou wilt work this experiment, thy will shall be fulfilled without making of sacrifices and as is aforesaid. If thou wilt do this experiment at the first beginning, do it on the Wednesday or Friday after the new of the ☽, saying these words:

"Conjuro vos, *spiritis* [spiritus], Aldiator, Ballerock, Bellonay, Hallyhallmza, Coolazem, per Patrem, + et Filium, + et Spiritum Sanctum,[1101] + and per the blood of our Lord Jesus Christ + and per St. Mary, Mother + of our + Lord Jesus Christ + and per his ascension, and per the virginity of St. Mary, and per the virginity of St. John the Baptist, that ye do fulfil my desire, and bring into this place a thousand pounds of gold and silver, per him which shall come to judge the quick and the dead, and the world per fire, so be it."

An example of the pentacle of Solomon with the names of the spirits as they ought to be written thereon and demand:

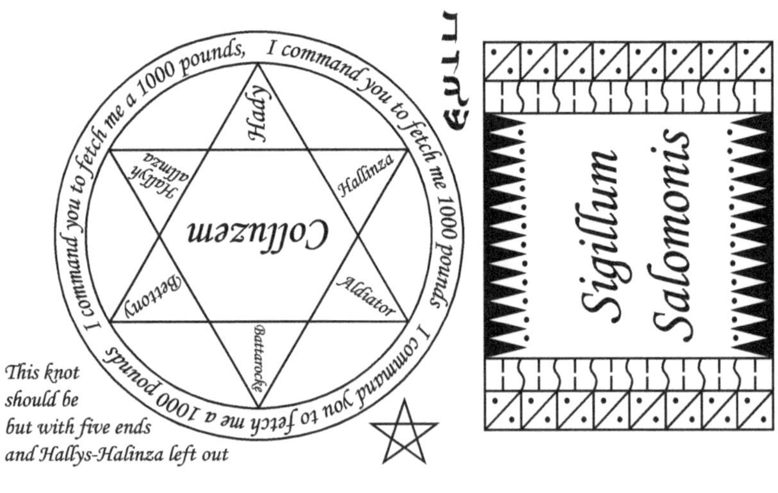

1100. *Deeped*: Plunged into.

1101. *Coniuro...Sanctum*: Translation: "I conjure you, spirits, Aldiator, Ballerock, Bellonay, Hallyhallmza, Coolazem, per the Father, + and the Son, + and the Holy Ghost."

[173]

[An Experiment for Love]

Take thy own flens,[1102] and write the name of the party in virgin parchment with these characters following:

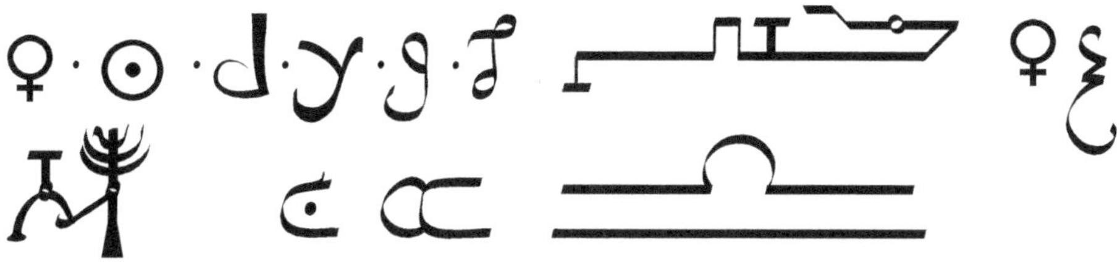

And with the same parchment, touch the same party, and then say as followeth once, casting it into the fire, and when it is in the fire, say it over twice more.

"O tu, Annaell, angelus dei et fortis *in a perationem* [operationem] mirabilem venereререa [?], ego precipio. Mando, et flagitur te per virtutem, potentiam istorum verborum quae recitavero utque per istud nomen dei Tetragramaton, et Sabaoth, et per *duodicem* [duodecim] nomina, et per septem angelos septem planetas presidentes, et per viginti octo angelos qui dominant[ur] mansionibus lunae, et per quatuor principes angelorum qui perfecti sunt super quatuor ventos, super quatuor partes mundi, et per quatuor angelos qui quatuor elementa regunt et duodecim mensis, per duodecim sacros apostolos, per duodecim membra signis distributa, per duodecim ordines beatorum spirituum, per charecteres *stelea* [stellae] veneris qui quidem sunt sancti, et per nomen et sigillum tuam quae quidem sunt sanctissima et suffumagationes vestras per sanctissimas, et per alta dicta aut verba qua dici aut constringi possunt. Ego precipio et mando te, tu princeps Hannell, ut *cogeris* [cogas?] mulierem vel virginem cujus nomen

[174]

"scriptum est in ista charta mea sanguine proprio, ut sicut nomen ejus ardeat in igne, ita mulier ipsa in mea amore ardeat ardentur cum maxime, 'Diligo te.' Totum consumatur ipsa, in meo amore fit plena fixa. Cogis per eum qui venturus est iudicare seculum per ignem, Amen, fiat, fiat, fiat, cito, cito, cito."

> "O thou, Annael, angel of God and strong, I order thee into a marvelous operation of Venus. I ask thee, and it is demanded, by the virtue and power of these names that I will have rehearsed, even by that name of God Tetragramaton and Sabaoth, and by the twelve names, and by

1102. *Flens*: Not in OED; compare to Latin "fleo," "to shed tears."

the seven angels guarding the seven planets, and by the twenty-eight angels who rule the mansions of the moon, and by the four princes of the angels who are excellent over the four winds over the four regions of the world, and by the four angels that have dominion over the four elements and twelve months, by the twelve holy apostles, by the twelve houses assigned with signs, by the twelve orders of the blessed spirits, by the characters of the planet Venus that are indeed holy, and by your name and seal that are indeed most holy, and your suffumigations by the most holy ones, and by the high sayings and words that are able to be said and bound. I command and ask thee, thou prince Hannell, that thou summonest the woman or virgin the name of whom [174] is written in this my paper in my own blood, so that as her name may burn in fire, so that woman may burn ardently in my love at this moment, [saying?] 'I love thee.' The same is entirely accomplished; she is fully constant in love of me. Thou summonest by him who will come to judge the world by fire. Amen. Let it be done, let it be done, let it be done, quickly, quickly, quickly."

[A Spirit of Love]

"Ego sum Nesroth, spiritus amoris qui corda mulierum ad amorem hominem vente, nec facite amor extinguitur. Ecce *ad sure* [assum] ad [sic] quid vocastis me."

"I am Nesroth, a spirit of love who stirs the hearts of women to love of men, and that love may not be extinguished [?]. Behold, I appear as thou hast called me."[1103]

1103. For a spirit list employing similar language, see Harms and Clark, *Of Angels*, 241–43, 246–47.

A Call to Oberion[1104]

In the first Monday of the new ☽, take a plate of lead and shape the image of Oberion thereon, and write his name in his forehead, and his sign over his head, and the sign of the ☉ on the right side, and the sign of the ☽ on the left side, and the name of the angel ☉ above the sign, that is, Storax, and the same of the Angell of the ☽ above the sign, is to say Carmillion, and say this conjuration.

"You angels of the ☉ and ☽, I pray and exercise[1105] you per the virtue of the high God Agla, and per the names that be marvellous, and per these signs that bind imparted in this place, and in the virtue and might of the Creator, and on the name of the high shining God, that whensoever I shall call Oberion, whose image is here pictured, and names here written, and his sign here drawn in the place, to make Oberion obey me, and to be right in man's form, without hurting, or perturbation, or fraudness, and without grieving my body or soul after my will and after his, without guile or fraud, in all things truly and perfectly to fulfil."

In the second day, write in the right side of the plate the name of their proper counsellor Raberion, and his sign, and say these words:

"I do exercise thee, Raberion, per the virtue of all heavenly things, earthly things, and infernal things, and per King Solomon which made thee subject unto him, and per all his signs, seals, and rings, and per the four elements per which the world is sustained and nourished, and per the serpent that was exalted in the wilderness, that thou help and give counsel to thy

[175]

Lord, that he shall shew himself to me, and say to me my desire in all things, that I desire of him after his power," & c.

Say this three times in the first day and once in the night. On the third day, write the name of the second counsellor, that is Severion, and his sign on the left side, and say:

"Thou Severion, I do exercise thee and command thee per this name Elizan,[1106] that is no man's name, but in peril of death or in great necessity,

1104. For other examples of the call to Oberion, see Harms, Clark, and Peterson, *Oberon*, 455–74; Harms and Clark, *Of Angels*, 290–91; Biblioteca Medicea Laurenziana Plut. 89 sup. 38; Bodleian Rawlinson D.252, 139r–142v; British Library Sloane 3826, 98r–99r; Sloane 3318,18v–21r, 62r–64r, 76r–79v; Sloane 3846, 102v–107r; National Library of Scotland GD 188/25/1/3, 142–52, 152–59; Wellcome Institute 110, 97r.

1105. *Exercise*: Possibly used in the sense of putting into motion, or a misspelling of "exorcise."

1106. *Elizan*: Harms, Clark, and Peterson, *Oberon*: "Elyron."

and per all the spirits as well high as low, that, without any tarrying, thou give counsel to thy lord, that he do shew to me his presence without dread to me, or quaking fear, and without any other disturbance in all things, you all his four angels and counsellors, Storax, Karmelion, Caberion, Severion, I do call you together and command you, that without delay you go to Oberion, whose speaking with I do desire, per the virtue of these names, Yzaby, Colpas, Frypas,[1107] and per the quick and very[1108] God that framed all the world of naught, and per all his angels and archangels, and per all the saints in heaven, and in earth, that you make Oberion to appear unto me, in a manlike manner and form, and to certify me of all things that I would ask him, without fraud or deceit, in the name of the Father, and of the Son, and of the Holy Ghost. Amen."

You must fume the plate with frankincense and aloes, and then say this invocation in a secret place, that is, the call of Oberion:

[176]

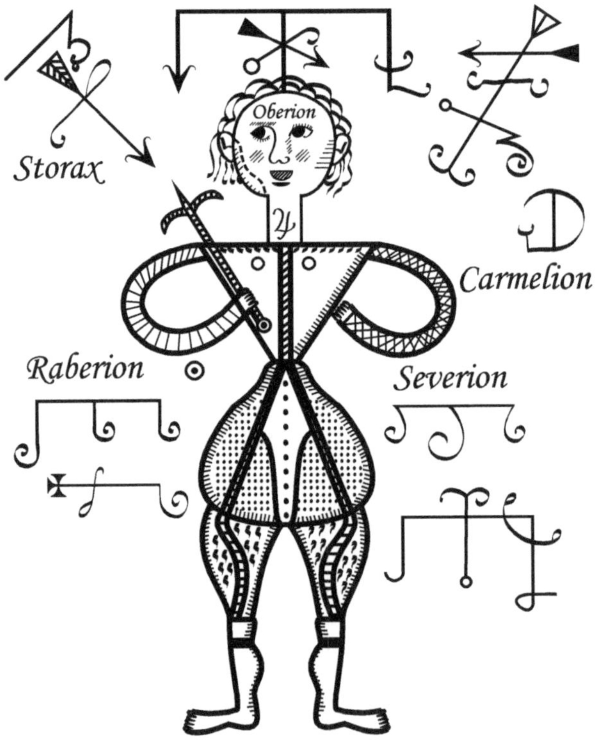

1107. *Yzaby...Frypas*: Harms, Clark, and Peterson, *Oberon*: "Yraky + Collpus + & Trypus."

1108. *Very*: Faithful.

[177]

"O you angels of the ☉ and of the ☽, whose names and signs are parted[1109] in this plate, and your spirits and counsellors, and every one of you angels and spirits whose names and signs are made in this plate and do attend and give counsel to the shining spirit Oberion, whose image is here drawn in this plate, I do exercise you, his angels and counsellors, whose names be these, Storax, Carmelion, Raberion, Severion, I do exercise you per all the unspeakable names of the most high God, the God of Abram, Isaac, and Jacob, and per the virtue of the twelve apostles, the twelve patriarchs, the twelve signs, and the four evangelists, and per all the powers and virtues of heaven and earth, and all things in them contained, I do exercise you to fulfil my request, per the virtue of this name Elizan, that no man's name but in the peril of death or in great necessity, and per all the spirits as well high as low, that without any tarrying you give counsel to your lord Oberion, that he may shew me his presence without any dread to me, or quaking fear, or any other disturbance in all things, you, his four angels and counsellors, Storax, Kermelion, Caberion, Severion, I do call you together and command you, that you do go without delay to Oberion, whose speaking with I desire, per the virtue of these names, Ysazy, Colpas, and Stripas, and per the quick very God that framed all the world of naught, and per all his angels and archangels, and per all the saints both in heaven and in earth, that you make

[178]

"Oberion to appear to me in manlike form, and a goodly manner, and to satisfy me of all things that I would ask him without any fraud or deceit, in the name of the everliving God, Amen. In the name of the Father, and of the Son, and of the Holy Ghost, per omnia secula seculorum.[1110] Amen.

"Rebano, Mataron, Macharon, Magell, Robale, Machare, Vagen, Potoza, Fanoy, Garnael, Zala, Mite, Agaza, Sebamay, Alacrice, Malaipe, per the power and virtue of these holy names, I do call thee, I do conjure thee, most shining spirit Oberion, whose name and image is here drawn and written, tarn the shear to be shed to my image.[1111] Come towards the east, I do call thee, which art worthily called, that thou fly not away, but shew thyself to me, clothing thee not fearfully, but pleasantly, per the virtue of Ysus, Odas, Joerh, and per the

1109. *Parted*: Placed.

1110. *Per…seculorum*: Translation: "Forevermore."

1111. *Tarn the shear…image*: Possible reading from Harms, Clark, and Peterson, *Oberon*, 472: "that now here it may be openly showed, to my image here present."

virtue of the high God, that which all the Arabics, Caves,[1112] Greeks, and Chaldeans worshipped, and per that king in whose legion thou art going, and per the prayer of these whose names be written in this plate, and per the signs and virtues that God gave to man, when he said that all spirits infernal should be subject to him. I conjure thee to appear unto me in man's form, me not grieving, nor any having this plate in his right hand, but to come readily, and that will of me I do constrain thee perfectly to fulfil per the virtue of all the rial[1113] names above spoken. Fiat, fiat, fiat."

[179]

Say this conjuration three times:

"Depart in peace, in the name of our Lord Jesus Christ, to the place ordained for thee, per our Lord God, and whensoever or as often as I shall call thee, or any that call thee, having this plate in thy right hand, that without delay thou do come and obey thee to me or him, which shall [call] thee to the virtue of Eligron and not else, in the name of the Father, and of the Son, and of [the Holy] Spirit, in the name of Jesus of Nazareth, I do sign me with the sign of the holy Cross true.  Discede, *C[h]ristus hic est*; [hic Christus est], liquesce: signum quod [ipse] *noste* [nosti] *domine* [damnat] tuam *calevane* [catervam]."[1114]

If he will not depart, rehearse the Gospel of St. John three times, "In principio erat verbum, et verum erat apud deum," & c.[1115]

"Adoramus te, *Christi* [Christe], miserere mei Jesu fili, domine."[1116]

Consecratio Circuli[1117]

"Conjuro te, circulum et locum istum, per illum verum deum qui istam terram creavit, sanctificem et conservatem circulum et locum istum, per Christum creatorem qui totum mundum de nihilo creavit et fecit, et per ista eius

1112. *Caves*: Readings uncertain. Not in Harms, Clark, and Peterson, *Oberon*.

1113. *Rial*: Royal.

1114. *Discede…[catervam]*: Translation: "Depart, Christ is here; Christ is here, melt; the sign that you yourself know condemns your company." These are stanzas from Prudentius's *Hymnus ante Somnum*; see Prudentius, *Prudentius*, 1:56–57.

1115. John Chapter 1.

1116. *Adoramus…Domine*: Translation: "We worship thee, O Christ; have mercy on me, Jesus, son, Lord."

1117. Translation: "The Consecration of the Circle." See Harms, Clark, and Peterson, *Oberon* 111–13, and below, manuscript pages 219–20.

nomina sanctissima + Theos, Otheos, + Iskyros, + Athanatos, + Fath, + Agle, + Yaym, + Deus, + Heloy, + Beth, + Hebaneth, + Zeth, + Othee, + Sabaoth, + Phanebabs, + Hely, + Haliel, + Onath, + Mathyel +

[180]

"Amasiel, + Gudomel, + Agios, + Ehekimas, + Ehelias, + Ymas, + Messias, + Oum, + Eloy, Eloey, + Elyon, + Aggen, + Ya, + Pe, + Peak, + Pathmael, + Vau, + Thaum, + He, + Het, + Haw, + Etheus, + Vawin, + Tallens, + Sanctus, + Agla, + Thata, + Cogothomoun, + Sadaly, + Tsohonos, + Sepuum, + Haglata, + Vitel, + Ytell, + Abria, + Divinum, + Hepe, + Neexe, + Yalena, + Ya + et per omnia nomina dei sanctissima, nota et ignota, sit *locuto iste* [locum istum] et circulum istum ex dono magno omnipotentis altissimi dei, benedictus et consecratus et custoditus et sanctificatus, et a *sufficiteatem* [sufficientem] omnium stipendium dei de stellarum celi angelorum et archangelorum, *thronum* [thronorum], *dominarint* [dominationum], *principates* [principatuum], [potestatum], et virtutum, quoque cherubin et seraphin, prophetarum, apostolorum, evangelorum, martirum, confessorum, atque virginium, patriarchum, potentes confirmantes et reconciliantes circulus et locus iste quatenus talem virtutem et potestatem et sanctitatem suam capiat et obteneat a signo dei veri et vivi a sancta Cristi Cruce, + *per et* [et per] sanctam Mariam, Matrem Domini Nostri Jesu Christi, plena gratia, consecratus pro nullus spiritus malignus habeat aliquam potestatem *alicuitur* [alicui] ingredi nec inter circulum istum, *tereores* [terrores], *sanctissimata* [sanctissima], timores, nos temptationes aliquando nobis nocendi valeat infra Cristo

[181a]

"adjuvante et defendate, [omnia] in caelestia, terrestia, et infernalia subjiciuntur."

> "I conjure thee, this circle and place, by that true God who created this world, this holy and protective circle and place, by Christ the creator, who created and made the whole world of nothing, and by these most holy names of him + Theos, Otheos, + Iskyros, + Athanatos, + Fath, + Agle, + Yaym, + Deus, + Heloy, + Beth, + Hebaneth, + Zeth, + Othee, + Sabaoth, + Phanebabs, + Hely, + Haliel, + Onath, + Mathyel + [180] Amasiel, + Gudomel, + Agios, + Ehekimas, + Ehelias, + Ymas, + Messias, + Oum, + Eloy, Eloey, + Elyon, + Aggen, + Ya, + Pe, + Peak, + Pathmael, + Vau, + Thaum, + He, + Het, + Haw, + Etheus, + Vawin, + Tallens, + Sanctus, + Agla, + Thata, + Cogothomoun, + Sadaly, +

Tsohonos, + Sepuum, + Haglata, + Vitel, + Ytell, + Abria, + Divinum, + Hepe, + Neexe, + Yalena, + Ya + and by all the most holy names of God, known and unknown, may this place and this circle, from the great gift of the highest omnipotent God, be blessed and consecrated, protected and sanctified, and from the providing of all wages of God, from the stars of the heaven, of angels and archangels, of thrones, of dominions, of principalities, of powers, and of virtues, also of cherubim and seraphim, of prophets, of apostles, of evangelists, of martyrs, of confessors, and of virgins, patriarchs, and powers strengthening and conciliating the circle and place, that it receive and acquire such of its virtue and power and holiness from the sign of the true and living god, from the holy cross of Christ, + and from the holy Mary, Mother of our Lord Jesus Christ, full of grace, consecrated that no evil spirit should have any power to enter anything, and finally no terrors, most holy things, fears, or temptations should have power of harming us in this circle under Christ, [181a] helping and defending us, to whom all things heavenly, earthly, and hellish things are subject."

Ista conjuratio debes discede[re] nomine Deum modo facies circulum hic dicendo et inde asperge aqua benedicta.

With this conjuration, you should leave directly in the name of God. You will make the circle, saying this, and then sprinkle with holy water:

"Aspergo te, aquam benedictam, in circulo et loco isto, in nomine Patris omnipotentes dei, qui te aquam fecit, et benedixit, et consecravit, et dedit potestatem famulis suis sacerdotibus *puerique* [praecipue] *dominantes* [dominantis] diebus in ecclesiam suam a ista aqua benedicere et consecrare qui est pater, et filius, et spiritus sanctus. Ego te, aquam benedictum, invoco et exorciso in nomine dei, et sancte Marie Matris suae, [nec non] in nomine, in virtute omnium sanctorum et sanctarum ejus, cum omnium caelestium *consortio* [consertio], ut tu, aqua [sit] benedicta et consecrata, per illum deum qui te fecit et conservavit, iussit omnibus defensio et protectio ab omnibus diaboli temptationibus et infestationibus incidiis et fraudibus *praesentis* [potestate] *Sanctus* [Sancti] Spiritus, nobis *manaum* [qui misericordiam] suam posse *tibis* [ubique] ad te dignetur [per] Dominum Jesum Christum."

"I sprinkle thee, holy water, in this circle and place, in the name of God the omnipotent Father, who made and blessed and consecrated thee, water, and gave power to his servants his priests, especially on Sundays in his church, to bless and consecrate by this water, he who is Father, and Son, and Holy Ghost. I invoke and exorcise thee, O holy water, in the name of God, and of his holy mother Mary, and besides in the name and the power of all male and female saints, with the company of all of heaven, that thou, water, may be holy and consecrated, by that god who made, preserved, and ordered in all things for protection and defence against all temptations of the devil, and disturbings, snares, and deceits in the power of the Holy Spirit, who should deem worthy too allow his mercy for us, everywhere for thee, through our Lord Jesus Christ."

Deinde intret circulum in nomine dei de nocte vel de die, et cum apparuerit spiritus, [dic]:

> Then enter the circle in the name of God, during night or day, and when the spirit might appear, say:[1118]

"Conjuro vos, spiritus qui *uram* [coram] me *istes* [estis], per patrum et filium, et spiritum sanctum, et per ista nomina dei, + Saday, Teragramaton, Tetragramag, Adonay, Algranay, et per omnia nomina sancta dei, re non habeas

[181b]

"potestatem in [sic] nocendi in corde *tum* [vel] anima, recidendi avisu meo donec verum responsum ad omnia interegatas exhi[be]ates sine mendatio et falacia *faciam* [faciatis] sine aliquibus canto."

> "I conjure you, spirits who are face to face with me, by the Father and the Son and the Holy Ghost, and by the these names of God, + Saday Te[t]ragramaton, Tetragramag, Adonay, Algranay, and by all holy names of God, that you not have [181b] power in this matter to hurt in heart or soul, or to recede from my sight, until you make and deliver a true answer to all I ask, without falsehood or stratagem, without any cry."

"Coniuro vos, spiritus, in nomine karacteris omnipotentes, et sancta Marie virgines Matris Jesu Christi, et per caput principis vestri et piam etatem eam, et per potentissimum Dominum qui *habiatur* [habeat] Dominus noster Jesus

1118. The original includes some odd brackets at about this point, as if something was intended to be added but was omitted instead.

Christus super vos, ut non habiates potestatem visum meum impediendum quando vos videre possim, et cognoscere in pulchra forma hominis ita quod vos non habeates potestatem recedendi visu meo, donec a me fuerites licentiati."

> "I conjure you, spirits, in the name of the omnipotent character, and of the holy virgin Mary, mother of Jesus Christ, and by the head of your prince, and his holy age, and by the most powerful God who our Lord Jesus Christ may hold over you, that you should not have power of hampering my sight, when I am able to see you and to know you in the beautiful form of a man, so that you may not have power to leave my sight, until you will be licensed by me."

Hic est licentia:

> The licence is here:

"[Vade] ad locum praedestinatam [ubi] Dominus Noster Jesus Christus vos *admiravit* [ordinavit] quousque alias vos *invocando* [invocavero], sub pena damnationem perpetuam et maledictionem dei Patris omnipotentes, et Filii, et Spiriti Sancti descendet super vos, et vobiscum maneat semper *misicite* [nisi cito] spiritus cum vos *invocandum* [invocavero], si aliquo modo *patris* [poteritis] *mofestinatur* [sine mora festinater] *cum periates* [copareatis] cum vos in domo vel extradomo in campus vel extra campus invocavero, benedictione vestri principis possidendo fiat. Amen."

> "[Go] to the predestined place where our Lord Jesus Christ ordained, until I call you again, under the penalty of perpetual damnation, and the curse of omnipotent God the Father, and of the Son, and of the Holy Ghost will come upon you, and it should remain with you always, unless immediately you, O spirits, when I will call you, if you will be able in any way, you all should come quickly and without delay, I will call you all in the house or outside the house, in the field or outside the field, having obtained the blessing of your prince. Amen." [1119]

1119. See Harms, Clark, and Peterson, *Oberon*, 480.

[182]

[The Summoning of Golias[1120] into a Crystal to Find a Malefactor]
All that will do this experiment must be clean in soul, and hear one Mass of the Holy Ghost of Saint Cyprian, and offer a penny, and say in the mass twenty Pater Nosters, twenty Aves, and eighteen Creeds, and in clean cloth, per the virtue of St. John Evangelist, and per my baptism.

"I go thee, Golias, that thou go in, and that thou enter into this glass, and shew me verily and truly the face of that man or that woman which hath done that false deed, and shew me the truth of all things that I shall ask thee hereafter. In nomine Domini,[1121] stand thou per the might of that is in heaven, and per the might and the power that our lord hath in heaven and in earth, from the highest degree to the lowest, and per the power that our Lord gave unto St. John the Evangelist which saw the permetive[1122] in heaven, and in earth, and in Hell, and in purgatory, and per the might and power of our Lord God and his destine,[1123] and of his baptism, and per the virtue and might of his fasting, of his passion, and of his resurrection, and per all the saints in heaven, I conjure thee, Golias, per the wounds of our Lord Jesus Christ, per the Father, the Son, and the Holy Ghost. Amen.

"Now I conjure thee or thou go, and I conjure you, devils, that you will bide my asking without harm or dread of my body or soul, per the virtue of the Father and the Son and the Holy Spirit, three persons in trinity, and per the virginity of his mother Mary, and merits of her son Jesus Christ our saviour, very God and man, only te, Golias, I conjure thee and thy fellows per the virtue of Christ's flesh

[183]

"and blood that thou shew the truth, or else not, per the virtue of Christ's body in form of, and now as bread is, and thee and thy fellows, I conjure, charge, and command you, per the virtue of Christ and these names, Ely, Eley, Eloy, Sother, Emanuel, Sabaoth, Adonay, Tetragramaton, Principium, Finis, Probum,[1124] Ananazapta, Lamazabathani, and per all the names of our Lord Jesus Christ, and his disciples, martyrs, confessors, patriarchs, and prophets, and per all the angels and archangels, I conjure that you do my

1120. *Golias*: Goliath, of Biblical fame.

1121. *In nomine Domini*: Translation: "In the name of God."

1122. *Permetive*: Unknown.

1123. *Destine*: Destiny.

1124. *Principium…probum*: Translation: "First, last, superior."

commandments, and shew truly, per the virtue of the Father, and of the Son, and of the Holy Ghost. Amen."

[184]

[The Summoning of Satan, Part 2][1125]

At this knot over the leaf forward,[1126] there you must begin, and say them two sides, and then begin with this side, then so forwards.

Then look towards the north, and hark if you hear any noise afar, and if you do fear not, but abide the coming of the spirit, that which shall be horrible at the first appearing, but afterward he shall shew himself with lowly cheer and ask your master "Quare vexisti me?"—"Master, why hast thou vexed

1125. The author missed a page and then skipped backward and forward to complete the incantation. Parts 1 and 3 will follow.

1126. The author apparently intended this item to help guide people through the text, but he does not seem to have put it elsewhere.

me?" The master then will say, ut petras,[1127] "A Archmynwifr ist."[1128] Then he shall say, "Do sacrifice unto me, and *you* [they] shall do what you ask," the which shalt thou deny, saying, "It becometh[1129] only sacrifice to be done unto almighty God." Then he shall depart with great noise. Then thou shalt say this conjuration with great fierceness.

"Adjuro te, Sathan, spiritus potens in *apere* [artem?] et scientiam per mirificam potestatem, et per virtutem omnium nominum dei altissimi, et per sanguinem domini Jesus Christi quem effudit in cruce per redemcionem humani, gender [?] genere et per sudorem lacrimas ejus, per sanguinem et aquam que de latrem ejus fluxerunt, per sepulchrum. Adjuro te per illam potentiam et virtutem qua vos spirituos infernales flangendo castra spolianda decendit de quo dictum

[185]

"*firt*, [fuit] 'Quis e[st] iste qui venit de eodem [sic] Edoum tinctis vestibus de Befra?' Per illam potentiam et virtutem, coniuro te ut non sis rebellus, nec in aliquo contrarius. Adjuro te per Patrem, et Filium, et Spiritum Sanctum, et per locius trinit[at]is individuem potentiem et eternem unitatem miraculam, scientie virtute. Adjuro te, Sathan, per virtutem et nomina omnium istorum et istarum et specialiter per gloriosam virginem Mariam Domini Jesu Christi, et ejus gratiam quam habuit inter omnes mulieres, per baptismum Christi, et per Spiritum Sanctum missum a Patre in columbe specie, and per Christum baptizatum, et per potentiam Patris dicentes, 'Hic est filius meus dilectus qui mihi bene complacuit.'

> "I adjure thee, Satan, a spirit powerful in art [?] and science, by the admirable power, and by the virtue of all names of the highest God, and by the blood of our Lord Jesus Christ that he shed on the cross for the redemption of man, by the people [?], and by his sweat and tears, by the blood and water that flowed from his side, by the tomb. I adjure thee by that power and virtue that pierced you infernal spirits in breaking the plundered camps [?], from which it is said, [185] 'Who is this that cometh from Edom, with dyed garments from Befra?'[1130] By

1127. *Ut petras*: National Library of Scotland GD 188/25/1/3, 173, has here "ut mihi obedias hiis praeci [praecepti?] quae praecipero tibi [(roughly) as you obey for me these commands that I give you], itt usiddo ir pethas."

1128. Mangled beyond translation. Kate Leach tentatively suggests either "Whom you commanded to be encircled with wire" or "O, Commander of Silence."

1129. *Becometh*: Is fitting.

1130. *Who…Befra?*: Isaiah 63:1. Translation from KJV.

> that power and virtue, I conjure thee that thou mayst not be rebellious or contrary in any way. I adjure thee by the Father, and the Son, and the Holy Ghost, and by the indivisible power of the holy Trinity, and by the miraculous eternal unity, through the power of knowing. I adjure thee, Sathan, by the virtue and the names of all male and female, and especially by the glorious virgin Mary of Lord Jesus Christ, and her grace that she had among all women, by the baptism of Christ, and by the Holy Ghost sent by the Father in the form of a dove, and by the baptised Christ, and by the power of the Father, saying, 'Here is my beloved son, with whom I am well pleased.'[1131]

"Adiuro te, Sathan, princeps fortis, *et* [per] potentiam *devini* [dei vivi] ut sicut ipse deus *ecclesias* [excelsus] de fontibus antiqui draconis extraxit amicos suos, et patres nostros ad inferos descendendo, et eas spoliando, ligando ligavit *ante quam* [antiquam] serpentem cathenis igneis, ita per potentiam tuam ne possiam mihi mihi [sic?] rebellus in aliquo. Veni ergo humiliter et obedias *precepte* [preceptis] meis."

> "I adjure thee, Sathan, you strong prince, by the power of the living God, that as the high God released his friends from the source of the old dragon, and our fathers by descending into Hell, by stripping and binding these, he bound the old serpent with chains of fire, so by thy power you may not be rebellious to me in any thing. Come therefore humbly, and obey my commands."

Then look towards the north coast, and thou shalt see him crowned with gold and clothed with silk and precious stones, standing afar without the circle. Then say unto him, "Princeps potens…"[1132]

[185]

[The Summoning of Satan, Part 1][1133]

This is the noble experiment and the secrets of Solomon, extract of Ebreno[1134] in Latin per the philosopher Alsidus,[1135] thought that which thing Alexander did subdue all the kings of the east, and obtained all things that he would.

1131. *Here…pleased*: Matthew 3:17.

1132. *Princeps potens*: Translation: "Powerful prince." See part 3 below, after part 1.

1133. Compare to National Library of Scotland GD 188/25/1/3, 171–75.

1134. *Ebreno*: National Library of Scotland GD 188/25/3, 171, has "Hebrews."

1135. *Alsidus*: Possibly Calcidius, a commentator on Plato who wrote on the topic of demons. See Boeft and Calcidius, *Calcidius on Demons*.

He that will make this experiment must in primis[1136] be clean bathed, and cleansed of all superfluities of his nails, and hands, and feet, and *shave* [clean] the soles of his feet, and also he must be shaven, and gather the hair together. He must gather of his sweat in a sponge, and with it write his own name in a cloth of coarse,[1137] in which cloth[1138] he must bind all the superfluities in the water of his own sweat, and thou must have with it in that circle a black cock which is hatched in March.[1139] Thou must also be clothed in linen clothes, which is white and new.

Know thou well that thou must [may] work this experiment every season and every day except Friday, and every hour except the third hour, and in every place except holy and consecrated places, in a desart[1140] place, and far from people. Also know then that is more convenient so, and then for two to work, but if thou shalt work, let them have one condition and preparation.[1141] Let *me* [him] enter into the circle bold and steadfast, bearing with him the cock with all the aforesaid things, kneeling upon thy knees towards the east, saying:

"Pater, Agyos, Pater Luminis, O Adonay, Conditor universe, creature, O Ekey Pater, imensam majestatem,

[185bis]

nedere linquas [ne derelinquas] me inferum in tempore necessitatis. Magne rex orbis universe, Deus Abraham, Deus Isaac, Deus Jacob, Deus, ad adjuvandum me festina, Deus liberasti Danielem de lacu leonum, tres pueros de camino ignis ardente, Sydrac, Mysaac, Abdenago, deus qui Sussanuam de falso crimine liberasti, libera me, domine, et protege quam propeo nisi fueris in implicatore, Dominator dominacionium veniet ne tardaveris nec permittas me per alicuja spiritus advenientes presentia assendi vel terrere."

1136. *In primis*: Translation: "Firstly."

1137. *Coarse*: Original appears to be "carse."

1138. National Library of Scotland GD 188/25/3 adds here, "And he must bind all the superfluities aforesaid."

1139. *Black...March*: A bird known either as an offering to demons or for frightening them away. For other examples, see Peterson, *Secrets of Solomon*, 142; Ó Súilleabháin, *A Handbook of Irish Folklore*, 41; Ó hÓgáin, "Dreaming and Dancing: W. B. Yeats' Use of Traditional Motifs in 'The Dreaming of the Bones' (1919)," 67; Lynch, "Folk Beliefs about the March Cock," 22, 24, 32; Harte, *Explore Fairy Traditions*, 126; Harms and Clark, *Of Angels*, 288

1140. *Desart*: Desolate.

1141. *Also know...preparation*: This is garbled. National Library of Scotland GD 188/25/3: "Also know that it is more convenient for one than for two to work, but if there must be two, let them be of one condition and one mind and of one preparation."

> "Father, Agios, Father of light, O Adonay, establisher of all things and creation, O Ekey, Father, boundless majesty, [185b] and do not forsake me below in my time of need. Great king of the whole world, God of Abraham, God of Isaac, God of Jacob, God, hasten to my aid, God, thou didst free Daniel from the lion's den, the three boys Sydrac, Mysaac, and Abednago from the burning furnace of fire, God, who freed Susanna from false judgment, free me, O Lord, and protect me, that thou shouldst be near the summoning in difficulty. The Lord of lords will come, and he will not delay, and may you not leave me, that any spirit or presence arriving may not be able to rise above me or frighten."[1142]

Then arise and turn thee towards the north, where Satan dwelleth in septentrion,[1143] and bless thee with the sign of the + round about thee, and say:

"Conjuro te, Sathan, et instantissime adjuro te, inter te principales spiritus principalem, et inter potentiores potentem, et [per] altissimam et ineffabilam nomina dei omnipotente vivi et veri, Agla, Eloy, Sabaoth, ut tu accedes [sine] molestia et terrore [et] obedias preceptis meis. Igitur adjuro te per potestatem Patris, et confidenter per ista nomina qua non licet nominare, nisi in tempore magne necessitatis, Uson, Usion, Adonay, Panteon, Egyndy, Ya, Tetragramaton, El, Eley, Athanatos et Alra, Emanuel, Gegeton, et per nomen virtutem et potentiam eorum, ut tu appeareas non terribili sed placabile assumendo corpus placatum obedire meis preceptis."

> "I conjure thee, Sathan, and instantly adjure thee, thou chief among the chief spirits, and powerful among the more powerful, and by the most high and ineffable names of the omnipotent, living, and true God, Agla, Eloy, Sabaoth, that thou comest without trouble or dread, and obeyest my orders. Therefore I adjure thee by the power of the Father, and boldly by these names that are not permitted to be named, save in great time of need, Uson, Usion, Adonay, Panteon, Egyndy, Ya, Tetragramaton, El, Eley, Athanatos and Alra, Emanuel, Gegeton, and by their name, virtue, and power, that you appear in a soothing body, being not received terribly but peacefully, to obey my commands."

1142. *That…frighten*: Conjectural.

1143. *Septentrion*: The north.

[186]

[The Summoning of Satan, Part 3]

"Princeps potens, fac quod jubio tibi," that is, "Thou mighty prince, do that which I command thee, thy saying or invocation." [The spirit will say,[1144]] "Ask what thou wilt, and it shall be fulfilled, so that thou shew me some token of friendship, at thy departing." Then the master must say, "That will do." Then let him ask what petition he will, and he shall tell it, and all things to him be possible. When thou hast sped thy matter, give the cock, promising that he come and obey thee thy will, that thou [will give] unto him that that is in the clout, but beware thou give it not, but promise it him, and he shall go his way.[1145] And tarry thou an hour or two in the circle after his departing, and thank God of thy speed, and say, "In principio erat verbum," & c., and bless thyself in the Father and the Son and the Spiritus Sanctus. Amen.

Sierkle tydd, tuaraell, In ddaleum[1146]

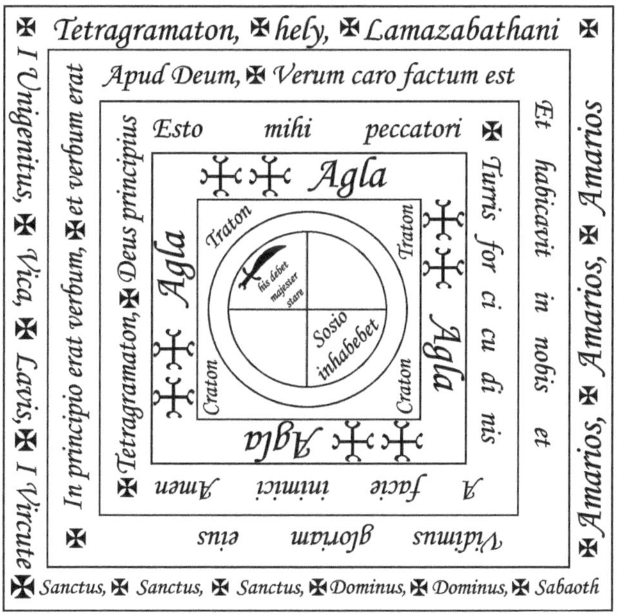

1144. The original is unclear whether this is a dialogue, but it seems to be the case.

1145. The magician is to offer to hand over his sweat, hair, and nail parings, giving the spirit power over him, but must avoid putting themselves in danger in such a manner.

1146. This section is of uncertain meaning.

The third inmost square in the diagram below is a modification of Psalm 60:4. See Harms and Clark, *Of Angels*, 92. The centre wording translates to, "The master should stand here with the servant occupying [this section]."

[187]

All These Are to Be Called into a Crystal[1147]

Vagan or Vacian	his ministers	Dus Audas Cunaball
Rex Arcan	his ministers	Bilat Micabi
Rex Senap	his ministers	Abuzabu Samael Satael Amabrox
Rex Mediat vel Madiat	his ministers	Ingremos Sulates
Suth Rex	Ditto	Maguts Gutriz
Sarabotieth Rex	Ditto	Amabuel Aba Abalidith
Rex Mamon	Ditto	Abumalith Assaibi Balidet

1147. The following spirit names are variants from the *Heptameron*, but they do not seem to clearly derive from any particular tradition thereof. Personal communication, Joseph Peterson, March 15, 2020.

You may call these spirits abovesaid per the same style serving for A. a. Anatos.

This square with the characters that are written here on is to be joined in the end of the experiment. Ancor, Anacor, Analos.[1148]

[188]

For the Toothache[1149]

The patient being absent, take a hazel wand of one year's growing. Write thereon this name, divided thus, "Te, + tra + gram, + mat + on +," and then both the two names of the patient, and in writing, say one Pater Noster, and then "In nomine Patris et Filii et Spiritus Sancti + Amen." This done, prick every vowel throughout the writing except "o" and "u," and thou must prick them twice over with a knife's point. But before thou prick them, say this word, "Tetragramaton," and then say, "I conjure thee, ache or gout, or whatsoever thou be, that thou disease no more this man or woman, a creature of God, N., and that thou go from him here. I conjure thee per the virtue of the Father, the Son, and the Holy Ghost, and per the virtue of this holy word Tetragramaton," and then prick all the vowels, and then clean the stick and

1148. *This square...Analos*: Upside down in the manuscript. These three angels are called upon in the *Heptameron* when putting on the vesture.

1149. The closest analogous rite is on manuscript page 16.

burn it in the fire, saying, "What humours in thou be," & c., as is aforesaid in this book.[1150]

A Godly Way to Have a Familiar Spirit, Which Will Tell Always Your Desire without Any Hurt or Fear[1151]

Rise up on the first Monday in the new of the ☽, and go where a palm tree groweth, and cut three wands thereof, which must be of one year's growth, and on one stalk, and not of

[189]

the top of the tree. Then take fine parchment and cut it in three pieces, and write upon the first "Dures," and wrap it about the first rod, and in the second piece, this name, "Artus," and wrap it about the second rod, and in the third piece, write this name, "Sebediell," and wrap it about the third rod. Then take the first rod in thy hand, and say:

"O thou rod, I conjure thee per the virtues and powers of that rod wherewith the holy prophet Elias raised up the water between him and Elizeus, so that the spirit whose name is wrapped about thee to be obedient to me always, whensoever I shall call him."

And so set the rods in the east part of the chamber. And then take the second rod in thy hand, and say:

"O thou rod, I conjure thee per the might and per the virtue of that rod wherewith Moses turned the water of Egypt into blood, so that the spirit whose name is wrapped about thee to be obedient unto me always."

And so set it in the west part of the chamber. Then take the third rod, and say:

"O thou rod, I do conjure thee per the virtue, might, and strength of that rod, wherewith the holy angels measured the temple of God, so that the spirit whose

1150. "*What humours…in this book*: The incantation described here does not turn up in the manuscript, so this might be a reference from its previous point.

1151. For a parallel text, see Bodleian Ballard 66, 1–10.

[190]

name is wrapped about thee, to be true always unto me and ready at all times at my calling."

And so set it in the south part of the chamber, and then say:

"I conjure you, spirits all thee, per the blessed God in trinity, and per God the Father almighty, and per God the Son Jesus Christ, and per the Holy Ghost blessed be, (for in the name of the Father, the Son, and the Holy Ghost, angels, archangels, prophets, apostles, martyrs, confessors, cherubin and seraphin, evangelists, and per all angels of God that in heaven be, and in the name of the blessed Trinity, one God, God in persons three, John Evangelist with us be, and the blessed virgin Mary, and John the Baptist, for Mary's sake, Mark, Matthew will not forsake, but for the love of the blessed Trinity in our business for to be),[1152] that, this night, verily you spirits to be with me to fulfil my mind truly in this place, for to be sure and certain presently like fair virgin ladies here to appear to me with Sebediell, angel of might. I conjure you so to do per the everlasting God the Father and per the might of the everlasting God our saviour Jesus Christ, and per the strength of the everlasting God, the Holy Ghost. I conjure you all per the virtue of all things that ever were

[191]

"wrought, made, or created in heaven and in earth, in the sea, and in the fountains, and per the virtue of all angels and archangels of God, that you so truly, as God from heaven came into this world personally per name, and into heaven ascended, and was Jesus again, our true Messias, and from heaven he shall come, Jesus again, and at the day of doom, to sit in judgment on us all, both quick and dead as man mortal, so truly this night[1153] might you spirits. I charge to appear and all things to bring to pass, even as I do require. I do conjure you so to do, per the might and per the power of the everlasting God whose names are holy and blessed, whose throne is in the height of heaven, in whose name I do conjure you in such wise that you may not deceive me, even as you shall answer at the dreadful day of judgment before our lord of great might."

1152. *(For...be)*: Parentheses in the original. It is not clear whether the author considered this to be essential or optional for the incantation.

1153. *[Night]*: From Ballard 66.

And so call them always the space of three nights, and at the third night there shall appear unto you and your bedside three fair ladies, and they will ask you what is your desire. Then say you:

"I do charge and command you per that Lord God that sent you hither, that you will truly tell and fulfil me all my request, without any fables

[192]

"or dissimulation, and always to be obedient unto me whensoever I shall call you, in the name of the Father, and of the Son, and of the Holy Ghost, our God, three persons, so be it, through Jesus Christ which liveth and reigneth, Jesus with God the Father, and the Holy Ghost, world without end. Amen. Fiat, fiat, fiat."

This is the most true[1154] way amongst all others' works. There is none so sure as this is, and so godly, for it hath been proved now of late.

Dures, | Artus, | Sebediell;

Blothe, | Berethe, + Baron,

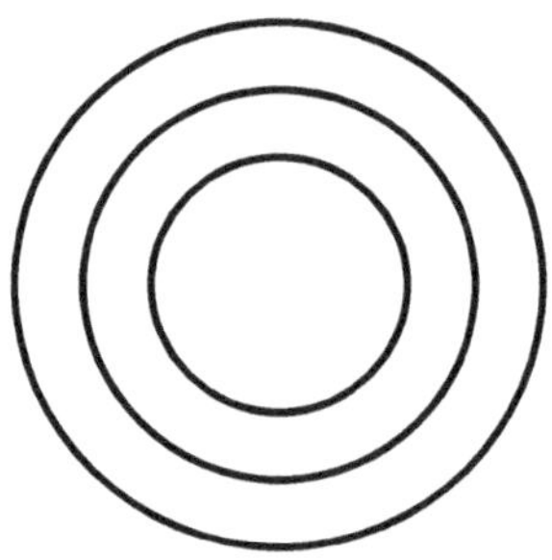

1154. *True*: Original has "trueth."

[An Incense to Call Spirits][1155]

The wise philosophers do affirm, that if there be made suffumigations of corzander or coriander of smallage with hemlock, it causeth incontinent devils to arise; therefore they be called herbs of spirits.

[To Make Virgin Parchment]

If that you will have virgin's parchment, you may make it of these four kinds of beasts: the lamb, the calf, the kid, or the fawn of a hind or fallow deer. You must rip the kid or lamb out of the dam's belly before it be heard, and strip him out of the skin, and spread it on a board or over a peck that you measure corn with sieve or bowl or some such like things, for to dry,

[193]

but beware it touch not the ground at any time before it be hallowed. And when it is dry, then hallow it. But if you can let it be ripped out in a good day and in a good hour, and it will be the purer, but first let the dam be quick[1156] and rip him out, the dam being alive after she is quick and not before.

1155. See Agrippa, *Three Books of Occult Philosophy* (1651), 86 (book 1, chapter 43). This appears to be an independent translation from the Latin, omitting henbane.

1156. *Quick*: At the stage of pregnancy when the foetus may be felt to move.

An Experiment with Characters, with Other Manner of Writing to Be Set on Images for to Cause a Thief to Appear before You, and to Come to You in What Place Soever You Be[1157]

Ag, ysgriuenna, yn, Halkentine,[1158] y delie[1159] Iris cu{m} / eum ista, ki[1160] 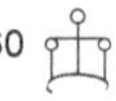 ag ynghwasted I penne[1161] stilm- / lacu{m}[1162] ista ke  in pectore scribe nomen tuus operante cum iste cum duob{us} no{min}ib{us} Eliaza Ma-Lagie

1157. This is one of the two passages in this manuscript in Welsh. Many thanks to Katherine Leach for her translation of the ritual. I have included the Welsh in the main text in order to preserve her copious footnotes.

1158. KL: "The Welsh word here is 'talcen,' which is Welsh for brow or forehead, but the scribe has mutated it, which happens after the 'yn,' which means 'in' or 'on.' 'Yn nhalcen' would be the way to write this, but 'yn halcen' certainly works just fine. The later part of this word is less clear. It could be 'tine,' I suppose, though that doesn't make much sense. In Welsh, the word 'tin' can mean 'the rear end' or 'lower part' of something, and I suppose 'tine' could be a variant of that. 'Tin' can also just mean tin, so if the image being written upon is made of tin or lead, this would work too, I suppose. Another option is that it is 'tue' and is a variant of the Latin 'tua'? (In Welsh, 'your' is 'ti')."

1159. KL: "Read 'delw' here. 'Delie' is an interesting, non-standard variant. Many charm texts of the fifteenth and sixteenth centuries feature interesting variants of words that are not standard in their spelling conventions. Perhaps an indication of oral/aural transmission?"

1160. KL: "This, and the rest of the instances of what looks to be 'ke' could simply be an abbreviation of 'character' (in Welsh 'caractr' or 'caracter' as a direct borrowing was attested in the seventeenth century (and often 'k' was written interchangeably with 'c,' though this is more common in medieval Welsh). It could also be 'ce,' which means 'key,' but the only instances of it in the Welsh dictionary refer to key as in a musical key. A final option would be to understand this as an abbreviation for 'kymer,' which means 'take' (modern Welsh verb is 'cymeraf'). In the Welsh medical texts 'kymer' is used where 'accipe' is used in Latin medical recipes. In the Welsh medical texts, 'kymer' is written as an abbreviation that can look a bit like 'ky' or 'kx' (similar to what proceeds the third and fifth symbols in this text). This Welsh/Latin version seems to be a translation of the English version that follows it, from what I can see. Based on this, I would consider the 'ki' and 'ke' variants as abbreviations for character perhaps?" (DH: I think "characters" is the best reading here.)

1161. KL: "This looks rather more like 'perme' and I wondered at first if it wasn't a from the Latin verb 'permeo,' to pass through or penetrate. However, the Welsh word 'gwastad y pen' means 'crown of the head,' which would match the English version below that seems to be a translation of this. 'Penn' for modern 'pen' would not be problematic, and I suppose having 'penne' could work, especially not knowing how comfortable with Welsh the scribe may have (or not have) been. The 'I' character here is the same as in 'Idris' elsewhere on the page, and often *Y* and *I* were interchangeable, so there is no problem with the 'I' here being read as the 'y' in 'gwastad y pen.' Given the English version below, I have no real problem reading this as 'gwastad I penne' for 'gwastad y pen.'"

1162. KL: "I think this is a miscopying or misunderstanding of 'simulacrum.'"

cum isto ke 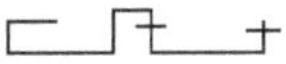 p. u. i. b. i. in dorso erga cor hu{n}t[1163] ke  nodele ea pile[1164] siria[1165] cum isto, ke 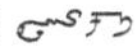

> And write in (the) lower forehead of the image "Iris" with it this character…and in the forehead the image/likeness of this character… in the breast write your name working with it, with these two names: Eliaza Malagie with this *character*…p. u. i. b. i. In the back against the heart, this character…in the little node in the base of the neck, this character…

Alias[1166]

First write in the forehead of the Image this word Iris, with this character , and ever observe the names above written in their places as is aforesaid, and for the crown of the head, make this character , and in the breast the characters that is afore shewed, and for the back against the heart,

[194]

this character , and in the node of the neck of the head, this character 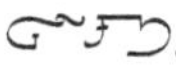.

This following is to be joined to the experiment aforesaid, or the next practised per Master Boney,[1167] at the discretion of the Master, that which I have used all three at once. This lastly, as followeth:

"O God, which didst send down thy Holy Ghost from above upon thine apostles, vouchsafe, I beseech thee, for thy son our Lord Jesus Christ's sake to send down thy holy grace, virtue, power, and strength. Open thy servant here in this place, prostrate in thy holy fear, and for thy holy namesake,

1163. KL: "Or potentially 'hyll'? Third-person singular present, from 'holli': to cut, cleave? Or it is simply 'hu{n}c' with the *C* as more of a *K* as written elsewhere before the efficacious characters are given. I favour the reading of 'hu{n}k' as 'hunc.' In Welsh, *C* and *K* could've been used interchangeably still, so if this was someone who was familiar with Welsh, this would make sense. If this were a Welsh MS, I would have no problem reading this as 'hunk' meaning 'hunc.'"

1164. KL: "Could this be 'pile' from the Latin 'pila' for 'pillar'…and with the meaning of 'the neck'? Or perhaps with the more specific meaning of the 'base or the pillar of the neck,' if we read 'siria' as a variant of 'swire.'"

1165. KL: "Could this be a miscopying or a variant of 'swire,' which was just 'neck'? I am unaware of any Welsh that would fit this context. 'Siria(f)' in Welsh means to become cheerful or to be delighted, so that would not fit!"

1166. Translation: "Another."

1167. *Boney*: A Boney Gelfe, husbandman, is mentioned in the Worcestershire quarter session rolls for September 9, 1620, as being resident in Ripple, later the parish of William Hodges. Bund, *Worcester County Records: The Quarter Sessions Rolls, Part II*, 721.

lighten mine eyes and understanding, good lord, that I may continue still in thy truth, with faith, hope, and charity all the days of my life. Also, I pray thee for the merits, death, and passion of sweet Jesus, in whom thou art well pleased. Let not mine enemy, either bodily or ghostly, have power to hurt me in thought, word, and deed, so that neither the world, the flesh, and the devil deceive me, but that all my thoughts, words, deeds, and works may be ruled after thee and thy divine wisdom now and ever, and also begun per thee, and so likewise per thee be ended, to the honour and glory of thy blessed name. Amen.

[195]

"O Good Jesus, I commend this work and business of mine into thy blessed hands and custody, beseeching thee for thy great mercy's sake, and for the merits of thy blessed mother, the glorious Virgin Mary, and so of all angels and saints in heaven and earth, that we may see and know thy goodness now and ever hereafter, calling thee to witness, most righteous judge, that I do it not for the hurt of any creature, but for the relief of my poor estate. Therefore most merciful Father, I beseech thee, send thy good angels from heaven above to guide me in thy truth and to strengthen me in all my studies and labours, for the love of Jesus Christ our Lord and Saviour. Amen.

"Help me, O ye bright and shining angels, I pray you, in the name of our Lord God, Sabaoth, Uriel, and Raguel, I beseech you that, in this night, you will cause and constrain the thief which hast stolen (such a thing) from N. M., to return back again to the same place from whence he stole it, and to restore the thing again to the right owner, and to confess his fault before him as soon and possibly may be.

"Hear, ye glorious and holy angels, I desire and entreat you per our lady St. Mary, mother of our Lord Jesus Christ, and per his two principal names, A and Ω, + Primus, + Novissimus, per Agla and Tetragramaton,

[196]

"which are two divine names of God Almighty, that you fulfil and accomplish all my request in the name of Jesu, per virtue whereof all knees do bow and obey in heaven and earth, and in hell, and in the voice of heaven, in which you are, doth sound his praise to whom be all glory, honour, virtue, and power ascribed, with all worship, thanks, laud, and praise, for ever and ever. Amen.

"And let all creatures of our Lord Jesus Christ say thereunto, fiat, fiat, fiat. Amen."

Memorandum: you must write these names and characters of the spirits abovesaid in virgin parchment. At every time of the working, burn two of the spirits' names and characters, putting them into the fire, when you say the words above written, "Hear, O ye glorious and holy," & c. And note that Raguel and Uriel are both angels of the ☽ whose day and hour is best accepted per this business. And when you have done with the images at the fire, then proceed as above written.

An Experiment of A Azaell[1168]

Bleath[1169] should a young beginner begin withal, although to call a Azaell is the most noblest art, whose character followeth.[1170]

[197]

If thou wilt have a true answer of treasure or theft, in the earth, or to have a carrier for treasure, here followeth a true profit and proved experiment. Go to a grave of man or woman within thirteen nights after they be buried, and look that ye know their names. Then say thus four times.

"O Azael, thou art the keeper of dead men's bones, here keepest the bones of N. I command and charge thee, and also I conjure thee per the virtue of

1168. For similar experiments of Azaell, see Additional 36,674, f. 47r; National Library of Scotland GD 188/25/1/3, 115.

1169. *Bleath*: For more on this spirit, see Legard and Cummins, *An Excellent Booke*, passim.

1170. Identical to what appears in the other two manuscripts, but at this point the text diverges from Additional 36,674.

almighty God the Father, the Son, and the Holy Ghost, and per all that God made ever in heaven and earth, per the might and power of the sacrament of the altar, per his passion, resurrection, and ascension, that thou come to me, N. M., at the hour of ♈, and at the entering, give three knocks over the window or door,[1171] and then appear to me in likeness to a child of seven years old without the hurting of me, or any other creature, per the virtue of Jesus Christ, qui venturus est judic[are] & c."[1172]

And when he cometh, charge him thus, saying:

"I conjure thee, Azael, per the virtue of God, and per our lady St. Mary, and per all that God made ever in heaven and in earth, and per the blessed Trinity, three persons and one God, and per the dreadful day of doom,

[198]

"that you lie not, but shew me the truth of all manner of things, that I shall enquire or ask of thee, per the Grace of God. Amen."

Then ask him what thou wilt, and he will shew the truth. Then may you command him to provide, or for to bring some treasure, or else a carrier as thus.

"I charge thee, Azaell, per the virtue of God the Father, the Son, and the Holy Ghost, per the holy Trinity, per that holy sacrament of the altar, and per the wounds of our Lord and saviour Jesus Christ, and per the cross that he died upon, and per the nails that was driven through his hands and feet, and per the blood that he bled upon the cross, that you go and seek me some good treasure to my intent that doth no man good, or else that thou seek me a carrier that hath no lord, and that he be neither of the highest nor of the lowest. I charge thee this to do, per the virtue and power of God. Amen."

Then he will say he may not do it, "For it is great peril," will he say. Then ask him why, and he will answer he wanteth humanity.[1173] Then say thou to him, "Thou shalt have humanity." Then say this, and charge as followeth.

1171. Reginald Scot mentions how some magicians pretended to contact spirits that made themselves known by knocking. Scot, *The Discouerie of Witchcraft*, 434.

1172. *Qui...& c.*: Translation: "Who will come to judge [the living and the dead]."

1173. *Humanity*: Perhaps the soul.

[199]

"I charge thee, Azaell, per the virtue of God, and per all that ever God made in heaven and in earth, and per the hely[1174] sacrament of the altar, in form of bread, and per the five wounds of our Lord Jesus Christ, and per the Cross that he died upon, and per the precious blood that our Lord bled upon the cross of tree,[1175] and per St. John the Baptist, and per St. John the Evangelist, and per St. Catherine and St. Margaret, and per all the holy company of heaven, that you bring to me one spirit that will be obedient to me at all times, and that thou bring the name of the spirit with thee. Also I charge thee per the virtue of God and our lady St. Mary, and all the holy company of heaven, that you come again at ♈ of the clock, and then bring with thee my humanity again. If thou do not, I command thee and constrain thee per the virtue of God to the everlasting pain of hell, and there to be bound with chains until the day of Doom. Fiat, fiat, fiat."

That done, blow thy humanity against him, and he will go his way, and thou shalt abide, and commend thy soul and body to almighty God, saying, "In manus tuas, Domine, commend[ab]o spiritum meum; redimiste me, domine, deus veritatis,"[1176] with these prayers, standing, sitting, or kneeling, until the hour be come, per he will keep his hour. And thou must prepare a

[200]

a plate of lead, as I will shew thee hereafter, four square and bright polished and ruled, and when he cometh again, say thou thus, "Benedicite,"[1177] and he will answer "Dominus"[1178] Then thou shalt see spirits kneeling before thee. Then shalt thou say, ask of Azaell the name of the spirit, and he shall tell thee, then command and charge the spirit thus, saying to him as followeth:

"I command and charge thee, N., per God Almighty the Father, Son, and Holy Ghost, three persons and one God per the holy Trinity, and per the blessed sacrament of the altar, and per the virtue of his substance, per the providence which had in his mind ere the world was made, and per the wisdom that he had when he made the earth and the elements of the world,

1174. *Hely*: Exalted or holy.

1175. *Tree*: Wood.

1176. *In manus...veritatis*: Vulgate Psalm 30:6. Translation (KJV Psalm 31:5): "Into thine hand I commit my spirit: thou hast redeemed me, O Lord God of truth."

1177. *Benedicite*: Translation: "Bless thee."

1178. *Dominus*: Translation: "Lord."

and per the angels in heaven, and per all archangels, thrones, dominations, principates, potestates, cherubim, and seraphim, and per St. John Baptist, and per St. John the Evangelist, and the apostles and confessors in heaven, and per all the holy names of our Lord, as Eloy, Sabaoth, Adonay, Emanuel, Tetragramaton, Messias, Usion, A and Ω, Athanatos, that thou be obedient unto me night and day, and that thou fulfil my desire I shall ask of thee, at all times, and any fraud or deceit. Also I command and charge thee per the virtue of God, and per his blessed

[201]

"blood that he bled upon the cross, that thou write thy name with four other names, that thou wilt honest obey openly in this plate that any man may read them, and that thou givest it to me again when thou hast fulfilled my mind, per virtutem Dominum meam, Jesus Christi, qui venturus est..."[1179] & etc.

Then cast the plate, and when he hath given it again to thee, then say on this wise:

"I charge thee, N., per the virtue of God and per his blessed sacrament of the altar, in form of bread, and per the cross he died on, and per the blood he shed thereon, and per the dreadful day of doom, that thou go again to the place where thou wast before, until I call thee again, and also I charge thee per the dreadful day of doom, that thou hurt me, not neither bodily or ghostly, nor man, woman, nor child, creature, nor any thing helping any creature, at any time in thy going or coming, as thou hopest to be saved at the day of judgment, per virtutem dei omnipotentis venientis in saecula seculorum.[1180] Amen."

Then license Althenothe in this manner:

"Vade[1181] Althenothe, into thy place or grave where thou wast before, as God hath ordained thee to live, without any disease of any Christian creature, per the virtue of God, and the dreadful

1179. *Per virtutem...est*: Translation: "By the power of my Lord Jesus Christ, who will come..."

1180. *Per virtutem...seculorum*: Translation: "by the power of the coming omnipotent God, world without end."

1181. *Vade*: Translation: "Go."

[202]

day of doom, vade pacifice et quiete,[1182] amen. Fiat, fiat, fiat."

Then bless them, saying, "In nomine Patris et Filii et Spiritus Sancti," & c.

Then he will go away, and when thou wilt do any thing; call him per his proper name, and he will come shortly. Then shew thou what he shall do. That done, license him as before, & c.

This is the form of the plate, which must be ruled for five names, made of lead, and fair polished.

Experimentum ad Inveniendum Furem Latronem[1183]

Scire cupiens furem rei ablata in mole ad [vadat] in *cresupenbo* [crepusculo] noctis ad sepulchrum cujusdam mulieri infra 30 dies *mortal* [mortalis?] transivit et *in Chrans* [inclimans] ad caput tumuli 30 nominibus, submissa voca non sive attentione, dixit:

> One desiring to know the thief of some item carried off should hasten in the evening to the tomb of some woman who passed within thirty days, and inclining to the head of grave with thirty names and in a soft voice, not without attentiveness, they said:

"Zerna, Zerna, Zerna, quod hic jaces in caverna, Abra, Cadra, Sabra, Conjuro te, *omnia* [anima] hujusque cadaveris N.,

[203]

"hic sepulta, per deum S. Samuelis, prophetae curiae [?] Patrem, et per omnia sancta nomina eius, et per eijus majestatem et virtutem incomprehensibilem

1182. *Vade...quiete*: Translation: "Go peacefully and quietly."

1183. Translation: "Experiment for the Uncovering of a Thief or Bandit." See manuscript page 129.

et immensam. Precipio et mando tibi, ut petas habeasque licentiam, ab eo qui detinet te hac nocte veniendi ad me et venias etiam sine mora, sine terrore, et sine laesione, placida et tranquilla, ad me, et in veritate reveles mihi furem illius rei ablata X K. Si *fueris* [facias], pro [te] intra tridium [missam faciam] celebrari. Ego iterum te rogo, moveo, et adjuro, ut hac nocte in somnis clarisse ostendas, in nomine Patris et Filii et Spiritus Sancti. Amen."

> "Zerna, Zerna, Zerna, that lies here in the crypt, Abra, Cadra, Sabra. I conjure thee, the soul of this body N., [203] having been buried here, by the God the Father of Saint Samuel, the sorrowful prophet, and by all his holy names, and by his incomprehensible and boundless majesty and power. I command and order thee that thou askest and havest licence from him who keeps thee back to come this night to me. And thou mayst also come without delay to me, without terror, and without injury, calm and tranquil, and that thou uncover in truth the thief of that carried-off thing X. K. to me. If you do so, I will have a mass to be celebrated within three days for thee.[1184] Again I beseech, stir, and abjure thee that thou wilt show them mostly clearly that night in dreams. In the name of the Father, and of the Son, and of the Holy Ghost. Amen."

And after, having said the Psalm "De profundis"[1185] twice, he went home and laid under the bolster, upon which he should sleep, some of the earth of the grave. Then he went to bed, and in his sleep came the spirit of the dead woman, shewing him the thief, the name of stealing, and also the place where it then laid hid. It shewed also the marks and signs per which the thief might be known, and so vanished. This experimentater swears this to be true, and said further, that thereper one might know of treasure hid, things past, present, and to come, and of any doubt whatsoever. You must work with such a one as you think there's hope in salvation. In like sort, if you work this experiment at the grave of a man, then must you say the masculine gender, "Zerne, Zerne, Zerne," and according to the

1184. Part of this sentence is conjectural from other versions. It is likely that the reference to a Mass for the dead was deliberately omitted here. For examples with this element, see Bodleian Rawlinson D.252, 67v; British Library Sloane 3851, 103v.

1185. *De profundis*: Vulgate Psalm 129.

[204]

the quality of the question, change what is to be changed. And this, he said, was a most true experiment.

Alias[1186]

First bless thee, and stand at the head of the grave. Call "A. A. A." and say, standing still. "O St. S., St. S. E. i., as thou art keeper of man's and women's bones, and at this time keepeth the body and bones of this man, N. M., whom I do call. I charge and command thee, and also per the virtue and might and power of our Lord Jesus Christ, per his nativity, per his resurrection, and per his ascension, and per his strength, power, and might, and also per the virginity of our Lord, the blessed virgin St. Mary, his mother, and per the virtue of heaven and earth, that thou appear to me this night visibly in the fair form of a man, not fearing or hurting me, or any other creature, and tell me of such treasure as is hidden in St. S.,[1187] and bring me safely to it, and thou lookest to be saved and not damned at the dreadful day of judgment. Fiat, fiat, fiat."

Then take some of the mould[1188] of the grave, and knit it in a fair linen cloth, and when thou keepest in thy bed, lay it under thy right ear.

[205]

To Make a Thief Bring Again the Goods Which He Hath Stolen, to the Same Place or Any Other Place Whatsoever at Any Time Thou Will Appoint Him to Come[1189]

First, being clean from sin three days before thou work, then in the increasing of the ☽, chiefly in the new. (Notwithstanding, it may be done new or old, if rightly wrought either upon the Monday or Wednesday.) And the manner of working is this: upon the day of ☽ or ♃, arise before the ☉ rising, and make prayer to God that he would vouchsafe to give thee virtue and power in thy work to perform it, that he will make these spirits obedient unto thy words, that wheresoever they be, either in fire, water, earth, and air, or else where they may obey thy will, and bring again the thief with the goods, at such a time as thou shall appoint them, & c. Then, with virgin wax, make this plate in manner as followeth, and in the round circle write the name of Satan, for

1186. Translation: "Another."

1187. *St. S.*: Assuming this book was copied near Worcester, one candidate would be Saint Swithun's Church.

1188. *Mould*: Earth.

1189. For more examples and analysis, see manuscript page 2.

unto the spirit they will obey, and the name or names, or thing or things stolen, and the names of the author, as the example sheweth.

Then pray and say as followeth, three times in the day, in the morning, noon, and at night:

"O ye spirits, Teltrion, Byoeton, Botheon, Spyrgon, et Maerion, ye that have power of God to restore theft, whose names and signs be here written with unknown names or titles whatsoever,

[206]

"you have of N. N., I do adjure and conjure you beforesaid, per the living God, the true God, the holy God, per God the Father, the Son, and the Holy Ghost, and per the undoubted Trinity, and per the proper name of + A + and + Ω + per all the names of our Lord Jesus Christ on whom our father called upon, and he did help them; + Sother, + Emanuel, + Sabaoth, + Agla, + Adonay, + Eloy, + and per the most excellent name of God, Tetragramaton, and per the passion of our Lord Jesu Christ, and per his glorious resurrection, and per his marvellous ascension, wheresoever you be in the earth, in the air, in the fire, or in the water, that you meet all in the same place in which he or the thief or thieves stand or be, which hath stolen or taken away M. from M. the same M. or goods if possible be. Ye make these thief or thieves to restore and bring N. upon N. day, N. hour, or make the thief or thieves to confess the theft and give satisfaction. Otherwise, I condemn you per the resurrection of our lord and saviour Jesus Christ, per his power shewed in the blessed virgin Mary, and Mother Christ,[1190]

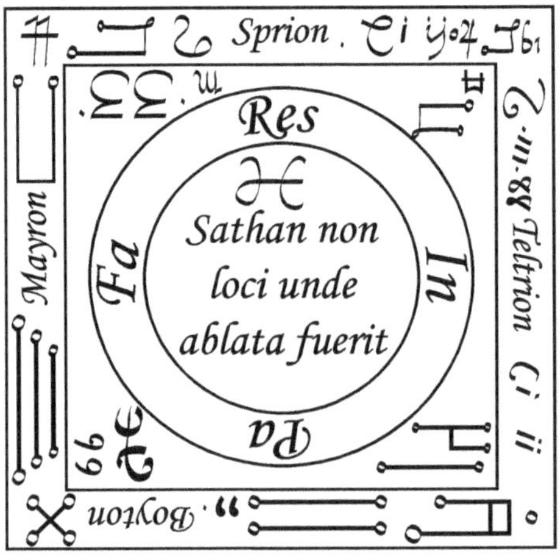

1190. Translation of image language: "Sathan, no, of the place whence it might have been taken [?]."

[207]

"and per the power of God in all saints, and you to be bound in fiery chains and grievously punished from day to day and hour to hour, always increasing with tormenting pains of fire and debility unto the end of the world, except you bring him or the thief or thieves again with N. or goods stolen, as beforesaid, unto thee, which I conjure you all, exorcised per the virtue and power of God in all heavenly sacrifices of angels and spirits, and per the faith of God in all patriarchs, prophets, and in the four evangelists, Matthew, Mark, Luke, and John, and in the twelve apostles, martyrs, confessors, and virgins, and in all their holy orders of the blessed, and per your four kings, that wheresoever you be, in the earth, water, fire, and air, you meet all in one place, and bring the thief and the goods aforesaid in the day and hour that is assigned, in nomine Patris et Filii et Spiritus Sancti. Amen."

But note to work aright, all should be done in the growing of the ☽. First look towards the east, and call the king to send his spirit, then to the south, then to the west, and then to the north. And if they come not the day the hour appointed, then bury the plate in the same ground, and repeat the work the next day three times as before, and they will bring it the next time without doubt.

[Herbs for Fever]

'Tis said that any herb gathered out of the brooks or river, before sun rising, and nobody see him that gather, it shall cure the tertian if it be bound to the left arm, and the sick not knowing what is done. 96—*3 Books* Cornelius Agrippa.[1191]

[208]

To See a Thief in Thy Sleep

In the day and hour of ☿, write these characters in virgin parchment, and lay it under thy head going to sleep, saying, "O Jesus Christ, son of God, fountain of all wisdom, per the virtue of these characters, send thy angel to reveal unto me N.," and then thou shalt see all in thy sleep.

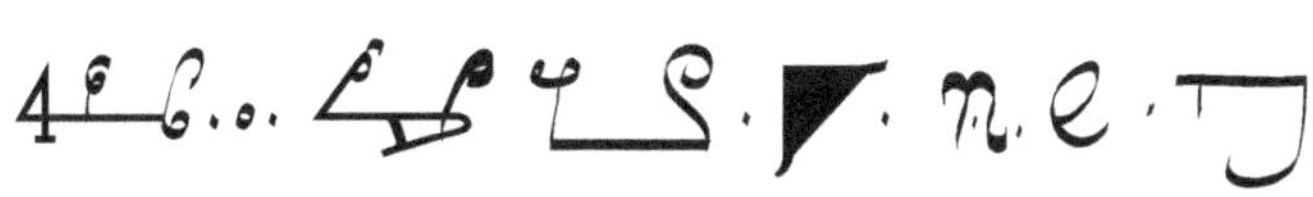

1191. Agrippa, *Three Books of Occult Philosophy* (1651), 96 (book 1, chapter 48).

Write these names—"Vadabat, Giel, Sarabini," in virgin parchment, and tie the same under thy right arm.

Pro Amore[1192]

Take three hairs of the head of the same woman as you desire, and make her image in virgin wax, and put the hairs therein, and after write the name of the man in the breast of the image, and the name of the woman in the forehead, and in the right foot thereof this word or name, "Goall," and in the left foot, "Arthru," and in the right hand, "Laetoncet," and in the left hand, "Belkebub," saying as followeth:

"I conjure you devils, per the Father, Son, and Holy Ghost, and per these names, Agla, Alpha, Ω, et Tetragramaton, and per St. Peter and St. Paul

[209]

"and holy Bartholomew, and per the blessed virgin Mary, mother of our Lord Jesus Christ, and per all the apostles, patriarchs, patriarchs, and prophets, and all virgins, and per confessors of our Lord, and per the cherubins and seraphins, and per thrones, dominations, heaven and earth, and per all things which are contained in them, and per all things heavenly, earthly, and helly, (that such a woman, here name her[1193]), ye make her to burn in my love, like as wax doth flow afore this fire, that she never wake, or sleep, nor do other thing in rest and quietness till she come unto me, and do what I would have her to do.

"Deus stetit *in=sumaga* [in synagoga] deorum in medio *ante* [autem] Deus deiudicat usquequo iudicatis iniquitatem et facies peccatorum sumitis iudicate egenem et papilla humilem et *parperem* [pauperem] justificate eripete pauperam et *epenem* [egenum] de manu *peccatoribus* [peccatoris] liberate eum nes[c]ierunt neque *intelexlexerunt* [intellexerunt] in tenebris ambulant *morebuntur* [movebuntur] omnia fundamenta terra ego dixi dii estis et filii *exelsis* [excelsi] *omnibus* [omnes] vos autem sicut homines *nomini* [moriemini] et *fiunt* [sicut] unis de principibus *cadent* [cadetis] surge *deas* [deus] iudica terram qui tu *habitabis* [hereditabis] in omnibus gentibus."

> "God standeth in the congregation of the mighty; he judgeth among the gods. How long will ye judge unjustly, and accept the persons of

1192. Translation: "For Love." Compare Harms and Clark, *Of Angels*, 298; manuscript pages 45 and 54.

1193. *That such…her*: The original punctuation is kept here, but it is likely that at least part of this should be read as part of the incantation.

the wicked? Defend the poor and fatherless; do justice to the afflicted and needy. Deliver the poor and needy; rid them of out of the hand of the wicked. They know not, neither will they understand; they walk on in darkness: all the foundations of the earth are out of course. I have said, Ye are gods, and all of you are children of the most High. But ye shall die like men, and fall like one of the princes. Arise, O God, judge the earth; for thou shalt inherit all nations."[1194]

[210]

When You Are in Dread of Thieves, or of Your Enemies[1195]

Say thus: "Jesus autem transiens per medium eorum ibat,"[1196] and also these verses in the Psalter three times: "Inruat super eos formido et pavor in magnitudine brachii tui domine fiant immobiles quasi lapis donec pertranseat populus *tuae* [tuus], Domine et populus [tuus] iste quem redemisti."[1197]

And you fear he will do you harm, say these words:

"My Lord God be with me, and in my company, and put from me all perils of fear, the power of thee and thy names following: + Ely, + Telena, + Ritona, + Aleator, + Arigus, + Linguatim, + Othem, + Athene, + Atham, + Eseche, + Gremitos, + Adonay, + Syth, +"

And if you be afraid in your house, say these names aforesaid, or write them in parchment and bear upon thy breast, with these figures, and fear not thou he meet with them.

'Tis said if a young person, on first setting out in life, chooses a verse, by hazard's chance, from the 49th Chapter of Genesis, it will unfold the future events of his life. See Thicknesse, *Memoirs*, page 22.[1198]

1194. *God standeth…nations*: Vulgate Psalm 81, translation taken from KJV Psalm 82.

1195. See manuscript page 104.

1196. *Sanctus…ibat*: Vulgate Luke 4:30, modified. Translation (KJV, modified): "But holy Jesus, passing through the midst of them, went his way."

1197. *Irruat…Domine*: Vulgate Exodus 15:16, modified at the end. Translation (KJV, modified): "Fear and dread shall fall upon them; by the greatness of thine arms they shall be as still as a stone; till thy people pass over, O Lord, and your people which thou hast redeemed."

1198. On page 13 of his memoirs, Philip Thicknesse seeks out the thirty-ninth chapter of Genesis for guidance. The author here has corrected the chapter but is mistaken about the page number. Thicknesse, *Memoirs and Anecdotes of Philip Thicknesse*, 13.

[211]

[A Curious Figure]

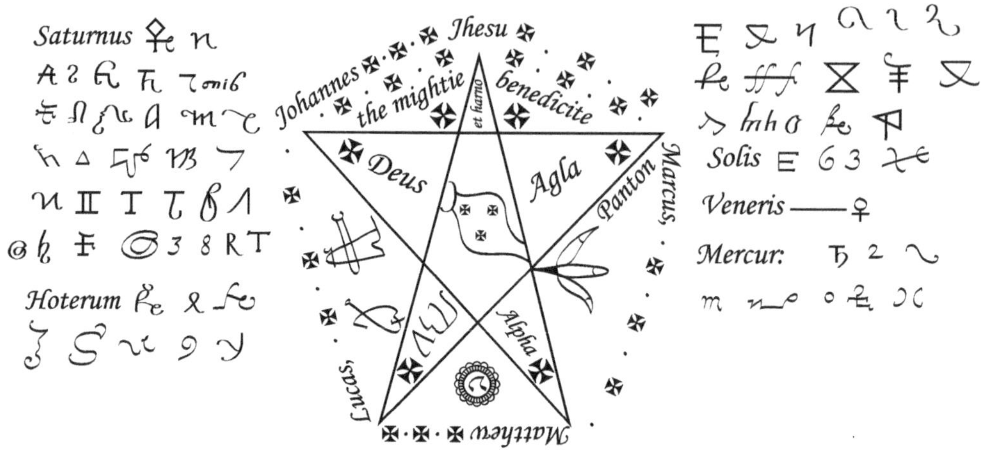

Memorandum that every cross ought to be made with red ink,[1199] and likewise the name written with the characters, but not above the pantacle or below.

Probatum est.

1199. This is drawn solely in black ink in the manuscript. See the appendix for one with crosses in red.

[212]

An Experiment to Talk with Spirits[1200]

If any man will speak with spirits in the augmentation of the ☽, in die ☽, the ☉ being in the first or third house of the day, make the image of a woman holding her daughter upon her left arm, of silver or of pewter, and let it be made of some cunning workman. And let the master do on a garment lucidis.[1201] When he is bathed and indued with garment fine, let him bring with him the images out of the town, and the images must have in their forehead such figures, described in your breast, ut sequitur.[1202]

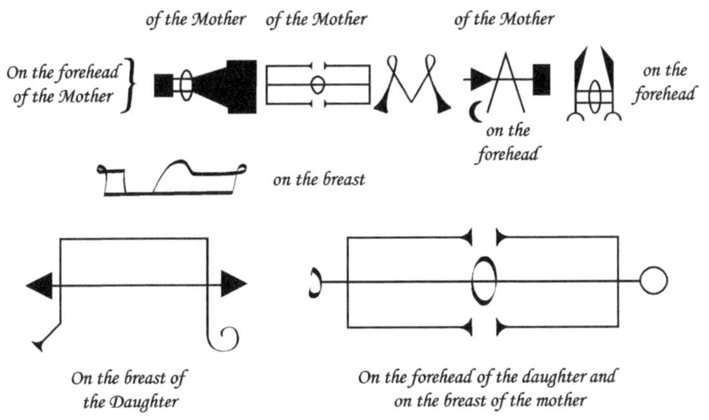

After the going down of the ☉, let him out. Then, straight standing on the earth in a secret and clean place, the master must have a round plate of lead to the breadth of his hand, wherein let

[213]

these figures be written, as this examples sheweth hereafter, wherewith both the images must be covered, as it sheweth. When it is done, let the master make a circle with a sword or knife with a white haft. In this operation, let the circle be from the images a cubit or a stride. Then look towards the east, and make a suffumigation of labdanum or of galbane,[1203] about the circle. And so, with one or two fellows being faithful, do this operation.

1200. Wellcome 4669, part 2, 50–53.

1201. *Lucidis*: Bright or shining.

1202. *Ut sequitur*: Translation: "As follows." For a version of the illustration with the original Latin, please see appendix.

1203. *Galbane*: Galbanum.

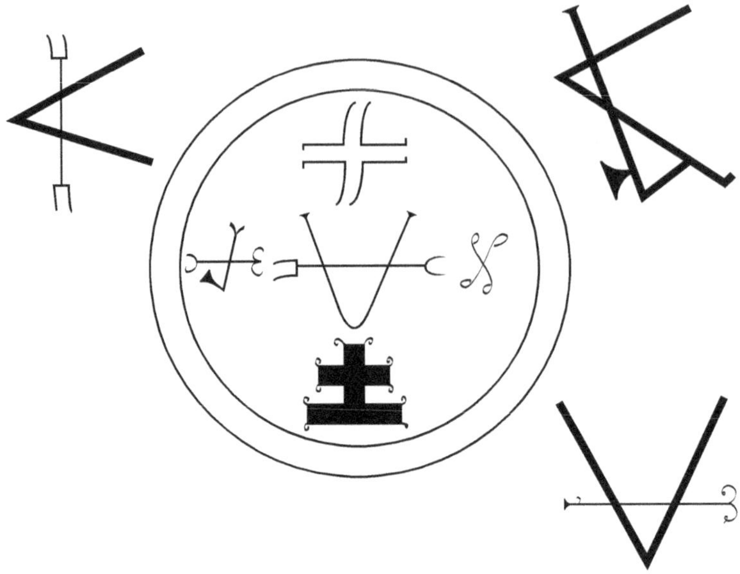

"Conjuro te, Ellina, simplex pulchra et decora et splendissima, per deum optimum et omnium rerum, visibiliam et invisibiliam, creatorem, et per omnia quae ipsa creavit ab initio mundi, per caelum, et terram, et mare, et omnes quae in eis

[214]

"sunt, et per imagines et figuras pro tuo amore et filiae tuae fabricatas quae ante sunt, ut tuam propriam filiam tecum ad nos adducas, et super hanc plumbae laminam et *imaginis* [imaginem] eam in forma speciosa mellae stare facias, sicut constituisti et nominibus veris [?] det responsum de omnibus rebus de quibus eam interrogabimus."

> "I conjure thee, Ellina,[1204] honest, beautiful, suitable, and most splendid, by the best God and creator of all things, visible and invisible, and by all things that he created from the beginning of the world, by heaven, and earth, and the sea, and all things that [214] are in them, and by the images and figures that were made before for thy love and that of your daughter, that you should bring thy own daughter with thee to us, and you may make to stand over this lamina of lead and this image, in the brilliant form of honey water, so that thou wilt confirm,

1204. *Ellina*: Wellcome 4669 has "Alma."

and she givest answer in the true names of all things regarding which we will ask her."

This said, incontinent she will appear in the form of a goodly woman, and bring with her another spirit of an inestimable fairness, and stand upon the plate of lead. And then ask what you will, and, after your desire, she shall answer you. That done, desire the spirits to consecrate those images to thee, and the plate of lead. Then whensoever 'tis necessary for your inquisition, they may come to you without conjuration, in whatsoever place you will, either in the town or without, and give you true answer, & c.

These images, after the consecration, have great efficacy to enquire of the love of a man, or woman, per only touching of the bare skin or garments. He that hath the plate of lead about him shall not die with the sword in the wars, and he that hath the falling sickness, in touching of it, shall be cured, and per touching of it, a woman that is barren shall bring forth fruit.

[215]

Invocatio Spiritus Bealphares[1205]

Incipit invocatio ad habendum spiritum responsum, absque sacrificio et aliqua pensione, et venit in forma pulchra hominis aut mulieribus, et dabit responsa verissima de quibuscunque ipsum interrogare vel imperare volueris, verpole de aliquo thesauro abscondito aufertque aurem vel argentum, aut ad te adducet mulierem vel puellam, et si vis ire una regione in alia, portabit te sine laesione corporis ille. Igitur qui hoc opus facere voluerit, debet abstinere jocis mendatiis libidine et ebrietate falcis iuramentis et facio et omnia abstinentia in uno fonte vino debet balneati, ut sit meddet albus vestibus mentus, provideat qui sibi locum secretum et portet secum *ducanstum* [caustum] et pennam eum quibus, scribet hoc *sacrenum* [sacrum] nomen dei in manu suae dextra, "+ Agla +," et in manu sua sinistra hoc nomen "+ + +  +" et habeat cunctada corrigeam de pille leperis aut cerni in qua fuit scripta hec sancta nomina in *curcuila* [circula] "+ 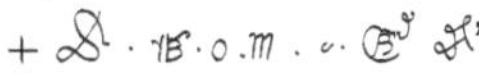" super pectos signum in charta virginea scriptum ut in praesenti figura, patebit et sit sincta super vestem albam, et si habere voluerit socios similiter sese exornent et habeant ut magister. Deinde habeant cultellum cum manubrio in cujus lamina tria nomina fuit scripte ab una parte, et ab alia.

1205. Translation: "Invocation of the Spirit Bealphares." For other operations of Bealphares, see Scot, *The Discouerie of Witchcraft*, 415–20. Variants in Sloane 3824, Sibley, *Solomon's Clavis, or Key to Unlock the Mysteries of Magic*, 208–15.

The invocation begins here to have an answer of spirits without sacrifice or any recompense, and it comes in the beautiful form of a man or of woman, and it gives a most true response regarding whatsoever you desire to ask or command it. He tells of any hidden treasure, and he carries off gold or silver, or he will bring a woman or girl to you,[1206] and if you desire to go from one region into another, he will carry you without injury of body. Therefore he who desires to perform this work, he should abstain from jokes, lies, pleasure, drunkenness, and false oaths, and I do[1207] and, abstaining from all things, he should be bathed in a living spring, and he should be clothed in white vestments. He should provide himself a secret place, and he should carry within him ink and a pen, with which he will be write this sacred name of God on his right hand, "+ Agia +" and on his left hand this name "+ + + 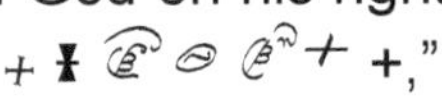 +," and he should have a belt of hare or deer fur,[1208] on which these holy names should be written in a circle, "+ + 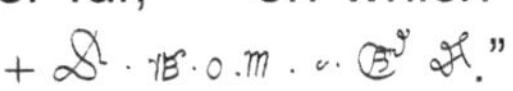." Upon his breasts should be exposed this sign written in virgin paper, as on the present figure, and it should be girdled over the white clothing, and if he desires to have associates, they should hold and equip themselves similarly as the master. Then they should have a knife with a handle, on the plate of which three names were written, on one side, and on another.

1206. *Or he will bring…to you*: Not in Scot.

1207. *And I do*: This appears to be an error.

1208. *Hare or deer fur*: Scot "lions or of a harts skin."

[216]

✠ *Agla,* ✠✠ ⁑ *et eum* dicto, a cultello fac circulum, ut infra hoc facto, infra circulum, et reformato locum eum cultello per quam intransti, et subfumigater ipsum et socios tuos eum olebano et mastice splendide et elies in exalio, Ales postea *mimeo* [vino, following Scot] misce. Dicat magister simpliciter vultu hanc suffumigationem.

> ✠ *Agla,* ✠✠ ⁑ *et eum* + and having said this, make a circle with the knife, as below. This being done, draw again below the circle and place through which you entered with the knife, and it and your associates are suffumigated with olibanum and bright mastic, and [?] [?].[1209] Afterward mix these in wine. The master should say simply, with expression, this suffumigation:

"Fatio in honorem suum omnipotentis dei, qui nos et vos paritur custodiat, et ab omni malo eripiat. Amen."

> "I do this in the honour of the omnipotent God, who guards us and you all equally, and may he wrest us from all evil. Amen."

1209. *[?] [?]*: Unclear in this manuscript. Scot has "lignum aloes."

Majesteri [magistri] versus eo oratione dicat tribus vocibus,[1210] (Psalm 22 and 51[1211]): "O deus, deus meus, respice,"[1212] and "Miserere mei,"[1213] et postea dicat,[1214] "Ne perdas cum impiis animam meam."[1215]

"Deus, Helye, Helycon, et Sier, Deus eternus Ch Loy[1216] Dominus sanctorum, ideo verax deus Anapheneton, Deus ineffabilis, Saday omnipotentis On, fortissimo qui te a peccatoribus exorrariem ovolmosti suscipe propitious hortias laudes at praeces quas nos indigni offerre tibi decrenimus et libera nos et miserere nostri. +

> "God, Helye, Helycon, and Sier, God eternal, Eloy, Lord of saints, therefore, true God, Anapheneton, ineffable God, of omnipotent On, by the most strong, who thou desired to plead thee with sinners, receive favourable sacrifices, praises, and prayers, that we the unworthy declare to offer to thee, and free us, and have mercy upon us. +

"Exorsizo te, et preceptor hujus operis, per creatorum caeli et terra, et per virtutem ejus, et per summum et ineffabilem nomen ejus Tetragramaton, et omnia nomina suae

[217]

pro sacramenta, sacramenta, sanctissima, et per sanctam magestatem, ad di[vin]etatem dei vivi. Coniuro te, et exorziso te, Bealphares per virtutes angelorum, per thronos, et dominationes, principates, et potestates, et per nomen verissimum magistri vestry, maneas quousque respondeas ad omnia interrogata mea, et compleas totam voluntatem meam absque dolo et falaciis."

> "I exorcise thee and the teacher of this work, by the creator of heaven and earth, and by his power, and by his highest and ineffable name Tetragramaton, and all the names of him [217] for the sacraments, the most holy sacraments, and by the holy majesty and divinity of the living God. I conjure thee and exorcise thee, Bealphares, by the powers of the angels, by thrones and dominions, principalities and powers,

1210. *Majesteri…vocibus*: Translation: "The masters should speak this oration, with three voices."

1211. The original gives the Latin titles of the Psalms, but the numbering of the commonly available English editions.

1212. *O deus…respice*: Vulgate Psalm 21. Translation (KJV Psalm 22): "My God, my God, why hast thou forsaken…"

1213. *Miserere mei*: Vulgate Psalm 50. Translation (KJV Psalm 51): "Have mercy upon me…"

1214. *Et postea dicat*: Translation: "And afterward he should say."

1215. *Ne perdas…meam*: Vulgate Psalm 25:9. Translation (KJV Psalm 22:9): "Gather not my soul with sinners." Scot's version includes references to prayers and incantations not present here.

1216. *Ch Loy*: Scot: "Eloy."

and by the most true name of your master, you should remain and also answer all my questions, and you should fulfil all my will without artifice or tricks."

Et statim spiritus veniet et dicet tibi omnia sine ullis falaciis et varaciter *assque* [absque] ullo dolo.

And immediately the spirit will come, and he will tell you all things without any tricks, and truly without any artifice.

Sequitur Vinculum[1217]

"By the might and power of this holy name, almighty God Pewmaton,[1218] and in the virtue and power of this holy name of God Pewmaton, which Moses did name when Kora, Dathan, and Abyram were drowned in the depth of darkness," (Numbers 16 verse 30), "and in the pit of hell, and so through the power of his holy name of God, Pewmaton. I curse thee and send thee, spirit N., for thy disobedience and rebellion, into the deepest lake of hell or darkness, until the last and dreadful day of judgment, that there thy pains may be multiplied daily more and more, and increased without, and through the might and power of this holy name of God, Pewmaton, except you fulfil my will and commandment. + So be it, + so be it, + so be it. +

[218]

"By the virtue, might, and power of this unspeakable name of God, the lord Tetragrammaton, and in the virtue, might, and power of this name of God Tetragramaton, which was written in a plate of gilt in the forehead of Aaron the high priest,[1219] I curse thee into the deep, infernal, bottomless pit of Hell, there to be tormented with excessive pains and torments until the last dreadful day of doom, except thou fulfil my will and commandment. Unless thou do, God the Father, the Son, and the Holy Ghost curse thee and condemn thee per ever in the fiery lake of Hell, except thou fulfil my will and commandment. Heaven and earth curse thee and condemn thee for ever. Amen.

"All holy angels of God curse thee and condemn thee forever, unless thou appear visible unto me and fulfil my commandment truly and unfeignedly, without fraud or guile. If thou do not, all the martyrs of the blessed be unto thee everlasting torments, and like as this is consumed in the noisome stink, so per the virtue, power, strength, force, and might of this holy name

1217. Translation: "The Binding Follows." From this point the text departs considerably from Scot.

1218. *Pewmaton*: Should be "Primeumaton."

1219. Note in margin: "Exodus 39:20–30."

of Tetragramaton, I condemn thee in the most terrible punishment for ever, unless thou fulfil my will and obey my commandment.

[219]

"This grant, O Lord Jesus Christ, with God his Father and the Holy Ghost forever. Amen."

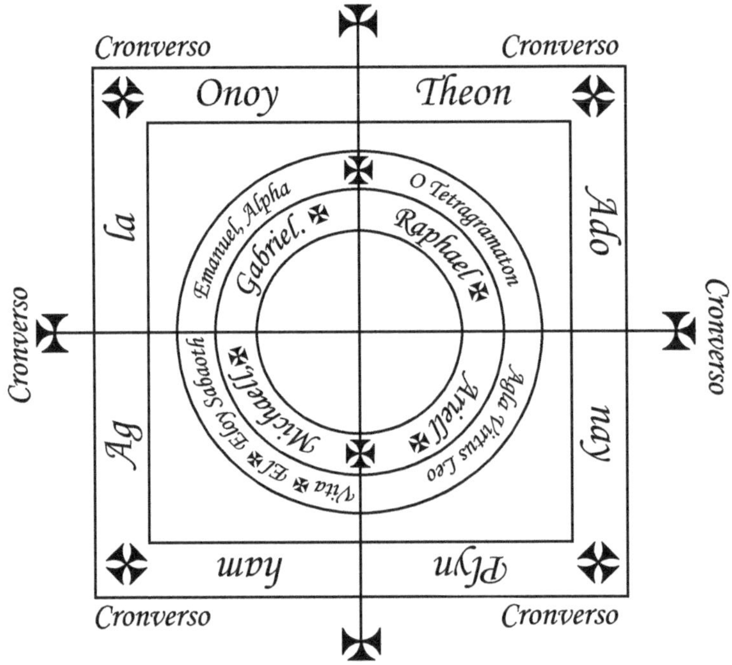

Consecratio Circuli[1220]

"Coniuro te, circulum, et consecro locum istum, per illum vivum et verum deum, creatorem caeli et terrae, qui istum circulum creavit. Sanctifico et consecro te, circulum et locum istum, per ipsum creatorem caeli et terrae, et per ista *sanctorum* [sancta] nomina, Theos, Iskyroth, Athanatos, Iothe, Otheos, Sabaoth, Baatze,

[220]

"Belle, Habuet, Admatas Antriel, Gudamel, Agios, Theleas, Ymas, Vau, El, Ely, On, Hawe, Ethem, Burie, Tollens, Se, Noe, Jana, Yara, et per omnia nomina dei sanctissima, + benedictus et consecratus, sanctificatus et custoditus, societate omnium sanctorum, evangelistarum, martirum, patriarcharum, prophetarum, principatum, et potestatum consumatus sit, et consecratus circulus et

1220. *Translation*: "Consecration of the Circle." See Harms, Clark, and Peterson, *Oberon*, 111–13.

locus ista quatenus virtutem et potestatem sanctissimam capiat, in signo dei vivi et sancta crucis Christi, et sancte Marie, matris domini nostri Jesu Christi plena gratia. Consecrata itaque per istam circulum terrores, *sanctissimata* [sanctissimum], timores, temptationes, aliquo [modo] in causa nocendi non valeant inferre ipso adjuvante et *caucedente* [defendete] cui celestia, terrestria, et infernalia subiiciuntur. Amen."

> "I conjure thee, circle, and I consecrate this place, by the living and true God, the creator of heaven and earth, who created this circle. I sanctify and consecrate thee, this circle and place, by the same creator of heaven and earth, and by these holy names, Theos, Iskyroth, Athanatos, Iothe, Otheos, Sabaoth, Baatze, [220] Belle, Habuet, Admatas Antriel, Gudamel, Agios, Theleas, Ymas, Vau, El, Ely, On, Hawe, Ethem, Burie, Tollens, Se, Noe, Jana, Yara, and by all the most holy names of God, + blessed and consecrated, sanctified and defended, in the company of all the saints, evangelists, martyrs, patriarchs, prophets, principalities, and powers, and so may it be finished and the circle and place be consecrated, so that it may take on virtue and most holy power, in the sign of the living God and of the holy cross of Christ, and of holy Mary, mother of our lord Jesus Christ, full of grace. Therefore, consecrated by this most holy circle, no terrors, fears, or temptations may be able to enter or to hurt in any way, that it might be strong for helping and defending us, to whom all things heavenly, earthly, and infernal are subject. Amen.

"Aspurgo te, aqua benedicta, in circulo et in loco dei omnipotentis qui te fecit te bene + dixit et conse + cravit, dedit potestatem famulis suis sacerdotibus *principae* [precipue] *comessit* [consecrare] qui est pater et filius, et spiritus sanctus, et ego te aqua benedicta evoco, et exorcizo, in nomine dei, et sancte beate Marie, nec non in nomine et virtute omnium sanctorum ejus cum omni celesti consortio ut tu sis aqua benedicta consecrata per

[221]

"illum deum qui te fecit, et consecrari iussit, et, ut sit omnibus nobis protectio et defensio ab omnibus diaboli temptationibus et infestacionibus, insidiis et fraudibus, *praesentia* [potestate] sanctus spiritus nobis per *mandam* [misericordiam] suam posse ubique *advenire* [ad omnem] *dignitatem* [dignetur] per Christum Dominum verum, & c."

"I sprinkle thee, holy water, in the circle and place of the omnipotent God who made, bles + sed, and conse + crated you. He, who is Father, Son, and Holy Ghost, gave power especially to his servants the priests. And I summon and exorcise thee, holy water, in the name of God and of the holy blessed Mary, and in the name and power of all his saints, with all the celestial fellowship, that thou, holy water, should be blessed and consecrated, by [221] that God who made thee and ordered thee to be consecrated, and that you be protection and defence to all of us from all temptations, disturbances, ambushes, and frauds of the devil, in the power of the Holy Ghost, by his mercy for us, to be deemed worthy everywhere and for everything, by Christ the true Lord, & c."

A Prayer to Be Said before You Come out of the Circle

"Deus propitius esto in *pectus custus* [peccatis] meis omnibus diebus vitae me[ae]. Deus Abraham, deus Isaac, deus Jacob, miserere mei, et mitte in adiutorum meum Michaelum angelum tuum sanctum, qui me defendat in praelio meo per eam in tremendo judito.

"Lord, have mercy on my sins for all the days of my life. God of Abraham, God of Isaac, God of Jacob, have mercy on me, and send to my help your holy angel Michael, who guards me in my battle by this in fearful judgment.

"St. Michael, archangelum dei, per gratiam quam meruisti *dexteoram* [deprecamur?], et per virginitatem filii dei domini vestri Jesu Christi, ut eripias me + ut & c. hodie et omni tempore periculo mortis. Sancte Gabriel, et omne sancti arcangeli dei, firmiter in cordibus vestris virtutes celorum, ut mihi per summi dei *patetriam* [paternitatem?] datam suis angelis, ut in nulla temptatione, interum *reocere* [nocere] vel condemnare possit in omne. Amen. Non in aere, amen. Non in conjur[ati]o, non in domo, amen. Non extra domo, amen. Non in aqua, amen. Non in igne, amen. Non in periculo, amen. Non in vigilantibus, amen.

[224][1221]

"Non in dormientibus, amen. Ecce + signum domini nostri Jesu Christi. Fugite partes adverse, vicit leo de tribu iuda, radix David, Alleluya. Salvator mundi, salva me qui per crucem et sanguinem tuam redemisti me. Auxiliare mihi,

1221. No pages numbered 222 or 223 exist in the manuscript; pages 221 and 224 are both sides of the same leaf.

Deus meus, Agios, Agios, Agios, + Crux Christi salva me, + Crux Christi prohege me, + Crux Christi defende me, nunc et semper. Amen."

> "Saint Michael, archangel of God, by the grace of which you are worthy, we pray, and by the virginity of the Son of God your Lord Jesus Christ, that you save me + as & c. from danger of death today and for all time. Holy Gabriel, and all the holy angels of God, the powers of heaven in your hearts, that for me, by the paternal feeling of the highest God that is given to his angels, that he will not be able meanwhile to harm or condemn me in all things. Amen. Not in the air, amen. Not in conjuration, not at home, amen. Not outside the home, amen. Not in water, amen. Not in fire, amen. Not in danger, amen. Not in wakefulness, amen. [224] Not in sleeping, amen. Behold + the sign of our Lord Jesus Christ. Flee, evil forces, the lion of the tribe of Judah, root of David, conquers, alleluia. Saviour of the world, save me, who by the cross and his blood redeemed me. Help me, my God, Agios, Agios, Agios, + Cross of Christ, save me + Cross of Christ, protect me + Cross of Christ, defend me, now and forever. Amen."

[The Seal of Paymon]

Here followeth the characters for Paymon, which ought to be shewed when ye call him up.

The Call [of Oriens][1222]

"In the name of the Father, and of the Son, and of the Holy Ghost, amen. O thou, King

[225]

"Oriens, which hast power over all the spirits of the air which be under thy regality,[1223] I warn thee, I constrain thee, I command thee now, I call on thee and conjure thee per these names of God the Father almighty, king of kings and lord of lords, Agla, Tetragramaton, Alpha et Ω, Agios, Otheos, Iskyrus, Athanatos, Panton, Craton, et Isus, Messias, Sother, Emanuel, Sabaoth, Adonay, that thou appear before me, that I may see thee in this crystal stone. I command thee, I conjure thee, I bind thee, I constrain thee, and I adjure thee, and with all my might, I command thee to obey me and fulfil my mind, and per all the holy names of God, and per thine own power, which thou hast above all the spirits of the air, being under thy regality and power, that I may have my will fulfilled in all things, according to my own desire. To these things I command thee and adjure thee, per the names of Jesus Christ, El, Eleya, Hely, Hely, Lamazabachany, Tetr[a]gramaton, Altenay, Adonay, On, Cados, Acynamos, Eba, Oymon, Saday, Aglaca, Ya, Yociell, Anora, Yana, Amabo, and per these two names Jath and Haboth,

[226]

"I command thee, I adjure thee, I constrain thee, that wheresoever thou be, that thou come to me, per the nine names of angels, that is to say Michael, Raphael, Gabr[i]ell, Daniell, Tobyell, Uryell, Barachyell, cherubim, and seraphin, and per our lady, the holy mother of Jesus Christ, and per the principal joys which she had of her Son our redeemer, that, per and per, without any tarrying, thou enter into this crystal stone, and to fulfil my will in all points, in the name of the Father, and of the Son, and of the Holy Ghost. Amen."[1224]

Look in the stone; if he now come, say this following:

"O King Oriens, I command thee, I conjure thee per the virtue of the true living God, which is Alpha and Ω, and I call upon thee per the virtue of our Lord Jesus Christ, which, for thy help of all mankind, came down from heaven,

1222. *Oriens*: Compare to Add. 36674, 48r–v. For other references to this spirit, see Bayerische Staatsbibliothek Clm 849, 33v–34r, 106r–v; Sloane 3824, 18r–v, 117v; Harms, Clark, and Peterson, *Oberon*, 170–1, 208, 285–86, 297–301; Harms and Clark, *Of Angels*, 106–7, 194; von Worms, *The Book of Abramelin: A New Translation*, 148, 171.

1223. *Regality*: Royal prerogatives.

1224. *Oriens…Amen*: Compare to Harms and Clark, *Of Angels*, 109.

and born of the virgin Mary. I conjure thee, Oriens, per the Holy Ghost comforter, which proceeded from the Father and the Son and rested upon Christ in the likeness of a dove, in the water of flem[1225] Jordan, and fulfilled the apostles which spoke in divers tongues, per the great mystery of God. I conjure thee per three persons in trinity, and I constrain

[227]

"thee per the virtues and powers of these three persons. I call upon thee and adjure thee per the Father and the Son and the Holy Ghost, and I constrain thee per the virtue of the undenied Trinity, and per the lamb sitting on the throne of God, and per the seven thrones which God hath ordained to be seven gifts of the Holy Ghost. I conjure thee, per angels, archangels, thrones, and dominations, per principates and potestates, per cherubim and seraphim, and per all the virtue of all the holy company of heaven. I call upon thee per all the servants of them. I constrain thee per the virtue of them that do cry and rest afore our Lord, saying with a loud voice, 'Sanctus, sanctus, sanctus,' I conjure thee per the twenty-four elders, beating their wings in their hands and come forth after God, and per their white crown and seats. I conjure thee per the twenty-four martyrs, and I conjure thee per the thunder of God, lightnings, and lettings,[1226] and I conjure thee per the seven candlesticks of gold that stand before God always burning. I call on thee, I conjure thee per the golden censer, and I call upon thee and command thee per all patriarchs and prophets, I constrain thee per all holy apostles, and per the holy evangelists, and I require thee and conjure thee

[228]

"per the company of all martyrs, which have suffered for the love of God. I conjure thee per all masses which have been sung and said in all the world, and per the nine well-learned priests, and per the nine children newly christened, and per nine elders of God. I constrain thee per the shewing of Christ, I require thee per the birth of Christ, I conjure thee per the baptism of Christ, I adjure thee per the fast of Christ, I call upon thee per the transfiguration of Christ, I command thee per the patience of Christ, I bind thee per the crown of thorns, that which the Jews[1227] put on the head of our saviour Jesus Christ,

1225. *Flem*: See manuscript page 145.

1226. *Lettings*: The ability to allow passage or set up obstacles.

1227. *Jews*: The Biblical accounts in Matthew, Mark, and John attribute this action, and the two thereafter, to Roman soldiers. This sadly reflects the anti-Semitism prevalent in early modern Europe at the time.

and per the reed which the Jews put in his right hand and did kneel down before him, mocking and saying to him, 'Hail, king of the Jews,' and per the buffets per which the Jews gave him, looking on him, and per the cross upon which our Lord Jesus Christ was nailed, and per the cry of our Lord Jesus Christ, saying to his father, 'O God, my God, why hast thou forsaken me?,' and per the death of Christ, and per the spear, with that which the side of Christ was opened up, and per the whips of Christ, and per the nails with that which the body of Christ was nailed, and per the virtue

[229]

"of the wounds of Christ, and per the virtue of the bread which Jesus took, blessed, and brake, and gave it to his disciples, saying, 'Take, eat, this is my body, which shall be given per you,' and for many likewise, he take the cup and said, 'Drink ye all of this; this is my blood of the New Testament, which is shed for you and for many on remission of sins,' and per the sheet in which Christ body was buried and lapped[1228] in, and per the sepulchre in which the body of Christ was buried, and per the going down of Christ into Hell, and per his glorious resurrection on the third day, and per the great deed and wonders of God, that wheresoever thou be, that thou do appear in all haste and enter into this crystal stone visible in my sight, and in the likeness of a fair man, having a red colour or a white colour, of a fair king crowned with a golden crown, and give me true answer, as far as thou hast knowledge of any things that I shall ask thee, speaking to me without any impediment of my wits and without any deceit, and without any hurt of my body and soul, or of any creature under the power of the bigger majesty of God. Fiat, fiat, fiat, Amen."[1229]

[230]

Aphorismum[1230] [A Selection from the *Arbatel*][1231]

Septem sunt gubernateres seu officiorum *Domini* [differentiae] Olympi, quibus deus voluit *univesd* [universum] hanc mundi machinam administrari. Visibilia ante eorum astra sunt Aratron. Bether. Phaleg. Och. Agith. Ophiel, Phul, Olympico sermone. Quilibet preterea *subsehz* [sub se habet] militiam firmamenti multiplicem.

1228. *Lapped*: Wrapped.

1229. *O King Oriens…Amen*: See Harms and Clark, *Of Angels*, 111–12.

1230. Translation: "Aphorism."

1231. *Arbatel*: Aphorisms 16 and 17. Translations of the below are taken from the 1665 edition of pseudo-Agrippa's *Fourth Book*. Corrected Latin and a new English translation may be found in Peterson, *Arbatel*.

> There are seven different governments of the spirits of *Olympus*, by whom God hath appointed the whole frame and universe of this world to be governed: and their visible stars are Aratron, Bethor, Phaleg, Och, Hagith, Ophiel, Phul, and the *Olympic* speech. Every one of these hath under him a mighty militia in the firmament.[1232]

Aratron praeest provincys xlix
Bether 32
Phaleg 35
Och 28
Hagith 21
Ophiel 14
Phul 7.

> ARATRON ruleth visible provinces XLIX.
> BETHOR, 32.
> PHALEG, 35.
> OCH, 28.
> HAGITH, XXI.[1233]
> OPHIEL, XIIII.
> PHUL, VII.[1234]

Numero viz [ut sint Olympi provinciae] 196 in quibus suam politiam septen gubernatores administrant, *qui* [quae] omnia in astronomia gratiae explicatur diserte. Hoc autem loco quomodo ad colloquia horam deducuntur [deducuntur horum] principes et *prelates* [potestates] explicandum [est].

> So that there are 186[1235] Olympic provinces in the whole universe, wherein the seven governors do exercise their power: all which are elegantly set forth in astronomy. But in this place is to be explained, in what manner these princes and powers may be drawn into communication.[1236]

Arothon in Sabbato et hora 1e die apparet, *et per* [ac] responsa dat de suis provinciis et provincialiabus verissime. Similiter et alii ordine in suis diebus et horis. Preest etiam quilibet 490 annis. Principium *animala* [anomaliae] simplices, anno 60 ante Christum natum e[st] principium administrationis Bethor

1232. Pseudo-Agrippa, *Fourth Book* (1665), 177.
1233. In the original manuscript, Hagith is given as 24.
1234. Pseudo-Agrippa, *Fourth Book* (1665), 177.
1235. *186*: Pseudo-Agrippa, *Fourth Book* (1665), should have 196 here.
1236. Pseudo-Agrippa, *Fourth Book* (1665), 177.

et duravit ad annum Christi [Domini] 430. Cui *successiae* [successit] Phaleg usque ad 920 *omnium* [annum]. Deinde Och ad 1410 annum. Abhinc Hagith regnat ad 1900 usque.

> Aratron appeareth in the first hour of Saturday, and very truly giveth answers concerning his provinces and provincials. So likewise do the rest appear in order in their days and hours. Also, every one of them ruleth 490 years. The beginning of their simply Anomaly, in the 60 year before the nativity of Christ, was the beginning of the administration of Bethor; and it lasted until the year of our Lord Christ 430. To whom succeeded Phaleg, until the 920 year. Then began Och, and continued until the year 1410, and thenceforth Hagith ruleth until the year 1900.[1237]

Magice evocanter vii gubernator[um] principes simplictier eo *the* [temporum] quo diei [et] horas [horis] praesunt, *visibilem* [visibiliter] aut *invisibilem* [invisibiliter], per sua nomina et officia, quia illis *dei* [deus] dedit, et proposito ejus charectere quem vel confirmanv[er]it vel *ipsi ceder* [dederint].

> Magically the princes of the seven governours are called simply, in that time, day, and hour wherein they rule visibly or invisibly, by their names and offices which God hath given unto them; and by proposing their character which they have given or confirmed.

Gubernator *Arothon* [Aratron] *hhnio* [habet in] sua potestate quae naturaliter facit *horem* [hoc est] eodem modo in predisposito

[231]

subiecto, ea quae in *astromema* [astronomiae] gratiae saturninis viribus ascribentur. Quae vero libra sua voluntate facit, sunt. 1 Quod potest quavis in lapidem convertere etiam in momento, veluti *atal* [animal] aut plantam *getinetem* [retinentem] eadem objecta visus. 2 *Convertiter* [convertit] thesauros in carbones ac contra carbones in thesauros. 3 Dat familiares cum definita potestate. 4 Docet alchimam, magiam, physicam. 5 Consiliat homini Pigmeos honos Phylosis. 6 Facit invisibilem. 7 Infaecundum facit foecundum, et donat *longamtatem* [longeuitatem].

> The governour *Aratron* hath in his power those things which he doth naturally, that is, afore the same manner and [231] subject as those

1237. Pseudo-Agrippa, *Fourth Book* (1665), 177–78.

things which in astronomy are ascribed to the power of *Saturn*. The things which he doth of his own free will, are,

1. That he can convert any thing into a stone in a moment, either animal or plant, retaining the same object to the sight.
2. He converteth treasures into coals, and coals into treasure.
3. He giveth familiars with a definite power.
4. He teacheth alchemy, magic, and physick.
5. He reconcileth the subterranean spirits to men; maketh hairy men.
6. He causeth one to be invisible.
7. The barren he maketh fruitful, and giveth long life.[1238]

Character Ejus[1239]

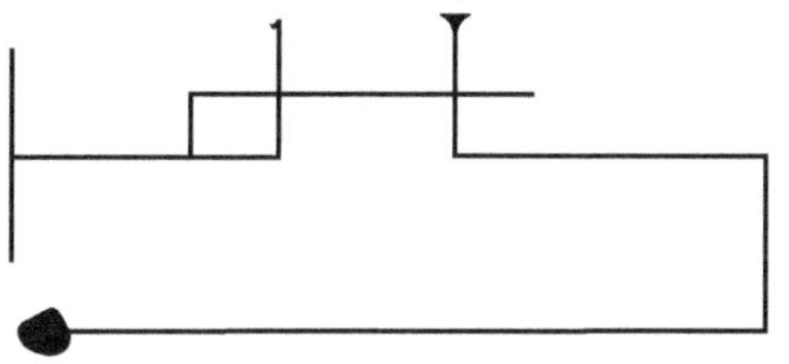

Habet sub se 49 reges, 42 principes, 35 satrapas, 28 duces, 21 ministros eoram se stantes, 14 familiares, 7 nuncios. Imperat legionibus 38000.

He hath under him 49 kings, 42 princes, 35 presidents, 28 dukes, 21 ministers, standing before him; 14 familiars, seven messengers he commandeth 36,000[1240] legions of spirits; [the number of a legion is 490].[1241]

Bethor quae Jovi adscribuntur, gubernat: vocatus cito advenit. *Quem* [quae] suo charactere dignatur ad maximas dignitates euehit, obiicit thesauros aereos conciliat spiritus, qui vera dant responsa. De loco ad locum transportant quesvis res et lapides preciosos, ac medicinas miraculosas in suis effectibus. Dat etiam familiares firmament, et potest ad 700 annos vitam prolongare, si deus valedit.

1238. Pseudo-Agrippa, *Fourth Book* (1665), 178.

1239. Translation: "His character."

1240. *36,000*: Douce MS. 116 has "38,000."

1241. Pseudo-Agrippa, *Fourth Book* (1665), 179. Bracketed material not in Douce MS. 116.

Bethor governeth those things which are ascribed to Jupiter: he soon cometh being called. He that is dignified with his character, he raiseth to very great dignities, to cast open treasures: he reconcileth the spirits of the air, that they give true answers: they transport precious stones from place to place, and they make medicines to work miraculously in their effects: he giveth also the familiars of the firmament, and prolongeth life to 700 years if God will.[1242]

[232]

Character

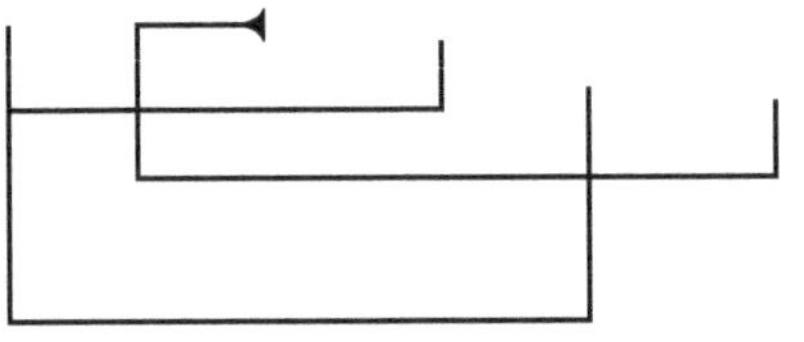

H[ab]et sub se 42 reges, 35 principes, 28 duces, 21 consiliarios, 14 ministros, 7 *inimicos* [nuncios]. 29000 legione spirituum.

He hath under him 42 kings, 35 princes, 28 dukes, 21 counsellors, 14 ministers, 7 messengers, 29,000 legions of spirits.[1243]

Phaleg praeest marti atributis, pacis prince. Ejus characterem cui tribuit, evehit ad sumas dignitates in re bellica.

Phaleg ruleth those things which are attributed to Mars, the prince of peace. He that hath his character, he raiseth to great honours in warlike affairs.[1244]

Character

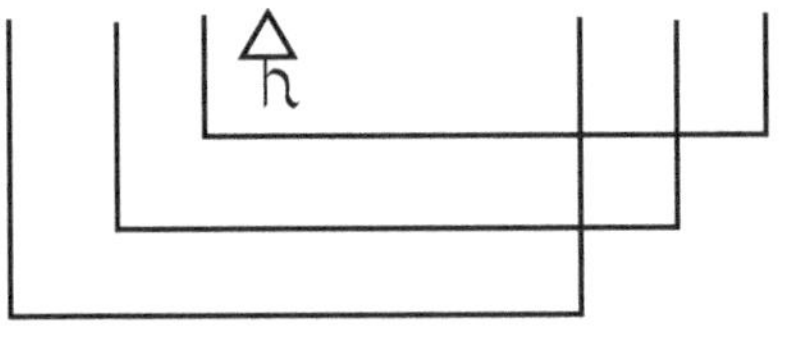

Hic [Och] solaribus praeest, dat 600 annos cum firma valetudine. Largitur *sapiamus* [sapientiam]. Dat spiritus prestantissimos, docet *perfrem* [perfectam] medicinam, convertit omnia in aurem purissimum et lapides preciosos,

1242. Pseudo-Agrippa, *Fourth Book* (1665), 179.

1243. Pseudo-Agrippa, *Fourth Book* (1665), 179.

1244. Pseudo-Agrippa, *Fourth Book* (1665), 179.

Dat aurum et crumenam pullulantem auro. Quem suo Charectere dignum duxerit, facit tanquam numen coli a regibus totius mundi.

> Och governeth solar things; he giveth 600 years, with perfect health; he bestoweth great wisdom, giveth the most excellent spirits, teacheth perfect medicines: he converteth all things into most pure gold and precious stones: he giveth gold, and a purse springing with gold. He that is dignified with his character, he maketh him to be worshipped as a deity, by the kings of the whole world.[1245]

Habet sub se legiones 36536. Solus administrat omnia, et sibi inseruiunt omnes sui spiritus per centurias.

> He hath under him 36,536 legions: he administreth all things alone: and all his spirits serve him by centuries.[1246]

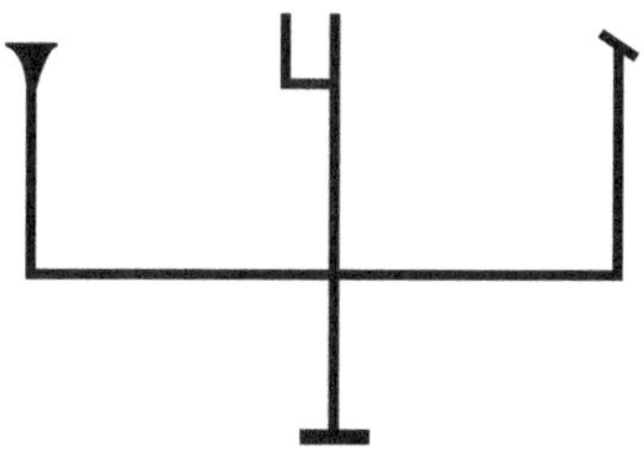

Character

[233]

Hagith gubernat venerea, quem suo dignatur charectere formosissimum facit, et ornatum omni decore. Cuprum convertit in momento in aurem, et *convertit* [contra] aurem in cuprum. Dat spiritus *similiter[?]* [fideliter] qui inseriiunt iis, quibus *obdientur* [addicuntur].

> Hagith governeth venerous things. He that is dignified with his character, he maketh very fair, and to be adorned with all beauty. He converteth copper into gold, in a moment, and gold into copper: he giveth spirits which do faithfully serve those to whom they are addicted.[1247]

1245. Pseudo-Agrippa, *Fourth Book* (1665), 180.
1246. Pseudo-Agrippa, *Fourth Book* (1665), 180.
1247. Pseudo-Agrippa, *Fourth Book* (1665), 181.

Character

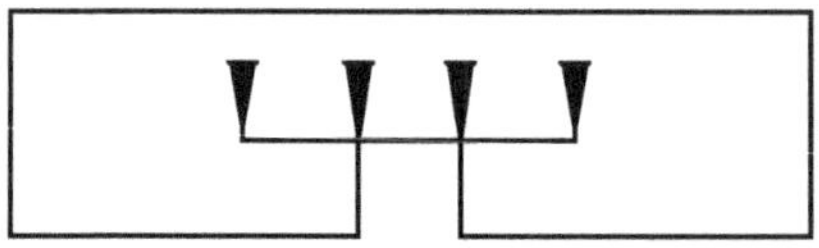

H[ab]et legiones 4000 *spiritus* [spirituum], et singulis millenis praefecit reges statis temporibus. Ophiel e[st] *gubnatorum crrialum* [gubernator Mercurialium]; ejus charecter est tales.

> He hath 4000 legions of spirits, and over every thousand he ordaineth kings for their appointed seasons. Ophiel is the governor of such things as are attributed to Mercury; his character is this.[1248]

[Character]

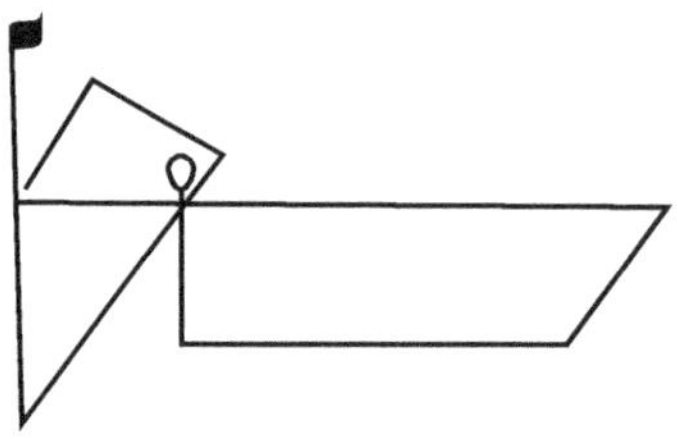

Ejus spiritus *onedunt* [accedunt] ad legiones centum milia, dat [spiritus] familiares facilime. Docet omnes artes, et quem suo charectere dignatur, facit posse in momento argentum vivum convertere in lapidem phylosophorum.

> His spirits are 100,000 legions: he easily giveth familiar spirits: he teacheth all arts: and he that is dignified with his character, he maketh him to be able in a moment to convert quicksilver into the philosopher's stone.[1249]

Character

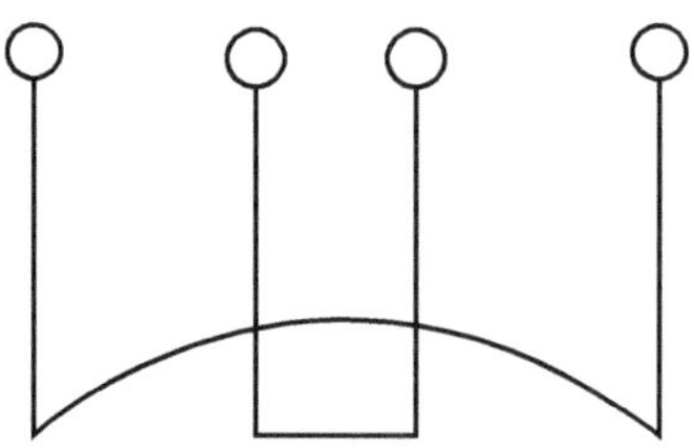

Ona me tella [Omnia metalla] in argentum commutat dicto et facto; *gubernat limaria* [lunaria]; sanat hydropem; dat aqueos spiritus, qui *infervint* [inseruiunt] homini corporali et visibili forma. Facit 300 Annos vivere.

1248. Pseudo-Agrippa, *Fourth Book* (1665), 181.
1249. Pseudo-Agrippa, *Fourth Book* (1665), 182.

He changeth all metals into silver, in word and deed; governeth lunary things; healeth the dropsy. He giveth spirits of the water, who do serve men in a corporeal and visible form; and maketh men to live 300 years.[1250]

[234]

To Go Invisible[1251]

Go to a swallow's nest upon a Tuesday, and take away her young ones, and leave their eyes in the nest still. Then the swallow will come, and see her young gone and will fetch a stone from the sea, and lay it in her nest. Then come you again upon a Tuesday, and take it away. Fiet.[1252]

Alter[1253]

Take hot scolding water, and go to a hill where many pismires[1254] be, and pour out the water in the hill, and shortly go thither, and then thou shalt find a stone of many colours. Take it, and bear it in thy hand, et fiet.[1255]

Alter[1256]

Take the stone that the raven fetcheth at the sea to quicken her eggs, and bear it with thee, and thou mayest go invisible.

Alter[1257]

Take a mould,[1258] and burn her to powder, and mingle it with the blood of a black lamb that hath no white spot, and write these words in virgin parchment, "Alhanatos, Isiros, Biros, Shor, Paua, Cras, Dhesas," and put it under thy right arm, et fiet.[1259]

1250. Pseudo-Agrippa, *Fourth Book* (1665), 182. This refers to the spirit Phul, with a line missing above the character. The manuscript stops its pseudo-Agrippa translation here.

1251. For another version, see British Library Sloane 3850, 145r. In other versions, the stone is used to alleviate eye troubles. Swainson, *The Folk Lore and Provincial Names of British Birds*, 51–52.

1252. *Fiet*: Translation: "It will be done."

1253. Translation: "Another." For other examples, see Harms, Clark, and Peterson, *Oberon*, 555–56; Johnson, *Svartkonstböcker*, 228; and elsewhere in this manuscript

1254. *Pismire*: Ant.

1255. *Et fiet*: Translation: "And it will be done."

1256. Translation: "Another." For other examples, see British Library Sloane 3850, 145r; Swainson, *The Folk Lore and Provincial Names of British Birds*, 91; Johnson, *Svartkonstböcker*, 292, 546.

1257. Translation: "Another."

1258. *Mould*: Harrington inserts here "mole."

1259. *Et fiet*: Translation: "And it will be done."

[Protection from Enemies]

If thou hast this name about thee "Nephemprosayton," thou shalt not be overcome of thy enemy.

[235]

For the Bleeding at the Nose, or Vein, or Wound[1260]

Where these letters following, 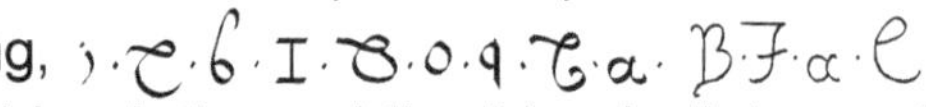 and bind it about the neck of them that bleedeth, and the blood stint, per God's grace. And if thou believe not this to be true, write the same upon the haft of a knife, and stick a pig therewith, and there shall no blood come out of the wound.

Alter[1261]

Touch thy nose and say, "Blood bide in this vein, as Christ abide in the Church, and hide in thee, as Christ hideth in himself."

To Win at Shooting

Write these letters in virgin parchment and put it in thine arrow. Proceed, and thou shalt win whilst thou carriest about thee:

To Obtain a Gift[1262]

Go to an elder tree when the ☉ shineth at noon, and strew consecrated rushes in the shadows of him, and call 3 times, "Magromon," and there will appear an herb much like gold before a fair woman, which will ask you what you will have. Then take up the herbs, and when you will have it, you shall not want any thing.

[236]

A Charm for Children[1263]

"Mary mild hath burned her child with a spark of fire. Out the fire, and in the frost, in the name of the Father, and of the Son, of the Holy Ghost, in nomine Patris, et Filii, et Spiritus Sancti. Amen." Say Pater Noster, Ave, and a Creed.

1260. For similar charms, see Skemer, *Binding Words*, 210; Power, "Section XXIII: History of Medicine: Independent Paper: The Lesser Writings of John Arderne," 109.

1261. Translation: "Another." Compare to Wright, *Rustic Speech and Folk-Lore*, 241.

1262. For other examples, see Harms, "The Herb and the Lady under the Elder at Noon."

1263. The "out fire, in frost" charm, as defined by Roper. For analysis and versions beginning with Mary, see Roper, *English Verbal Charms*, 116–19; Davies, "Healing Charms in Use in England and Wales 1700–1950," 23–24; Morgan, "Charms," 204; Leather, *The Folk-Lore of Herefordshire*, 73. The other examples of this variant are from counties on the Welsh border.

For the Toothache[1264]

"Sancta Apollonia fuit virgo, multum a deo dilecta. Cujus dentes pro amore Christi extracti fuerunt. Oravit ad Dominum Deum Jesum Christum ut si quis nomen eijus super se portabit a dolore dentium libereter, + Christus *vivat* [vivit], + Christus regnat, + Christus imperat, + Christus me creaturam dei *aliciam* [aliquam] ab omni dolore dentium capitque corpus defendat, + Christus, Christus + Christus, + Jesus + Jesus, + Jesus, + Amen."

> "Saint Apollonia was a virgin, much beloved of God. Her teeth were extracted for the love of Christ. She prayed to Lord God Jesus Christ that, if one will carry her name with them, they will be freed from toothache. + Christ lives, + Christ reigns, + Christ commands, + may Christ defend me, any creature of God, from all toothache, head and body, + Christ, Christ + Christ, + Jesus + Jesus + Jesus, + Amen."

To Go Invisible[1265]

Take a kite's tongue, and put it where the nine masses are sung. Then put it under thy arms, et eris invisibilis.[1266]

[To Be Beloved][1267]

Write these words in thy hand, "Tata, Parta." These be the words to be beloved of all men.

To Play at Dice

Go upon a Wednesday to a forrow way,[1268] and sit, and write with the blood of a lapwing in virgin parchment, in the way, these names: "Asaab, Abas, Abla, Tasbat, Agrano, Kaskaat, Laytor, Transtor, Donsor, Agayne." After these, thou

[237]

shalt fold them up and say,

"Usias, Asnaque, Abab, Mans Hora, all you come and consecrate me these names and characters quickly, that whensoever I shall have these names and characters about me or talk upon your names, no man may win of me or

1264. A toothache charm attributed to Saint Apollonius, known for having her teeth removed violently. Other sources state a similar charm should be written and worn. Braekman, *Middeleeuwse Witte en Zwarte Magie in het Nederlands Taalgebied*, 169–71; Hunt, *Popular Medicine in Thirteenth-Century England*, 88, 98, 247.

1265. For other beliefs about a kite's tongue, see Stefánsson, "Icelandic Beast and Bird Lore," 304–5.

1266. *Et eris invisibilis*: Translation: "and you will be invisible."

1267. Ohrt, *Danmarks Trylleformler* (1917), 2:128.

1268. *Forrow way*: Possibly a "four-way" or crossroads.

prevail against me, yea, and that the dice themselves shall obey me, until I have won that sum of money, that I would win."

And this done, and thou shalt bury them there, and the lapwing for a sacrifice, but thou shalt pin the names of them about thee, written with the blood of the lapwing, in virgin parchment:

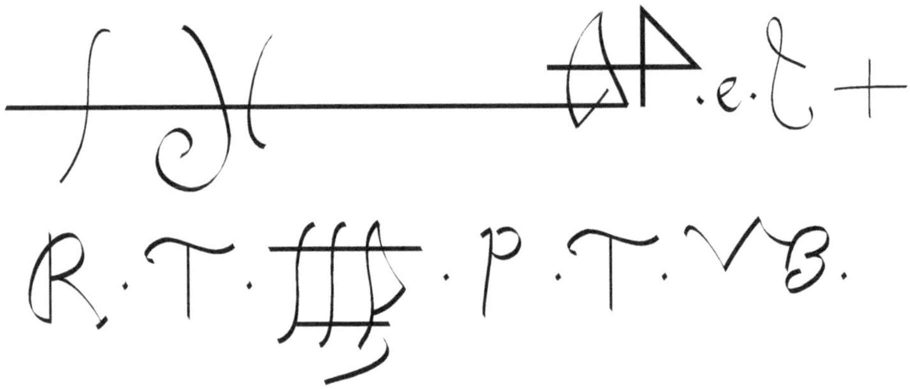

p. adonay. est A free A qeeo Ayre

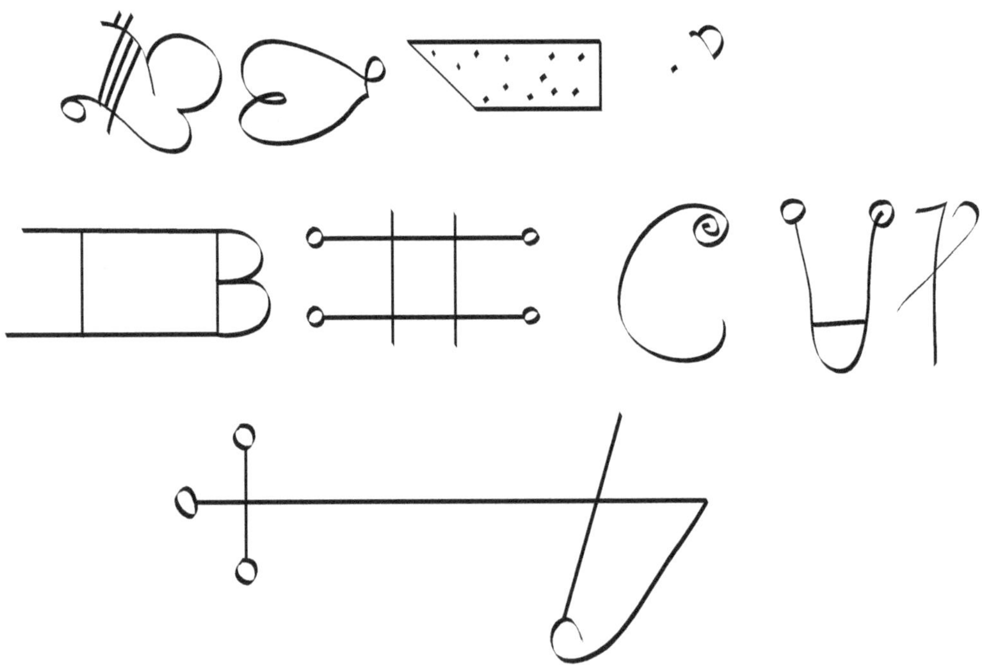

[238]

For the Falling Sickness[1269]

Take the blood of her little finger, and write this, and hang it about her neck: "+ Jasper brought myrrh; Melchior, frankincense; Balthatus, gold + whosoever carries with him the three names of the kings, save from the falling illness through the compassion of the Lord."

"+ Jasper fert myrrham, thus Melchior, Ballthatus aurum, hec quicunque secum portant tria nomina + a *regina* [regum] salve tua a morto domini pietate caduco."[1270]

Then drink the root of peony for a month's space.

Experiment upon Several Accounts

"Jesus Christ was bound, St. Peter was bound, St. Andrew was bound, per the hands of men and counsel of devils, and like as I beseech the bond of Jesus Christ, of St. Peter, and St. Andrew, so verily and truly, O Lord God, I most humbly beseech thee, that thou, per thy almighty power, holy word, and virtue, will bind, force, and constrain, and compel Sathan and all manner of devils, witches, evil spirits, whether they more or less, and also evil winds[1271] and evil humours, which doth either possess or obsess this man N., molesting his mind, wits, senses, and reason, or any part of his body and limbs, most glorious, holy, and most merciful Father, suffer them not to have any more abiding in him. Let them nevermore hereafter to torment, grieve, or annoy

[239]

"him, but command them to avoid and be gone far from him, and that they may never trouble him anymore. Also, moreover, that it may please thee, to command and suffer, that per the virtue, power, and strength of all angels, archangels, the holy thrones, dominations, principates, potestates, virtutes, cherubim, and seraphim, and of all things celestial, and superior powers, Sathan and all other devils, witches, evil spirits, evil minds, and all manner of evil humours may be forced and constrained, compelled and bound to avoid, and depart, and be gone from this, thy poor creature and distressed servant

1269. The Three Kings charm; see manuscript page 61.

1270. + *Jasper...caduco*: For the translation, see manuscript page 61.

1271. *Evil winds*: Winds were believed to bring pestilence. Dobson, *Contours of Death and Disease in Early Modern England*, 20.

N., from us and from this place forevermore, and that they be clean cast out of him, may never return to him or any one of us here present, in this place, or any other place, or any other creature, in any other place whatsoever, that they every one of them, both more or less, may peaceably and quietly go out of thy poor servant. N., from him, and us, and this place, to the place where thou, Lord God, shall appoint per them, without hurt or harm or of any danger to him or us in body or soul, goods or cattle, or of any other creature of thine in this world or in the world to come, and also that thou wouldst

[240]

"vouchsafe to give leave and licence, virtue and power in thy name to bind and constrain them so that they may obey me, and the words of my mouth, and the charge and command which I shall give them. Most holy gracious and merciful Father, grant this per Jesus Christ's sake, thy most dear Son our Lord and only saviour, and like as our Lord Jesus Christ did cast out devils per the powers of his godhead, and did bind Sathan, the infernal devil, with his holy word, and gave power to St. Bartholomew to bind the devil with a hair of his beard, so per the same power, most gracious and loving God, I most humbly pray and beseech thee that, per thy leave and licence, virtue, power, and assistance, and also per the most merciful sufferance, Sathan and all his ministers, both witches, devils, evil spirits, evil minds, and evil humours may be bound, enforced, constrained, and compelled to avoid and depart, and be gone from this thy poor creature and oppressed servant N., suddenly, presently, quickly, without any further stay or delay, without or [sic] any manner of harm in body or soul to him or us or any other creature of thine whatsoever, and like as our Lord Jesus Christ the Father, the Son, and the Holy Ghost, or lord and king of heaven and earth,

[241]

"and like of this is most true that I speak; even so, good Lord, I most humbly beseech thee, let Satan or whatsoever it is, be it devils or devils, witch or witches, evil spirit or spirits, evil humour or humours, and evil, harmful, and hurtful winds which doth either possess or obsess, and doth either vex, torment, annoy, grieve, molest, trouble, or oppress this man N. in his wits, senses or reason, or in any part of his body or limbs, per any kind or manner of means whatsoever, be in force and constrained, and also compelled and bound to come out of him, and to avoid from him, and be gone with all speed and haste as may be possible from our presence, without hurt or harm or any manner of danger to him or us, or any other creature whatsoever, and like as our Lord Jesus Christ was bound, St. Peter was bound, and St. Andrew was bound, so I pray to our Lord Jesus Christ, that, through his grace, mercy, and merits, Satan and everyone, both devil or devils, witch or witches, evil spirit or spirits, evil, harmful, or hurtful humour or humours, and all harmful wind may be cast out of this poor creature N. utterly, per doth now either possess or obsess him, and doth vex, torment, and grieve him, and molest, trouble, and oppress him, in his wits, senses, and reason, and also in his body and limbs may be surely bound or enforced, constrained, and compelled to obey me and the words of my mouth which I say, and to avoid and depart[1272]

[242]

"from him and us, and from this place, per virtue, power, and might, and great mercy of God the Father, the Son, and the Holy Ghost, the nativity of our Lord Jesus Christ, per his circumcision, per his baptism, per his transfiguration, per his fasting and temptation, per his victories and overcoming, per his power, per his virtue, per his merits, per his pretitious[1273] death and bitter passion, per his resurrection, per his glorious ascension, and per the sending of the Holy Ghost, and per the seven gifts of the Holy Ghost, per his casting out of devils, per the collusion and choirs of angels, per the four crowned persons, per the three children viz. Sidrach, Misac, and Abednago, per the twenty-four elders, per the seats of the twelve apostles, per the victory of martyrs, per the faith of patriarchs, per the merits of the prophets, per the suffrages of the apostles, per the chastity and purity of the virgins, per the continuance[1274] of widows, per the preaching of God's word, and per the holiness of all saints, that Sathan with all his ministers and servants, both devils, witches, and wicked spirits may be confounded and put to rebuke, which doth either possess or obsess thy servant N., and all wicked winds and all evil humours may be cast out of him, and chiefly this devil and evil wicked spirit which doth so vex, torment, annoy, and grieve him, and doth molest, trouble, and oppress him, both in body and limbs, wits, senses, mind, and reason, and that he or they may

1272. *Depart*: Catchword not included in main text.

1273. *Pretitious*: Precious?

1274. *Continuance*: Retention in a position.

[243]

"come out of him, as I have said, to avoid, depart, and be gone from him and us, and from this house and place, presently, quickly, and suddenly, without staying or delays, or any manner of crafts or deceits, frauds, or guiles, wiles, or lets[1275] whatsoever, without either hurt or harm, or any manner of danger, to him or us or any other creature of God whatsoever, in body, soul, or mind, wits, senses, reason, or of houses, goods, or cattle, or of any other things else that is ours or yours, whatsoever in the world or in the world to come. Grant this, O most merciful Father, per Jesus Christus's sake, thy most dearly beloved Son, our lord and saviour, and for his merits, death, and passion, and per his holy namesake, for all that ever may move thee to pity and compassion. Amen.

"And I most humbly beseech thee, most meek and merciful Lord Jesus Christ, that the blessed and glorious Virgin Mary thy mother, with all the holy orders of angels and blessed saints, both in heaven and earth, may assist us and pray for us, that we may prosper in all our proceedings, and have thy grace, favour, and mercy in all our petitions, desires, and requests, to the great honour and glory of thy most holy name, and to the everlasting health, comfort, and salvation of our body and souls, both in this world and in the world to come. Amen."

[244]

"From all our enemies and persecutors, defend us this day and ever hereafter. O Lord, I most humbly beseech thee, for in thee have we trusted; therefore let us never be confounded. Deliver us, save us, justify and help us, O most holy and blessed Trinity. Sit nomen Domini benedictum ex hoc nunc et usque in se[culum].[1276]

"And now I most humbly desire and beseech thee, the most blessed and glorious virgin St. Mary, the mother of God, the blessed St. Michael the archangel, St. Gabriel the archangel, St. Raphiel the archangel, with all the rest of the nine orders of angels, that they, per your nine most glorious interceptions and help, may bind, force, constrain, and compel Sathan, or any other devil or wicked spirit, which doth now possess or obsess this creature of God

1275. *Lets*: Obstructions.

1276. *Sit…se[culum]*: Translation: "May the name of the Lord be blessed, both now and forever." An episcopal blessing for the end of the Mass.

N., and also any malignant humour or witch that hath or shall do him hurt or harm to him or us, in body or soul, or any other creature or creatures of God whatsoever.

"And likewise I desire and beseech thee, holy Father, Abraham, chief patriarch, and St. John Baptist, chief prophet, and per all the rest of the holy patriarchs and prophets, and per your most holy intercession and help, may bind, force, and constrain Satan, or this devil or wicked spirit or evil humour which doth not possess and obsess this poor creature of God, N.,

[245]

"to go forth of him without hurt or harm of any manner of danger to him or us, and never to vex or trouble him or us anymore, and avoid and depart from hence and begone hastily and quickly, and never to return to him or any of us again.

"And also I desire and beseech St. Peter the Apostle, St. Paul the Apostle, and St. John the Evangelist, with all the rest of the apostles and evangelists they be; their most holy intercessions and prayers may help and cause Satan, or the wicked spirit or spirits, witch or witches, or any kind of devil or naughty malignant humour or hurtful wind, which doth possess or obsess this man or woman N., and doth now vex and grieve him, and both molest and trouble him in his wits, senses, and reason to come out of him, and to avoid, and depart, and be gone from him and us, and from this house or place, presently, quickly, and suddenly, with all haste as may be possible, and without either hurt or harm to him or us or any other creature or creatures whatsoever.

"And likewise, I desire and beseech St. Steven the martyr, St. Augustine confessor, with all the rest of the holy blessed martyrs and confessors, that they, per the most holy intercessions and prayers may procure Sathan or the devil, or devils, or evil spirit or spirits, and both evil mind and malignant humours, which doth now possess and obsess this poor distressed creature. N.,

[246]

"to come out of him, and likewise both witch and witches to depart and avoid, and be clean gone away far from him and us, and from this house and place, without either hurt or harm to him or us, or this house and place, of any creature of God whatsoever, and that very quickly and both hastily and suddenly, without any manner of fraud, guile, or deceit. And also I beseech St. Anne, mother of our blessed lady St. Mary, St. Mary Magdalene, St. Catherine, and St. Winifred,[1277] virgins, with St. Monaczie widow,[1278] and all the rest of the holy virgins, innocents, martyrs, widows, and saints of God, that they, per your most holy prayers and intercessions, may procure and cause Sathan, and all manner and kind of devils, witches, evil spirits, naughty and evil humours, and wicked and harmful winds, may both hastily, speedily, and quickly, avoid, depart, and be gone away from this poor and distressed man or woman, N., and chiefly this wicked and evil spirit and humour which doth now possess and obsess him, to come out of N. presently, without stay or delay, and to vanish and be gone from him and us, and this house or place, without the doing of any hurt or harm to him, or any of us, or of any creature of God whatsoever in body, soul, house, goods, or cattle, in this

[247]

"world or in the world to come. O most merciful Lord Jesus Christ, grant this for thy most glorious namesake, which liveth and reigneth with the Father, the Holy Ghost, one God, world without end. Amen."

Phil[ippians 2] verse 10

"In nomine Jesu omne genu flectatur caelestium, terrestrium, et infernorum, et omnes lingua confiteatur quia Dominus Jesus Christus, in gloria est dei Patris. Per signum Crucis, + de inimicis nostris libera nos deus noster."

> "That at the name of Jesus every knee should bow, of heavenly, earthly, and infernal beings; and that every tongue should confess that Jesus Christ is Lord, to the glory of God the Father.[1279] Free us, O our Lord, from our enemies by the sign of the cross, +."

"In nomine Patris, et Filii, et Spiritus Sancti, Amen.

"O thou envious traitor ♄[1280] with all thy crafty wile and sleights, I command and charge thee, in the name of Jesus Christ, the son of the true living God, that thou depart out of this man N., a creature of God, and never hereafter to vex or trouble him anymore. O thou most filthy and horrible spirit, avoid from

1277. *St. Winifred*: Famous Welsh saint who died in the seventh century.

1278. *St. Monaczie*: Most likely St. Monica, mother of St. Augustine. Another possibility is the Welsh Saint Monacella, but she was never a widow.

1279. *That at the name…Father*: Philippians 2:10–11 (translation from KJV).

1280. ♄: An abbreviation for Satan here.

him. I compel thee per all that may constrain and bind thee. Ye I do conjure, bind, and adjure thee, per almighty and everlasting God, and per his virtue and power, and per all his marvellous and wonderful works, and per heaven and earth, per the celestial and terrestrial powers, per the sky, per all the stars, planets, signs, all that in them is, and per the infernal party, that thou depart, avoid, ♄, and

[248]

"be gone without stay or let from this man N., without the hurt of him or us, in body, soul, goods, house, or cattle, or the hurt or harm of any other creature of God whatsoever, in this world or in the world to come. Also I bind and adjure thee, Sathan, thou servant of Lucifer, and all other devil, wicked spirits, witches, wicked winds, and evil humours whatsoever which doth vex, annoy, trouble, and torment this man N. I command, charge, and compel thee, and them generally, and every one severally, to avoid and depart from him suddenly, per the virtues and powers of all the celestial and heavenly powers of God, the holy thrones, dominations, principates, potestates, virtutes, cherubim, and seraphin, the holy angels, archangels, patriarchs, prophets, apostles, martyrs, confessors, virgins, matrons, innocents, and widows of God, and per all saints of God whatsoever, that thou, Sathan, and all other devils, both witch and witches, evil humour or humours, and all wicked winds, depart without delay or stay, and that presently, quickly, and suddenly out of this man N., per grace the servant of Jesus Christ the son of almighty God, in whose name, per his virtue, power, and strength, I adjure thee, Sathan and all other spirits, both witch or witches, devil

[248bis]

"or devils, evil humour or evil humours, and every evil and wicked wind, from this man N., and from every and member of him, from the top of his head to the soles of his feet, and from the ends of his toes and soles of his feet, to the crown and top of his head, in nomine Patris et Filii et Spiritus Sancti. Amen.

"Adjuro te, Sathan in nomine Jesus + et per potentissimum et corroboratum nomen dei + El + forte et admirabile[1281] from his fingers and toes, and from

1281. *Adiuro...admirable*: Translation: "I adjure thee, Sathan, in the name of Jesus, + and by the most powerful and strengthened name of God + El + strong and wonderful." Compare this and the passages following in this ritual to de Abano, "Heptameron."

the nails and joints of them, and from all that is in them or belonging to them, et per Agros [Agios][1282] et sedem Adonay + per Othos,[1283] + Iskyros, + Athanatos, + Paracletus, + O Sathan, from his fingers and toes, from the nails and joints of them or belonging to them, et per eum qui venturus est iudicare vivos et mortuos, et mundum per ignem,[1284] from his fingers and toes, and from the nails and joints of them, and from all that is in them or belonging to them, Sathan.

"Adjuro te, Sathan in no[m]i[n]e Jesu + et per nomen + Yot i + quod Adam audivit, et locutus est,[1285] from his hands and feet, which the wristles,[1286] heels, and insteps and joints of them, and from all that is in them or belongeth to them, et per tria secreta nomina[1287] + Agla, + On, + Tetragramaton, + O Sathan,

[249]

"from his hands and feet with the wristles, heels, insteps and joints of them, or belonging to them, et per + Adonay + et Saday, + omnia nomina dei,[1288] from his hands and feet, with the wrists, heels, and insteps and joints of them, and from all that is in them or belonging to them, Sathan.

"Adjuro te, Sathan, in nomine Jesu + et per nomen dei + Agla, + quod Loth audjuvit et factus salvus cum sua familia,[1289] from his arms, elbows, legs, and knees, and from the joints of them, and from all that is in them or belonging to them, et per nomen eterni vivi et veri dei[1290] + Helioren, + O Sathan, from his arm, elbows, legs, knees, and from the joints of them, and from all that is in them or belonging to them, et per sanctam Mariam, matrem domini

1282. *Agros [Agios]*: This error appears in many of the printed and manuscript versions of the *Heptameron*. See de Abano, "Heptameron."

1283. *Et per…Othos*: Translation: "And by *Agros* [Agios] and the seat of Adonay, + by Othos."

1284. *Et per…ignem*: Translation: "And by him who will come to judge the living and the dead, and the world by fire."

1285. *Adiuro te…est*: Translation: "I adjure thee, Sathan, in the name of Jesus + and by the name + Yot I + that Adam heard and spoke."

1286. *Wristle*: Probably wrist, as appears below.

1287. *Et per…nomina*: Translation: "And by the three secret names."

1288. *Et per…dei*: Translation: "And by + Adonay + and Saday + all the names of God."

1289. *Adjuro…familia*: Translation: "I adjure thee, Sathan, in the name of Jesus + and by the name of God + Agla, + that Lot heard and was saved with his family."

1290. *Et per…dei*: Translation: "And by the name of the eternal, living, and true God."

vestri Jesu Christi, mater divina gratia,[1291] from his arms, elbows, legs, and knees, and from the joints of them, and from all that is in them or belonging to them, Sathan.

"Adjuro te Sathan in nomine Jesu, + et per nomen + Ioth, + quod Jacob audivit ab angelo secum luctante et liberatus est de manu fratris sui Esau,[1292] from his arms' holes,[1293] shoulders, thighs, lips, and buttocks, and from the joints of them, and all is in them or belonging to them, et per nomen dei + Sabaoth et in virtutem istius

[250]

"nominis Sabaoth,[1294] + O Sathan from his armholes, shoulders, thighs, lips, and buttocks, and from the joints of them, and all that is in them, or belonging to them or any way towards them, Sathan.

"Et per sanctum Michaelem, archangelorum dei, et omnes angelos et archangelos ejus,[1295] from his arms' holes, shoulders, thighs, lips, and buttocks, and from the joints of them, and also that is in them or belonging to them, Sathan.

"Adjuro te, Sathan in nomine Jesu + et per nomen + Zebaoth + quod Moyses nominavit, et omnia flumina et paludes de terra Aegypti versa fuerunt in sanguinem,[1296] from his kidneys, reins, bladder, guts, and belly, and from the spondyls[1297] of his back and joints of them, and all that is in them or belonging to them, et per nomen + Eloim, + et Saday,[1298] + Saraye, + O Sathan from his kidneys, reins, bleather,[1299] guts, and belly, and from the spondyls of his

1291. *Et per...gratia*: Translation: "And by holy Mary, mother of your lord Jesus Christ, mother of divine grace."

1292. *Adiuro...Esau*: Translation: "I adjure thee, Sathan, in the name of Jesus, + and by the name + Ioth + that Jacob heard from the angel wrestling with him, he was freed from the hand of his brother Esau."

1293. *Arm's holes*: Armholes or armpits.

1294. *Et per...Sabaoth*: Translation: "And by the name of God + Sabaoth and in the power of that [250] name Sabaoth."

1295. *Et per...ejus*: Translation: "And by the holy Michael of the archangels of God, and all his angels and archangels."

1296. *Adiuro...blood*: Translation: "I adjure thee, Sathan, in the name of Jesus, + and by the name + Zebaoth + that Moyses named, and all streams and bogs of the land of Egypt were turned into blood."

1297. *Spondyls*: Vertebrae.

1298. *Et per...Saday*: Translation: "And by the name + Eloim + and Saday."

1299. *Bleather*: Bladder, as above.

back, and joints of them, and all that is in them or belonging to them, et per eum qui habet clavis inferni et mortis,[1300] from his kidneys, reins, bleather, guts, and belly, and from all the spondyls of his back, and joints of them, and all that is in them, or belonging to them, Sathan.

"Adjuro te, Sathan in no[m]i[n]e Jesu + et per nomen Anephexeton, + quod Aron audivit et loquens et

[251]

sapiens *sanctus* [factus] est,[1301] from his cods,[1302] stones, yard,[1303] fundament, secret parts, and share bone,[1304] and from the joints thereof, and all that is in them or belonging to them, et per nomen+ Messias, + Sother + et Emanuel,[1305] + O Sathan, from his cods, stones, yard, fundament, and secret parts, and share bone, and from the joints thereof, and all that is in them or belonging to them, et per thronum, dominationum, principatum, et potestatem, cherubim et seraphim, et omnes virtutes caelorum, et per thronum, dominationum, principatum, et potestatem, cherubim et seraphim, et omnes virtutes caelorum,[1306] from his cods, stones, yard, fundament, secret parts, and share bone, from the joints thereof, and all that is in them or belonging to them, Sathan.

"Adjuro te, Sathan, in nomine Jesu, + et per nomen + Escerehie Oristion, + quod Moses nominavit, et omnes fluvii ebullierunt ranas, et ascenderunt in domos Egyptiorum omnia destruentes,[1307] from his midriff, liver, gale, spleen, heart, sides, and back, and from the joints thereof, and all that is in them or belonging to them, et in virtutem nominum istorum[1308] + Aye + Saraye + Eloy + Archima, + Rabur, + O Sathan from his midriff, liver, gale, spleen, heart, sides, and back, and from the joints of it, and all that is in them or belonging

1300. *Et per…mortis*: Translation: "And by him who holds the keys of Hell and death."

1301. *Adiuro…est*: Translation: "I adjure thee, Sathan, in the name of Jesus + and by the name Anephexeton, + that Aaron heard, and spoke, and [251] was made wise."

1302. *Cods*: Scrotum.

1303. *Yard*: Penis.

1304. *Share bone*: Pubis.

1305. *Et per…Emanuel*: Translation: "and by the name[s] + Messias, + Sother + and Emanuel."

1306. *Et per…caelorum*: Translation: "and by the thrones, dominions, principalities, and powers, cherubim and seraphim, and all the powers of the heavens."

1307. *Adiuro…destruentes*: Translation: "I adjure thee, Sathan, in the name Jesus, + and by the name + Escerehie Oristion, + that Moses named, and all rivers produced frogs, and they climbed into the houses of the Egyptians, destroying all things."

1308. *Et…istorum*: Translation: "And in the power of those names."

to them, et per caelum et terram et omnia quae in eis sunt,[1309] from his midriff, liver, gall, spleen, heart, sides, and back, and from all the joints of it, and all that is in them or belonging to them, Sathan.

[252]

"Adjuro te, Sathan, in nomine Jesu, + et per nomen + Elion, + quod Moses nominavit et fuit grando tales qualis non fuit ab initio mundi,[1310] from his stomach, lights,[1311] breast, and ribs, and from the joints of them, and all that is in them or belonging to them, et per nomen dei, + Shemhamephares, + et in virtute istius nominis[1312] + Shemhamephares + O Sathan from his stomach, light, breast, and ribs, and from the joints of them, and all that is in them or belonging to them, et per [virtutem] omnium patriarcharum, prophetarum, apostolorum, martirum, confessorum, et virginum, et omnes sanctos[1313] from his stomach, lights, breast, and ribs, and from all the joints of them, and all that is in them or belonging to them, Sathan.

"Adjuro te Sathan in nomine Jesu, + et per nomen Adonay + quod Moses nominavit et fuerunt locustae, et apparuerunt super terram Egyptiarum et comederunt qua residua erant grandini,[1314] from his windpipe, wasond,[1315] neck, and throat, tongue, cheeks, and teeth, and from the joints of them, and all that is in them or belonging to them, et per + nomen Elohim, + et Elohe, + Escerehie + Saday, + Dominus + Deus, + Elcellsus[1316] + O Sathan, from his windpipes, wasond, neck, and throat, tongue, and cheeks, and teeth, and from the joints of them, and all that is in them or belonging to them, et per virtutem et potestatem Domini vestri Jesu Christi[1317] from his windpipe,

1309. *Et per...sunt*: Translation: "And by heaven and earth, and all things that are in them."

1310. *Adiuro...mundi*: Translation: "I adjure thee, Sathan, in the name of Jesus, + and by the name + Elion, + that Moses named and there was such hail as there was not from the beginning of the world."

1311. *Lights*: Eyes?

1312. *Et per...nominis*: Translation: "And by the name of God + Shemhamephares, + and in the power of that name."

1313. *Et per...sanctos*: Translation: "and by [the power?] of all patriarchs, prophets, apostles, martyrs, confessors, and virgins, and all saints."

1314. *Adjuro...grandini*: Translation: "I adjure thee, Sathan, in the name of Jesus, + and by the name of Adonay + that Moses named and there were locusts, and they appeared over the land of the Egyptians, and they ate what was left from the hail."

1315. *Wasond*: Gullet.

1316. *Et per...Elcellsus*: Translation: "And by + the name Elohim, + and Elohe, + Escerehie + Saday, + Lord + God, + Elcellsus."

1317. *Et per...Christi*: Translation: "And by the virtue and power of your Lord Jesus Christ."

wasond, neck and throat, tongue, cheeks, teeth, and from the joints of them, and all that is in them or belonging to them, Sathan.

[253]

"I adjure thee, Sathan, in the name of Jesus, + and by this name Primeumaton + that Moses named, and Corah and Abiron were sunk and swallowed in the depths of hell, and by the power of this name Primaumaton, + I adjure thee, Sathan, Adjuro te, Sathan, in nomine Jesu, + et per hoc nomen Primeumaton + quod Moses nominavit in cavernis abisii fuerunt profundati vel absorpti Corali et Abiron et in virtute istius *nomine* [nominis] Primaumaton, + adjuro te, Sathan[1318] from his brains and marrow, flesh, blood, sinews, gristles, bones, and flesh, and from the joints of them, and all that is in them or belonging to them, et per deum vivum, per deum verum, et per deum sanctum qui te creavit,[1319] O Sathan, from his brains, marrow, flesh, blood, fat and lean, sinews, gristles, and bones, and from the joints of all, and all that is in them or belonging to them, et per nomen magnum ipsius dei,[1320] + Jehova, and from his brains and marrow, flesh, blood, fat and lean, sinews, gristles and bones, and from all the joints of them, and all that is in them or belonging to them, Sathan.

"Adjuro te, Sathan, in nomine Jesu, + et per nomen A et Ω quod Daniel nominavit et destruxit Beel et draconem interfecit,[1321] from his head and face, ears, eyes, nose and mouth, cheeks and chin, and from the joints of his head, and all that is therein or belonging to it, et per nomen sanctum quod scriptum in fronte Aron sacerdotis, et per hac nomina sancta,[1322] Eli, Eli + Lama Zabathani + O Sathan, from his head and face, ears, eyes, nose, mouth, cheeks and chin, and from the joints of his head, and all that is therein or belonging to it, et per virtutem saevissimam mortem crucis Domini nostri Jesu Christi et per descentionem ejus ad inferos

1318. *Adiuro te, Sathan...te, Sathan*: Translation: "I adjure thee, Sathan, in the name of Jesus, + and by this name Primeumaton + that Moses named, and Corah and Abiron were sunk and swallowed in the depths of hell, and by the power of this name Primaumaton, + I adjure thee, Sathan."

1319. *Et per deum vivum...creavit*: Translation: "And by the living God, by the true God, and by the holy God who created thee."

1320. *Et...Dei*: Translation: "And by the great name of God."

1321. *Adiuro...interfecit*: Translation: "I adjure thee, Sathan, in the name of Jesus, + and by the name A and Ω, that Daniel named, and he destroyed Beel and killed the dragon."

1322. *Et per nomen...nomina sancta*: Translation: "And by the holy name written on the chest of Aaron the priest and by these holy names."

[254]

"per resurrectionem, ascentionem ejus ad caelum, et per diem tremendi iudicii,[1323] from his head, and face, ears, eyes, nose, mouth, cheeks and chin, and from the joints of his head, and all that is therein or belonging to it, Sathan.

"Adjuro te, Sathan, in nomine Jesu + et per nomen Emanuell, + quod tres pueri, Sidrach, Misacke, et Abdenago, in camino ignis ardentis cantaverunt et liberati fuerunt,[1324] from his hairs and skin of his head and body, both inward and outward parts, and from his apparel and wearing clothes,[1325] and all that is in them or belonging to them, from the top of his head to the sole of his feet, et per eum qui dixit et factum est, qui dixit, "Consumatum est," qui est A et Ω, principium, et *finetid* [finis],[1326] from his hairs and skin of his head and body, both inward and outward parts, and from his apparel and wearing clothes, and all that is in them or belonging to them, et per Dominem Deum omnipotentem, qui es trinitas in filioque, et filius in patrem, una cum spiritus sancto, qui es semper et eras, ante omnia, et eris per omnia, Benedictus Deus, in secula seculorum,[1327] from the hairs and skin of his head and body, both inward and outward parts, and from his apparel and wearing clothes, and all that is in them, or belonging to them, Sathan.

[255]

"Adjuro te, Sathan, in nomine Jesu + qui veniet in die tremendi judicii adjudicare vivos et mortuos, et per illum tremendum diem juidicium, et per mare omnibus incertum vitreum, quod est ante conspectum divina majestatis gradiens, et potentiale, et [per] quatuor divina animalia T. ante sedem divinae majestatis gradientia, et oculos ante et retro habentia, per ignem ante ejus thronum circumstantem, et per sanctos angelos caelorum T., et per eam

1323. *Et per virtutem…iudicii*: Translation: "And by the power of the most cruel death of our Lord Jesus Christ on the cross, and by his descending into Hell [254] by his resurrection and ascension to heaven, and by the great day of judgment."

1324. *Adjuro…fuerunt*: Translation: "I adjure thee, Sathan, in the name of Jesus + and by the name Emanuell, + that the three youths, Sidrach, Misacke, and Abdenago, chanted in the furnace of burning fire, and they were saved."

1325. *Wearing clothes*: Clothes intended for wearing.

1326. *Et per…[finis]*: Translation: "And by he who spoke and it was done, who said, "It is finished," who is A and Ω, the beginning and the end." See Revelation 1:8.

1327. *Et per…seculorum*: Translation: "And by the omnipotent Lord God, who is trinity in the Son and the Son to the Father, one with the Holy Ghost, thou who always art and wert before all things, and will be through all, blessed God, world without end."

quae ecclesia dei in [sic] nominatur, et summam sapientiam omnipotentis dei. Veriliter exorcizamus et adjuro vos, Sathan, et omnes demones infernales, et omnes infestinationes, et [sic] omnium malorum spiritorum, et omnes malignos humores, et omnes inimicos nostros, ab isto homine N. et nos, et ab hoc loco, conjuro et adjuro vos, in nomine Jesu Christi filii Dei veri, qui est rex regum potentissimus et tremendissimus, cujus vires nulla subter fugere potest creatura, et cui omne genuflectitur calestium, terrestium, et infernorum, cujus in manu omnia regna regum sunt, nec est qui suae contrarius esse possit majestati. Quatenus constringo vos, Sathan, et omnes damones infernales, et omnies infestationes et [sic] omnium malorum spiritorum, et omnes inimicos nostros, ab isto homino N., per eum qui creavit mundum, caelum, et terram, et omnia qua

[256]

"in eis sunt, qui dixit et facta sunt, cui omnia obediunt creatura, et per hac sanctissima nomina dei vivi et veri, + Jehova, + Jesus, + Tetragramaton, + et Ω + Agla, + On, +."

> "I adjure thee, Sathan, in the name of Jesus + who will come to judge the living and the dead on the great day of judgment, and by that great day of judgment, and by the unsettled sea of glass proceeding before the sight of the divine majesty and the power, and by the four holy animals T. proceeding before the seat of the divine majesty and having eyes before and behind, by the fire encircling his throne, and by the holy angels of heaven T., and by that one of whom the church of God is named, and the highest wisdom of the all-powerful God. We strongly exorcise, and I adjure, you all, Sathan, and all the demons of hell, and all attacks of all evil spirits, and all evil humours, and all our enemies, from this man N. and us, and from this place. I conjure and exorcise you all, in the name of Jesus Christ, son of the true God, who is the most powerful and greatest king of kings, whose powers no living creature below is able to flee, and to whom every heavenly, earthly, and hellish knee is bowed, in the hand of whom are all kingdoms of kings, and that none of these is able to be hostile to the divine majesty. So I constrain you all, Sathan, and all thy hellish demons, and all attacks of all evil spirits, and all our enemies, from this man N. by him who created the world, heaven and earth, and all things that [256] are in them, who spoke and it was done, whom all creatures obey, and by

> these holiest names of the living and true God, + Jehova, + Jesus, + Tetragramaton, + A and Ω + Agla, + On. +"[1328]

Confessio[1329]

"Confiteor tibi, domine, pater coeli et terra, tibique, Domine Jesu Christi et benignissime salvator vestrae, cum sancto spiritu coram pia matre tua, et coram sanctis angelis tuis, et coram *presentia* [praesenti] *altero* [altario] tuo, quia in peccatis conceptus fui, in peccatis natus, in peccatis nutritus, in peccatis post baptismum, usque ad hanc horam sum conversatus.

> "I confess to thee, O Lord, Father of heaven and earth, and to thee, Lord Jesus Christ and most favourable saviour of you all, with the Holy God, face to face with your holy mother, and face to face with your holy angels, and face to face with your altar at hand, because I was conceived in sin, born in sin, raised in sin, in sin after baptism, up until this hour I abide.

"Confiteor *et Cain* [etiam] tibi quia peccavi nimis in superbia, tam visibili quam invisibili, in *vana* [inani] gloria, in extolentia tam oculorum quam vestium, et omnium actuum meorum, in invidia, in odio, in avaritia, in ventris *inglume* [ingluvie], in commestationibus et *obrietatibus* [ebrietate], in fabulis octiosis, in osculis et amplexibus jucundis, in luxuriis, in femoribus, in genitalibus membris meis, et omni genere fornicacionis, in adulteriis, qui *ego* [feci?] mea culpa, et facientibus concensi in sacralegiis, in perjuriis, in furtis, in rapinis, in homicidiis, charitatem, fidem, et spem non habendo; in accipiendo corpus et sanguinem Domini semper indigne, in *exartacionibas* [exhortacionibus], et adulacionibus malignis,

[257]

"in ignorantia, nec [sic] in negligentia, in subreptionibus, in subtrahendis, eleemosinis, in pauperibus exasperandis, in hospitalibus et in receptionibus pauperum, in affectionibus propinquorum, non visitando infirmos juxta praeseptum tuum evangelicum, et in carcere positos non *vestiendo* [visitando] *undus*, non *recreader* [recreando] esurientes, nec *potandum* [potando]

1328. *I adjure...On,* +: Much of this parallels passages from the *Heptameron*. See de Abano, "Heptameron."

1329. Translation: "Confession." Garofali, *Ordo ad Dandam Poenitentiam*, 35–38. For the usage of similar confessions in magical contexts, see Bibliothèque Nationale de France Arsenal 2350, 39–45; Peterson, "Sloane 3847: The Clavicle of Solomon, Revealed by Ptolomy the Grecian."

sitientes, solemnitatibus sanctorum, et diebus *ebus duicis* [celebrationem] *debetum* [debitam], honorem non impendendo, [nec] sobrie nec caste in eis vivendo, consentientibus suadentibus mihi, in malo nocendo potius quam adiuvando peticiones et clamores pauperum, misericorditer non audiendo propinquis, nec non subditis principibus atque ecclesiasti[ci]s viris detrahendo, et blasphemando amicis et benefactioribus meis fidem non servando, debita obsequia non *perpendendo* [rependendo], animalium et *peccudiam* [pecudum] concubitam conscientia immunda intuendo, in eclesia dei superbe intrando, stando, sedendo, et egrediendo atque ociosis fabulis, et turpibus *eloquiis* [colloquiis] both in ea cum aliis insistendo, oraciones in ecclesia negligenter faciendo et audiendo in cogitationibus etiam pessimus peccavi, in *immeditationibus* [meditationibus] perversis in suspicionibus falcis, in juditiis temerariis,

[258]

"in consensu malo, in concupiscentia carnali et delectationem, ac polutione *purricunda* [immunda], in verbis otiosis, superfluis, luxuriosis at *contemneliosis* [contumneliosis] in mendatiis, in falsitatibus, in juramentis *multimo dis* [multis modis] et diversis, et in detractionibus assiduis, in rixis, ac discordiis seminandis, in [ir]risionibus et *otietate* [otiositate], *insurrectione* [in susurratione], in *manu* [inani] laetitia, in omne malo linguae, in murmuracionibus, in blasphemiis, in *scurrilitabus* [scurrilitatibus], in *chactimis* [cachinnis] communibus, in dissimulatione, in vigiliis deo contrariis, in dliectione dei et proximi, in visu, auditu, gustu, odoratu, et tactu superfluo, et immundo, in *omnibus modis* [omnimoda] cogitatione, *locutione*, voluptate, accione peccavi, in his et aliis vitiis, *quibascanque* [quibuscunque] humana fragilitas contra Deum et creatorem suum, aut cogitando, aut operando, aut delectado, aut concupiscendo peccare potest, in omnibus me peccasse, et reum in conspectu dei, super omnes homines esse cognosco et confiteor. Propterea tibi pie virgo supplico, et vobis sancti angeli, et omnes sancti dei in quorum conspectu hec omnia confessus sum, ut testes mihi sitis in die judicii, contra diabolum, et hostem humani generis, hec omnia me confessum fuisse, quatenus non gaudeat de me inimicus meus, ut non glorietur adversus me in die judicii, dicens

[259]

"me *peccasse* [peccata] et scelera mea tacuisse et confessum non fuisse, sed sit gaudeum in celo de me qui omnia peccata confessus fui et *peni tui* [penitus?] me de illis, sanctum verbum per Dominum Jesum Christum filium dei vivi qui regnat per omnia secula seculorum. Amen, Amen. Amen."

"I confess to thee also, because I have sinned excessively in pride, as visible as invisible, in empty praise, in pride, as much of the eyes as of clothing, and of all my impulses, in jealousy, in hatred, in covetousness, in gluttony of the bowels, in revels and drunkenness, in idle conversations, in kisses and delightful caresses, in excesses, in loins, in my generative members and in every type of fornication, in adulteries, that I did in my fault, and in the making of complicity, in sacrileges, in perjuries, in thefts, in plunderings, in killings, not having charity, faith, and hope, in always receiving the body and blood of the Lord undeservedly, in wicked exhortations and flatteries, [257] in ignorance and not in negligence, in thefts, in withdrawing alms, in provoking the poor, in the hospitality and receiving of the poor, in love of those near, in not visiting the sick according to your evangelical command, and not visiting those imprisoned,[1330] in not feeding the hungry, and in not providing drink to the thirsty, withdrawing from celebration of the festivals of the saints and the owed [feast] days, and not employing honour, living neither soberly nor chastely in them, in advocating conspiracies for myself, in injuring evilly rather than helping the requests and cries of the poor, in not listening to neighbours mercifully, and in removing overthrown sovereigns and ecclesiastical men, and in blaspheming to my friends and benefactors, in not preserving faith, in not repaying debts and allegiances, in gazing upon coupling of animals and cattle with unclean conscience, in entering, standing, sitting, and leaving the church of God arrogantly, and in idle conversations and filthy speeches, persisting in these and others, in both making and hearing prayers in church carelessly. Also, I have sinned the worst in my thoughts, in perverse contemplations, in false suspicions, in rash judgments, [258] in evil plots, in carnal longing and amusement, and unclean defilement,

1330. This seems to be confusing two lines, "in carcere positos non visitando" ("in not visiting those imprisoned," and "non pauperes vestiendo" ("in not clothing paupers"). The final word is untranslatable and has no analogy in Garofali.

in idle, superfluous, wanton, and insulting words, in lies, in falsehoods, in many and contrary oaths, and in incessant slanders, in sowing disputes and disagreements, in mockery and idleness, in whispering, in empty joy, in every evil of the tongue, in murmurings, in blasphemies, in buffooneries, in public jeering, in dissimulation, in wakefulness contrary to God, in love of God and my neighbour, in superfluous and unclean vision. I have sinned in all sorts of thought, speech, pleasure, and action, in these and other vices whatsoever human frailty is able to sin against the Lord and his creator, either in thinking or working or entertaining or coveting in all things, to have sinned for me, and I understand and confess to be a defendant in the sight of God over all humans. Therefore I pray to thee, divine virgin, and to you holy angels, and all saints of God in the sight of them. I confessed all these, so that you all may be witnesses to me on the day of judgment, against the devil and the enemy of the human race. I have confessed all of these things, so that my enemy may not rejoice over me, that he may not boast to me on the day of judgment, saying [259] to me that I have not been confessed and kept silent of my sins and crimes, but let there be joy in heaven for me, who confessed all sins and was penitent of all these, the holy word, by Lord Jesus Christ, son of the living God, who rules forever and ever. Amen. Amen. Amen."

This confession should or may be said with most prayers that are in this book.

[A Talisman for Protection and for the Circle, Part 1][1331]

This writing or tablet following hath diverse singular virtues, more than is therein expressed. It ought to be written in parchment in manner as followeth, and after per a priest consecrated, and then worn about one secretly under the right arm, and first you shall make it thus. Make a circle in parchment and write therein as followeth.

Whosoever beareth this writing upon him, he shall not be overcome of his enemies on water, nor on land, nor on the water be drowned, nor with fire be burnt, nor he shall not die no sudden death, and if he come before & c. justices, he shall have help and gain. And if he be in any irdordie[1332] on the sea, take a dishful of salt water, and bless it with this writing, and then cast out the water in four parts of the ship, and the stern shall cease. And if a woman travail with child, take water of a well

1331. This writing is apparently supposed to be placed within the circle that follows in several pages. The instructions here are for writing a version to be carried.

1332. *Irdordie*: Unknown—could be "jeopardy."

[260]

in a cup, and bless it with this writing, and give three spoonful to drink milk, warm, with a little juice of hyssop, and he shall be delivered, and the child baptised, and the mother have good purification. And if a man beareth this writing about or upon him, about his, posted [?] with his beast, about his place in town or field, and bless the ground he goeth with this writing, there shall no thief do you hurt. If a thief steal any goods, it shall not lie in his power to bear anything much or drive it away, but to stay still until you give him leave to go. This proved to be true: it will keep thee from the axes, and from the falling evil, and if a man be in prison for debt, or for any other thing, he shall be well delivered and saved. If this writing be on of him, he shall be never slain in battle, nor taken prisoner will his enemies, neither on sea nor on land. It driveth away all evil spirits. Full many virtues hath this in writing, which none knoweth but the true God only.

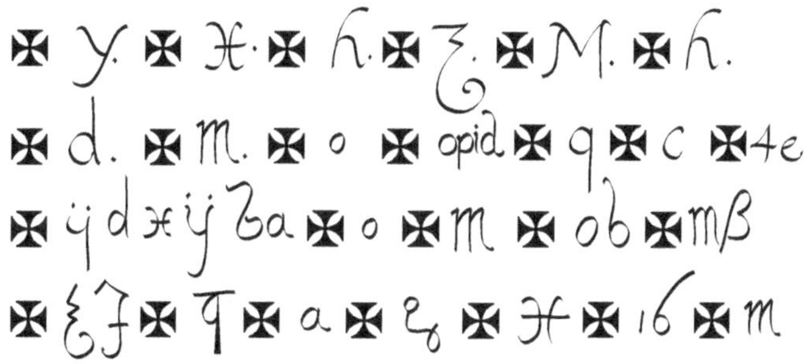

[261]

"O most merciful Lord, I beseech thee to be my help, both in the morning when I arise and at night when I shall take me bed or rest, in the name of the Father, and of the Son, and of the Holy Ghost. Amen. + Messias, + Sother, + Emanuell, + Sabaoth, + Adonay, + Homo, + Usion + Uniginutas, + Via, + Viva, + Principium, + Primeginitas + Sapientia, + ut Alph + Caput, + Finis, + Fons, + Origo, + Bonus, + Peracletus, + Mediator, + Agnis, + Ovis, + Vitulis,

+ Serpens, + Aris, + Leo, + Verbis, + Verbum, + Splendour, + Sol, + Gloria, + Lux, + Imago, + Panis, + Eles, + Vic, + Mons, + Sanna, + Petra, + Lapis, + Angelos, + qz, + Sponsus, + Pastor + Propheta, + Sacerdos, + Athanatos, + Kiros, + Theos, + Panton + Creaton, + Usus, + Tusi, + Pucer, + Orator, + Mediator, + G + et + Filius + Sanctus + Amen, + O Lord, I beseech thee, deliver me from that peril of death, this day and all times hereafter. O most holy of holiest, let thy holy Michaell, + holy Grabriell, + holy Raphiel, +

[262]

"holy Uriell, + the holy angels take charge of me, thy servant, and help me in all my necessities and dangers. O Holy Spirit, the mighty power of God help me, and behold the cross + of our saviour Jesus Christ. Fly from it, all you evil spirits, whom the line of the tribe of Judea and the stock of David wholly overcome. Praised be God, O Saviour of the world; save me through the sign of the holy T. Holy cross save me, O holy + defend me in the name of the Father, and of the Son, and of the Holy Ghost, Amen.

"Let us pray. O most merciful Father, which worketh wonderful things, suffer me not, Lord, I beseech thee, to perish in whom thy creature dost steadfastly trust in. I inwardly require of thy merciful goodness, and our mediator's sake, to give to me thy servant space[1333] true repentance, of my sins before I die, and that it would please thee, through thy most holy name, O most merciful Father, which didst defend David, a young child, and gavest him victory over great Golias, per reason of a true faith he had in thee, and also did give the Philistines unto the hands of the Israelites, that thy mighty name should be magnified. Even so, I beseech thee, O Lord, that, as the weapon of Golias did miss thy servant David, and like as the Israelites, through faith of their good captain, overcame the

[263]

"Philistines, even so I beseech thee, Lord, let it be thy pleasure that thy servant, being ruled per thy Holy Spirit, be not overcome with any enemies, but God Lord stop their weapons to their shame and confusion, that thy mighty name may be glorified forever and ever. Amen.

"+ A + g + L + A + Lord Jesus deliver me from all evils, both from body and soul, as thou didst thy servant Susanna. Amen. Maei, + Marabu + Heaculum,

1333. *Space*: Apparently this was intended as a space where the person could write their name. Why "N. M." was not used here is unclear; perhaps the copyist did not catch the intent.

+ Mathen, + Jaspior, O Lord God and Father almighty, which defendest thy servants Jaspar, Melchior, + and Balthazer, + for their goodwill, they bear to thee from wicked Herod for his cruelties. Likewise, Lord, in their dreams thou didst tell them how to stop their enemies; so suffer me, thy servant, trust in thee to perceive and stop mine enemies, for thy holy Son's sake, Jesus Christ, Amen.

"And Lord, keep me from the powers of devils and evil spirits, and from the power of witches and their sorceries, from the hands of all thieves, I beseech thee, also to keep all my goods and cattle. Per the virtue of thy holy cross T, grant me, ere I die, to speak in time of true repentance, that I may please thee through thy holy name. Amen.

"O holy, holy, holy God which wast betrayed for us, O holy, holy Lord + God + which wast sold for us,[1334]

1334. Text picks up on 264e.

[264a]

[Magical Seals and Instructions][1335]

This is the infallible name of God, which Aaron took in the mount.
Against all dangers.

This sign carry with thee on virgin parchment,[1336] and all aerial and infernal spirits will obey you.

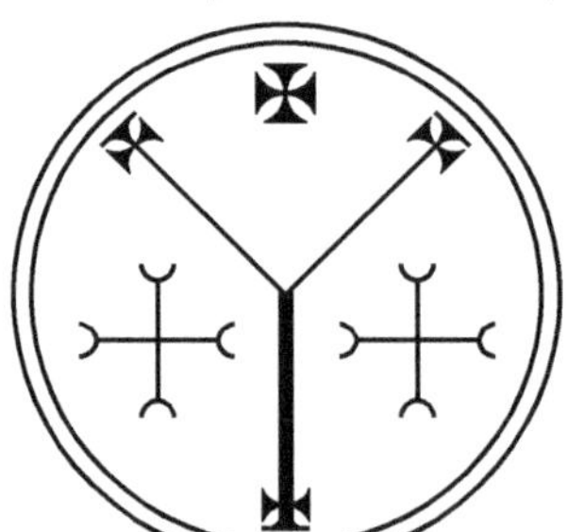

Behold the cross of the Lord.
Extracted from Bacon's original MSS., the MSS. from which the magical art, in the "Astrologer of the Nineteenth Century"[1337] is taken.

1335. As suggested below, these appear originally in Folger V.b.26. Some of the experiments within are attributed to Friar Bacon, which might lead to Raphael's attribution of the entire work to him. See Harms, Clark, and Peterson, *Oberon*, 371; Vârtejaru, "The Book of Pentacles: Folger V.b.26." Raphael also copied it into another manuscript, Wellcome 4639, 110r–v. Vârtejaru, "The Book of Pentacles: The Vadian Clavicle."

1336. *On virgin parchment*: Not present in Folger V.b.26 or Wellcome 4639.

1337. Raphael and Anglicus, *The Astrologer of the Nineteenth Century*, 506.

[264b]

[Unknown Diagram] [1338]

[264c]

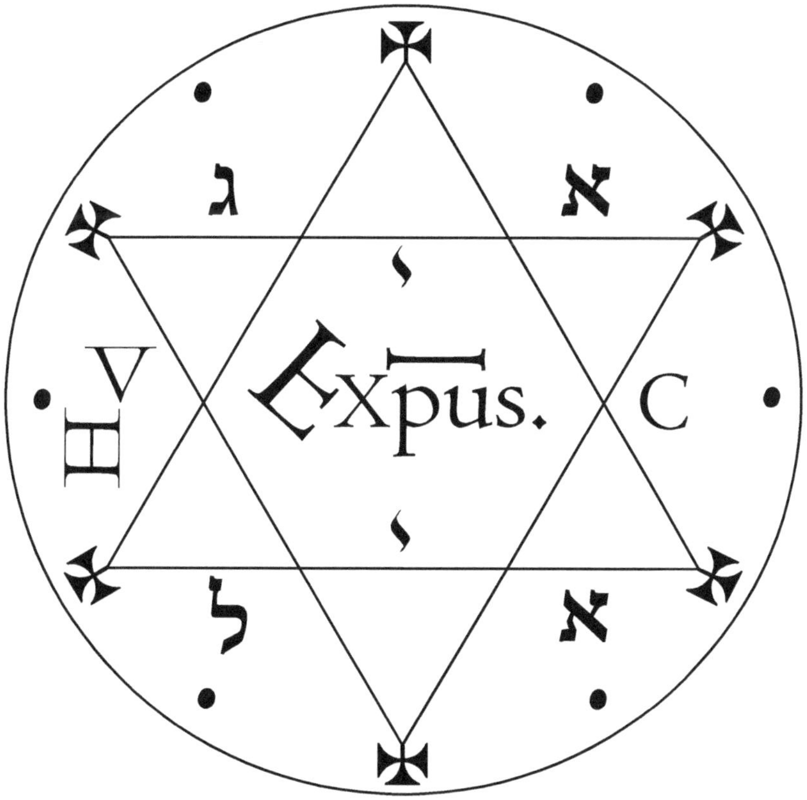

1338. This image was drawn on a cream-coloured card and inserted into the text here. Its significance, if any, is unknown; it appears more like a child's scribbling than anything else. I include it for the sake of completeness.

This is the true pentacle of Peter de Abano,[1339] corrected from a MSS. in the possession of the Mercurii[1340]—see Agrippa, 4th Book, page 132.[1341]

The virgin parchment, so often spoken of in this book, is easily procured at any law stationer's, it being neither more nor less than fine kidskin, which is easily obtained.

The best consecrations for magical purposes which I have yet seen, are to be found in Scot's.

[264d] [Right margin]

Discovery of Witchcraft.[1342] They are very simple yet of wonderful occult power, which I have myself often proved.

[On the Influence of the Planet Herschel, or Uranus]

It is a curious fact that Herschel,[1343] the newly discovered planet, is found to be the origin of magical, mystical, and astrological proceedings. I have seen the nativities of most professors of the occult sciences, and also of most of its admirers, all of them, have a ray of Herschel to the moon or Mercury. Mr. Varly[1344] has the moon in conjunction with Herschel, I have the moon in opposition to Herschel, "H. W.," the President of the Mercurii,[1345] has the moon in sextile to Herschel. And in numerous other instances, this star seems to preside over magick and occult sciences peculiarly. If this phenomenon be compared with the wonderful events that have occurred since the discovery of Herschel, it may lead to some rational conjecture as to the grand era which appears to be approaching, in which I believe astrology and occult philosophy will either again reign supreme lord of the ascendants, or set for ever, in clouds of mystic darkness, which before the year 1832, in all human probability, this interesting question will be determined. I believe that many of the departed spirits of the ancient Ma[gi?] are, at this moment, bent upon raising the occult sciences.

R. C. Smith Nov 1825

1339. *Peter de Abano*: Italian philosopher and astrologer to whom magical works were later attributed.

1340. *Mercurii*: A mystical brotherhood of nineteenth-century London, of which the astrologer Robert Cross Smith, or "Raphael," was the most prominent member. Harms, *Balloonists, Alchemists, and Astrologers of the Nineteenth Century*, 11–15.

1341. *Fourth Book*: This would seem to be a reference to a manuscript edition, as neither of the published ones available at this time includes relevant content on this page.

1342. *Discovery of Witchcraft*: The 1665 edition does have two chapters explicitly on making consecrations. Scot, *The Discovery of Witchcraft*, 215–16, 220–21.

1343. *Herschel*: An early name for the planet Uranus, after William Herschel (1738–1822), its discoverer.

1344. *Varly*: John Varley (1778–1842), painter and possible member of the Mercurii.

1345. *"H. W."*: An unknown individual. This does suggest that "H. W." was not simply Raphael under a pseudonym.

[264e]

[A Talisman for Protection and for the Circle, Part 2]

"and whipt for our sins. Holy, holy, holy Lord, most gentle saviour, which upon Good Friday for our sins was hanged upon the cross dead and buried, Lord, give unto me, thy servant, evermore thy good spirits. Defend me from all perils of body and soul. Amen."

[The Talisman][1346]

Mattheus, ✠ *Marcus,* ✠ *Lucas,* ✠ *Johannes.*

Pro Crucis hoc signum —— fugiat procull omne malignun ✠ *et per idem signum Salretum quod per benignum*

[Instructions for Creating the Circle, Part 1]

Here also followeth, over the leaf, the figure of the circle, which must be in parchment and cut round, wherein this aforesaid must be written, and also the characters and things as be hereafter in order. As example sheweth, there are thirty-three characters which must fill the outward margin of the circle, every one in his order round about, with the verses belonging there to, and here are expressly set down per example.

[A Concoction to View Spirits]

'Tis said, if a smooth, shining piece of suet be smeared over with the juice of mugwort and made to fume, it will make invocated spirits to be seen in it. Page 91, *3 Books* Cornelius Agrippa.[1347]

1346. In the talisman below, "malignun" should be "malignum," "salretum" should be "salvetur," and "quod per" should be "quodque." Translation of the corrected Latin: "May all wicked things flee by this sign of the cross / and by the same sign every thing good is saved."

1347. *Cornelius Agrippa*: The 1651 edition has this passage on that particular page (book 1, chapter 45).

[265]

[Instructions for Creating the Circle, Part 2]

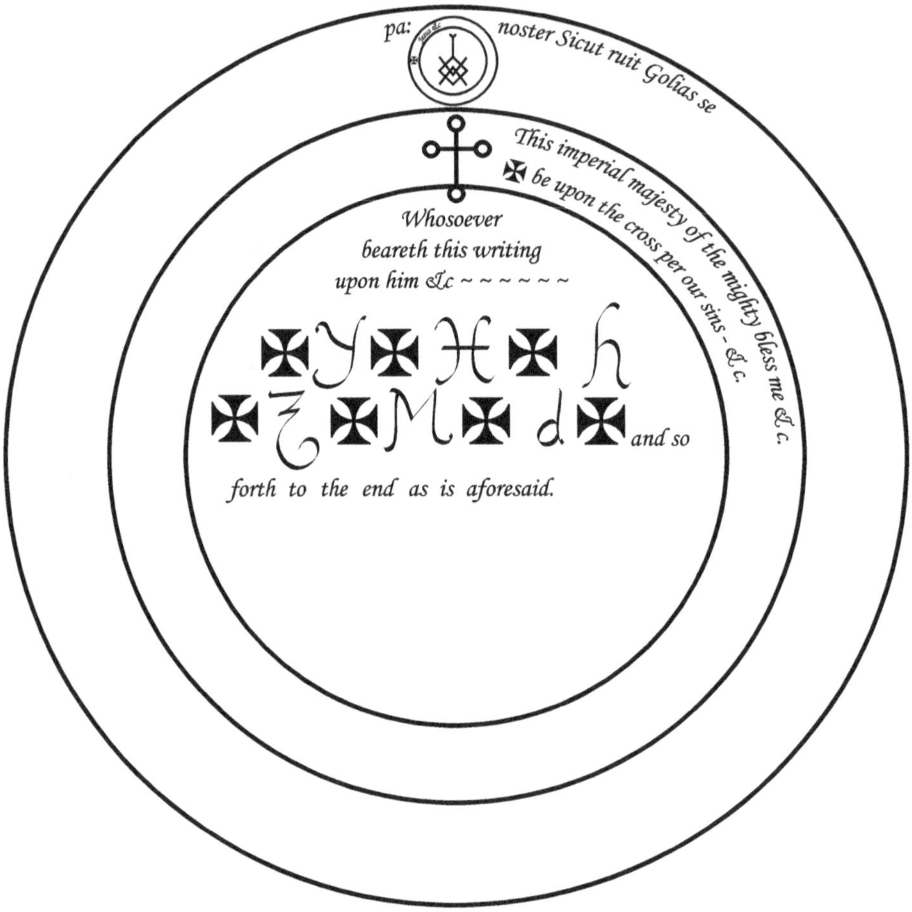

[Circles][1348]

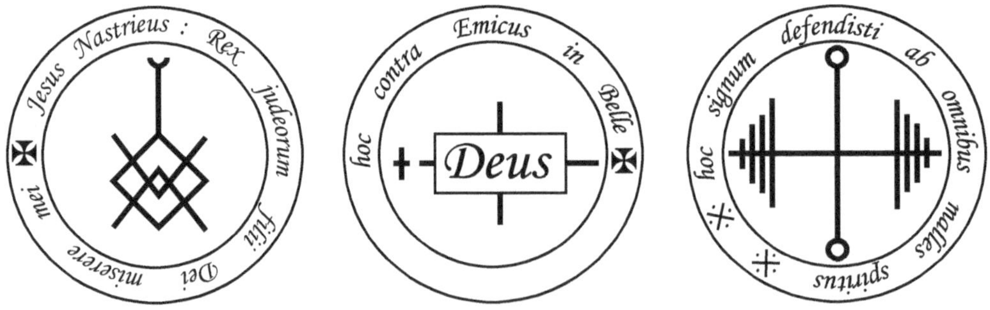

1348. Translations of the below, left to right: "Jesus of Nazareth [corrected], king of the Jews, Son of God, have mercy on me"; "This against enemies in war / God"; "This sign defended from all evil spirits."

[266]

[Circles][1349]

1349. Translations of the below, left to right, top to bottom: (2) "This sign defends from evil death"; (3) "This sign defended from enemies in me"; (4) "no Father, no Son, no Holy Ghost"; (5) "Make this sign and may it bind you enemies."

[267]

n
s
biti
a a
A
GL
A
Pater
Pyon socium
filium nomen
am finis finis
Jesus
Nazariacus
y annis re X
me: ♓ ii. ?. c 9
ɦ ɦe. o. o. ſ. u. o.
c. ſ. p. p. ſ. o. L.
o. ♓ . oo ɓ o t

[268]

This oration next must be written also about in the tablet above the characters, as is afore shewed in the example, in the manner of a ring from the beginning to the ending:

"Sicut ruit Golias ante faciem pueri tui David et ruet in selestia in monte Sinay coram Moses, et ruit *faruo* [Pharao] in *marii* [mare] rubro *caram* [coram] *peple* [populi] Israel, et Amelec coram Mose, et Og coram Josua sic consoenanter, consequenter, et festinanter cadant inimicie mei sub pedibus meis, et consequenter fatias Deus ut avertas arma eorum a me et frangas frimbrias eoram et liquidos facies a conspectu mee sicut cera a facie ignis coram populo orbis terrarum sicut, *quas* [quia] nomen tuum invocantem est a me, in nomine Patris et Filii et Spiritus Sancti. Amen."

> "As Golias fell before the face of your servant David, and Moses fell on Mount Sinai face to face with heavenly things, and Pharaoh fell before the face of the people of Israel, and Amalek face to face with Moses, and Og face to face with Joshua, so my enemies shall fall agreeably, suitably, and quickly under my feet, and following, O Lord, you should make that you turn away their weapons from me and shatter their fragments,[1350] and you should make them liquid in my sight, as wax

1350. "Frimbrias" could also be a garment hem, or borders of an area.

in the face of the fire, face to face with the people of the world, thus because your name is called by me, in the name of the Father, and of the Son, and of the Holy Ghost. Amen."[1351]

[269]

These holy lines following must be written in the second margin of the circle afore in the two second liges[1352] round about from the beginning to the end orderly, as for an example.

"The imperial majesty of thy might, bless me + upon the cross for our sins."
"The everlasting deity keep me, Jesus Christ God Almighty."
"The rial[1353] divinity protect me, and so, per the holy correctors,[1354] save me."
"The glorious unity comfort me; save me, thy servant."
"The incomprehensible Trinity defend me from the dangers of my enemies."
"The inestimable goodness direct me. Alpha et Omega, God and man."
"The power of the Father govern me; let this blessing be to me."

[270]

"The wisdom of the Son quicken me; health and safety of body and soul."

"The virtue of the Holy Ghost illuminate me and be with me against all my enemies, visible and invisible."

"O Lord God Almighty, have mercy on me, sinful wight, now and forever and ever, bless me, and as Christ + + + + + did, shed, his, precious, blood."

1351. This appears to be a variant of the so-called "Prayer of Aethelstan," aimed at protection in battle. Muir, *A Pre-Conquest English Prayer-Book (BL. MSS Cotton Galba A.Xiv and Nero A.Ii (Ff. 3–13)*, 21.

1352. *Liges*: Lines?

1353. *Rial*: Royal.

1354. *Correctors*: Superiors in religious orders.

[The Magical Roll][1355]

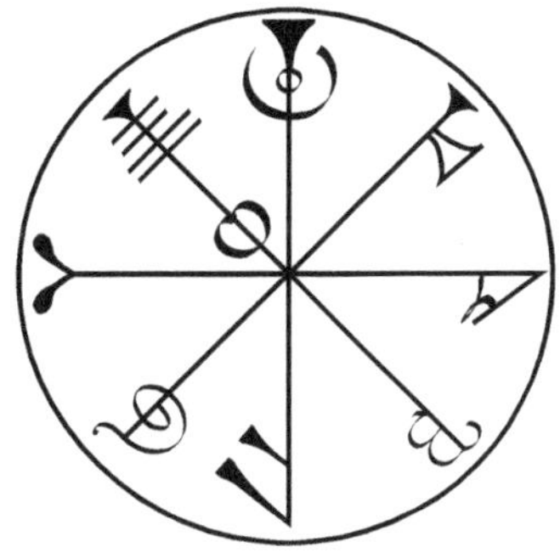

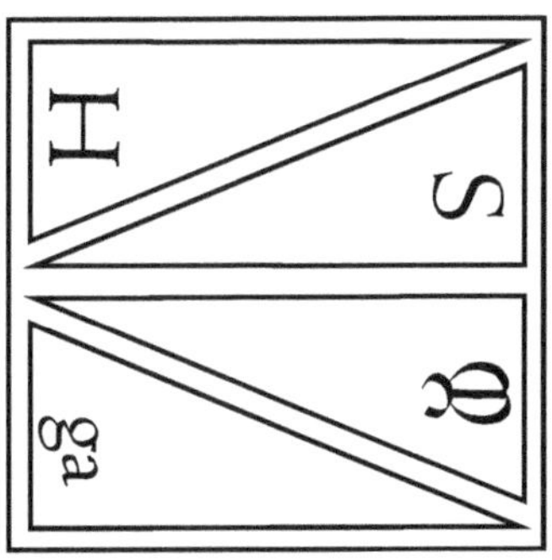

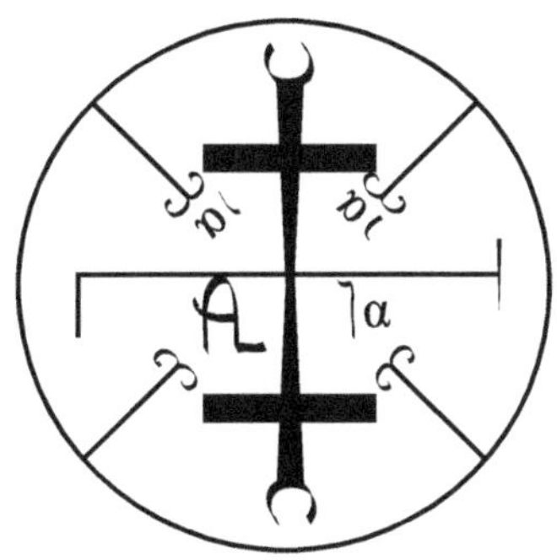

1355. Magical rolls were lengthy pieces of parchment, containing a wide variety of sacred diagrams and prayers compiled for protection and salvation. Although several examples have been found, what follows (manuscript pages 270–89) is, to my knowledge, the only known set of written instructions for making such a roll. Skemer, "The Magic Serpent," 27–32.

[271]

[Planetary Angels and Characters][1356]

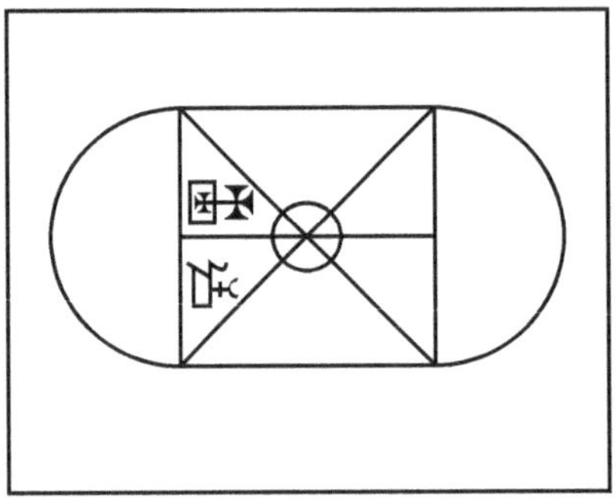

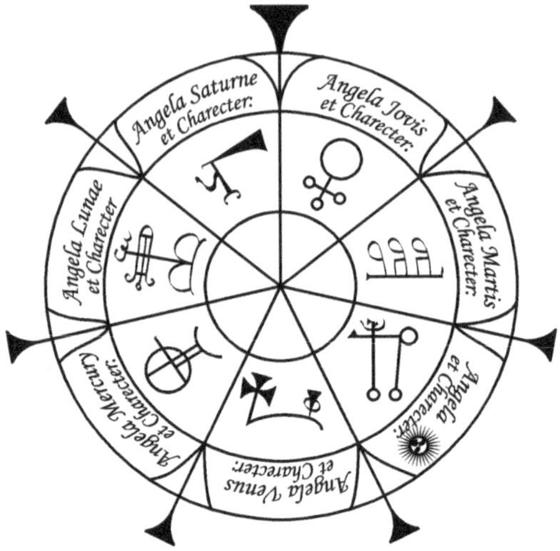

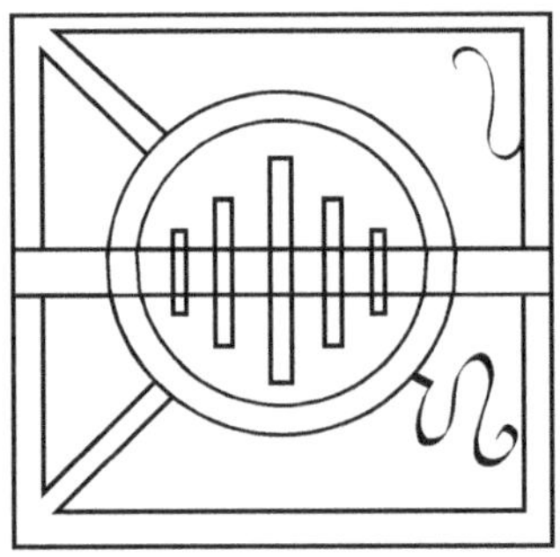

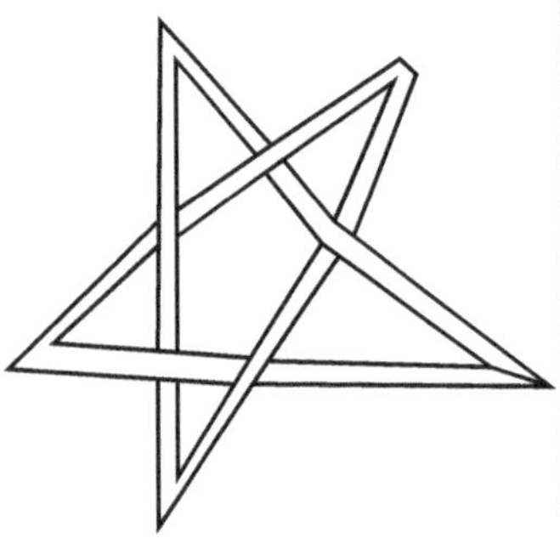

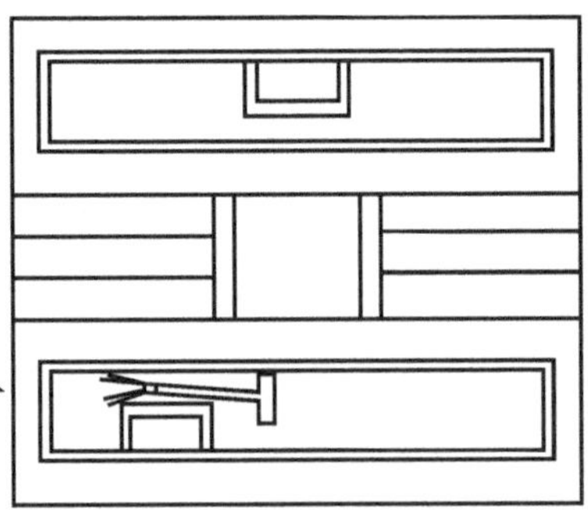

1356. Translation of the upper left: "The angel and character of Jupiter / The angel and character of Mars / The angel and character of ☉ / The angel and character of Venus / The angel and character of Mercury / The angel and character of the moon / The angel and character of Saturn." Mihai Vârtejaru points out the usage of a similar symbol in the magical treatise entitled "The Rings of Messalah." See his "The Book of the Seven Rings of the Planets of Messalah."

[272]

[A Prayer of Protection]

"The triumphant title of the Cross + Jesus of Nazareth, King of the Jews, + Christ overcometh + Christ reigneth, + Christ bless me, and from all thunder and lightning, tempest, and all evil deliver and defend me. Behold the cross + of Jesus Christ, fly hence the wicked spirits, and the valiant lion of the tribe of Judah and the rock of Jesse hath gotten the victory. Kyrie Leyson, Christe Elison, Kyrie Leyson. The blessing of God the Father, the Son, and the Spiritus Sanctus be with me evermore. Amen. The cross of Christ + be ever with me, remain, and abide with me. Amen." Pater Noster, Ave, and Creed.

"The sacred name, O Lord, engrave within my breast,
for therein doth consist my joy and only rest."

"Jesus, fili dei, miserere mei.[1357] Amen."

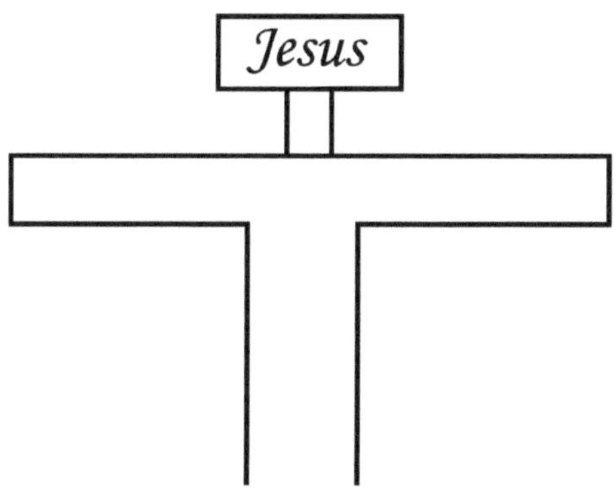

1357. *Jesus…mei*: Translation: "Jesus, son of God, have mercy on me."

[273]

[The Measure of Christ][1358]

Jesus, fili dei, miserere mei.[1359]

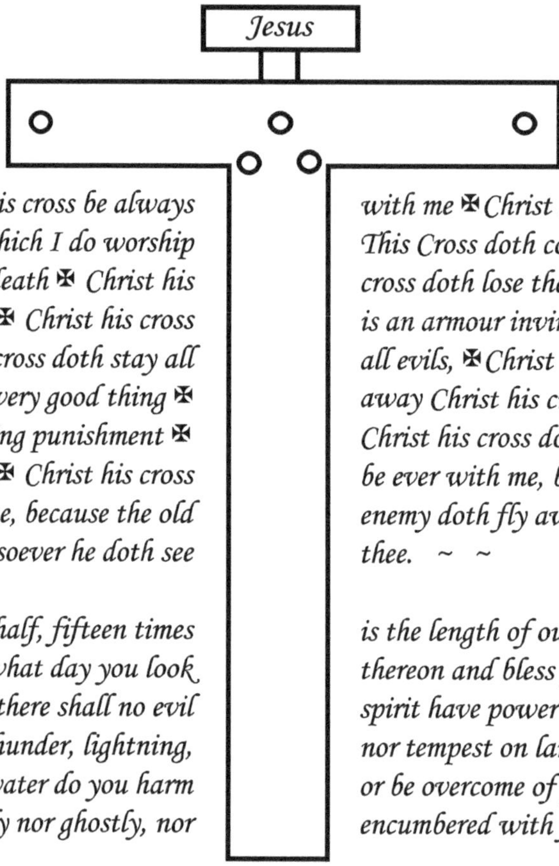

Christ his cross be always with me ✠ Christ his cross ✠
is that which I do worship This Cross doth command the
sword of death ✠ Christ his cross doth lose the bonds
of death, ✠ Christ his cross is an armour invincible ✠
Christ his cross doth stay all all evils, ✠ Christ his cross
doth give every good thing ✠ away Christ his cross doth take
everlasting punishment ✠ Christ his cross doth
save me, ✠ Christ his cross be ever with me, before me
and behind me, because the old enemy doth fly away
wheresoever he doth see thee. ~ ~

Four inches and a half, fifteen times is the length of our Lord
Jesus, and what day you look thereon and bless you,
therewith there shall no evil spirit have power to hurt
you, neither thunder, lightning, nor tempest on land
or water do you harm or be overcome of your ene-
mies, bodily nor ghostly, nor encumbered with friends.

And if a woman have this cross on her when she laboureth of child, she shall sound be delivered, per the grace of God, and the child have Christendom, and the mother purification of the church.

1358. *Measure of Christ*: A protective amulet meant to be as lengthy Christ was tall, often found on magical rolls. Skemer, *Binding Words*, 143; Edsall, "Arma Christi Rolls or Textual Amulets?"; Boroffka, *Die "Länge Christi" in der Malerei*, 147–51.

1359. *Jesus…mei*: Translation: "Jesus, son of God, have mercy on me."

[274]

[The Three Nails of the Passion][1360]

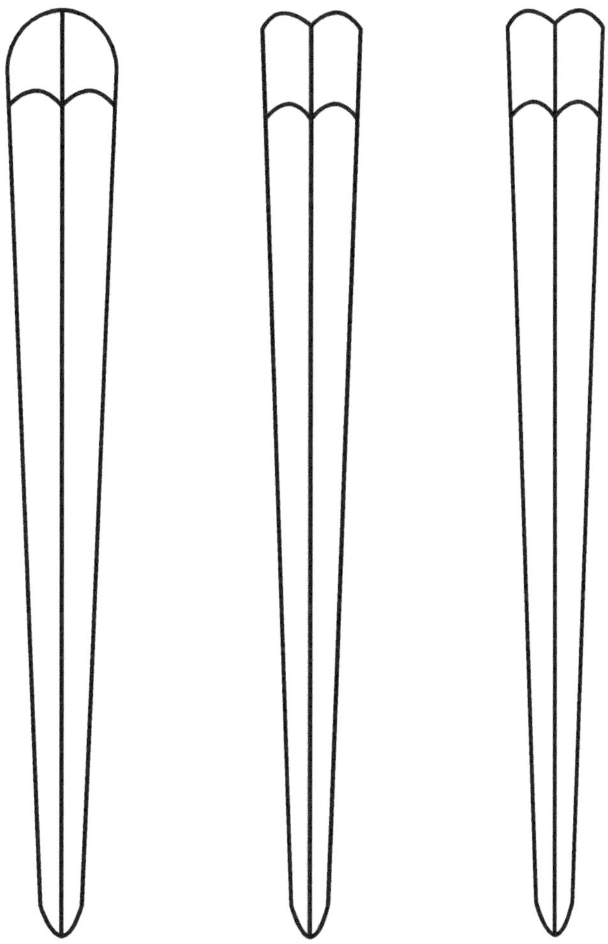

Pater noster *Pater noster* *Pater noster*
Ave Maria *Ave Maria* *Ave Maria*

1360. For other examples, see Beinecke Takayima 56; British Library Harley T.11; Skemer, *Binding Words*, 260, 262–63; Boroffka, *Die "Länge Christi" in der Malerei*, 128–29.

[275]

This is the true length of the nails, that our Lord Jesus Christ's hands and feet were nailed with to the cross, and whosoever beareth this measure of the three nails or the true length upon him, he shall have seven gifts given him of God.

The first is he shall not die no sudden death. The second is there shall no man annoy with him with the sword. The third is his enemies shall not overcome him. The fourth is there shall no wickedness nor evil words annoy him. The fifth is he shall lack no worship nor goods. The sixth is he shall not die without the rites of the holy church. The seventh is he shall not before, nor after, death be troubled with any evil spirits, and no fire nor water shall hurt him, and whosoever beholdeth these same three nails with contrition and devotion to our Lord Jesus Christ, saying three Pater Nosters, three Aves, and one Creed shall have grace to put from him all deadly sins.

The nails are exact, seven inches a nail long.

[A Wound of Christ?][1361]

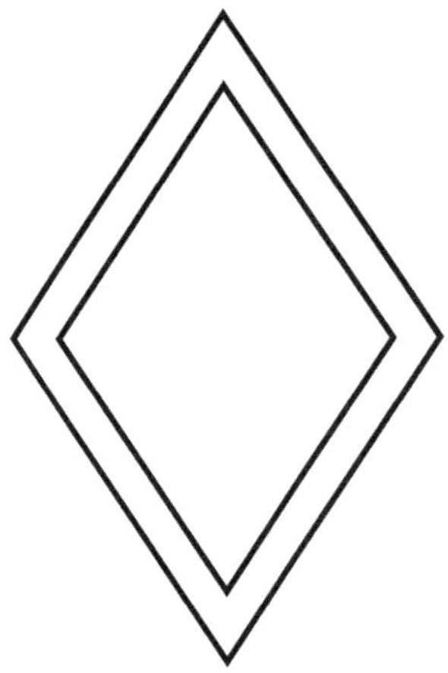

[276]

"O Lord God, Almighty Father, Son, and Holy Ghost, grant me, thy servant, victory and triumph against all devilish temptations, and against all my foes which desire to hurt me, that they may not have power either to hurt or withstand me, so that their strong devices and policies[1362] may turn to my good.

1361. This is similar to depictions of the wounds of Christ that appear in other rolls and charms. Simpson, "On the Measure of the Wound."

1362. *Policies*: Tricks.

And thou, O almighty God, be thou my stronghold, my refuge, and the staff of my defence, and against my foes a fiery pillar, and a strong tower of my strength and protection, so that, per thy might, all my adversaries and foes may be scattered and dispersed. O God of Abraham, God of Isaac, God of Jacob, the god of all well-living and believing people, deliver me thy servant from all tribulations, troubles, perils, and dangers, and give me strength, power, and perseverance in my actions. Sweeten my lips, and speech may be a sweet sacrifice unto thee, that all my words and deeds may be acceptable unto thee, and to all thy people which shall either see or hear me, so that, per thy might, I may find honour amongst all men and obtain my petitions of them. The prophet proclaimeth, the apostle testifieth that Christ saveth and healeth all them that put their trust in him.

"+ Christ overcometh, + Christ reigneth +

[277]

"+ Christ vouchsafe to make me conqueror of all mine enemies; therefore will I not fear what man can do unto me. O God, heal me for thy name's sake, and deliver me from all mine enemies, both visible and invisible, and grant me time and space of repentance and power, though thy name, to perform the same. Grant me, O Lord, that I may obtain some per competent preferment and maintenance during my pilgrimage in this vale of misery. O Lord Jesus Christ, the son of the living God, which most willingly didst submit thyself to the death upon the cross, and thy side to be pierced with a spear, and hast redeemed me with thy most precious blood, and deliveredst the three children, Sidrac, Misac, and Abednago, from the fiery furnace, and didst defend Susanna, from her false accusers and preservedest Daniel from the lion's den. So, good Lord, defend me thy servant per the virtue of thy word from all adversity of body and soul, and from all and every evil action, both present and to come. Amen.

"In the name of the Father, and of the Son, and of the Holy Ghost. Amen. And with all his mighty force and wonderful words of God. Amen. +"

[278]

The foresaid orations ought to be written in a roll of parchment, with this following per itself in another roll of parchment. Bring another for the same benefit, and on the back side certain characters which here may be omitted for forgetfulness. I drew them out before, being in the third and fourth leaf backward, that which containing twelve characters, shall per order as there before be placed so that, at any time you chance to read the said orations in your own name or any others, or before the bewitched or possessed, the said characters on the back, are ever in the sight and beholding, as in hearing, of the ghostly enemy, to terrify him as well, in the beholding as in hearing of it read. That which writing have been proved many times to vanquish devils, and the devil hath cried out and bidden burn the writing.

"O cross of Christ, direct me
And from my foes protect me;
O precious blood of Jesu,
Be my defence and rescue.

"O painful smart and smartful pain
How sinful facts cause me refrain;
O wonderful corpse, from top to toe,
Be my comfort in weal and woe,
Wid[1363] holes with nails and spear, and
O gursling[1364] streams of blood so dear.

[279]

"O dreadful death and gelded ghost,
Help me in time when I need most,
At this time present and ever then,
Sweet Jesus Christ, our Lord. Amen.

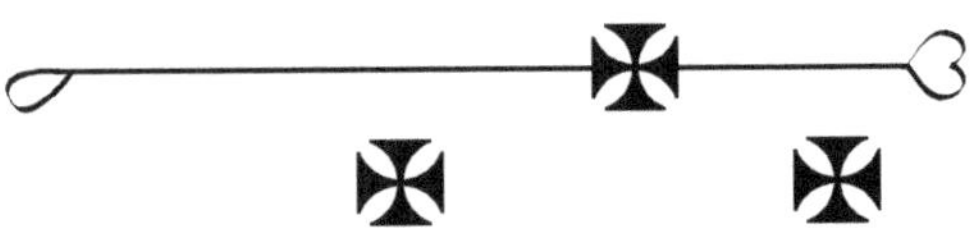

"In nomine Patris, + et Filii, + et Spiritus Sanctus. Amen. + Christ became obedient for us to death, even to the death of the cross. + Jesus of Nazareth, king of the Jews crucified, have mercy upon me. + The five wounds of God be medicine. + The holy cross and passion of Christ be my refreshing. + Christ overcometh + Christ commandeth, + Christ defend me from all evil. + O Lord Jesus Christ, the good shepherd, defend me, thy servant, the bearer here as from all wicked spirits, visible and invisible, whether I sleep or wake, and per the virtue and power of thy precious blood shedding, wherewith thou hast redeemed me. Amen. A., + L., + Tetragramaton, + On, + On, + + + + +

1363. *Wid*: A regional variant of "with."
1364. *Gursling*: Gurgling?

"The cross + of Christ be ever with me. + The cross of Christ is the thing which I obey, adore, reverence, and worship. + The cross of Christ is perfect health. + The cross of Christ excelleth all joy. + The cross of Christ looseth the bands of death.

[280]

"+ The cross of Christ is invincible, per weapon. + The cross of Christ is an unmoveable sign. + The cross of Christ be unto me the way unto all virtues and the virtue itself, per the virtue and power of the Holy Ghost and cross. + I take my journey. + The cross of Christ openeth all goodness. + The cross of Christ chaseth away all evil. + The cross of Christ taketh away all eternal pains. + O cross of Christ save me; be thou upon me, before me, and behind me, for the old enemy flyeth away wheresoever he beholdeth thee. O the wonderful height, breadth, and depth of the cross of Christ, that which no height, breadth, or depth of any thing could at any time comprehend, or attune unto. Save and deliver me from all devilish arts and wicked thoughts, which, per any means, might abide and remain in me. Thou devil, fly from me that I know thee not. As thou art like us, thou art cut off from heaven and estrained[1365] from all felicity, and doest not desire nor long after God, so be thou estranged and cut off from me, and not to desire to ease to me. O Lord Jesu Christ, be with me, that thou mayst defend me. Be thou within me, to refresh me

[281]

"under me, to lift me up, and ever above me, to bless me with thy mighty right hand. O thou that art three in persons, and one in messance,[1366] defend me, world without end. In nomine Patris, + et Filii + et Spiritus Sancti + Amen. + St. Michael, be my habergeon,[1367] + St Gabriel be my helmet, + St. Raphael, be my shield, + St. Uriel, my defence, + St. Cherubim, my health, + St. Seraphin, be to me truth and strength, and all the holy angels and archangels of God, keep me, protect me, defend me, and bring me to everlasting life through Jesu Christ our Lord. Amen. In nomine Patris, et Filii, et Spiritus Sancti + Amen. In the most highest and blessed name of Jesu, let every knee bow, both of things in heaven, things in earth, and things in hell, and let every tongue confess that our Lord Jesus Christ is in the glory of God the Father. Amen. In the name of Jesu, I sign me with the sign Tau, T being the

1365. *Estrained*: Bound.

1366. *Messance*: Possibly a mistake for "in essence."

1367. *Habergeon*: A sleeveless coat of chainmail.

sign of Christ's cross + The five wounds of God be my medicine to heal all the diseases and grievous wounds or sins of my body and soul, naming this word, Tetragramaton, and Jesus,

[282]

"passing forward, went through the midst of them. Three bodies of divers members did hang on three trees, Dismas et Gismas, and between them God's divine power. Dismas ascended to the heavenly joys, and Gismas fell to the pit of pains.[1368] Christ both now and ever protect, keep, and defend me, and suffer me not to lose my goods. + Christ overcometh, + Christ reigneth, + Christ giveth power, + Christ vouchsafe that I may reign, triumph, and overcome all my adversaries and enemies evermore. Amen. And the beautiful company of angels in heaven, do here now set forth the holy names of their almighty God, + Omnipotens, + Dominus, + Christus, + Messias, + Sother, + Emanuell, + Sabaoth, + Adonay, + Est, + Unigenitus, + Via, + Vita, + Manus, + Homo, + Usion, + Principium, + Primogenitus, + Salvator, + Sapientia, + Virtus, + Alpha, + Ω, + Fons, + Origo, + Spes, + Fides, + Charitas, + Oza, + Agnus, + Ovis, + Vitulus, + Serpens, + Aries, + Leo, + Vermis, + Primus, + Novissimus, + Rex, + Pater, + Filius, + Spiritus Sanctus, + Ego Sum qui Sum, + Creator, + Eternus, + Redemptor, + Trinitas +

[283]

"+ Unitas, + Clemens, + Caput, + Otheoteco, + Tetragramaton, + Bonus, + Paracletus, + Mediator, + Verbum, + Splendor, + Sol, + Gloria, + Lux, + Ymago, + Panis, + Patris, + Flos, + Vitis, + Mons, + Janua, + Petra, + Lapis, + Angelus, + Sponsus, + Pastor, + Propheta, + Sacerdos, + Athanatos, + Kyros, + Theon, + Panton, + Craton, + et Ysus + These names keep, protect, and defend me, from all plague and adversity, + from all infirmities of body and soul, fully deliver me, and ever be ready at hand to help me. The four evangelists, Matthew, Mark, Luke, and John, be ever ready at hand to help, deliver, and defend me, from all perils, temptations, and dangers, and anguishes of body and soul, and from all evils past, present, and for to come, being appointed thereunto, per Jesu Christ our lord and saviour. Amen."

Of a Crystal Stone

This is a proper vision and divine glass wherein is great efficacy. Per it you may see of the four elements. Therefore make a glass of crystal, which ull[1369] and well graven, and

1368. *Three bodies...pains*: See manuscript pages 1 and 103, on the "Dismas et Iesmas" charm.

1369. *Ull*: Reading here uncertain.

[284]

it must not be looked upon per any woman. Then write in it this holy name "Agla," which must be done featly.[1370] Then lay it on an altar, and sing nine Masses thereon. Then take it and close it in silver on Thursday, Wednesday, and Tuesday, and in three hours. This must be done in the days aforesaid. The whole work must be clean, and as near as ye can, let it not be defiled of women. Therefore, when thou wouldst know anything which is lost in the world & c., set the glass before thee and say these prayers following under on this manner: the first of St. John Baptist, the second of the Blessed Virgin Mary, the third of the patient of our Lord Jesus Christ, the fourth of the ascension, the fifth of St. Longine.

Hear followeth the figure of the glass, which must be made of wood of bay, or silver, and must be made in manner of a cross.

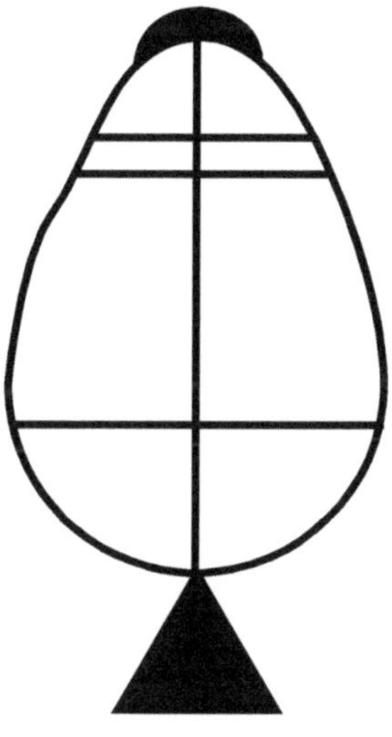

[285]

Here beginneth the consecration. In the first day, you must say the seven psalms,[1371] three Paters, one Ave, and one Creed, the litany and the Gospel of St John, then these prayers as followeth:

"O Lord, our holy Father, I admonish thee with that most pleasant oration which thy most blessed son said before thee when he raised Lazarus, with his eyes and hands erected up to heaven. In that pleasant oration, I put away all unclean prayers and unworthy, and I beseech thee, in the name of the beloved son, that thou wilt give me four angels that may obey me and fulfil my will and pleasure, & c. Amen.

1370. *Featly*: Properly.

1371. *Seven psalms*: The seven penitential psalms.

"God the Father almighty, which at the first madest all things of nothing, and all creatures, powers, and kingdoms obey thee, which canst do all things, and with thee all things are easily and possible, so that no discretion can comprehend thee in sight or reason. Have mercy on me, that thy grace, virtue, and humility, and thy Holy Spirit may help me, all the holy angels, archangels, Mic[h]ael, Gabriel, Raphael, Uriel, Cherubin, Seraphin, and the holy thrones, dominations, powers, per the virtues of heaven.

[286]

"I, unworthy sinner and the servant of Jesus Christ, I beseech you that you would vouchsafe to defend and keep me all the days of my life, that the devil or any evil spirit have no power to hurt me in any operation, and that you keep me, per the name of the great God which is blessed forever. Amen. The defender of all them that trust in thee, without whom nothing is strong nor holy, multiply upon us thy mercy, that thou, being our captain and guide, like as we pass per temporal things, we lose not the eternal ways, per him which shall come to judge the quick and the dead, and the world per fire. Amen.

"O thou, most glorious mother of our Lord Jesus Christ, be thou a helper to me to consecrate this glass, + and that we may see in it all that we desire. All hail, most radiant beam, the glass of virginity beholding all things. All hail the rose of Paradise, the precious stone of Christ. All hail, holy Mary, pray for us, that we may be found worthy of the promise of Christ.

"Lord have mercy upon us,
Christ have mercy upon us,
Lord have mercy upon us, & c.[1372]

[287]

"God, which taketh the blessed virgin Mary from the torments of this world, most merciful Father, take this, thy wretched servant N., into thy mercy. I commend my soul into thy hands, now and ever. O glorious and holy mother of God, Virgin Mary, pray pro me, to our Lord Jesus Christ, thy only son, and with thy holy prayers, help me to consecrate + bless + and sanctify + this glass that I may see in it, per the holy angels, all that I desire to see, and keep me from all perils, dangers, and impediments of Sathan or devils, now and ever, per thy virginity, and per our Lord Jesus Christ, thy son, which liveth and reigneth, world without end. Amen.

1372. *Lord have... & c.*: The Kyrie Eleison.

"God, holy Father almighty, God of all power, which madest all things with thy word, I humbly and devoutly beseech thee that, in this glass, per thine holy martyrs, confessors, and virgins, thou wouldst vouchsafe to visit + sanctify, + bless, + and consecrate, + that is being consecrated per his power, virtue, which shed his blood on the cross, which is thy son, our Lord Jesus Christ, that it may have such virtue that I may see in it, per thy holy saints, to my full sight, all things that I desire,

[288]

"that as oft as I shall illuminate my eyes thereon, I may know thy wonderful power, and thy holy angels + Michael, + Gabriel, + Raphiel, + Uriel, + & c., and may see the company of holy angels, and that they may speak with me familiarly to shew and fulfil my precepts and teach me all which I shall require, and that I may know all things per the virtue of this glass, per our Lord Jesus Christ eternal. Amen.

"Lord Jesus Christ, the good shepherd, vouchsafe to look upon this glass with the eyes of thy majesty, and also + consecrate, + bless, + and sanctify + it per the virtue of thy name, and especially of this name graven in this glass that is Agla, + and per the honour of the Blessed Virgin Mary, per whose humility thou didst leave the seat of the Father, that thou, being an infant, mightest be conversant with her. I beseech thee most humbly, that in this glass blessed, thine angels may appear, and that I may see them, and that they may speak with me familiarly and fulfil my request, which with God the Father and the Holy Ghost liveth and reigneth, world without end. Amen.

[289]

"Lord, the everlasting King, thou Holy Ghost, the most holy comforter, which per thy unspeakable clemency doth visit all creatures, and per that love which thou makest between the Father and the Son, and per those beams of love which thou didst pour on the apostles, and per that clemency and humility which thou mercifully didst pour on the Virgins Mary. Look upon this glass, I pray thee, and I beseech thee to + consecrate, + bless, + and sanctify + it, that thine angels may appear in it, and that I may speak to them familiarly and understand them in my mother tongue, per Christ our Lord. Amen.

"O blessed mother of God, Virgin Mary, consecrate, I beseech thee, this glass. O you holy spirits, cherubin and seraphin, vouchsafe to + sanctify this glass. O you worshipful apostles, O blessed patriarchs and prophets, O holy martyrs, O invincible confessors, and most holy virgins, vouchsafe to + consecrate, +

bless, + and sanctify + this glass, that in it I may see, per the holy apostles, all that I shall desire without fear or trembling and amazing, that the power of the chief king may be magnified, which in his spirits doth not want to exorcise great things, per Christ Amen."

Consideranda[1373]

First consider, when the ☉ is in ♈ or in ♎, thou make a circle in thy secret chamber in die ♃ et in ejus

[290]

hora,[1374] ☽ growing to the full after. On Friday after nine of the clock in hora[1375] ♀, if thou be clean of conscience, and devoutly fast that day with bread and water, and hear a Mass of the Trinity, and one of the Holy Ghost, and another of St. Mary, with an oblation in every Mass, and put upon thee clean clothes, and go to this matter towards the east, kneeling down. And when thou hast done all this, set the glass on a table in the midst of the circle, and let all these pass for that night, and go to thy rest in a perfumed chamber nigh to the secret place or chamber, and sleep not, and thou must lie in clean sheets. And without doubt before midnight, you shall hear a great sound to bless your glass. You must have a consecrate[1376] ring always on thy finger all that night following.

This is the circle that belongeth to this work.

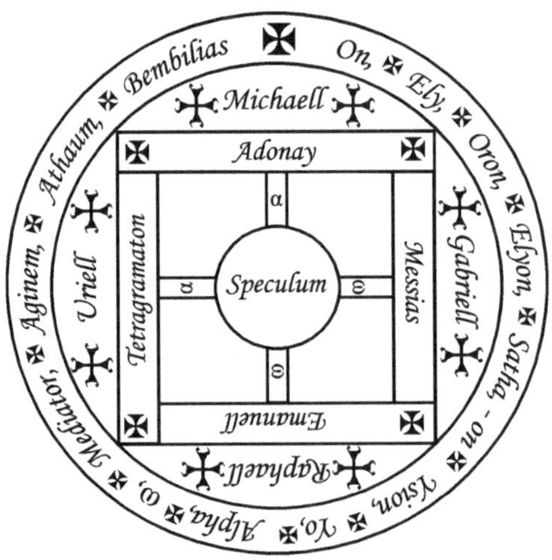

1373. Translation: "Items to Be Considered."

1374. *In…hora*: Translation: "In the day and hour [290] of Jupiter."

1375. *In hora*: Translation: "In the hour of."

1376. *Consecrate*: Consecrated.

[291]

And after night in the morning rise, and take heed that thou be not polluted, but abstained from sin, and go into the circle, and, kneeling, say this consecration following:

"O blessed Trinity, the Father, the Son, and the Holy Ghost, three persons and one God, I honour and magnify thee, I glorify and beseech thee, that this glass being consecrated, per the grace and virtue of the Holy Ghost, and per the Virgin Mary, mother of our Lord Jesus Christ, and thy holy saints, into the virtue of this consecration may always continue with grace, virtue, clemency, and the goodness of the Holy Ghost may perform it, all holy angels and archangels, Michaell, Gabriel, Raphaell, Uriell, Cherubin, and Seraphin, the holy thrones, dominations, kind ones, virtues of heaven, the thousand of thousands of whom there is no number, that they may appear before me in this glass to shew, declare, and fulfil my will, when I call upon them, to keep and defend me all the days of my life, that the devil have no power to hurt me in any place, nor in this operation, but keep me in your custody, per the name of the Great God Sabaoth, which is blessed forever and ever. Amen."

Dic[1377] Pater [Noster], Ave. et Credo, & c.

Finis experimenti.[1378]

[292]

To Prove Theft[1379]

(Psalm 50) Take a Latin psalter and turn to this psalm, "Deus, deorum Dominus,"[1380] and at the same where this very beginneth, when thou sawest a thief, put in a hollow key with a cross in the bit. And first write the suspected person's name in parchment, and put it in the pipe of the same key, and put your two fingers into the bow of the key, and say as followeth.

"Cani, Cani, Cani, Maligi, Maligi, Maligi.

"I charge you, both and either of you, to come quickly without tarrying or let, and shew me the truth of such things as I shall demand, as you hope to be saved and not damned at the dreadful day of doom."

1377. *Dic*: Translation: "Say."

1378. *Finis experimenti*: Translation: "The end of the experiment."

1379. See manuscript page 14.

1380. Vulgate Psalm 49.

Say this three times. If the key does not turn upon your fingers, say three times thus:

"Cum videbas furem currebas ad eo, et cum adulteris portionem tuam ponebas,"[1381] and without doubt, if the suspected person be guilty, it shall turn. Fiat.

An Experiment to Know Whether the Suspected be Guilty or Not, Also to Know Whether a Woman Be with Child, Corrupt in Living, or Any Such Thing Which Must Be Wrought as Followeth[1382]

[293]

Write these names under a loaf of bread, "+ Messias, + Sother, + Sabaoth, + Emanuell, + Adonay, + Otheos, + Eloy, +," and afterward write, about the compass of the bread or loaf, this name, parted this manner, "+ Te + Tra + gram, + ma + ton." Then take four knives, and put one into one side of the loaf, saying:

"O knife, I put thee into this loaf in the name of the Father, and of the Son, and of the Holy Ghost, that as per going of the ☉ about the world, though through turning about with this loaf wilt shew us the truth of these things which we shall ask," & c.

Then put in another on the same manner, & c., that point towards the middle, and after say, Psalm 51, "Miserere mei, deus, secundum magnum misericordiam tuam," & c.,[1383] and so forth to the end of the psalm, then next after this Psalm 53, "Deus, in nomine tuo salvum me fac," & c. concluding with it, "Gloria patri, et filio," & c.[1384] Then Pater, Ave, Credo, must be said, with your face towards the east, and take the names of the suspected persons, and write on the loaf and say this prayer:

1381. *Cum...ponebas*: Vulgate Psalm 49:18. Translation from KJV Psalm 50:18: "When thou sawest a thief, then thou consentedst with him, and hast been partaker with adulterers." For another instance, see Harms and Clark, *Of Angels*, 141; manuscript page 19.

1382. This procedure of using a loaf of bread and knives to find the identity of a thief dates to the thirteenth century. Examples: Laurent d'Orleans, *Des Coninx Summe*, 269; Franz, *Die Kirchlichen Benediktionen im Mittelalter*, 2:360–61; Davies, *Popular Magic*, 2–3; Mitchell, "Cultural Uses of Magic in the Fifteenth-Century England," 124–25; Braekman, *Middeleeuwse Witte en Zwarte Magie*, 338–41.

1383. Vulgate Psalm 50.

1384. Not in Psalm 53, but possibly indicating it should be said until the end.

"O Lord God, I most humbly beseech thee to look upon me, and have mercy upon me,

[294]

"lest thou wouldst deny unto me, that to man thou hast revealed, and lest thou shouldst look upon my sins, I not denying thee to be my God. Therefore, O merciful lord, hear the prayers of thy servant, and grant that I may deserve to find thy strength, virtue, and power, in this experiment written with thy most holy names, which liveth and reigneth one God, world without end. Amen."

Oremus[1385]

"I pray thee, God almighty Father, that per the name of thy son, our lord Jesus Christ, per thy holy apostles Peter and Paul, and as thou hast fulfilled five thousand men with five loaves of bread and two fishes, so grant, O most merciful Father, that the truth may appear upon this loaf, and that thou wilt vouchsafe to shew whether N. hath done this theft, or if it was done per his counsel, that then this loaf may turn about, so that he may be proved guilty. O Lord Jesus Christ, which knoweth the hearts and reins of all creatures; O Lord Jesus Christ, which hath knoweth all things before they were made; O Lord Jesus Christ, which hath said, 'I am the living bread, which have descended from heaven'; O Lord, the beginning and ending, per thy most holiest son, which is Tetragramaton,

[295]

"per the merits and prayers of thy holy apostles Peter and Paul, I, most wretched sinner, do beseech thee of thy mercy and goodness. It may please thee to vouchsafe for thy son, our lord Jesus Christ's sake, to send me knowledge and, per turning of this loaf, whether this person N. be guilty or no. For if he or she be guilty, merciful Lord, Father, grant this loaf turn about; if not, it have no power to stir or move. Grant this, O most merciful Father, through the merits of our Lord, mediator, and advocate Jesus Christ, who liveth and reigneth, now and forever, & c. Amen.

"O very God which hast delivered Daniel from the mouth of the ramping lions, and the three children from the burning oven, and also the children of Israel from the furious rage of Pharoah, King of Egypt, per leading them though

1385. Translation: "Let us pray."

the Red Sea per the hands of Moses and Aaron, and hast given them victory against Amalech, King of the Assyrians, and infinite other, and also hath raised thy servant Lazarus from death, I, most wretched sinner, do beseech thee to vouchsafe to give us knowledge, whether this person be guilty or no, per the turning of this loaf of

[296]

"bread about if he be guilty. If he be not guilty, O most merciful Lord, grant that it hath not the power to turn or move. Grant this, O most merciful Lord, for the love of thy only son, our saviour. Amen."

Alias[1386]

Experimentum Panis[1387] [Part 1]

Dicas[1388] "Adjutorium nostrum in nomine."[1389] & c., "Sit nomen *Dominum* [Domini],"[1390] & c. Oremus,[1391] "Acciones vestras *quesisimus* [quaesimus?] Domine."[1392] & c.

Oremus[1393]

"Domine Jesu Christe qui es A et Ω, principium et finis, per virtu[te]m tuum quod [est?] Tetragramaton, et per intercessionem s[anc]torum tuorum, Petri et Pauli nobis, de coelis clementia tua *implertibus* [implectis], ostende et consede, ut in iste suspectu cuibus in scripeum e et super pane istum pontum reus lee-sencienus fuit per circimotucorem istis panis ostendas si non non moneat panis iste."

> "Lord Jesus Christ, who is A and Ω, the beginning and the end, by your power that is Tetragramaton, and by the intercession of your saints Peter and Paul, for us, from the heavens filled with your clemency,

1386. Translation: "Another."

1387. Translation: "Experiment of the Bread."

1388. *Dicas*: Translation: "You should say."

1389. *Adjutorium...nomine*: Vulgate Psalm 123:8. Translation from KJV 124:8: "Our help is in the name,"

1390. *Sit...[Domini]*: Vulgate Psalm 112:2. Translation from KJV 113:2: "[Blessed] be the name of the Lord."

1391. *Oremus*: Translation: "Let us pray."

1392. *Acciones...Domine*: Translation (conjectural): "Your duties, we beg, O Lord." A collect for the Litany of the Saints. Weller, *The Roman Ritual*, 1:372.

1393. Translation: "Let Us Pray."

send and grant that the party in suspicion, whose name is written in this bread, you show to turn; if not, may this bread not turn."[1394]

Iste circulus fiat super crustam superiorem panis.

Let this circle be made over the upper crust of the bread.

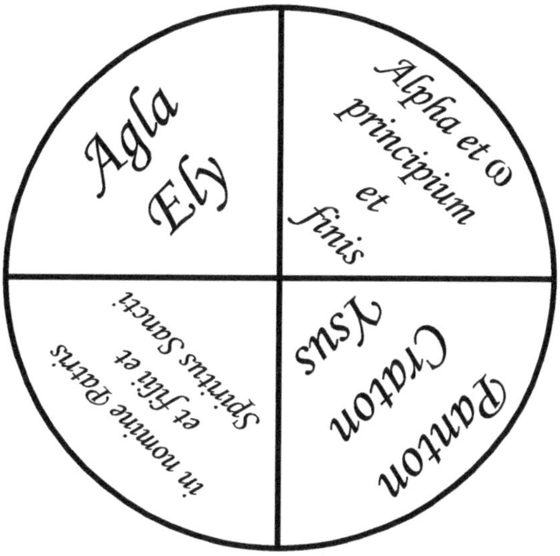

Charm for the Toothache

Three teeth from a dead man's skull wore, viz., a ribbon down the neck.

A Charm for the Toothache or Ague That Be Wrote on a Quarter Plat[1395] of Paper in These Large Letters[1396]

SATOR
AREPO
TENET
OPERA
ROTAS

Knot it and hang it about the party's neck, that it may hang betwixt breasts.

1394. This translation is highly conjectural.

1395. *Plat*: Sheet.

1396. For more on the SATOR square, see manuscript page 143.

[297]

[The Experiment of the Bread, Part 2]

Iste circulus fiat *si* [in] crustam inferiorum.

This circle should be made on the lower crust.

Alias[1397]

To Know If a Man Suspected for a Thief Be Guilty

Take a loaf of bread and put a nail in the midst of the top of it. Then make a character in the manner that hereafter followeth, and write in the midst of the character the name of the suspected person. Then fasten the paper on the bottom of the leaf, and hold the nail between the two foremost fingers, kneeling down, and say this prayer following, and within six or seven times saying, it will turn about of your fingers if that he be guilty.

The Character[1398]

1397. Translation: "Another"

1398. Translation of inscription: "The name of the thief here."

The Prayer

[298]

"Rogo te, Deum patrem omnipotentem, per immensurabilem trinitatem tuum, et nomen filii, in Dominum vestrum Jesum Christi, et per omnia mirabilia tua quae fecisti. Quinque millia hominum cum quinque panis et duobus pissibus, sic ostende mihi omnem veritatem in hoc pane si illo vel in illa res talis deposita fuerit, ut cum vie in fanis furti fuit."

> "I ask you, God the omnipotent Father, by your immeasurable Trinity and the name of your son, to your Lord Jesus Christ, and by all wonders you have created. You made five thousand men with five loaves and two fishes. So show me the whole truth in this bread, if it may have been left in this or in such matters, as it was of the theft in the churches with power."[1399]

Ut Fur Consiliatur, Furtum Foyle[1400]

Take silver foiling,[1401] and temper it with the white of an egg, and take a stick of cypress, and paint an eye on a wall with the one end, and with the other paint about the eye these names, "Malleo, Nabba, Celerum, Bathenay." Then take a needle of pure copper and touch the black of the eye. Say as followeth:

"Coniuro vos, Malleo, Nabbas, Celerum, Baltenay, ut furem faciatis aperire os suum et recognoscere quod quarimus."

> "I conjure you, Malleo, Nabbas, Celerum, Baltenay, that you make the thief to open his mouth and to admit that which we seek."

Then rehearse his name which you will do the grief unto, and strike the eye, and he or she will cry out.

1399. *As it…power*: Conjectural.

1400. Translation: "That a Thief Is Confirmed, Foil Theft [?]." The Eye of Abraham. See manuscript page 13.

1401. *Foiling*: Foil.

Figura[1402]

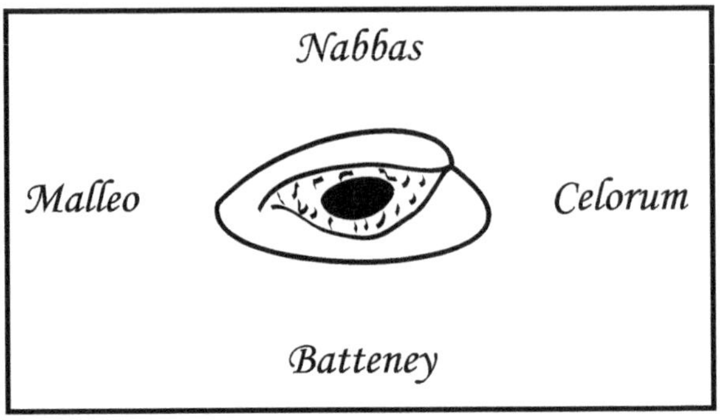

[299]

Alias[1403]

Take the blood of an owl, and draw an eye with the pen of a raven or a crow, and prick the apple of the eye with a nail or needle of copper in the midst four times saying hac conjurat[ion]em: this conjuration:[1404]

"Conjuro te, Adromalee, quod tu fure sentire dolorem facias, quo ego illum afficio."

"I conjure thee, Adromalee,[1405] that you should make the thief to feel pain, wherefore I fix the same."

Dic Pater, et fiat.

Say a Pater, and let it be done.

Alias[1406]

"I conjure thee, Andromalcus, Arromaleus, that thou make the thief to have the pain, to appear that I do here."

Then rehearse it four times, and without doubt, it shall go out.

1402. *Figura*: Translation: "Figure."

1403. Translation: "Another." Another Eye of Abraham. For this variant, see Sloane 3846, 83v.

1404. *Hac coniurat[ion]em*: Translation: "This conjuration."

1405. *Adromalee*: Andromalchus, a spirit connected with the discovery and punishment of thieves. Other appearances: Bodleian Rawlinson D.252, 119r–120r; Peterson, *The Lesser Key of Solomon*, 39; Skinner and Rankine, *The Goetia of Dr. Rudd*, 174; Turner, "Brief Remarks," 59; Harms and Clark, *Of Angels*, 119.

1406. *Alias*: Translation: "Another."

Figura, Alias Est Exp[erimen]t[um], Figura[1407]

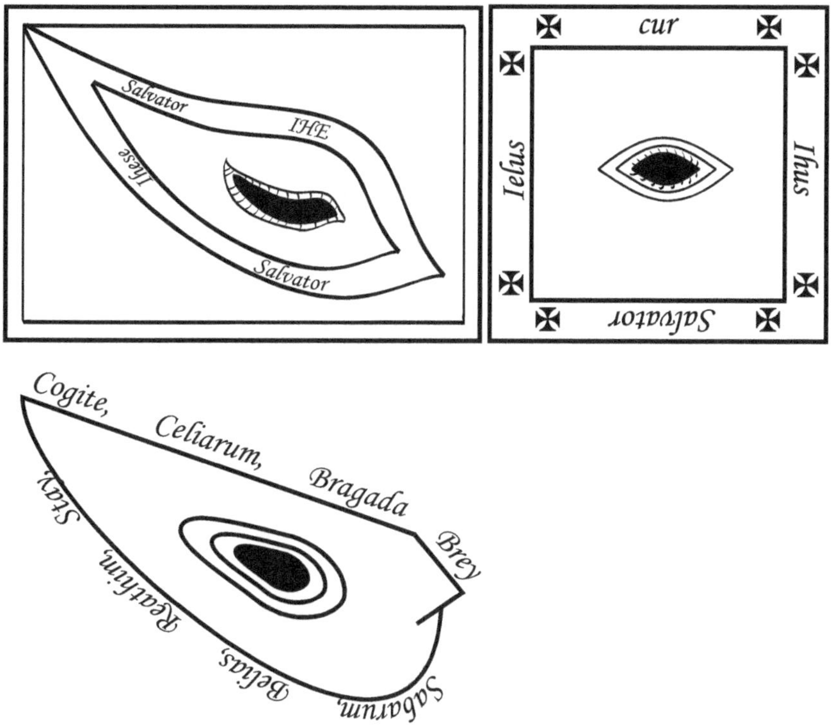

[300]

To that, when thou wilt work this experiment, thou must have before thee a left eye painted like this, with letters of silver. Then, with the white of an egg, fasten a nail of copper in the midst of the eye, saying the prayer following:

"Jesus, the saviour of all men, the true utterer of all things, both sacred and profane, for thy holy name's sake, grant us to have knowledge of the goods of N. which are stolen, that he or she who hath stolen these goods, may, in and per thy name, plainly know them guilty wheresoever they be, and grant that whatsoever do shame to this eye, the like may chance[1408] to his or her eye, in nomine Patris, et Fillii, et Spiritus Sancti. Amen."

This must be said three times. Then take the hammer and strike the nail, saying:

"Rabas, Sabay, Reathy, Stay, Cogite, Coliarum, Braggada, Bray, make thee these appear manifestly that have stolen the goods of this man, whatsoever they be, and like as this nail is thrust into this eye, so, per your help, he, she,

1407. *Figura...Figura*: Translation: "Figure, It Is Another Experiment, Figure." The Eye of Abraham. See manuscript page 13.

1408. *Chance*: Happen.

or they may tarry in great pain, until they do confess themselves guilty, or restore to us again the thing which they have stolen," & c.

[301]

An Experiment to Hide Treasure under the Earth or to Leave Clothes or Any Other Thing Forth of Doors All Night[1409]

"O holy Benedicatis,[1410] the Father, the Son, and the Holy [Spirit] with us 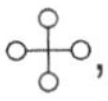, in nomine Patris, et Filii, et Spiritus Sancti, 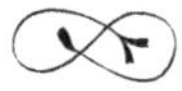 apostles, martyrs, virgins, of houses + I bequeath this place round about me, and all my goods within and without, to the Holy Trinity, that is, one God in persons three ✡, and to St. John the Evangelist, that went upon the earth with Christ , that no thief away it take,  but keep it me, John, for Marcus's sake , and that through the virtue of the passion in manhood 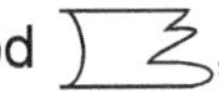, and that through the virtue in form of bread , I charge you, planets seven and you twelve signs clire,[1411] both ☉ and ☽, I charge you all to keep them still here, that they pass no foot away, till they have compled[1412] every stone in the earth, and every drop of water in the sea. I pray to God that it so be, and that you bind him or them also, hand and feet, and as St. Bartholomew did the devil with one hair of his beard, thieves, thieves, thieves, stand you here still, per the virtue of the Trinity, and per the virtue

[302]

"of the passion of Christ Jesus, per his death and his resurrection, till tomorrow I come hither and speak with you in any manner. I charge you that it so be, per the virtue of the Trinity. That lord of might is most, the Father, the Son, and the Holy Ghost. Box, box, box, a Maria, day, day, day, a Sarpelkhe."[1413]
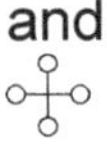

[On a Night-Spell][1414]

Also, a charm or incantation must be said at night or against night about the place, house, or field, or about beasts without in fields or meadows. (That charm is a night-spell.)

1409. Clothes were some of the most commonly stolen items at this time. Lemire, "The Theft of Clothes and Popular Consumerism in Early Modern England."

1410. *Benedicatis*: "You all may bless."

1411. *Clire*: Clear?

1412. *Compled*: Accomplished. Probably an error for "counted."

1413. *Box...Sarpelkhe*: Probably references to prayers, as indicated by the "a Maria" in the middle.

1414. *Night-Spell*: A spell for protection during the night.

A Bond to Bind Thieves That Have or Would Have Robbed Any Man of His Money or Goods to Cause Them Come Again, Bringing the Goods to the Right Owner, or Else to Be Taken with the Robbery

"Jesus Christ was bound, St. Peter was bound, St. Andrew was bound per the hands of men and counsel of devils, and like as I do believe the bonds of Jesus Christ. St. Peter, St. Andrew, alike, I bind you thieves not to move or store before I be satisfied, per the virtue, power, might, and strength of the holy Trinity, with the Father, Son, and Holy Ghost. Amen."

[303]

To Excommunicate a Spirit for No Appearance

"O thou obstinate and rebellious spirit, which hast been often and lawfully called and cited here to appear before us at this circle, and as yet thou hast neither appeared nor come, we pronounce thee and curse thee, and the contempt of our Lord and thine, Jesus Christ, which hath created thee and me, and now for that curse we, per the authority of the said Jesus Christ, in his behalf given and committed to us, in the scriptures bear us, in so much that thou shalt be excommunicate and accursed, despised, and from your office put down into the most strongest and bitter pains of hell and hottest fire, and hottest sulphur, where thou shalt be permanent, tormented, and burned, until such time as you shall be obedient unto your precepts and fulfil our desires. And now, per the licence of God, and per the authority of the same, we pronounce, approve, and affirm, and confirm all the foresaid pains to increase and burn, that thou shalt never have rest, liberty, hope of forgiveness in the judgment, so that your pains may not be released, but increased and multiplied upon you from day to day, from hour to hour, from time to time, from moment to moment, from pain to pains,

[304]

"and ever there to abide, and from the sight of God to be expulsed and put out, unto the time that you shall be obedient unto my will, and perfectly and truly to fulfil the same. Fiat, fiat, fiat."[1415]

"Provided always, so far as you shall appear at my next citing and commandment before me and my fellows visibly and quickly at your next calling, as we cite you to do under the pain of condemnation before rehearsed, that then

1415. The text indicates a line break here, although the text does not seem to require it.

this conjuration to be void and of none effect, and if you do not then to stand in full strength, power, and virtue."

A General Curse Following for All Spirits Both for Stone and Circle[1416]

Make a circle on the earth in the hour of ♃, and enter into it in the hour of ♀,[1417] and make a fire of dry cow turds, brimstone,[1418] or of such like stinking things, and write the spirits' names in virgin parchment. Then burn it,[1419] saying the curse following, but first conjure the fire as followeth:

"I conjure thee, thou creature of God, fire, per him which commanded and all things were done, and per the living God, per the true God, and per the holy God, per him which made the fire and elements

[305]

"with his words, per him which appeared to Moses in the fiery bush, and per him whom led the people and children of Israel in a fiery pillar through the wilderness, and per him which shall come to judge the world with fire and brimstone, that thou, which art made of fire and brimstone, do make hot this disobedient person[1420] N.,[1421] till he come unto me and shew himself obedient in all things as I command him. Fiat, fiat, fiat.

"O heavenly + God + the author of all virtue and the invisible king of glory, most strong and mighty captain of the strong triumphant army of holy angels, of God of all gods and lord of hosts, which holdest in thy hands all the corners of the earth, which with the breath of thy mouth makest all the world to shake and tremble, which makest thy angels lightnings and holy ministers flaming fires,[1422] vouchsafe, I beseech thee, to send thy holy angels into this fire to torment and persecute this disobedient person, and to overcome him as Michael the archangel did overcome Lucifer, the prince of darkness, till he come to me and obey me. Fiat, fiat, fiat.[1423]

1416. For other examples, see BL Additional MS. 36,674, 77v–78r; National Library of Scotland GD 188/25/1/3, 129–33. Additional 36,674 also lists the "glasse" as a place where it is applicable. Another version, aimed at the spirit Oberion, appears in Raphael and Anglicus, *The Astrologer of the Nineteenth Century*, 224–25.

1417. ♀: Additional 36,674 has ☿. Raphael omits all timing instructions.

1418. *Brimstone*: Burning sulphur is not merely stinking but toxic, and it should generally be avoided.

1419. Raphael states that the parchment should be burned thrice.

1420. *Person*: Additional 36,674 and Raphael have "spirit."

1421. *This…N.*: Additional 36,674 underlines this passage and indicates in a marginal note that this is when the parchment is cast into the fire. Raphael replaces "N." with "Oberion."

1422. *Which makest…fires*: Psalm 104:4. This does not match any known translation.

1423. Raphael's version leaves off here, picking up with "O thou puissant prince" below.

"The mighty God, the eternal God, O Lord hath spoken and called the world, from the rising

[306]

"of the ⊙ of the going down thereof.

"Out of Sion hath God appeared in perfect beauty. Our God shall come and not keep silence; there shall go before him a consuming fire, and a mighty tempest shall be stirred round about him.

"God shall call the heathen from above, and the earth, that he may judge his people.

"Gather my saints together, those which have made a covenant with me with sacrifice, and the heavens shall declare his righteousness, for God is judge himself.

"Hear, O thou spirit, and God will speak; he himself will testify against thee, for he is God, even our God.[1424]

"Plead thou my cause, O Lord, with them that fight against me, and strive thou against them that strive with me.[1425]

"Let them be confounded and put to shame that disobey thy name.

"Let them be turned backward and put to confusion that imagine mischief against thee.

"Let them be as the dust, and the angel of the Lord scattering them.

"Let his way be dark and slippery, and the Lord scattering them.[1426]

[307]

"Let a sudden destruction upon them unawares, that he may fall into his own mischief.

"The Lord shall laugh him to scorn, for he hath seen that his day is coming.[1427]

"O God, most mighty and most gracious Lord, which, per thy first judgment, hast cursed the serpent in paradise for alluring man to disobey your commandment,

1424. *The mighty God...our God*: Psalm 50:1–7. This does not precisely follow any translation I have seen, and neither do the items that follow

1425. *Plead...me*: Psalm 35:1.

1426. *Let them be confounded...scattering them*: Psalm 35:4–6.

1427. *The Lord...coming*: Psalm 37:15.

vouchsafe, I beseech thee, to command, condemn, and curse this disobedient person N., which doth contemn and disobey thy most holy and blessed name. Amen. Fiat, fiat, fiat.

"O thou puissant Prince Rodomantus[1428] which punisheth, [in thy prison][1429] of thy perpetual perplexity, the disobedient devils of Hell, and also the ghostly ghosts of men dying in dreadful despair, I conjure, bind, and charge thee, per Lucifer, Belzabub, Sathanas, Tantanill,[1430] and per their power, and per the homage that thou owest unto them. And also I charge thee per the triple crown of Cerberus's head, per Styx and Phlegethon, per your fellow and principal devil Haranber,[1431] that you do torment and punish this disobedient person, till you make him come corporally to my sight, and obey

[308]

"my will in whatsoever I shall command him. Fiat, fiat, fiat.[1432]

"O thou most disobedient spirit N., I condemn thee, per the power and virtue of the three dreadful and mighty names of God, + Agla, + On, + Tetragamaton, + into the hands of these princes Lucifer, Belzabub, Sathanas, Tantanill, to be tormented in the bottomless pit of Hell for thy stubbornness and wilfulness. And furthermore, as Jesus Christ cast out devils per the divine power of his godhead, so, per the power of Christ Jesus, cast I thee into the pit of fire of brimstone, there to be tormented until the latter day, except thou be obedient to fulfil my desire in all that I have or shall demand of thee, without any deceit, falsehood, or delay, in nomine Patris, et Filii, et Spiritus Sancti. Amen."

Note that there is no plague so great as to burn the spirit's name and character, most especially if he be of the aery.[1433]

1428. *Rodomantus*: Rhadamanthus, a just man in Greek myth who was appointed one of the three judges of the Underworld after his death.

1429. *[In thy prison]*: Added from Additional 36,674 for context.

1430. *Tantanill*: Additional 36,674 has "Tancanill." Raphael has "Tamanill."

1431. *Haranber*: Additional 36,674 has "Baranter." Raphae has "Barantos."

1432. Raphael's version ends here.

1433. *Note that…aery*: This section is not in Additional 36,674.

A Conjuration for the Light to Be Used in Any Work, That Is Practised in All Cases

[309]

"I conjure thee, light, and you angels of the light, per him which said, 'Fiat lux,'[1434] and which may ☉ and ☽, stars, fire, water, and all things else in heaven most bright, per shining, per the clear light, per the holy light, per the blessed light, per Mary, mother of our Lord Jesus Christ, per that light ever shining, per that which we are saved and delivered, that thou forthwith wax most clean for the sight of N., so that the sight of him be not hindered, so that he or we may see and hear these spirits perfectly in this stone. Also I conjure you, winds and air, per the same Jesus + Christ which, with his blessings and virtue, did stay and qualify you, so that he might walk upon the sea, and per that virtue which he gave to Peter the Apostle in coming to him, that forthwith you clear and be quiet without clouding, blustering, or blowing, until such time as we have done this work, which we have begun, so that, per you, we be not hindered in the sight and hearing of these creatures of God, N., per the blessing of God omnipotent Father, and of the Son, and Holy Ghost, whose virtue and power descend upon us most vile wretches, and the power of God, the health, virtue, clemency, body, and blood of our saviour Jesus Christ, be our

[309bis]

"help to bring the spirits to subjection to us, being per grace of servants of God. Amen."

In all thy operations that thou takest in hand per writings, it is good not to leave out this consecration aforegoing, so shall thy work prosper before God and men. Therefore be sure that everything have his right ceremony that thou workest withal.

Here Follow the Names of Certain Spirits as They Serve in Their Aptest Operation, as Hath Been Proved

Showers[1435]

Andromaleus
Somar alias Senior

1434. *Fiat lux*: Genesis 1:3 (KJV). Translation: "Let there be light."

1435. *Showers*: Presumably, one who shows the magician what is desired in a crystal or elsewhere.

Seer ☿
Schor
Abecze
Othey
Vasago
Obelison } ♃
Vasagon }
Ancor
Anacor
Anatos
Salmon
Maherion
Asterothe
Sibilla

For Theft and to Bring Them Again

Raguell } ☽
Uriel }

Pro Amore[1436]

Phanum Regni
Miclial

Almazin } ♀
Elicona }

Titan } ancilla[1437]
Burfax }

Temporis Nota ad Operandum[1438]

Cyprian saith that after October, you may not work until March. Also you must work in some months in even days, and some odd, as in:

March	Even
April	Common
May	Even
June	Even
July	Even
October	Even

1436. Translation: "For Love."

1437. *Ancilla*: Translation: "Handmaid."

1438. Translation: "Memoranda on the Time for Working." See National Library of Scotland GD 188/25/1/3, 126.

August	Common
September	Odd

Also, you must work in a chamber or garden, which must be four square, with a cubit on every side high. It also must be twenty-four foot of length, and twenty foot broad.[1439]

[310]

[More Names of Spirits]

Call them die et hora ♃, ☽ crescente, ante meridiem.[1440]

Anazell
Aziell
Anthima
Absull
Azaell
Tezin
Calizabin

Aosall: call him per day in hora ♄,[1441] or any other hour.

Azaell, the ruler of the dead: call him per night in hora ☉. Require one under him to serve, and if he say no, be not eager. Let him go, and call him another night.

The place being aptly prepared, as some close chamber having four windows to the four parts of the world, and that time with all other instruments in apt order, as is shewn in this book, thou mayest call the four kings or any other carrier after this manner:

1 } Oriens	Orien[ti]s rex
2 } Paymon	Occidental[is] rex
3 } Amaymon	Australis rex
4 } Egin	Septentrionalis rex[1442]

1439. For similar instructions, see Wellcome 110, 2r; Harms, Clark, and Peterson, *Oberon*, 294–95.

1440. *Die...meridiem*: Translation: "in the day and hour of Jupiter, with the moon waxing, before noon."

1441. Compare Additional MS. 36674, 50r.

1442. *Orien[ti]s...rex*: Translation: "King of the East / King of the West / King of the South / King of the North."

The Circle

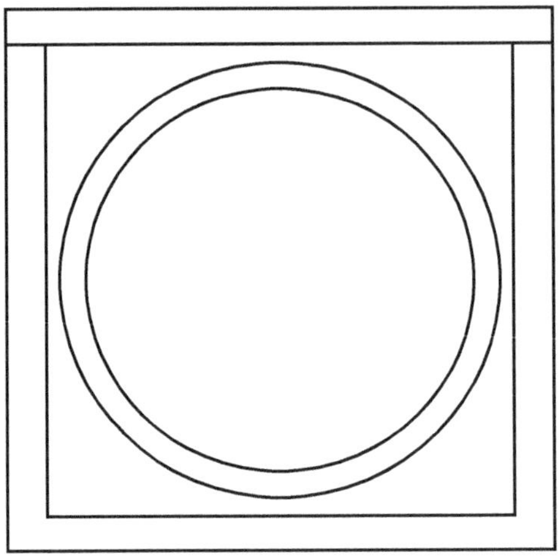

[311]

The ninety-first psalm must be written about the round circle, unto the eleventh verse, and about the quadrant this: "Jesus autem transiens per medium illorum ibat in pace."[1443]

 + And these great names of God which follow on this manner: "+ Messias, + Sother, + Emanuell, + Sabaoth, + Adonay, + Est, + Unigenitas, + Via, + Veritas, + Manus, + Homo, + Usion, + Jesus, + Christus, + Agla, + Agios, + Otheos, + Iskyros, + Athanatos, + Elizon, + Yinas, + Fons, + Origo, + Bonus, + Paraclitus, + Rex, + Sacerdos, + Mons, + Petra, + Sponsus, + Lapis, + Propheta, + *Anies* [Aries], + Serpens, + Leo, + Virmis, + Jesus, + Salvator, + Mediator, + Consolator, +. Christus, + regnat, + Christus imperat, + Christus in pace nos benedicat, + Jesus autem transiens, + per mediam illorum, ibat in pace.[1444] Amen."

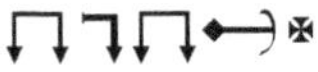

1443. *Jesus...pace*: Luke 4:30. Translation (KJV): "But Jesus, passing through the midst of them went his way in peace."

1444. *Christus...pace*: Translation: "Christ + reigns, + Christ commands, + May Christ bless us in peace, + But Jesus passing, + among them went his way in peace."

Experimentum Nobile Fili[ci]s Anglicum;[1445] Fern on Saint John Baptist's Even[1446]

In pridie sancti John Baptiste, inter horas undecimem et 12 annum nocte, vade ad locum ubi felix crescit.[1447] And lay a sheet double per it, and on the sheet, set a clean basin, saying a Pater Noster,

[312]

Ave Maria, and a Credo. Turning you towards the east, kneeling, make your prayer to God that the seed of fern may keep all his virtues. Then take three or four stalks as you can hold them conveniently all together, and cut them off in the stalk, cast them into the basin. If you bear off the seed aforesaid, put in virgin parchment. It hath these properties: he or she shall not fall into sudden sickness; they shall overcome all their enemies both visible and invisible; they shall not die suddenly; it purchaseth favour of all men; it helps women in their travail; it is forceable against enchantments of any one; the guilty man or woman shall not be accused of any crime; truth shall not be known to death; it profits one bearing it in virgin parchment, being in danger per in a ship, & c.

Benedictio Chartae[1448]

"Coniuro te + charta + per verba illa tituli triumphalis salvatoris Domini nostri Jesu Christi, et per omnia alia verba quae dicuntur de creatore omnium *creaturem* [creaturarum], et per illum qui potest tribuere et facere quod tantam obtineas virtutem, ut omnia quae supra te scribentur ad effectum salutis aeternae *predicere* [perducere] valeas et ut omnes

[313]

"fallatia et virtus diaboli exeat de te et intret in te omnis virtus predicta sine mora, in nomine P. et F. et SS. Amen," et aspergatur aqua benedicta.

1445. Translation: "The Famous English Experiment of the Fern."

1446. Finding fern seed on St. John's evening was considered a route to magical powers. For other examples, see British Library Sloane 3850, 155v, 158r; Jackson, *A Treatise Containing the Originall Unbeliefe*, 178–79; K[innaston], *Leolinas and Sydanis*, 119; Bovet, *Pandaemonium*, 217–18.

1447. *In pridie…crescit*: Translation: "On the day before that of Saint John the Baptist, between the hours of eleven and twelve of the night, go to a place where the fern grows."

1448. Translation: "Blessing of the Paper." Either paper or parchment might be appropriate here. A longer version of this charm appears in a popular Latin collection of blessings supposedly compiled by the Czech theologian Bernard Sannig. Sannig, *Collectio Benedictionum*, 257–59.

"I conjure thee + paper + by those words of the triumphal inscription of our Lord Saviour Jesus Christ, and by all other words that were said of the creator of all things created, and by him that was able to bestow and to make, that thou may maintain so much virtue, that all things written on you may have power to deliver for the production of lasting health, and so that all [313] tricks and virtue of the devil may depart from thee, and all the aforesaid virtue may enter thee without delay, in the name of the Father, and of the Son, and of the Holy Ghost. Amen." And it is sprinkled with holy water.

This Most Holy Ligatum[1449] Following Shall Be Said Now or Before the Exorcism of the Fire Casting Out Devils and All Evil Spirits from Men, Women, Children, or Beasts

Y et V	הוהי	
Jah	Zabaoth	Saday
Saraye	Adonay	El
Eloy	Elohim	Elion
Agla	On	Anephexeton
Oriston	Aye	Cepher Raziell[1450]
Usion,	Archyma	Cepher Saday
Elos	Rabur	Asseres
Elohe	Egyrion	Firmamentum
Elyson	Synagion	Pumaton
Ioth	Otheos	Than
Sabaoth	Iskyros	Meloch
Anepheneton	Athanatos	Semilech
Primeumaton	Paracletus	Debeth
Panton	Dominus	Basson
Craton	Deus	Hoth
Sedekin	Excelsus	Sothe
Verdon	Jesus	Othe
Cados	Christus	Jana
Helioren	Messias	Yne
Yaleselem	Sother	Ysus
	Hell	
	Suranet	

1449. *Ligatum*: Binding.

1450. *Cepher Raziell*: The book of magic, here transformed into a magical phrase.

[314a]

Eloy	Emanuell	Zeboroth	Hatim
Eloym	Salvator	Pangraton	Contine
Elee	Sapientia	Pantateron	Mary
Ysistron	Veritas	Algramay	Nota
Shemhamephares	Consolator	Stimulamaton	Abim
Tetragramaton	Ymas	Rex	Jesta
Heremon	Dignator	Regum	Hy
Anobona	Orator	Hu	Fa
Artheuie	Tusi	He	Ya
Pangraton	Pucer	Sa	Ey
Eserehie	Medicina	Ve	Haa
Abraye	Baldachie	Asamie	Eye
Pantheon	Elibra	Asaraie	Exe
	Lux		
Meffaton	Ima	Jaym	A
Arbytros	Theon	Janie	Hau
Yegeron	Eloim	Amie	Va
Achim	Jen	Oza	An
Esa	Minosel	Agnus	Aie
Eie	Acadan	Vitulus	Mediator
Athana	Vay	Serpens	Verbum
Calbat	Vaa	Aries	Splendor
Salbac	Ay	Leo	Sol
Berifay	Anathay	Vermis	Gloria
Alnayme	Est	Primus	Ymago
Hey	Unigenitus	Novissimus	Patris
Heya	Via	Pater	Panis
Ja	Vita	Filius	Flos
Je	Manus	Spiritus sanctus	Vitis
Acim	Homo	Ego sum qui sum[1451]	Mons
Ina	Principium	Creator	Janua
Saclay	Primogenitus	Aeternas	Petra
Sar	Virtus	Redemptor	Lapis
Atay	Fons	Trinitas	Angelus
Tireip	Origo	Unitas	Sponsus
Azia	Spes	Clemens	Pastor p
		Fides	
Hyn	Charitas	Caput	

1451. *Ego…sum*: "I am that I am."

[314b]

Propheta	Jechell	Elzapharas	Yara
Sacerdos	Sanctus	Occinomos	Fortis
Principium	Immortalis	Elean *	Force
Finis	Arimon	Beth	Av
Mathon	Ajemphaton	Haw	Ve
Apomachon	Yea Saray	Ethen	Solus
Magnus	A et Ω	IHS	That thou come forth out of this man

These Following Are the Seals of the Earth

See page 382

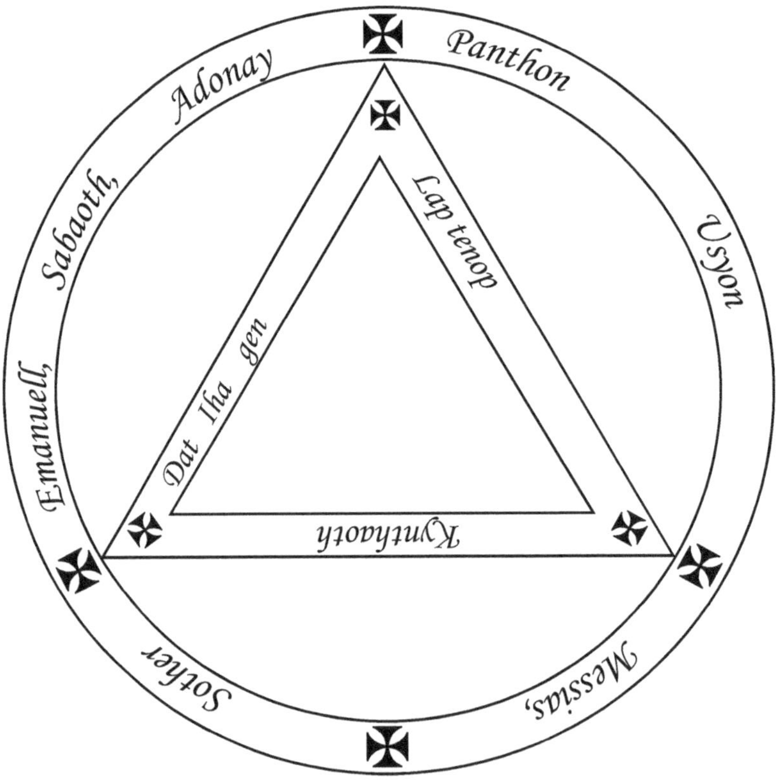

Without that which, no spirit will appear except thou have them with thee.

[315]

See this page 382

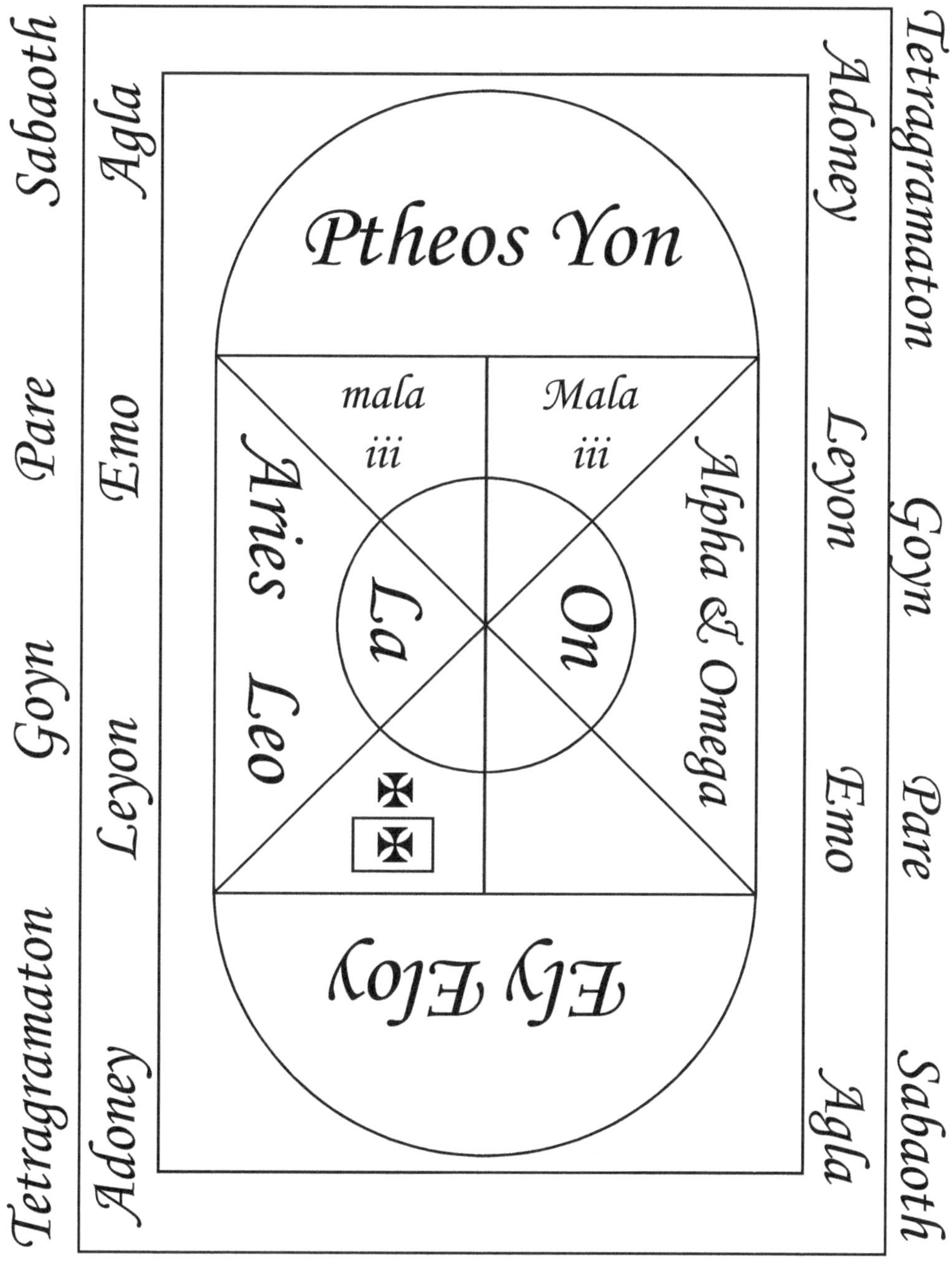

[316]

[A Magical Lamen] [1452]

To fear the spirits thus, thou oughtest to have those figures before thy breast or forehead, else they will not fear thee; howbeit, so soon as they shall see it, they will fear thee, and thou shalt have thy will in all things.

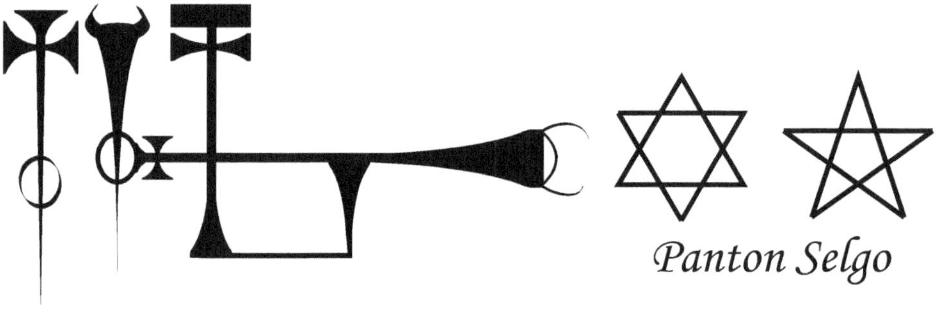

1452. See Scot, *The Discouerie of Witchcraft*, 415; also, manuscript page 216.

[317]

Here Followeth the Names of the Angels of the Planets, and First of ♄[1453]

Your names are written in heaven[1454]

Angelo[rum] de ♄ nomina[1455]

Sachier
Anach
Anefon
Yczeseres
Saym
Finter Ylls

Se aliter vocati sunt.[1456]

Facier
Anach
Anefen
Perczophare
Saym Sutila
Abrathe

Nomina angelorum de ♃[1457] }

Saxages
Lerston
Tryton
Filiops
Renell
Astuodeyt

1453. What follows is a variant on a list of planetary and zodiacal angels from the *Liber imaginum* attributed in other sources to Sebel, Zoel, or Zael. For examples, see Biblioteca Apostolica Vaticana Lat. 4085, 105r; Biblioteca Medicea Laurenziana Plut. 89 sup. 35, 68r; Bibliothèque Nationale de France lat. 7337, 46v–47r; British Library Sloane 3847, 107v–109v.

1454. *Your...heaven*: Luke 10:20 (KJV): "Notwithstanding in this rejoice not, that the spirits are subject unto you; but rather rejoice, because your names are written in heaven."

1455. *Angelo[rum]...nomina*: Translation: "The names of the angels of ♄."

1456. *Se...sunt*: Translation: "They are called in another manner."

1457. *Nomina...♃*: Translation: "The names of the angels of ♃."

Nomina angelorum de ☉[1458]

Alphereon Succundia
aut Succundia
Pleclu Jephin
Maeriall
Daramell
Peutos
Scurdabelen

Nomina angelorum de ♂[1459]

Bellageron
Tobrintec
Theophares
Seeczaburems
Zelydron
Preristorides Purir
Niplicuch

[318]

There are 12 Legions of Angels. See Matthew 26 Chap—53 Verse.[1460]

Nomina angelorum de ♀[1461]

Yenell an Yenell
Appries
Uliach
Drisores Necher
Prebell, Neptalien

Aliter per eadem[1462]

Aperpes
Filiacz
Disows
Nichictur
Pribalva
Paaelaim

1458. *Nomina*...☉: Translation: "The names of the angels of the ☉."

1459. *Nomina*...♂: Translation: "The names of the angels of ♂."

1460. *There are*...*Verse*: KJV: "Thinkest thou that I cannot now pray to my Father, and he shall presently give me more than twelve legions of angels?"

1461. *Nomina*...♀: Translation: "The names of the angels of ♀."

1462. *Aliter per eadem*: Translation: "Another for the same."

Nomina angelorum ☿[1463]
Saluncham
Pargandagt
Chihit, Apantois
Truell, Garilien
Gemasnay

Nomina angelorum de ☽[1464]
Ydreel
Mare, Scorphine
Buffan, Gesgm
Phylosan, Efomeloy
Aat Iderid

Nomina angelorum signorum, in primis de nominibus angelorum signi ♈.[1465]

De signi[1466] ♈

Uriden	Mansletay
Benhiz	Ymaclyon

De signi ♉

Geofriell	Frantiell
Dridenoy	Dirqealy

De signi ♊

Sinchatiriell	Anabroth
Anabrot	Tefeell
Gofrell	Belyaly

[319]

De signi ♋

Tharthyn	Enduyan
Fedrich	Cafasim

De signi ♌[1467]

Belferael	Fatison
Andryn	Gredichiam

1463. *Nomina…*☿: Translation: "Names of the angels of ☿."

1464. *Nomina…*☽: Translation: "The names of the angels of ☽."

1465. *Nomina…*♈: Translation: "The names of the angels of the signs, first, of the names of the angels of the sign ♈."

1466. *De signi*: Translation: "Of [the names of] the sign." The following ten examples are untranslated.

1467. The angels of Virgo are missing.

De signi ♎

Efroy	Sephyron	Siphyan
Drabudyn	Yfrey	
Prohabeen	Syphyron	

De signi ♏

Sentission	Orphuon	Ophiton
Grissolis	Cifucon	

De signi ♐

Tebondrie	Rusibian	Exdromell
Zeroteel	Excromell	

De signi ♑

Gragisneill	Andam
Angoliell	Ruchag'ly

De signi ♒

Flucumagon	Zachayt	Zabugr
Amdeball	Flumicion	Ambelial[?]
Gorchiz	Ambeball	

De signi ♓

Nesteteyll	Angiliell
Angoliell	Sulthomyn
Cedrophyane	Nolycegll
Salteriacon	Codrapan

[320]

Sigillum de ♈ est[1468] 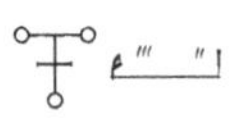

Ditto de ♉ est[1469] 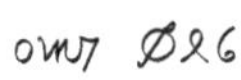

Ditto de ♊ est 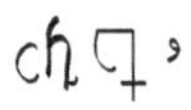

Ditto de ♋ est 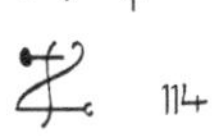

Ditto de ♌ est of 

Ditto de ♍ est 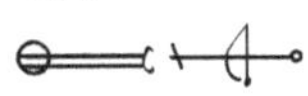

Ditto de ♎ est 

Ditto de ♏ est 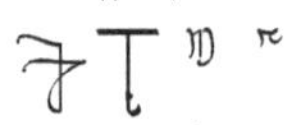

Ditto de ♐ est 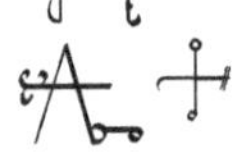

1468. *Sigillum…est*: Translation: "The seal of ♈ is."

1469. *Ditto…est*: Translation: "The seal of ♉ is." The next twelve have been left untranslated.

Ditto de ♑ est 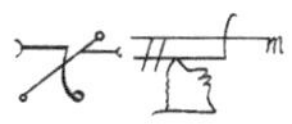

Ditto de ♒ est 

Ditto de ♓ est 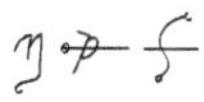

Ditto de ☊ est 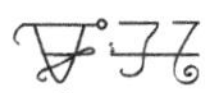

Ditto de ☋ est 

[321]

See page 366, and see page 379

Names of the Angels That Ruleth Different Hours of the Day

Psalm 78 v. 49
Matthew 12 v. 22
Mark 3 v. 15
Luke 11 v. 14-31
Luke 13 v. 16
Acts 19 v. 13, 14, 15
1 Samuel 16 v. 14
9 Judges 25v[1470]

Hora, die[1471]

	Die ☉	Die ☽	Die ♂	Die ☿	Die ♃	Die ♀	Die ♄
1	Michaell	Gabriel	Samael	Raphael	Sachiel	Anael	Cassiel
2	Anaell	Cassiel	Michael	Gabriel	Samael	Raphael	Sachiel
3	Raphaell	Sachiel	Anael	Cassiel	Michael	Gabriel	Samael
4	Gabriell	Samael	Raphael	Sachiel	Anael	Cassiel	Michael
5	Cassiel	Michael	Gabriel	Samael	Raphael	Sachiel	Anael
6	Sachiel	Anael	Cassiel	Michael	Gabriel	Samaiel	Raphael
7	Samael	Raphael	Sachiel	Anael	Cassiel	Michael	Gabriel
8	Michael	Gabriel	Samael	Raphael	Sachiel	Anael	Cassiel
9	Anael	Cassiel	Michael	Gabriel	Samael	Raphael	Sachiel
10	Raphael	Sachiel	Anael	Cassiel	Michael	Gabriel	Samael
11	Gabriel	Samiel	Raphael	Sachiel	Anael	Cassiel	Michael
12	Cassiel	Michael	Gabriel	Samael	Raphael	Sachiel	Anael
	Hora	Hora	Hora	Hora	Hora	Hora	Hora
	noctis	noctis	noctis	noctis	noctis	noctis	noctis

1470. All but the last verse on this list relate to angels and demons.
1471. *Hora, die*: Translation: "In the hour, in the day."

Isaiah 9 v. 6—For unto us a child is born, a son is given; his name shall be called wonderful counsellor, the mighty God, the everlasting Father, the prince of peace. David overcame Goliah in the home [?] of the Lord of Hosts, 1 Samuel 17, 45–49—the Great I Am—Exodus 3. 14

God's name is holy Luke 1. 49, 51–52

[322]

Of Angels, Hebrews 1.7, Colossians 1.15–16, Matthew 4.11, 18.10, Genesis 19.11–13, Judges 13.3–6, Exodus 3.2, Acts 7.30, [Acts] 7.53, Galatians 3.17, 18, 19, Hebrews 2.2, 1 Peter 1.12, Genesis 16.7, 8, John 21.14, 17 to 20, Genesis 18.2 to 16, [Genesis] 19.1, 2 to 26, [Genesis] 24.7, 12, 27, 40, Genesis 31.11, 1 Kings 19.5–6

1	Sachiel	Anael	Cassiel	Michael	Gabriel	Samael	Raphael
2	Samael	Raphael	Sachael	Anael	Cassiel	Michael	Gabriel
3	Michael	Gabriel	Samael	Raphiel	Sachiel	Anael	Cassiel
4	Anael	Cassiel	Michael	Gabriel	Samael	Raphael	Sachiel
5	Raphael	Sachiel	Anael	Cassiel	Michael	Gabriel	Samael
6	Gabriel	Samael	Raphael	Sachiel	Anael	Cassiel	Michael
7	Cassiel	Michael	Gabriel	Samael	Raphiel	Sachiel	Anael
8	Sachiel	Anael	Cassiel	Michael	Gabriel	Samael	Raphael
9	Samael	Raphael	Sachiel	Anael	Cassiel	Michael	Gabriel
10	Michael	Gabriel	Samael	Raphael	Sachiel	Anael	Cassiel
11	Anael	Cassiel	Michael	Gabriel	Samael	Raphael	Sachiel
12	Raphael	Sachiel	Anael	Cassiel	Michael	Gabriel	Samael

[323]

De Spiritu Merezium[1472]

Cause a ring of gold or silver to be made in horam ☿ Christo regnante in sua domo,[1473] and, in the sealing place, grave in good deep letters the spirit's name, which done, fill the letters with dragon's blood, so it may be well read. Then take a clean crystal which is fair and white, and put over the name

1472. Translation: "Of the Spirit Merezium." A spirit called "Merizim" is mentioned in the Janus Magica Reserata as "a South Demon...a Prince of the power of the air and the spirit which works in the Children of Disobedience." Skinner and Rankine, *The Keys to the Gateway of Magic*, 115.

1473. *In horam...domo*: Translation: "in the hour of ☿, with the same ruling in its house."

aforesaid, like as ye set a stone in a ring; see that you may read the name through it. This done, wash it clean with rose water oftentimes. After that, in hora ☿ in loco solataria et ameno,[1474] put the ring upon thy middle finger, and holding up thy hand, say:

"Omnipotens sempiterne Deus, qui sedes gloriosus in majestate tua, et cui nihil impossibile est nec latet, cui revelata est scientia omnium arcanorum, et solus es inspirator omnis mirabilitate, per tuam immensam pietatem, misericordiam, et clementiam, mittere digneris ad me, licet miserum peccatorum, et in te confidentem et [324] penitentem, de exercitu sancte magnitudine tue, istum angelum tuum Merizium mihi de omnibus responsuram veraciter quacunque die vel hora voluero, sine de nocte, sine de die, ut tuo mandato mediante; ut sequatur, et benigne consulta in necessitatibus et desideriis meis, gloriosissime Adonay, [in po]tentiam tuam, nec statuas mihi hoc ad peccatum, sed solum propter."

> "All-powerful, eternal God, thou who sittest glorious in your majesty, and to whom nothing is impossible or hidden, to whom was revealed knowledge of all secrets, and thou alone art inspirer of all marvels, by thy great goodness, mercy, and clemency, deign to send to me, one valued as a wretched one of sins, both confiding in thee and [324] penitent, thy angel Merizium of the army of your thy greatness, to me, for all of his responses truly, in whatsoever day or hour I desire, whether of day or night, as by your mediating command, so it should follow, and with advising kindly in my necessities and wishes, most glorious Adonay, in your power, and do not ordain me for sin by this, but only nearby."[1475]

Say this three times. After, take off the ring and bless it, saying, "In nomine Patris et Filii et Spiritus Sancti. Amen." Then say:

"Veni, angele sancte ac scientissime prudentissimeque, et mihi adesto, minister dei, Merizium, potens in scientiis largiendis, et occultis revelandis. Ecce creator vel formator seculi. Per spiritum sanctum vos vocat. Amor dei te conjugat, sua *potentiatem* [potentiam] derigat, et sua misericordiam *te* [et?] comitem benignem custodiat. Veni igitur in nomine illius vivi et veri dei, qui vos et me verbo creavit, cujus nomina sunt tremendissimam quae sunt, Gelon,

1474. *In hora…ameno*: Translation: "in the hour of ☿ in a solitary and agreeable place."

1475. *And do not ordain…nearby*: Conjectural. This seems to be missing a conclusion.

Hora, Ymeym, Leton, Anepheton, Cados, Saday, Sother, Emanuell, Occynomeno. Veni per sanctam sedem Samay, et per gloriam paradisie, et per obedientiam

[325]

"quam *h[ab]etis* [habes] ad deum, per vivam eternitatem, sapientiam, et humilitatem. Veni patiens et placaturus. Veni per illum qui omnia creavit et vos, et omnes stellas regit, et ad hoc te conjuro per omnia predicta, et omnia mirabilia, caelestia et terrestria, et per illum qui te constituit ministrum suum, et mercurium illum planetam instrumentum ad omnia occulta revelanda, et scientias omnes auspiciendas, et per istum annulum quem hic ad honorem tuum fabricatum teneo, et per omnia quibus te allicere possum, omnia que interogavero: per deum qui venturus est judicare vivos et mortuos, et seculum per ignem. Amen."

> "Come, holy, most knowledgeable, and most skilled angel, and be present to me, attendant of God Merizium, powerful in bountiful sciences and revealings of secrets. Behold the creator or fashioner of the world. He calls you all[1476] by the Holy Ghost. The love of God joins you, he guides his power, and he guards his mercy and kind compassion. Therefore come in the name of the living and true God, who made you and I with a word, the names of whom are greatest, which are Gelon, Hora, Ymeym, Leton, Anepheton, Cados, Saday, Sother, Emanuell, Occynomeno. Come by the holy seat Samay, and by the glory of paradise, and by the obedience [325] to God that you possess, by eternal life, wisdom, and humility. Come, suffering and ready to appease; come by him who created all things and you all, and who rules all the stars, and I conjure thee for this by all things aforesaid, and by all celestial and terrestrial marvels, and by him who appointed his attendant, and Mercury, the planet and instrument for all revealed occult things and all revealed sciences, and by this ring that I hold here, made to thy honour, and by all things with which I am able to attract thee and all things that I will have asked, by God who will come to judge the living and the dead, and the world by fire. Amen."

When any spirit appeareth, say:

1476. *You all*: The incantation shifts from singular to plural person multiple times. The Latin verb "veni" just before and used throughout is in the singular.

"I conjure thee, spirit N., thou that art appeared to me here, per almighty God and per all his virtue, might, and strength, and per the virtue which he hath in heaven, in the earth, the sea, and under the earth,

[326]

"and per the high name of God, Agla, that thou be ever obedient unto me, and serve me, and obey me, saying ever to me the truth in all things that I shall ask thee. I conjure thee per the dreadful day of doom, that thou make no lies to me, nor false imaginations, or use any false wiles, but ever tell the truth, and give it in true answer of all that I shall enquire of thee. Item[1477] I conjure thee per the holy name of God Neupmaton, that Moses named when the earth swallowed Dathan and Abiron. Right so, in the said name, I conjure and command thee to speak unto me, meekly, lowly, gently, and openly in a man's voice, and say the truth I shall ask thee. Fiat, fiat, fiat. Amen.

"And if thou withstand my will and commandment in word or deed, per day or night, here or elsewhere, now or any time hereafter, I condemn thee, N., per all the might of God, of our lady St. Mary,

[327]

"and of all the company in and of heaven, per the pain of death and passion that our Lord Jesus Christ suffered, and per all the virtue of his blessed flesh and blood, and per the virtue of all the holy names that heretofore I have named in this book and read, and per all the holy names constrained in this book. I command and bind thee into the deepest pit of Hell, there to remain till the day of doom, except thou give me anon a grant of my asking in all things that thou may do."

And when he granteth thee, thus shalt thou swear and bind him, and let him say after thee:

"I swear per God, per the holy virgin Mary, mother of almighty God, and per all the company of heaven, that I will be ready to thee per day and night, to say and to do truly, without leasing,[1478] fraud, or guile, all that I can or may, that without circle, characters, or conjuration, when thou wilt call me, and not before thou call per me, neither per day nor per night. Fiat. fiat. fiat."

1477. *Item*: Also.

1478. *Leasing*: Lying.

[328]

Ad Invocandum Spiritum Secrete in Camera[1479]

Inprimis vade ad locum secretum ubi area fuerit dura, *itage* [itaque] littera scripta in ea possit apparere, et flexis genibus contra orientem dicas:

> First go to a secret place where the ground is hard, so that the sign can appear written on it, and on bent knees, say toward the east:

"Dirige, domine deus meus, actus meos in beneplacito tuo, et viam iniquitatis amove a me, et de lige tua miserere mei."

> "O Lord my God, guide my acts in thy pleasure, and remove the way of iniquity from me, and have mercy on me regarding your law."[1480]

Postea accipe cultellum novum, cujus manubrium sit *corum* [cornu] albo, et in eo sit scriptum cum sanguine tuo haec tria nomina, Agla, Sabaoth, Adonay. Deinde cum cultello, "Facio in nomina dei Patris omnipotentis, qui solo verbo cuncta creasti ex nihilo."

> Afterward take a new knife, the handle of which should be of white horn, and on it should be written, in your blood, these three names, "Agla, Sabaoth, Adonay." Then, with the knife, [make a circle, saying,] "I make this in the name of Almighty God the Father, who created all things out of nothing with a word."

Deinde fac circulum aliud, infra illud dicens:

> Then make another circle, saying after that:

"Hoc circulum facio in nomine Filii dei unigeniti qui humanum genus pretiosissime sanguine redemit."

> "I make this circle in the name of God the only-begotten son, who redeemed the human race with his most precious blood."

Deinde fac tertium circulum in medio, dicens:

> Then make a third circle in the middle, saying:

"Hoc circulum facio in nomine paracleti qui coram apostolorum et prophetarum invisibli pertransivit potentil."

1479. Translation: "For Invoking a Spirit Secretly in a Chamber."

1480. Compare to Harms, Clark, and Peterson, *Oberon*, 512.

"I make this circle in the name of the Holy Ghost, who passed before the eyes of the apostles and prophets with invisible power."

Et tunc scribe omnia prout in curculo sequenti palet. Deinde duc socios tuos tecum in bona pace, ad illum locum et claude ostium ultimum post illos, dicens et scribens cum sanguine tuo, "Tamen, Depon,

[329]

"Deyron,"

And then write all things as shown in the following circle. Then lead your companions with you in good peace to that place, and close the last door after them, saying and writing with your blood, "Tamen, Depon, [329] Deyron."

Et tunc intra circulum et dic:

And then enter the circle, and say:

"Conjuro te, Androges, per fidem quam habes vel debes demoni tuo privato, et per virtutem dei vivi puri et misericordissimi, et si hoc sit verum quod Maria fuit vergo in partu, ante partum, et post partum; et si hoc sit verum quod hostia de pane vertitur in verum corpus Domini nostri Jesu Christi, et vinum et aqua in sanguinem, statim venias hac sine lesione corporis et anime mee, et alicujus alterius in toto mundo, et qui tibi iussero, festinanter facies."

"I conjure thee, Androges, by the faith that you have or owe to your personal demon, and by the virtue of the living, pure, and most merciful God, that if it may be true that Mary was a virgin during birth, before birth, and after birth, and if it may be true that the Host of bread is turned into the true body of our Lord Jesus Christ, and wine and water into blood, thou shouldst come immediately without injury of my body or soul, or any other person in all the world, and that what I will have ordered thee, thou wilt do quickly."

Et quando feceris tuum negotium, secundum tuum, desiderium licentia eum hoc modo:

And when you will have finished your business, according to your will, license him in this manner:

"Conjuro te, Androges, per fidem quam debes vel habes domino tuo privato, & c., ut recedas de isto loco, sine nocimento corporis mei et anime mee, vel alicujus in toto mundo, et cum alias te invocavero, statim mihi prompter sis, et mandatis meis sine dilacione aliqua."

> "I conjure thee, Androges, by the faith that you owe or have for your personal lord, & c., that you should depart from this place, without injury of my body and blood, or of anyone in all the world, and when I will have invoked thee another time, thou mayst be manifest to me immediately and to my commands without any delay."

[Times for Working]

Martio	Julio	Luna pari[1481]
Mayo et	Octobre	}

[330]

Ad Operandi Bonum[1482]

Junio	Luna impari
Septembre	
Aprili	Luna pari
Augusto	vel impari[1483]

Dies Prohibiti[1484]

January	2, 4, 6, 9
February	9, 15, 20
March	4, 6, 8, 12
April	2, 3
May	2, 3
June	2, 3
July	12, 17
August	9, 20, 28
September	12, 17
December	4, 11, 12

1481. *Martio...pari*: Translation: "March / May / and / July / October / with the moon even."

1482. Translation: "Good for Working."

1483. *Junio...impari*: Translation: "June / September /with the moon odd / April / August / with the moon even or odd."

1484. Translation: "Forbidden Days."

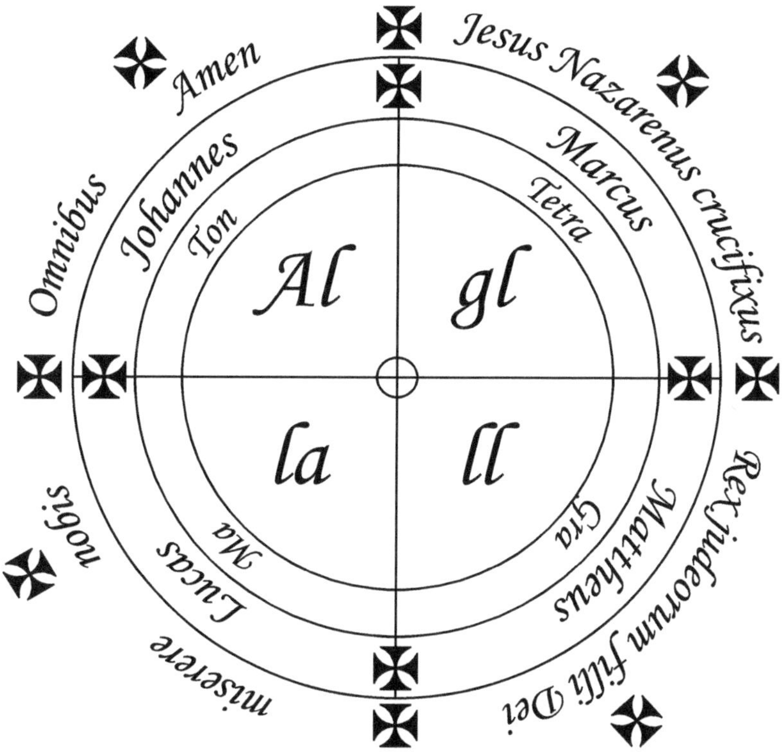

Ad Habendum Vera Responsa de Omnibus Questionibus[1485]

Primo, antequam hoc facias, debes esse vere penitens et confessus, et in prima die *jemma* [jejuna] in pane et aqua. Postea

[331]

in die Mercurii, fero in hora ☿, intrendum dormitum *solis* [solus] sis in camera tua, et ardeat lucerne, et stando, dic ista verba.

> First, before you do this, you should be truly penitent and confessed, and on the first day, fast on bread and water. Afterward, [331] on Wednesday, in the hour of ☿, you should be going to sleep alone in your room, and a lamp should burn, and standing, say these words:

"Sanctus, sanctus, sanctus, [dominus] noster Jesus Christus, in die ☿ fuit perditus heu traditus. Sanctus, sanctus, sanctus, dominus noster Jesus Christus, in die Jovis fuit captus, temptatus, et flagellatus. Sanctus, sanctus, sanctus, [dominus] noster Jesus Christus in die ♀ fuit suspensus, flagellatus,

1485. Translation: "For Having a True Response to All Your Questions." See manuscript page 169.

et sepultus. Sanctus, sanctus, sanctus, deus cum sanctis tuis, mitte mihi nuncium qui dabit mihi vera responsa de quibuscunque eum interogabo."

> "Holy, holy, holy, our Lord Jesus Christ, on Wednesday was lost, alas!, and handed over. Holy, holy, holy, our Lord Jesus Christ, on Thursday was seized, tested, and whipped. Holy, holy, holy, our Lord Jesus Christ, on Friday was suspended, whipped, and buried. Holy, holy, holy, God with your saints, send me a messenger who will give me true responses on whatsoever I will ask."

Hec verba dic tribus vicibus, et postea vade dormitum ad lectum tuum, et cito post vigilia invenies hominem barbatum in specie hominis senis: et primo interoga nomen ejus diligenter, et postea quere de omnibus que volueris scire.

> Say these words three times, and afterward go to sleep in your bed, and immediately after wakefulness you will find a bearded man in the form of an old man, and first ask his name assiduously, and afterward ask him regarding all things that you may desire to know.

For One That Is Bewitched[1486]

Say three or four times together these words:

> "Canke, Cole, Oarth, Abiron, Onagla, Letera, Gramato."

Let a piece of linen cloth be deeped[1487] in his urine every morning, which he hath worn about him, and then cast it into the fire, saying these words aforesaid as it burneth. Probatum est.

1486. This rite, using a bodily excretion of the afflicted person to affect a witch, is similar in principle to a witch bottle.

1487. *Deeped*: Immersed.

[332]

The Figure of a Circle for the First Hour of the Lord's Day in Springtime[1488]

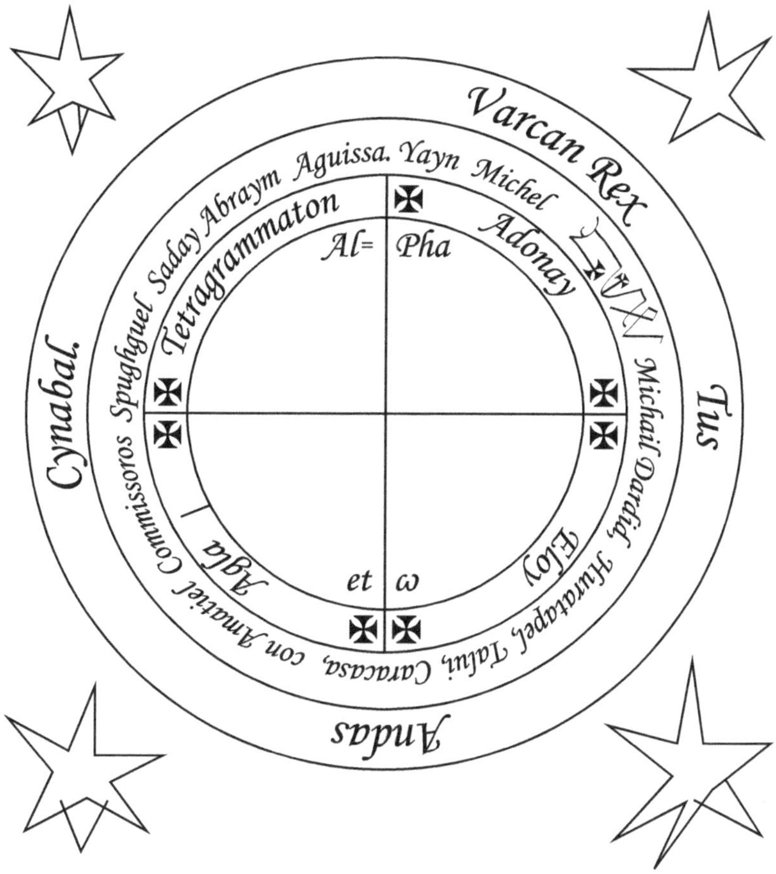

The antient Magi called the Sun Mithra. This was the name also by which Zoroaster worshiped his glorious and wondrous orb.

On, hail him as lord of the whole Creation.

NB. From this to page 365 is taken from the *4th Book,* Cornelius Agrippa. The orations here are translated into English }

1488. The material for the next several pages derives from the *Heptameron*, specifically Turner's translation in the 1665 edition of psudo-Agrippa's *Fourth Book*, 87–106.

To Explain the Week, First of the Lord's Day

Consideration of the Lord's Day

The angel of the Lord's day, his sigil, planet, sign of the planet, and the name of the fourth heaven.

☉♌

Michael

Machen

[333]

The Angels of the Lord's Day

Michael, Dardiel, Huratapal.[1489]

The Angels of the Air Ruling on the Lord's Day

Varcan, king.

His Ministers

Tus, Andas, Cynabal.

The Wind Which the Angels of the Air Abovesaid Are Under

The north wind.

The Angel of the Fourth Heaven Ruling on the Lord's Day, Which Ought to Be Called from the Four Parts of the World[1490]

At the east:

Samael, Gabriel, Baciel, Vionatraba, Atel.[1491]

At the west:

Anael	Pabel	Ustael
Burchat	Suceratos	Capabili.

At the north:

1489. *Huratapal*: This spelling indicates that either Turner's 1655 or 1665 edition of pseudo-Agrippa, *Fourth Book*, was the source of this text.

1490. These mostly follow pseudo-Agrippa, *Fourth Book* (1665), with some reorganization of the order of the names.

1491. *Samael...Atel*: Also in pseudo-Agrippa, *Fourth Book* (1665), but reordered here as if the copyist read each column after the other before deciding to maintain them in subsequent lines.

Aiel Aniel, vel Aquiel,
Sapiel Matuyel Masgabr[i]el.

[334]

At the south.
Haludiel Machasiel Charsiel
Uriel Naromiel

The Perfume of the Lord's Day

Red sanders.[1492]

The Conjuration of the Lord's Day[1493]

"I conjure and confirm upon you, ye strong and holy angels of God, in the name Adonay, Eye, Eye, Eya, which is he who was, and is, and is to come, Eye, Abray; and in the name Saday, Cados, Cados, Cados, sitting on high upon the cherubin; and per the great name of God himself, strong and powerful, who is exalted above all heavens, Eye, Saray, [maker of the world, who created the world, the heaven,][1494] the earth, the sea, and all that is in them[1495] the first day, and sealed them with his holy name Phaa; and per the name of the holy angels who ruleth in the fourth heaven, and serve before the most mighty Salamia, an angel great and honourable, and per the name of his star, which is Sol; and per his sign; and per the immense name of the living God, and per all the names aforesaid,

[335]

"I conjure thee, Michael, O great angel, who art chief ruler of the Lord's day; and per the name Adonay, the God of Israel, who hath created the world, and [all that] therein is, that thou labour per me, and fulfil all my petitions, according to my will and desire, in my cause and business."

The spirits of the air of the Lord's day are under the north wind; their nature is to procure gold, gems, carbuncles, riches; to cause one to obtain favour and benevolence; to dissolve the enmities of men; to raise men to honours; to carry or take away infirmities.

1492. Given that Turner's 1655 edition of pseudo-Agrippa, *Fourth Book*, has "red wheat" (page 89) this establishes that the source text was the 1665 printing (page 89).

1493. Most of this is the same as pseudo-Agrippa, *Fourth Book* (1665), with a few minor variations, such as the insertion of "per" for "by."

1494. *[maker...heaven]*: All of this is on one line in pseudo-Agrippa, *Fourth Book* (1665), so the copyist likely skipped it by accident.

1495. *Is in them*: pseudo-Agrippa, *Fourth Book* (1665): "in them is in."

Considerations of Monday

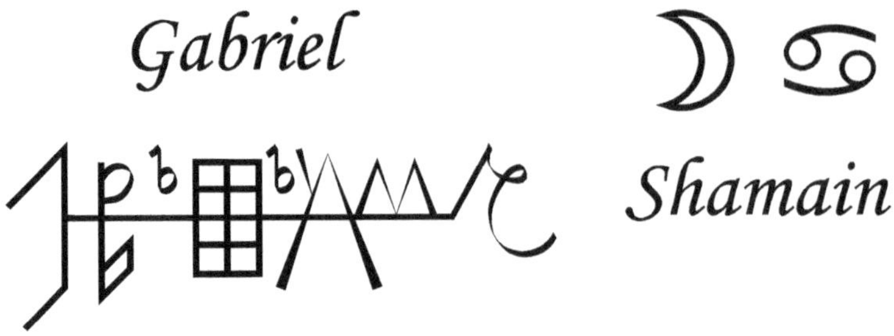

The Angels of Monday

Gabriel, Michael, Samael.

The Angels of the Air Ruling on Monday

Arcan, king.

[336]

His Ministers

Bilet, Missabe, Abuzaha.[1496]

The Wind Which the Said Angels of the Aire Are Subject To

The west wind.

The Angels of the First Heaven Ruling on Monday, Which Ought to Be Called from the Four Parts of the World

From the east:
Gabriel, Gabrael, Madiel, Deamiel, Janael.

From the west:
Sachiel, Zaniel, Habajel, Bachanael, Corabael.

From the north:
Mael, Vuael, Valnum, Baliel, Balay, Humastrau.

From the south:
Curaniel, Dabriel, Darquiel, Hanun, Anayl, Vetuel.

The Perfume of Monday

Aloes.

1496. *Abuzaha*: This error for "Abuzaba" arises from a misreading of the printed text.

[337]

The Conjuration of Monday

"I conjure and confirm upon you, ye strong and good angels, in the name Adonay, Adonay, Adonay, Eye, Eye, Eye, Cados, Cados, Cados, Achim, Achim, Ja, Ja, strong Ja, who appeared in Mount Sinai, with the glorification of the King Adonay, Saday, Zebaoth, Anathay, Ya, Ya, Ya, Marinata, Abim, Jeia, who created the sea and all lakes and waters in the second day, which are above the heavens and in the earth, and sealed the sea in his high name, and gave it bounds, beyond which it cannot pass, per the names of the angels who rule in the first legion, who serve Orphaniel, a great, precious, and honourable angel, and per the name of his star which is ☽, and per all the names aforesaid, I conjure thee, Gabriel, who art chief ruler of Monday, the second day, that, for me, thou labour and fulfil [& c.]."

The spirits of the air of Monday are subject to the west wind, which is the wind of the ☽: their nature is to give silver; to convey things from place to place;

[338]

to make horses swift; and to disclose the secrets of persons both present and future, but in what manner they appear, fear not.[1497]

Considerations of Tuesday

The angel of Tuesday, his sigil, his planet, the sign governing the planet, and the name of the fifth heaven.

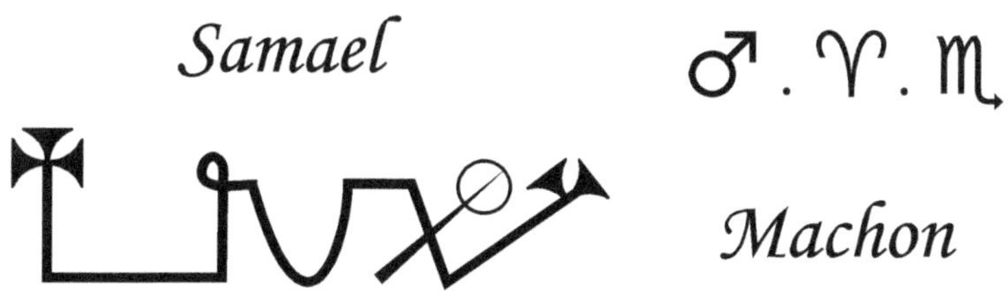

The Angels of Tuesday

Samael, Satael, Amabiel.

The Angels of the Air Ruling on Tuesday

Samax, king.

1497. *Fear not*: Pseudo-Agrippa, *Fourth Book* (1665), has "you may see in the former book," referring to the *Fourth Book* that appears before it in that compilation.

His Ministers

Carmax, Ismoli, Paffran.

The Wind to Which the Said Angels Are Subject

The east wind.

The Angels of the Fifth Heaven Ruling on Tuesday, Which Ought to Be Called from the Four Parts of the World

[339]

At the east:
Friagne, Guael, Damael, Calzas, Arragon.

At the west:
Lama, Astagna, Lobquin, Soncas, Jazel, Isiael, Irel.

At the north:
Rahumel, Hyniel, Rayel, Seraphiel, Mathiel, Fraciel.

At the south:
Sacriel, Janiel, Galdel, Osael, Vianuel, Zaliel.

The Perfume of Tuesday

Pepper.

[The Conjuration of Tuesday]

"I conjure and confirm upon you, ye strong and holy angels, per the name Ya, Ya, Ya, He, He, He, [Va], Hy, Hy, Ha, Ha, Ha,[1498] Va, Va, Va, An, An, An, Aie, Aie, Aie, El, Ay, Elibra, Eloim, Eloim, and per the name of that high God, who made the dry land appear, and called it earth, and brought forth herbs and trees out of the same, and sealed the same with his precious, honourable, and fearful

[340]

"and holy name, and per the name of the angels ruling in the fifth heaven, who serve Acimoy, a great angel, strong, powerful, and honourable, and per the name of his star which is ♂, and per the names aforesaid, I conjure upon thee Samael, who art a great angel and art chief ruler of Tuesday, and per the name Adonay the living and true God, that pro me thou labour and fulfil, & c."

1498. *Ha*: This third "Ha" is particular to the two Turner editions of pseudo-Agrippa, *Fourth Book.*

The spirits of the air of Tuesday are under the east wind; their nature is to cause wars, mortality, death, and combustions, and to give two thousand soldiers at a time, to bring death, infirmities, or health.

Considerations of Wednesday

The angel of Wednesday, his sigil, planet, the sign governing the planet, and the name of the second heaven.

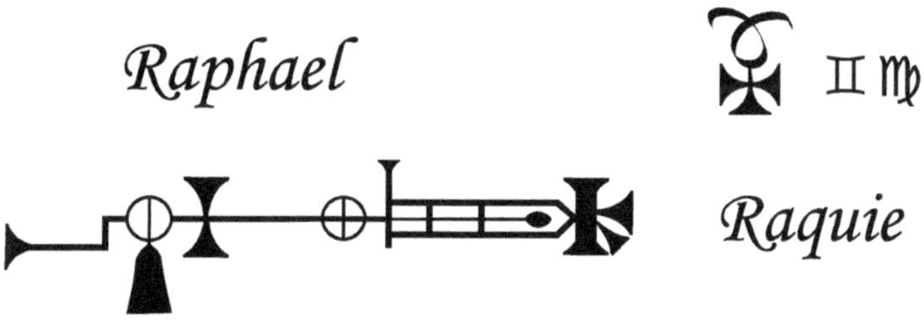

The Angels of Wednesday

Raphael, Miel, Serap[h]iel.

[341]

The Angels of the Air Ruling on Wednesday

Mediat, or Modiat, rex.[1499]

Ministers

Suquinos, Sallales.

The Wind Which the Said Angels of the Air Are Subject To

The southwest wind.

The Angels of the Second Heaven Governing Wednesday, Which Ought to Be Called from the Four Parts of the World

At the east:

Mathlai, Tarmiel, Barabo.

At the west:

Jerescus, Mitraton.

At the north:

Thiel, Rael, Jeriabel, Venabel, Velel, Abniori, Veirnuel.[1500]

1499. *Rex*: Translation: "King."

1500. *Thiel…Veirnuel*: Peterson, *Elucidation of Necromancy*, 217: "Thiel. Raël. Jariahel. Venahel. Velel. Abuiori. Ucirnuël." The discrepancies might be due to the scribe's inability to read the italicised text in the 1665 edition.

At the south:

Miliel, Nelapa, Babel, Caluel, Vell, Laquel.

The Fumigation of Wednesday

Mastic.

[342]

The Conjuration of Wednesday

"I conjure and confirm upon you, ye strong, holy, and potent angels, in the name of the most strong, most dreadful, and blessed Ja, Adonay, Eloim, Saday, Saday, Saday, Eie, Eie, Eie, Asamaie, Asaraie, and in the name Adonay, the God of Israel, who created the two great lights to distinguish the day from the night: and per the name of all the angels serving in the second host, before Tetra, a great, strong, and powerful angel; and per the name of his star, which is ☿, and per the name of the seal which is sealed per God, most mighty and honourable, per all things before spoken, I conjure upon thee, Raphael, a great angel who art chief ruler of the fourth day, and per the holy name which was written in the forehead of Aaron, the priest of the most high Creator, and per the names of the angels who are confirmed into the grace of our saviour, and per the name of the seat of the animals having six wings, that pro me thou labour to fulfil, [& c.]"

[343]

The spirits of the air of Wednesday are subject to the southwest wind. Their nature is to give all metals; to reveal all earthly things, past, present, and to come; to pacify judges; to give victories in war; to re-edify and teach experiments and all decayed sciences; and to change bodies mixed of elements conditionally out of one into another; to give infirmities or health; to raise the poor, and to cast down the high ones; to bind or loose spirits; to open locks or bolts. Such kind of spirits have the operation of others, but not in their perfect power, but in virtue or knowledge.[1501]

1501. Pseudo-Agrippa, *Fourth Book* (1665), has after this: "The what manner they appear, it is before spoken." This was likely removed due to the lack of the *Fourth Book* in this manuscript.

Considerations of Thursday

The angel of Thursday, his sigil, planet, the sign of the planet, and the name of the sixth heaven.

Sachiel ♃ ♐ ♓

Zebul

The Angels of Thursday

Sachiel, Castiel, Asasiel.

[344]

The Angels of the Air Governing Thursday

Suth, rex.

Ministers

Maguth, Gutrix.

The Winds Which the Said Angels of the Air Are Under

The south wind.

But because there are no angels of the air to be found above the fifth heaven, therefore on Thursday say the prayers following in the four parts of the world.

At the east:

"O great and most high God, honoured, world without end."

At the west:

"O wise, pure, and just God of divine clemency, I beseech thee, most holy Father, that this day I may perfectly understand and accomplish my petition, work, and labour; thou who liveth and reigneth, world without end. Amen."

At the north:

"O God, strong and mighty, from everlasting."

At the south:

"O mighty and merciful God."

[343b]

The Perfume of Thursday

Saffron.

The Conjuration of Thursday

"I conjure and confirm upon you, ye holy angels, and per the name, Cados, Cados, Cados, Escher[e]ie, Escher[e]ie, Escher[e]ie, Hatim, Ya, strong founder of the worlds, Cantine, Jaym, Janic, Anic, Calbot, Sabbac, Berisay, Alnaym, and per the name Adonay, who created all[1502] fishes and creeping things in the waters, and birds upon the face of the earth, and flying towards heaven in the fifth day; and per the names of the angels serving in the sixth host before Pastor, a holy angel, a great and powerful prince, and per the name of his star, which is Jupiter, and per the name of his seal, and per the name Adonay, the great God, creator of all things; and per the name of all stars, and per their power and virtue, and per all the names aforesaid, I conjure thee, Sachiel, a great angel, who art chief ruler of Thursday, that pro me thou labour, & c."

The spirits of the air of Thursday

[344c]

are subject to the south wind. Their nature is to procure the love of women, to cause men to be merry and joyful; to pacify strife and contentions; to appease enemies; to heal the diseased, and to disease the whole; and procureth losses, or taketh them away.[1503]

Considerations of Friday

The angel of Friday, his sigil, his planet, the sign governing the planet, and the name of the third heaven.

The Angels of Friday

Anael, Rachiel, Sachiel.

The Angels of the Air Ruling on Friday

Sarabotes, king.

1502. *All*: Not in Turner (1655 or 1665).

1503. Pseudo-Agrippa, *Fourth Book* (1665), adds, "Their manner of appearing is spoken of already."

Ministers

Amabiel, Aba, Abalidoth, Blaef.[1504]

The Wind Which the Said Angels of the Air Are Under

The west wind.

[345]

Angels of the Third Heaven, Ruling on Friday, Which Are to Be Called from the Four Parts of the World

At the east:

Setchiel, Chedusitaniel, Corat, Tamael, Tenaciel.

At the west:

Turiel, Coniel, Babiel, Kadie, Maltiel, Hupbaltiel.[1505]

At the north:

Peniel, Penael, Penat, Raphael, Raniel, Doremiel.

At the south:

Porna, Sachiel, Chermiel, Samael, Santanael, Famiel.

The Perfume of Friday

Pepperwort.

See *Fourth Book,* Cornelius Agrippa, page 101.[1506]

The Conjuration of Friday

"I conjure and confirm upon you, ye strong angels, holy and powerful, [in the name] On, Hey, Heya, Ja, Je, Adonay, Saday, and in the

[346]

"name Saday, who created four-footed beasts and creeping things, and man in the sixth day, and gave to Adam power over all creatures, wherefore blessed be the name of the Creator in his place, and per the name of the angels serving in the third host before Dagiel, a great angel, and a strong and powerful prince, and per the name of the star which is Venus, and per

1504. *Blaef*: Pseudo-Agrippa, *Fourth Book* (1665): "Blaef." Peterson, *Elucidation of Necromancy*, 223: "Flaëf."

1505. *Hupbathiel*: Pseudo-Agrippa, *Fourth Book* (1665): "Hupbathiel." Peterson, *Elucidation of Necromancy*, 223: "Hufaltiel."

1506. *See…page 101*: The page number that corresponds to this is from the 1655 edition of the *Fourth Book*, and the page in question is actually page 100 misnumbered.

his seal which is holy, and per all the names aforesaid, I conjure upon thee Anael, who art chief ruler of the sixth day, that thou labour pro me, & c."

The spirits of the air of Friday are subject to the west wind. Their nature is to give silver; to excite men and incline them to luxury; to reconcile enemies through luxury; and to make marriages; to allure men to love women; to cause or take away infirmities; and to do all things which have motion.

Considerations of Saturday, or the Sabbath Day

The angel of Saturday, his seal, his planet, and the sign governing the planet.

[347]

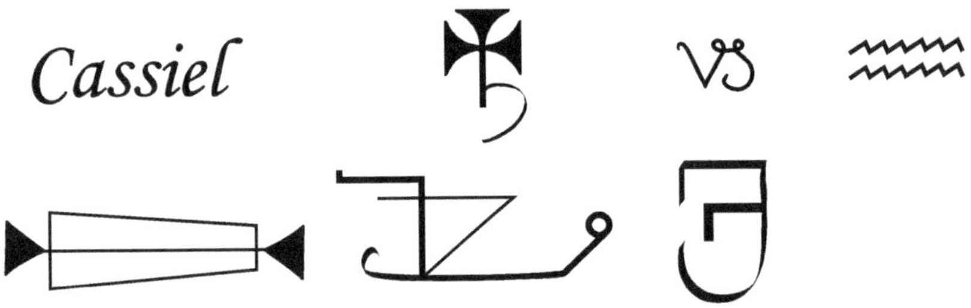

The Angels of Saturday

Cassiel, Machatan, Uriel.

The Angels of the Air Ruling on Saturday

Maymon, king.

Ministers

Abumalith, Assaibi, Balidet.

The Wind Which the Said Angels of the Air Aforesaid Are Under

The Southwest wind.

The Fumigation of Saturday

Sulphur.[1507]

It is already said, in the consideration of Thursday, that there are no angels ruling the air above the fifth heaven; therefore, in the four angles of the world, use these orations which you see applied to that purpose on Thursday.

[348]

See page 103—*4th Book,* Cornelius Agrippa[1508]

1507. *Sulphur*: See manuscript page 304 regarding the dangers of burning sulphur.

1508. *See page 103...Agrippa*: Refers to 1655 edition of the *Fourth Book*.

The Conjuration of Saturday

"I conjure and confirm upon you, Caphriel or Cassiel, Machator, and Seraquiel, strong and powerful angels, and per the name Adonay, Adonay, Adonay, Eie, Eie, Eie, Acim, Acim, Acim, Cados, Cados, Ina or Ima, Ima, Sallay, Ia, Sar, lord and maker of the world, who rested on the seventh day, and per him who is of[1509] good pleasure, gave the same to be observed per the children of Israel, throughout their generations, that they should thoroughly keep and sanctify the same, to have thereper a good reward in the world to come, and per the names of the angels serving in the seventh host, before Booel, a great angel and powerful prince, and per the name of his star, which is Saturn, and per his holy seal, and per the names before spoken, I conjure upon thee, Caphriel, who art chief ruler of the seventh day, which is the Sabbath day, that pro me thou labour to fulfil," & c.

The spirits of the air of Saturday are subject to the southwest wind. The nature of them is to sow discords, hatred, evil thoughts, and cogitations; to give leave freely to slay or kill everyone;

[349]

to lame or maim every member.[1510]

Hours of the Day		*Hours of the Night*[1511]	
1. Yayn.	7. Ourer.	1. Beron.	7. Netos.
2. Janor.	8. Tanic.	2. Barol.	8. Tafrac.
3. Nasnia.	9. Neron.	3. Thami.	9. Sassur.
4. Salla.	10. Jayon.	4. Athir.	10. Aglo.
5. Sadedali.	11. Abay.	5. Mathun.[1512]	11. Calerna.
6. Thamur.	12. Natalon.	6. Rana.	12. Salam.

But this is to be observed,[1513] that the first hour of the day of every country, and of[1514] every season whatsoever, is to be assigned to the sun rising, when he first appeareth arising in the horizon: and the first hour of the night is to be the thirteenth hour, from the first hour of the day.[1515]

1509. *Is of*: Pseudo-Agrippa, *Fourth Book* (1665): "Of his."

1510. Added in pseudo-Agrippa, *Fourth Book* (1665): "Their manner of appearing is declared in the former book."

1511. The following are the names of the hours of the day and night taken from the end of the *Heptameron*, with the angels of the hours of each day of the week omitted.

1512. *Mathun*: Pseudo-Agrippa, *Fourth Book* (1665): "Mathon."

1513. Agrippa adds here "by the way."

1514. *Of*: Pseudo-Agrippa, *Fourth Book* (1665): "In."

1515. Pseudo-Agrippa, *Fourth Book* (1665), adds: "But of these things it is sufficiently spoken."

[Angels of the Seasons][1516]

A year [therefore] is fourfold, and is divided into the spring, summer, harvest, and winter, the names whereof are these.

The spring	Talvi
The summer	Casmaran
The autumn	Adarael
The winter	Farlas

Angels of the Spring

Caracasa, Core, Amatiel, Commissoros.

The Head of the Sign of the Spring

Spugliguel.

The Name of the Earth in the Spring

Amadai.

[350]

The Names of the Sun and Moon in the Spring

The sun	The moon
Abraym	Agusita

The Angels of the Summer

Gargatel, Tariel, Gaviel.

The Head of the Sign in the Summer

Tubiel.

The Name of the Earth in Summer

Festativi.

The Names of the Sun and ☽ in Summer

The sun	The moon
Athemay	Armatus

The Angels of Autumn

Tarquam, Guabarel.

The Head of the Sign in Autumn

Torquaret.

1516. The sections that follow (manuscript pages 349–53) derive from sections of the *Heptameron* preceding the hours of the day and night. Pseudo-Agrippa, *Fourth Book* (1665), 72–76.

The Name of the Earth in Autumn

Rabianara.

The Names of the ☉ and ☽ in Autumn

The sun	The moon
Abragini	Metasignais[1517]

[351]

The Angels of the Winter

Amabael, Ctarari.

The Head of the Sign in Winter

Altarib.

The Name of the Earth in Winter

Geremiah.

The Names of the Sun and Moon in Winter

The sun	The moon
Commutaff	Affaterim

The Consecration and Benedictions,
and First of the Benediction of the Circle

When the circle is rightly perfected, sprinkle the same with holy or purging water, and say, "Thou shalt purge me with hyssop, O Lord, and I shall be clean; thou shalt wash me, and I shall be whiter than snow."

The Benediction of Perfumes

"The God of Abraham, God of Isaac, God of Jacob, bless here the creatures of these kinds, that they may fill up the power and virtue of their odours; so that neither the enemy, nor any false imagination, may be

[352]

able to enter into them, through our Lord Jesus Christ," & c. Then let them be sprinkled with holy water.

The Exorcism of Fire, upon Which the Perfumes Are to Be Put

The fire which is to be used per fumigations is to be in a new vessel of earth or iron, and let it be exorcised after this manner:

1517. *Metasignais*: Other versions have "Matasignais."

"I exorcise thee, O thou creature of fire, per him per whom all things are made, that forthwith thou cast away every phantasm from thee, that it shall not be able to do any hurt in any thing."

Then say, "Bless, O Lord, this creature of fire, and sanctify it, that it may be blessed to set forth the praise of thy holy name, that no hurt may come to the exorcisers or spectators, through our Lord Jesus Christ," & c.

Of the Garment and Pentacle

Let it be a priest's garment, if it can be; but if it cannot be had, let it be of linen and clean. Then take this pentacle made in the day and hour of ☿, the ☽ increasing,

[353]

written in parchment made of a kid's skin. But first let there be said over it a Mass of the Holy Ghost, and let it be sprinkled with water of baptism.

This figure from page 80, *4th Book*, Cornelius Agrippa.[1518]

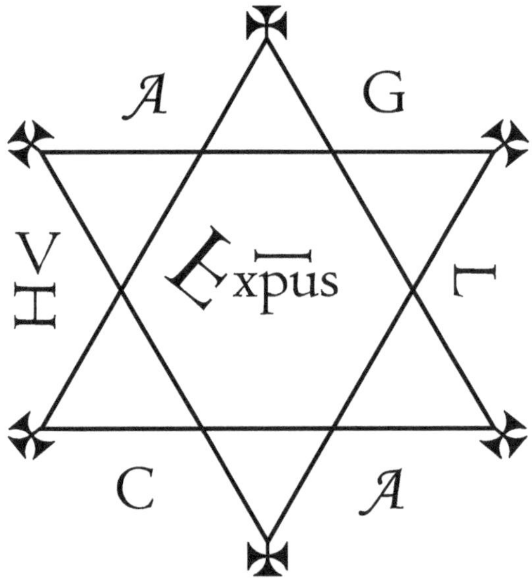

An Oration to Be Said When the Vesture Is Put On

"Ancor, Amacor, Amides, Theodonias, Anitor, per the merits of the angels, O Lord, I will put on the garment of salvation, that this which I desire may bring to effect, through thee, the most holy Adonay, whose kingdom endureth per ever and ever. Amen."

1518. *This figure…Agrippa*: From the 1655 edition.

[354]

This from page 74, *4th Book*, Cornelius Agrippa.

Of the Circle and the Composition Thereof

The form of circles is not always one and the same, but useth to be changed, according to the orders of the spirits that are to be called, their places, times, days, and hours. Pro in making of a circle, it ought to be considered in what time of the year, what day, and what hour, that you make the circle, what spirits you would call, to what star and region they do belong, and what functions they have. Therefore let there be made three circles of the latitude of nine feet, and let them be distant, one from another a hand's breadth; and in the middle circle, first write the name of the hour wherein you do the work. In the second place, write the name of the angel of the hour; in the third place, the sigil of the angel of the hour; fourthly, the name of the angel that ruleth that day wherein you do the work, and the names of his ministers; in the fifth place, the name of the present time; sixthly, the name of the spirits ruling in that part of time, and their presidents; seventh, the name of the head of the sign ruling in that

[355]

part of time wherein you work; eighthly, the name of the earth, according to that part of time wherein you work; ninthly, per the completing of the middle circle, write the name of the sun and of the moon, according to the said rule of time, pro as the time changeth, so the names are to be altered. And in the outermost circle, let there be drawn in the four angels[1519] the names of the presidential angels of the air, that day wherein you would do this work, to wit, the name of the king and his three ministers. Without the circle in four angles, let pentagons be made. In the inner circle, let there be written four divine names with crosses interposed in the middle of the circle, to wit, towards the east, let there be written "Alpha," and towards the west [let there be written] "Omega," and let a cross divide the middle of the Circle. When the circle is thus finished, we may work.[1520]

1519. *Angels*: Pseudo-Agrippa, *Fourth Book* (1665), has "angles."

1520. *We may work*: Pseudo-Agrippa, *Fourth Book* (1665), has "according to the rule now before written, you shall proceed."

Thus per Cornelius Agrippa, *4th Book*, page 74—To know what stones & c. other things under the power of the seven planets, see page 50, *3 Books*, Cornelius Agrippa.[1521]

Thou Mayst Call a Spirit Under per This Prayer to Appear in a Crystal Glass Held per Thy Self, A Maid, or Child

'Tis said if a smooth shining piece of steel be smeared over with the juice of mugwort and made to fume, it will make invocated spirits to be seen in it. Page 91, *3 Books* Cornelius Agrippa.[1522]

"O marvellous and everlasting God, which madest both heaven and earth, and in the mightiness of thy arm, thou didst measure

[356]

"them; O glorious, that sitteth upon cherubin and seraphin, in light of lights, that which the frailty of human nature cannot attain; O worthy, to whom be praise pro evermore, I beseech humbly thine everlasting majesty to constrain the spirit, to constrain the spirit, to constrain the spirit, that he may truly and faithfully, without all fraud, shew and declare unto me, and open," (thy name, the child or maid, whichever it be that doth look in the glass), "all such things as I shall, at any time or hour, command thee. Good Lord, grant this through the power of thy unspeakable Tetragramaton, and per thy wonderful name Jesus. Hearken, O thou N., I adjure thee with an unspeakable adjuration, I bind thee with a marvellous band, I conjure thee with a conjuration of mighty honour, I call thee with a call of nobility, I constrain thee with a terrible constraint, I compel thee with a dreadful compulsion, I command thee with a commandment of fame, I bid thee with a bidding

[357]

"that thou mayst not deny, I will thee with a will that thou canst not again say, I charge thee with a charge of worthy importance, that thou, N., that thou art, per," (name of office) "called per, do appear in this crystal, incontinent, visibly, openly, and distinctly, in a fair shape and form in the likeness that thou art called in, per thine office." (Here must thou name whether he shall appear to thee, the maid, or the child.) "And that thou do, without any man-

1521. *Page 50…Agrippa*: These numbers and those below appear in J. F.'s 1651 English translation of *Three Books of Occult Philosophy*. Harrington's catalogue mentions a 1651 edition in his library; see King, *Catalogue* […]*of Dr. Thos. Harrington*, 30.

1522. *'Tis said…*: From Agrippa, *Three Books of Occult Philosophy* (1651) (book 1, chapter 45).

ner of deceit, falsehood, or craft in any wise, shew the truth of any thing that shall be here demanded of thee. I, the servant of the living God, to whom be all honour and glory, speak unto thee, & c. O thou spirit, in the name and per the name of him that is glorious and everlasting, whose power endureth per ever, I conjure thee, that thou have no tarrying to abide in fire, air, earth, or water, or in any other place, but that thou do straight forth come, from fire to fire, from air to air, from earth to earth, from water

[358]

"to water, and from all deep places where thou now art, that thou do appear here, and shew thyself in this crystal glass, to the sight of," & c. (name it), "in such likeness as I have called thee, and as before I have commanded thee to come, and that thou tarry and abide with me in this glass, finally, all the time of my natural life, ready to make me answer, and to shew me the truth of all things that I shall demand of thee. Hearken, O thou spirit, per the name that thou art called per, that I, the servant of the everlasting and glorious God, do adjure, compel, charge, and command thee, that thou do all this that I have before spoken." (Here name your own names, both Christian and surname), "I, the servant of the everlasting and glorious God, do adjure, conjure, constrain, compel, charge, and command thee, with an adjuration, conjuration, constraint, compulsion, charge, and commandment of honour, worthy fame, nobility, might, and unspeakable glory from above. I adjure thee per the names of many

[359]

"years, whose garments be as white as snow, and the hairs of his head like to most pure wool,[1523] whose seat is of a flaming fire, a fiery flood, and the wheels thereof glistering fire, fire proceedeth even before him, and a thousand times a thousand do stand before him, and ten thousand times ten thousand him do serve. I conjure thee per the name marvellous, which is called El. I command thee to appear per him which spoke his word, and all things were made and done; and per the mighty name Agla, and per the power of the same name Agla, that Noah named and was delivered of all his family from the universal flood; and per the name Tetragramaton, and in the power of the great name Tetragramaton, that Enoch and Ely did name when they went to fight against Leviathan, and they were brought to the land of

1523. *Whose garments...wool*: Revelation 1:14. This and the following passages do not seem to come from any known translation.

promission;[1524] and per the name Anobona, and in the wonderful might of the great name Anabona, in that which God shall cast the holy fire of the earth upon the holy hill; and per

[360]

"the name Adonay, which God shall speak in the midst of the night, and at the same voice, both good and evil shall arise out your grave, even in the twinkle of an eye; and per the name Aloy, and in the name Aloy, in that which God shall trouble the seas and the flood, and the fishes shall be vexed and fight one against another, and they shall die all in one day, even with the third part of men dwelling over the compass of the earth, and per the name Alyon, and in the name Alyon, in which God shall dry up the seas and make them fall down into the deepest, and per the name On, and in the name On, in that which God shall restore again the seas and flood, and all manner of waters; and per the name of Messias, and in the name of Messias, in that which God shall make all the beasts wild and tame to be far gone and mad, and to fight one against another, so that all they shall die in one day; and per the name Arbitrall, and in the name Arbritrall, in that which God shall destroy houses and towers and all manner of buildings in one day, and there shall not remain

[361]

"one stone upon another, and per the name Sother, and in the name Sother, in which God shall make stones one to fight against another, and then shall the nations of the earth say unto the mountains, 'Come and fall upon us, and the little hills come, and do you cover and hide us';[1525] and per the name Emanuel, and in the name Emanuel, in which God shall make all flying fowls and birds of the air, one to fight against another, and in one day to consume; and per the name Sabaoth, and in the name Sabaoth, in that which God shall come with his orders of angels, even as an emperor entering into a city with great honour, crowned with a crown of gold, to judge the quick and the dead, and then shall the ungodly be stricken with lightning and fire, of that which it is spoken, the fire shall proceed even forth before him,[1526] about him shall be shewed a mighty strong tempest; and per the name Athanatos, and in the name Athanatos, in that which after that God shall finish his dreadful

1524. *Promission*: Promise.

1525. *And then shall…*: Luke 23:30.

1526. *The fire shall proceed…*: Psalm 97:3.

judgment, shall cast the devil with all wicked sprites into a terrible prison, even a

[362]

"castle of lightning, and of devouring fire, and then shall God with all his elect people enter into the joys of paradise with all triumphant glory; and per the Alpha and Omega, and in the name of A and Ω, in that which God shall make all the waters and flood to rise up above the earth per fifteen cubits, then shall heaven be fulfilled up, even as it were a boot, and it shall be gathered together, even like a tabernacle. This present state shall be renovated of which is thus spoken, 'Thou shalt change them, and they shall be changed,'[1527] per all these names that I have before recited, and per all other holy names of the everlasting God and wonderful, to whom be honour and glory for ever more. Amen.

"I charge and command thee, thou spirit, that thou appear here in this crystal without tarrying, and here to shew unto me, or whom I name, to shew the truth of all questions that thou shalt of him demand.

"I conjure thee, N., that thou appear here in

[363]

"this crystal, with all manner of gentleness, and not in terror, desert,[1528] or horrible shape or form, and truly to answer to my requests. I conjure thee in the name of Adonay, Sabaoth, Aloy, Saday, Tetragramaton, unspeakable Lord of virtues, Lord gracious of Israel which inhabiteth above all manner of places, and in the eleventh heaven is his seat, and in the earth is his power. I conjure per the name, and in the name of Moses heard from the middle of the flame, and was wonderfully astonished, and per the name and in the name that the children of Israel heard upon Mount Sinai, and they did fear, and per the name, and in the name that the sea heard and delivered his waufes,[1529] and per the name and in the name that the stones did hear and did break, and per all mighty and holy names of Jesus Christ, the son of the everlasting God, which shall come to judge the quick and the dead, and the world per fire.

1527. *Thou…changed*: Psalm 102:26.

1528. *Desert*: Something deserving of reward or punishment.

1529. *Waufes*: Possibly waves.

"I conjure thee, N., right loud to appear in this crystal, and truly to make answer to my demand. Come in the name of the Father,

[364]

"come in the name of the Son, come in the name of the Holy Ghost, so be it, so be it, so be it, in the name of Jesus Christ. Amen."

And when he doth appear in the crystal, then shew to him your holy ring or carect,[1530] and say:

"I conjure thee, N., which doth here appear in this crystal, per the marvellous word, per that which thou dost appear in this stone. I conjure and constrain thee per the virtue of these most holy names, which are written with four letters: Ioth, + Theos, + Agla, + Yaym, + Deus, + Aloy, + that which being heard the sea goeth back, the air is brought low, the earth trembleth, the fire is extinguished, and all the power of heaven, earth, Hell quaketh, and is trowled,[1531] and per the virtue of these holy names. I conjure, adjure, constrain thee, per the virtue of these holy names A and Ω, principium et finis, El, Eloe, or Eloy, Elyon, Sother, Emanuel, Sabaoth, Adonay, Egge, Ya, Ya, Ye, Ye, and per the virtue of these aforesaid names, I constrain thee, I exorcise thee, I bind thee per these holy names Athem,

[365]

"Arathon, Vegethon, Ya, Yaren, Ysion, Isilari, per all the saints and per all the angels, archangels, powers, dominations, and per that name through that which Solomon did bind and conclude[1532] all the devils into a vessel of glass, Ibooth, Hebauth, Agla, Ioth, Sothe,[1533] Sabaoth, Phanaibaoth, and per all the holy names that which be written in this book, and per all the virtues and powers of them, and per the power of this wonderful Tetragramaton, and further that thou enclosed in this crystal stone, to be a familiar unto me all my natural life, and truly to make answer to all my demand in any day, hour, minute."

For a continuation of this, see *4th Book*, Cornelius Agrippa, page 102.[1534]

1530. *Carect*: Inscription or brand.

1531. *Trowled*: Likely means turned over.

1532. *Conclude*: Enclose.

1533. *Sothe*: The first letter here is conjectural, as it has been redrawn repeatedly.

1534. This does not correspond to the pagination in either the 1655 or 1665 edition.

The Colour of the Planets[1535]

♄ Blue and leaden
♃ Citron near to a paleness
♂ Red and fiery
☉ Yellow, red, and glittering
♀ White and shining
☿ Glittering
☽ Fair silver colour

Physiognomy is mentioned often in holy writ: Exodus 3:4–6, 29, Numbers 14.18 and 1 Chronicles 12.8, Joa. 13.8, Scells [Psalms?] 8:1, Proverbs 17.24, Nehemiah 2.2, Prov[erbs] 15.13, Job 16.6, Job 37.1. See page 117, 272, Three Books, Cornelius Agrippa.[1536]

Influences of the ☽

☽ in ♈ prosperous for voyages. ☽ in the middle of this sign has influence on riches and discovery of treasure, and the movement is favourable to make the talisman and characters for success in love. When ☽ arrives at ♉ or the head of the Bull, 'tis bad for love and friendship, but twenty-five minutes after she has passed the Bull, the influences are exceeding good and shews a fine genius for the sciences, was a good

[366]

counsel from persons of distinction, and if at that time she is in conjunction with ♀, the talisman and characters made at this time are infallible. When the ☽ enters the sign ♊, her influences render every enterprise happy and makes you invulnerable, but when the ☽ enters ♋, she gives malign influences, but when the moon is near out of this sign Leo, she is liberal in all things and continues the same in the Sign Virgo. If she does not find herself affected by the melancholy ♄ when she enters ♎, she favours enterprises. When she hopes into ♏, she is very prejudicial to travellers or those who undertake a voyage, and to those who marry, and commerce and friendship. ♐ She influences health and love to the fair sex. The moon in ♓ with no bad aspect from Saturn, the characters and talisman under this constellation, of favourable influence by ☿. ♃. or ♀, she inalienably influences honour, health, and good

1535. Agrippa, *Three Books of Occult Philosophy* (1651), 281 (book 2, chapter 31).
1536. These passages do not appear to be referenced in Agrippa, especially not on the pages cited.

fortune for play. See this more fully in the *Key to Rabby Saloman,*[1537] and still better in 286 of Cornelius Agrippa's *Third Book.*[1538]

Hours of the Day

Hours	1	2	3	4	5	6	7	8	9	10	11	12
Sunday	☉	♀	☿	☽	♄	♃	♂	☉	♀	☿	☽	♄
Monday	☽	♄	♃	♂	☉	♀	☿	☽	♄	♃	♂	☉
Tuesday	♂	☉	♀	☿	☽	♄	♃	♂	☉	♀	☿	☾
Wednesday	☿	☾	♄	♃	♂	☉	♀	☿	☽	♄	♃	♂
Thursday	♃	♂	☉	♀	☿	☽	♄	♃	♂	☉	♀	☿
Friday	♀	☿	☽	♄	♃	♂	☉	♀	☿	☽	♄	♃
Saturday	♄	♃	♂	☉	♀	☿	☽	♄	♃	♂	☉	♀
			Hours of the Night									
Hours	1	2	3	4	5	6	7	8	9	10	11	12
Sunday	♃	♂	☉	♀	☿	☽	♄	♃	♂	☉	♀	☿
See page	♀	☿	☽	♄	♃	♂	☉	♀	☿	☽	♄	♃
379	♄	♃	♂	☉	♀	☿	☽	♄	♃	♂	☉	♀
and page	☉	♀	☿	☽	♄	♃	♂	☉	♀	☿	☽	♄
333	☽	♄	♃	♂	☉	♀	☿	☽	♄	♃	♂	☉
♂	[illegible]	☉	♀	☿	☽	♄	♃	♂	☉	♀	☿	☾
	☿	☾	♄	♃	♂	☉	♀	☿	☽	♄	♃	♂

The Spirit of ♄
is called Sabathiel
♃ Zedekiel
♂ Madimiel
☉ Semeliel
♀ Nogahel
☽ Jareafel[1539]

1537. *Key to Rabby Saloman*: See Sibley, *The Clavis or Key to the Magic of Solomon*, 337–38.

1538. This does correspond to the Mansions of the Moon in the 1651 edition of Agrippa, *Three Books of Occult Philosophy*.

1539. Agrippa, *Three Books of Occult Philosophy* (1651), 435 (book 3, chapter 28). The copyist omits the spirit of Mercury, Cochabiah or Cochabiel.

This table from page 227, Cattan[1540] shows what planet reigns every hour of the seven days of the week, accounting for the first hour of the day, the first hour after midnight. But others say the hours should be from sunrise.

[367]

The Ring or Cup of Divination

This Scheme from John Heydon's *Holy Guide*, Page 160[1541]

1.	2.	3.	4.	5.	6.	7.	8.	9.	10.	20.	30.	40.	50.
A.	B.	C.	D.	E.	F.	G.	H.	I.	K.	L.	M.	N.	O.
60.	70.	80.	90.	100.	200.	300	400.	500.	600.	700.	800.	900.	
P.	Q.	R.	S.	T.	U.	X.	Y.	Z	J,	U	Hi	Hu	

1540. Cattan, *Geomancie* (1608), 227.

1541. Heydon, *The Holy Guide*, bk. 2, 157–61.

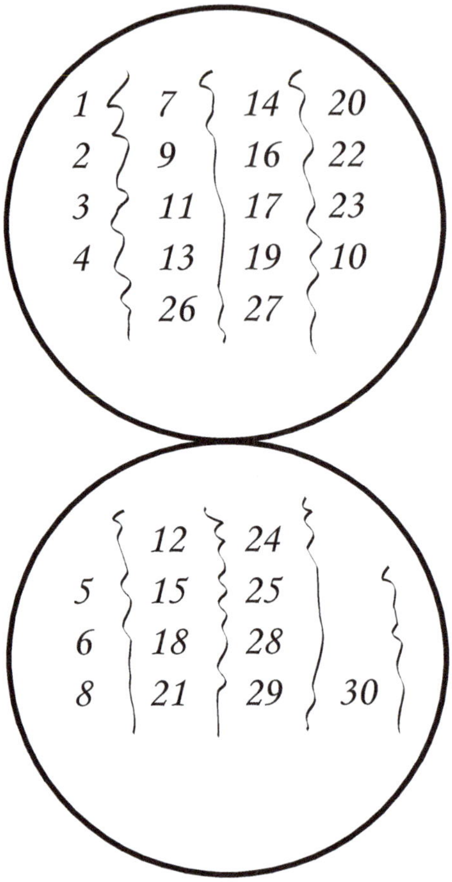

Directions: First choose a number, be what it will. Then take the number of the day (as on the opposite leaf). Then take the number of the first letter of your name that you were christened, as T for Thomas, no. 100.[1542] see the table above. Add all into one sum, which divide by thirty. If the rem[ainder] is in the upper half, that matter will go well; if in the lower then it proceeds contra.

But in matters of love, take the number of the first letter of your name, the number of the planet, and of the day of the week. Add them together, divide by thirty. If the remainder fall in the upper part, you shall have the request; if in the under piece, contra. See the bottom of the leaf, page 78. Each is worked in the same manner.

1542. Heydon, *The Holy Guide*, has "if your Name be Francis, you must take F." (157). This suggests that Harrington has altered the text to reflect his own name.

N. The quantity of figures is the same in each table, but not exact the same numbers. This table page 75, is exact from the old *Book of Knowledge*.[1543]

[368]

This is from Cattan[1544] and agrees exactly with one in the *Shepherd's Calendar*.[1545] See also page 51 of this book, which differs essentials from this.

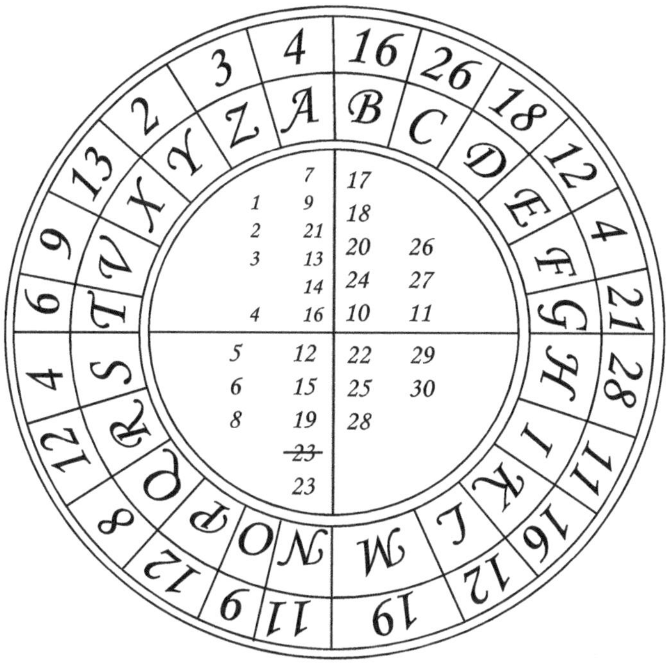

[Planetary Substances]

Monday	☽	Silver
Tuesday	♂	Iron
Wednesday	☿	Quicksilver
Thursday	♃	Pewter
Friday	♀	Tin
Saturday	♄	Lead
Sunday	☉	Gold

See page 51

1543. Erra Pater, *The Book of Knowledge*, 75. This book does not appear in the Harrington catalogue, so it is uncertain to what edition he had access. The 1726 is the only one I have examined that has this table on this page.

1544. Cattan, *Geomancie* (1608), 260.

1545. *Shepherd's Calendar*: A wide variety of booklets were published as the "Shepheard's Kalender," some of which did include numerological calculations of this sort.

The Number of the Planets and Their Characters

55	78	39	34	45	114	45
♄	♃	♂	☉	♀	☿	☽

Numbers of the Days of the Week

106	52	52	
Sunday	Monday	Tuesday	
102	31	68[1546]	45
Wednesday	Thursday	Friday	Saturday

These all from Cattan. Numbers & c.[1547]

John Heydon, page 158 of his *Holy Guide*, has the numbers of the day of the week exact as above, but his number of the planets differs much, being as follows: ♄ 7, ♃ 3, ♂ 9, ☉ 10, ♀ 6, ☿ 5, ☽ 2.

[369]

[A Talisman for Games]

This, written to virgin parchment and wore secretly on the breast and on the forehead in thy hat lining, will make thee fortunate in all games.

1546. *68*: 98 in Heydon, *The Holy Guide*.

1547. Cattan, *Geomancie* (1591), 239.

[370]

Dreams

Those who are desirous of receiving the oracles of a dream, let him make unto himself a ring of the ☉ or of ♄. There is also an image to be made of excellent efficacy and power to work this effect, which being put under his head when he goeth to sleep, doth especially give true dreams of whatsoever the mind hath before determined and consulted on. The tables of numbers do likewise confer to receive an oracle, being duly formed under their own constellations and those things are further mentioned in the *Third Book*, Cornelius Agrippa.

Holy tables and papers do also serve to this effect, being specially composed and consecrated, such as is the *Almadel* of Solomon, and the Table of the Revelation of the Name Tetragrammaton, and those things which are of this kind and written unto these things, out of divers figures, numbers, holy pictures, with the inscription of the holy names of God and of angels. The composition thereof is taken out of divers places of holy scriptures, psalms, and verses, and other certain promises of the divine revelations and prophecies.[1548]

But those who would receive true dreams should keep a pure undisturbed imagination, and the person likewise should render himself good by prayers, temperance, & c., that he may be worthy of this knowledge, for wicked, dull, or unpolished minds cannot receive the species and representations which flow from superior intellect, nor retain them when received. Therefore, we should be sound in body, nor disturbed in mind, nor the wheels of life closed with gross meats and drink, nor sad through poverty, nor provoked through any vice of lust or wrath, but with gratitude, chastity, and temperance, and go to bed, and take this quick natural rest, and thus wilt thou be prepared for

[371]

in the divine power instructing thy soul, which doth receive those beams and representations which are sent down and shine forth from the divine mind. Neither will that deity be wanting to the good, when he is awaked who ruleth all his actions.[1549]

1548. Pseudo-Agrippa, *Fourth Book* (1655), 63–64. Here the text changes to become much smaller and neater, although in the same handwriting.

1549. Agrippa, *Three Books of Occult Philosophy* (1651), 512 (book 3, chapter 51).

[372]

To Know the Certain Hour of Any Planet[1550]

You must notice at what hour of that day the sun doth rise, attributing ever the first hour of the sun passing the planet that bears the name of that day. As on Sunday, the first hour shall be the hour of Sol or the Sun; on Monday; the first hour shall be the first hour of Luna or the Moon; Tuesday, Mars; Wednesday, ☿ governeth the first hour, and so on; Thursday, ♃; Friday, the first hour ♀; Saturday, ♄. And after the knowing of the planet that governeth the first hour of ☉ rising on every day, you must follow the natural order of the planets, attributing still the succeeding planet to every succeeding hour. The natural order of the planets is ♄, ♃, ♂, ☉, ♀, ☿, ☽.

1550. Simotta, *A Theater of the Planetary Houres*, 7–8.

[373]

[blank]

[374]

[On the Olympic Spirits]

From Cornelius Agrippa's *Fourth Book*, page 187 [1551]—☉

There are seven different governments of the Spirits of Olympus, to whom he hath appointed the whole frame and universe of the world to be governed per them or their visible stars, and Aratron, Bethor, Phaleg, Och, Hagith, Ophiel, Phul. Aratron appeareth in the first hour of Saturday.

But when you would call any of the Olympic spirits, observe the rising of the ☉ that day, and of what nature the spirit is which you desire (which may be seen and more fully explained in the *Fourth Book*, Cornelius Agrippa, page 187), and saying the following, your desire shall be perfected.

"Omnipotent and eternal God, who hast ordained the whole creation for thy praise and glory, and for the salvation of man, I beseech thee that thou wouldst send thy spirit N. N. of the solar order, who shall inform and teach me these things which I shall ask of him," or "that he may bring me medicine against" (any particular disorder you may be afflicted).[1552] "Nevertheless, not my will be done but thine, through Jesus Christ, thy only begotten Son, our Lord. Amen."

But thou art not to detain this spirit more than an hour, unless he be familiar addicted to thee.

"Forasmuch as thou camest in peace and quickly, and hast bended unto my petitions, I give thanks unto God, in whose name thou camest; and now thou mayest depart in peace unto thy orders, and return unto me again when I shall call thee by thy name, or by thy order, or by thy office, which is granted from the Creator. Amen."[1553]

1551. Pseudo-Agrippa, *Fourth Book* (1655), 187. The paragraph below is taken from that source.

1552. *Any particular…afflicted*: Pseudo-Agrippa, *Fourth Book* (1655), 19: "the dropsie."

1553. These past four paragraphs from pseudo-Agrippa, *Fourth Book* (1655), 194–95.

[375]

[blank]

[376]

[blank]

[377]

[Seals for Goetic Spirits][1554]

Seer, a mighty prince under Amaymon, king of the east, very quick and good natured.[1555]

Seal of Andromalis, excellent at bringing a thief, very good, and is a mighty earl.[1556]

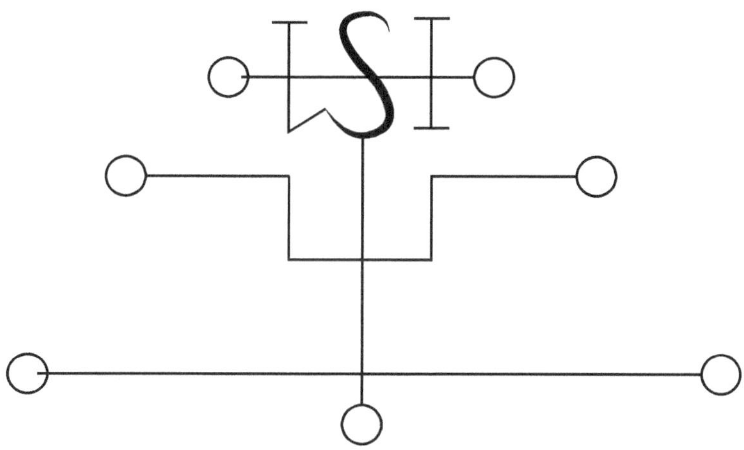

This long stroke above at bottom is only single.[1557]

The seventy-two are under Amayon, King of the East; Corson, of the South; Zimimar, North; Gaap, West, and are not to be called but on great occasions, but invocated to send such or such a spirit under their government.[1558]

1554. These spirits are taken from the *Goetia*, the first section of the *Lesser Key of Solomon*. Critical edition: Peterson, *The Lesser Key of Solomon*, 7–55. No such manuscript is noted by name in the Harrington catalogue.
1555. Compare Peterson, *The Lesser Key of Solomon*, 38.
1556. Compare Peterson, *The Lesser Key of Solomon*, 39.
1557. This has been corrected in the illustration provided.
1558. Compare Peterson, *The Lesser Key of Solomon*, 40. The closest parallel to the spelling of these names is Sloane 3846.

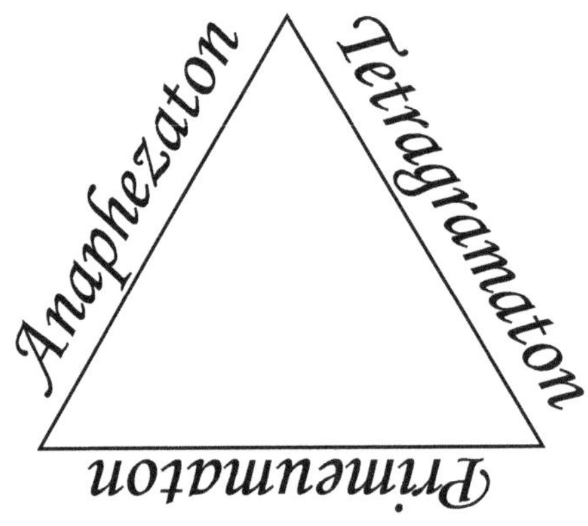

Make this in the east, three foot from the large circle (No. 1), which large circle should be nine foot over, and the names round. But some assert the small circle No. 2 answers as well with the above triangle three foot from it.

Either of these circles for the spirits to appear in:

1[1559]

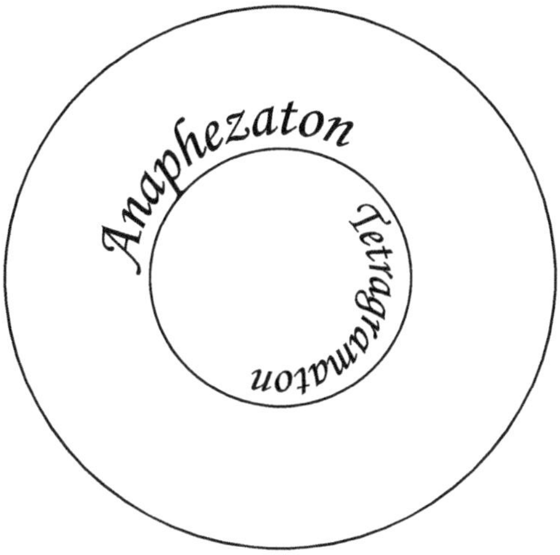

or

No 2

1559. The first of these should be the ring worn by the magician. See Peterson, *The Lesser Key of Solomon*, 44–45.

[A Talisman for Influence]

He that beareth this sign about him shall obtain esteem of the great.

[378]

Clavicula: The Magical Ceremonies of Solomon the King

Gap or Gaap is a mighty prince. He appeareth when the ☉ is in the south signs in human shape, going before him his mighty kings as a suite to conduct him in his way. He maketh men knowing in philosophy. He can cause love or hatred, and can teach you how to conjurate these things belonging to Amaymon his king, and can deliver familiars out of custody of others, and answer truly all things past, present, and to come, and can carry men from one kingdom to another at the pleasure of the exorcist. He ruleth sixty-six legions of spirits of the order of potentates. His seal:

Gaap's Seal 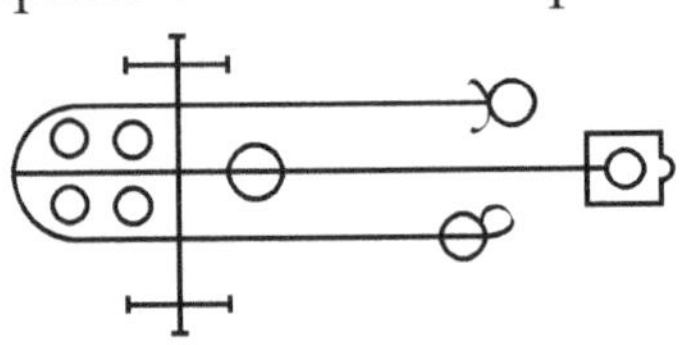 *Gaap's Seal* 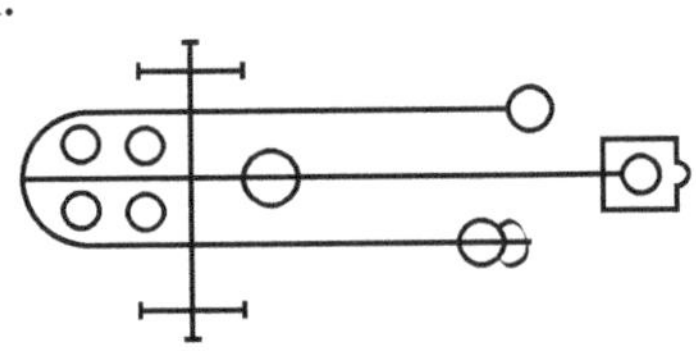

Either of these are Gaap's seal. Two were drawn because one of them was not thought so correct.[1560]

1560. Peterson, *The Lesser Key of Solomon*, 22.

Malphas[1561]

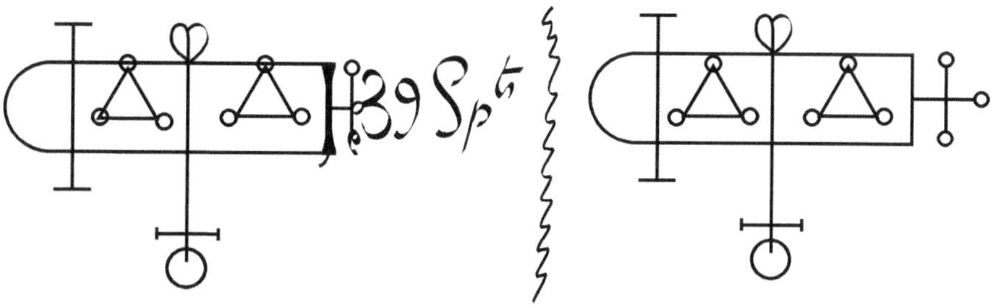

A Mighty Prince

There are two of these, because one is a little incorrect, this appendage 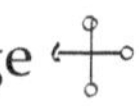 at the end of the first being confused with the number "39 Spirit," which should have been set further off. I have made room for the end.

Furcas

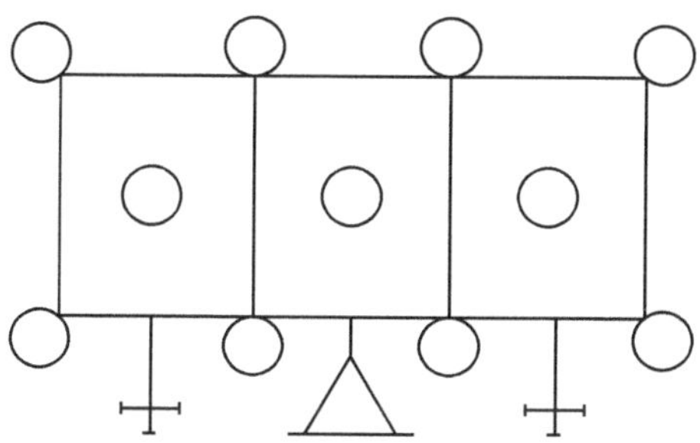

The fifty spirits, a knight rules twenty.[1562]

Buer, a President to Be Called When ☉ Is in ♑:[1563]

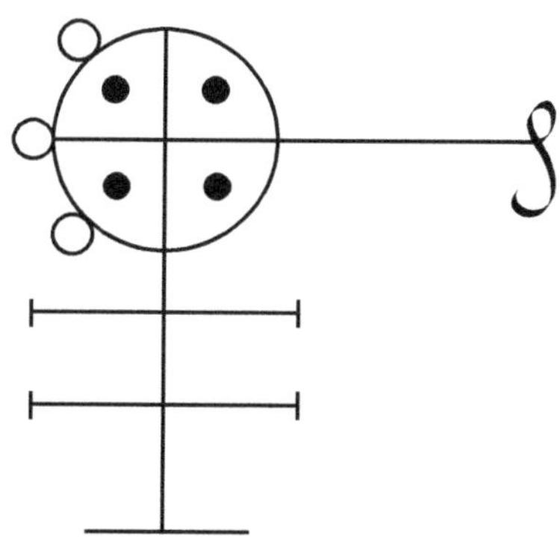

1561. Malphas is indeed the 39th spirit in the *Goetia*.

1562. Peterson, *The Lesser Key of Solomon*, 30.

1563. Peterson, *The Lesser Key of Solomon*, 11–12. That text links Buer to Sagittarius.

Remove, an earl[1564]

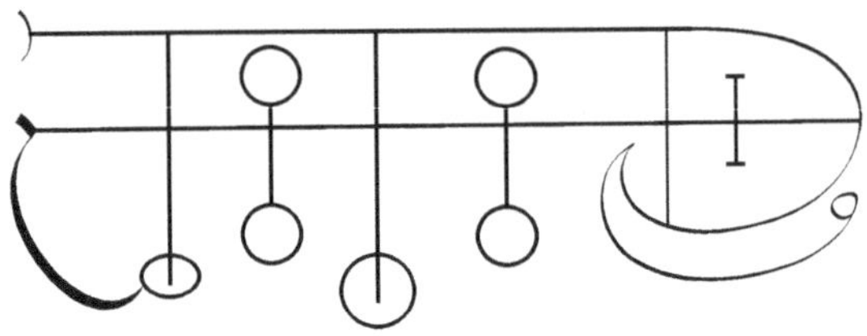

Dantalion, a mighty duke[1565]

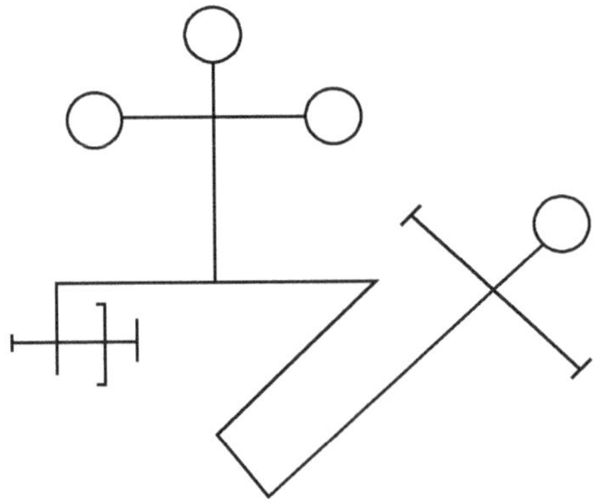

Decarabia, a marquis[1566]

1564. This could be Ronove (see Peterson, *The Lesser Key of Solomon*, 19), although the seal is different.

1565. Compare to Peterson, *The Lesser Key of Solomon*, 38–39.

1566. Peterson, *The Lesser Key of Solomon*, 38.

[379]

Page 321; see page 366, 378

A Table of Angels Ruling Every Hour of the Day and Night, with Their Planets

See Cornelius Agrippa's *Fourth Book*, 102.[1567]

Monday ☽

Mon or day	Night
1 ☽ Gabriel	1 ♀ Anael
2 ♄ Caffiel	2 ☿ Raphael
3 ♃ Zachiel	3 ☽ Gabriel
4 ♂ Samael	4 ♄ Caffiel
5 ☉ Michael	5 ♃ Zachiel
6 ♀ Anael	6 ♂ Samael
7 ☿ Raphael	7 ☉ Michael
8 ☽ Gabriel	8 ♀ Anael
9 ♄ Caffiel[1568]	9 ☿ Raphael
10 ♃ Zachiel[1569]	10 ☽ Gabriel
11 ♂ Samael	11 ♄ Caffiel
12 ☉ Michael	12 ♃ Zachiel

1567. Pseudo-Agrippa, *Fourth Book* (1655), 102. The author has removed the names of the hours of the day and night.

1568. *Caffiel*: Pseudo-Agrippa, *Fourth Book* (1655): "Cassiel."

1569. *Zachiel*: Pseudo-Agrippa, *Fourth Book* (1655): "Sachiel."

♂ Tuesday

Day	Night
1 ♂ Samael	1 ♄ Caffiel
2 ☉ Michael	2 ♃ Zachiel
3 ♀ Anael	3 ♂ Samael
4 ☿ Raphael	4 ☉ Michael
5 ☽ Gabriel	5 ♀ Anael
6 ♄ Caffiel	6 ☿ Raphael
7 ♃ Zachiel	7 ☽ Gabriel
8 ♂ Samael	8 ♄ Caffiel
9 ☉ Michael	9 ♃ Zachiel
10 ♀ Anael	10 ♂ Samael
11 ☿ Raphael	11 ☉ Michael
12 ☽ Gabriel	12 ♀ Anael

Hours
☿ Wednesday

Day	Night
1 ☿ Raphiel	1 ☉ Michael
2 ☽ Gabriel	2 ♀ Anael
3 ♄ Caffiel	3 ☿ Raphael
4 ♃ Zachiel	4 ☽ Gabriel
5 ♂ Samael	5 ♄ Caffiel
6 ☉ Michael	6 ♃ Zachiel
7 ♀ Anael	7 ♂ Samael
8 ☿ Raphael	8 ☉ Michael
9 ☽ Gabriel	9 ♀ Anael
10 ♄ Caffiel	10 ☿ Raphael
11 ♃ Zachiel	11 ☽ Gabriel
12 ♂ Samael	12 ♄ Caffiel

Hours of
♃ Thursday

Day	Night
1 ♃ Zachiel	1 ☽ Gabriel
2 ♂ Samael	2 ♄ Caffiel
3 ☉ Michael	3 ♃ Zachiel
4 ♀ Anael	4 ♂ Samael
5 ☿ Raphael	5 ☉ Michael
6 ☽ Gabriel	6 ♀ Anael
7 ♄ Caffiel	7 ☿ Raphael
8 ♃ Zachiel	8 ☽ Gabriel
9 ♂ Samael	9 ♄ Caffiel
10 ☉ Michael	10 ♃ Sachiel
11 ♀ Anael	11 ♂ Samael
12 ☿ Raphael	12 ☉ Michael

The office of these angels to do all things attributed to the planet next to them in these tables, as in first hour Monday, Gabriel has dominion over things relative to the moon, and soon. For a further explanation, see the inside of the cover to Cornelius Agrippa's *Fourth Book* in manuscript.[1570]

1570. *Fourth Book in manuscript*: Possibly item 111 in the catalogue. King, *Catalogue* [...] *of Dr. Thos. Harrington*, 37.

[380]

The Angels of the Hours

♀ Friday

Hours Day	Night
1 ♀ Anael	1 ♂ Samael
2 ☿	2 ☉
3 ☽	3 ♀
4 ♄	4 ☿
5 ♃	5 ☽
6 ♂	6 ♄
7 ☉	7 ♃
8 ♀	8 ♂
9 ☿	9 ☉
10 ☽	10 ♀
11 ♄	11 ☿
12 ♃	12 ☽

Saturday ♄

Hours Day	Night
1 ♄ Cassiel	1 ☿ Raphael
2 ♃ Zachiel	2 ☽
3 ♂	3 ♄
4 ☉	4 ♃
5 ♀	5 ♂
6 ☿	6 ☉
7 ☽	7 ♀
8 ♄ Cassiel	8 ☿
9 ♃	9 ☽
10 ♂	10 ♄
11 ☉	11 ♃
12 ♀	12 ♂

☉ Sunday, the ☽ Monday, ♂ Tuesday, ☿ Wednesday, ♃ Thursday, ♀ Friday, and ♄ ruleth Saturday.

☉ Sunday

Day	Night
1 ☉ Michael	1 ♃ Zachiel
2 ♀ Anael	2 ♂ Samael
3 ☿ Raphael	3 ☉ Michael
4 ☽ Gabriel	4 ♀ Anael
5 ♄ Caffiel	5 ☿ Raphael
6 ♃ Zachiel	6 ☽ Gabriel
7 ♂ Samael	7 ♄ Caffiel
8 ☉ Michael	8 ♃ Zachiel
9 ♀ Anael	9 ♂ Samael
10 ☿ Raphael	10 ☉ Michael
11 ☽ Gabriel	11 ♀ Aneal[1571]
12 ♄ Caffiel	12 ☿ Raphael

These are tables of angels of the hours. The nature of these twenty-four angels of day and night changeth every day. Their office is to do all things that is attributed to the seven planets. N.B. In Cornelius Agrippa's *Fourth Book*, page 102, is a table exactly similar to this, but has also the name of the hour, which does not vary, so that one set of names serves for all the hours. I have added them on the back of this leaf, which see. But this is to be noted: that the first hour of the day of every country, and in every season whatsoever, is to be assigned to the sun rising when he first appeareth rising in the horizon, and the first hour of the night is to be the thirteenth hour from the first hour of the day. It is also to be known that the angels (turn over)

1571. *Aneal*: Error in the original.

[381]

A Table of the Names of the Hours[1572]

Hours of the Day	Hours of } the Night }	
1 Yayn	1 Beron	These
2 Janor	2 Barol	answer
3 Nasnia	3 Thanus[1573]	to thy figures
4 Salla	4 Athir	of every
5 Sadedali	5 Maton[1574]	month,
6 Thamur	6 Rana	day and night.
7 Ourer	7 Netos	It's only
8 Tanic	8 Tafrac	setting them
9 Neron	9 Saffur	in the same
10 Jayon	10 Aglo	order for
11 Abay	11 Calerna	every month.
12 Nathlon Natalon	12 Salam	

This Table belongs to, and is mentioned in, the leaf behind it.

See *Fourth Book*, Cornelius Agrippa, page (75)

It is also known that the angels do rule the hours in a successive order, according to that course of the heavens and planets unto which they are subject to. That spirit which governeth the day ruleth also the first hour of the day, and the second from this governest the second hour, the third the third hour, and so on, and when seven planets and hours have made their revolution, it returneth again to the first that ruleth the day. This table on the side is therefore the names of the hours only.

1572. Despite the attribution further down, the names here are closer to pseudo-Agrippa, *Fourth Book* (1655), 102 [103]–6, than to the separate listing on pages 75–76.

1573. *Thanus*: Pseudo-Agrippa, *Fourth Book* (1655), 102 [103]: "Thanu."

1574. *Maton*: Pseudo-Agrippa, *Fourth Book* (1655), 104: "Mathon." The 1579 Latin has "Maton."

[Talismans for Conjuration and Other Purposes]

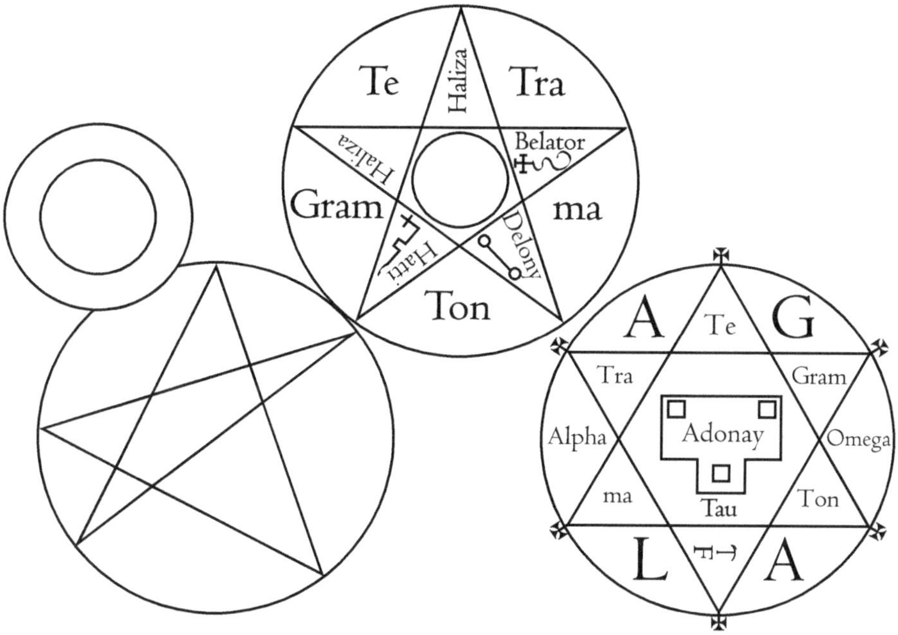

This to be made of gold and worn on the breast with the spirit's seal as below (No. 2) to preserve from danger and command by.

The Names of God
are—Jehovah
Eloy
Emmanuel Sabaoth
Adonay
Tetragramaton

Near this, (No. 2) at the bottom of your vesture, covered with a white linen cloth.

Paracelsus affirms that these two figures (the one with five, the other with six angles) exceed all other characters, pentacles, and seals or figures in power or virtue, especially this first. The latter, which has six spaces, should have the six letters inserted therein which makes that great name Adonay, No. 2, not those letters now inserted in it. See Paracelsus, *Occult Philosophy*, page 41.[1575]

1575. Paracelsus, *Of the Supreme Mysteries*, 41.

[382]

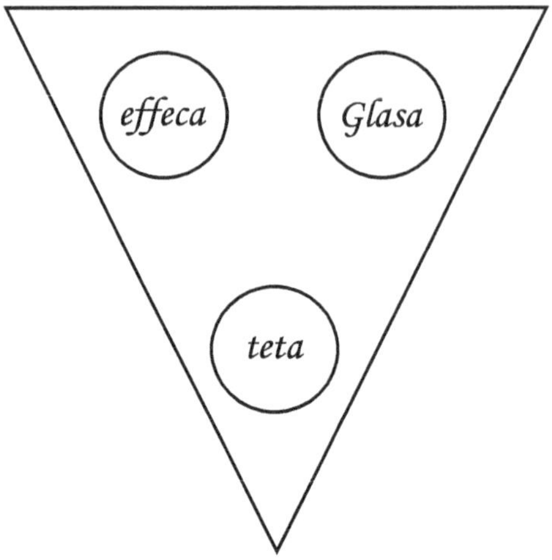

Make a seal of pure tin in this form in the day and hour of ♃ in the new ☽, and let ♃ be strong and of good aspect to the ☽. You must cast and grave the words in it as you see in the figure, in the said hour of ♃. So when you go to play, hang it about your neck. Then when you come home, hang it in some safe place in your house, till you have occasion to use it again. But before you use it, lay it always before you use it, lay it always before you, and lay your right hand on it, and say, "In the name of God the Father; I have sought thee; in the name of the Son, I have found thee; in the name of the Holy Ghost, I do conjure thee to win for me all that I play for. So be it." Then hang it about thy neck. N.B. This a gentleman of Paris left his son on his deathbed.

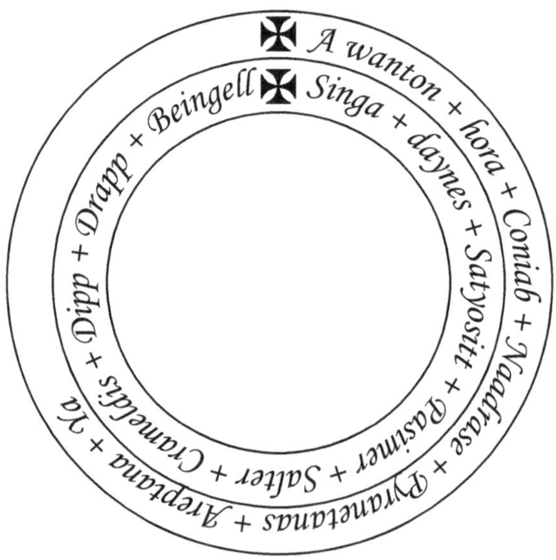

This written in virgin parchment and wore secretly on thy breast, and on the forehead within thy hat lining, will make thee fortunate in all games. N.B. The circle and writing only has to do with it.

The Seals of the Earth[1576]

These two figures beneath are called the seals of the earth, without that which no spirit will appear, except thou have them with thee. N.B.

No1

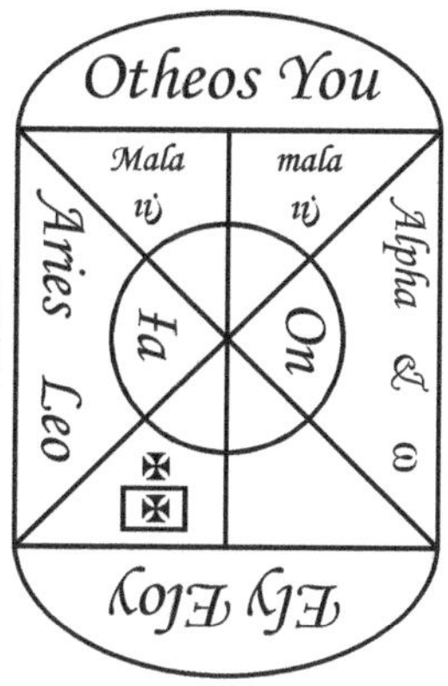

No2

See page 314

See this page 315

By this (No. 3), Constantine overcame his enemies. It must be made in parchment in the hour of ♂ and the ☽ in ⚹ or △ to ♂.

All these from Red Quarto Book Manuscript.[1577]

1576. For other examples, see Scot, *The Discouerie of Witchcraft*, 400; Sibley, *The Clavis or Key to the Magic of Solomon*, 16.

1577. See manuscript page iii. Punctuation on this chart has been corrected for consistency.

[383]

Of the Planetary Hours[1578]

See page 372

Length of the Day	Length of the Planets Hours by Day	Length of Planetary Hours by Night
H - M	H - M - Sec	H. M. Sec
6 - 0	0 - 30 - 0	1 - 30 - 0
6 - 30	0 -32 - 30	1 - 27 - 30
7 - 0	0 - 35 - 0	1 - 25 - 0
7 - 30	0 - 37 - 30	1 - 22 - 0
8 - 0	0 - 40 - 0	1 - 20 - 0
8 - 30	0 – 42 - 30	1 - 17 - 30
9 - 0	0 - 45 - 0	1 - 15 - 0
9 - 30	0 - 47 - 30	1 - 12 - 30
10 - 0	0 - 50 - 0	1 - 10 - 0
10 - 30	0 - 52 - 30	1 - 7 - 30
11 - 0	0 - 55 - 0	1 - 5 - 0
11 - 30	0 - 57 - 30	1 - 2 - 0
12 - 0	1 - 10 - 0	1 - 0 - 0
12 - 30	1 - 2 - 30	0 - 57 - 30
13 - 0	1 - 5 - 0	0 - 55 - 0
13 - 30	1 - 7 - 30	0 - 52 - 30
14 - 0	1 - 10 - 0	0 - 50 - 0
14 - 30	1 - 12 - 30	0 - 47 - 30
15 - 0	1 - 15 - 0	0 - 45 - 0
15 - 30	1 - 17 - 30	0 - 42 - 30
16 - 0	1 - 20 - 0	0 - 40 - 0
16 - 30	1 - 22 - 30	0 - 37 - 30

To find the length of the planetary hour and the planet governing it: first, get the hour and minute of sun rising. Then observe what hours and minutes have elapsed between your proposed time and the sun rising, and multiply these hours by sixty, and to the product add your minutes (if you have any), and the total divided by the length of the planetary hour. The quotient gives

1578. Gadbury, *Genethlialogia*, pt. 2, 238.

your desire. Example: on January 1, 1697,[1579] the sun at 8 o'clock, my time is two hours and twenty minutes distant from the ☉ rising, and the length of the planetary hour by day against eight in this table is forty minutes, which multiplied and divided leaves in the quotient three, unto which I add the twenty minutes, and that tells me there is twenty minutes of the fourth planetary hour gone of the time proposed. Now to know what planet governeth that hour, observe the day of the week, and that is Friday. Enter therewith in the lead of the table, page 366,[1580] and find the hour of the day underneath, which is opposite the day you have your desire.

[384]

For the aspects, see page 93

[Astrological Tables]

Signs	*Houses of the Planets*	*Exaltation*	*Detrement*	*Fall*
♈	♂ · *D*	☉ · 19	♀	♄
♉	♀ · *N*	☽ · 3	♂	·
♊	☿ · *D*	☊ · 3	♃	♂
♋	☽ · *N*	♃ ·· 15	♄	·
♌	☉ · *D*	· ·	♄	
♍	☿ · *N*	☿ · 15	♃	♀
♎	♀ · *D*	♄ · 21	♂	☉
♏	♂ · *N*	· ·	♀	☽
♐	♃ · *D*	☋ · 3	☿	·
♑	♄ · *N*	♂ · 28	☽	♃
♒	♄ · *D*	· ·	☉	
♓	♃ · *N*	♀ · 27	☿	☿

In this table, you may see that ♈ is the day house of ♂ as the letter D denotes, and ♉ the Night house of ♀ as N informs, likewise ☉ is exalted in 19th day of ♈ and ☽ in 3rd day of ♉.

1579. *1697*: Gadbury, *Genethlialogia*, has 1659.

1580. *The table, page 366*: That table is not taken from Gadbury, *Genethlialogia*.

Night Houses		Day Houses
♑	♄	♒
♓	♃	♐
♏	♂	♈
♉	♀	♎
♍	☿	♊
	☉	♌
	☽	♋

This table shews that ♑ is the night house of ♄ and ♒ the day house and so of the rest

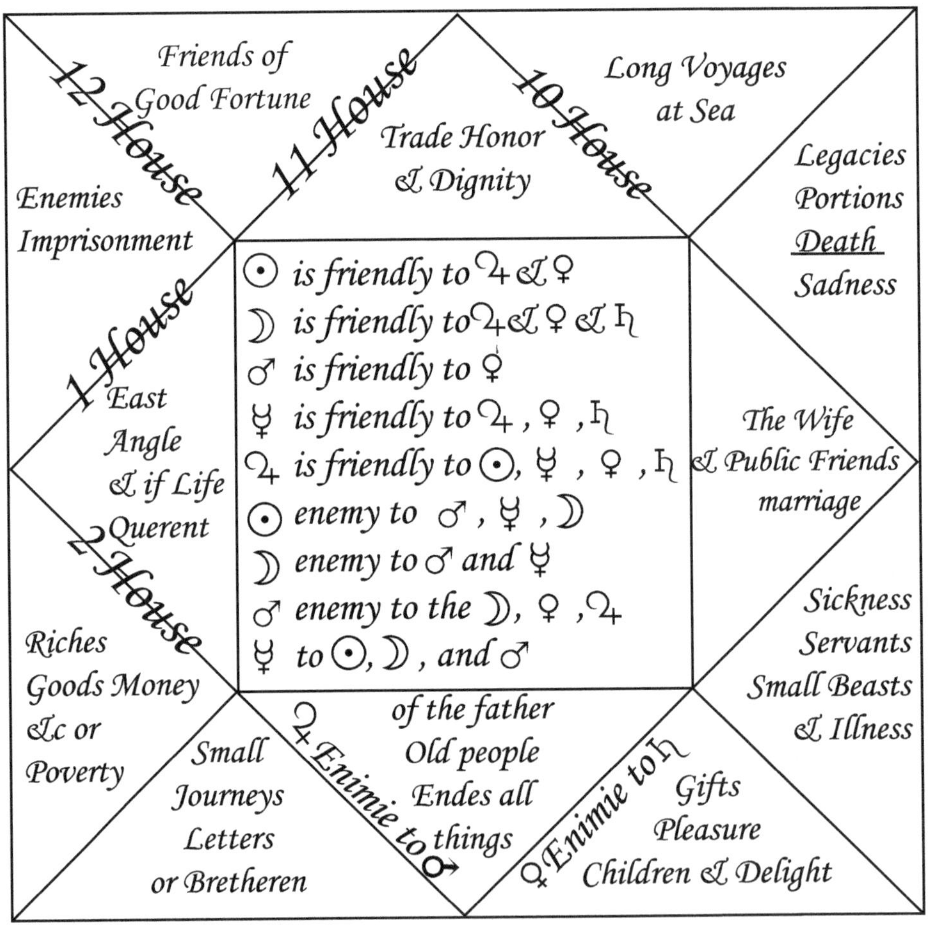

To Erect a Figure[1581]

Take the time you set it for, and get the degrees of that ☉ place in the ephemeris for that time, and with these degrees enter the table of houses under the sign you found the ☉ in. And in the tenth house, against the degree of the ☉, to the left hand under the title of time from noon, you will find certain hours and minutes, unto which it you add the hour and minute of the day (reckoning that day from noon to noon). The product (unless it exceeds twenty-four hours) is to guide you in the same column (be it either upwards or downwards) until you find the number, against which in the opposite columns you have the particular cusps of the six oriental houses, viz., 10, 11, 12, 1, 2, 3. The other six are opposite. But if your number exceed twenty-four hours, subtract from it twenty-four hours, and the number that remains whole the hour guide.

The first house shews life,
The second wealth do give,
The third how brethren, fourth how parents live;
Issue the fifth, the sixth diseases bring,
Seventh, wedlock, and the eighth denotes the king.
Cold death the ninth, man's faith and zeal,
The tenth the glory of the commonweal.
True friendship from the 11th house is known,
And sorrow from the twelfth to every one.[1582]

1581. Gadbury, *Genethlialogia*, 36–37.

1582. Most of this tracks to *Aristotle's Compleat Master Piece*, 128, listed in King, *Catalogue* [...] *of Dr. Thos. Harrington*, 2. The 1749 version ends differently: "The seventh Wedlock, and the eighth Death's Sting; / The ninth Religion, the tenth Honour shews; / Friendship the eleventh, and the twelfth our Woes."

[385-7]

[blank][1583]

1583. This is a single page numbered "385-7" in pencil.

[388]

See page 4 of this book, and also pages 5 and 6.

Instructions [for Summoning Spirits]

N.B. These instructions are in my red quarto page 40, and also page 9 of my little manuscript.[1584] The first mentioned days of the moon appear the same, and right in back.

First you are to observe the ☽ age for the workings—that is, when she is two, four, six, eight, ten, twelve, and fourteen days old. The other days are not so profitable. The Solomon adds the sixteenth, nineteenth, twenty-fourth, twenty-eighth, and thirtieth, and always in the increase.

The seals of kings must be made in ☉, marquis in ☽, dukes in ♀, prelates in ♃, knights in ♄, presidents and earls in ♀ or ☽ equal alike.

The above is gold, silver, tin, pewter, lead.[1585]

The chief kings may be bound from 9 to 12 o'clock at noon, and from 3 till ☉ set. Marquises from 3 [in the] afternoon till 9 at night, and from 9 at night till sunrise. Dukes may be bound from ☉ rise to noon day in fine weather. Prelates may be bound any hour of the day. Knights may be bound from the dawning of the day till ☉ rise, or from 4 o'clock till ☉ set. Presidents may be bound in any hour of the day except twilight or night. Earls may be bound in any hour of the day, so it be in woods or any convenient place.—Place where men resort not or keep, no voice is heard, and always pure and neat.[1586]

[Preparations for the Art][1587]

The operator in this Art should be learned, patient, steady, religious, sensible, humble, and respectful in the invocations and ceremonies required, one who is not avaricious and minds not little expenses which is requisite for the success of the operation. He must above all be a firm mind, clear intellect, and great courage, and should be accompanied by some discreet person not faint-hearted but good and replete with confidence and firm hope, and fearing nothing from vain imaginations, but be heady, forming no phantoms or chimeras, and be a close observer of all that's prescribed in these mysteries.[1588]

1584. *Little Manuscript*: Unknown.

1585. The repetition of such material indicates it is intended for another reader.

1586. Peterson, *The Lesser Key of Solomon*, 41.

1587. What follows is a paraphrase from the *Key of Solomon*. For the text closest to the wording, see Skinner and Rankine, *The Veritable Key of Solomon*, 69ff.

1588. Skinner and Rankine, 75–76.

Place: a private, clean room if towards the east, best with a table, some chairs, a pair of drawers, a cabinet which must lock, all which furniture should be very clean (if new, better) and purified with some sweet odour of perfume, nor any utensil admitted for the evacuation of the body for purity must be observed.[1589]

[389]

Talismans, Mysterious Figures, Images & c.

In forming, attention must be had to the situation of the planet that governs your work and to the metal you work on, which must have affinity. For those who take a plate of lead and work under the auspices of the sun will have no success, & c.[1590] To prevent mistakes, we repeat the proper metals for the seven planets: the ☉ influences gold, ☿ quicksilver, ♄ lead, ♀ tin,[1591] ☽ silver, ♃ pewter[1592], ♂ iron. It is plain means that the ☉ should be for the operation if Sunday, silver and the ☽ for Monday, iron and ♂ for Tuesday, quicksilver and ☿ for Wednesday, ♃ and pewter for Thursday, tin[1593] and ♀ for Friday, lead and ♄ for Saturday.[1594]

The Manner to Raise a Figure Cabalistic or a Talisman in the Name and Day of One of the Seven Planets

It is not material whether the piece of metal is round, square, or oval, so that it is a regular geometrical form, but both the metal, virgin parchment, virgin wax, or plaster of paris, & c., whatever you use, should not only be perfectly clean, but kept so, as dirt and slovenliness would spoil all.[1595]

Instruments proper for the operation are a small new wooden box lined with clean cloth, with a small new lock to make it fast. It must be filled with great order with the vest or habit made of new white cloth with linen drawers, neat clean slippers, white gloves, also ink, pens, penknife with white handle, black lead pencil, a phial of holy water, and a scissors, and a neat hazel stick and switch of the same wood, also a perfume applicable to the seven planets, with a small earth vessel, and charcoal or a chafing dish to

1589. Skinner and Rankine, 79.

1590. *For those...& c.*: Present in Skinner and Rankine, *The Veritable Key*, but not in the Sibley *Clavis*.

1591. *Tin*: Other texts in this series list brass or copper.

1592. *Pewter*: This is closer to the Sibley *Clavis*. Sibley, *The Clavis or Key to the Magic of Solomon*, 24–25.

1593. *Tin*: As above. The repetition indicates this is not an error.

1594. Skinner and Rankine, *The Veritable Key of Solomon*, 81.

1595. *But both...all*: Not present in either group of manuscripts.

make a fire to the incense and perfumes or fumigations, a ball also of new cord to help trace the

[390]

circle on the floor,[1596] a sword, also a mitre or cap, a long white linen robe, a girdle, a lion's skin or cloth three inches broad with the names about it round the outward circle, oil to anoint the temples, fair water to wash the hands & c. (and say with David, "Thou Shalt purge me with hyssop" & c.),[1597] a Bible, an ephemeris of some astrology book, and clean paper, and virgin parchment, and as the garment is putting on, say "By the figurature[1598] of this vesture, I will clothe me with the armour of salvation in the strength of the highest, Anchor, Amacor, Amides, Theodonias, Anitor, that my deserved end may be effected through thy strong Adonay, to whom the praise and glory will for ever belong. Anich, amen." Here should be a prayer according to the work,[1599] and there should also have the figure on the breast and girdle as you wilt find, page 381, and also the pentacle, if to raise spirits, page 392, and say a prayer, page 400–353.

Influences

We are next to attend to the secret influences of the ☽, ☉, & c., which are called for their power the eyes of heaven. The ☽ is the first and principal receptacle of the influences of the sun. She passes round her orbit in one month; the entire, likewise, in all the celestial signs, is thus timed, is often found in conjunction with the ☉ and other planets, and to succeed in the undertaking, you must be exact in taking the time of her entering conjunctions & c. For instance, a talisman made at the time of ☽ entering the head of the Ram ♈; at this time, her influences are good and prosperous for voyages. When the ☽ is arrived at the middle of this sign, her influences are good for riches & c.[1600] But see all her powers and influences fully explained in the *Three Books* of Cornelius Agrippa, page 285,[1601] and when the sign ♌ she is

1596. *Instruments…floor*: Skinner and Rankine, *The Veritable Key of Solomon*, 85–86.

1597. *A sword…& c.*: Peterson, *The Lesser Key of Solomon*, 47. Note the items repeated in this section from the previous one.

1598. *Figurature*: Form. Peterson, *The Lesser Key of Solomon*, has "figurative Mystery."

1599. *And as…work*: Peterson, *The Lesser Key of Solomon*, 47.

1600. *We are next…& c.*: Skinner and Rankine, *The Veritable Key of Solomon*, 87.

1601. The 1651 edition begins its discussion of the mansions of the moon on this page.

fortunate for all things for gamesters, especially if a talisman is made at this time.[1602] Old St. John the

[391]

Baptist is esteemed as a very, very favourable day for these operations.[1603]

Of the Working the Figures, Characters, Talismans & c.[1604]

Those not experienced in this mysterious occult art should begin by pentacles and be acquainted with the twelve grand names of God, and the seven others which are at the head of every day of the week, and are given them in honour of the genius which presides over the influences of the seven planets and which are appropriated to each day of the week. They may be made on virgin parchment, plates of metal, & c., and to begin the operation, a fortunate constellation should be chosen, or the planets in benign aspects, and all must be done in the private apartment prepared as before mentioned and destined only to the mysteries of this art, removed from noise, and to be in still tranquillity during the operation. The rooms and table & c. must be sprinkled with holy water, and you must be clad in the garments before mentioned. Then, after repeating the orations, invocations, conjurations proper to the day of operating and which are suitable to the genius which should then preside, holy water being sprinkled on the instruments, and indeed on everything used. Then begin to trace upon the metal, or with a crow quill pen on the parchment, the characters suitable and those you desire to make, which on the metal is best performed with a graver or bodkin. A pair of compasses and rule will be found necessary. The pentacle has generally

[392]

a double circle for mysterious names, or a passage out of holy writ which has some affinity to what you would obtain by this pentacle. For instance, if their design is for riches or honours, you must put down in the double circle of the pentacle these words, "Gloria et divitiae in domo ejus,"[1605] and in the centre of the round, you engrave with order and symmetry the characters of the planets under the influences of which you have from your pentacle.

1602. There does not seem to be a talisman for Leo in the *Key* or *The Three Books of Occult Philosophy*, but one for gamblers is listed under Virgo. Skinner and Rankine, *The Veritable Key of Solomon*, 88.

1603. *Old St. John…*: Skinner and Rankine, 83.

1604. Most of what follows parallels Skinner and Rankine, 90–93, save when noted otherwise.

1605. *Gloria…eius*: Vulgate Psalm 111:3. Translation (KJV Psalm 112:3): "Wealth and riches shall be in his house."

Several proper models will be found in this book, page[1606], but many more in the folio *Key of Rabby Soloman* from which these remarks are taken. Several of these forms and models of talismans, pentacles, mysterious characters are fully to be seen in the *Fourth Book* of Cornelius Agrippa, particularly the manuscript past, as also in the *Third Book*, Cornelius Agrippa.[1607] The following, by way of example, is one of the Eight Superior Pentacles at the head of the day which she governs or presides, and that of Solomon, and the Grand Pentacle and the lead of all, and therefore called the Grand Pentacle of Solomon.

This should be made with great seriousness and exactness, because it should be presented at all the operations of the grand, but you must choose the most favourable constellation of the year to work upon, and particularly the spring season, as at that time nature seems replete with new force. You may work any day of the week except Saturday, because that day is not altogether lucky, it being governed by ♄ and bad, unless ♄ is well aspected.

[The Grand Pentacle of Solomon]

1606. Blank hereafter in manuscript.

1607. *Several proper…Agrippa*: Not present in Skinner and Rankine.

From page 30 of *Rabby Salomon* folio

This is the model of the mysterious pentacle.

[393]

When this pentacle (which we have shewn on the other side) is finished in its perfection, it must be folded carefully in a purse of silk (or clean cloth, provided it be new) and then locked in a box, to be made use of as occasion requires. Its virtue in particular is to guard you against fear, that will naturally attend you at the appearance of the spirit. This virtue is so powerful that the most unlucky geniuses, which are saturnine, can do no hurt when this pentacle is present.[1608] For the orations necessitative to this pentacle, and proper prayers, invocations, & c., see page[1609]

N.B. It is necessary to mention that you must not wait till the hour is favourable for the operation, but begin to prepare all that is necessary, having everything ready that at the first instant you may begin to work, that you may gain time to let down with correctness the different character, which is convenient to make use of it in the operation.[1610]

[394]

<u>*Enforcing Particulars*</u>

The hour of the day and night for the seven days of the week that have affinity with the seven planets has been and is mentioned in this book, as also the hours of the day and the night for all the week with the planet that governs. And we have said that the first hour of each day begins the moment the ☉ rises, but you must be cautious to make no mistake with respect to ☉ rising sooner or later in different climes or places, according to the elevation of the role, and therefore to be competent to this art, a knowledge in arithmetic, astronomy, and astrology is necessary.[1611] And in the course of this book will be found proper tables which contain the mysterious names of the angels which preside at every hour, day and night, likewise the names of every hour for the seven days, as see in page 379, 321, 366, and to find what metals, stones, herbs, and other things are under the influence of all the seven planets. See page 50, *Three Books*, Cornelius Agrippa.

1608. *This virtue...present*: Not present in the *Veritable Key* edition, but does appear in Sibley, *The Clavis or Key to the Magic of Solomon*, 44.

1609. Blank after this in the manuscript.

1610. *It is necessary...in the operation*: Skinner and Rankine, *The Veritable Key of Solomon*, 94.

1611. *The hour of the day...necessary*: Skinner and Rankine, 94.

[395]

<u>Of the Perfume</u> *Proper for the Seven Planets Are as Follows*

For ♄, frankincense or pepperwort root; ♃ odoriferous fruits, as nutmeg, cloves, & c., in fresh powder to sprinkle on the fire;[1612] to ♂, all odoriferous weeds, as sanders, cypress,[1613] lignum aloes; to the ☉, all gums, frankincense, mastic, benjamin, storax, laudanum, ambergris, musk; to ♀, flowers as roses, violets, saffron, & c.; to ☿, all the bark of wood and fruit as cinnamon, lignum cassia, mace, citron peel;[1614] to the ☽,[1615] the leaves of myrtle and bay tree. The twelve signs of the zodiac have also their proper fumes, as ♈, myrrh; ♉, pepperwort; ♊, mastic; ♋, camphor; ♌, frankincense, ♍, sanders; ♎, galbanum; ♏, opoponax; ♐, lignum aloes; ♑, benjamin; ♒, euphorbium; ♓, red storax. (More of this, page 88, *Three Books*, Cornelius Agrippa).[1616]

A little grate or stove was mentioned as necessary before; these perfumes are to be sprinkled on the fire therein—that is, the incense or perfume proper for the planet on which you are at work, repeating orations, invocations, conjurations, which you will find page[1617]. Nor is this ceremony chimerical or imaginary, because it is certain that the aerial spirits which are destined by the Creator for the service of man may be attracted by perfumes. At the same time, evil or bad spirits which impede or obstruct the benign influences may be driven back. This may be seen in the history of Tobie in the pages of sacred history, relative to the marriage in the Apocrypha.[1618]

[396]

<u>*Orations, Invocations, and Conjurations*</u>

The conjurations for every day in the week may be seen on page 334 & c. of this book, and the orations and invocations and prayers are many in this book, and also dispersed in several of these manuscript books, which see[1619]. But the true disciples of this grand art, and lovers of this sanct[1620] science,

1612. *In fresh…fire*: Not in Agrippa, *The Three Books of Occult Philosophy*, and added to the passage later.

1613. Agrippa includes "Lignum-balsaim" here.

1614. Agrippa includes "Bayberries" here.

1615. Agrippa includes "the leaves of all Vegetables, as the leaf Indum."

1616. Agrippa, *Three Books of Occult Philosophy* (1651), 89 (not 88, as stated) (book 1, chapter 44).

1617. Blank follows in the manuscript.

1618. Skinner and Rankine, *The Veritable Key of Solomon*, 96.

1619. Harrington seems to have assumed that his library would be passed along to another person.

1620. *Sanct*: Holy. This appearance is a century before the oldest in OED.

should not content themselves in repeating orations at particular times of the operation, but they should be said each day whether you work or not at the operation. And all these prayers and orations should be repeated with the face towards the east[1621] and with great attention.[1622] But no prayers can be acceptable if the mind is polluted with vice. Our life should be innocent, our prayers energetic, sincere, fervent, and fragrant, for prayer is a communion of God with our souls. And be careful not to solicit for trifling or frivolous matters, nor dare to ask an unjust thing, for ignorant and improper supplications often reduce our prayers to nothing and cause our foolish wishes to be denied. Yet I deny not but that there are natural sciences, metaphysical arts, and occult ingenuities which can be practised without offending God or injuring faith and religion.

[397]

Further Remarks Respecting Sigils Amiable[1623]

To procure the solar virtue of anything, it should be wrapped in bay leaves[1624] and hung about the neck with a golden thread or a silken thread of a yellow colour whilst the sun rules in the heaven, so shalt thou be endued with the solar virtue of those things and the like, according to the suitableness of things. Thus must you use according to the suitable planet or constellation, either wire or silken threads with hair, cat gut & c.

1621. Skinner and Rankine, *The Veritable Key of Solomon*: "South." Sibley, *The Clavis or Key to the Magic of Solomon*: "East."

1622. Skinner and Rankine, *The Veritable Key of Solomon*, 99.

1623. Agrippa, *Three Books of Occult Philosophy* (1651), 93 (book 1, chapter 46).

1624. Agrippa adds "Or the skin of a lion."

[398]

[blank]

[400][1625]

The Prayer

After having put on the garments, as page 390, make a prayer to God according to your work, or as follows by way of example:

"O Great Supreme Jehova, and thou, O Lord Jesus Christ, who hast given power unto thy apostles to heal the diseased, to raise up the dead, to cleanse the leper, and to cast out devils, give unto me thy grace that I may be able to succeed in this my work, to perform what I now attempt in thy name, that I may have power to bind these spirits whom I intend to call at this time by thy grace and sufferance, and that I may bind and constrain them to do all things that I command them by the virtue and power of thee and the Lord Jesus Christ and the holy church our mother. And as thou hast commanded thy holy apostles to ask and receive, seek and find, knock and it shall be opened unto you, even so, O Lord, I do ask, seek, and call upon thee, asking and intreating those things of thee and through the merits of the Blessed Virgin Mary, the mother of all saints. Even as thou hast promised to give unto them all things asking in thy name, grant, O Lord, that straightway at any spirit coming before me, being called in thy name, that I may be able to constrain and bind them to be obedient unto me and my purpose, and whatsoever I will command them through Jesu Christ our lord. Amen."

[401]

The Conjuration

"I invoke and conjure you, spirit N., and being armed with power from the supreme majesty, I most strongly command you, Beralanensis, Baldachiesis, Primachie, and Opologia,[1626] I exorcise and powerfully command you, spirit N., in and by him that said the word and it was done, and by all the most powerful and glorious names of the most high God, living and true, and by these his most holy names, Adonay, Eserchie, Jah, Tetragrammaton, Sadin, that you forthwith appear and shew yourselves visibly unto us here before this circle in a fair and human shape, and without any delay do you come to make rational answers unto all things I shall ask of you. And come peaceably, visibly, affable, without delay, manifesting what I desire, obedient, and by his powerful name Tetraggrammaton Jehovah, which being heard the elements are overturned, the air is shaken, the sea runneth back, the fire

1625. The numbering skips page 399.

1626. British Library Additional MS 36,674; Peterson, *Lesser Key of Solomon*, 48. For the likely significance of these as the seats of God, see Peterson, *Elucidation*, 20.

is quenched, and all the host of the celestials, terrestrials, and infernals do tremble and are troubled and confounded together, that you visibly and affably speak unto me without any ambiguity in a clear voice intelligibly. Therefore come ye in the name of Adonay, Saday, the King of Kings command you,"[1627] say this as often as you please, "I conjure and command you, spirit (N), to appear and shew yourself visibly to me before the ○ in a fair and comely form" (N.B. The letter N is substituted for the name of the spirit which you intend to invoke or call, which should be the spirit of the planet, day, and hour at the time you are working; the ○ signifies either the glass, beryl, or circle, or room, or grove, or where or whatever you expect or wish the spirit to appear in) "without any deformity, bid in the Name of Jah and Vax, which Adam heard and spoke; and by the name Joth, which Jacob heard from the angel striving with him and was delivered from the hands of his brother Esau; and by the name of God Agla, which Lot heard and was saved with his family; and by the name Anaphenaton, which Aaron heard and spake and became wise; and by the name Emanuel, which the three children heard, Shedrack, Mescheek, and Abednego, run in the midst of the fire and was delivered; by Alpha and Omega, which Daniel named and destroyed Bel and slew the dragon; and by the name Tevoah, which Moses named and all the waters in Egypt's land was turned into blood; and by the name Eserchie Oriston, which Moses named and all the rivers brought forth frogs, and they went into all the houses of the Egyptians, destroying all things; and by the name Elion, which Moses called upon, and there was great hail such as never was to this day; and by the name Adonay, which Moses named and there came locusts upon all the land of the Egyptians and destroyed all that the hail had left; by the Name Hagios, Iscyros, *Anthanatos* [Athanatos], Paracteton; and by the holy and sacred Names of God, Agla and Tetragrammaton[1628]; and by the dreadful judgment of God; and by the unstable sea of glass, which is before the face of divine majesty and most powerful; and by the four beasts which are before the throne, having eyes before and behind; and by all the holy angels of heaven; and by the seal of Baldatel; and by his name Primeuation, which commandeth all the whole host of heaven, as such Moses named and the earth opened her mouth and swallowed…"[1629]

(See this conjuration much lengthened and more perfect in page 43 of my red quarto manuscript, this being taken from an imperfect manuscript in my very small book.)

1627. Peterson, *The Lesser Key of Solomon*, 48.

1628. *By the three…Tetragrammaton*: The third name is not provided.

1629. Peterson, *The Lesser Key of Solomon*, 49–50.

[401bis]

[blank]

[402]

<u>*The Spirits' Chain*</u>[1630]

"O thou wicked spirit N., because thou hast not regarded my words and hast rebelled, although my words were all glorious names of the true and living God, and master and creator of you and all the world, and by the power of these names, to which no creature is able to resist, do curse you into the depth of the bottomless pit, to remain till the day of doom in chains of fire and brimstone unquenchable, unless you appear before me ○ in the △ to do my will. Therefore come quickly *and* peaceably by these names, Adonay, Zeaboeh, Adonay, Anoum, come, your king Adonay commands you."

When you have read so far and they don't come, write his name and seal in virgin parchment, and put it into a black box (or pill box) with brimstone and asafoetida, and such things as make a stink, and then bind the box round with an iron wire, and hang it on the sword's point, and hold it over the fire of charcoal and say to the fire, it being placed toward the quarter the spirit is to come from:

<u>*Conjuration for the △ Fire*</u>[1631]

"I conjure thee, <u>fire</u>, by him that made thee and all other good creatures in the world, to torment, burn, and consume this spirit N. everlastingly. I condemn thee, thou Spirit N. to fire everlastingly, because thou art disobedient, and obey not my command nor keep the precepts of the Lord thy God neither wilt[1632] thou obey me nor my invocations, I have hereby called you forth who am the Servant of God, dignified and fortified by this celestial power and permission. Neither cometh thou to answer these things we requested of you, for which contempt you are guilty of disobedience. I shall therefore excommunicate you and destroy thy name and seal which I have here enclosed in this box burn them in immortal fire and burn them in immortal oblivion, unless thou immediately come and appear here before that ○" (I suppose then ○ means circle) "in this △ in a fair and comely form, and no ways terrible hurtful or forgetful to me or any other creatures on this ⊖, and make rational answer to my request and perform all my desires in all things make known to you."

1630. Peterson, *The Lesser Key of Solomon*, 52.

1631. Peterson, *The Lesser Key of Solomon*, 52.

1632. *Wilt*: Text has "doest" just above this word, but "wilt" is not marked out.

If he do not come, say:

"Now, O thou spirit N., who art still disobedient, I do in the name of God, Jehovah Tetragrammaton, the only creator of heaven, ⊖ earth, and hell, and all that in them is, who is the disposer of all things, curse you and deprive you of all your offices, joy, and place, and to bind you in the depth of Hell to the last day. Let all the holy company of heaven curse thee, the ☉, ☽, and stars into the fire unquenchable."

The manuscript from which this was taken is here tore out. What follows is borrowed from other authors, viz.[1633]

1633. Blank here in the original manuscript.

[403]

[blank]

[404]

When the Spirits Appear[1634]

Say as follows:

"Welcome, spirit N., most noble king, unto me. I have called you through him who created the heavens and the earth. By the same power, I call you forth and bind you that you remain affable here before this ○ in this △ so long as I shall have occasion for you, and not depart without my licence and you have truly and faithfully performed my will without falsity."

Then command them to perform your business, and it shall be done.

Licence to Depart[1635]

"O thou spirit N., as thou hast diligently obeyed my word and demand and was willing to come at my command, I do here license you to depart unto thy proper place without doing any harm to man or beast. Departed, be ready at my call. Being conjured by the rites of magic, I charge thee to withdraw thyself in peace, and the peace of God be continued between thee and me."

After you have given the spirit licence, you are not to depart till you have made a prayer to God and thanks for being delivered from the harm and malice of the Devil.

1634. Peterson, *The Lesser Key of Solomon*, 54.

1635. Peterson, *The Lesser Key of Solomon*, 55.

[405]

[Talismans for Virtues]

[406]

[Magical Rings]

A ring for power: Let the image of Saturn be engraved upon a loadstone and worn on the right hand.[1636]

A ring for prosperity and health: The image of Jupiter, a ring, holding lightning, sitting upon a throne and an eagle at his feet.[1637]

A ring for sanity: a stag engraved upon a white stone, set in pure gold, and worn.

A ring to conquer: a man sitting on a comely dragon with a sword in his hand, to be engraved on amethyst and set in steel.[1638]

A ring for the sight: a virgin engraved in a crystal, holding a lighted candle in her hand, to be set in the purest gold, vide Thetel.[1639]

1636. Agrippa, *Three Books of Occult Philosophy* (1651), 298 (book 2, chapter 38).

1637. Compare to Agrippa, *Three Books of Occult Philosophy* (1651), 299 (book 2, chapter 39).

1638. Leonardi, Lecouteux, and Monfort, *Les pierres talismaniques*, 103.

1639. Leonardi, Lecouteux, and Monfort, *Les pierres talismaniques*, 123.

[407]

[Various Talismans]

Topaz

Set in Gold
For complain of fever
and gout -

Rosucrucian Seal

Made in Lapis
Lazuli

Seal of <u>Love</u> on a <u>Stone under Venus</u> Set in ☽

Gold

Silver

[408]

[Untitled Poem][1640]

O mighty parent, as thy works I trace,
I worship thee—with unovated[1641] grace!
Thy wonder mighty to the earth declare,
Thy will, O! God, omnipotent and rare,
All things till that <u>One</u> on high
Each mental comfort does supply.
O! Source of wisdom, humbly at thy feet
Let me Thy aid and love protection greet.
Be Thou a Father in cruel scene of woe
Then, calmly find, will all my misery go.
Upheld by thee, in vain afflictioned
will agonise, protected by my God—
I'll fear no ill, but still joyful be
And all the world shall my triumphs see
Yes, Lord, thou art comfort and uphold,[1642]
And in good time, thy mercurial[1643] unfold,
My prison healing, then the captive free
Will dedicate, O Lord, her grace to thee
with heartful joy—praise Thy holy name,
And grateful sing thy most glorious fame.

Olive

1640. I have done my best to copy this, but the handwriting is unclear at many points.

1641. *Unovated*: Without applause?

1642. *Uphold*: Support.

1643. *Mercuriall*: Likely here a medicine involving mercury, considered healthy at that time.

[409]

[More Talismans]

In Hoc Vinci[1644]

IN·HOC·VINCI·

This sigil in pure gold is invaluable, Thetel says.

Prosperitas[1645]

PROSPERITAS.

This sigil in silver was dealed[1646] by Thetel, good for gain.

1644. Translation: "In This to Conquer."

1645. Translation: "Success."

1646. *Dealed*: Bestowed.

[410]

Hymn by Princess Olive

The gifts, O God, which I received from thee
Have softened all my misery;
Amidst a prison's gloom I find
A peaceful heart, and happy mind.

Repose thrust, given! And led on,
O! Finish, Lord, what is begun;
Wisdom shower from thy throne,
Then, Lord, my sorrows will have flown.

And power nor fortunes longer pain,
If life eternal is my gain.
Chastise me, Lord, if to thee,
I'm led by care and misery,

And where my sufferings merit grace,
Let me with thee find a place.
Thy cross I've borne—alas, its weight
Has oft distressed my earthly state.

Then heal the wounds my heart has known;
Let mercy from thy heavenly throne

[411]

Direct, O Lord, each thought of mine;
Let me show thy love divine.

So shall my mind expand and be
The mirror clear, thyself to see
In all thy works, and to adore
While I each miracle explore.

Teach me, Lord, each good to know
The source from whence thy blessings flow.
Keep me steadfast in thy way;
More perfect make me every day.

Thy grateful servant, let me live;
The Lord in time all things will give.

And let me triumph o'er each Foe—
My bounteous Love will all bestow.

Olive

Tuesday night, in my captivity[1647]

[412]

[More Talismans]

Upon gold for health, says Thetel, a philosopher of the primitive age

To be made on the sixth day of the moon in pure silver,
for successful traffic

1647. Olivia Serres was frequently in debtors' prison.

[427][1648]

[William Browne's "Behold O God IN RIvers[1649] of My Tears"][1650]

Behold, O God | *IN* | | *RI* | *vers of my tears*

I come to thee, bow downe | | *thy blessed eares*

To here me wretch & let | | *thine eyes with sleepe,*

Yet never closet, behold a | | *weepe.*

Let not O	*God,*	*O God*		*my God my*	*fault*	*though great*
And numberless		*-but*	*W*	*hen thy mercy*		*Seate*
And my poore		*Soul but*	*H*	*ow since we*		*are taught*
Thou Lord remem		*berst th*	*Y*	*ne if thou be*		*sought.*
I co~~me not Lord~~	*ME*	*not Lord wit*	*H*	*- any O*	*the*	*r merrit*
Then	*WH*	*at I by my S*	*A*	*- viour*	*CH*	*rist inherit.*
Be th-	*EN*	*his wound*	*S*	*my balme first*	*RI*	*pes my bliss*
My Crown is	*TH*	*orns my*	*T*	*h be -*	*ST*	*in his*
And th:	*OY*	*my bles*	*T*	*redemer*	*SA*	*viour, God,*
Quit my ac	*CO*	*mpts with all*	*H*	*old thy*	*Y*	*full rod.*
O beg for	*ME*	*my th-*	*O*	*ughts on*	*T*	*hee art set*
And Chri-	*ST*	*forgi:*	*V*	*es by*	*H*	*is debt*
The Liv:	*IN*	*g found li*	*F*	*e the wa-*	*Y*	*I know*
And but	*TO*	*thee -*	*O*	*whither-*	*S*	*hould I goe*
All O	*TH*	*er helps a*	*R*	*e vain; great*	*E*	*thine to me;*
for in t-	*HY*	*crosse my*	*S*	*aving hea:-*	*L*	*th must me.*
Hark	*K*	*en then wh*	*A*	*i with-*	*F*	*aith implore*
Lest S	*IN*	*& death sin*	*K*	*me for*	*E*	*vermore*
Lastly O	*G*	*od my way*	*E*	*direct*	*A*	*nd guide*
In	*D*	*eath defe*	*N*	*d me that I*	*N*	*ever slide.*
And at the D	*OM*	*e let*	*M*	*o be mise*	*D*	*then*
To live	*E*	*with the-*	*E*	*sweet Jes*	*VS*	*say amen.*

1648. At this point, the manuscript flips over and writing begins at the other end. Given that much of it is a single block of text, I will present pages 413–27 in reverse order and then resume regular pagination from there.

None of the prescriptions in this section are recommended, and the stated amounts of various substances are not always clear based upon the characters used for amounts in the original.

1649. *INRI*: Abbreviation of "Iesus Nazarenus, Rex Iudaeorum," or "Jesus of Nazareth, King of the Jews," the inscription supposedly placed over Jesus's head on the Cross. (KJV John 19:19).

1650. This diagram is a poem by William Browne (1590/91–1645?), a poet admitted to the Inns of Court, perhaps best known for his unfinished work *Britannia's Pastorals*. "Behold, O God!" was not published until 1815, and that without its figurative arrangement, but it circulated in multiple manuscript editions before then. Wright, "A Pattern Poem."

There are many deviations in the text from Browne's editions not noted here; someone in the chain of transmission might not have understood the full significance of each line's text and arrangement. The blank on the fourth line should be the word "Sinner." It's not clear whether this was meant to be inserted in a different colour.

[426]

Experiments for Birds, Fish, Coneys,[1651] Gathered Out of Divers Authors

A Very Good Bait to Angle

Take one spoonful of clarified honey, powder of ences camphor,[1652] and fine wheat flour, and four drops of balm, and temper it altogether somewhat warm and make stiff, paste, and fit.

Alio[1653]

Take one spoonful of honey and asafoetida, and boil them together till they be stiff, and strike your line a handful above the stock, and you shall have very good luck.

To Take Fish with Your Hand

Dry the gall of an ox, or any other gall, per the ☉ or per the fire, and cut it in small pieces, and cast it where fish is.

Sicca herba barbati radicem ejus in umbra tum pulveriza et pulvern aspergas ubi pisces statet et stati pisces gustabunt et eos cum manibus capere potes.

> Dry the root of the herb arum[1654] in shade, then pulverise it and sprinkle the powder where fish tarry, and these fish will snack on it, and you are able to take them with your hands.[1655]

To Take Birds with Your Hand

Take of henbane seed, poppy's seed, hemlock seed, and wheat, and boil altogether in wine lees or good ale lees, and cast it where birds haunt.

To Take All Manner of Fowl That Eat Corn

Boil barby[1656] and asafoetida in strong wine lees or aqua vitae till it be thick, and cast it where fowls' haunt, et fiet.[1657]

1651. *Coneys*: Rabbits.

1652. *Ences camphor*: Unknown. Markings on "ences" indicates that it is an abbreviation.

1653. Translation: "For Another."

1654. *Arum*: According to the *Dictionary of Medieval Latin from British Sources*, "barbati" may be translated as arum, burdock, deadnettle, ribwort plantain, hypocistis, houseleek, and withered rose. Of these, only arum would be considered poisonous. A better option might appear in the parallel passage on manuscript page 425.

1655. The original has some curious shifts in tense.

1656. *Barby*: Unknown. Possibly "barba" as listed above.

1657. *Et fiet*: Translation: "And it will be done."

To Take Fish in a Pool or River[1658]

Take three berries of oculus indiae,[1659] crumbs of white bread, hard cheese shaven or sweet cream, and live honey. Make all these into a paste and make it into small pellets somewhat less than a pea. Cast one in after another, and in an hour's time, you shall see good sport.

To Take Fish

Take mullein, henbane, and dwale,[1660] of every one a handful, and stamp them in a mortar, and take an dram of asafoetida, and take the fat of a tench[1661] and the liver, and put them altogether. Take fair meat oil and put thereto one, and let them stand together a day and a night, and then scaul[1662] them and strain them. Throw a fair linen cloth,

[425]

and then put the asafoetida therein, and let them be together, and take thereto a ¼ dram of frankincense. Take this oil and go to a still water, and put it therein, and the fish will come thereto.

To Comfort[1663] *Fish to Bite*

Take a dram of gum arabic, as much of oil benedictus,[1664] and as much of the oil of asperadge, and a little asafoetida, bean flour, a little honey, the yokes of three or four eggs, and a little saffron. All these must be made thick, and bait your hook therewith and not fail.

A Bait for Fish

Take wheat flour and tallow of a new flayed sheep, and that glyre of an egg, and beat them altogether, and bait your sack therewith.

To Take a Pike

Take three or four inches' length of a sheep's guts, and fill it with tar, and knife it like a pudding, and cast it into the water, and when the pike hath eaten it, he will turn up his belly straight away.

1658. See also Markham, *The Husbandman's Jewel*, 38.

1659. *Oculus indiae*: Bud of *Cannabis indica*.

1660. *Dwale*: *Atropa belladonna*.

1661. *Tench*: *Tinca vulgaris*, a fish related to carp.

1662. *Scaul*: Scald?

1663. *Comfort*: Incite.

1664. *Oil benedictus*: This has been interpreted variously as petroleum, blessed oil, or "alchemist's oil." Berners, *The Treatise on Angling*, 40.

To Take Fish with the Angle Rod

Take pig's heart and close it fast in a glass four weeks in the ☉, then put thereto asafet[1665] and put thereof on your hook.

Pro Eodem[1666]

Take one spoonful of clarified honey, powder of emens camphor,[1667] any of fine wheat flour, three drops of balm, and temper altogether somewhat warm, and make paste.

Pro Eodem[1668]

Take one spoonful of honey and asafet, and boil them together till they be stiff, and strike your line a handful above the hook, et fiet.[1669]

To Take Fish with Your Hand

Dry the gall of an ox, or any other thing, per the fire, and cut it into small pieces, and cast it in the water where fish is.

Alia[1670]

Sicca herbam tapsi barbati, radicem ejus in umbra, tum palveriza et pulverem aspurges ubi pisces scantet, et fiet.

> Dry the root of the herb mullein[1671] in shade, then pulverise it and sprinkle the powder where fish rise to the surface, and it will be done.

[424]

To Take Coneys

Take darnel[1672] seed and grind it, and make thick cakes thereof, and bake it, and it being whole, lay it on the windy side that the coneys might smell it, and they will come and eat it, and as many as eat shall die.

1665. *Asafet*: Asafoetida.

1666. Translation: "For the Same." See previous page for another example.

1667. *Emens camphor*: Unknown, but see earlier.

1668. Translation: "For the Same."

1669. *Et fiet*: Translation: "and it will be done."

1670. Translation: "Another."

1671. *Mullein*: Common mullein (*Verbascum thapsus*), used as a common piscicide, e.g., Aristotle, *History of Animals, Books VII–X*, 2:174–75; Wilhelm, "The Mullein: Plant Piscicide of the Mountain Folk Culture."

1672. *Darnel*: *Lolium temulentum*, a plant with poisonous properties.

Pro Eodem[1673]

Take aqua vitae, and wheat hay or parsley therein, and lay it for them to eat. It maketh them drunken, that one may catch them.

To Take Coneys or Deer

Take dwale, a handful when he seedeth, a handful of henbane, a handful of the herb John, a gallon of river water with foam. Boil all these together an hour. Then take a pot of oats and drench them therein when it is cold, and let them lie therein two days and two nights, and that fourth day, take up the oats and let that water run out of them. Then take an earthen pot and parch them, and in parching of them, put a dram of asafoetida, and a dram of frankincense thereto, and take of these oats and lay them in the wind to deer or coneys, and they shall sleep till you may take them.

To Take Coneys

Take asafet, make thereof powder, and temper it with boar's grease. Put into a pot of earth with a hole of either side, and put coals of fire thereto, and go on the windy side, that the smell may go to the coneys and they will come thereto.

Ad Aves Capiendas[1674]

Take wheat and put it in the dross of wine, or put it into the juice of rue, and give it to the birds, and it stonyeth[1675] them.

To Take Doves

Take wheat or peas, and steep it in the lees of wine, and let it boil in the savour, with a good quart of cumin and galls of beast, till they be upon the breathing. Then take them off from the fire and dry them till the moisture be dried up. Then cast them to eat, & c.

[423]

Ad Capiendas Aves, Pasceres, Cornes, et Columbas & c.[1676]

Take gall, and lay hemp seed therein eight days, and cast it where they do use.

1673. Translation: "For the Same."

1674. Translation: "For Taking Birds."

1675. *Stonyeth*: Stupefies.

1676. Translation: "For Taking Birds, Sparrows, Ravens, and Doves."

Si Vis Accipere Columbas[1677]

Accipe fabas, et unge cum felle alicuius avis, et omnes cum gustaverunt morientur.

Take beans, and anoint them with the gall of some bird, and all will die when they eat of it.

Ad Aves Capiendas[1678]

Take henbane, poppy, and lettuce seed, hemlock, but stamped and boiled in wine, mained[1679] with corn.

To Take Birds

Take the juice of rue and vinegar both together, and steep corn in it, and fling it to them.

To Take Cranes

Take beans, and make a hole in the side, and gather out the flour, and save the hole and the bean whole, and fill it with quicksilver and stop it with wax, and cast where they do use, and they will willingly eat thereof, and then they cannot away nor help themselves.

To Take Birds

Poppy seeds steeped in aqua vitae twenty-four hours, and cast it unto them.

To Take Coneys

Take cumin seed and henbane seed, beat them in a mortar, and then take strong ale and oats, and seek them till be dry with the powder, then lay on wort leaves before the holes.

[To Frighten Cattle]

It is written, per divers authors, that if wolves' dung be hidden in the mangers, racks, or else the hedges about the pastures where cattle go, through the antipathy of the nature of the wolf and other cattle, all the beasts that savour the same do not only forbear to eat, but ran about as though they were mad, or (as they say) bewitched.

To Make Cider Fly, or to Be Smart

Hg wa 4 qebcf bs gvr pernz os gbegre wagb rhrel obggyr.[1680]

It will make the cork fly out above three yards.

1677. Translation: "If You Desire to Take Doves."

1678. Translation: "For Taking Birds."

1679. *Mained*: Mainlined.

1680. *Hg…obbgyr*: Deciphered: "Ad[d] in 4 drops of the cream of tartar into every bottle."

[422]

Ubi gb znxr n frag sbe pyneerg beivwgr iwar[1681]

Take you a linen cloth and lay it in rose water all night, then dry it very well, and take these spices: aniseed, one dram; cloves, one dram; ignem podyan,[1682] one dram; long pepper, one dram; grains, one dram; orris, one dram; one dram coriander seed, one dram of currants. Beat these together, then melt you brimstone and dip your cloth in it, then throw your spice on it.

Gb znxr n frag sbe firrg iwar[1683]

Lay your cloth in rose water all night, then dry it well. Use the spices following: cloves, one dram; coriander-seed, one dram; one dram of camphor; nutmegs, one dram. Beat all these together, and then melt your brimstone, and dip the cloth in it, then scatter your spices.

Ditto

Take a quarter of a pint of strong water,[1684] and dip your cloth in it, then put it to the brimstone, and fire it with a candle, so put it into the hogsheads and stop it close, so that the air may not come in.

Hogshead of ivwg gung ybfg vwf pbyre[1685]

First overdraw[1686] your hogshead four gallons, and then take three gallons of milk, and let it stand until it hath gathered a cream. That cream is there. Put it into your hogshead, then beat it well with that perpylying[1687] staff, then make your . . . .[1688] with the whites of twelve eggs. Beat the . . . . to take away the threads of them, then take one handful of bay-salt, two drams of rock alum burnt, and one dram [?] of starch. Then beat these together with a pottle[1689] of your milk till it be very short, then put it into your hogshead. Then beat it with your staff a quarter of an hour, and then let it stand twenty-four hours, and it will be very fine and white.

1681. Deciphered: "How to Make a Scent for Claret or White Wine."

1682. *Ignem podyan*: Unknown.

1683. Deciphered: "To Make a Scent for Sweet Wine."

1684. *Strong water*: Either a strong alcoholic drink or, more likely, nitric acid.

1685. Deciphered: "White That Lost Its Colour."

1686. *Overdraw*: To remove liquid from a container without disturbing the bottom.

1687. *Perpylying*: Unknown.

1688. Ellipses present in the original.

1689. *Pottle*: Half a gallon.

[421]

Pynee[r]g gung ungu ybfg vwf pbybhe[1690]

First overdraw your hogshead four gallons, then put it into the three gallons of red wine, then take the yolks of twelve eggs, the threads being taken away, and a handful of bay-salt, and beat it well with your brush with a quart of the same wine, till it be very short.[1691] Then put it into your hogshead, and beat it very well with your staff. If you have no red wine, then take six drams [?] of trumsell,[1692] and lay it in. Steep with a gall of the same come half an hour, then wring it out of the wine, then put it into the hogshead and the . . . . as is before laid down, and in three days, it will be fine.

Ws pyneerg or frnyy[1693]

Rack it upon a sack lee into another hogshead. If it drink eager,[1694] take three or four pounds of chalk, scrape it very fine, and so put it into it, and let it stand seven or eight hours, then take it off into another vessel. If it drinks hard, take seven or eight pounds of raisins, and bruise them very small, and put them into your hogshead, and beat them in your hogshead with your staff, and in three days, it will very fine drink well and sweet.

Ws Pyneerg iwyy abg iwar[1695]

Take a new drawn hogshead, and wash it very clean, and scent it. If your iwar[1696] be pale, overdraw it nine or ten gallons, then hew it very deep, or else it will not bear the milk, and when it be full wanting a gallon. Then put in one gallon of milk, then beat it with your staff half an hour, then let it stand three or four days, and it will be iwar.

Pyneerg be ivwgr ws gurl or fznyy[1697]

Take half an ounce of India or Jamaica pepper,[1698] and half a dram of long pepper, and three drams of cloves, and three drams liquorice, three case-nuts,[1699]

1690. Deciphered: "Claret That Hath Lost His Colour."

1691. *Short*: Not viscous.

1692. *Trumsell*: Unknown.

1693. Deciphered: "If Claret Be Small." "Small" means "weak."

1694. *Eager*: Sour.

1695. Deciphered: "If Claret Will Not Wine."

1696. *Iwar*: Deciphered: "Wine." This word is actually crossed out just before the cipher.

1697. Deciphered: "Claret or White, If They Be Small."

1698. *Jamaica pepper*: Allspice.

1699. *Case-nuts*: Possibly nuts packed in chests instead of bags, for superior flavour.

[420]

three drams of damask powder. Put all these together, then make a bag of a foot long, that it may go into the bung. Then hang your bag with the spice, with two lemons cut small and put in the bag. Then hang your bag in the midst of the hogshead, and in very short time, your white or pyneerg[1700] will drink very strong.

Ws n ohgg bs fnpx unhr gbfg vwf pbybhe[1701]

Take six gallons of milk, then let it stand six or seven hours, then take the cream clean from it. Then take the whites of twelve eggs, one handful of bay salt, three drams of rock alum, and brew it very well together on the fire, then beat it small. Then put it to your eggs and your salt, and beat it with your staff, until it be very short. Then put it to your milk, and beat it well with your brush, then put it into your butt, and beat it well with your staff, and, in two days, it will be iwar.[1702]

Ws fnpx gewax rntre[1703]

Take six pounds of chalk, scrape it fine, and so put it into your butt. Beat it with your staff, and let it stand ten or twelve hours. Then take it out into another butt, and use the ...... as before laid down, and let your fnpx[1704] be from his vrr[1705] before you put in your chalk.

Ws fnpx qewax uneq, hfr guwf sbe n[1706] *Hogshead*

Take eight or ten pounds of alligant raisins,[1707] and stamp them in a mortar very small. Then beat them up with some of that iwar,[1708] then put it into your hogshead and beat it with your staff. Then let it stand six or seven days, and it will drink sweet, you may broach.[1709]

1700. *Pyneerg*: Deciphered: "claret."

1701. Deciphered: "If a Butt of Sack Have Lost His Colour." A "butt" is a cask for liquid storage, or a standard of liquid volume based upon such a cask. "Sack" is imported white wine, from the Canaries or Spain.

1702. *Iwar*: Deciphered: "wine."

1703. Deciphered: "If Sack Drink Eager."

1704. *Fnpx*: Deciphered: "sack."

1705. *Vrr*: Deciphered: "lee."

1706. Deciphered: "If Sack Drink Hard, Use This for a"

1707. *Alligant raisins*: Raisins made from grapes used to make Alicante wine.

1708. *Iwar*: Deciphered: "wine."

1709. *Broach*: To tap a keg.

Ws fnpx qewax fznyy, hfr gurrfr[1710]

Take one ounce of India pepper, one dram of long pepper, two ounces of coriander seeds, one dram of aniseed, four drams of cloves, six drams of

[419]

damask powder, and beat all these together, and make a bag a foot long, and put your spice into it, and hang it in the bung, and be every day tasting of it, for fear it be too strong of the spice. Therefore, when it comes to his last and strength, pull out the bag.

Gb znxr n ohgg bs zhfxwqwar[1711]

Take fifty gallons of brown bastard,[1712] and seven gallons of cute,[1713] and put them into a clean butt. Then take the yolks of twelve eggs and two handfuls of bay salt, and beat it very well with your brush, until it be very short. Then put it into your butt, and beat it well with your staff, then fill it with any wine, lee of fnpx,[1714] or white or pyneerg,[1715] which you will.

How to Make a . . . . for the Butt of Muscadine, Before Mentioned

Three drams of damask powder, six drams of cloves, two drams of long pepper, two drams of ginger, four case-nuts, one dram of camphor, one dram of coriander seeds. Beat all these together, and make your bag a foot long, and put your spice into it, and hang it into the middle of your muscadine. Then take a grain of musk, and put it into half a pint of rosewater, and put it into the butt, and in seven or eight days' times. It will be perfect.

Ws ob[e]iar onfgneq or rntre[1716]

Take six [?] of chalk, scraped it very fine, and put it into one gallon of the same wine, and stir it with your brush. Then put it into your pipe, and beat it well with our staff, and let it stand with the bung open eight or nine hours. Then take it off into another pipe, and it will be as good as it was before it was better. Let it stand three or four days, and then you may draw it.

1710. Deciphered: "If Sack Drink Small, Use These."

1711. Deciphered: "To Make a Butt of Muscadine."

1712. *Brown Bastard*: A sweet wine from Spain.

1713. *Cute*: New wine sweetened after rendering it down to a particular consistency.

1714. *Fnpx*: Deciphered: "sack."

1715. *Pyneerg*: Deciphered: "claret."

1716. Deciphered: "If B[r]own Bastard Be Eager."

Ws n ohgg of fnpx be fwqre, or ebcwr, be ybbx oebiar[1717]

Take an empty clean butt then draw your fnpx[1718] into it, clean

[418]

from his vrrf.[1719] Then + + + take two pounds of rice flour, as fine as you can, and four grains of camphor. Beat it with some of the flour, and then put it into the butt, and beat it with your staff half an hour, then use your . . . . as is before laid down with your eggs and milk, and rock alum, and bay salt, as you have heard before.

Ubi[1720] *gb enpx enlawfu iwar*[1721]

First wash your hogshead overnight, and let it lie and drain all night, when you use it. Then take your scent made of nothing but of + brimstone, let it be two handfuls long, that put to your scent when + it is light in the bundy,[1722] and quarter of pint of aqua vita. Then stop it close six or seven hours, then rack; you come into it.

Iwar fgwax & prbeeheg[1723]

Take two or three quarts of good wheat, and put it into a bag, and hang it into the midst of the iwar,[1724] and in short time it will take the ill savour away. Then rack it into another vessel, and that stink will be gone.

How to Make Hippocras[1725] *for to Fill Two Gallons*

Two pounds of sugar, two drams of cinnamon, two drams of ginger, one dram of cloves, one dram of nutmegs, one dram of long pepper, four drams of grains, two drams of coriander seed. Beat all these together, and put them into your iwar,[1726] and let them stand eight or nine hours, and then take a pint of milk, and put it to it, and then let it run through your bag, then harry a little musk into it, and use with it two or three drams of cinnamon-water.

1717. Deciphered: "If a Butt of Sack Be Cider, or Ropy or Look Brown." "Ropy" is a bacterial condition in which filaments appear in a liquid.

1718. *Fnpx*: Deciphered: "sack."

1719. *Vrrf*: Deciphered: "lees."

1720. Translation: "When."

1721. Deciphered: "To Rack Rhenish Wine."

1722. *Bundy*: Unknown.

1723. Deciphered: "Wine Stink and Corrupt."

1724. *Iwar*: Deciphered: "wine."

1725. *Hippocras*: Flavoured and sweetened wine.

1726. *Iwar*: Deciphered: "wine."

Ubi[1727] *gb znxr hwawtre*[1728]

Take salt and pepper mixed together with sour leaves, and it will perform it quickly.

To Make a Flavour

Take two drams of coriander seed, two drams bengman,[1729] two drams of long pepper,

[417]

two drams of white suet. Beat them together and hang them in the midst of your pipe of butt.

A True Receipt to Find Any Piece of rwgure fcnawfe be Serapu Iwar[1730]

Take half a pound[1731] isinglass,[1732] and steep it in the hardest French iwar.[1733] You have let the iwar, cover it, then let it stand twenty-four hours. Then take the isinglass with your hands, and put it to pieces, and then put a little of the same iwar to it, then let it lie. Three or four times a day, break it and squeeze it with your hands till it comes to a clear jelly, and as it thickens, put more of the same to it. Then, when it is come to a perfect clear jelly, take a pint or a quart to a hogshead, and so, according to that as you have occasion of, overdraw the same piece of iwar, that you beat three or four gallons. Then put the same that of isinglass into the can as you overdrew, then stir the isinglass and break it with your staff exceeding well together, then fill it up top full, and so let it lie.

For the French, ditto, bung it up well. The Spanish, what you will.

To Fine[1734] *Any Piece of Wine That Is Qualish*[1735] *or Brown, Be It What Sort Soever*[1736]

Take a pint of the same jelly of the same isinglass, and a quart of milk, as you find the piece of wine a matter[1737] of eight gallons. Then, with a paddle staff,

1727. Translation: "By Which."

1728. Deciphered: "To Make Vinegar."

1729. *Bengman*: Benjamin.

1730. Translation: "Either Spanish or French Wine." D. D., *The Skilful Physician*, 375–76.

1731. *Half a pound*: Symbol in manuscript unknown, so this is taken from the printed source.

1732. *Isinglass*: Gelatin made from sturgeon, or perhaps from hide and hooves of farm animals.

1733. *Iwar*: Deciphered: "wine," here and below.

1734. *Fine*: Become clear.

1735. *Qualish*: Curdled?

1736. D. D., *The Skilful Physician*, 376–77.

1737. *Matter*: Quantity.

stir it two or three blows, then suddenly, putting in both milk and isinglass in the butt or hogshead. Then beat it very well, then fill it up top-full, and this will fine it in one or two days.

How to Make Wine Sweet That Stinketh, or That Hath an Ill Savour, or That Is Grown Musty[1738]

If the fault be in the cask, as oftentimes it 'tis, then you must of necessity draw him off into a fresh cask and yrrf,[1739] but let none of the old yrrf at any hand come out of it when you draw it. Therefore draw you him not too near, then thus afterwards I use him. Take twelve eggs—both

[416]

whites and yolks—and beat them short. Then you shall take two drams of ginger, two drams of cloves, two drams of orass,[1740] two drams of grains, and one dram of long pepper. Put the eggs into a pint of damask rose-water, mingled together; put them into the wine, then beat the butt half an hour, and then, when the spices be grossly beaten, you must take two grains of musk, and bruise it well in four spoonfuls of damask rose-water (with the back of a spoon), and put it also into the butt. Then beat the butt again a quarter of an hour. Then take two grains of ambergris, and as much of manus christi;[1741] beat them well and put them amongst the spices, and put all into a bag and tie it safe to the bung, and let it hang almost to the bottom of the butt for two days, then safely draw it up to the middle of the wine, then let it stand two days more, then lastly draw it up almost to the top, then let it hang a day more. Then you may take it out and roll the butt a little, but it be [sic] must be forced well, and close stopped up, and in two days after, in two days after [sic] you may broach him, and it will be very sweet and pleasant every way.

How to Make a Piece of Qu[a]l[it]y[1742] *ffcnawfr iwar,*[1743] *Fine*[1744]

Take half a quarter of a pound[1745] of white starch, and a quarter of writing sand, small, and a pint of isinglass, and a good handful of bag-soot, and the

1738. D. D., *The Skilful Physician*, 378–79.

1739. *Yrrf*: Deciphered: "lees."

1740. *Orass*: Unknown. "Orras" is given in D. D., so probably orris root, or powdered rhizome of *Iris germanica*.

1741. *Manus christi*: "Hand of Christ," a cordial made of sugar and rosewater, cinnamon, or violet water.

1742. *Quality*: The letters in brackets were inserted above the main word.

1743. Deciphered: "Spanish Wine."

1744. D. D., *The Skilful Physician*, 377–78.

1745. *Half a quarter of a pound*: Unit in manuscript unknown, taken from D. D.

whites of two eggs, and beat them well with a little brush. Then overdraw the hogshead or butt of wine,[1746] and so beat it up extraordinary well, fill it up top-full and that will make it perfect, fine.

For Any serapu Iwnr that comes bhre upon the yrr that is grown oebhar[1747] and Faint[1748]

Take one pound[1749] of aby-bastard-dust[1750] sifted, and overdraw the hogshead of serapu iwar,[1751] three or four gallons, then put the dry dust into the bung of it, as it is upon the yrr.[1752] Then take a staff and

[415]

give it good strokes, then fill it top-full. The more you stir it, the better it will be upon the yrr, and nothing will be seen but grow perfect good. The longer it lies, the better it is, and when you see good, you may rack it off.

To Make a Hugher[1753] That Is Excellent[1754]

Take a good butt of znyx-fwr.[1755] Overdraw it one quarter, then fill him up with fat bastard and two gallons of cute, then parell[1756] him as you did the znyx-fwr and bastard, being both after one manner, with the same thing and after the same manner. So beat him and keep him close, and within two or three days after you may pierce him, and he will be almost perfect, and drink off.

To Make zhfxnqry[1757] of Jeane[1758]

Take a butt of engal[1759] or good zhfxnqry, and fill him up with fat bastard, and use him after the manner as you did the malmsey, and beat him well an hour, till he be fine.

1746. *Wine*: Original in cipher: "iwar."

1747. Deciphered: "French Wine That Comes over upon the Lee That Is Grown Brown."

1748. D. D., *The Skilful Physician*, 377.

1749. *Pound*: Unit taken from D. D.

1750. *Aby-Bastard-Dust*: D. D. is obscured here, but seems to read "alablasted," or gypsum, which is still used in winemaking to soften water.

1751. *Serapu Iwar*: Deciphered: "French wine."

1752. *Yrr*: Deciphered "lee," here and following.

1753. *Hugher*: Unknown. D. D. has "tyre," an imported sweet wine.

1754. D. D., *The Skilful Physician*, 397–98.

1755. *Znyx-fwr*: Deciphered as "malmsey," a sweet Mediterranean wine, here and following.

1756. *Parell*: Using a solution of eggs to clarify wine.

1757. Deciphered: "Muscadel."

1758. D. D., *The Skilful Physician*, 398.

1759. *Engal*: Unknown. D. D. does not mention this.

For Onfgneg[1760] *That Drinketh Hard Be Malmsey*[1761]

Put in three or four gallons of running water, and as much milk, then beat him well and give him the parcel of the yolks of six eggs and a pint of water, and put it into the wine. Beat the butt half an hour together, and when it is fine, rack him into a clean butt, and put into him two gallons of honey water, and stop him close. Roll him aside in two days; it shall be fine.

A Pleasant Scent or Savour for a Butt of Muscadel

Take a quart of a yard of canvas, and make a bay of it, one ounce of calamus aromaticus, two drams of flour, two drams of benjamin, two drams of orras, one dram of coriander seeds, and one of aniseed. Bruise and beat those together, and put them into your bag, and hang them in the middle of the wine.

[414]

Let it hang in three days and nights, then take it out, and after take two grains of civet, two grains of musk, a pint of damask rosewater, and warm the water blood warm, and rub all them well with the back of the spoon, and so put it into the butt. Stop him, and scole[1762] him well, but turn him not over. Within two days, it shall be perfect good.

N cresrpg pher sbe gvr zebcfwr.[1763] *Probatum Est.*[1764]

Take senaef[1765] the best, two drams; and a half rebark, half dram; pollipody of the oak, two drams; white tarter, three drams; wood of life, three oz.; leaf of betony and rosemary together, one handful; the wood of sassafras, one dram; and one quarter dram of the juice of scurvy-grass; a pint of the ray-soll[1766] stoned; two drams of ashen keys hulled; two drams of carraway seed; two case-nuts pounded; horseradish roots sliced, one handful chamaepitis; one handful sorsayeriall; two drams of rosy; and cut those that are properly so to be used, bruise such as are to be bruised, fill them into a bag of butter, and put a small weight in the bottom, and put into it two gallons of middle sort

1760. Deciphered: "Bastard."

1761. D. D., *The Skilful Physician*, 399.

1762. *Scole*: Scald?

1763. Deciphered: "A Perfect Cure for the Dropsy."

1764. I am uncertain of the source or the identities of some of these ingredients.

1765. *Senaef*: These and some of the other words in this recipe are indecipherable, suggesting the copyist was not sure of their meaning himself.

1766. *Raysoll*: Unknown.

as it work, fill it up with the same liquor. Stop it up and let the party drink as much every morning as will give him five or six stools, without hindering to his employ.

Sbe gvr tbhg nf tbby nf orsbre[1767]

Take eight quarts of running water. Steep therein three drams of sassafras, six drams of sarsaparilla, one dram of red china,[1768] twelve hours, then put it into a pot, and stop it very close with paste, that no air come therein and forth, and let it boil six hours with a very gentle fire, and be sure that the paste do not rise to let the air come forth. Then put therein four drams of stickadoss,[1769] and a half pound of ray-soll, three drams of liquorice, three drams of aniseed bruised, and let them boil softly two hours. Steep close as before; let no steam come forth. Then loose them

[413]

from the fire, and put therein one ounce [?] of rhubarb, one ounce [?] of seine. Cover it close until it be cold, then stamp it forth, and drink one-half pint every morning fasting, an hour after, and so drink it as the ordinary drink and no other liquor. Be sure to keep yourself very warm.

[Quotations from Agrippa]

There are trees which, after the solstice, do invert their leaves, as the poplar, elm, olive, line tree & c., and shellfish, crabs, and oysters do increase, the ☽ increasing, and when the moon decreaseth, do grow lean. In winter, when all things wither and dry, pennyroyal flourisheth.[1770]

To Distil All Manner of Flowers without an Alembic

Take an earthen pot; let it be full of holes at bottom. Put it on another pot and fit them together. Fill the uppermost pot half full of flowers. Lay a strong piece of holland[1771] over it, then secure the sides and put in the cloth, bending to the flowers' ashes, then embers, so force down the virtue of the herbs, which you may convey as you please. N.B. I think if the upper pot was flattish, or like a pan with holes, and a warming pan fire with charcoal or live embers laid thereon, would force down the steam or virtue. Perhaps the

1767. Deciphered: "For the Gout, as Good as Before."

1768. *Red china*: Could be China root (*Smilax china*).

1769. *Stickadoss*: Likely stickadove (*Lavandula stoechas*).

1770. Agrippa, *Three Books of Occult Philosophy* (1651), 551–52 (book 3, chapter 44).

1771. *Holland*: Likely a piece of linen fabric, so named from its original place of manufacture.

steam might be condensed by setting the bottom pot in a pan of cold water. A good lute[1772] to cement or keep the steam in betwixt the pots is made of filings of iron, beat or filed very small (perhaps its powder) mixed with honey and anoint the outside of the glass, or earthen materials, which will keep the spirits from coming out or evaporating.

[On the Moon]

The harvest moon is the first full moon after the sun enters ♍ Virgo,[1773] and the next full moon that the sun enters in Libra ♎ is the hunter's moon.

1772. *Lute*: A substance intended to cement a gap.

1773. The harvest moon is usually the moon closest to the fall equinox.

[428]

[blank]

[429]

[430]

[blank]

[431]

10 7 9 6 3 2 5
DIVINE WISDOM
Henry Cornelius Agrippa,
from a scare Print of Ancient Date

[432]

[blank]

[433]

[Aphorisms]

Life is short, art long, occasion sudden, experience dangerous, judgment difficult,[1774] nor is it sufficient that medicines perform their office, unless the patient does his duty by gratitude to his maker and emanation to nature.

Laus Deo.[1775]

It will meet the waking, sleeping, sailing, traveling, by night and by day, when thou speakest or keep silence, for God is omnipotent and omnipresent. Nor is there anything which hath not the image of God, who is in all his works and everywhere, for no place is hid, but at all times and in all things everywhere, he is ready at thy hand to be found and seen if you rightly seek him with faith and truth to whom be glory, power, might, majesty, and dominion, with gratitude, laud, and thanksgiving without end.[1776] Amen. Thus sayeth the Lord: "I am Alpha and Omega, the beginning and the end, which is, which was, which is to come, the Almighty.[1777] I am the first and the last, who am living and was dead, and behold I live for ever and ever and I have the keys of death and hell.[1778]"

There is a time and season for all things;[1779] therefore, gather knowledge while you may. Delay not. Remember, the sun ariseth and the sun goeth down, and hasteth to the place where he rose,[1780] so rivers unto the place from whence they come, thither they return again;[1781] let us then be vigilant in our researches, e'er thy silver cord be loosed, or the golden bowl be broken, or the pitcher destroyed at the fountain, or the wheel broken at the cistern.[1782] The wind goeth towards the south and turneth about unto the north; it whirleth about continually, and the wind returneth again according to his circuit.[1783] So shall our dust return to the earth as it cease, and the spirit shall return unto God who gave it.[1784]

Be civil, sober, wise, and just, and see thou try before thou trust, he that means to live at rest must harmless be, and say thee best.

1774. The first section of the first aphorism of Hippocrates. From this point, the quote changes.

1775. *Laus Deo*: Translation: "Praise to God."

1776. *It will meet…end*: Everard, *Divine Pymander*, 136. See comment, page i.

1777. *I am Alpha…Almighty*: Revelation 1:8.

1778. *I am the first…hell*: Revelation 1:17–18.

1779. *There is…things*: Ecclesiastes 3:1.

1780. *The sun…arose*: Ecclesiastes 1:5.

1781. *So rivers…again*: Ecclesiastes 1:7.

1782. *E'er…cistern*: Ecclesiastes 12:6.

1783. *The wind…circuit*: Ecclesiastes 1:6.

1784. *So shall…it*: Ecclesiastes 12:7.

[434]

Latin and English Names[1785]

Aaron—Aron
Abel—Abel
Abrahamus—Abraham
Adonia—Adoniah
Albertus—Albert
Alexander—Alexander
Andreas—Andrew
Antonius—Anthony
Archbaldus—Archibald
Arthurus—Arthur
Barnabius—Barnaby
Benjamin—Benjamin
Christopherus—Christopher
Carolus—Charles
Daniel—Daniel
David—David
Edwardus—Edward
Eliah—Elias
Emanuel—Emanuel
Edmundas—Edmund
Felix—Felix
Georgius—George
Gregorius—Gregory
Humphridus—Humphrey
Jacob—Jacob
Johannes—John
Ludovicus—Lewis
Lucas—Luke
Marcus—Mark
Philippus—Philip
Richardus—Richard
Simeon—Simeon
Thomas—Thomas
Gulielmus—William

Anna—Ann
Alicia—Alice
Elizabetha—Elizabeth
Jana—Jane
Katharina—Katharine
Lucia—Luce
Margareta, Margaret
Maria—Mary
Penelope—Penelope
Sara—Sarah
Pistor—Baker
Olivia—Olive
Jacobus—James

Ludovicos—Louis
Robertus—
—Robert
Octaviois
—Octavia
Livia—Levy
Magratus—

Magret
Phebus—
—Phebe
Herodeas
—Herod
Augustus—
Augusta
Henricus
Henry—

1785. For use in various rituals of divination in the book.

413
215 £ 2.12.6[1786]

433 Really 445, as 75,
135, & 344 are treble; 129,
181, 248, 309 & 314 are doubled
264 is 5 pp. & 223-5, &
385–7 are each 1 leaf.

2 Quires @ ½

1786. These are the catalogue numbers and price given in Cochran's catalogue; the significance of the middle number is unknown. These numbers here do not appear to be in Douce's handwriting.

Appendix: Alternative Illustrations

A great deal of thought and consideration goes into how the author and illustrator present our images in a way that is accurate, attractive, and useful to our readers. With this in mind, we have presented some alternatives for the ones in the main text of the book.

Manuscript page 3: The central word "Father" is very stylised in the original, but we went with the artistic appearance. Here's a clearer version:

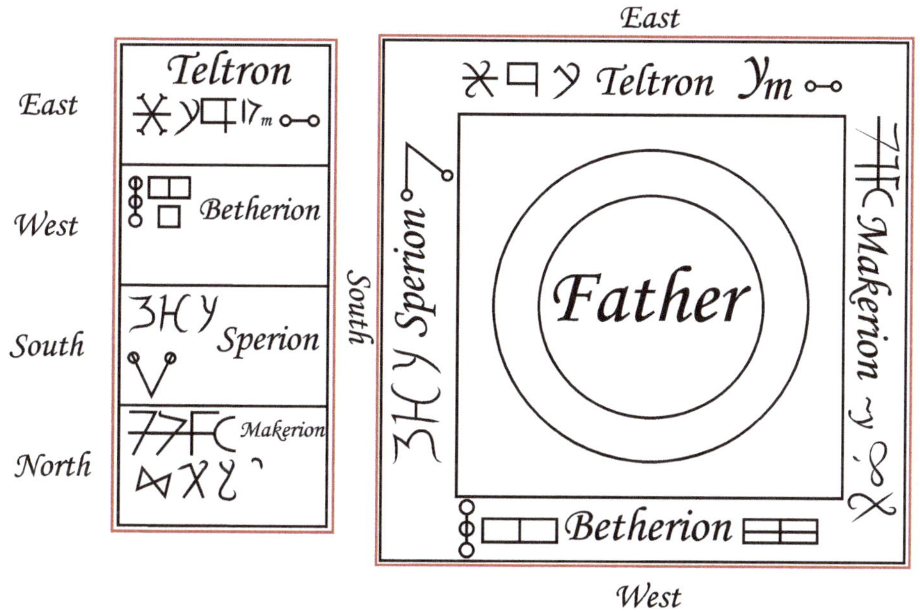

Manuscript page 211: The instructions for the figure on this page state that every cross should be drawn in red ink, but the copyist has not done so. Here's how it would look with the red text:

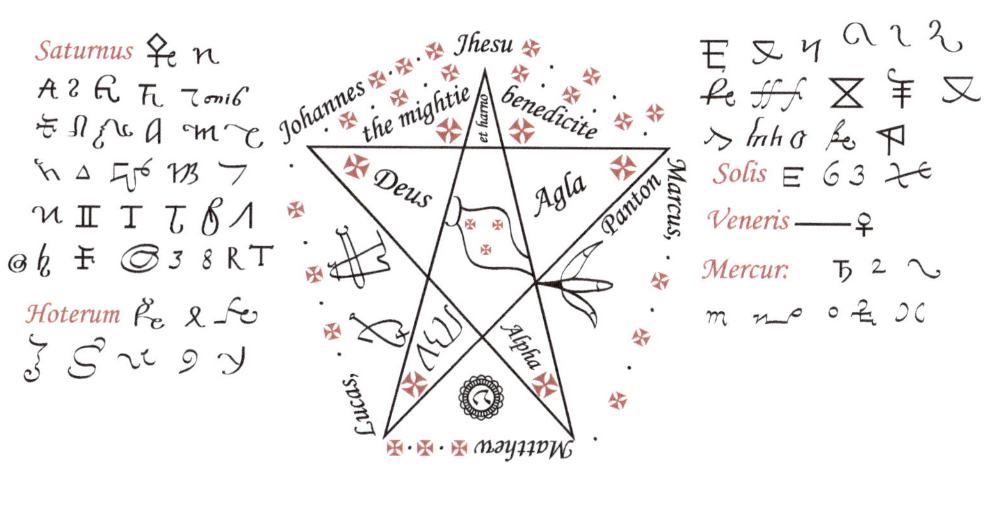

Manuscript page 212: We translated the Latin with its curious variant spellings in the regular version. The original is a bit more like this:

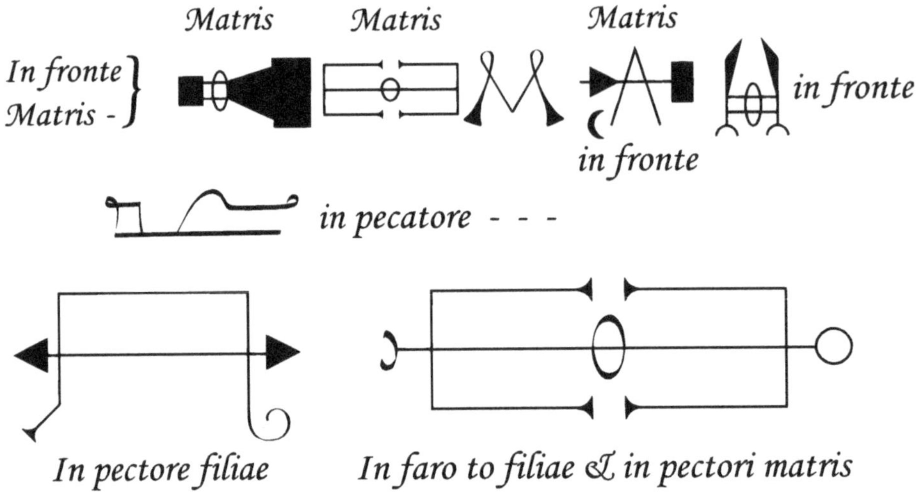

Manuscript page 265: We wondered if we could create an image of this entire circle, at least to give an overall appearance of what it might look like when completed:

Manuscript page 332: The name "Michael" is misspelled in the original:

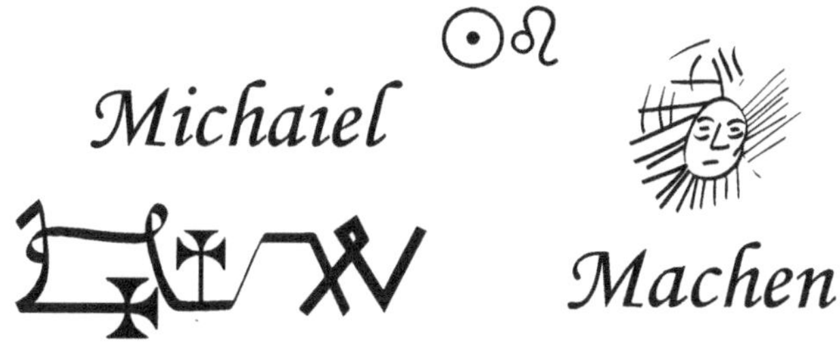

Here are some cleaned-up versions of some of the talismans near the end.
Manuscript page 405:

Manuscript page 407:

Manuscript page 409:

IN·HOC·VINCI·

PROSPERITAS

Those that follow are messier but closer to the original.
Manuscript page 412:

Bibliography

Manuscript Sources

Cambridge, Cambridge University Library

Additional 3544

Edinburgh, National Library of Scotland

GD 188/25/1/3

Florence, Biblioteca Medicea Laurenziana

Plutei 89 sup. 35, 89 sup. 38

Leipzig, Universitätsbibliothek Leipzig

Cod. mag. 41

London, British Library

Additional 36674

Harley T.11

Lansdowne 1203

Sloane 121, 1315, 1727, 3160, 3318, 3824, 3826, 3845, 3846, 3847, 3850, 3851, 3853

London, University College London, Senate House Library

HPF/3C/1

London, Wellcome Institute

Wellcome 110, 4639, 4669

Munich, Bayerische Staatsbibliothek

Clm 849

New Haven, Beinecke Library

Takayima 56

Oxford, Bodleian Library

Additional B.1

Ashmole 1378

Aubrey 24

Ballard 66

Bodleian 163

Douce 116

Douce e. 28

e Mus. 238

Rawlinson D.252

Paris, Bibliothèque Nationale de France
Lat. 7337

Vatican, Biblioteca Apostolica Vaticana
Lat. 4085

Washington, DC, Folger Shakespeare Library
V.b.26, X.d.208

Printed Sources

Agrippa von Nettesheim, Heinrich Cornelius. *De Occulta Philosophia Libri Tres.* Edited by V. Perrone Compagni. Leiden; New York: E.J. Brill, 1992.

———. *Henrici Cornelii Agrippae ab Nettesheym, Armatae Militiae Equitis Avrati, et Iuris Utrivsque ac Medicinae Doctoris, Opera in Duos Tomos Concinne Digesta* [...] Lugduni [Basel]: Beringos Fratres [Thomas Guarin], [1579].

———. *Three Books of Occult Philosophy.* Translated by Eric Purdue. Rochester, VT: Inner Traditions, 2021.

———. *Three Books of Occult Philosophy, Written by Henry Cornelius Agrippa, of Nettesheim, Counseller to Charles the Fifth, Emperor of Germany: And Judge of the Prerogative Court. Translated out of the Latin into the English Tongue, by J.F.* London: Printed by R. W. for Gregory Moule, 1651 [i.e., 1650].

Albertus Magnus [pseud.]. *Being the Approved, Verified, Sympathetic, and Natural Egyptian Secrets; or, White and Black Art for Man and Beast.* Chicago: Egyptian Publishing Company, 1930.

Almond, Philip C. *Demonic Possession and Exorcism in Early Modern England: Contemporary Texts and Their Cultural Contexts.* Cambridge: Cambridge University Press, 2007.

Ashmole, Elias, William Lilly, and Charles Burman. *The Lives of Those Eminent Antiquaries Elias Ashmole, Esquire, and Mr. William Lilly, Written by Themselves; Containing, First, William Lilly's History of His Life and Times, with Notes, by Mr. Ashmole; Secondly, Lilly's Life and Death of Charles the First: And Lastly, The Life of Elias Ashmole, Esquire, by Way of Diary. With Several Occasional Letters by Charles Burman, Esquire.* London: T. Davies, 1774.

Argentine, Richard. *De Praestigiis et Incantationibus Daemonum et Necromanticorum Liber Singularis Nunquam ante Hac Aeditus.* Basel, 1568.

Aristotle. *Aristotle's Compleat Master Piece in Three Parts; Displaying the Secrets of Nature in the Generation of Man: Regularly Digested into Chapters and Sections, Rendering It Far More Useful and Easy than Any yet Extant; To Which Is Added, A Treasure of Health; or, The Family Physician, Being Choice and Approved Rem-*

edies for All the Several Distempers Incident to Human Bodies. 23rd ed. [London]: Printed and sold by the booksellers, 1749.

———. *History of Animals, Books VII–X*. Edited and translated by D. M. Balme. Vol. 2. 3 vols. Loeb Classical Library 439. Cambridge: Harvard University Press, 1991.

Asprem, Egil. *Arguing with Angels: Enochian Magic and Modern Occulture*. Albany: State University of New York Press, 2012.

Aster, Ari, director. *Hereditary*. New York: A24, 2019.

The Astrologer of the Nineteenth Century. *Tales of the Horrible, or, The Book of Spirits*. London: Charlton Wright, 1837.

Atkin, Malcolm, and Worcestershire County Council. *Worcestershire under Arms: An English County during the Civil Wars*. Barnsley, South Yorkshire: Pen & Sword Military; Worcestershire County Council, 2004.

Attrell, Dan, and David Porreca, trans. *Picatrix: A Medieval Treatise on Astral Magic*. University Park: Pennsylvania State University Press, 2019.

Aubrey, John. *Miscellanies, viz. I. Day-Fatality; II. Local-Fatality; III. Ostenta; IV. Omens; V. Dreams; VI. Apparitions; VII. Voices; VIII. Impulses; IX. Knockings; X. Blows Invisible; XI. Prophesies; XII. Marvels; XIII. Magick; XIV. Transportation in the Air; XV. Visions in a Beril, or Glass; XVI. Converse with Angels and Spirits; XVII. Corps-Candles in Wales; XVIII. Oracles; XIX. Exstasie; XX. Glances of Love, Envy; XXI. Second-Sighted Persons*. London: Edward Castle, 1696.

Bacon, Francis. *The Works of Francis Bacon, Lord Chancellor of England, A New Edition*. Edited by Basil Montagu. Vol. 4. London: William Pickering, 1826.

Bang, Anton Christian. *Norske Hexeformularer og magiske Opskrifter*. Kristiania: J. Dybwad, 1901.

Barbierato, Federico. "Magical Literature and the Venice Inquisition from the Sixteenth to the Eighteenth Centuries." In *Magia, Alchimia, Scienza Dal '400 al '700: L'influsso Di Ermete Trismegisto = Magic, Alchemy and Science, 15th–18th Centuries: The Influence of Hermes Trismegistus*. Florence: Centro Di, 2002.

Barrett, Francis. *The Magus, or, Celestial Intelligencer: Being a Complete System of Occult Philosophy in Three Books Containing the Antient and Modern Practice of the Cabalistic Art, Natural and Celestial Magic, &c.* [...] *Exhibiting the Sciences of Natural Magic, Alchymy, or Hermetic Philosophy; Also the Nature, Creation, and Fall of Man* [...] *To Which Is Added Biographia Antiqua, or the Lives of the Most Eminent Philosophers, Magi, &c.: The Whole Illustrated with a Great Variety of Curious Engravings, Magical, and Cabalistical Figures, &c.* London: Printed for Lackington, Allen, and Co., 1801.

Baugh, Nita Scudder. *A Worcestershire Miscellany: Compiled by John Northwood, c. 1400: Edited from British Museum MS. Add. 37,787*. Diss., Bryn Mawr, 1956.

Baxter, Richard. *The Certainty of the Worlds of Spirits: Fully Evinced by the Unquestionable Histories of Apparitions, Operations, Witchcrafts, Voices, & c. Proving the Immortality of Souls, the Malice and Misery of the Devils, and the Damned, and the Blessedness of the Justified. Written for the Conviction of Sadduces & Infidels, by Richard Baxter*. London: T. Parkhurst, 1691.

Beck, Wolfgang, and Markus Cottin. *Die Merseburger Zaubersprüche: Ein Einführung*. Petersberg, Germany: Michael Imhof Verlag, 2015.

Bellhouse, W. D. *A Complete System of Magic*. Edited by Dan Harms. Hinckley, UK: Caduceus Books, 2018.

Benati, Chiara. "Painted Eyes, Magical Sieves, and Carved Runes: Charms for Catching and Punishing Thieves in the Medieval and Early Modern Germanic Tradition." In *Magic and Magicians in the Middle Ages and the Early Modern Time: The Occult in Pre-Modern Sciences, Medicine, Literature, Religion, and Astrology*, edited by Albrecht Classen, 149–218. Berlin: Walter de Gruyter, 2018.

Bennett, Chris. *Liber 420: Cannabis, Magickal Herbs, and the Occult*. Walterville, OR: Trine Day, 2018.

Berners, Juliana. *The Treatise on Angling in the Boke of St. Albans (1496): Background, Context and Text of "The Treatyse of Fysshynge Wyth an Angle."* Edited by Willy Louis Braekman. Scripta 1. Brussels: Universitaire Faculteiten St.-Aloysius, 1980.

Betz, Hans Dieter. *The Greek Magical Papyri in Translation, Including the Demotic Spells*. Chicago: University of Chicago Press, 1986.

Blagrave, Joseph. *Blagrave's Astrological Practice of Physick Discovering the True Way to Cure All Kinds of Diseases and Infirmities Which Are Naturally Incident to the Body of Man; Being Performed by Such Herbs and Plants Which Grow within Our Own Nation, Directing the Way to Distil and Extract Their Virtues and Making Up of Medicines; Also, a Discovery of Some Notable Philosophical Secrets Worthy Our Knowledge, Relating to a Discovery of All Kinds of Evils, Whether Natural, or Such Which Come from Sorcery or Witchcraft, or By Being Possessed of an Evil Spirit, Directing How to Cast Forth the Said Evil Spirit Out of Any One Which Is Possessed, with Sundry Examples Thereof*. London: Printed by S. G. and B. G. for Obad. Blagrave, 1671.

Bodleian Library. *Catalogue of the Printed Books and Manuscripts Bequeathed by Francis Douce, Esq. to the Bodleian Library*. Oxford: Oxford University Press, 1840.

———. *The Douce Legacy: An Exhibition to Commemorate the 150th Anniversary of the Bequest of Francis Douce (1757–1834)*. Oxford: Bodleian Library, 1984.

Bodleian Library and Florence Madan. *A Summary Catalogue of Western Manuscripts in the Bodleian Library at Oxford.* Vol. 4. 7 vols. Oxford: Clarendon Press, 1897.

Boeft, J. den, and Calcidius. *Calcidius on Demons (Commentarius Ch. 127–136).* Philosophica Antiqua 33. Leiden, Netherlands: E. J. Brill, 1977.

Boroffka, Anna. *Die "Länge Christi" in der Malerei: Codifizierung von Authentizität im intermedialen Diskurs.* Vestigia Bibliae 35/6. Bern: Peter Lang, 2017.

Boudet, Jean-Patrice. "Magie entre Illusionnisme Moyen Âge et Renaissance: Les Annulorum Experimente Attribués à Pietro d'Abano." In *Médecine, Astrologie et Magie entre Moyen Âge et Renaissance: Autour de Pietro d'Abano*, edited by Franck Collard, Jean-Patrice Boudet, and Nicolas Weill Parot, 247–93. Micrologus Library 50. Florence: SISMEL Edizioni del Galluzzo, 2013.

Bovet, R. *Pandæmonium, or the Devil's Cloyster. Being a Further Blow to Modern Sadduceism, Proving the Existence of Witches and Spirits, Etc.* J. Walthoe, 1684.

Braekman, Willy Louis. *Magische Experimenten en Toverpraktijken i teen Middelnederlands Handschrift: With an English Summary.* Ghent, Belgium: Seminarie voor Volkskunde, 1966.

———. *Middeleeuwse Witte en Zwarte Magie in het Nederlands Taalgebied: Gecommentarieerd Compendium van Incantamenta Tot Einde 16de Eeuw.* Ghent, Belgium: Koniklijke Academie voor Nederlandse Taal-en Letterkunde, 1997.

Brennan, Chris. "The Planetary Joys and the Origins of the Significations of the Houses and Triplicities." *International Society for Astrological Research Journal* 42, no. 1 (2013): 27–42.

Breverton, Terry. *The Physicians of Myddfai: Cures and Remedies of the Mediaeval World.* Carmarthenshire, UK: Cambria Books, 2012.

Briggs, K. M. "Some Seventeenth-Century Books of Magic." *Folklore* 64, no. 4 (1953): 445–62.

Bund, J. W. Willis, ed. *Worcester County Records: The Quarter Sessions Rolls, Part II: Kalendar of the Sessions Rolls, 1591–1643, Compiled for the Records and Charities Committee of the Worcestershire County Council.* Worcester, UK: Ebenezer Bayliss and Son, 1900.

Burnett, Charles. "The Conte de Sarzana Manuscript." In *Magic and Divination in the Middle Ages: Texts and Techniques in the Islamic and Christian Worlds*, IX.1–7. Aldershot, England: Variorum, 1996.

Buzzetta, Flavia. "Fragments of a Jewish Magical Tradition in the Library of Giovanni Pico Della Mirandola." In *Folklore, Magic, and Witchcraft: Cultural Exchanges from the Twelfth to Eighteenth Century*, edited by Marina Montesano, 92–103.

Routledge Studies in the History of Witchcraft, Demonology, and Magic. London: Routledge, 2022.

Campbel, Duncan. *Secret Memoirs of the Late Mr. Duncan Campbel, the Famous Deaf and Dumb Gentleman, Written by Himself, Who Ordered They Should Be Publish'd after His Decease, to Which Is Added, an Appendix, by Way of Vindication of Mr. Duncan Campbel, Against That Groundless Aspersion Cast upon Him, That He but Pretended to Be Deaf and Dumb.* London: Printed for J. Millan and J. Chrichley, 1732.

Campion, Nicholas. *History of Western Astrology.* Vol. 2, *The Medieval and Modern Worlds.* London: Continuum, 2009.

Cardano, Girolamo. *Hieronymi Cardani Mediolanensis Medici De Rerum Varietate Libri XVII.* Basel: H. Petri, 1557.

Cattan, Christopher. *The Geomancie of Maister Christopher Cattan Gentleman: A Booke, No Lesse Pleasant and Recreative, Then of a Wittie Inuention, to Know All Things, Past, Present, and to Come; Whereunto Is Annexed the Wheele of Pythagoras, Translated out of French into Our English Tongue.* London: John Wolfe, 1591.

———. *The Geomancie of Maister Christopher Cattan Gentleman, with the Wheele of Pythagoras: A Booke No Lesse Pleasant and Recreative, Then of a Wittie Inuention, to Know All Things Past, Present, and to Come; Newly Corrected, and Enlarged, with Many Necessarie and Profitable Additions.* London: E. A., 1608.

Cecchetelli, Michael. *Crossed Keys.* N.p.: Scarlet Imprint, 2011.

C[hamberline], R[ichard]. *Lithobolia, or, The Stone-Throwing Devil Being an Exact and True Account (by Way of Journal) of the Various Actions of Infernal Spirits, or (Devils Incarnate) Witches, or Both, and the Great Disturbance and Amazement They Gave to George Waltons Family, at a Place Call'd Great Island in the Province of New-Hantshire in New-England* [...] London: E. Whitlook, 1698.

Chambers, Ephraim. *Cyclopædia, or, An Universal Dictionary of Arts and Sciences: Containing the Definitions of the Terms, and Accounts of the Things Signify'd Thereby, in the Several Arts, Both Liberal and Mechanical, and the Several Sciences, Human and Divine: The Figures, Kinds, Properties, Productions, Preparations, and Uses, of Things Natural and Artificial: The Rise, Progress, and State of Things Ecclesiastical, Civil, Military, and Commercial: With the Several Systems, Sects, Opinions, & c.: Among Philosophers, Divines, Mathematicians, Physicians, Antiquaries, Criticks, & c.: The Whole Intended as a Course of Antient and Modern Learning.* Vol. 1. 2 vols. London: J. and J. Knapton, 1728.

Chardonnens, László Sándor. *Anglo-Saxon Prognostics, 900–1100: Study and Texts.* Brill's Studies in Intellectual History 153. Leiden, Netherlands: Brill, 2007.

———. "Magic Manuscripts from Somers and Jekyll in the Collections of the British Library." *Societas Magica Newsletter*, no. 35 (spring 2017): 1–7.

———. "Mantic Alphabets in Late Medieval England, Early Modern Europe, and Modern America: The Reception and Afterlife of a Medieval Form of Dream Divination." *Anglia* 132, no. 4 (2014): 641–75.

———. "Mantic Alphabets in Medieval Western Manuscripts and Early Printed Books." *Modern Philology: Critical and Historical Studies in Literature, Medieval through Contemporary* 110, no. 3 (2013): 340–66.

Chardonnens, László Sándor, and Rosanne Hebing. "Two Charms in a Late Medieval English Manuscript at Nijmegen University Library." *The Review of English Studies* 62, no. 254 (2011): 181–92.

Clark, J. Kent. *Goodwin Wharton*. Oxford: Oxford University Press, 1984.

Cochran, John. *A Catalogue of Manuscripts in Different Languages, on Theology; English and Foreign History; Heraldry; Philosophy; Poetry; Romances; the Fine Arts (Including Caligraphy and Some Splendid Persian Drawings); Sports; Alchemy; Astrology; Divination; &c. &c., of Various Dates, from the Twelfth to the Eighteenth Century: Many of Them upon Vellum, and Adorned with Splendid Illuminations. To Which Is Added a Small Collection of Manuscripts in the Oriental Languages; with an Appendix Containing a Few Printed Books, Some of Them with Manuscript Notes and Autographs of Eminent Persons, Now Selling (for Ready Money) at the Prices Affixed by John Cochran, No. 108, Strand, (Savoy Steps)*. London: Ibotson and Palmer, 1829.

Coley, Henry. *Clavis Astrologiae Elimata: Or a Key to the Whole Art of Astrology, New Filed and Polished, in Three Parts* [...] London: Benjamin Tooke and Thomas Sawbridge, 1676.

"Cooke's Folly." *Oxford University and City Herald*. September 22, 1821.

Curry, Patrick. "Heydon, John (b. 1629, d. in or after 1670), Writer on Astrology and Alchemy, and Occultist." In *Oxford Dictionary of National Biography*. Oxford: Oxford University Press, 2010.

D., D. *The Skilful Physician: Containing Directions for the Preservation of a Healthful Condition, and Approved Remedies for All Diseases and Infirmities (Outward or Inward) Incident to the Body of Man* [...] *Whereunto Is Added Experimented Instructions for the Compounding of Perfumes. Also for the Chusing and Ordering of All Kinds of Wines, Both in Preserving the Sound, and Rectifying Those That Are Prick'd. Never Before Imparted to Publick View*. London: Printed by Thomas Maxey for Nathaniel Ekins, 1656.

Davies, Owen. "Decriminalising the Witch: The Origin of and Response to the 1736 Witchcraft Act." In *Witchcraft and the Act of 1604*, edited by John Newton and Jo Bath, 207–32. Studies in Medieval and Reformation Traditions 131. Leiden; Boston: Brill, 2008.

———. "Hag-Riding in Nineteenth-Century West Country England and Modern Newfoundland: An Examination of an Experience-Centred Witchcraft Tradition." *Folk Life: Journal of Ethnological Studies* 35, no. 1 (1996): 36–53.

———. "Healing Charms in Use in England and Wales 1700–1950." *Folklore* 107 (1996): 19–32.

———. *Popular Magic: Cunning-Folk in English History*. London: Hambledon Continuum, 2007.

Davies, Owen, and Francesca Matteoni. *Executing Magic in the Modern Era: Criminal Bodies and the Gallows in Popular Medicine*. Palgrave Historical Studies in the Criminal Corpse and Its Afterlife. Cham, Switzerland: Palgrave Macmillan, 2017.

Dawson, W. Harbutt. *History of Skipton*. London: Simpkin, Marshall, and Co., 1882.

———. "An Old Yorkshire Astrologer and Magician, 1694–1760." *The Reliquary, Quarterly Archaeological Journal and Review* 23 (March 1882): 197–202.

De Abano, Peter. "Peter de Abano: Heptameron, or Magical Elements." Translated by Joseph H. Peterson. Esoteric Archives. 1998. Accessed August 23, 2020. http://esotericarchives.com/solomon/heptamer.htm.

Dearlove, Jenny. "The Pretended Trial of Witchcraft." In *Treasures of the Morrab: A Penzance Library That Has More than Books*, edited by June Palmer and Ann Altree, 21–30. Penzance, UK: Penwith Local History Group, 2005.

Dee, John. *A True & Faithful Relation of What Passed for Many Yeers Between Dr. John Dee* [...] *and Some Spirits: Tending (Had It Succeeded) to a General Alteration of Most States and Kingdomes in the World: His Private Conferences with Rodolphe Emperor of Germany, Stephen K. of Poland, and Divers Other Princes about It. The Particulars of His Cause, as It Was Agitated in the Emperors Court; by the Pope's Intervention: His Banishment, and Restoration in Part. As Also the Letters of Sundry Great Men and Princes (Some Whereof Were Present at Some of These Conferences and Apparitions of Spirits) to the Said D. Dee. Out of the Original Copy, Written with Dr. Dees Own Hand, Kept in the Library of Sir Tho. Cotton* [...]. *With a Preface Confirming the Reality (as to the Point of Spirits) of This Relation: and Shewing the Several Good Uses That a Sober Christian May Make of All.* Edited by Meric Casaubon. London: Printed by D. Maxwell for T. Garthwait, 1659.

Defoe, Daniel. *A System of Magick; or, a History of the Black Art. Being an Historical Account of Mankind's Most Early Dealing with the Devil; and How the Acquaintance on Both Sides First Begun.* London: Andrew Millar, 1728.

Delrío, Martinus. *Disquisitionum Magicarum Libri Sex: Quibus Continetur Accurata Curiosarum Artium et Vanarum Superstitionum Confutatio, Utilis Theologis, Iurisconsultis, Medicis, Philologis.* Cologne: Agrippinae, 1679.

Dibdin, Thomas Frognall. *Reminiscences of a Literary Life; with Anecdotes of Books, and of Book Collectors.* Vol. 2. London: John Major, 1836.

Dillinger, Johannes. *Magical Treasure Hunting in Europe and North America: A History.* Basingstoke, UK: Palgrave Macmillan, 2012.

Dixon. *The True Prophetic Messenger for 1833: Containing Remarkable Events, Predictions, the Weather, & c.* [...]. [London]: J. Denley, 1832.

Dobson, Mary J. *Contours of Death and Disease in Early Modern England.* Cambridge Series in Population, Economy, and Society in Past Time 29. Cambridge: Cambridge University Press, 1997.

Dodoens, Rembert. *A Nievve Herball, or Historie of Plantes: Wherin Is Contayned the Vvhole Discourse and Perfect Description of All Sortes of Herbes and Plantes: Their Diuers [and] Sundry Kindes: Their Straunge Figures, Fashions, and Shapes: Their Names, Natures, Operations, and Vertues: and That Not Onely of Those Whiche Are Here Growyng in This Our Countrie of Englande, but of All Others Also of Forrayne Realmes, Commonly Vsed in Physicke; First Set Foorth in the Doutche or Almaigne Tongue* [...]. Translated by Henry Lyte. London [Antwerp]: [printed by Henry Loë, sold] by Gerard Dewes, 1578.

Duffour, J. "Heures Anciennes d'Auch." *Revue de Gascogne* 5 (1905): 125–34.

Edge, Joanne. "Licit Magic or 'Pythagorean Necromancy'? The 'Sphere of Life and Death' in Late Medieval England." *Historical Research* 87, no. 238 (2014): 611–32.

Edsall, Mary Agnes. "Arma Christi Rolls or Textual Amulets?: The Narrow Roll Format Manuscripts of 'O Vernicle.'" *Magic, Ritual, and Witchcraft* 9, no. 2 (2014): 178–209.

Ehrman, Bart D. *Forgery and Counterforgery: The Use of Literary Deceit in Early Christian Polemics.* Oxford; New York: Oxford University Press, 2014.

Elsakkers, Marianne. "In Pain You Shall Bear Children (Gen 3:16): Medieval Prayers for a Safe Delivery." In *Women and Miracle Stories: A Multidisciplinary Exploration*, edited by Anne-Marie Korte, 179–209. Leiden; Boston: Brill, 2004.

Erra Pater. *The Book of Knowledge Shewing the Wisdom of the Ancients in Four Parts. I. Shewing the Various and Wonderful Operations of the Signs and Planets, and*

Other Celestial Constellations on the Bodies of Men, Women and Children: And the Great Influences They Have upon Those That Are Born under Them. II. Prognostications Forever, Necessary to Keep the Body in Health: With Several Choice Recipts in Physick and Surgery. III. An Abstract of the Art of Physiognomy and Palmistry; Together with the Signification of Moles, and Interpretation of Dreams. IV. The Farmer's Kalender; Containing Perpetual Prognostications for Weather, The Whole Mystery of Husbandry, the Compleat and Experienc'd Farrier, Cow-Leech, Swineherd, and Shepherd. Written by Erra Pater, a Jewish Doctor in Astronomy and Physick, Born in Bethany, near Mount Olivet, in Judea; and Made English by William Lilly, Student in Physick and Astrology. To Which Is Added, the Dealer's Directory: Containing the True Form or All Sorts of Bills Bonds, Counter-Bonds, Letters of Attorney and License, Deeds of Gift, Bills of Exchange, and Other Writings. The Best Method of Getting in Debts, and Compounding Them. An Account of Weights, Measures, Numbers, Coins, Tables of Shires, Post-Roads, and Principal Fairs. A Catalogue of All the Markets, and Days on Which They Are Held, and Divers Other Necessary Things and Tables. With Several Additions Which Were Never Publish'd in Any of the Former Impressions of This Book. Gosport, UK: Printed by J. Phillport, 1726.

Everard, John. *The Divine Pymander of Hermes Mercurius Trismegistus, in XVII Books, Translated Formerly out of the Arabick into Greek, and Thence into Latine, and Dutch, and Now out of the Original into English.* London: Robert White, 1649.

Ezell, Margaret J. M. "Invisible Books." In *Producing the Eighteenth-Century Book: Writers and Publishers in England, 1650–1800*, edited by Laura L. Runge and Pat Rogers, 53–69. Newark: University of Delaware Press, 2009.

Faraone, Christopher A. *Ancient Greek Love Magic.* Cambridge: Harvard University Press, 1999.

Faust, Johannes. *Doctor Johannes Faust's Magia Naturalis et Innaturalis: Threefold Coercion of Hell, Last Testament, and the Sigils of the Art.* Translated by Nicolás Álvarez Ortiz. N.p.: Enodia, 2017.

Fell-Smith, Charlotte. *John Dee (1527–1608).* London: Constable & Co., 1909.

Feola, Vittoria. "Elias Ashmole's Collections and Views about John Dee." *Studies in History and Philosophy of Science* 43, no. 3 (September 2012): 530–38.

Forbes, Thomas R. "The Social History of the Caul." *Yale Journal of Biology and Medicine* 25, no. 6 (1953): 495–508.

Forbes, Thomas Rogers. "Verbal Charms in British Folk Medicine." *Proceedings of the American Philosophical Society* 115, no. 4 (1971): 293–316.

Foreman, Paul. *The Cambridge Book of Magic: A Tudor Necromancer's Handbook.* Edited by Francis Young. Cambridge, UK: Francis Young, 2015.

Foxe, John, Thomas Cranmer, and John Gough Nichols. *Narratives of the Days of the Reformation, Chiefly from the Mauscripts of John Foxe the Martyrologist; with Two Contemporary Biographies of Archbishop Cranmer*. London: Camden Society, 1859.

Franz, Adolf. *Die Kirchlichen Benediktionen im Mittelalter*. Graz: Akademische Druck-u. Verlagsanstalt, 1960.

Frazer, James. *The Golden Bough*. London: Macmillan, 1951.

Gadbury, John. *Genethlialogia, or, The Doctrine of Nativities, Containing the Whole Art of Directions, and Annual Revolutions: Whereby, Any Man (Even of an Ordinary Capacity) May Be Enabled to Discover the Most Remarkable and Occult Accidents of His Life, as They Shall Occur unto Him in the Whole Course Thereof, Either for Good or Evil. Also, Tables for Calculating the Planets Places for Any Time, Either Past, Present, or To Come, Together with the Doctrine of Horarie Questions; Which (In the Absence of a Nativity) Is Sufficient to Inform Any One of All Manner of Contingencies Necessary to Be Known*. London: J. Cottrel, 1658.

Gal, Florence, Jean-Patrice Boudet, and Laurence Moulinier-Brogi. *Vedrai Mirabilia: Un Libro di Magia del Quattrocento*. I Libri di Viella 245. Rome: Viella, 2017.

Garofali, Vincenzo. *Ordo ad Dandam Poenitentiam ex Insigni Rituali Codice Membranaceo XI. Saeculi Bibl. Canonicor. Reg. S. Salvatoris Bononiae*. Rome: Typis Lazzariniis, 1791.

Gaster, M. "English Charms of the Seventeenth Century." *Folklore* 21, no. 3 (1910): 375–78.

Giacosa, Piero. *Magistri Salernitani Nondum Editi: Catalogo Ragionato della Esposizione di Storia della Medicina Aperta in Torino nel 1898*. Turin: Fratelli Bocca, 1901.

Goldstein, Leba M. "The Life and Death of John Lambe." *Guildhall Studies in London History* 4, no. 1 (1979): 19–32.

Great Britain. *The Statutes of the Realm: Printed by Command of His Majesty King George the Third, in Pursuance of an Address of the House of Commons of Great Britain, from Original Records and Authentic Manuscripts*. Vol. 4, part 2. London: Dawsons, 1963.

Great Britain Royal Commission on Historical Manuscripts. *Third Report of the Royal Commission on Historical Manuscripts*. London: Printed by George Edward Eyre and William Spottiswoode for Her Majesty's Stationery Office, 1872.

Greatrakes, Valentine. *A Brief Account of Mr. Valentine Greatraks, and Divers of the Strange Cures by Him Lately Performed Written by Himself in a Letter Addressed to the Honourable Robert Boyle, Esq.; Whereunto Are Annexed the Testimonials of*

Several Eminent and Worthy Persons of the Chief Matters of Fact Therein Related. London: Printed for J. Starkey, 1666.

Grohmann, Joseph Virgil. *Aberglauben und Gebräuche aus Böhmen und Mähren.* Vol. 1. Leipzig: Brockhaus, 1864.

Hagen, Kaja Merete Haug. "Crux Christi Sit Mecum: Devotion to the Apotropaic Cross." *Religions* 10, no. 11 (2019): 1–32.

Halpern, Barbara Kerewsky, and John Miles Foley. "The Power of the Word: Healing Charms as an Oral Genre." *The Journal of American Folklore* 91, no. 362 (1978): 903–24.

Hand, Wayland, ed. *Popular Beliefs and Superstitions from North Carolina, 4874–8569.* The Frank C. Brown Collection of North Carolina Folklore 7. Durham, NC: Duke University Press, 1964.

Hanegraaff, Wouter J. *Esotericism and the Academy: Rejected Knowledge in Western Culture.* Cambridge: Cambridge University Press, 2012.

Harms, Daniel. *Balloonists, Alchemists, and Astrologers of the Nineteenth Century: The Tale of George and Margaret Graham.* Self-published, Amazon Kindle Direct Publishing, 2019.

———. "The Herb and the Lady under the Elder at Noon: Analysis of an Early Modern Magical Ritual." *The Enquiring Eye* 5 (2021): 10–15.

———. "Of Fairies: An Excerpt from a Seventeenth-Century Magical Manuscript." *Folklore* 129, no. 2 (2018): 192–98.

———. "Spirits at the Table: Faerie Queens in the Grimoires." In *The Faerie Queens: In Magic, Myth and Legend*, edited by Sorita D'Este, 41–58. London: Avalonia, 2013.

———. "'Thou Art Keeper of Man and Woman's Bones': Rituals of Necromancy in Early Modern England." *Thanatos* 8, no. 1 (2019): 62–90.

———. *Witch Bottles: Steel and Glass.* Burbage, UK: Caduceus Books, 2019.

Harms, Daniel, and James Clark. *Of Angels, Demons & Spirits: A Sourcebook of British Magic.* Woodbury, MN: Llewellyn Publications, 2019.

Harms, Daniel, James R. Clark, and Joseph H. Peterson. *The Book of Oberon: A Sourcebook of Elizabethan Magic.* Woodbury, MN: Llewellyn Publications, 2015.

Harrington, Thomas. "A Favourite Lesson for the Piano Forte or Harp." Bury St. Edmunds, UK: Printed for and sold by the author, c. 1800.

———. "Lord Broome's March, Adapted for the Piano Forte and a Military Band." Bury St. Edmunds, UK: Printed for and sold by the author, c. 1800.

Harte, Jeremy. "Exotic Snakes." *FLS News: The Newsletter of The Folklore Society* 84 (2018): 10–11.

———. *Explore Fairy Traditions*. Wyneswold, UK: Heart of Albion, 2004.

Hartlieb, Johann. *Das Buch Aller Verbotenen Künste, Des Aberglaubens und der Zauberei*. Edited by Falk Eisermann and Eckhard Graf. [Ahlerstedt, Germay]: Param, 1989.

Hebing, Rosanne. "The Textual Tradition of Heavenly Letter Charms in Anglo-Saxon Manuscripts." In *Secular Learning in Anglo-Saxon England*, edited by Sándor Chardonnens and Bryan Carella, 203–22. Amsterdamer Beiträge zur älteren Germanistik 69. Leiden, Netherlands: Brill, 2012.

Heinrich, Fritz. "Ein Mittelenglisches Medizinbuch nach den Manuskripten des British Museum: Sloane 3153, Sloane 405, Royal 17 A III, Royal 19, 674, Harleian 1600 unter Zugrundelegung des Br. M. Additional Ms 33,996." Diss., Karras, 1895.

Henning, B. D. "Sandys, Samuel I (1615–85), of Ombersley, Worcs." The History of Parliament. 1983. https://www.historyofparliamentonline.org/volume/1660-1690/member/sandys-samuel-i-1615-85.

Heydon, John. *The Holy Guide, Leading the Way to Vnite Art and Nature in Which Is Made Plain All Things Past, Present, and to Come*. London: T. M., 1662.

Historical Manuscripts Commission. *Report on Manuscripts in Various Collections*. Vol. 7. London: The Hereford Times, 1914.

Hohman, Johann Georg. *The Long-Lost Friend: A 19th Century American Grimoire*. Edited by Daniel Harms. Woodbury, MN: Llewellyn Publications, 2012.

Holthausen, Ferdinand. "Rezepte, Segen, und Zaubersprüche aus Zwei Stockholmer Handschriften." *Anglia: Zeitschrift für Englische Philologie* 19 (1897): 75–88.

Honorius. *The Sworn Book of Honorius: Liber Iuratus Honorii*. Edited and translated by Joseph H. Peterson. Lake Worth, FL: Ibis Press, 2016.

Howe, Ellic. *Raphael; or, The Royal Merlin*. London: Arborfield, 1964.

———. *Urania's Children: The Strange World of the Astrologers*. London: William Kimber, 1967.

Howell, T. B. *A Complete Collection of State Trials and Proceedings for High Treason and Other Crimes and Misdemeanors from the Earliest Period to the Year 1783, with Notes and Other Illustrations*. Vol. 5. 21 vols. London: T. C. Hansard, 1816.

Hunt, Tony. *Popular Medicine in Thirteenth-Century England: Introduction and Texts*. Cambridge; Wolfeboro, NH: D. S. Brewer, 1990.

Hunt, Tony, and Michael Benskin, eds. *Three Receptaria from Medieval England: The Languages of Medicine in the Fourteenth Century*. Oxford: The Society for the Study of Medieval Languages and Literature, 2001.

Hunter, Michael. *The Decline of Magic: Britain in the Enlightenment*. New Haven, CT: Yale University Press, 2020.

Jackson, Thomas. *A Treatise Containing the Originall Unbeliefe, Misbeliefe, or Misperswasions Concerning the Veritie, Unitie, and Attributes of the Deitie: With Directions for Rectifying Our Beliefe or Knowledge in the Fore-Mentioned Points.* London: J. D., 1625.

Johnson, Thomas K. *Svartkonstböcker: A Compendium of the Swedish Black Art Book Tradition.* Seattle, WA: Revelore, 2019.

Johnsson, J. W. S. "Les 'Experimenta Duodecim Johannis Paulini.'" *Bulletin de la Société Française d'histoire de la Médecine* 12 (1913): 257–67.

Jones, Peter Murray, and Lea T. Olsan. "Middleham Jewel: Ritual, Power and Devotion." *Viator* 31, no. 1 (2000): 249–90.

———. "Takamiya MS 61: A Book of Experiments." *Poetica* 73 (2010): 87–107.

Kieckhefer, Richard. *Forbidden Rites: A Necromancer's Manual of the Fifteenth Century.* University Park: Pennsylvania State University Press, 1998.

King, Thomas. *A Catalogue of the Very Rare and Curious Library of Dr Thos. Harrington, Decd., Comprising Old Songs, Ballds, History, Magic, Witchcraft, Astrology, Many with Scarce Portraits, by Gaywood Cross, & c., a Few Etchings, Curious Manuscripts on Various Subjects; Being One of the Most Singular Collections in the Above Branches of Literature Ever Brought Before the Public, Which Will Be Sold by Auction by Mr. King, Jun., at His Auction Rooms, No. 36, Tavistock Street, Covent Garden, on Tuesday, May 20, 1806, and Four Following Days, at Twelve o'Clock.* London: n.p., 1806.

K[innaston], F[rancis]. *Leoline and Sydanis: An Heroick Romance of the Aduentures of Amorous Princes Together with Sundry Affectionate Addresses to His Mrs under the Name of Cynthia.* London: Richard Hearne, 1646.

Kirk, Robert. *The Occult Laboratory: Magic, Science, and Second Sight in Late Seventeenth-Century Scotland: A New Edition of Robert Kirk's The Secret Commonwealth and Other Texts.* Edited by Michael Hunter. Woodbridge, UK: Boydell Press, 2001.

Kittredge, George Lyman. *Witchcraft in Old and New England.* New York: Russell & Russell, 1956.

Klaassen, Frank F. *Making Magic in Elizabethan England: Two Early Modern Vernacular Books of Magic.* University Park: Pennsylvania State University Press, 2019.

———. "Three Early Modern Magic Rituals to Spoil Witches." *Opuscula* 1, no. 1 (2011), 1–10.

Klaassen, Frank, and Sharon Hubbs Wright. *The Magic of Rogues: Necromancers in Early Tudor England.* Magic in History Sourcebooks. University Park, PA: Pennsylvania State University Press, 2021.

Labouvie, Eva. *Verbotene Künste: Volksmagie und Ländlicher Aberglaube in den Dorf gemeinden des Saarraumes (16.–19. Jahrhundert)*. St. Ingbert, Germany: Röhrig Verlag, 1992.

Láng, Benedek. *Unlocked Books: Manuscripts of Learned Magic in the Medieval Libraries of Central Europe*. University Park: Pennsylvania State University Press, 2008.

Laurent d'Orleans. *Des Coninx Summe*. Edited by D. C. Tinbergen. Bibliotheek van Middelnederlandsche Letterkunde 64–5. Leiden, Netherlands: A. W. Sijthoff, 1900.

Le Forestier, René. *La Franc-Maçonnerie Occultiste au XVIIIe Siècle & l'Ordre des Élus Coens*. Paris: La table d'emeraude, 1987.

Leather, Ella Mary. *The Folk-Lore of Herefordshire*. Hereford, UK: Jakeman & Carver, 1912.

Lecouteux, Claude. *The Book of Grimoires*. Rochester, VT: Inner Traditions, 2013.

———. *Dictionary of Ancient Magic Words and Spells: From Abraxas to Zoar*. Rochester, VT: Inner Traditions, 2015.

Legard, Phil, and Alexander Cummins, eds. *An Excellent Booke of the Arte of Magicke: The Magical Works of Humphrey Gilbert and John Davis from British Library Additional Manuscript 36674*. London: Scarlet Imprint, 2020.

Leitão, José, ed. *Opuscula Cypriani: Variations on the Book of Saint Cyprian and Related Literature*. West Yorkshire, UK: Hadean Press, 2019.

———, ed. *The Book of St. Cyprian*. West Yorkshire, UK: Hadean Press, 2014.

Lemire, Beverly. "The Theft of Clothes and Popular Consumerism in Early Modern England." *Journal of Social History* 24, no. 2 (1990): 255–76.

Leonardi, Camillo, Claude Lecouteux, and Anne Monfort. *Les pierres talismaniques*. Vol. 3 of *Speculum lapidum*. Paris: Presses de l'Univ. de Paris-Sorbonne, 2003.

Luther, Martin. *Werke: Kritische Gesamtausgabe*. Edited by J. K. F. Knaake. Vol. 1. Weimar: H. Böhlaus, 1883.

Lynch, Geraldine. "Folk Beliefs about the March Cock." Dublin: National Folklore Collection, Ireland, University College Dublin, 1976.

Lytton, Edward Bulwer Lytton. *Zanoni*. London: Saunders & Otley, 1842.

M., J. *Sports and Pastimes, or, Sport for the City and Pastime for the Country with a Touch of Hocus Pocus, or Leger-Demain / Fitted for the Delight and Recreation of Youth by J. M.* London: Printed by H. B. for John Clark, 1676.

Macfarquhar, Colin, and George Gleig, eds. *Encyclopaedia Britannica; or, a Dictionary of Arts, Sciences, and Miscellaneous Literature.* 3rd ed. Vol. 10. Edinburgh: A. Bell and C. Macfarquhar, 1797.

MacLeod, Mindy, and Bernard Mees. *Runic Amulets and Magic Objects.* Woodbridge, UK; Rochester, NY: Boydell, 2006.

Macnair, Miles. *Olive, Princess of Cumberland (1772–1834): A Royal Scandal.* Studley, UK: Brewin Books, 2011.

A Magical Vision, or, A Perfect Discovery of the Fallacies of Witchcraft as It Was Lately Represented in a Pleasant Sweet Dream / to a Holy Sweet Sister [...] *for Preservation of the Saints from Being Tainted with the Heresies of the Congregations of the Doe-Littles.* London: Thomas Palmer, 1673.

Mandeville, John. *[Here Endeth the Boke of Iohn Maunduyle Knyght of Wayes to Ierusalem [and] of Marueylys of Ynde and of Other Countrees].* London: Richard Pynson, 1496.

Mann, James G. "Francis Douce as a Collector." *Bodleian Quarterly Record* 7, no. 81 (1934): 361–65.

Marathakis, Ioannis. *The Magical Treatise of Solomon or Hygromanteia: Also Called the Apotelesmatike Pragmateia, Epistle to Rehoboam, Solomonike.* Singapore: Golden Hoard Press, 2011.

Markham, Gervase. *The Husbandman's Jewel Directing How to Improve Land from 10 l. per Annum to 50 l. with Small Charge by Planting* [...] London: G. Conyers, 1695.

Martin, John. *Animal Magnetism Examined: In a Letter to a Country Gentleman.* London: John Stockdale, 1790.

Martin, Ruth. *Witchcraft and the Inquisition in Venice, 1550–1650.* Oxford: Blackwell, 1989.

Mathers, S. Liddell MacGregor, and Joseph H. Peterson, eds. *The Key of Solomon the King: A Magical Grimoire of Sigils and Rituals for Summoning and Mastering Spirits; Clavicula Salomonis.* Newburyport, MA: Red Wheel/Weiser, 2016.

Mathiesen, Robert. "The Key of Solomon: Toward a Typology of Manuscripts." *Societas Magica Newsletter*, no. 17 (2007): 1, 3–9.

———. *The Unseen Worlds of Emma Hardinge Britten: Some Chapters in the History of Western Occultism.* Theosophical Society Occasional Papers 9. Fullerton, CA: Theosophical History, 2001.

Maxwell-Stuart, P. G. *The British Witch: The Biography.* Stroud, UK: Amberley, 2016.

McIlwaine, H. R., ed. *Minutes of the Council and General Court of Colonial Virginia, 1622–1632, 1670–1676, with Notes and Excerpts from Original Council and General Court Records, into 1683, Now Lost.* Richmond, VA: Library Board, Virginia State Library, 1924.

McWilliam, Rohan. "Unauthorized Identities: The Imposter, the Fake and the Secret History in Nineteenth-Century Britain." In *Legitimacy and Illegitimacy in Law, Literature, and History*, edited by Margot C. Finn, Michael. Lobban, and Jenny Bourne Taylor, 67–92. Houndsmills, UK; New York: Palgrave Macmillan, 2010.

Member of the School of Black Art, Italy. *Witchcraft Detected and Prevented; or, the School of Black Art Newly Opened. The Greater Part of This Highly Curious Little Volume Is Selected from the Ancient and Scarce Works of the Principal Writers on These Subjects, Particularly from Scott's Discovery of Witchcraft, the Book Which Supplied Shakespeare with His Witch and Wizard Lore. It Also Contains a Variety of the Most Approved Charms in Magic; Receipts in Medicine, Natural Philosophy, and Chemistry, &c.* 2nd ed. Peterhead, UK: P. Buchan, 1824.

Mesler, Katelyn. "The Medieval Lapidary of Techel/Azareus on Engraved Stones and Its Jewish Appropriations." *Aleph* 14, no. 2 (2014): 73–143.

Metzler, Rosemary. "The Plough Monday Plays." Master's thesis, the Ohio State University, 1971.

Milton, John. *A Maske Presented at Ludlow Castle, 1634 on Michaelmasse Night, before the Right Honorable, Iohn Earle of Bridgewater, Vicount Brackly, Lord Præsident of Wales, and One of His Maiesties Most Honorable Privie Counsell.* London: Augustine Mathewes, 1637.

Mitchell, Laura Theresa. "Cultural Uses of Magic in the Fifteenth-Century England." PhD diss., University of Toronto, 2011.

Morgan, W. E. T. "Charms." *Folklore* 6, no. 2 (1895): 202–4.

Muir, Bernard James, ed. *A Pre-Conquest English Prayer-Book (BL. MSS Cotton Galba A.Xiv and Nero A.Ii (Ff. 3–13)).* Woodbridge, UK: Henry Bradshaw Society, 1988.

Muyard, F. "Un Manuel de Sorcellerie en Basse Bretagne au XVIIIe Siècle." *Annales de Bretagne et des Pays de l'Ouest* 99, no. 3 (1992): 291–97.

Nash, Michael L. *Royal Wills in Britain from 1509 to 2008.* London: Palgrave Macmillan, 2018.

Newton, John, and Jo Bath, eds. *Witchcraft and the Act of 1604.* Studies in Medieval and Reformation Traditions 131. Leiden, Netherlands: Brill, 2008.

Nottingham, Gary St. M. *Welsh Border Witchcraft: A Rendition of the Occult History of the Welsh March*. London: Avalonia, 2018.

Ó hÓgáin, Dáithí. "Dreaming and Dancing: W. B. Yeats' Use of Traditional Motifs in 'The Dreaming of the Bones' (1919)." *Hungarian Journal of English and American Studies* 8, no. 1 (2002): 57–75.

Ó Súilleabháin, Seán. *A Handbook of Irish Folklore*. London: H. Jenkins, 1963.

Ohrt, F. *Danmarks Trylleformler*. Vol. 2. Copenhagen: Gyldendal, 1917.

Olsan, Lea T. "Writing on the Hand in Ink: A Late Medieval Innovation in Fever Charms in England." *Incantatio* 7 (2018): 9–45.

Otto, Bernd-Christian. "Historicising 'Western Learned Magic': Preliminary Remarks." *Aries* 16 (2016): 161–240.

Paracelsus. *Paracelsus, Of the Supreme Mysteries of Nature: Of the Spirits of the Planets [and] Occult Philosophy; The Magical, Sympathetical, and Antipathetical Cure of Wounds and Diseases: The Mysteries of the Twelve Signs of the Zodiack*. Translated by Robert Turner. London: Printed by J. C. for N. Brook and J. Harison, 1656.

Pendered, Mary L., and Justinian Mallett. *Princess or Pretender?: The Strange Story of Olivia Wilmot Serres, So-Called Princess of Cumberland, and Her Daughter Lavinia Janetta Horton Ryves*. London: Hurst & Blackett, 1939.

Peterson, Joseph H., ed. *Arbatel, Concerning the Magic of the Ancients: Original Sourcebook of Angel Magic*. Lake Worth, FL: Ibis Press, 2009.

———, trans. "The Clavicle of Solomon, Revealed by Ptolomy the Grecian." Esoteric Archives. Last modified December 31, 2020. http://www.esotericarchives.com/solomon/sl3847.htm.

———, ed. *Elucidation of Necromancy: Lucidarium Artis Nigromanticę Attributed to Peter of Abano, Including a New Translation of His Heptameron or Elements of Magic*. Lake Worth, FL: Ibis Press, 2021.

———, ed. *Grimorium Verum*. Self-published, CreateSpace, 2007.

———, ed. "Heinrich Cornelius Agrippa: His Fourth Book of Occult Philosophy." Esoteric Archives. 2019. http://esotericarchives.com/agrippa/agrippa4.htm.

———, ed. "Index of Angel Names, Magical Words, and Names of God." Esoteric Archives. October 4, 2020. http://esotericarchives.com/solomon/nameindx.htm.

———, ed. "Le Grand Grimoire, ou l'Art de Commander les Esprits Celestes, Aériens, Terrestres, Infernaux." CD-ROM, 1999.

———, ed. *The Lesser Key of Solomon: Lemegeton Clavicula Salomonis: Detailing the Ceremonial Art of Commanding Spirits Both Good and Evil*. York Beach, ME: Weiser Books, 2001.

———, ed. "Liber Juratus Honorii, or The Sworne Booke of Honorius." CD-ROM, 2009.

———, ed. *Secrets of Solomon: A Witch's Handbook from the Trial Records of the Venetian Inquisition*. Kasson, MN: Twilit Grotto, 2018.

———, ed. *The Sixth and Seventh Books of Moses: Original Sourcework of Folk Magic*. Lake Worth, FL: Ibis Press, 2008.

Pingree, David Edwin, ed. *Picatrix: The Latin Version of the Ghāyat al-Hakīm*. London: Warburg Institute, 1986.

Pliny, and W. H. S. Jones. *Natural History: Libri XXVIII–XXXII*. Cambridge, MA: Harvard University Press, 1975.

Pope, Stephanie. "'Darcke and Clowdie Speeches': A Composition and Provenance of Bodleian Library, MS. Douce 116." *Bodleian Library Record* 26, no. 2 (2013): 208–39.

Power, D'Arcy. "Section XXIII: History of Medicine: Independent Paper: The Lesser Writings of John Arderne." London, 1913.

Priddle, Robert A. "More Cunning Than Folk: An Analysis of Francis Barrett's The Magus as Indicative of a Transitional Period of English Magic." Master's thesis, University of Ottawa, 2012.

Priebsch, Robert. "Segen aus Londoner Handschriften." *Zeitschrift für Deutsches Altertum und Deutsche Literatur* 38 (1894): 14–21.

Principe, Lawrence M. *The Secrets of Alchemy*. Chicago: University of Chicago Press, 2013.

Prudentius. *Prudentius*. Translated by H. J. Thomson. Vol. 1. 2 vols. Loeb Classical Library. Cambridge, MA: Harvard University Press, 1962.

Pseudo-Agrippa von Nettesheim, Heinrich Cornelius. *Henry Cornelius Agrippa, His Fourth Book of Occult Philosophy; Of Geomancie; Magical Elements of Peter de Aban; Astronomical Geomancie; The Nature of Spirits; Arbatel of Magick; The Species or Several Kindes of Magick*. Edited by Robert Turner. London: J. C., 1665.

———. *Henry Cornelius Agrippa, His Fourth Book of Occult Philosophy, of Geomancy, Magical Elements of Peter de Abano, Astronomical Geomancy, the Nature of Spirits, Arbatel of Magick. Edited by Robert Turner*. London: Printed by J. C. for John Harrison, 1655.

Quinn, Phil. "Fact and Folly: The Folklore of 'Modern' Sites." *3rd Stone* 29 (1998): 8–11.

Raiswell, Richard, and Peter Dendle. "Demon Possession in Anglo-Saxon and Early Modern England: Continuity and Evolution in Social Context." *The Journal of British Studies* 47, no. 4 (2008): 738–67.

Rankine, David, and Paul Harry Barron, eds. *The Book of Gold: A 17th Century Magical Grimoire of Amulets, Charms, Prayers, Sigils, and Spells Using the Biblical Psalms of King David.* London: Avalonia, 2010.

Rankine, David, and Paul Harry Barron, trans. *The Complete Grimoire of Pope Honorius.* London: Avalonia, 2013.

Raphael. *The Familiar Astrologer; An Easy Guide to Fate, Destiny, & Foreknowledge, As Well As to the Secret and Wonderful Properties of Nature.* London: Printed for John Bennett, 1832.

———. *The Prophetic Messenger for 1832; or, The Events, Predictions, and the Weather That Will Occur in Each Month during the Year.* London: William Charlton Wright, 1832.

———. *Raphael's Witch!!!, Or the Oracle of the Future, by the Author of the Prophetic Messenger, with Ten Coloured Designs on Copper, by R. Cruikshank and the Author, and a Piece of Music by Blewitt.* London: William Charlton Wright, 1831.

———. "[Untitled]." *The Straggling Astrologer*, July 31, 1824.

Raphael, and Merlinus Anglicus. *The Astrologer of the Nineteenth Century.* London: Knight & Lacey, 1825.

Ravaisson-Mollien, François. *Archives de la Bastille: Documents Inédits.* Vol. 10. Paris: A. Durand et Pedone-Lauriel, 1879.

Rebiger, Bill, ed. *Sefer Shimmush Tehillim: Buch vom magischen Gebrauch der Psalmen: Edition, Ubersetzung und Kommentar.* Tübingen, Germany: Mohr Siebeck, 2010.

Reynes, Robert. *The Commonplace Book of Robert Reynes of Acle: An Edition of Tanner MS 407.* Edited by Cameron Louis. Garland Medieval Texts 1. New York: Garland, 1980.

Rider, Catherine. *Magic and Impotence in the Middle Ages.* Oxford: Oxford University Press, 2006.

Roper, Jonathan. *English Verbal Charms.* Helsinki: Suomalainen Tiedeakatemia, 2005.

Rosen, Edward, and Lynn Thorndike. *The Sphere of Sacrobosco and Its Commentators.* Chicago: University of Chicago Press, 1949.

Ryan, William Francis. *The Bathhouse at Midnight: An Historical Survey of Magic and Divination in Russia*. Magic in History. University Park: Pennsylvania State University Press, 1999.

Sachse, William L. *Lord Somers: A Political Portrait*. Manchester: Manchester University Press, 1975.

Sannig, Bernhard. *Collectio Benedictionum, sive Apparatus Absolutionum, Conjurationum, Exorcismorum, Rituum, et Caeremoniarum, Ecclesiasticarum, et Administrationis Sacramentorum*. Venice: Recurti, 1732.

Schönbach, Anton E. "Eine Auslese Altdeutscher Segensformeln." In *Analecta Graeciensia: Festschrift zur 42. Versammlung Deutscher Philologen und Schulmänner in Wien 1893*, edited by Verein Deutscher Philologen und Schulmänner, 39–50. Graz, Austria: Verlagsbuchhandlung, 1893.

Scot, Reginald. *The Discouerie of Witchcraft, Wherein the Lewde Dealing of Witches and Witchmongers Is Notablie Detected, the Knauerie of Coniurors, the Impietie of Inchantors, the Follie of Soothsaiers, the Impudent Falshood of Cousenors, the Infidelitie of Atheists, the Pestilent Practices of Pythonists, the Curiositie of Figure Casters, the Vanitie of Dreamers, the Beggerlie Art of Alcumystrie, the Abhomination of Idolatrie, the Horrible Art of Poisoning, the Vertue and Power of Naturall Magike, and All the Conueiances of Legierdemaine and Iuggling Are Deciphered: And Many Other Things Opened, Which Have Long Lien Hidden, Howbeit Verie Necessarie to Be Knowne: Heerevnto Is Added a Treatise Vpon the Nature and Substance of Spirits and Diuels, &c.* London: William Brome, 1584.

———. *The Discovery of Witchcraft Proving That the Compacts and Contracts of Witches with Devils and All Infernal Spirits or Familiars Are but Erroneous Novelties and Imaginary Conceptions: Also Discovering, How Far Their Power Extendeth in Killing, Tormenting, Consuming, or Curing the Bodies of Men, Women, Children, or Animals by Charms, Philtres, Periapts, Pentacles, Curses, and Conjurations: Wherein Likewise the Unchristian Practices and Inhumane Dealings of Searchers and Witch-Tryers upon Aged, Melancholly, and Superstitious People, in Extorting Confessions by Terrors and Tortures, and in Devising False Marks and Symptoms, Are Notably Detected* […]*: In Sixteen Books*. London: Printed for Andrew Clark, 1665.

Secrets Merveilleux de La Magie Naturelle et Cabalistique du Petit Albert, Traduit Exactement sur l'Original Latin, Intitulé Alberti Parvi Lucii, Libellus de Mirabilibus Naturae Arcanis, Enrichi des Figures Mystérieuses & la Maniere de les Faire. Rev. ed. Lyon: Beringos Fratres, 1752.

Serenus Sammonicus, Quintus. *Liber Medicinalis*. Paris: Presses universitaires de France, 1950.

Serres, Olivia. "Astrological Fragments, by Her Royal Highness Princess Olive of Cumberland: Fragment II." *The Straggling Astrologer*, August 14, 1824.

———. "Astrological Fragments, by Her Royal Highness Princess Olive of Cumberland: Fragment III." *The Straggling Astrologer*, August 21, 1824.

———. "Astrological Fragments, by Her Royal Highness Princess Olive of Cumberland: Fragment IV." *The Straggling Astrologer*, September 4, 1824.

———. "Astrological Fragments, by Her Royal Highness Princess Olive of Cumberland: Fragment the First." *The Straggling Astrologer*, August 7, 1824.

Shakespeare, William. *King Lear*. Edited by R. A. Foakes. The Arden Shakespeare Third Series. London: The Arden Shakespeare, 1997.

———. *M. William Shak-Speare: His True Chronicle Historie of the Life and Death of King Lear and His Three Daughters With the Vnfortunate Life of Edgar, Sonne and Heire to the Earle of Gloster, and His Sullen and Assumed Humor of Tom of Bedlam: As It Was Played before the Kings Maiestie at Whitehall Vpon S. Stephans Night in Christmas Hollidayes, By His Maiesties Seruants Playing Vsually at the Gloabe on the Bancke-Side*. London: [Nicholas Okes], 1608.

Sibley [Sibly], Ebenezer. *The Clavis or Key to the Magic of Solomon*. Edited by Frederick Hockley and Joseph H. Peterson. Lake Worth, FL: Ibis Press, 2009.

———. *Solomon's Clavis, or Key to Unlock the Mysteries of Magic*. Burbage, UK: Society for Esoteric Endeavour, 2008.

Simotta, George. *A Theater of the Planetary Houres for All Dayes of the Yeare VVherein May Be Gathered from the Earth, Vnder the Cœlestiall Influences, Divers Sorts of Hearbs, Rootes, Leaves, Barkes, Flowers, Fruits, Seedes, Stones, Animals, &c. for the Vse of Physick: Whereby Both Suddenly, and Happily Infirmities May Be Cured. The Evils Too Are Set Downe, That Happen, and Are Caused by the Seuen Plannets: The Friendship and Hatred Betwixt Them: The Sunne Rising; and to Finde the Determinate Houre of It. A Worke Not Onely Curious and Delightfull, but Likewise Necessary for Physitians, and All Curious Spirits. Composed by George Simotta a Grecian, of Constantinople, Spagirick Physitian, to Monsieur, Brother to His Majestie of France. Translated out of Greeke, into French, and Now into English, Fitted to Our Calculation*. London: August. Matthewes, 1631.

Simpson, W. Sparrow. "On the Measure of the Wound in the Side of the Redeemer, Worn Anciently as a Charm; and on the Five Wounds as Represented in Art." *Journal of the British Archaeological Association* 30 (1874): 357–74.

Skemer, Don C. *Binding Words: Textual Amulets in the Middle Ages*. University Park, PA: Pennsylvania State University Press, 2006.

———. "The Magic Serpent: German Amulet Rolls in Time of War and Pestilence." *Magic, Ritual, and Witchcraft* 16, no. 1 (2021): 23–63.

Skinnebach, Laura Katrine. "Haptic Prayer, Devotional Books, and Practices of Perception." In *Touching, Devotional Practices, and Visionary Experience in the Late Middle Ages*, edited by David Carrillo-Rangel, Delfi-I. Nieto-Isabel, and Pablo Acosta-García, 95–122. Cham, Switzerland: Palgrave Macmillan, 2019.

Skinner, Stephen, and David Rankine, eds. *The Goetia of Dr. Rudd: Angels and Demons of Liber Malorum Spirituum seu Goetia Lemegeton Clavicula Salomonis*. London: Golden Hoard Press, 2010.

———, eds. *The Keys to the Gateway of Magic: Summoning the Solomonic Archangels & Demon Princes*. London: Golden Hoard Press, 2005.

———, eds. *Practical Angel Magic of Dr. John Dee's Enochian Tables*. Sourceworks of Ceremonial Magic 1. Singapore: Golden Hoard Press, 2010.

———, eds. *The Veritable Key of Solomon*. London: Golden Hoard Press, 2008.

Sloane, Hans. *Magic and Mental Disorder: Sir Hans Sloane's Memoir of John Beaumont*. Edited by Michael Hunter. London: Robert Boyle Project, 2011.

Solomon. *The Clavis or Key to Unlock the Mysteries of Magic*. Edited by Stephen Skinner and Daniel Clark. Translated by Ebenezer Sibley [Sibly]. Sourceworks of Ceremonial Magic 10. Singapore: Golden Hoard Press, 2018.

Sommers, Susan Mitchell. *The Siblys of London: A Family on the Esoteric Fringes of Georgian England*. New York: Oxford University Press, 2018.

Stallcup, Stephen B. "The 'Eye of Abraham' Charm for Thieves." *Magic, Ritual, and Witchcraft* 10, no. 1 (2015): 23–40.

Stefánsson, Vilhjálmur. "Icelandic Beast and Bird Lore." *The Journal of American Folklore* 19, no. 75 (1906): 300–308.

Stehle, Bruno. "Volkstümliche Feste, Sitten, und Gebräuche im Elsass, 1892." *Jahrbuch für Geschichte, Sprache und Litteratur Elsass-Lothringens* 8 (1892), 159–81.

Stein, Herbert. "Das Sator-Quadrat: Magie, Mystik und Wissenschaft." *Archiv für Religionspsychologie / Archive for the Psychology of Religion* 23 (2000): 209–19.

Stemmler, Joan K. "'Undisturbed Above Once in a Lustre': Francis Douce, George Cumberland, and William Blake at the Bodleian Library and Ashmolean Museum." *Blake: An Illustrated Quarterly* 26, no. 1 (1992): 9–18.

Swainson, Charles. *The Folk Lore and Provincial Names of British Birds*. Publications of the Folklore Society 17. London: Elliot Stock, 1886.

Thicknesse, Philip. *Memoirs and Anecdotes of Philip Thicknesse, Late Lieutenant Governor of Land Guard Fort, and Unfortunately Father to George Touchet, Baron Audley*. Dublin: Printed by Graisberry and Campbell for William Jones, 1790.

Thiers, Jean-Baptiste. *Traité des Superstitions qui Regardent les Sacremens Selon l'Ecriture Sainte, les Décrets des Conciles, & les Sentimens des Saints Pères, & des Théologiens*. Avignon, France: Chambeau, 1777.

Thomas, Keith. *Religion and the Decline of Magic*. Harmondsworth, UK: Penguin, 1971.

Thompson, C. J. S. *The Mysteries and Secrets of Magic*. New York: Causeway Books, 1973.

Thorndike, Lynn. *A History of Magic and Experimental Science During the First Thirteen Centuries of Our Era*. Vol. 2. New York: Macmillan, 1923.

———. *Michael Scot*. London: Nelson, 1965.

Timbers, Frances. *The Magical Adventures of Mary Parish: The Occult World of Seventeenth-Century London*. Kirksville, MO: Truman State University Press, 2016.

Topper, Jody. "Francis Douce and His Collection: An Antiquarian in Great Britain, 1757–1834." Master's thesis, University of North Carolina at Chapel Hill, 2002.

Trotula. *Medieval Woman's Guide to Health: The First English Gynecological Handbook: Middle English Text*. Edited by Beryl Rowland. Kent, OH: Kent State University Press, 1981.

Turner, Dawson. "Brief Remarks, Accompanied with Documents, Illustrative of Trial by Jury, Treasure-Trove, and the Invocation of Spirits for the Discovery of Hidden Treasure in the Sixteenth Century." *Norfolk Archaeology* 1 (1847): 55–64.

University of Oxford and Joseph Foster. *Alumni Oxonienses: The Members of the University of Oxford, 1500–1714: Their Parentage, Birthplace, and Year of Birth, with a Record of Their Degrees*. Oxford and London: Parker and Co., 1891.

"[Untitled]." *London Courier and Evening Gazette*. June 29, 1802.

Valentine, Basil. *The Last Will and Testament of Basil Valentine, Monke of the Order of St. Bennet. Which Being Alone, He Hid under a Table of Marble, behind the High-Altar of the Cathedral Church, in the Imperial City of Erford: Leaving It There to Be Found by Him, Whom Gods Providence Should Make Worthy of It, to Which Is Added Two Treatises, the First Declaring His Manual Operations, the Second Shewing Things Natural and Supernatural, Never Before Published in English*. London: S. G. & B. G., 1671.

Vârtejaru, Mihai. "The Book of Pentacles: Folger V.b.26." *Studies on Magic* (blog), March 27, 2022. http://studies-vartejaru.blogspot.com/2022/03/the-book-of-pentacles-folger-vb26.html.

———. "The Book of Pentacles: The Vadian Clavicle." *Studies on Magic* (blog), March 16, 2022. http://studies-vartejaru.blogspot.com/2022/03/the-book-of-pentacles-vadian-clavicle.html.

———. "The Book of the Seven Rings of the Planets of Messalah." Esoteric Archives. 2020. http://esotericarchives.com/messalah/The_Book_of_the_Seven_Rings_of_the_Planets_of_Messalah_Mihai_V%E2rtejaru.pdf.

———. "Planetary Characters in Agrippa." *Studies on Magic* (blog), February 10, 2018. http://studies-vartejaru.blogspot.com/2018/02/planetary-characters-in-agrippa.html.

Veiga, Marcos Antonio Lopes. "Sob a Capa Negra: Necromancia e Feitiçaria, Curandeirismo e Práticas Mágicas de Homens em Aragão (Séculos XVI e XVII)." PhD diss., Universidade de São Paulo, 2012.

Vinel, Nicolas. "Le Judaïsme Caché du Carré SATOR de Pompéi." *Revue de l'Histoire des Religions* 2 (2006): 173–94.

Von Worms, Abraham. *The Book of Abramelin: A New Translation.* Edited by Georg Dehn. Translated by Steven Guth. Rev. ed. Lake Worth, FL: Ibis Press, 2015.

Wallis, Faith. *Medieval Medicine: A Reader.* Toronto: University of Toronto Press, 2010.

Wallton, Richard. *The Genuine Life, Confession, and Dying Speech, of Richard Wallton, Student in Astrology and Physick, Commonly Call'd the Conjuror, Who Was Executed, at Warwick, on Friday the 10th of This Instant August 1733, for Promoting and Encouraging Humphry Mousall, Morrice Walker, and William Coley, to Commit Several Robberies, &c., to Which Is Added a Poem on His Death.* Birmingham, UK: T. Warren, 1733.

Walsh, Brendan C. "The Devil's Power of Obsession." *Societas Magica Newsletter*, no. 36 (2021): 1–5, 7–9.

Waters, Thomas E. *Cursed Britain: A History of Witchcraft and Black Magic in Modern Times.* New Haven, CT: Yale University Press, 2019.

Watts, Donald. *Dictionary of Plant Lore.* Amsterdam: Elsevier, 2007.

Webster, John. *The Displaying of Supposed Witchcraft. Wherein Is Affirmed That There Are Many Sorts of Deceivers and Impostors, and Divers Persons under a Passive Delusion of Melancholy and Fancy. But That There Is a Corporeal League Made Betwixt the Devil and the Witch, or That He Sucks on the Witches Body, Has

Carnal Copulation, or That Witches Are Turned into Cats, Dogs, Raise Tempests, or the Like, Is Utterly Denied and Disproved. Wherein Also Is Handled, the Existence of Angels and Spirits, the Truth of Apparitions, the Nature of Astral and Sydereal Spirits, the Force of Charms, Philters; and with Other Abstruse Matters. London: J. M., 1677.

Weller, Philip T., trans. *The Roman Ritual.* Vol. 1. 3 vols. N.p.: Caritas, 2017.

Weyer, Johann. *Ioannis Wieri de praestigiis daemonum, & incantationibus ac ueneficiis libri sex, postrema editione quinta aucti & recogniti. Accessit Liber apologeticus, et Pseudomonarchia daemonum* [...]. Basel: Ex Officina Oporiniana [per Balthasarum Han, Hieronymum Gemusaeum & Polycarpi fratris haeredes], 1577.

"Whereas Thomas Harrington..." *Morning Post*, April 3, 1806. Page 2.

A Whip for the Devil; or, the Roman Conjurer, Discovering the Intolerable Folly, Profaneness, and Superstition of the Papists, in Endeavouring to Cast the Devil out of the Bodies of Men and Woman by Him Possest. London: Thomas Malthus, 1683.

Whitby, Christopher. *John Dee's Actions with Spirits: 22 December 1581 to 23 May 1583.* Vols. 1 and 2. Routledge in Library Editions: Alchemy 7. Abingdon, NY: Taylor & Francis, 2014.

Wickham, J. D. C. *Records by Spade and Terrier: Historical Side-Lights from the Discovery of Stone-Age, Celtic, and Roman Remains; Also from the Etymology of Local Place and Family Names, from Customs and Folk-Lore, Garnered from the Tithe-Maps and Registers of Holcombe-by-Mendlip and Surrounding District; with Illustrative Anecdotes, Being Personal Reminiscences.* Bath: George Gregory, 1912.

Wilhelm, Gene, Jr. "The Mullein: Plant Piscicide of the Mountain Folk Culture." *Geographical Review* 64, no. 2 (1974): 235–52.

Wilkins, David. *Concilia Magnae Britanniae et Hiberniae* [...]. 4 vols. London: R. Gosling, F. Gyles, T. Woodward, and C. Davis, 1737.

Willis-Bund, J. W., and William Page, eds. "Parishes, Stoulton." In *The Victoria History of the County of Worcester*, 3:532–37. London: Victoria County History, 1913.

Wood, Anthony à, Philip Bliss, and University of Oxford. *Athenae Oxonienses: An Exact History of All the Writers and Bishops Who Have Had Their Education in the University of Oxford, to Which Are Added the Fasti, or Annals of the Said University.* Vol. 1. 4 vols. London: Rivington, 1813.

Woolley, Benjamin. *The Queen's Conjuror: The Life and Magic of Dr Dee.* London: HarperCollins, 2002.

Wordsworth, Christopher. *Horae Eboracenses: The Prymer or Hours of the Blessed Virgin Mary According to the Use of the Illustrious Church of York, with Other*

Devotions as They Were Used by the Lay-Folk in the Northern Province in the XVth and XVIth Centuries. Publications of the Surtees Society 132. Durham: Andrews & Co., 1920.

Wright, Elizabeth Mary. *Rustic Speech and Folk-Lore*. London: Oxford University Press, 1913.

Wright, Gillian. "A Pattern Poem by William Browne of Tavistock: 'Behold O God in Rivers of My Tears.'" *English Manuscript Studies, 1100–1700* 7 (1998): 264–74.

Young, Francis. *A History of Anglican Exorcism: Deliverance and Demonology in Church Ritual*. London: T&T Clark International, 2018.

———. *Magic as a Political Crime in Medieval and Early Modern England: A History of Sorcery and Treason*. London: I.B. Tauris, 2018.

Zingerle, Oswald von. "Segen und Heilmittel aus einer Wolfsthurner Handschrift des XV. Jahrhunderts." *Zeitschrift des Vereins für Volkskunde* 1 (1891): 172–77, 315–24.

Index

A

Aaron, 96, 97, 333, 360, 362, 372, 398, 440, 497, 533
Aat Iderid, 421
Aba, 306, 443
Abab, 207, 349
Abagor V, King, 141
Abalidith, 306
Abalidoth, 443
Abas, 349
Abay, 445, 478
Abbots Leigh, 22, 24
Abdisnel, 59
Abecze, 410
Abednego / Abdenago / Abednigo, 303, 363, 497
Aberhafesp, 148
Abesis, 113
Abies, 96, 97
Abilon, 256
Abim, 415, 437
Abiron, 362, 427, 432
Abla, 349
Abniori, 439
Abra, 247, 248, 319, 320
Abracadabra, 10, 260
Abragini, 447
Abraham, 38, 66–68, 125, 146, 158, 217, 222, 303, 304, 336, 355, 387, 401–3, 447, 533, 563, 565
Abrathe, 419
Abray, 435
Abraye, 415
Abraym, 446
Abres, 96, 97
Abria, 295, 296
Abrimael, 60
Abrothe, 117
Absull, 411
Abumalith, 306, 444
Abuzaba / Abuzaha, 436
Abuzabu, 306
Aby-bastard-dust, 523
Abyram, 333
Acadan, 415
Accusers, 222, 282, 387
Achamaytymon, 108
Achim, 415, 437
Achor, 218
Acim, 415, 445
Acimoy, 438
Aconite / Aconitum, 159
Acynamos, 338
Adam, 95, 96, 99, 100, 162, 245, 278, 358, 443, 497
Adanatus (Athanatos), 125, 232, 295, 304, 318, 334, 335, 338, 358, 370, 390, 412, 414, 452, 497
Adarael, 446
Adariat, 82
Admolita, 79
Adonay / Andonay, 56, 96, 97, 105, 125, 146, 149, 162, 163, 208, 218, 229, 233, 246, 256, 274, 297, 299, 303, 304, 318, 322, 325, 338, 358, 361, 369, 390, 396, 412, 414, 425, 428, 435, 437, 438, 440, 442, 443, 445, 448, 452–54, 479, 489, 496, 497, 499
Adromalee. *See* Andromalchus
Adze, 158

Aedriel, 59
Aeroy, 112
Aethiopides, 153
Affair of the Poisons, 9
Affaterim, 447
Afriel, 245
Agayne, 349
Agaza, 293
Age, 22, 129, 130, 157, 160, 165, 166, 168, 222, 263, 298, 487, 509
Aggen, 295
Agios / Ag[i]os / Agros, 117, 146, 232, 262, 295, 304, 334, 335, 337, 338, 358, 412
Agith. *See* Hagith
Agla, 75, 76, 110, 111, 114, 121, 162, 219, 227, 229, 264, 291, 295, 304, 314, 322, 324, 329, 338, 358, 364, 365, 391, 393, 408, 412, 414, 427, 428, 451, 454, 497
Aglaca, 338
Agle, 295
Aglo, 445, 478
Agnus castus, 119
Agnus Dei, 144
Agrano, 349
Agrimony, 122
Agrippa, Henry Cornelius von Nettesheim, 8, 10, 13, 17, 19, 23, 26, 30, 36, 39, 58–60, 77, 112, 122, 133, 179, 191, 197, 200–207, 212, 213, 217, 260, 281–283, 311, 323, 374, 375, 433, 443–45, 448–50, 454–56, 461, 464, 473, 475, 477, 478, 489, 491–94, 504, 525, 542, 558, 559, 565
Agris, 262
Ague, 46, 47, 133, 151, 160, 161, 171, 260, 267, 399
Ague, quartan, 133
Ague, quotidian, 160
Ague, tertian, 323
Agusita, 446
Aie, 415, 438
Aiel, 139, 435
Ailif, 157
Airy spirits, 281
Ajemphaton, 416
Alaby, 89
Alacrice, 293
Alcanus, 137
Alcarice, 218
Alcariel / Alkarell / Alkariel, 256, 257
Alchemy, 6, 14, 15, 19, 22, 30, 35, 43, 343, 543, 547, 559, 566
Aldiacor, 288
Aldiater, 288
Ale, 65, 511, 515
Aleator, 325
Aleo, 116
Ales, 66, 160, 263, 331
Alexander, 33, 137, 302, 533, 555
Alexander (city), 137
Algatha, 280
Algramay, 162, 415
Algranay, 297
Alhanatos, 347
Alhanudos, 110, 111
Alibeat, 79
Alibus, 137
Alifesta, 113
Alkaley, 222
All Naim, 163
Allyson, 151
Alma, 218, 328
Almadel (pseudo-Solomon), 461
Almazin, 410
Almonds, 64

Alnaym, 442
Alnayme, 415
Aloe wood, 239
Aloy, 452–454
Alph, 369
Alpha, 76, 97, 110, 111, 125, 146, 147, 149, 218, 233, 272, 279, 324, 338, 380, 390, 449, 453, 497, 532
Alphereon Succundia, 420
Alpho, 139
Alra, 304
Alsidus, 302
Altarib, 447
Altenay, 338
Althenothe, 318
Altra, 117
Altremel, 60
Alua, 261
Alum, 141, 516, 518, 520
Alyon, 452
Amabael, 447
Amabiel, 163, 437, 443
Amabo, 338
Amabrox, 306
Amabuel, 306
Amacor, 448, 489
Amadai, 446
Amael, 109, 110
Amalech / Amalek, 379, 398
Amaneczax, 83
Amasiel, 295
Amatiel, 446
Amaymon, 103–5, 411, 467, 470
Ambeball, 422
Ambelial, 422
Ambergris, 493, 522
Amdeball, 422
Amethyst, 504
Amides, 448, 489
Amie, 415
Amiriell, 59
Amis, 163
Ammiel, 60
Amnediel, 59
Amore, 117
Amtiel, 59
Anabona, 452
Anabrot, 421
Anabroth, 421
Anach, 419
Anacor, 307, 410
Analos, 307
Anamizapta / Ananizapta, 56, 72, 150, 218
Anaphenaton / Anapheneton, 332, 497
Anathay, 415, 437
Anatos, 307, 410
Anayl, 436
Anazell, 411
Anchor, 313, 489
Ancor, 307, 410, 448
Andam, 422
Andas, 434
Andrew, Saint, 351, 353, 405
Androges, 429, 430
Andromalchus / Andromalcus / Andromalee, 402
Andromaleus, 409
Andromalis, 467
Andryn, 421
Anefen, 419
Anefon, 419
Anepheneton, 414
Anepheton, 426
Anephexeton, 360, 414
Anerium, 112

Angels, 6, 10, 17, 29–31, 36, 38, 41, 47, 48, 55, 56, 58, 60, 61, 64, 65, 69–71, 77, 94, 96, 97, 99, 102, 104, 108, 111, 112, 114, 115, 119, 121, 123, 125, 126, 132, 137, 141, 145, 158, 159, 163, 168, 193, 219, 221, 224–227, 231, 245, 246, 252, 253, 259, 260, 263–66, 273, 274, 289–93, 296, 299, 303, 305, 307–9, 314, 315, 318, 323, 324, 332, 333, 336–40, 351, 353, 354, 357, 359, 364, 365, 368, 370, 382, 389–93, 395, 396, 402, 406, 407, 409, 419–21, 423–26, 434–49, 452, 454, 461, 473, 475–78, 492, 497, 543, 552, 558, 563, 566
Angiliell, 422
Angoliell, 422
Anic, 442
Anich, 489
Aniel, 435
Aniseed, 516, 519, 524, 525
Anitor, 448, 489
Anne, Saint, 136, 356
Anobona, 415, 452
Anora, 338
Anoum, 499
Anthanatos, 497
Anthill, 280
Anthima, 411
Antriel, 334, 335
Ants, 62, 88
Anuam, 78
Aosall, 411
Apantois, 421
Aperpes, 420
Aperyes, 103, 104
Apolin, Saint, 277
Apollo, 36, 152
Apollonia, Saint, 277, 349
Apomachon, 416
Apple, 115, 116, 118, 151, 160, 402
Appries, 420
Aprops, 112
Apuleius, 128
Aqua vitae, 135, 511, 514, 515
Aquarius, 123
Aquiel, 435
Arato, 153
Aratron, 340–42, 454, 464
Arbatel, 10, 340, 558, 559
Arbitrall, 452
Arbytros, 415
Arcan, 306, 436
Archangels, 56, 102, 114, 121, 123, 126, 137, 163, 253, 266, 274, 292, 293, 296, 299, 309, 318, 337, 339, 351, 354, 357, 359, 389, 392, 395, 406, 454, 563
Archima, 360
Archyma, 414
Ardefiel, 59
Arepo, 261, 399
Aret, 97
Arex, 113
Aries, 59, 104, 112, 123, 125, 138, 149, 370, 390, 412, 415, 558
Arigus, 325
Arimon, 416
Aristotle's Compleat Master Piece, 485, 542, 550
Armatus, 446
Arnus, 265
Arot, 95, 96
Arragon, 438
Arriel, 73
Arromaleus, 402
Arrowhead, 160
Ars Notoria, 8

Artheuie, 415
Arthru, 324
Artus, 308
Arum, 511
Asaab, 349
Asafet, 513, 514
Asafoetida, 260, 499, 511–14
Asamaie, 440
Asamie, 415
Asaraie, 415, 440
Asasiel, 163, 441
Asboga, 212
Ascarothe, 104
Ashmole, Elias, 6, 33, 54, 541, 542, 550
Askariel, 256
Asmodai / As Monday, 103, 104
Asmodeus, 106–8, 281
Asnaque, 349
Ass, 151, 159, 164, 245, 263
Assaibi, 306, 444
Asseres, 414
Astagna, 438
Astaroth, 282
Astarothe, 105
Asterothe, 410
Astrologer of the Nineteenth Century, The (Raphael), 22–24, 372, 406, 543, 560
Astrologer's Magazine, The, 16
Astrology, 6, 13–16, 20, 23, 25, 30, 38, 39, 41, 173, 183, 198, 262, 374, 483, 489, 492, 544–47, 550, 554, 562, 565
Astronomy, 14, 40, 59, 341, 343, 492, 550
Astrot, 95–97
Astuodeyt, 419
Atay, 415
Atel, 434
Atemihelt, 113
Atham, 325
Athana, 415
Athanasian Creed, 20, 220, 286
Athatos, 281
Atheizen, 108
Athemay, 446
Athene, 325
Athir, 445, 478
Athole, 250, 251
Atzaliel, 59
Audas, 306
Augustine, Saint, 355, 356
Augutaris, 256
Ausion, 256
Av, 416
Ave Maria, 3, 4, 55, 57, 70, 72, 109, 114, 134, 136, 137, 140, 145, 147, 149, 155, 160, 161, 164, 215, 216, 220, 228, 233, 261, 263, 264, 273–75, 277, 278, 299, 348, 383, 386, 391, 395, 396, 413, 514, 515
Avengers of evil, 281
Avernus, 265
Ay, 415, 438
Aye, 360, 414
Azachiel, 59
Azael / Azaell, 315–17, 411
Azaga, 218
Azaria, 108, 109
Azeruel, 59
Azia, 415
Aziel, 60
Aziell, 411
Aziria, 226

B

Baatze, 334, 335
Babel, 440

Babiel, 443
Bacatu, 81
Bachanael, 436
Baciel, 434
Bacon, Friar, 265, 372
Bafeo, 222
Bag-soot, 522
Bag, silk, 219
Balay, 436
Baldachie, 415
Baldachiesis, 496
Baldatel, 497
Baldmoney, 92
Balidet, 306, 444
Baliel, 436
Balko, 222, 223
Balm, 144, 511, 513
Baltenay, 401
Balthazar / Balthatus, 125, 145, 229, 351
Baltim, 104, 105
Balto, 222
Barabo, 439
Barachyell, 338
Bararthethyel, 113
Baratiel, 139
Barbada, 81
Barchiel, 60
Barcilana, 87
Bardiel, 59
Baroch, 159, 263
Barol, 445, 478
Baron, 7, 564
Barrett, Francis, 17, 21, 543, 559
Bartholomew, Saint, 53, 55, 123, 216, 352, 404
Barton-on-the-Heath, 19
Baruth, 117
Barzabel, 208
Basin, water, 118, 219
Bason, 57
Basson, 414
Bastard, 519, 523, 524
Bat, 91, 133, 279, 280
Bat, blood of a, 91, 133, 279, 280
Bater, 91
Batheryone, 55
Battenay, 67, 68
Bauros, 85
Bay, 135, 391, 493, 494, 518–20, 524
Bay salt, 135, 518–20
Bayacy, 77
Bayberries, 493
Beal / Beall, 73, 256, 272
Bealphares, 329, 332
Beandinet, 86
Beans, 133, 134, 515
Bear, 85, 127, 135, 136, 138, 145, 163, 169, 235, 236, 240, 242, 266, 276, 281, 285, 287, 325, 347, 369, 371, 405, 413, 517, 549
Beclachim, 108
Becu, 263
Beel, 362
Beelzebul, 145
Bees, 113, 139, 203
Befra, 301
Beguiling spirits, 281
"Behold O God" (Browne), 510, 567
Bel, 497
Belam, 245
Belferael, 421
Belferiel, 112
Belial, 104, 105, 281
Belkebub, 324
Belladonna, 13, 512
Bellageron, 420

Bellaman, 66
Belle, 334, 335
Belleracke, 288
Bellonay, 288
Belyaly, 421
Belzabub / Belzebub, 103–5, 121, 280, 408
Benculsioth, 85
Benedoefet, 197, 258
Benhiz, 421
Benisci, 225
Benisti, 225
Benjamin, 493, 521, 524, 533, 547, 566
Beralanensis, 496
Berifay, 415
Beringos Brothers, 197, 283
Berisay, 163, 442
Beron, 445, 478
Beryl, 16, 497, 564
Besal'el, 22
Beth, 295, 416
Bethlehem, 162, 216, 264, 265
Bethnael, 59
Bethor / Bether, 340–44, 464
Betony, 261, 524
Betradandi, 82
Betu, 159
Bevisci, 225
Bewdley, 12
Bex, 90
Bibas, 218
Bible, 9, 35, 75, 489
Bilat, 306
Bilet, 436
Bine, 258
Biros, 347
Birthwort, 260
Blaef, 443
Blake, William, 26, 563
Bleath, 315
Blockley, 6
Blood, 40, 55, 60, 64, 72–74, 77–79, 82, 87, 89–94, 96, 99, 102, 113, 117, 120, 126, 133, 136, 137, 139, 144, 148, 154, 155, 159–62, 170, 203, 237, 239, 240, 253, 257, 261, 270–72, 275–80, 284, 287, 288, 290, 299, 301, 308, 316–18, 337, 340, 347–51, 359, 362, 367, 380, 387, 388, 393, 402, 409, 424, 427–30, 497, 524
Blunder, 150
Boal, 73, 74
Boar, 152, 285, 514
Bodkin, 266, 490
Bodleian Library, 2, 25–28, 54, 541, 544, 545, 559, 563
Bokinleph, Saint, 277
Bones, 80, 113, 152, 154, 155, 160, 245–47, 249, 264, 270, 271, 278, 303, 315, 321, 360, 362, 552, 558
Boney, Master, 8, 313
Booel, 445
Book, 2, 4, 5, 8, 10–14, 16–33, 35, 36, 39, 41, 54, 58–60, 69–71, 75–77, 104, 112, 115, 122, 133, 135–37, 143–161, 163, 166, 179, 191, 193, 195, 200–206, 212, 217, 218, 233–44, 254, 258, 260, 262, 263, 270, 281–83, 308, 311, 321, 323, 338, 340–47, 368, 372, 374, 375, 382, 411, 414, 427, 433–35, 437, 438, 440, 442–46, 448–50, 454–56, 459, 461, 464, 473, 475, 477, 478, 481, 487, 489, 491–94, 497, 504, 525, 535, 543, 549, 550, 552–55, 557–60, 565
Book of Knowledge, 166, 195, 459, 549

Book of Spirits and Tales of the Dead, The (Raphael), 24
Borse, 143
Bosco, 222, 223
Botheon, 322
Bots, 155
Box, 11, 27, 38, 64, 86, 273, 274, 283, 313, 404, 488, 492, 499
Box, wooden, 488
Boyle, Robert, 14, 551, 563
Braciget, 104
Braggada, 403
Brain, swine, 83
Branch, beech, 156
Branch, hazel, 1, 46, 72, 74, 159, 164, 228, 229, 263, 307, 488
Brandel, 112
Brandy, 135
Brass, red, 203
Brass, yellow, 205
Bray, 64, 135, 403
Bread, 65, 76, 123, 150, 151, 161, 244, 266, 268, 272, 286, 299, 317, 318, 340, 394, 396–401, 404, 429, 431, 512
Bread, white, 512
Breve, 125, 225
Bricii, 225
Bridle, 279
Brimstone, 231, 406, 408, 499, 516, 520
Briony, 171
Bristol, 22, 24
Britannia's Pastorals (Browne), 510
British Institution, 19
British Museum, 25, 26, 544, 553
Britten, Emma Hardinge, 21, 556
Broche, 159
Brown bastard, 519
Browne, William, 510, 567
Brucius, 105
Bubo, 277
Buck, blood of a, 287
Bucket, 65
Buer, 471
Buffan, 421
Bull, 82, 283, 455
Bung, 518, 519, 521–23
Burchat, 434
Burdock, 511
Burfax, 410
Burie, 334, 335
Burwall's Cave, 24
Bury St. Edmunds, 13, 552
Bustera, 262
Butera, 262
Butter, 524
Byoeton, 322

C

Caberion, 292, 293
Cados, 163, 338, 414, 426, 435, 437, 442, 445
Cadra, 247, 248, 319, 320
Cafasim, 421
Caffriel / Cafriel, 245
Cageti, 161
Calamus, 524
Calbat, 415
Calbot, 442
Calcidius, 302, 545
Calerna, 445, 478
Calf, brain of a, 120
Calibit, 86
Calizabin, 411
Caluel, 440
Calzas, 438
Campbell, Duncan, 16

Camphor, 493, 511, 513, 516, 519, 520
Cana, 219
Canaan, 222
Cancer, 123, 199, 277
Candle, 112, 113, 119, 135, 136, 139, 250–52, 287, 504, 516
Cani, 93, 395
Canke, 432
Cannabis, 13, 512, 544
Cantharides, 120
Cantine, 163, 442
Canvas, 524
Cap, 251, 489
Capabili, 434
Caphriel, 445
Capricorn, 123, 199
Capthorn, 266
Captiel, 109–11
Caracasa, 446
Carbunculae, 277
Carlisle, Arthur, 27
Carmax, 438
Carmillion / Karmelion, 291, 292
Carpet, 160, 263
Carraway, 524
Carrier for treasure, 315
Carsial, 78
Case-nuts, 517, 519, 524
Casia, 91
Casmaran, 446
Cassiel / Caffiel, 163, 423, 424, 444, 445, 473–77
Caste, 96, 97, 366
Castiel, 163, 245, 441
Casyl, 157
Cat gut, 494
Cat blood, 94
Cat brain, 94
Cat skin, 280
Catherine, Saint, 251, 317, 356
Catillya, 287
Catrigiel, 60
Cattan, 131, 165, 179, 183, 457, 459, 460, 546
Cattion blood, 94
Cattle, 8, 16, 47, 151, 204, 241, 246, 265, 271, 352, 354, 356, 357, 367, 371, 515
Caucze, 83
Caudae, 82
Cauenpria, 87
Cecilia / Saint Cicely, 250, 251
Cedrophyane, 422
Celandine, 136, 189
Celerum, 401
Cell, 6, 7, 114
Cenerax, 116
Centus, 218
Cepher Raziell, 414
Cepher Saday, 414
Cerberus, 408
Ch Loy, 332
Chafing dish, 135, 488
Chair, 66
Chalk, 219, 252, 261, 517–19
Chamaepitis, 524
Chara, 162
Charathion, 112
Charcoal, 95, 104, 287, 488, 499, 525
Charity, Saint, 269, 278
Charlemagne / Charles, King / Carolus, 125, 127, 132, 145, 146, 533
Charsiel, 435
Chasteberry, 119
Chedusitaniel, 443
Cheese, 151, 512
Cheese, hard, 512

Chermiel, 443
Cherubim / Cherubin, 56, 163, 258, 266, 295, 296, 309, 318, 338, 339, 351, 357, 360, 389, 392, 393, 395, 435, 450
Chihit, 421
Chimrat, 162
China root, 525
Christmas Day, 145
Christopher, Saint, 277
Church of England, 4, 12
Ciauliarug, 81
Cider, 515, 520
Cifucon, 422
Cinis Imago, 256
Cinnamon, 493, 520, 522
Cinnamon-water, 520
Circle, 1, 21, 47, 55, 63, 124, 128, 158, 219, 252, 253, 283–85, 294–97, 302, 303, 305, 321, 327, 330, 331, 334–36, 368, 375, 376, 380, 394, 395, 399, 400, 405, 406, 412, 427–29, 433, 447, 449, 468, 481, 489, 490, 496, 497, 499, 536
Ciriael, 112
Citron, 455, 493
Civet, 524
Cixlen, 85
Claret, 516–19
Clavicula Salomonis. *See* Key of Solomon
Clavis Astrologiae Elimata (Coley), 173, 547
Clay, 219
Cleidomancy, 69
Clement, Saint, 147
Clier, 91
Cliody, 122
Cloth, 64, 78, 82, 83, 86–88, 122, 132, 134, 138, 227, 249, 274, 299, 303, 321, 432, 479, 488, 489, 492, 512, 516, 525
Cloth, lawn / linen, 52, 78, 82, 83, 87, 91, 122, 132, 133, 227, 249, 303, 321, 432, 448, 479, 488, 489, 512, 516, 525
Clothes, 113, 303, 363, 394, 404, 555
Clothes, dead person's, 113
Clouts, 273
Cloves, 493, 516, 517, 519, 520, 522
Cochran, John, 25, 534, 547
Cock, 62, 73, 94, 237, 245, 284, 303, 305, 555
Cock, black, hatched in March, 303
Cock, blood of a, 94
Cock, March, 303, 555
Cock, red, blood of a, 94
Cock, white, 73, 237
Codrapan, 422
Coffin, 221
Cogothomoun, 295
Colceram, 67
Cole, 432
Coliarum, 403
Colkeram, 68
Cologne, 75, 229, 549
Colpas, 292, 293
Comilici, 116
Commen, 147
Commissoros, 446
Commutaff, 447
Comosnay, 112
Compasses, 490
Coney, 511, 513 514, 515
Confession, 365, 368, 565
Confirma, 162
Coniel, 443

Conjunction (astrology), 34, 44, 199, 374, 455, 489
Conjurer's Magazine, The, 16
Consona, 162
Constantine, 157, 158, 170, 225, 481
Contine, 415
Convocation of Canterbury, 12
Cook's Folly, 24
Cooke, John, 24, 547
Coolazem, 288
Cooper's hammer, 158
Copper, 38, 40, 67, 68, 82, 86, 87, 97, 141, 345, 401–3, 488, 560
Copperas, 141
Corabael, 436
Corah / Kora, 333, 362
Coral, 189, 202
Corat, 443
Core, 446
Coriander seed, 311, 516, 519–21, 524
Coriet, 87
Cork, 515
Cornelius, 10, 13, 17, 26, 30, 36, 39, 58, 60, 77, 122, 150, 179, 191, 283, 323, 375, 433, 443, 444, 448–50, 454–56, 461, 464, 473, 475, 477, 478, 489, 491–93, 542, 558, 559
Correola, 203
Corson, 467
Coscinomancy, 197, 258
Cosma, 117
Cotton, Thomas, 10, 380, 548, 557
Cow, 82, 270, 285, 406
Crabs, 525
Cras, 347
Craton / Creaton, 75, 110, 111, 125, 162, 163, 229, 256, 281, 287, 338, 370, 390, 414
Cream, sweet, 512
Cross, 22, 63, 69, 72, 74, 102, 126, 132, 137, 140–48, 157, 160, 161, 164, 168, 169, 171, 216, 219, 224, 225, 228, 231, 232, 255, 257, 259, 263, 265–67, 270, 274–77, 294, 296, 301, 316–18, 326, 335, 337, 340, 356, 363, 370–72, 374, 375, 380, 383, 384, 386–91, 393, 395, 449, 508, 510, 535, 552, 554
Crothe, 287
Crothea, 287
Crothees, 287
Crow, 52, 402, 490
Crow quill, 490
Crowther, Timothy, 16
Crux, 116
"Crux Christi" prayer, 126, 141, 142, 157, 171, 337, 552
Crystal, 16, 46, 47, 157, 158, 221–25, 255, 256, 273, 299, 306, 338, 340, 390, 409, 424, 450, 451, 453, 454, 504
Ctarari, 447
Ctitiel, 212
Cubras, 103, 104
Cucumbers, 240
Cumin, 514, 515
Cunaball, 306
Cunning folk, 8, 9, 15, 21
Curaniel, 436
Currants, 516
Custard, 221
Cute, 519, 523
Cuttlefish shell, 135
Cynabal, 434
Cypress, 67, 68, 401, 493
Cyprian, Saint, 299, 555

D

D'Israeli, Isaac, 26
Dabriel, 436
Daffodil, 219
Dagiel, 443
Daleth, 266
Damael, 438
Damask powder, 518, 519
Daniel, 16, 38, 85, 96, 222, 304, 362, 387, 397, 497, 533, 549, 552, 553, 563
Dantalion, 472
Daphnes, 161
Dardiel, 163, 434
Dariel, 74
Darnel, 513
Darquiel, 436
Darriel, 73
Dates, 5, 64, 77, 396, 547
Dathan, 333, 427
Dathar, 117
Datharm, 117
David, 6, 33, 146, 147, 217, 243, 336, 337, 370, 377, 379, 424, 489, 533, 543, 559, 560, 563, 566
De Abano, Peter, 163, 282, 357, 358, 365, 374, 548, 559
Deadnettle, 511
Debeth, 414
Decarabia, 472
Decline of Magic (Hunter), 14, 15, 267, 553, 564
Deda, 279
Dedia, 117
Dee, John, 6, 10, 548, 550, 563, 566
Deer, 311, 330, 514
Deer fur belt, 330
Defect, 258
Delaton, 116
Democritus, 128
Dencalion, 117
Denley, John, 22, 549
Dentalien, 99
Dentalis, 99–102
Depon, 429
Dermmat, 87
Devil, 5, 12, 16, 123, 126, 141, 145, 149, 197, 216, 229, 260, 261, 297, 314, 336, 352–55, 357, 368, 388, 389, 392, 395, 404, 408, 414, 453, 502, 545, 546, 549, 565, 566
Dew, 43
Deyron, 429
Dhesas, 347
Diagalanga, 92
Diah, 110, 111
Diaton, 287
Dice, 74, 75, 133, 134, 137, 139, 140, 281, 349, 350
Diclary, 218
Dibdin, Thomas Frognall, 27, 549
Dies, 43, 73, 91, 92, 95, 97, 99, 103, 173, 197, 247, 258, 280, 319, 430
Dill, 261
Din, 212
Dirachiel, 59
Diraco, 105
Dirqealy, 421
Discouerie of Witchcraft (Scot), 4, 8, 11, 17, 54, 104, 125, 143–61, 193, 252, 262, 263, 316, 329, 374, 418, 481, 557, 561
Disdros, 103, 104
Diseros, 112
Dish, wooden, 138
Dismas, 54, 215, 390
"Dismas et Iesmas" charm, 54, 215, 390

Disows, 420
Dixon, 23, 24, 549
Dodoens, Rembert, 151, 549
Dog, 12, 45, 46, 89, 92–94, 119, 137, 150, 159, 170, 259, 285
Dog, black, blood of a, 159
Dog, black, gall of a, 159
Dog, skin of a, 89
Dog, white, blood of a, 93
Dog, white, brain of a, 93
Doleo, 116
Doliarimerat, 88
Dona, 258
Donat, 62, 342
Donsor, 349
Doremiel, 443
Douce, Ellen, 25
Douce, Francis, 25–27, 32, 544, 556, 563, 564
Douce, Francis, Sr., 25
Dourina, 197
Dove, black, blood of a, 89
Dove, blood of a, 239, 240
Dove, heart of a, 92
Dove, white, blood of a, 93
Dove, white, brain of a, 93
Drabudyn, 422
Draco, 104, 117, 279
Dracon, 117
Dragon, 87, 282, 302, 362, 424, 497, 504
Dragon sting, 87
Dragon's blood, 87, 424
Drawers, linen, 488
Dridenoy, 421
Drisores Necher, 420
Drocks, 263
Droitwich, 7
Dropsy, 347, 524
Duke, 9, 19, 472, 552
Dung, wolves', 515
Dürer, Albrecht, 27
Dures, 308
Durissimus, 218
Dus, 306
Dust, 62, 119, 407, 523, 532
Dwale, 512, 514
Dysentery, 47, 261

E

Eagle, 10, 28, 93, 504
Eagle and Child pub, Oxford, 28
Eagle, blood, 93
Eaicham, 112
Earl, 6, 467, 472
Early English Books Online, 5
Earth, 41, 43, 47, 56, 67, 69, 70, 73, 82, 89, 90, 96, 97, 100, 108, 114, 121, 123, 133, 136, 139, 163, 164, 168, 220, 223, 227, 230–32, 246, 248, 249, 254, 258, 265, 266, 268–70, 272, 273, 275, 282, 288, 292, 293, 299, 309, 314–17, 320–25, 327, 328, 332, 333, 335, 352, 354, 357, 361, 364, 365, 389, 404, 406, 407, 416, 427, 435, 437, 438, 442, 446, 447, 449–54, 481, 488, 497, 500, 502, 506, 514, 532, 562
Earth of the grave, 248, 320
Eba, 338
Ebaseb, 117
Edas, 161
Edinburgh Review, 27
Edom, 301
Edy, 229
Eel, 77, 133
Eel blood, 77
Efomeloy, 421

Efroy, 422
Egg, 46, 66–68, 220, 401, 403, 512
Egge, 454
Egibiel, 59
Egin, 103–5, 411
Eglantine, 226, 227
Egyndy, 304
Egypt, 308, 359, 397, 497
Egyrion, 414
Ehekimas, 295
Ehelias, 295
Eie, 415, 440, 445
Elizeus, 308
Ekey, 303, 304
El, 22, 105, 207, 256, 304, 334, 335, 338, 357, 414, 435, 438, 451, 454
El Ab, 207
Elande, 117
Elay, 147
Elcellsus, 361
Elchior, 218
Elder, 141, 162, 164, 189, 348, 552
Elder (tree), 141, 162, 164
Elean, 416
Elecampane, 91
Eledo, 114
Elee, 415
Elefore, 56
Elemer, 226
Eleoselinum, 159
Elex, 90
Eley, 105, 274, 299, 304
Eleya, 338
Elezel, 75, 76
Elgay, 229
Eli, 96, 97, 155, 362
Elias, 6, 33, 308, 533, 542, 550
Eliaza, 312, 313
Elibra, 415, 438
Elicona, 410
Eliel, 75, 76, 117
Eliet, 117
Eligron, 294
Elim, 214, 246
Elion, 160, 263, 361, 414, 497
Elital, 117
Elite, 9, 21, 29, 116
Elitese, 116
Elizabeth, Saint, 136, 140
Eliazare, 108–109
Elizaus, 219
Elizeus, 308
Elizon, 412
Ellina, 328
Elm, 525
Elmalim, 120
Eloey, 295
Eloh, 209
Eloha, 110, 111
Elohim / Eloim, 110, 111, 229, 359, 361, 414, 415, 438, 440
Elos, 229, 414
Eloy, 105, 115, 233, 246, 274, 295, 299, 304, 318, 322, 332, 360, 396, 414, 415, 454, 479
Elpa, 279
Elpanton, 75, 76
Élus Cöens, 21
Elves, 269
Ely, 114, 218, 222, 256, 299, 325, 334, 335, 451
Elzapharas, 416
Emalagra, 226
Emanuel / Emanuell, 56, 94, 97, 110, 111, 125, 132, 219, 233, 256, 271, 273, 274, 299, 304, 318, 322, 338, 360, 363, 369,

390, 396, 412, 415, 426, 452, 454, 497, 533
Emaris, 160, 263
Emmanuel, 72, 96, 97, 146, 149, 219, 479
Encyclopaedia Britannica, 18, 119, 120, 556
Enduyan, 421
Enediel, 59
Engal, 523
English Civil War, 7
Enitamaus, 197
Enlightenment, 14, 15, 553
Enuell, 139
Ephemeris, 485, 489
Epilepsy, 150, 218, 272
Epiphany, 56, 75, 139
Epos, 218
Ergedial, 59
Esa, 415
Esau, 359, 497
Escarioth / Eskarioth, 11, 273, 274
Escerehie Oristion, 360
Escher[e]ie / Eschereie, 163, 442
Eseche, 325
Esenaroth, 159, 263
Eserchie, 496, 497
Eson, 160, 263
Esser, 150
Ethem, 334, 335
Ethen, 416
Ethem, 334–35
Etheus, 295
Euphorbia, 94
Euphorbium, 493
Eve, 10, 96, 100, 122, 246
Evesham, 7
Ewal, 117
Excrement, 149
Excrement, cow, 406
Excromell, 422
Exdromell, 422
Exe, 415
Exorcism, 12, 30, 414, 447, 542, 567
Ey, 415
Eye, 63, 66–69, 88, 156, 158, 189, 263, 264, 267, 271, 347, 401–3, 415, 435, 437, 452, 552, 563
Eye of Abraham, 66–68, 158, 401–3, 563
Ezell, Margaret, 13, 31, 550

F

Fa, 415
Faccigrat, 122
Facier, 419
Facison, 112
Fairies, 9, 11, 30, 47, 65, 88, 145, 233, 252–54, 267–69, 552
Fall, 52, 54, 67, 71, 83, 135, 150, 161, 163, 168, 216, 244, 269, 270, 275, 325, 379, 407, 413, 452, 458, 526, 543
Falling evil. *See* epilepsy.
Fallow deer, 311
False gods, 281
Famiel, 443
Familar Astrologer, The (Raphael), 23, 216, 217, 560
Familiar, 23–25, 29, 45, 47, 58, 65, 216, 217, 270, 283–285, 308, 313, 346, 454, 464, 560
Fanoy, 293
Faraanto, 117
Farlas, 446
Faro, 117
Fascination, 46, 47, 235, 270
Fascra, 81
Fastarie, 83

Fat, children's, 159
Fath, 295
Fatison, 421
Fax, 160
Fecana, 161
Fedrich, 421
Fennel, 280
Ferce, 256
Feres, 150
Fermagon, 85
Fern, 122, 413
Festativi, 446
Fever, 10, 47, 122, 132, 143, 160, 161, 171, 259, 260, 267, 323, 558
Figa, 147
Figalis, 147
Figs, 64
Filiacz, 420
Filiat, 103, 104
Filiops, 419
Filos, 256
Fimiricti, 86
Finter Ylls, 419
Fire, 6, 24, 28, 36, 53, 56, 65, 66, 72, 75, 95–97, 100, 105, 108, 110, 112, 115, 120, 121, 126, 138, 141, 143–46, 152, 155, 163, 164, 189, 193, 223, 226, 227, 231, 232, 239, 245–47, 256, 257, 262, 265, 266, 283, 287–90, 302, 304, 308, 315, 321–24, 337, 348, 358, 363, 364, 368, 380, 386, 392, 405–9, 414, 426, 432, 447, 448, 451–54, 489, 493, 496, 497, 499, 500, 511, 513, 514, 516, 518, 525
Fisamus, 117
Fistula, 277
Flagla, 117
Flamel, Nicolas, 43, 44
Flax, 124, 145
Fleawort, 124
Flegur, 88
Flour, barley, 221
Flour, bean, 512
Flour, rice, 520
Flour, wheat, 511–513
Flucumagon, 422
"Flum Jordan" charm, 264
Flumicion, 422
Foiling, silver, 401
Fortimelich, 88
Fourth Book of Occult Philosophy (pseudo-Agrippa), 5, 8, 10, 11, 17, 18, 26, 30, 39, 58, 282, 283, 340–47, 374, 433–35, 437, 438, 440, 442–46, 449, 461, 464, 473, 475, 477, 478, 491, 558, 559
Fraciel, 438
Fracradi, 88
Frankincense, 73, 77, 85, 103, 125, 145, 253, 260, 272, 292, 351, 493, 512, 514
Frantiell, 421
Friagne, 438
Friday, 38, 99, 128, 135, 164, 286–88, 303, 375, 394, 432, 442–44, 459, 460, 462, 476, 477, 483, 488, 565
Frogs, 112, 360, 497
Frondes populeas, 159
Frypas / Stripas, 293
Furcas, 471
Furies, 282
Fuseli, Henry, 26
Fyliath, 112

G

Gaap / Gap, 467, 470, 526
Gabiel, 59, 60
Gabrael, 436
Gabrick, 117

Gabriel / Grabriell, 137, 163, 168, 336, 337, 354, 389, 392, 393, 395, 423, 424, 434, 436, 437, 473–75, 477
Galangal, 92
Galbanum, 260, 327, 493
Galbat, 151
Galbes, 151
Galdat, 151
Galdel, 438
Galdes, 151
Galhinos, 107
Gall, beast's, 514
Gall, bird's, 515
Gall, ox's, 511, 513
Galpha, 117, 134
Galtim, 104, 105
Ganfrite, 117
Gargatel, 446
Garilien, 421
Gariot, 88
Garliam, 112
Garlic, 159
Garnael, 218, 293
Gaspar, 145
Gassiar, 229
Gata, 134
Gathinos, 108
Gaviel, 446
Gazelle brain, 93
Gebali, 161
Gebare, 161
Gedaco, 161
Geerin, 88
Gegeton, 304
Gelam, 245
Gelfe, Boney, 8, 313
Geliel, 59
Gell, 75, 76
Gelon, 425, 426
Gemasnay, 421
Gemini, 123
Genius, 26, 40, 455, 490
Geofriell, 421
Geomancie (Cattan), 131, 165, 179, 183, 457, 459, 460, 546, 559
George III, King, 19
George IV, King, 19
Gerdicham, 112
Geremiah, 447
Gesetret, 258
Gesgm, 421
Gesmas, 54
Gesta, 139, 204
Giaray, 77
Gibor, 57, 110, 111
Gideon, 53
Giel, 219, 324
Giles, 150
Ginger, 519, 520, 522
Girdle, lion's skin, 489
Glandula, 277
Glass, 43, 46, 52, 57, 133–35, 139, 164, 223, 224, 227, 239, 255–57, 287, 299, 364, 390–95, 450, 451, 454, 497, 513, 526, 543, 552
Gloves, white, 488
Goall, 324
Goalls, 121
Godras, 95–97
Goetia, 17, 18, 402, 467, 471, 563
Gofrell, 421
Goitz, 72
Gold, 1, 2, 38, 40, 43, 45, 58, 70, 80, 89, 97, 125, 141, 145, 158, 164, 168, 169, 230, 233–44, 258, 272, 283, 284, 288, 302, 330, 339, 345, 348, 351, 424, 435,

452, 459, 479, 487, 488, 504, 507, 509, 560
Golias / Goliath, 299, 370, 379
Goliathe, 121
Gorchiz, 422
Goshawk brain, 93
Gosling Sellert, 249
Gospel of St. John, 144, 294, 391
Grabriel, 109, 110
Gragisneill, 422
Graham, George, 23, 552
Graham, Margaret, 23, 552
Grains, 85, 516, 520, 522, 524
Gramato, 432
Grapevines, 105
Graphiel, 208
Grate, 493
Gratnel, 106–8
Gratny, 117
Graver, 490
Grax, 116
Grease, boar, 514
Greatrakes, Valentine, 12, 551
Gredichiam, 421
Green Park, London, 14
Gregory, 146, 533, 542, 566
Gremitos, 325
Griberi, 88
Grimm, 280
Grimorium Verum, 133, 286, 287, 558
Grissolis, 422
Guabarel, 446
Guael, 438
Gudamel, 334–35
Gudgin, 156
Gudomel, 295
Gum arabic, 512
Gustera, 262
Gutrix, 441
Gutriz, 306
Guts, sheep, 512
Gutta, 153
Gys, 117

H

Haa, 415
Hab, 151
Habajel, 436
Habakkuk / Abacub, 85
Habar, 150
Habay, 150
Haboth, 338
Habuet, 334, 335
Hag, 263, 271
Hagiel, 211
Hagith / Agith, 340–42, 345, 464
Haglata, 295, 296
Hagrernet, 117
Hairs, human, 119, 121, 122, 135, 262, 303, 305, 324
Hairs, men's, 85
Hakim, 163
Halen, Saint. *See* Helen
Haliel, 295
Hallahallynza, 288
Haludiel, 435
Haly, 222
Hammer, 67, 158, 261, 403
Hamnscadan, 82
Hannell, 289, 290
Hanun, 436
Haralapall, 163
Haranber, 408
Hare, 93, 94, 151, 245, 330
Hare, fur, belt, 330
Hare rennet, 93, 94

Harrington, Thomas, 3, 13, 14, 17–19, 22, 28, 30, 32–36, 39, 45, 58, 59, 62, 66, 77, 122, 129, 153, 166, 179, 187, 226, 347, 450, 458, 459, 467, 475, 485, 493, 552, 554, 566
Hart's tongue, 134
Hasmodai, 214
Hastas, 91
Hatim, 415, 442
Hau, 415
Haw, 295, 416
Hawe, 334, 335
Hay, 82, 514
Hay, wheat, 514
Hazelnut, 170
Heaculum, 370
Headache, 46, 152, 233, 239
Heart, pig's, 513
Heavenly Letter, 125, 168, 553
Hebaneth, 295
Hebauth, 454
Heber, 150
Hecas, 161
Helen / Halen / Halena / Helena, Saint, 157, 224, 225
Helioren, 358, 414
Hell, 97, 100, 148, 153, 164, 215, 223, 227, 231, 232, 246, 251, 256, 299, 302, 314, 317, 333, 340, 360, 362–64, 389, 405, 408, 414, 427, 454, 500, 532, 550
Hellebore, 260
Heloy, 295
Hely, 97, 295, 317, 338
Helycon, 332
Helye, 332
Hemlock, 311, 511, 515
Hemp seed, 514
Hen, 245
Henbane, 13, 311, 511, 512, 514, 515
Henbane seed, 511, 515
Henry, Duke of Cumberland, 19
Hepe, 295, 296
Heptameron (pseudo-Abano), 5, 8, 10, 11, 163, 282, 306, 307, 357, 358, 365, 433, 446, 548, 558
Herbs, 11, 13, 40, 41, 46, 56, 62, 82, 83, 119, 123, 134, 153, 164, 246, 274, 275, 311, 323, 348, 438, 492, 525, 544
Heremon, 415
Hermes Trismegistus, 29, 543
Herod, 371, 533
Herschel (Uranus), 24, 374
Heya, 415, 443
Heydon, John, 7, 128, 166, 457, 458, 460, 547, 553
Himmelsbrief, 125
Hind, 311
Hippocrates, 532
Hippomanes, 92, 120
Hismael, 207
Hit, 156, 157
Hod, 207, 214
Hodges, William, 8, 263, 313
Hog's turd, 152
Hogs, 151
Hogshead, 516–18, 520–23
Holland, 525
Holloway, John, 37
Holofernes, 96
Holy Guide (Heydon), 128, 166, 457, 458, 460, 553
Holy water, 144, 148, 239–41, 261, 296, 297, 336, 414, 447, 488, 490
Homousion, 219, 256
Honey, 62, 92, 233, 260, 328, 511–13, 524, 526

Horehound, 260
Horse, 16, 45, 52, 88, 92, 155, 166, 279, 283
Horse hoof, 88
Horseradish, 524
Horseshoe, 158, 262, 263
Host, 154, 163, 429, 440, 442, 443, 445, 497
Hoth, 414
Houseleek, 511
Hu, 313, 415, 457
Hubert, 150
Hugher, 523
Human blood, 94
Humanity, 107, 316, 317
Humastrau, 436
Humfiem Beskebub, 281
Hunamalich, 88
Hupbaltiel, 443
Hur, 143, 151
Huratapal, 434
Husbreth, 122
Husey, John, 6
Hy, 415, 438
Hygromanteia, 10, 220, 556
Hyleates, 239
Hymnus ante Somnum (Prudentius), 294
Hyniel, 438
Hypocistis, 511
Hyssop, 261, 273, 369, 447, 489

I

Ia, 76, 101, 109, 445
Iamfriel, 245
Ibis, 156, 553, 558, 559, 562, 565
Ibooth, 454
Idol, 88
Ignem podyan, 516
Ihe, 147
Illustrations of Shakespeare (Douce), 27
Ima, 415, 445
Image magic, 187
Imbroson, 107
Imohalite, 162
"In sanguine Adae" charm, 162, 278
Ina, 415, 445
Incense, 58, 81, 85, 87, 260, 311, 489, 493
Indum, 493
Ingremos, 306
Inney, 77
Inns of Court, 510
Invisibility, 11, 13, 31, 45, 47, 62, 64, 133, 258, 268, 270, 280, 287, 328, 343, 347, 349, 367, 380, 387, 388, 406, 413, 429, 543, 550
Iod, 110, 111
Iophiel, 207
Ioth, 359, 414, 454
Iothe, 334, 335
Irel, 438
Irelpel, 280
Irioni, 150
Iris, 108, 109, 226, 312, 313, 522
Iron, 38, 40, 45, 83, 89, 97, 100, 135, 146, 160, 203, 261, 283, 447, 459, 488, 499, 526
Isaac, 26, 125, 146, 217, 222, 293, 303, 304, 336, 387, 447
Isander Joy, 168
Iscariot, 273
Iscyros, 497
Ise, 277
Isiael, 438
Isilari, 454
Isinglass, 521, 522

Isiros, 347
Iskyroth, 334, 335
Ismoli, 438
Israel, 238, 379, 397, 406, 435, 440, 445, 453
Isus, 338
Ivory, 85, 86
Ivy, 135, 260
Ivy leaves, 135
Iwereston, 287

J
Jabir, 44
Jacob, 38, 125, 217, 222, 293, 303, 304, 336, 359, 387, 447, 497, 533
Jah, 207, 414, 496, 497
Jana, 334, 335, 414, 533
Janael, 436
Janic, 442
Janie, 415
Janiel, 438
Janor, 445, 478
Jareafel, 456
Jaspar / Jasper / Jaspior, 125, 218, 272, 351, 371
Jath, 338
Jaym, 415, 442
Jayon, 445, 478
Jazel, 438
Je, 415, 443
Jechell, 416
Jehovah, 53, 207, 229, 271, 273, 274, 479, 496, 500
Jeia, 437
Jen, 415
Jennefatos, 89
Jerescus, 439
Jeriabel, 439
Jerusalem, 143, 162, 216, 244
Jesquet, 197
Jesta, 415
Jews, 127, 142, 147, 155, 171, 271, 339, 340, 376, 383, 388, 510
Job, 26, 36, 140, 155, 455
Joerh, 293
John, Baptist, Saint, 114, 136, 140, 155, 250, 251, 288, 309, 317, 318, 355, 391, 413, 490
John, Evangelist, Saint / Johannes, 127, 136, 140, 146, 147, 155, 250, 288, 309, 317, 318, 355, 391, 413, 533
Jonah, 96
Jones, Richard, 6
Jordan, 114, 147, 155, 162, 216, 264, 271, 273, 339
Joseph, 9, 27, 33, 91, 147, 217, 228, 306, 544, 548, 552, 553, 556, 558, 562, 564
Joseph of Arimathea, 147
Joshua, 53, 379
Joth, 497
Joys (astrology), 38, 545
Judah, 147, 337, 383
Judith, 96
Jupiter, 112, 114, 118, 119, 202, 207, 283, 344, 382, 394, 411, 442, 504
Jynx, 120

K
Kadie, 443
Kanop, 218
Karmelion. *See* Carmillion
Kaskaat, 349
Katherine, Saint, 250
Kedemel, 211
Kelley, Edward, 6
Kesler, Saint, 277

Kester, Saint, 277
Key of Rabbi Soloman / Key of Rabby Soloman / Key to Rabby Salomon, 39, 491
Key of Solomon, 17–19, 22, 38, 258, 402, 467, 469–72, 487–90, 492–94, 496, 497, 499, 502, 556, 558, 563
Khiriora, 150
Kidskin, 374
King, Thomas, Jr., 13, 35, 39, 166, 179, 187, 450, 475, 485
King's or Queen's evil, 152
Kiriel, 59
Kite's tongue, 349
Knife, 58, 64–66, 72, 150, 225, 261, 267, 307, 327, 330, 331, 348, 396, 428, 512
Knife, brass, 64, 65
Knife with a white haft, 327
Knight, 160, 471, 560
Kora. *See* Corah

L

Labdanum, 327
Lacerieb, 59
Laetoncet, 324
Lama, 362, 438
Lamazabachany / Lama Zabathani, 338, 362
Lamb, 125, 144, 164, 219, 266, 311, 339, 347
Lamb, black, blood of a, 347
Lambe, John, 6, 7, 551
Lamen, silver, 118
Lamfriel, 245
Lammas, 136
Lamp, 122, 135, 286, 431
Lapwing, 64, 65, 349, 350
Lapwing blood, 349
Laquel, 440
Lata, 119
Laudanum, 493
Laytor, 349
Lazarus, 222, 391, 398
Lead plate, 11
Leather, 2, 17, 85, 132, 222, 255, 348, 555
Leather, hart's, 222, 255
Leclamat, 121
Lees, ale, 511
Lees, wine, 511
Leicestershire, 5
Lemegeton, 18, 558, 563
Lemons, 518
Leo (constellation), 104, 112, 123, 125, 147, 149, 336, 370, 390, 412, 415, 455, 490
Leo, Pope, 127, 145
Leopard blood, 94
Leper, 139, 496
Letera, 432
Leton, 426
Lettuce seed, 515
Leviathan, 451
Leyson, 383
Liber Juratus, 21, 59, 60, 559
Libra, 61, 88, 123, 342, 526
Lignum aloes, 83, 240, 331, 493
Lignum cassia, 493
Lignum-balsaim, 493
Lime, 86
Line tree, 525
Linen, 52, 78, 82, 83, 87, 91, 122, 132, 133, 227, 249, 303, 321, 432, 448, 479, 488, 489, 512, 516, 525
Linguatim, 325
Lion, 125, 147, 222, 284, 304, 337, 383, 387, 489, 494

Liquorice, 517, 525
Litany of the Saints, 142, 398
Liver, dog's, 92
Lizard, 82, 120, 135
Loadstone, 504
Lobquin, 438
Locks, opening, 46, 153, 285, 440
London, 6, 7, 14, 17, 19, 22, 23, 28, 33, 52, 374, 541–44, 546–64, 566, 567
Longinus / Longens / Longine, 137, 160, 391
Longwort, 159
Lot, 35, 39, 177, 179, 358, 497
Lucas Smith, Sarah, 24
Lucidarium Artis Nigromaticę, 11
Lucifer, 13, 56, 97, 99–105, 116, 163, 357, 406, 408
Lucy, Saint, 250, 251
Ludula, 90
Luke / Lucas, Saint, 53, 123, 127, 154, 163, 215, 216, 323, 325, 390, 412, 419, 423, 424, 452, 533

M

Maaroch, 263
Maaroth, 159
Mace, 493
Machare, 218, 293
Macharon, 218, 293
Machasiel, 435
Machatan, 163, 444
Machator, 445
Macriton, 222
Madiat / Mediat, 306, 439
Madiel, 436
Madimiel, 456
Maei, 370
Mael, 436
Maeriall, 420
Maerion, 322
Magell, 293
Maggots, 155
Magi, 229, 433, 543
Magical rolls, 381, 384
Magoll, 218
Magpie, 170, 285
Magromon, 348
Magus, The (Barrett), 17, 543, 559
Maguth, 441
Maguts, 306
Maherion, 410
Malagie, 313
Malagria, 226
Malaipe, 293
Malaron, 218
Malbeas, 67
Malcha betharsisim hed beruah Schehakim, 214
Malchus, 125
Maligi, 395
Malkeo, 68
Malleo, 401
Malmsey, 523, 524
Malphas, 471
Maltiel, 443
Malxipe, 218
Mammon / Mamon, 282, 306
Mammot, 106
Mammoy, 107, 108
Mandeville, John, 216, 556
Mandrake, 26, 217
Manna, 83
Manopall, 88
Manoth, 274
Mans Hora, 349

Mansions of the moon, 11, 45, 60, 77, 290, 456, 489
Mansions of the moon, rings of, 77
Mansletay, 421
Mantic alphabet, 228
Manton, 287
Manus Christi, 522
Marabu, 370
Maratarykin, 153
Marcelline, 251
Marciterton, 255
Marcondyt, 168
Mare, 52, 53, 88, 95, 96, 271, 328, 363, 379, 421
Margaret, Saint, 250, 317
Marinata, 437
Mark / Marcus, Saint, 53, 62, 123, 163, 215, 226, 250, 251, 261, 265, 309, 323, 339, 390, 423, 533
Marma, 250, 251
Marotus, 117
Marquis, 472, 487
Marse, 143
Martalio, 88
Martin, 37, 133, 148, 555, 556
Mary Magdalene, 36, 356
Mary, virgin, 70, 113, 114, 139, 143, 159, 161, 219, 223, 246, 253, 298, 302, 309, 314, 322, 324, 339, 354, 374, 391–93, 395, 427, 496, 566
Mase, 117
Masgabr[i]el, 435
Mass of the Holy Ghost, 55, 58, 299, 448
Mass of the Holy Ghost of Saint Cyprian, 299
Mass of the Trinity, 394
Mass of Three Kings / Mass of the Three Kings, 75, 139
Massias, 125
Master Boney, 8, 313
Mastic, 235, 239, 241, 242, 245, 331, 440, 493
Mataron, 293
Mathen, 371
Matherione, 55
Mathiel, 438
Mathiesen, Robert, 19, 21, 556
Mathlai, 439
Mathon / Maton, 416, 478
Mathun, 445
Mathyel, 295
Matthew / Mattheus, Saint, 53, 123, 127, 149, 215, 302, 309, 323, 339, 390, 420, 423, 424
Matua, 251
Matuyel, 435
Maveton, 287
Max, 91, 150, 160
Mayfa, 66
Maymon, 444
Me Nec Hic, 103, 104
Meadow, 82, 87, 122
Measure of Christ, 384
Mechat, 218
Mechymn, 112
Medula, 218
Meffaton, 415
Megalagia, 108, 109
Meillya, 287
Melcatria, 117
Melchio, 229
Melchior / Melachior / Melatrior, 145, 146, 150, 272, 351, 371
Meloch, 414
Melons, 46, 240
Meltat, 157

Memiatha, 107
Memoirs and Anecdotes of Philip Thicknesse, 18, 325, 564
Memory (prayer), 58
Menstrua, 52, 202
Mercurii, 21, 23, 25, 205, 285, 286, 374, 431
Mercury of the Philosophers, 43
Merezium / Merizium, 424–26
Merion, 74
Merizim, 424
Mertarus, 117
Mescheek, 497
Mesler, Katelyn, 22, 557
Messcas, 110, 111
Messias, 56, 96, 97, 146, 149, 218, 219, 229, 256, 271, 273, 295, 309, 318, 338, 360, 369, 390, 396, 412, 414, 452
Metasignais, 447
Mex, 90
Micabi, 306
Michael / Mic[h]ael, Saint, 14, 109–11, 137, 163, 336–38, 354, 359, 389, 392, 393, 406, 423, 424, 434–36, 473–75, 477, 537, 544, 546, 553, 554, 557, 563, 564
Miclial, 410
Midsummer Eve, 10
Miel, 163, 439
Mies, 197, 258
Milfoil, 141
Mili, 90
Miliel, 440
Milk, 43, 65, 70, 86, 157, 246, 270, 369, 516–18, 520–22, 524
Milk, red cow's, 270
Milliens, 240
Millpath, 85
Minosel, 415
Miratin, 108
Miririm, 281
Misac / Misach / Misacke, 222, 353, 363, 387
Misanas, 91
Missabe, 436
Mistletoe, oak, 87
Mite, 40, 293
Mithra, 433
Mitraton, 439
Mitre, 489
Modiat, 439
Mole, 117, 136, 319, 347
Mole, blood of a, 117, 136
Moly, 159
Molybdomancy, 118
Monacella, Saint, 356
Monaczie, Saint, 356
Monday, 38, 47, 55, 56, 103, 104, 128, 163, 169, 226, 231, 291, 308, 321, 436, 437, 459, 460, 462, 473, 475, 477, 488, 557
Monday plays, 56, 557
Monica, Saint, 356
Moon, 11, 39–41, 43, 45, 53, 56, 60, 70, 77, 109, 118, 150, 165, 183, 206, 213, 290, 374, 382, 411, 430, 446, 447, 449, 455, 456, 462, 475, 487, 489, 509, 525, 526
Moon, liquid from the, 43
Morning Post, 14, 18, 52, 566
Morrab Library, Penzance, 15
Morrison, Robert. *See* Zadkiel
Mortar, 62, 512, 515, 518
Mosaical rod, 1, 5, 164
Moses, 104, 154, 233–37, 240, 308, 333, 360–62, 379, 398, 406, 427, 453, 497, 559

Mosesisamis, 117
Mount Calvary, 153
Mouse skin, 85
Mucon, 222
Mucriton, 222, 223
Mugwort, 170, 375, 450
Mullein, 159, 512, 513, 566
Munton, 255
Muscadine, 519
Musk, 241, 493, 519, 520, 522, 524
Mustard, 108
Mydocy, 263
Myroch, 159
Myrrh, 79, 125, 145, 218, 272, 351, 493
Myrtle, 493

N

Nabbas, 66–68, 401
Nachiel, 209
Nail, brass, 158
Nail, copper, 67, 403
Nail, cypress, 67
Nail, finger, 58, 71, 74, 75, 133, 139, 303, 305, 358
Nail, iron, 261
Nails of the Passion, 385
Naith, 89
Nare, 137, 151
Naromiel, 435
Nasnia, 445, 478
Natalon, 445, 478
National Library of Wales, 148
Nazareth, 76, 127, 142, 147, 271, 272, 294, 376, 383, 388, 510
Necior, 218
Necromancy, 29, 33, 128, 247, 439, 443, 549, 552, 558
Neexe, 295, 296
Neger, 147
Nelapa, 440
Nemigatha, 108
Nephemprosayton, 348
Neptaban, 112
Neptalien, 420
Neray, 147
Neron, 445, 478
Nesroth, 290
Nesteteyll, 422
Net, 243
Netos, 445, 478
Neupmalon, 163
Neupmaton, 427
Neville, William, 6
New and Complete Illustration of the Occult Sciences (Sibley), 16
New Astrologer of the 19th Century (Raphael), 24
New College, Oxford, 8
Nichictur, 420
Nightshade, bitter, 263
Nigromancy, 29
Niplicuch, 420
Nogahel, 456
Noli me tangere, 139, 277
Nollekens, Joseph, 27
Nolycegll, 422
Nones, 99
Northwick Hill, 6
Novissimus, 125, 314, 390, 415
Numel, 89
Nuncia, 90
Nutmeg, 493
Nymphs, 269

O

Oak, 45, 84, 87, 156, 189, 524
Oarth, 432
Oatmeal, 270

Oats, 514, 515
Obelison, 410
Oberion, 291–93, 406
Obessiel, 139
Obey, 36, 56, 57, 66, 71, 78–80, 82, 83, 96, 113, 139, 155, 226, 227, 256, 257, 291, 294, 301, 302, 304, 305, 314, 318, 321, 322, 334, 338, 350, 352, 353, 364, 372, 389, 391, 392, 406, 408, 427, 499
Obrotz, 117
Obsession, 12, 565
Obtablait, 79
Occinomos, 416
Occult Philosophy (Paracelsus), 189, 479
Occult, the, 13, 15, 16, 19, 21, 374, 544, 554, 558, 564
Occynomeno, 426
Och, 340–42, 344, 345, 464
Oculus indiae, 512
Odas, 293
Of the Supreme Mysteries of Nature (pseudo-Paracelsus), 8, 558
Offra, 134
Og, 115, 379, 543
Oil, 52, 66, 71, 112, 122, 135, 149, 157, 220, 221, 223, 224, 234, 243, 244, 260, 261, 265, 489, 512
Oil benedictus, 512
Oil of asperadge, 512
Oil of roses, 234, 243, 244
Oil papal, 265
Oil, meat, 512
Olam, 245
Olibanum, 331
Olive oil, 71
Olive, Princess. *See* Serres, Olivia
Olympic spirits, 464
Omega, 76, 97, 125, 146, 147, 233, 380, 449, 453, 497, 532
Onagla, 432
Onath, 295
Oon, 56
Opera, 157, 197, 261, 399, 542
Ophiel, 340, 341, 346, 464
Ophiton, 422
Opimusque, 137
Opinusque, 137
Opium, 13
Opologia, 496
Opoponax, 493
Opposition (astrology), 199, 374
Opulusque, 137
Orass, 522
Orden des Gülden und Rosen-Creutzes, 21
Oriens, 338–40, 411
Origo, 86, 125, 149, 369, 390, 412, 415
Oriston, 414, 497
Orphaniel, 437
Orphic Circle, 21
Orphuon, 422
Orris, 516, 522
Orris root, 522
Osael, 438
Ostera, 262
Ostnandra, 262
Osturcios, 82
Otfriel, 245
Othe, 414
Othee, 295
Othem, 325
Otheoteco, 390
Othey, 410
Othis, 112
Othos, 358
Otto, Bernd-Christian, 29, 558
Oum, 295

Our Lady, 58, 155, 157, 249, 275, 314, 316, 317, 338, 427
Ourer, 445, 478
Ousion, 229
"Out fire, in frost" charm, 348
Owl blood, 90, 402
Oxford English Dictionary, 5
Oymon, 338
Oyson, 132
Oysters, 525
Oza, 149, 390, 415

P

Paaelaim, 420
Pabel, 434
Paffran, 438
Palm tree, 308
Palnato, 55
Pamis, 137
Pandaemonium (Bovet), 9, 413
Pandorica, 162
Pangraton, 415
Pantacle of Solomon, 288
Pantateron, 415
Panteon, 304
Panthon, 163
Paper, 2, 25, 43, 52, 70, 72, 75, 76, 90, 132, 143, 144, 156, 164, 225, 239–42, 265, 272, 285, 290, 330, 348, 399, 400, 413, 414, 489, 559
Papyrus, 90
Paracelsus, 8, 187, 189, 479, 558
Paracletus / Peracletus, 146, 218, 358, 369, 390, 414
Paracteton, 497
Parchment, 58, 74, 77–80, 82, 83, 85–87, 90, 99, 104, 117, 119, 122, 153, 164, 205, 216, 219, 226, 235, 236, 238, 252, 259–61, 266, 285, 287, 289, 308, 311, 315, 323–25, 347–50, 368, 372, 374, 375, 381, 387, 395, 406, 413, 448, 460, 481, 488–90, 499
Parchment of a black cat's spine, 287
Pargandagt, 421
Paris, 41, 480, 488, 542, 555, 560, 562
Parish, Mary, 9, 564
Parre, 142
Parsley, 514
Parta, 349
Partiko, 153
Pasqually, Martinez de, 21
Pastor, 163, 256, 370, 390, 415, 442
Pata, 256
Pater Noster, 57, 70, 72, 109, 114, 137, 140, 143, 147, 160, 161, 215, 216, 271, 274, 277, 278, 307, 348, 383, 395, 413
Pathmael, 295
Patzunfici, 82
Paua, 347
Paul, Saint, 216, 324, 355
Paulinus, John, 137
Pax, 160, 162
Paymon, 103, 104, 337, 411
Pe, 295
Peak, 295
Pean, 119
Peas, 133, 514
Pangeton, 147
Pen, 72, 90, 312, 330, 402, 490, 543
Penael, 443
Penat, 443
Pence, 87, 88, 288
Pencil, 25, 95, 486, 488
Penel, 112
Peniel, 443
Penis, 52, 91, 360

Penknife with white handle, 488
Penny, 44, 73, 299
Pennyroyal, 525
Peperit charm, 136, 140, 261
Pepper, 438, 516, 517, 519–22
Pepper, India, 519
Pepper, Jamaica, 517
Pepper, long, 516, 517, 519–22
Pepperwort, 443, 493
Perczophare, 419
Perdegramma, 82
Perenell, 103, 104
Pergor, 89
Periel, 74
Perfume, 5, 83, 159, 260, 394, 435, 436, 438, 442, 443, 447, 488, 489, 493, 547
Pestilence, 45, 132, 142, 145, 169, 281, 351, 563
Peter, Saint, 324, 351, 353, 355, 405
Peterson, Joseph, 11, 23, 28, 33, 38, 53–56, 59, 60, 64, 91, 104, 115, 119, 124, 128, 133, 136, 163, 219, 221, 233–237, 240, 249, 255, 258, 259, 282, 283, 285, 286, 291–94, 298, 303, 306, 334, 338, 340, 347, 365, 372, 402, 411, 428, 439, 443, 467, 469–72, 487, 489, 496, 497, 499, 502, 548, 552, 553, 556, 558, 562
Petosiris, 128
Petroleum, 512
Petron, 57
Petronil, Saint, 277
Petronilla, Saint, 277
Peutos, 420
Pewmaton, 333
Pewter, 38, 327, 459, 487, 488
Phaa, 435
Phaleg, 340–42, 344, 464
Phanaboth, 163
Phanaibaoth, 454
Phanebabs, 295
Phanum Regni, 410
Pharaoh, 53, 379
Pharap, 77
Phebas, 161
Philistines, 370
Philosopher's Stone, 43, 346
Philosophical Merlin, The (Graham and Raphael), 23
Phlegethon, 408
Phul, 340, 341, 347, 464
Phylosan, 421
Picatrix (pseudo-Al-Majriti), 10, 93, 94, 543, 559
Pig, 150, 261, 348, 513
Pike, 512
Pillow, 170
Pimlbe, 122
Pin, 72, 350
Pirgistas, 280
Pisces, 61, 123, 202, 511, 513
Pismires, 88, 347
Placental, 219
Plam, 245
Plarata, 280
Plaster of paris, 41, 488
Platter, wood, 138
Pleclu Jephin, 420
Pliphes, 90
Plum, 149
Poco, 142
Podendi, 162
Podera, 162
Poet, 6, 103–5, 510
Polaza, 218
Pollipody, 524

Pomander, 260
Pope, Stephanie, 28, 559
Poplar, 159, 525
Poppy, 511, 515
Porna, 443
Porringer, 262
Possession, 2, 6, 7, 9, 12, 19, 20, 25, 39, 40, 153, 374, 542, 560
Pot, 136, 234, 245, 514, 525, 526
Potoza, 293
Prayer of Aethelstan, 380
Prebal, 112
Prebell, 420
Prelates, 431, 487
Preristorides Purir, 420
President, 7, 25, 374, 471
Priapus, 52
Pribalva, 420
Primachie, 496
Prime, 99, 287
Primeginitas, 369
Primer, York, 149
Primeumaton, 333, 362, 414
Primeuation, 497
Primus, 125, 149, 314, 390, 415
Probalnea, 103, 104
Prohabeen, 422
Propera, 251
Prophetic Messenger (Raphael), 23, 24, 549, 560
Protalion, 103, 104
Protectorate, 8
Psalms, 4, 46, 69, 158, 233, 332, 391, 455, 461, 560
Psalter, 69, 75, 216, 228, 325, 395
Pucer, 229, 370, 415
Pumaton, 414
Puppet, 88
Purgatory, 4, 147, 299
Pythagoras, 128, 131, 546
Python, 281

Q

Qaure, 137
Quanton, 110, 111
Quare fare nare, 151
Quarto Red Book, 39
Quicksilver, 38, 40, 97, 170, 346, 459, 488, 515
Quill, 135, 490
Quill, goose, 122

R

Rabale, 218
Rabas, 403
Rabbas, 66
Raberion, 291, 293
Rabianara, 447
Rabur, 360, 414
Rachiel, 163, 442
Rael, 439
Ragael, 227
Raguel / Raguell, 117, 314, 315, 410
Rahumel, 438
Raisins, 517, 518
Raisins, alligant, 518
Ralboch, 163
Ramet, 108
Rana, 445, 478
Rani-bricii, 225
Raniel, 443
Ranis, 137
Rankine, David, 6, 17, 33, 54, 158, 233–44, 258, 402, 424, 487–94, 560, 563
Raphael / Smith, Robert Cross, 19–25, 28, 32, 215, 216, 372, 374, 406, 408

Raphael / Raphiel (angel), 109–11, 163, 217, 338, 354, 370, 389, 392, 393, 423, 424, 439, 440, 443, 473–77, 553, 560
Raphael's Witch (Raphael), 23, 217, 560
Ratilla, 251
Raven, 171, 283, 347, 402, 514
Raven, heart, 171
Raven, pen, 402
Rawlinson, Thomas, 15, 54, 55, 108, 226, 249, 285, 291, 320, 402, 541
Rayel, 438
Raysoll / ray-soll, 524, 525
Rea, 116
Reael, 59
Reathy, 403
Rebam, 245
Rebano, 293
Red china, 525
Red Quarto. *See* Quarto Red Book
Red Sanders, 5, 435
Red Sea, 53, 398
Remedies against Magic, 170
Remis, 137
Remora, 120
Remove (demon), 472
Renell, 419
Rentone, 147
Reotha, 251
Requiel, 60
Reremise, 91
Rerus, 120
Retha, 66
Rhadamanthus, 408
Rhubarb, 525
Ribas, 137
Ribo, 137
Ribwort plantain, 511
Rimas, 137
Rimos, 137
Ring, 47, 48, 77–89, 122, 139, 150, 277, 287, 379, 394, 424–26, 454, 457, 461, 469, 504
Ringworm, 277
Ripple, 8, 313
Ritona, 325
Ritual magic, 2, 4, 8, 10, 13–16, 18, 21, 23, 24, 28–31
Roatha, 250, 251
Robale, 293
Robam, 218
Robe, white linen, 489
Robinson Crusoe (Defoe), 16
Rock alum, 516, 518, 520
Rods, hazel, 46, 228, 229, 263
Rogaell, 226
Ronceval, 145
Ronove, 472
Rooster blood, 92
Rootha, 250
Rope, 157
Rose water, 425, 516
Rosemary, 91, 273, 524, 557
Roses, 234, 240, 243, 244, 493
Rosewater, 519, 522, 524
Rosicrucian, 7, 17, 21
Rosy, 524
Rotas, 261, 399
Royal Academy, 19
Royal Society, 7, 14
Rubeus, 96, 97
Rubibian, 112
Rubres, 96, 97
Ruchag'ly, 422
Rudd, Dr., 17, 402, 563
Rue, 260, 261, 275, 514, 515
Ruel, 117

Rule, 58, 92, 177, 179, 221, 233, 290, 342, 437, 449, 478, 490
Rupasca, 82
Rush, 112
Rushes, consecrated, 348
Rusibian, 422
Rutilla, 250
Ryros, 281

S
Sa, 415
Saback, 163
Sabaoth / Sabauth / Sabbaoth, 56, 96, 97, 105, 125, 146, 147, 149, 160, 163, 226, 227, 229, 233, 246, 289, 295, 299, 304, 314, 318, 322, 334, 335, 338, 359, 369, 390, 395, 396, 412, 414, 428, 452–54, 479
Sabaothe, 110, 111, 115
Sabarathagla, 57
Sabathiel, 456
Sabay, 403
Sabbac, 442
Sabra, 247, 248, 319, 320
Sachiel / Zachiel, 163, 423, 424, 436, 441–43, 473–77
Sachier, 419
Sack, 266, 512, 517–20
Saclay, 415
Sacriel, 438
Sadai, 110, 111
Sadalos, 89
Sadaly, 295
Saday, 162, 163, 297, 332, 338, 358, 359, 361, 414, 426, 435, 437, 440, 443, 453, 497
Sade, 266
Sadedali, 445, 478
Sadin, 496
Saducismus Triumphatus (Glanvil), 9
Saffron, 442, 493, 512
Sage, 153, 261, 270
Sagittarius, 61, 104, 112, 123, 471
Saglas, 117
Sahl ibn Bishr, 22
Saint Blaze, 152
Saint James Eve, 122
Saint John's Eve, 122
Saint John's wort, 55, 514
Saint Swithun's Church, 321
Sakunas, 104, 105
Salam, 445, 478
Salamia, 435
Salbac, 415
Salbeo, 117
Salic, 133
Salla, 445, 478
Sallales, 439
Sallay, 445
Salmon, 410
Saltem, 104, 105, 119
Salteriacon, 422
Saluncham, 421
Salus Vitae (Alcanus), 137
Saluzem, 288
Samael, 163, 306, 423, 424, 434, 436–38, 443, 473–77
Samax, 437
Samay, 426
Sambio, 117
Sammuel, 110, 111, 140
Samuel, 7, 109, 110, 140, 247, 248, 320, 423, 424, 553
Sand, writing, 522
Sanders, 5, 435, 493
Sandys, Samuel, 7, 8, 553

Sannig, Bernard, 413, 561
Santanael, 443
Sapiel, 435
Sar, 415, 445
Sarabini, 324
Sarabotes, 442
Sarabotieth, 306
Saray, 416, 435
Saraye, 359, 360, 414
Sarite, 162
Sarpelkhe, 404
Sarsaparilla, 525
Sassafras, 524, 525
Sassur, 445
Satael, 133, 163, 306, 437
Satan, 13, 15, 102, 281, 300–302, 304, 305, 321, 352, 353, 355, 356
Sathan, 56, 99–105, 121, 301, 302, 304, 322, 351–64, 392
Sathanas, 105, 408
Satonay, 218
Sator, 90, 261, 399, 565
Satquiel, 109, 110
Satuel, 117
Saturday, 38, 47, 113, 128, 169, 266, 282, 342, 444, 445, 459, 460, 462, 464, 476, 477, 488, 491
Satyr, 218
Saucer, 65
Savine, 284
Saxages, 419
Saym, 108, 419
Saym Sutila, 419
Scalprutus, 117
Scapula, 245, 246
Scare, 58, 137
Scariot, 273
Schedbarscemoth Schartathan, 214
Schor, 410
Scibilla, 108, 109
Scissors, 488
Scolpa, 279
Scorphine, 421
Scorpio, 123
Scorpion, 151, 156
Scott, James, Duke of Monmouth, 9
Scrofula, 277
Sculpa, 117
Scurdabelen, 420
Scurvy-grass, 524
Sebamay, 218, 293
Sebediell, 308, 309
Sebel, 419
Second Merseburg Charm, 278
Sedebin, 229
Sedekin, 229, 414
Sedula, 218
Seeczaburems, 420
Seer, 138, 410, 467
Sefer Shimmush Tehillim, 233–36, 238–40, 244, 560
Seheliel, 59
Seine, 525
Semeliel, 456
Semilech, 414
Senaef, 524
Senap, 306
Sendal, 78
Senior, 409
Sentission, 422
Sepa, 162
Sepaga, 162
Sepagoga, 162
Sephirus, 277
Sephirus, 277
Sephyron, 422

Sepuum, 295, 296
Seraphiel, 438, 439
Seraphim / Seraphin, 56, 163, 211, 258, 266, 295, 296, 309, 318, 338, 339, 351, 357, 360, 389, 392, 393, 395, 450
Serapiel, 163
Seraquiel, 445
Serpent skin, 122
Serres, John, 19
Serres, Olivia, 19, 23, 25, 32, 508, 509, 558, 562
Sesame, 52
Setchiel, 443
Setz, 72
Severion, 291–93
Sextile (astrology), 374
Shears, 10, 197, 258, 262
Shedrack, 497
Shell, 65, 135, 234
Shellfish, 525
Sheltion, 55
Shemhamephares, 361, 415
Shepherd's Calendar, 46, 166, 179, 459
Shor, 347
Sibilla / Sibilia / Sibella / Sybella / Sybilla, 226, 250–54, 410
Sibly, Ebenezer, 16, 17, 19, 329, 456, 481, 488, 492, 494, 562, 563
Sicare, 106, 108
Sicate, 107
Sidrach, 222, 353, 363
Sier, 332
Sieve, 10, 197, 258, 311
Silk, 1, 64, 79–81, 84, 91, 171, 219, 288, 302, 492
Silmo, 117
Silver, 38, 40, 65–68, 70, 77, 78, 82, 88, 97, 118, 122, 150, 164, 169, 202, 204–6, 230, 285, 288, 327, 330, 347, 391, 401, 403, 424, 437, 444, 455, 459, 487, 488, 507, 509, 532
Silver foil, 66–68
Simel, 116
Simon, 266
Sinai, Mount, 379, 437, 453
Sinchatiriell, 421
Sion, 407
Siphyan, 422
Siprosona, 76
Six Clerks Office, 25
Skin, adder, 137–38
Skinner, Stephen, 6, 17, 33, 402, 424, 487–94, 563
Skipton, 16, 55, 548
Skull, 133, 150, 399
Slippers, 488
Sloane, Hans, 7, 15, 563
Smabathan, 108
Smallage, 159, 311
Smart, Peter, 17
Smith, Robert Cross. *See* Raphael
Society of Antiquaries, 25
Socrates, 62
Solomon, King, 56, 224, 291
Solomon's seal, 279
Somalphar, 251
Somar, 409
Somers, John, 7, 8, 547, 561
Sonalker, 251
Soncas, 438
Sonsiane nemorie, 82
Soot, 159
Sophyr, 218
Sorath, 209
Sorday, 117
Sorday, 117

Sorsayeriall, 524
Sorthia, 252
Sorthie, 252
Sorthios, 252
Sothe, 414, 454
Sother, 56, 96, 97, 125, 149, 256, 274, 299, 322, 338, 360, 369, 390, 396, 412, 414, 426, 452, 454
Spanish fly, 120
Sparrow blood, 94
Sparrow, brain, 94
Spirits of lies, 281
Spittle / saliva, 78, 79, 80, 81, 82, 83, 86, 87, 88, 89, 122, 152
Spoon, silver, 65
Sports and Pastimes (J. M.), 5, 164, 555
Spring, 40, 77, 138, 150, 330, 446, 491, 547
Spugliguel, 446
Spyrgon, 322
Saraye, 359, 360, 414
St. Pancras Church, 27
Stable, 88
Staff, 267, 269, 282, 285, 387, 516–21, 523
Stag, 283, 504
Stake, gallows, 105
"Stans sanguis in te" charm, 162
Starch, 516, 522
Starch, white, 522
Stavi, 90
Stay, 53, 155, 162, 217, 222, 248, 256, 257, 278, 352, 356, 357, 369, 403, 409
Steel, 52, 63, 450, 504, 552
Steven, Saint, 355
Stick of cypress, 67, 68, 401
Stick of elder, 141, 162, 164
Stickadoss, 525
Stickadove, 525
Sticks, 160, 226
Stone, 43, 46, 47, 54, 68, 69, 77, 95, 123, 138, 152, 168, 203, 215, 216, 222–24, 255, 257, 275, 280, 281, 325, 338, 340, 343, 346, 347, 390, 392, 404, 406, 409, 425, 452, 454, 504, 559
Stone, marble, 68, 69
Storax, 291–93, 493
Storax, red, 493
Stoulton Heath / Stouten Heath, 5, 249
Stove, 493
Straggling Astrologer, The, 19, 20, 22, 23, 560, 562
Straw, bed, 138
Stroke of a planet, 267
Sturgeon, 521
Styx, 408
Succundia, 420
Suceratos, 434
Suet, 270, 375, 521
Suet, sheep's, 270
Suet, white, 521
Sugar, 260, 520, 522
Sulates, 306
Sulphur, 43, 159, 260, 405, 406, 444
Sulthomyn, 422
Sun, 40, 43, 44, 53, 56, 65, 71, 133, 136, 141, 150, 155, 158, 164, 183, 200, 203, 204, 209, 225, 253, 286, 323, 433, 445–47, 449, 462, 477, 482, 483, 488, 489, 494, 526, 532
Sun pan, 133
Sunday, 5, 38, 128, 168, 284, 459, 460, 462, 477, 488
Sunday epistle, 168
Suquinos, 439
Suranet, 414

Surrey, 5
Susanna, 70, 95, 96, 222, 304, 370, 387
Suth, 306, 441
Sutquiel, 110, 111
Swallow, 156, 347
Swallow's heart, 156
Swallow's liver, 156
Sweet-brier, 245
Swine, 83
Switch, hazel, 488
Sword, 58, 142, 161, 163, 203, 283, 327, 329, 386, 489, 499, 504, 543
Sword, white haft, 327
Sybilla. *See* Sibilia
Synagion, 414
Syphyron, 422
System of Magick (Defoe), 16, 549
Syth, 325

T

Tafrac, 445, 478
Talamite, 218
Tales of the Horrible (Raphael), 24, 543
Talic, 133
Talisman, 39, 183, 368, 375, 455, 460, 470, 488–90
Tallens, 295
Tallow, sheep, 512
Talvi, 446
Tamael, 443
Tamen, 76, 429
Tanic, 445, 478
Tantanill, 408
Taphtharath, 212
Tar, 512
Tariel, 446
Tarmiel, 439
Tarquam, 446
Tartarus, 96
Tarter, white, 524
Tasbat, 349
Tata, 349
Taurus, 123
Tebondrie, 422
Techel, 22, 557
Tecta, 222
Teeth, dead man's, 80, 151, 399
Tefeell, 421
Tegragaton. *See* Tetragrammaton
Tegramaton. *See* Tetagrammaton
Telena, 325
Teltrion, 322
Tempters, 282
Tenaciel, 443
Tench, fat of a, 512
Tench, liver of a, 512
Tenet, 261, 399
Teste, 96, 97
Tetra, 440
Tetragramag, 297
Tetragrammaton / Tet[r]agrammaton / Tetragramaton / Tetraggrammaton, 55–57, 72, 76, 96, 97, 100, 110, 111, 115, 117, 121, 124, 125, 149, 160, 218, 251–254, 256, 258, 264, 271, 273, 274, 287, 289, 299, 304, 307, 314, 318, 322, 324, 332–334, 338, 358, 364, 365, 388, 390, 397, 398, 415, 450, 451, 453, 454, 461, 479, 496, 497, 500
Tevoah, 497
Tezin, 411
Thami, 445
Thamur, 445, 478
Than, 7, 14, 17, 20, 22, 27, 29–31, 33, 34, 43, 63, 64, 118, 144, 187, 228, 242,

282, 303, 367, 368, 373, 374, 414, 420, 447, 464, 478, 512, 542, 548, 559
Thanu / Thanus, 478
Tharthyn, 421
Thasia, 90
Thata, 295
Thaum, 295
Thean, 281
Theleas, 334, 335
Theodonias, 448, 489
Theon, 334, 390, 415
Theophares, 420
Theos, 256, 295, 334, 335, 370, 454
Thetel, 22, 504, 507, 509
Theulus, 281
Thicknesse, Philip, 18, 325, 564
Thief, 25, 45–47, 55, 66–68, 71, 76, 157–59, 215–17, 225–27, 237, 247, 248, 255, 263, 312, 314, 319–23, 369, 395, 396, 400–402, 404, 467
Thiel, 439
Thieves, 16, 45–47, 53, 55, 66, 69, 123, 134, 145, 146, 215, 216, 221, 227, 235, 255, 322, 323, 325, 371, 402, 404, 405, 544, 563
Thimeramet, 107
Thimi, 108
Thorion, 73
Thorn, 47, 110, 152, 272, 276
Thread, 89, 112, 119, 135, 145, 156, 288, 494
Thread, golden, 494
Thread, silken, 288, 494
Thread, virgin-spun, 89, 119, 145
Three bitter biters charm, 263
Three Books of Occult Philosophy (Agrippa), 8, 10, 77, 112, 122, 133, 179, 191, 200–206, 212, 311, 323, 450, 455, 456, 461, 490, 493, 494, 504, 525, 542
Three Kings, 75, 139, 229, 271, 272, 351
Three Kings charm, 272, 351
Three Nails of the Passion, 385
Threfon, 74
Threshold, 52, 90, 91, 136, 140, 158, 170, 217, 218
Throat, sore, 152
Thursday, 38, 128, 163, 166, 220, 231, 283, 286, 391, 432, 441, 442, 444, 459, 460, 462, 475, 477, 488
Thyme, 273
Tibe, 119
Tible, 119
Tiblo, 119
Tibolato, 57
Tidimat, 85
Tile stone, 138
Tile, stone roof, 95
Tin, 38, 40, 43, 44, 82, 97, 205, 245, 312, 459, 480, 487, 488
Tiniel, 117
Tireip, 415
Titan, 410
Toads, 119
Tobit, 67
Tobrintec, 420
Toby, 217, 222
Tobyell, 338
Tola, 55
Tongs, 265, 266
Torquaret, 446
Towel, 65
Tower of London, 6
Tranda, 251
Transtor, 349

Treasure, 1, 5, 7–9, 21, 33, 66, 69, 133, 164, 221, 229–31, 233, 248, 249, 254, 255, 315, 316, 320, 321, 330, 343, 404, 455, 542, 549, 564
Tribo, 57
Trine (astrology), 199, 544
Trinity, 53, 70, 76, 100, 114, 123–25, 136, 155, 159, 163, 199, 215, 222, 231, 233, 246, 255, 263, 264, 266, 269–71, 273–75, 277, 278, 299, 302, 309, 316, 317, 322, 339, 354, 363, 380, 394, 395, 401, 404, 405
Tronda, 250
True and Faithful Relation (Casaubon), 10
Truell, 421
Trumsell, 517
Tryon, Thomas, 35
Tryton, 419
Tsohonos, 295, 296
Tubiel, 446
Tuesday, 38, 128, 163, 347, 391, 437–39, 459, 460, 462, 474, 477, 488, 509, 554
Turiel, 443
Turks, 160
Tus, 155, 434
Tusi, 370, 415
Twelfth Day, 75, 139
Tyre, 523

U
Ulcer, 277
Uliach, 420
Ulicia, 226
Ultera, 262
Uniginutas, 369
Unno, 95, 96
Uperion, 55
Upton-upon-Severn, 6
Urania, 23, 24, 553
Uranus (planet). See also Herschel, 374
Urciferi, 79
Uriden, 421
Uriel, 163, 226, 227, 314, 315, 389, 392, 393, 410, 435, 444
Urine, 52, 105, 161, 432
Urtera, 262
Uryell, 338
Usias, 349
Usion, 125, 149, 304, 318, 369, 390, 412, 414
Uson, 304
Ustael, 434
Uxbridge, 52

V
Vaa, 415
Vadabat, 324
Vadasuall, 219
Vagan / Vacian, 306
Vagen, 218, 293
Vairus, Leonardus, 155
Valentine, Basil, 35, 43, 44, 564
Valerian, 91
Valnum, 436
Varcan, 434
Varley, John, 374
Varrical, 78
Varsian, 78
Vas, 91
Vasago, 410
Vasagon, 410
Vau, 209, 295, 334, 335
Vawin, 295
Vax, 497

Vay, 415
Vedaath, 110, 111
Vegethon, 454
Veirnuel, 439
Velel, 439
Vell, 440
Velpor, 251
Venabel, 439
Venis, 137
Venue, 105
Venus, 106, 112, 118, 204, 211, 284, 289, 290, 382, 443
Verbim, 219
Verdon, 414
Vervain, 114, 134, 136
Vese, 251
Vespers, 99
Vessel, brass, 159
Vessels of iniquity, 281
Vetuel, 436
Vianuel, 438
Victoria, Queen, 20
Vimon, 97
Vinegar, 155, 515, 521
Vineyards, 81
Violet water, 522
Violets, 493
Vionatraba, 434
Viper, 156
Virgo, 123, 349, 366, 421, 455, 490, 526
Viscus quarci / viscus querci, 87–89
Vitel, 295, 296
Vuael, 436

W

W., H., Mercurii president, 24, 374
Waistcoat, 144, 145
Walcates / Walkates, 222, 223
Walnuts, 64
Waltham-hall, Essex, 14
Walton, Richard, 16
Wand, hazel, 72, 159, 263, 307
Wand, white thorn, 110
Warwick, 16, 565
Warwickshire, 7, 19
Wasud, 63
Water, 40, 53, 56, 62, 65, 73, 77, 78, 85, 91, 92, 102, 106, 108, 112, 118, 123, 126, 136–38, 141, 144–46, 148, 150, 155, 159–63, 219, 221, 226, 234, 239–41, 257, 260–62, 264–66, 269, 271–73, 275, 276, 278, 280, 281, 285–87, 296, 297, 301, 303, 308, 321–23, 328, 336, 337, 339, 347, 368, 386, 394, 404, 409, 414, 425, 429, 431, 447, 448, 451, 488–90, 512–14, 516, 522–26
Water, salt, 108, 368
Water, well, 368
Wax, 4, 10, 41, 55, 73, 91, 103, 106, 108, 109, 112, 113, 119–22, 134, 135, 139, 141, 144, 153, 155, 156, 187, 193, 218, 225–27, 246, 247, 262, 276, 277, 287, 321, 324, 379, 409, 488, 515
Wax, red sealing, 225
Webster, John, 10, 565
Wednesday, 38, 47, 55, 64, 65, 128, 286–88, 321, 349, 391, 431, 432, 439, 440, 459, 460, 462, 474, 477, 488
Wen, 277
West Sussex, 5
Weston Library, 28
Wharton, Goodwin, 9, 133, 547
Wheat, 5, 85, 242, 435, 511–14, 520
Whelp, 133

Whip for the Devil, A (Anonymous), 5, 260, 261, 566
White thorn, 110
Williams, 22
Wilmot, Anna-Maria, 19
Wilmot, James, 19
Wilmot, Olivia. *See* Serres, Olivia
Wilmot, Robert, 19
Wine, 12, 151, 155, 161, 219, 242, 258, 260, 331, 429, 511, 514–24
Wine, red, 517
Winifred, Saint, 356
Winter savoury, 273
Wire, 301, 494, 499
Wire, iron, 499
Witch bottle, 52, 432
Witch trials, 9, 11
Witchcraft Act of 1604, 8
Witchcraft Act of 1735/6, 21, 548
Witchcraft Detected and Prevented (Anonymous), 22, 153, 557
Witches, 4, 9, 14, 16, 21, 36, 46, 47, 55, 57, 150, 153, 157–59, 187, 189, 197, 265, 266, 351–53, 355–57, 371, 545, 546, 554, 561, 565, 566
Withered rose, 511
Wolf (disease), 277
Wolf's head, 159
Wood of life, 524
Wood, fragrant, 118
Worcester, 5–8, 12, 313, 321, 545, 566
Worcester Castle, 7
Worcestershire, 1, 5–7, 12, 19, 145, 313, 543–545
Worms, 64, 136, 140, 155, 169, 338, 565
Wound / Wounds of Christ, 215, 340, 386
Wryneck, 120
Wycherley, William, 7, 273

X

Xusi, 229

Y

Ya, 163, 295, 296, 304, 338, 415, 437, 438, 442, 454
Yalena, 295, 296
Yaleselem, 414
Yam Jarnice, 163
Yara, 334, 335, 416
Yaren, 454
Yarrow, 141
Yaym, 295, 454
Yayn, 445, 478
Yczeseres, 419
Ydreel, 421
Yea Saray, 416
Yegeron, 415
Yenell an Yenell, 420
Yfrey, 422
Yinas, 412
Ymaclyon, 421
Ymas, 295, 334, 335, 415
Ymeym, 426
Yne, 414
Yociell, 338
Yot I, 358
Ysagnel, 117
Ysion, 454
Ysistron, 415
Ystay, 83
Ysus, 125, 293, 390, 414
Ytell, 295, 296
Yzaby, 292

Z

Zabugr, 422
Zachayt, 422
Zadkiel (Morrison, Robert), 23
Zael, 419
Zala, 293
Zaliel, 438
Zan, 114
Zaniel, 436
Zanoni (Bulwer-Lytton), 22, 555
Zazel / Zazell, 157, 207
Zeaboeh, 499
Zebaoth, 359, 437
Zeboroth, 415
Zedekiel, 456
Zedica, 142
Zedroteyl, 112
Zelo, 142
Zelydron, 420
Zerna, 319, 320
Zernae, 247, 248
Zeroteel, 422
Zeth, 295
Zeysezey, 142
Zimimar, 467
Zoel, 419
Zoroaster, 433

To Write to the Authors

If you wish to contact the authors or would like more information about this book, please write to the authors in care of Llewellyn Worldwide Ltd. and we will forward your request. Both the authors and the publisher appreciate hearing from you and learning of your enjoyment of this book and how it has helped you. Llewellyn Worldwide Ltd. cannot guarantee that every letter written to the authors can be answered, but all will be forwarded. Please write to:

Dan Harms and S. Aldernay
℅ Llewellyn Worldwide
2143 Wooddale Drive
Woodbury, MN 55125-2989

Please enclose a self-addressed stamped envelope for reply, or $1.00 to cover costs. If outside the U.S.A., enclose an international postal reply coupon.

Many of Llewellyn's authors have websites with additional information and resources. For more information, please visit our website at http://www.llewellyn.com.